E&L 19 (03/09)

Renfrewshire
Council

(CE)

EDUCATION AND LEISURE SERVICES
LIBRARIES

Thank you for using ————————————
Library. Please return by the last date below. Renewals can be requested in person, by telephone or via our website www.renfrewshire.gov.uk/libraries

19 NOV 0.		
18 JUN 11.		
17 JAN 1?		
12 MARCH		

RED MEN

RED MEN

LIVERPOOL FOOTBALL CLUB
THE BIOGRAPHY

John Williams

MAINSTREAM
PUBLISHING

EDINBURGH AND LONDON

First published in Great Britain in 2010 by
MAINSTREAM PUBLISHING COMPANY
(EDINBURGH) LTD
7 Albany Street
Edinburgh EH1 3UG

ISBN 9781845965570

A catalogue record for this book is available
from the British Library

Typeset in Caslon and Franklin Gothic

Printed in Great Britain by
Clays Ltd, St Ives plc

1 3 5 7 9 10 8 6 4 2

ACKNOWLEDGEMENTS

This book has taken much longer to produce than I thought it would. I want to thank those who have been waiting patiently for it to be born. But many more thanks are also in order. Much of the research for this text was undertaken by ploughing through the Liverpool press and connected sources, and my dedicated researcher David Gould did as much of this crucial spadework as anyone else. I want to thank him for his excellent job, and I hope that his beloved Stoke City continue to survive – and more – in the heady Premier League. We both want to thank the staff at the Liverpool Central Library for looking after us so well during our many visits there between 2006 and 2008. I must also thank my dear friend Cathy Long for letting me stay over in her flat in Liverpool when I most needed to. I could not have completed this work without my Liverpool base.

My friends and colleagues David Gould, Andrew Ward, Stephen Hopkins, Neil Carter, Viet-Hai Phung and Alec McAuley all read early versions of some of these chapters and offered many useful comments and scholarly support. Andrew Ward, especially, is a terrific writer and researcher as well as being a very good friend. Andrew helped me restructure chapters when I was in danger of losing my way. I also 'entertained' some of my fellow Liverpool supporters in the Flat Iron pub in Liverpool with ad hoc and often obscure stories taken from the text, and even the occasional historical football quiz about Liverpool FC. I thank them, as always, for their tolerance, humour and interest. They are the very best of knowledgeable Liverpool supporters. James Cleary and Adrian Killen gave me great advice on pictures and Liverpool FC's past, and Ken Rogers at Trinity Mirror was kind enough, initially, to ask me to write this book. When the book transferred to Mainstream Publishing, Bill Campbell, Claire Rose and Graeme Blaikie performed heroics in keeping the whole thing on track. Finally, Stephen Done at the Liverpool FC museum read an early version of the text, and he offered many priceless correctives and pieces of sound guidance and advice. He also allowed me to look at the surviving official Liverpool FC minute books (1914–56), for which I am eternally grateful.

At home, as I tried valiantly to pull all this material together, my partner Sylvia offered her usual love, patience and encouragement, and my precious toddler granddaughters, Millie and Sasha, kept me amused and full of energy when things started to flag. They were even joined later on in the piece by little Esmée. Despite her US heritage, Sasha will be well schooled by her mother in the Reds tradition, and at just three years of age Millie can already sing whole sections of the Fernando Torres song and is now busy learning 'You'll Never Walk Alone' – though her sudden and strange obsession with sharks and other matters has proved a distraction to her much more important Liverpool FC schooling. Her uncle Seb will help keep her focused on the main task.

I also want to say here that a number of sources, in particular, were completely invaluable as I tried to make sense of Liverpool FC's extraordinary history. Tony Matthews' *Who's Who of Liverpool* is an excellent and comprehensive starting point for pen pictures of Liverpool players, going right back to the earliest days of the club. All Liverpool fans should own a copy. As he will no doubt notice, I used his research so frequently I could not always attribute it, and I give my heartfelt thanks (and sheepish apologies) to him here. Likewise, Brian Pead's *Liverpool: A Complete Record 1892–1990* is a very useful guide to the club's early formations and playing records, and Eric Doig and Alex Murphy's *The Essential History of Liverpool* is indispensable for its accuracy and detail. Vital too is the club website lfchistory.net for providing lots of crucial historical information about the club and its players.

The *Football League Players' Records 1888–1939* by Michael Joyce got me out of many tight spots in trying to establish the identities of early opponents of Liverpool Football Club and to track their careers, and Jack Rollin's *Rothmans Book of Football Records* did the same for crowd data information and for relevant Football League tables. Simon Inglis's terrific account of the history of the Football League, *League Football and the Men Who Made It*, was exceptionally useful for keeping me up to date with wider developments in the game as we lurched, uncertainly, towards the present. Finally, John Belchem's wonderful edited collection in celebration of the city of Liverpool, *Liverpool 800: Culture, Character and History*, gave me plenty to contemplate – and to rely upon – concerning history, culture and social change in the city. I hope I have done no gross disservice in the text to any of these indispensable works.

When I use a source directly and extensively, I have indicated this fact in the text, though I must reiterate I used the standard Liverpool FC reference books and sites rather more liberally than such formal referencing suggests. Finally, I have tried to report on events covered in this book quite critically, as a researcher, and not simply with a supporter's feverish eye: the reader will have to judge how well (or how badly) I have done in this respect. Needless to say, all the errors in the text – though only some of the insights – are mine and mine alone.

For the lost 135, Heysel and Hillsborough

CONTENTS

Introduction *11*

1 Football in Liverpool – From the Very Beginning *17*

2 Liverpool Out of Everton – One Seed, Two Clubs *33*

3 Turning Ice Into Fire – Tom Watson, the First Great Liverpool Manager *59*

4 As Many Downs as Ups – The Topsy-Turvy 1900s *87*

5 The First FA Cup Final – 1914 at the Palace, and Then War *117*

6 The Roaring Twenties – Liverpool Back on the Title Trail *143*

7 'Where's Liverpool?' – 'Top of the League!' *161*

8 They Shall Be Our Teachers – The First Internationalisation of Liverpool FC *177*

9 Lisha! Lisha! – Elisha Scott and the Liverpool Kop *195*

10 Football Life During Wartime – Surviving the Conflict and Emerging Stronger *213*

11 1946–47, Champions Again – George Kay and the Willie and Albert Show *225*

12 The Almost Seasons – The Double Frustration of 1950 *245*

13 The Rocky Road to Glenbuck – The Bleak 1950s *269*

14 Bill Shankly and the New Liverpool – Or How the Liverpool Board Finally Learned How to Spend Money *295*

15 Ee-Aye-Addio, the FA Cup at Last! – Liverpool FC at Wembley and in Europe *317*

16 Nothing but Blue Skies – Bob Paisley in Charge at Anfield *339*

17 At the Dark End of the Street – Heysel and Hillsborough *367*

18 Continental Drift – The New Liverpool Technocrats *387*

Epilogue: There Must Be Some Way Out of Here – The Liverpool Ownership Crisis *405*

Bibliography – Sources and Useful Reading *420*

Index *425*

INTRODUCTION

For the year 2008, and despite its many doubters, the city of Liverpool was a spectacularly successful European Capital of Culture. This is a fitting reason, in itself, for the production of a book during that halcyon period that celebrates the history and cultural significance of football and of Liverpool Football Club in the city. Without doubt, football is as much a feature of the cultural heritage and artistic landscape of the city of Liverpool as any theatre production, media installation or art exhibition.

As many people have noted, Liverpool is something of a city on the edge, both geographically and culturally. Despite its considerable Welsh and Scottish in-migrations, Liverpool has typically looked westwards, to Ireland and the United States, rather than back to Britain or southwards to Continental Europe, for its inspiration and for much of its cultural history. It has many of the independent and distinctive characteristics of a city on the margins, a place at the end of the line even. Rather like other great peripheral cities of Europe that have football at their cultural heart, such as Marseille and Naples, Liverpool has an uneasy and shifting relationship with its national host, often preferring to look inwards rather than to national forms of identification. In this sense, T-shirts that describe Liverpool football supporters in the city as 'Scouse not English' are making rather more than a joke.

Accordingly, the city of Liverpool has a highly idiosyncratic set of cultural reference points, whether they be the city's Irish, Welsh or Scottish cultural influences; its old traveller stories and sea shanties; its bastardised versions of American jazz and soul music; the beat traditions of the Beatles and their many imitators; the deep creativity of the shoal of Liverpool poets and artists, past and present; or else the incredible native imagination of local football supporters in their endless task of producing new songs and banners in praise of their heroes on and off the football pitch. Indeed, there can be few places in the world where complex football songs are created so prodigiously or sung with such gusto. And there is nowhere – anywhere – in the world where one minute these anthems are likely to be pumping out to the rhythms of rousing Irish Republican choruses and then, the next, being delivered to the strains of deeply Loyalist hymns or other melodies assiduously collected from around the globe. Football in Liverpool is, quite simply, a text constructed as much by the club's avid supporters as it is by its players, managers and even directors. It is much more important today than any religious or political divide, or indeed any other schism shaped by difference, fashion or creed. But it is also interesting to note, as I have frequently done in this text, that *playing* weekend football, in Liverpool's parks and public spaces, has often been opposed fiercely by local religious leaders and for much longer than was the case in many other major English cities.

There can be few places other than in Liverpool, too, where football has quite the specific cultural-political resonances that it has – and has had – in the city. As this book, I hope, shows, football on Merseyside has variously been a focus for civic rivalry and celebration, as in the early 1900s; a local bulwark against the effects of economic depression, as in the 1920s and 1930s, and in many periods that followed; a crucial site for the recovery of local pride and a sense of community, as in the post-war reconstruction period of the 1940s and 1950s; part of a celebration of the youthful energy and the brief creative world dominance of popular culture on Merseyside in the 1960s; a potential escape, abroad, from the privations of central government meddling and cruelty and a focus for mutual community support, as in the successful and tragic 1980s; and a site for global fusion, as it increasingly seems to be in the 2000s.

But football is also important in Liverpool – perhaps most important of all – in its own terms: as an individual and collective physical performance and a local class and masculinity rite. In this last respect, I have tried to chart the near constant struggle of women in the city to play and watch the game, often against the fiercest male opposition. This fight, thankfully, is still being waged, though it is far from won. Football in England offers a very specific, but also a highly complex, range of traditional working-class aesthetic archetypes – the brave and rugged defender; the powerful and constructive midfielder; the creative and elegant winger; the cool and nerveless striker – in addition to a set of collective and individual cultural practices that many men – and increasingly women – in the city of Liverpool continue to identify with very strongly. As the author Arthur Hopcraft points out in his brilliant 1968 book on the game, *The Football Man*, football in cities such as Liverpool is not just a sport people take to, like cricket or tennis – it has both conflict and beauty and is inherent in the people. Football is something that is built into the urban psyche, and in Liverpool it really *matters* to the people who live there. It does so as poetry or fine art matters for some people and alcohol does to others. A *combined* love of alcohol and football as occurs in Liverpool and similar cities, it goes without saying, is an especially potent mix.

There are certainly few more informed, animated, articulate and passionate forums in the city than at the tables and bars in north Liverpool pubs as kick-off approaches at Anfield. The same has been true for more than 100 years and will doubtless continue to be the case for decades to come. And this huge passion remains despite the awful disasters that beset football in the 1980s, in which Liverpool Football Club and its fans played no small role as both perpetrators and victims. It has also survived the recent hyper-commercialisation of the game and its movement – because of price and restricted access to tickets – out of the reach of many of those local people who used regularly to attend football. Instead, Liverpool supporters now travel to the city from far and wide – I was born and raised in the nearby borough of Bootle but now drive in from the East Midlands for home games – and new groups of supporters including British Asians and Continental Liverpool followers now find their places on the Kop, as well as on websites and in Internet chat rooms. This is while bars and pubs in and around Liverpool are packed on Saturday and Sunday afternoons to watch the local football clubs play live on television. This new media consumption of top-level football in cities such as Liverpool often occurs via jerky TV 'feeds' usually illegally procured from mysterious countries from around the globe. It is all part of the contradictory new globalisation and democratisation of football support, in an era when the price of a seat for a top-level game in England is now forbidding for many supporters.

Nor is football an arena today simply for the celebration of *local* talent – as if this was ever the case. In the first Liverpool v. Everton Football League derby match, way back in 1894, the Liverpool side was packed with alien Scots, and the local press in the city was full of complaints about the lack of opportunity for young men from the area to play for the top Merseyside clubs. Very few would make it into the Liverpool team before the First World War. Not much has changed in over a century, except that the clubs' players are now drawn in not just from over the border but from around the world, and that top-level footballers today can earn more in a *week* than many people would take five years, or more, to accumulate. Gone are the pre-celebrity football days when Liverpool players walked to the ground with the crowds that worshipped them. Or – as the great Billy Liddell did in the 1950s – they caught the tram to Anfield to undertake their (part-time) jobs as football professionals for Liverpool. Football today has its transient mercenaries, of course. But, we might also ask, are some of today's football millionaires – Jamie Carragher, for one – or even the recent international Liverpool heroes – Germany's Didi Hamann or Finland's Sami

Hyypiä, for example – *really* any less 'of' the city of Liverpool, or less typical of its football traditions and dedication, than earlier Reds heroes who may have been more local and earned peanuts by comparison? I wonder.

This book deals in some detail with periods when ordinary professional footballers were not especially high earners, nor nationally known. I am especially interested here in the span of almost 90 years from the late 1870s, when football began to emerge on Merseyside from diverse political roots, up to 1965 when Liverpool Football Club under Bill Shankly finally managed to win the FA Cup for the first time. This long period takes up much of the first part of the main text, and here I introduce readers to great names in the club's past, such as its first successful manager Tom Watson, the wonderful all-rounder Alex Raisbeck, and the totemic Reds goalkeeper for three decades Elisha Scott. I also explore great Liverpool sides of the past, such as the 1901 and 1906 championship teams and the Liverpool squad containing Scott that won back-to-back league titles in 1922 and 1923. But the FA Cup had certainly been Liverpool Football Club's central concern almost since the club was formed in 1892, and this was especially the case after the first Liverpool Football League championship was won near the beginning of the twentieth century.

From that point on, the FA Cup was the holy grail, *the* prime target for the Anfield board and probably for most of the club's players and supporters. Liverpool had actually come much closer to succeeding in this grand quest, at various moments, than its two losing FA Cup finals before 1965 (1914 and 1950) might suggest. But finally winning the FA Cup in 1965 seemed like something of the end of a journey, a 'natural' point of closure to the early part of the story of Liverpool FC and the people who made it. The long period before 1965 – lengthy stretches of aspiration and hope, flecked by occasional moments of real success – is much less well known to most of the club's followers, for obvious reasons. After 1965, the footballing landscape of Europe opened up to Liverpool and set quite a different set of challenges.

I also cover, of course, the great years of Shankly and Paisley, and these will be quite well known to most Liverpool supporters. There is a fixation with managers at Liverpool that it is difficult to trace anywhere else in England. I deal with the main reasons for the decline of the club after the end of the boot-room era and with the terrible disasters at both Heysel (1985) and Hillsborough (1989) that played a major part in shaping that decline and the recent supporter traditions around the club. I discuss the successes and problems of the new Continental influences at Liverpool in recent years and try to bring the Anfield story right up to date in the closing chapters, and especially in the epilogue, by looking at aspects of the new ownership arrangements at Liverpool. Throughout the text, I have tried to provide some wider cultural and economic context for football in the city by offering brief descriptions of events and debates that were going on in and around the city at the time. This is in order better to locate developments at Liverpool Football Club in both time and space. This seems to me what a real football club history that dwells on the sport's local cultural significance should try to do.

I also try, wherever possible, to draw on the contemporaneous voices of football supporters and other people in Liverpool, admittedly taken mainly from the letters pages of the local press. This, I think, adds more cogency to the story and tells us something about how people saw relations with the club and football in the city at that time. I do, necessarily, begin my account of the history of Liverpool FC, briefly, with a discussion of the early years of *Everton* Football Club, especially when the Blues played at Anfield. This is done in order to cover the origins of association football itself, and to try to tell the reader something about how and why organised football overtook rugby in the city of Liverpool in the late nineteenth century. I also describe here, of course, how Liverpool Football Club emerged following the famous split from Everton in 1892, and how the emerging character of the two clubs has developed and differed ever since.

At the very end of the book, I say something about the possibilities of choosing a 'best-ever' Liverpool side. In many ways, this is a rather fatuous task, for obvious reasons, but it is also a very entertaining and diverting one. I have spent many happy hours in Liverpool pubs and elsewhere doing just this kind of thing, and I would guess many other readers have done the same. Most of us are constrained in this task to choosing players we have seen live or glimpsed on television. Arguments will continue to rage on this score, and rightly so. Limits of space have meant that I have said very little in support of my own choices, but I think the main text does this for me. What I try to do in this final section is to show just how limiting most discussions currently are about the 'greatest-ever' Liverpool team. This is simply because they tend to ignore the first 70 years, or so, of the club's history.

My selections consciously try to counter that tendency, and they are aimed at getting the reader at least to think about earlier periods in the history of the club. A number of my own selections come from the era before Bill Shankly produced his first great Liverpool side in the early 1960s and before Bob Paisley produced a team to dominate the game from the mid-1970s. This may surprise and even appal some readers, but there are players from earlier periods who also have their claims to be considered among the club's greatest-ever servants. I hope this book convinces on this matter. It should go at least some way to explaining why clearly exceptional Liverpool players of more recent eras, such as Ian St John, Ray Clemence, Phil Neal, Kevin Keegan, John Barnes, Graeme Souness, Ian Rush and also many other past and recent stars, have not made it into my own all-time 'best' Liverpool XI. Readers will have to make up their own minds on this and on many other issues I try to cover. At least we can all agree that the story of Liverpool Football Club – and of football in the city of Liverpool – has been a joyous and remarkable one, if one also characterised by vital moments of real human drama and occasional terrible loss. This is, of course, what makes the modern Liverpool Football Club precisely what it is. Come on, you Red Men!

John Williams
April 2010

1

FOOTBALL IN LIVERPOOL
From the Very Beginning

STIRRINGS DOWN SOUTH

Despite what many Scousers and other Liverpool fans might like to think, association football didn't actually originate in Liverpool at all. In fact, the first of a series of meetings about establishing football as the national game took place in the Freemason's Tavern in Great Queen Street, London, on 26 October 1863. A group of ex-public schoolboys were trying to agree on a common set of laws for football by setting up the Football Association (FA). The meeting barely raised a murmur in the great Victorian city of Liverpool. It was certainly not reported in the local press. Why should it be? Here, after all, was a small group of southern-based toffs mulling over ideas originally coined by Cambridge University graduates. They wanted a common set of laws for a ball game – association football – to be played in Harrow, Eton and a selection of England's elite public schools. Why on earth should this little sporting cabal register even a blip of interest in the resplendent, prosperous great working port of Liverpool of the north?

Folk versions of something called 'football' had existed for centuries in England, of course. Rivers, streams and other local landmarks mapped out the playing areas. Essentially, these were brutal, public-holiday free-for-alls for local young bucks – a sort of legitimised mass brawl over possession of a ball or keg. Occasionally, they ended fatally for some of those involved. Lancashire was a special site for sporting matches organised by pub landlords for gambling purposes. The city of Liverpool was dominated by a slightly milder version of this anarchic ritual that came codified from the English public schools. In fact, the first recorded non-school football match played under Rugby School rules in the north of England took place at the Edge Hill cricket ground, Liverpool, in 1857. It was played between men from Liverpool and Manchester but was described extravagantly as a fixture that pitched 'Rugby School' against 'the World'. Fifty players were involved, most of them ex-Rugby public schoolboys and sons of Liverpool's merchant class. Signs of what would become the association game there were none. Although early versions of 'football' often meant a mixing and matching of handling and kicking, rugby was king in mid-nineteenth-century Liverpool. The Liverpool Rugby Union Club was founded in 1862, and rugby in the city seemed just as its elite supporters wanted it to be: upper or middle class in personnel, and violent and uncompromising in play. Manchester opponents (always keen rivals for Liverpudlians, even then) commented a few years later, after a trip to the city to play rugby football, that, 'Anyone who played in the match at Queen's Park [Liverpool] in or about 1865 would remember it, as we were overmatched and roughly handled. Some of us had to be helped out of the railway carriage on arrival at Manchester Victoria station.'[1] Great stuff.

The association men at the FA did seem to have a rather more democratic view than their rugby opponents about the possibilities of spreading a new common football code *downwards* among working people in cities such as Liverpool, as well as to the new urban middle classes. This would only be possible, of course, as long as football could be stripped of some of the violent excesses of the past. They were determined to get their way, even fiddling the votes at early meetings in order to keep their vision on track.[2] With a little more diplomacy or tact, the FA might have successfully compromised with its opponents by agreeing to establish *two* football codes: one for association football and the other for rugby football. This strategy would have boosted FA membership and increased its early national importance. Instead, the hackers and handlers would eventually set up their own rival body, outside the FA. Nor did the FA men do much even to try to *explain* or spread their modest new football laws. In any case, people in the city of Liverpool seemed largely disinterested in them. Elsewhere, the new laws served to confuse early FA members and other football clubs rather than offer any real clarity. In fact, many existing football clubs chose to adopt *some* aspects of the FA laws and to reject others, thus producing a bewildering series of hybrid football codes.[3] It looked as if this obscure new southern sporting body – and its fancy new association-football code – was actually going nowhere fast.

In 1871, the embryonic world of football was turned on its head. The Rugby Football Union was formed, and, partly as a response, the FA launched the world's first national sporting knockout competition: the FA Cup was born. Two thousand fans, drawn mainly from the London social elites, watched the first FA Cup final at the Kennington Oval in 1872. A team of ex-public schoolboys from Wanderers defeated ex-public schoolboys representing Royal Engineers, 1–0. Predictably, there were no reports of this historic southern encounter in the Liverpool press. But by the late 1870s the first real *northern* working-class football hero, Fergus Suter, a Scottish stonemason, had already emerged – not in Liverpool but in East Lancashire. Football in this part of the north seemed to be a continuation of local traditions rather than something especially encouraged by the public schools or the FA.

As football was being dragged kicking and screaming into the mainstream of English public life, the great seaport of Liverpool remained resolutely a cricket and rugby city. In Yorkshire, and in some parts of Lancashire, cup competitions for largely working-class northern rugby were established in the late 1870s. But the controlling elitist ex-public school rugby clubs in the great cities of Liverpool and Manchester refused, point blank, to play any competitive cup rugby football. Their argument was that 'gentlemen' should play only friendly sporting fixtures, 'for the good of the game'. More importantly, these social elites feared being drawn to play against their social inferiors in a cup competition. They might even come across veiled professionals. This kind of social superiority (or rank snobbery, if you like) provided just the sort of social and cultural sporting vacuum that association football would eventually rush to fill in Liverpool. Over the next decade or so, ordinary working-class people in the north and Midlands increasingly began to link up with social reformers, employers and middle-class patrons to form association football clubs in and around cities such as Sheffield, Birmingham and Nottingham.

LEFT BEHIND LIVERPOOL

But why was association football for working people in the 1870s already well established in places such as East Lancashire, South Yorkshire and the Midlands, but not so at all in Liverpool? By 1880, for example, the local press in Birmingham was reporting on eight hundred and eleven local football contests while the Liverpool press could find only two on Merseyside. For one thing, the Liverpool area lacked the folk forms of football that had been common in East Lancashire and around Sheffield. For another, the incredible economic and cultural span between Liverpool's elite rich, its ranks of clerks in the middle and the squalid, urban poor at the bottom meant that there was much less of the sort of social mixing and paternalism that was now common in other British cities. There were plenty of returning ex-Harrow public schoolboys living in Liverpool who might have been expected to spread association football. But because of the stark divisions between rich and poor in the city, sport could not be so easily passed down from local social elites, as had happened elsewhere. And, in any case, the poor in Liverpool's docklands had neither the space nor the good health to play sport.[4]

In the 1860s and early 1870s, northern and Midlands association football clubs had been made up mainly of players from the upper and middle classes. Then, from the middle of the 1870s, as the sport mushroomed from the bottom up, new football clubs began to develop for working people out of existing institutions, such as cricket clubs and churches. New football clubs were often inspired by the Victorian doctrine of 'Muscular Christianity', a form of community engineering from above aimed at combining the restraint and sobriety of Methodism with the obvious benefits of physical activity and healthy competition for working people. Football was seen by liberal elites as an improving form of 'moral cleansing' for the urban poor. It might even help 'save' the souls of the working class, people who could otherwise be easily tempted by the connected evils of fecklessness, crime, drinking and gambling.

Some of her critics – and even her friends – might well have argued that the Liverpool of the 1870s and 1880s was in urgent need of a good dose of moral cleansing. This heaving and turbulent nineteenth-century English seaport probably seemed a rather odd place compared to the average English provincial town of the time. But it fitted perfectly well with the outlook in transient Continental seaports such as Hamburg and Marseille, or great cities across the Atlantic. An American visitor of the time thought Liverpool to be a modern marvel, 'the Chicago of England', and the *London Illustrated News* on 15 May 1886 described it as 'the New York of Europe, a world city rather than merely British provincial'. Many of Liverpool's Victorian residents were moulded, for good or ill, by this same sense of being cosmopolitans, authentic citizens of the world.[5]

Liverpool's selective affluence, its nod to cosmopolitanism and its flamboyant identity as a thriving global port was also reflected in the conviviality and sheer liveliness of the city centre – and in the fact that by 1874 there was a grand total of 2,585 places in the city from which beer and spirits were sold. But this largesse also meant that public drunkenness – especially among Merseyside street children, criminals and the poor – was a regular local focus for moral concern and regulation among those who were occasionally forced into rubbing shoulders with the lower orders. This included the city's civic leaders and members of the press. Liverpool's wonderful municipal Victorian finery, its extensive programme of public lectures, an impulse for self improvement and its sheer commercial dynamism stood cheek by jowl with incredible levels of desperation and deprivation. One overseas visitor to the city remarked that he had seen such vast wealth and poverty in other cities but 'never before had I seen the two so jammed together'.[6]

Among the worst affected by poverty and poor health was Liverpool's Irish community, especially Catholic families who were originally from the south and west of Ireland and who were part of the group of 580,000 Irish who passed through the port at the height of the great potato famine in 1846 and 1847. Many of the Irish who then settled in Liverpool drew attention to themselves in the northern end of the city mainly through their sheer numbers and levels of unemployment and poverty, and the diseases they suffered, caused by malnutrition and overcrowded and unsanitary housing conditions. With one of the highest mortality rates in Britain, Liverpool in the mid-nineteenth century was publicly labelled as 'the Black Spot on the Mersey'.[7] Amidst the deprivation, squalor and filth, idle hands inevitably turned to gangs, violence and crime. The so-called 'cornermen' who stood outside Liverpool pubs or on street corners demanding money for beer from passers-by became notorious. Public panics about the alleged existence of organised criminal gangs in the city, including the 'High Rip Gang', the 'Bridge Boys' and the 'Canal Bankers', all contributed, periodically, in the wider public's mind to a sense that Victorian Liverpool was a violent, chaotic and potentially lawless place. The city of Liverpool was now already established as a place of extremes: it hosted high culture and global commerce but also crime and destitution in an uneasy and often seemingly unequal balance. It was a stigma that would prove difficult to shift.

As well as divisions of poverty and ill health, the peculiar occupational structure of Liverpool also held back the spread of football on Merseyside. It was shaped by the port and its processing industries, and it meant that it was much more difficult for the vast majority of working people in the city to find free time for playing and supporting *any* sport. The Liverpool workforce had to lobby long and persistently for change in this area, with even most skilled workers in the city being unable to attain a shorter working week until as late as 1872. By contrast, beginning with the Ten Hours Act of 1847, East Lancashire textile workers had been granted a two o'clock end to work on Saturdays by 1850, reduced to one o'clock in 1874. The Ten Hours Act meant that cotton spinners now worked 55 hours rather than 70 hours, and for these workers 'it became a practice, mostly on Saturdays, to play football and cricket, which had never been done before'.[8] Most men in Birmingham did not have to work Saturday afternoons from the 1870s.

By contrast, because of the casual nature of their employment practices and the lack of care shown by dock employers for their workers, the mass of Liverpool's dockworkers had much less power to bargain with their bosses, and they would only gain Saturday afternoons off from work in April 1890 – fully two years *after* the formation of the Football League.[9] Conditions for working people in Liverpool lagged behind as the profits poured into the city coffers.

RED MEN

TURNING RUGBY MEN TO FOOTBALL

Another reason for the late uptake of football in Liverpool was probably the fact that rugby remained such a powerful force in the city and that it continued to be so jealously guarded by its local social elites. But things were changing fast, and not just on Merseyside. With the establishment of the Lancashire FA Cup and other local football competitions from 1879 onwards, and especially after the national FA Cup successes of the working-class clubs of Blackburn in the late 1870s and early 1880s, previously exclusively rugby-playing areas of the north-west of England were now rapidly converting, en masse, to football. Preston and Burnley – later, founder members of the Football League – were originally staunch rugby towns, but by the early 1880s both had become football strongholds. Previously high-profile supporters of the rugby code, including the great Fergus Suter himself, by now had turned from rugby to association football.[10] The spread of football in what were previously rugby havens was like a bush fire. Local football derbies between Liverpool's emerging association clubs, such as Everton FC and Bootle FC, now began to be reported on at some length by the Liverpool press. By 1882, exhibition football matches were being staged on Stanley Park, featuring teams selected by top local footballers – one match attracted one thousand four hundred fans. By 1883, the *Liverpool Daily Post* was routinely carrying results of the national FA Cup ties, and it even ran an account of an FA meeting in London on law changes for the association game. How times had changed. Finally, football was stirring on Merseyside.

As the association game began to challenge rugby's dominance in the parks and in the sporting press on Merseyside, another man to turn away from rugby in order to champion football was to play a crucial role in developing football in the city. Irishman and future Everton FC, Liverpool FC and Football League stalwart 'Honest' John McKenna would help shape the modern game, but his conversion from rugby was also a vital moment in the history of Liverpool Football Club. John McKenna had arrived in the city in 1854 as part of the great Irish diaspora that flooded into the sprawling mix of chaos and opportunity that was mid-nineteenth-century Liverpool. At the age of 17, McKenna had become a grocer's boy and then a vaccination officer before later becoming a sergeant major in the Lancashire Artillery military regiment. A keen rugby man when the sport was still dominant in Liverpool, this 'man of action' McKenna was eventually dismayed by rugby's avowed elitism and violence. But he was immediately impressed by the sheer competitiveness and the spectator potential of the new football cup competitions that were sweeping the north-west of England in the late 1870s. Football, with its simplicity, more civilised laws, its mixed constituents and its

22

wider social appeal, certainly chimed well with McKenna's keen entrepreneurial instincts. He noticed that in 1880 an East Lancashire football derby between Blackburn Rovers and Darwen was already attracting an extraordinary 10,000 spectators, many of them cotton workers. He reasoned that there was money to be made by smart businessmen in association football on Merseyside.

But football was much more than a commercial proposition for McKenna. He had his values – he worked with the poor and destitute for the West Derby Union and he deplored gambling – and he was also openly envious of the way the national football cup successes of the clubs of East Lancashire, Blackburn Olympic and Rovers, drew great publicity and brass-band welcome-home parties in these small towns for winning the southerners' FA Cup. He now desperately wanted to bring this sort of national sporting triumph to his adopted city of Liverpool. He would not have to wait too long. After a late start, by the early 1880s Liverpool had a stock of new association clubs, including Everton, Stanley Park, the ex-public school Liverpool Ramblers, Bootle FC, Druids, Bootle Wanderers, Anfield, Tranmere, Toxteth Wanderers, St Peters and Liverpool Linden. More were forming all the time. McKenna would throw his lot in with the rising Everton club and its charismatic president, 'King' John Houlding. By 1886, the new Liverpool Cup competition could attract 20 clubs from inside the city in its inaugural season. Within one extraordinary decade, between 1878 and the launch of the Football League in 1888, the city of Liverpool would move from having no association football at all to attracting the largest crowds to football matches anywhere in the world.

THE MYSTERIOUS BIRTH OF EVERTON FC AND THE COURT OF KING JOHN

In this place of extreme contrasts, boasting both plenty and abject poverty, local association clubs now rapidly started to form on Merseyside. Everton FC was established in a slightly more affluent area of the north end of Liverpool after a meeting in the Queen's Head Hotel in November 1879. The Anglican Everton United Church Football Club had been set up earlier that year by a group of curates from St John's College in Cambridge University led by the 25-year-old Reverend Alfred Keely. Keely had been spreading the virtues of Muscular Christianity via football in both Bootle and Liverpool. St Saviour's Church had provided the core of the United team, Methodism its values.

The exact origins of Everton FC remain contentious. The club is popularly believed to have grown out of a club at the St Domingo's New Connexion Methodist Chapel, which was supposedly formed in 1878 and which initially played cricket. The Reverend Ben Swift Chambers, a Yorkshire Methodist, is thought to have coaxed young men into playing football for St Domingo's. Leading early Everton committee members George Mahon and Will Cuff were prominent New Connexion Methodists. But one recent historian can find no trace of the St Domingo's Football Club, suggesting that the St Domingo's football team might have been a clever fiction invented later by Everton's directors in order to undermine the early role played at Everton by local brewer and Liverpool FC founder John Houlding.[11] But there is at least one reference in the *Liverpool Courier*, on 20 October 1879, to St Domingo's actually playing an association fixture against the Everton Church Club on Stanley Park. This was just before Everton FC was formed.[12] John Houlding, a prominent local Conservative politician and Orangeman, had been on the lay vestry at St Saviour's, and, through Everton United, he could have been involved in the early days of Everton FC before 1881, by which time he had become the club's first president. Houlding, no doubt, already had plans to exploit his links with the new football club for commercial and political gain, aspirations which were very out of tune with the ideals of both Cambridge curates and Merseyside Methodists.

Clerks dominated these early Merseyside sports clubs – Liverpool was a financial hub so was full of them – and by 1881 Everton FC had regular fixtures against local clubs and teams from nearby Lancashire and Cheshire, as well as matches with clubs from Manchester. In September 1882, the *Liverpool Courier* was already suggesting that football was overtaking rugby in Liverpool in terms of its popularity, and it was now seen as an entertainment by fans and players, even if it was still regarded by some of its patrons as a bulwark against drink and crime. By 1885, twenty-five out of the one hundred and twelve football clubs playing in the city had connections with religious organisations, and the origins of four out of five of the Merseyside clubs that eventually played professional football were in religious groups.

The growing ambitions of Everton were signalled by the appointment of John Houlding to the office of club president. Houlding owned a house and a pub – the Sandon Hotel – virtually overlooking Everton's home patch on Stanley Park. The Everton-born brewer and politician, now approaching 50, had been educated to no great level at Liverpool College and had begun his working life at 11 years of age as a lowly errand boy in a customs house. He followed this with a spell as a cowman's assistant; his father was a cowman, but the plague had damaged the milk business, and the impatient young Houlding soon moved on. He then became a drayman and later a foreman and chief brewer in the Clarkson Brewery – all before he had reached 21 years of age. Houlding eventually set up his own successful brewing business in the city, the Tynemouth Street Brewery in Everton, producing Houlding's Sparkling Ales. There were few people in 1880s Liverpool – certainly few drinkers or politicians, or few of the poor of the Everton district – who had not heard of Councillor John Houlding.

There were some obvious early tensions inside the Everton club. Its original philosophies – about sobriety, Methodism and liberalism – clashed somewhat with those of the self-made and charismatic patrician Tory politician and businessman John Houlding. The latter's political antennae for identifying compassionately with the grassroots, and his honed commercial interests in cashing in on the obvious connections between working people, drink and sport, were already well known in the city. Houlding, according to the *Liverpool Mercury*, was 'one of the most remarkable of men for, while not possessing any great educational advantages . . . he read and studied to such an extent that there was not a topic of conversation that he was unable to hold his own and give an intelligent opinion on'. Houlding was also chairman of the Everton Conservative Association, a leading Freemason and a staunch Unionist at a time when the city of Liverpool, like most other places in England, was effectively subject to one-party rule.

Houlding's reliable local political and cultural contacts, his 'common touch' shown by his poor-law work with young people in the city and with the elderly stuck in poverty, and his work as a great publicist for the asssociation game (and especially for Everton FC) all meant that, despite his many failings, what he had to offer football clubs in Liverpool seemed like an unbeatable combination. Houlding appeared unstoppable. He was such a major public personality and positive force for the club, a man who talked in a language that ordinary people could understand, that the local press soon dubbed him 'Honest' John or 'King John of Everton'.[13] Eventually, however, Houlding's commercial and political instincts, his lingering suspicions of Methodism and his powerful Liberal opponents on the Everton board would end King John's football reign in this half of Liverpool. But it would also help start, from scratch, another football dynasty in the city at a new association club.[14]

Like many local parks' clubs, most of Everton's early games were friendly affairs and fixtures in local cup competitions fought out on Stanley Park. Everton even met a football club called 'Liverpool' at Walton Stiles in the Liverpool Cup in January 1883, defeating their hapless hosts 8–0. But Everton's fiercest rivals by now were certainly north-end neighbours Bootle FC. Their keenly fought-out local contests often spilled over into disputes and crowd disturbances. Even the *Liverpool Echo* was by now picking up on the significance of these local rivalries and on the wider national impact of the 'football fever'. The *Echo* carried a major report on 2 April 1883 on the history-making FA Cup final at the Oval between Old Etonians and Blackburn Olympic. Sensationally, Olympic had won 2–1, and the *Echo* made much of the sharp contrast between the elite followers of the public-school club and those of the Lancastrian tribe, the 'artisan class', who followed their Blackburn heroes to London. 'Co'om Olympics, put on another shovelful!' the visiting spectators reportedly urged on their team, much to the *Echo*'s amusement. But such passion seemed to do the trick: the northern working classes at last began to colonise what would become *their* sport.

HERE COME THE PROFESSIONALS

Because of their FA Cup exploits, Olympic were now offered hard cash to take up new fixtures around the country. Eyeing up this East Lancashire success and its obvious commercial possibilities, John Houlding wanted to develop the Everton club for their own place in the FA Cup (achieved in 1886) by collecting gate money from the few hundred regular fans who followed the club, free of charge, on Stanley Park. In 1883, and for one season only, Everton hired an enclosed field, Coney Green, off Priory Road, near the Anfield Cemetery. The club won the Liverpool Cup and also played some of the top Lancashire clubs, but the noise from home supporters disturbed the club's new landlord William Cruitt and probably those who were paying their last respects next door. Everton FC were turfed out, and the club moved to a field owned by John Orrell on the other side of Stanley Park, much closer to Houlding's Sandon Hotel and wedged between Anfield Road and Walton Breck Road. John Houlding negotiated the deal and acted as representative tenant. Everton players would get changed and drink afterwards in the Sandon Hotel, a pub named by Houlding after a local Tory grandee. The *Daily Post* reported on 29 September 1884 that 'Everton has had to seek a new home during the recess and have been fortunate to secure a capital one near to the Sandon Hotel, the headquarters of the club . . . Today the new ground will be opened with a match against Earlestown, the runners-up for the last cup contest.'

Everton easily disposed of Earlestown, 5–0. Association football had finally arrived at what would later become Liverpool's Anfield Road ground. King John would now build up the club's crowds and the stadium facilities. Until, that is, the great Merseyside football split of 1892 effectively handed all this over to a new Liverpool Football Club – controlled by the same John Houlding.

The city of Liverpool had few skilled footballers at this time. As we have seen, the sport had arrived very late to Merseyside, and it would take time to become embedded among working people. As football crowds grew and matches became more important in the north of England, so recruiting and holding on to the best talent – and keeping it fresh, especially for big FA Cup matches – meant that football clubs had to scout more intensively and also 'invent' jobs for migrant footballers, whilst also paying them to play.

Professionalism in football was opposed, mainly in the south, because it was feared that business values would soon supersede sporting ones if payment for play became the norm. Paying footballers in this way did not especially concern ordinary working people in the north. But many local spectators and commentators *were* strongly opposed to the notion that players should be brought in from *outside* the area to represent their clubs. Why not give local talent a chance? This was certainly the position taken by the *Daily Post* on 25 October 1884 when it pointed out that professionalism and local English players worked perfectly well in cricket. Professionalism was not the problem for the *Post* and the rest of the Liverpool press – it was 'foreign' recruits. Such debates about football 'outsiders' would continue, no less passionately of course, more than 100 years later.

When Everton opened up their 1886–87 roster of 'friendly' fixtures at Anfield against Glasgow Rangers, the money that was now in the sport had begun to show its face. The *Daily Post* on 30 October 1886 reported, 'The Everton committee are doing their level best for the comfort and accommodation of their patrons.' Certainly, the Anfield ground had undergone considerable redevelopment and was already taking shape as a recognisable modern football stadium – even including some seating provision for football writers, as the *Post* reported:

> The ground is now completely enclosed, a stand capable of seating about 400 persons has been erected, and for one hundred yards on the opposite side a substantial wooden terrace has been constructed with standing room for 800, whilst just behind the rails a bench has been run the whole length of the ground . . . The members of the Fourth Estate have not been forgotten either, as a space has been allotted to that body on the front bench of the stand.

More than 5,000 people attended the Rangers match (including, no doubt, some local Irish Catholic Everton followers from the north end), and with Everton recent winners of the Liverpool Senior Cup, and capable of attracting big gates, the club urgently needed new challenges. Entry into the FA Cup signalled some important progress, and in 1887 a crowd in excess of 8,000 fans watched the club's FA Cup third-replay victory against Bolton at Anfield. All human life was here, according to the local press, as 'the immense concourse of spectators swarmed across the ground after the final whistle had sounded' and '800 colleens . . . dainty maids, clad in minks and victorines . . . came rushing through the portals – a sight for gods and mortals'. To their female fans' delight, Everton won the tie, but seven of their Scottish players were later deemed to be 'veiled professionals', and the club forfeited the win and was suspended from all football for one month. Also, because of the length of time it had taken to complete the tie, Everton had been forced to postpone valuable friendly fixtures with other clubs, including with a fuming Bootle FC. Football clubs of the size and ambition of Everton and Bootle needed a new structure, a fixed and reliable list of contests for which they could offer fans season tickets. They needed a football league.

McGREGOR'S 1888 UNION OF CLUBS

It was William McGregor, a Scottish Methodist draper and director of Aston Villa, who, at 41 years of age, first dreamed up the idea of a football league. Some suggested that he borrowed the concept from unofficial press tables for English cricket's County Championship. Others thought the idea might have come from the baseball leagues in the USA, which had been operating since 1876. Whatever the source, McGregor toured football clubs in the north and Midlands in the summer of 1887 to try to gather support for his project. But he received only a mixed reception: not everyone shared his enthusiasm for radical change. Unimpressed by the response from his travels – football clubs were worried by travel costs and losing valued local contests, and were unsure a league would even work – McGregor then sent a letter to the nation's top professional clubs (professionalism had been reluctantly sanctioned in a limited way by the FA in 1885). He had just two replies, although representatives from seven clubs eventually met for further discussions at the Anderton Hotel in London on 22 March 1888. The northern giants, Preston and Bolton Wanderers, were absent but apparently still keen on the league concept. Preston and Bolton, along with all the other clubs at this first meeting – Stoke, West Bromich Albion, Burnley, Wolverhampton Wanderers, Blackburn Rovers, Notts County and Aston Villa – became founder members of the new Football League. Nine clubs were now tied up: just three more to find. Everton, Accrington and Derby County were then invited to a second meeting, at the Royal Street Hotel in Manchester on 17 April at 6.30 p.m. Here the new league was formed, and McGregor's 'Football Union' was renamed the Football League. There was no club from Sheffield or anywhere in Yorkshire involved, and none at all from the south of England.

Why invite modest Accrington to join, and why seek out Everton? Why, indeed? *Athletic News* commented, acidly, that some of the chosen 12 had been 'knocked into smithereens by teams who, so far, have been left out in the cold'. Bootle Football Club was surely one of these.[15] Accrington's league claims were supported by the other Lancashire clubs, and the town was at least easy to reach by rail, an important consideration. *Both* Merseyside clubs could not be invited to join, because McGregor had decided it should be only one club per local area. Bootle FC was a better bet on the playing side than Everton, but Everton had better facilities and was attracting bigger crowds at Anfield. Everton's gates were already worth twice those of Bootle.[16] In 1888, Bootle had already beaten three proposed Football League clubs – Blackburn Rovers, Accrington and Burnley – in the run up to the new league's formation. But it made no odds: Bootle were out and the more commercially attractive Everton were in.

Everton made a raft of signings in the summer of 1888, including the brilliant Scot Nick Ross from Preston North End. Ross had teeth that were 'discoloured almost green to the gums and he hissed through them as he played' yet he was described as 'the champion back of the world'.[17] His defensive kicks were legendary, routinely clearing the Kemlyn Road chimney pots. Ross could also be difficult: he wanted a hand in coaching and selection, but he was 'just another player' to the Everton hierarchy. 'Too many cooks have spoiled the Everton broth,' opined the Lancashire press, 'and Ross has done quite right in showing his independence and his contempt for the childish mismanagement.'

With Ross and other signings newly on board on the first day of Football League fixtures on 8 September 1888, it was the Anfield ground that drew the biggest crowd of the day as an estimated 10,000 watched Everton beat Accrington 2–1. Anfield stadium security was sorely tested, as one 'hulking fellow tore down a portion of hoarding and 50 followed him through the breach'. Later, 'a little urchin trespassed on the grass and got a "free kick" from an elderly steward'. Then, a 'little young fellow went for the official without ceremony, leaving him prostrate with blood streaming from his face'.[18] Welcome, indeed, to league football in Liverpool.

Everton were widely chided in the Lancashire press in these early days for their spendthrift ways and their alleged player poaching, but also for their on-pitch aggression. Their approach was described locally as a kind of 'football forcing . . . the most expensive, the dearest lot of players that has ever been got together'. The club recruited 36 professionals, paying more than £100 per week for them. They certainly showed the necessary ruthlessness. The Scottish full-back Alec Dick was known as a 'savage' defender. His hack on an Aston Villa forward produced a punch missed by the officials, and Dick was routinely involved in fist fights on the field. Dick also allegedly once butted a spectator, and his bad language on the pitch was notorious. He was the first Football League player officially cautioned and then suspended. Everton, it was said, in this first, turbulent season, were 'singularly disliked in official quarters'.

Everton struggled in this first season, and after an Anfield defeat 0–1 to West Bromwich Albion, 'hero' Nick Ross got home later that night to find that Everton supporters had smashed all the windows in his house. The local press described the affair as 'rag-tag and bobtail footballism with a vengeance'. Ross might have escaped lightly in the circumstances, because some British football fans were already showing that they could be frighteningly critical. For example, around this time the Glasgow Rangers captain Donald Gow received a parcel at Ibrox Park from an anonymous fan following a bad run of results. Its message needed little decoding: the package contained the neatly arranged carcasses of 11 dead mice.[19]

Everton's apparent chaos was sometimes matched by that of the Football League itself in its first season. Matches often seemed to be as badly organised as the old friendly fixtures before them, because clubs frequently turned up late for matches and some had even 'lost' players en route. Everton played a total of 61 matches in the first league season, only 22 of them in the Football League. John Houlding ensured that they also played 41 of those games at Anfield, thus raking in the receipts.

The new Football League worked essentially because of the good sense of its members and the commitment of the clubs to make it work – but also because of British engineering and the existence of the Lancashire and Yorkshire railways to take players and spectators to matches: they covered five hundred and ninety miles and three hundred and nine stations, none more than two miles apart. On 19 January 1889, Everton hosted champions-elect Preston North End in a match between the best and the best supported of all the original league clubs. Everton lost 0–2 in front of 15,000 fans, the largest Football League crowd that first season. The local press described the Anfield grandeur as a 'huge circus, with its two immense galleries, rising tier after tier, and its covered stands, stretching the length of the ground'. Liverpool was rapidly becoming unrivalled as the country's premier centre for supporting association football. But as Bootle Football Club began to ail, so Everton FC now needed a credible local rival to really get the competitive sporting juices working in the city. Although no one yet knew it, King John Houlding of Everton was about to provide his colleagues on the Everton board with just what they desired.

CHAPTER 1 REFERENCES

1. Booth, *The Father of Modern Sport*, p. 39
2. Harvey, *Football: The First Hundred Years – The Untold Story*
3. Harvey, *Football: The First Hundred Years – The Untold Story*
4. Preston, 'The Origins and Development of Association Football in the Liverpool District, *c*.1879–*c*.1915'
5. Milne, 'Maritime Liverpool', p. 257
6. Marne, 'Whose Public Space Was It Anyway? Class, Gender and Ethnicity in the Creation of Sefton and Stanley Parks, Liverpool: 1858–1872', p. 425
7. Pooley, 'Living in Liverpool: The Modern City', pp. 173 and 187
8. Williams, *The Code War*, p. 49
9. Physick, *Played in Liverpool*, p. 15; Mason, *Association Football and English Society 1863–1915*
10. Collins, *Rugby's Great Split*, p. 38
11. Preston, 'The Origins and Development of Association Football in the Liverpool District, *c*.1879–*c*.1915', pp. 103–5
12. Lupson, *Across the Park*, p. 17
13. Lupson, *Thank God for Football!*, p. 59
14. Kennedy and Kennedy, 'Ambiguity, Complexity and Convergence: The Evolution of Liverpool's Irish Football Clubs'
15. Inglis, *League Football and the Men Who Made It*, p. 8
16. Preston, 'The Origins and Development of Association Football in the Liverpool District, *c*.1879–*c*.1915', p. 67
17. Sanders, *Beastly Fury*, p. 113
18. Taw, *Football's Twelve Apostles*, pp. 127 and 146
19. Taw, *Football's Twelve Apostles*, p. 179

2

LIVERPOOL OUT OF EVERTON
One Seed, Two Clubs

THE GREAT SPLIT: 1892 AND ALL THAT

Recovering successfully from their various trials in 1889, Everton Football Club actually fulfilled one of King John Houlding's great football ambitions by winning the 1891 Football League championship and with it the newly bought league-championship trophy. But it was not exactly a vintage year for football. High-spending Everton lost seven times and secured just twenty-nine points from twenty-two matches. Like any good modern chairman, Houlding was reportedly 'much disgusted' with his players for losing the final 'dead' league match against Burnley, especially in light of the reported substantial players' wage bill at Everton of some £80 or £90 a week. Couldn't these guys start to *earn* what they were paid? Houlding himself had reportedly loaned Everton more than £2,300 over the previous five years so had cause to demand more.

But 1891 *was* a vintage football year on Merseyside in another important sense. It signalled the official adoption by the sport of an authentic Liverpool invention: the goal-net. Liverpool city engineer J.A. Brodie had first considered the problem of a mechanism for confirming goals scored in August 1889. Matches between Everton and Bootle especially had supporters crammed into grounds and inevitably balanced along the touchlines. They could trip or baulk players, and, standing behind the goals, they sometimes loitered with the intention of keeping opposing shots out. Everton had even had a clear goal ruled out at an early Football League match against Accrington. By November 1890, after a trial on Stanley Park, the new goal-net was approved by the Patent Office. In September 1891, both the Lancashire League and the Football League made goal-nets compulsory, and they were also used at international and FA Cup final matches.[1] But despite Brodie's ingenuity, more than a century later even some professional football clubs have still not worked out how to design nets to avoid the ball rebounding out and embarrassing some half-awake referee.

There were also, in 1891, already the beginnings of administrative and financial rumblings from inside the Everton club. After a defeat by West Bromwich Albion in September 1891, the *Liverpool Review* reported on Houlding's plans to convert the Everton club into a limited company, with shares valued at £12,000: 'The players will have to do better if the shares are to be taken up at all quickly.' Houlding, as the representative tenant at Anfield, had effectively been Everton's landlord, and he was charging the club rent, which had increased from a figure of £100 to a weighty £240 a year by 1888 – and was still rising. Houlding saw this arrangement as a reasonable business deal: the success of the Football League had raised the value of the rent at Anfield. Everton's committee, led by George Mahon, an accountant, now asked for a long-term lease, which Houlding refused. Houlding claimed, instead, the rights for himself to the exclusive sale of refreshments to the club's fans. This was some nerve – and King John was some businessman and local politician. Houlding now proposed that Everton must also use adjacent land he owned for training, which would raise the total club rent to £370 a year. Either that or the club could convert to a limited company and purchase the land owned by Houlding and Orrell, including the stands and offices, for a total of just over £8,737. Otherwise, Orrell insisted that the Anfield land would be used for building and that Everton FC would have to move to a new site.

Understandably, all this left a rather bad taste in the mouth of Everton's Methodist founders, led by Mahon, who had been exploring the possibility of renting nearby land for just £50. After initially seeming to accept Houlding's corporate solution to the Everton 'problem', finally, on 15 September 1891, a general meeting was held in the Royal Street Hotel, at which the president produced a valuation and prospectus for the purchase of the Anfield land. The prospect of being faced with buying Anfield from John Houlding and his associates was too much for the growing band of men inside Everton who disliked King John's brewing businesses and his corporate style. Another solution would have to be sought for this problem. The *Liverpool Echo* reported that an Everton member had told a shareholders' meeting that 'it seemed to him we could expect nothing but the policy of Shylock from Mr Houlding. He was determined to have his pound of flesh, or intimidate the club into accepting his scheme.' George Mahon, leading for Houlding's opponents at Everton, put forward the motion that this proposal 'should not be entertained'. It was comfortably passed, and Houlding threatened to evict the club from Anfield. Time was now fast running out to patch things up. The anti-Houlding men at Everton were effectively looking to establish their own limited liability company so that they could purchase land for a new stadium. They even thought they had seen a suitable site, some wasteland just on the other side of Stanley Park at Mere Green Field. It would later be known, of course, as Goodison Park.[2]

This angry stand-off between Houlding and his rivals inside Everton was definitely heading for a fall, though on 8 January 1892 the Houlding-loyal *Liverpool Review* still felt able to report that 'The malcontents in the Everton club are climbing down nicely to the King of Everton's ideas. Seemingly, they were ill advised to quarrel with him.' This was overly optimistic. John McKenna was by now, with vice chair William Barclay, one of a dwindling number of Houlding allies around Everton. For local-born entrepreneurs and public figures such as John Houlding, involvement in football was part of the wider moral and political appeal that local elites felt they had to make to working people. But, frankly, he just didn't need all these football problems, because he had real difficulties with national and local party politics. The death of a local Conservative MP in the Everton division had made Houlding seem like a local shoo-in for the job. All seemed set, especially as the brewer epitomised popular Toryism in his support for male working-class leisure interests – sport and the pub – against the fanaticism of the Liverpool abstentionists.[3] But then the tide turned; temperance reformers began to gain ground in the city, especially around the issue of 'drunken children'. It was no help when Houlding's dispute inside Everton began to turn publicly sour at the same time. King John was also perhaps too much of a maverick and just *too* popular locally among working people for the national Tory bigwigs. Perhaps because of his obvious personal local popularity, he was strongly opposed by the Tory hierarchy and the constituency party in Liverpool, and Houlding was eventually forced to withdraw his candidacy to avoid splitting the party.

By now John Houlding's prominent position at Everton Football Club was also fading fast for lack of internal support. His opponents attempted to set up a new limited liability company using the Everton name, only to find that Houlding had mischievously registered 'Everton Football Club and Athletics Grounds Company, Limited' just 24 hours before. On 15 March, Houlding was ejected from Everton's ruling committee at a meeting at a Presbyterian school in Royal Street. He refused to chair the meeting as club president, and he learned that the Football League had sided with his opponents in the matter of company name. His arrival was cheered, but out of the five hundred Everton members present 'only eighteen or twenty stood by the King', reported the *Liverpool Review* on 19 March 1892. But the newspaper also rubbished rumours that Houlding had been undone in his sporting business by political radicals inside the club, arguing that, 'If the Everton football club was polled tomorrow, it is safe to say that the majority would be found Tory to the backbone.'

Others suggested otherwise: that it was Liberals and Methodist non-conformists at Everton – Mahon and club director and church choirmaster Will Cuff, especially – who were opposed to Houlding's commercial brewing interests and who most wanted Everton distanced from the drinks trade. It also seems clear that Houlding's opponents at Everton FC probably wanted to establish a much more democratic ownership and membership structure for their club, whereas, for all his good works with the poor in the city, the Tory King John wanted to tap into local working-class community support whilst still maintaining overall corporate control of the club. The *Liverpool Echo*, no great fan, had described Houlding, disparagingly, as a 'one man government' at Everton. The later, rather uneven, spread of share ownership at the two clubs rather confirmed this view of Houlding's dictatorial tendencies, with Liverpool FC's shares being concentrated in the hands of far fewer shareholders than were Everton's.[4] This meant much more autocratic control of the club by its directors than typically existed at Goodison Park, where it was one share, one vote and much more of a members' club than a corporate business. Everton's shares were also well spread among manual workers (36 per cent), whilst Liverpool FC could claim very few obviously working-class shareholders (just 5 per cent) under John Houlding.[5]

The *Review* also carried, on 26 March 1892, a *Private Eye*-like near-spoof account, provided by an 'insider', of the raucous special general meeting (officially closed to the press) that finally ejected Houlding and his followers from the Everton club. It starts with a preamble and a brief account of director Tom Howarth's pro-Houlding speech, and then things really began to hot up:

9.30 [John] McKenna rises and is received with terrible howls of execration and cries of 'Lie down McKenna!' 'Traitor!', etc. This is kept up all the time he is on his feet. Is cried down. Cheers, jumps up again. Howled down. Ditto. Howarth resumes, but is again interrupted. Members say he is only spouting to waste time.

9.45 Vote taken for Goodison Road. No question as to the majority.

9.50 Clayton moved that Mr Houlding, Mr Howarth and Mr Nisbet be removed. [William] Barclay (secretary) says he would like to hear Mr Houlding defend himself.

10.10 Houlding's speech (the chairman hopes members will give him a silent hearing because he has been ill). This is given with but few exceptions.

General opinion of speech is that he should have communicated as a gentleman should and have acknowledged them.

10.25 Mr Houlding's speech lasted a quarter of an hour. Wilson deeply regrets having to leave the [Anfield] ground though the majority of the committee have his entire sympathy. Loud cheers and cries of 'Good old Bob!', etc. Motion put to meeting. Honestly think there were not fifty voted against it. Howarth wants to speak, as regards being removed from the committee. But meeting will not hear him . . .

10.35 Members in hurry to close as there are only a few minutes to sup ale. Vote to chairman and loud cheering.

The whole sorry affair took just over an hour. When ale had been supped by the members and the dust had finally settled on what had been a poisonous dispute, Houlding claimed that it was not his business plans for Everton but the 'teetotal fanaticism' of his opponents that had forced his actions and produced the split. In truth, it had probably been both. His very public face in the city, his drinks firm and his 'direct' methods in business and public relations never seemed quite to fit at Everton. The dispute over rental charges also marked Houlding as an obvious 'outsider' in the Everton camp: he sometimes seemed to treat the club, at least in the eyes of his opponents, in a high-handed way as just another business client.

Was it greed or politics or drink or even personality clashes that forced Houlding out of Everton FC? The local politician certainly had many enemies in the Merseyside press. The temperance-supporting *Daily Post* of 19 March, for example, congratulated the board for 'trying to rid the Everton Club of an influence that had apparently grown stronger year after year'. The *Liverpool Echo* argued that Houlding was both autocratic and patronising, a man who liked to lead his colleagues 'by the nose'. Not unreasonably, Houlding felt unjustly treated in these accounts, and he also proved something of a poor loser, obstructing the Everton officials as they tried to remove their property from Anfield. The ever-loyal *Liverpool Review* of 19 March offered its own, much more misty-eyed, assessment of Houlding's recent treatment and decline and his considerable contribution to the Everton club. In a lengthy editorial lament, entitled 'Houlding Kicked Offside', the *Review* also offered its views of the possible future for both Houlding and the now vacant Anfield ground:

Oh, football. There seems to be as much gratitude in you in so far as 'King Houlding' is concerned as there is in politics . . . Years ago, 'King Houlding' advanced the then struggling but rising Everton Football Club funds at a small rate of interest. He also assisted the organisation in other ways, for which the members were righteously thankful. As a landlord he lent the club a ground, at a moderate rental, to play on. He advanced money to erect grandstands and provide all the rest of the paraphernalia of a first-class football club. Things went on swimmingly and the Everton players made a name second to none, hardly, in the football world. Then came a change o'er the scene. Things were not what they seemed.

As the club prospered the rental of the ground was increased and the interest asked by the landlord for money advanced increased perceptively. There were mumblings and grumblings and finally the storm burst . . . The King has been kicked and the victorious host has elected to migrate to a fresh field and pastures new . . . All this is very sad and, a large number of onlookers think, very stupid . . . And it really is a pity that a man like 'King Houlding' should be mixed up in such an unseemly tangle as that which has been going on at Everton Football Club. Perhaps 'King Houlding' will run a new football club in the present ground at Oakfield Road? If he does, the migrators to the new ground in Goodison Road will have a rival to beat.

There was much to support in this spirited defence. After all, it was Houlding who had provided Everton with the use of the Anfield Road ground, and he had later followed it with loans at excellent rates for ground improvements. Now, as Everton began to achieve some financial success, he surely had a right to expect some return on his investment. But Houlding's sometimes lofty approach to the club's affairs, coupled with his brewing interests, had brought him into direct conflict with Liberal opponents on the Everton board, and at a time when politics in the city were changing.[6] Houlding was astute enough to know very well the importance of football to local politics in a bubbling working-class Victorian city such as Liverpool – which is one reason why he was determined to form *another* professional football club just as soon as he possibly could.

LIVERPOOL FC IS BORN – BUT REJECTED BY THE FOOTBALL LEAGUE

Though the *Liverpool Review* might have had an inside track on John Houlding's future plans, paradoxically, on 28 May 1892, it also criticised Houlding for spending just too much of his time on football-related business. But almost from the outset of the dispute at Anfield, King John seemed to have designs on forming a new club at Oakfield Road. After all, he had a ready-made football stadium at cost, and Anfield might offer the rump of a new supporter base, too. He could run the new club as he liked, without interference. After failing to hold on to the Everton name, Houlding arguably trumped his erstwhile colleagues by choosing a club name much more in keeping with modern times and the emerging town and *city* rivalries that were now keenly promoted by the Football League. Anticipating the use of the Orrell-owned land for other sports, he adopted the rather grand name of Liverpool Football Club and Athletic Grounds Company Limited. Typically, he charged his new club £100 in rent – this was still business after all – but then donated £500 to its empty coffers.

Unsurprisingly, Liverpool's new board would be largely free from the sorts of Liberal influence that had plagued Houlding at Everton, and it would also be Catholic-free, dominated by prominent local Conservatives, Protestant Unionists and Freemasons and people involved in overlapping local civic, political and business organisations. Initially, it also involved Houlding's son William and his son-in-law Thomas Knowles, who came from a Wigan family with brewing and mining interests. Out of the original forty-six subscribers who established Liverpool FC, seventeen were Freemasons, and of the original six directors of the club, four were of the same persuasion – between 1892 and 1914, fifteen out of twenty-three Liverpool directors were members of the Masonic order.[7] Houlding clearly wanted his own people around him. But, unlike the situation in Glasgow prior to the formation of Celtic FC, the existing major football clubs on Merseyside were never entirely closed to local Irish influence – both Liverpool and Everton had Irish shareholders. Despite the obvious marginalisation, and the discrimination aimed at the Liverpool Irish, the major football clubs in the city were never fated to carry quite the weight of sectarian identification and enmity as they would in Glasgow. There was also, partly as a consequence, no real groundswell of popular support in Liverpool for the specifically *Irish* football clubs that were formed in the city but which soon went under because of financial and organisational problems and lack of local support.[8]

A new football chapter was now beginning at Oakfield Road, Anfield. The embryonic Liverpool Football Club was born into a city with the keenest possible rivals any sporting club could possibly have: a club whose owners positively hated Liverpool FC's hierarchy and its politics, and who were now digging the foundations of a new stadium in a field less than a mile away. Everybody in the city of Liverpool knew this was going to be some sporting rivalry. The irrepressible Houlding immediately applied to the Football League for membership for his new Liverpool club. It seemed like perfect timing. For the 1892–93 season, the league was expanding from 14 to 16 clubs in the First Division, with the creation of a whole new Second Division made up of 12 clubs. On the face of it, then, possibly *fourteen* new league places were up for grabs, and none of the competition looked particularly strong. But the new Liverpool club was turned down flat by the league, on the mysterious grounds that they 'did not comply to regulations'.

What could this mean? The Liverpool stadium could not be at fault: it was first class for the time, with four seasons of First Division football already behind it. And Houlding had quickly sent John McKenna off to Scotland (where else?) to find a team worthy of playing league football for Liverpool. Merseyside certainly seemed well capable of supporting another Football League club, so there could be few complaints about Liverpool lacking a local spectator base. It has been suggested that Liverpool was rejected by the league because it refused to consider joining any competition other than the First Division.[9] But objections orchestrated by Houlding's opponents at Everton FC were probably the crucial factor in blocking Liverpool's application to join the Football League.[10]

The new football war in Liverpool had started – and it was already a dirty business. The men from the Football League also probably wanted to teach the uppity Houlding a lesson on Everton's behalf – Methodists stick together. But there were other factors involved. The Football League had a membership application for the Second Division from Bootle FC to consider. Accepting Bootle and holding up the new Liverpool Football Club probably carried some moral force with William McGregor and his Football League management committee. These must have seemed like the obvious cards to play. Finally, the Football League also wanted to expand *outside* of its original Lancashire/ Liverpool and Midlands bases, so accepting *three* clubs from the Merseyside area might have seemed a little excessive. So, in 1892, while rejecting Houlding's Liverpool, the Football League reached for the first time into Manchester, Cheshire, Lincolnshire and South Yorkshire for new members.

At Anfield, Houlding had kept with him at least a few loyal supporters from the old Everton club: directors Frank Brettle and Sam Crosbie went right back to the old Stanley Park days, and William Barclay and Edwin Berry had also stayed loyal to King John. But pretty much all the decent players had moved across to Goodison Park – they were, after all, contracted to the recent Football League champions. And who knew at what level the new Anfield club might be playing? With John McKenna ostensibly acting as main scout, player recruiter and club manager, there was at least the basis for the administration of a new football club, especially given some much needed time to sort things out while fiddling about in the Lancashire League. The Liverpool press was convinced that when the names of these new Anfield signings were revealed they would prove 'to include some of the best known and cleverest exponents of the game'. Time would tell.

THE TEAM OF THE MACS

The highly capable right-back Andrew Hannah had joined Everton in 1889 and had captained the side, winning a league-championship medal for Everton at Anfield in 1891. Now he signed for John McKenna and Liverpool, and he would be captain for them, too, a unique feat: captain of *both* of the senior Liverpool clubs when each was based at Anfield. Hannah was experienced, reliable and mentally strong and was still only 27 years old when he joined Liverpool in July 1892. He was a leader and just the sort of solid character required to offer continuity, backbone and on-field direction to the new Liverpool side. He played in front of Liverpool-born goalkeeper Sid Ross. On the left side of defence was an ex-Everton and Scotland international full-back, the 'flaming, big burly' Duncan McLean, a no-nonsense, wide-of-girth stopper described later as a 'champion back' in the Football League. Joe McQue, a 22-year-old centre-half from Glasgow, was signed by McKenna from Celtic's reserves. Good in the air, he liked to score the occasional goal (14 in 142 appearances), but his main strength was in his defensive resolve: Liverpool would concede only 18 goals in their first season in the Second Division of the Football League in 1893–94, with McQue invariably a formidable barrier at the back.

From Leith Athletic, McKenna picked up the McQueen brothers, Matt and Hugh. Half-back Matt McQueen eventually played one hundred and three times for Liverpool whilst winning two Second Division titles in the process. He was an extraordinarily versatile player, an intelligent man who could play anywhere – including 20 times in goal for Liverpool in the Football League. He later qualified as a referee. A real Liverpool servant, McQueen later became a Liverpool director and also managed the club to the 1923 league title before ill health forced his retirement. Unlike Matt, younger brother Hugh, a clever winger with an accurate shot, was something of a maverick off the field. He once leapt from a Southport springboard during a Liverpool training camp and had to be hauled out of the water spluttering for breath – he couldn't swim. John McCartney, a tough-tackling, elegant-passing ex-cotton worker from Ayrshire, anchored the Liverpool midfield for five years until he left for New Brighton Tower, and another Scot, right-winger Tom Wyllie, came from Everton and was reputedly Liverpool FC's first professional player. Malcolm

McVean signed as a semi-professional from Third Lanark and played in all five forward positions for the Liverpool club between 1892 and 1897. He scored in Liverpool's first competitive fixture, in 1892, and also claimed the club's first Football League goal, in September 1893, in a 2–0 victory over Middlesbrough Ironopolis. He died, still a young man, in 1907.

The city of Liverpool to which these Scottish signings had migrated echoed aspects of Glasgow and its environs. Although not quite hosting the pernicious sectarian divide that existed north of the border, Catholic v. Protestant riots were still a pretty routine feature of Liverpool life. However, a survey of one hundred and six houses in the Everton area in January 1893 found that only four heads of households claimed any connection with church or chapel. Meanwhile, the Broughton Terrace mosque and its members in Liverpool were routinely attacked by so-called 'respectable' Christians. One unfortunate Muslim worshipper was stabbed in the face.

While poverty and squalor continued to characterise much of the north end of the city, the Scottish-rooted Liverpool Caledonian football club was now established at 'a grand ground' at Woodcroft Park in Wavertree in the south of the city. It was reported in the local press to represent 'Scotia's sons in Liverpool'. Caledonian were obviously well backed, and they were reportedly 'determined to make the winter game in Liverpool their own' as the game expanded. 'Football in Liverpool is rapidly becoming a national kind of business,' reported the *Liverpool Review* in an editorial on 11 June 1892. From £2 a week or up to £300 a year – 'and for eight months' work only' – Liverpool FC's own agents were reported by the local press to be seeking a nucleus of a new team north of the border among the 'Scottish Professors', 'to the extent of £1,000 for the season'.

The *Review* calculated that Scotland might provide up to one-quarter of the new Liverpool FC team – it would be much more, of course – and thus that as much as £4,000 would be needed to pay for the whole of John McKenna's squad. Here was serious money being spent on sport. Cue a new local media panic about football wages and 'foreign' players in the city: 'Football appears to pay professional players better than running a bank,' complained the *Liverpool Review*. All this was before Liverpool FC had even played its first friendly fixture. The *Liverpool Review* editorial continued with questions about 'outsiders' and wages that would still be asked in press columns and public houses in the city and elsewhere almost 120 years later:

> How long is this kind of thing to go on? Liverpool is very fond of football,
> but are local football devotees likely to pay for it at this price? Next season

we will have Everton, the Liverpool Caledonians, Liverpool and Bootle in full swing as the leading quartet of local clubs, besides many smaller fry. In nearly every football club of any pretensions, some, if not all, of the players are paid. It is no exaggeration to say that Liverpool's football bill for players during the 1892–93 season will reach to between £12,000 and £15,000. And the men who will take the vast bulk of the coin will be Scotchmen, who are still *the* exponents of the game. That is Liverpool football up to date.

A few days later, the *Review* concluded, glumly, that 'footballers are becoming of more importance than prime ministers'. John Houlding was reported to be prepared to pay his new recruits some £300 a year on average, which the newspaper equated, uncertainly, to the extraordinary payment of three shillings a minute for their football services. Local charities were also argued to be losing money as football crowds grew: 'Do the coppers and the sixpences now go to princely paid footballers?' it asked. The *Review* reminded its readers that Liverpool was an impoverished city full of 'ragged urchins' and neglected 'offal', a place where 'children of the gutter huddle together hungry and unwashed'. Officially, the average proportion of paupers to population in Liverpool was one in twenty-four, compared to one in sixty-one for the county, and one in forty-one for the whole of England and Wales. The city, it was claimed locally, was invaded in 1892 by 'habitual drunks, indigent paupers from foreign lands and . . . stowaway sailors', not to mention prostitutes in the guise of the alleged '10,000 loose women of Liverpool'. Could such wages for mere footballers be justified alongside this kind of want, chaos and depravity?

By 27 August 1892, a 'Liverpool Football War' was predicted in the local press. The four premier local clubs now began to take shape, thus replacing the tired old Everton–Bootle duopoly as the new Goodison Park was officially opened for business. 'War will be waged until the end of April. How many dead and wounded there will be during the eight months of carnage remains to be seen.' Clearly, tabloid newspaper reporting styles pre-date the rise of the rapacious British red tops. 'Everybody is talking about it,' continued the *Liverpool Review*, arguing strongly that football had a unique cross-class appeal in the city: 'The mechanic is as enthusiastic as the hobbledehoy and the schoolboy. Practice games on the several grounds during the past few nights have been followed with unwonted, almost feverish, excitement. How tenaciously will the actual warfare be followed?' How tenaciously, indeed.

AN EVERTON AND LIVERPOOL FOOTBALL TAKEOVER

On Thursday, 1 September 1892, Liverpool, playing in blue-and-white quarters, hosted Midland League champions Rotherham Town in a friendly match, the club's first-ever fixture at Anfield. Would anyone turn up to see Houlding's new project, especially after all the antagonism at Everton? Despite the new club's claim that 'no better game will be held in any plot in the neighbourhood', Anfield contained no more than a handful of curious fans, who witnessed a 7–1 home drubbing of the visitors.[11] Preston's Higher Walton club was Liverpool's first Lancashire League opponents just two days later. A couple of hundred local supporters turned up to watch an 8–0 Liverpool landslide. There were no *English* players in the Liverpool team, let alone any Scousers. Perhaps this was one of the reasons why the fans were staying away. But with two points gained and fifteen home goals scored in two fixtures, it was not for the lack of entertainment that home support was still reluctant. But things can soon change in football.

Middlesbrough Ironopolis crushed an outclassed Liverpool 0–5 in their next away fixture, another friendly match. It was a result mitigated for the Liverpool press by a 'railway journey of 140 miles and a heavy meal afterwards . . . not exactly the kind of things to prepare eleven men for an hour and a half of football'. It seemed like a fair point.

'The football madness has again bitten us badly – *very* badly this year,' commented an overheated *Liverpool Review* on 10 September 1892, noting that as far as spectators were concerned 'on present form, Everton and the Caledonians appear to have the pull'. This may have been because, according to the press at least, 'spectators on the Everton ground have made some mutual compact not to support the Liverpool club when playing away, but to patronise Bootle'.

Cunning John Houlding had his own plans to overcome these negative sentiments from across Stanley Park. Recalling his very modest origins in the north end of the city where he had once 'bathed in pits' with other local boys, he sent complimentary Anfield season tickets 'to a number of gentlemen who, for the past few years, have done their best towards assisting association football in Liverpool and the neighbourhood'. He was using his 'common touch' again to try to launch his new football club, as well as attempting to revive his ailing political career. This marketing strategy might even have helped do the trick, because later in September a remarkable 6,000 fans (it was probably more like 4,000) were reported by the Liverpool press to have turned up at a match at Anfield. In December 1892, some 4,000 fans were present to watch the visitors Blackpool claim the first away victory against

Liverpool at Anfield, a 0–2 defeat for their hosts. This was hardly a shock. The Seasiders had already crushed the Reds on the northern coast by an even more convincing score of 0–3.

Despite this first deflating home loss, the crowd figures suggested that perhaps the new football club at Oakfield Road really did have a future in the city. Indeed, estimated average crowds at Liverpool in this first Lancashire League championship season reached a very healthy 5,217, compared to 13,230 at First Division Everton. The average gate for Everton had also actually *grown* by 3,000 from the previous season, suggesting that most Evertonians had remained just that: loyal to Everton. A substantial proportion of the crowds now following Liverpool were probably entirely *new* football fans, or perhaps football supporters who had previously followed other local clubs in the city.

'At all events,' the *Liverpool Review* commented on Liverpool FC in its first season, 'the team is growing in public favour. All the unsportsmanlike talk about "boycott" is likely to be falsified. And why should it not?' Moreover, all the Liverpool FC company shares had been taken up, and the Anfield ground was now owned freehold, meaning that the new club's financial position 'need scarcely be discussed'. John Houlding had exactly what he wanted: undisputed control of a financially sound football club, which was also potentially a popular political base. Prestigious southern clubs, such as the public-school Corinthians, were already turning to the barely established Liverpool Football Club for their lucrative friendly fixtures in the area. 'How is it, may I ask,' mused 'Centre' rhetorically in the *Liverpool Review*, 'that the Corinthians approached *Liverpool* before Everton for dates? Are the ex-champions of the league getting into bad repute?'

All of this conjecture and 'puffing up' of Liverpool FC must have really riled Everton and their followers. As must another local story: that the Goodison club was making a 'handsome present' to a local pressman who had 'materially assisted in the club's welfare'. This reporter must surely be 'the best scribe at the game in this district', stated Centre, archly. Were the mighty Everton really trying to *buy* local press favours in the face of the early successes of these Anfield upstarts?

Everton sensitivities were also on show in the anger expressed when the two club committees could not agree on the venue for the annual Christmas theatrical charity match to be played in the city in 1892 to raise funds for local hospitals. The match, involving top local players, had previously been played at Anfield, of course. But then it had always been hosted by Everton – who, not unreasonably as the senior club, now wanted it staged at their new Goodison Park home. A reported 'slanging match' ensued between the rival committees, with Everton resisting any compromise suggestion from Houlding that the fixture should now be staged at a neutral venue, or even at each of the major grounds in alternate years. The affair was dubbed 'childishly absurd' and 'football foolery' by the *Liverpool Review*, which concluded that 'the selfishness seems to be largely on the side of the Everton committee'. The enmity between Mahon's followers and Houlding and his allies was obviously holding fast.

By this early stage, too, King John told the local press that the new Liverpool already had 30 players to call upon, with 16 reported to be of 'first XI' potential. This strong squad was now starting to perform, even beating the mighty Aston Villa in Birmingham in a friendly fixture on a Monday early in November 1892, thus producing a reported 'great rejoicing' on the Anfield side of the city.

As Liverpool FC grew ever more powerful, and especially as its rather spiteful rivalry with Everton began to capture the local public imagination, so the other two clubs among the premier four in the city – Bootle FC and Liverpool Caledonian – began to fall on harder times. Caledonian could not even make it intact to Christmas 1892, with much of its traditional local Scottish support now draining towards the developing 'team of the Macs' over at Anfield. Bootle resigned from the Football League the following year. Liverpool FC had also had the advantage over these two rivals inasmuch as the population around the Anfield stadium showed a sizeable proportion of residents drawn from the relatively affluent middle and lower-middle classes, key constituencies in building up support for early professional football clubs.[12] In short, the residential site for Bootle FC probably lacked some of the crucial demographics for sustainable Victorian football-club growth, which depended initially more on the presence and patronage of clerks and bookkeepers than it did on the keenness of manual workers.

Evidence of the scale of early travelling football support, of rival fan exchanges and also of the growing interest in football among the higher classes in the city was provided by the *Liverpool Review* of 11 February 1893, on the eve of First Division Everton hosting Nottingham Forest:

> At about midday, a tram heavily laden with Notts. Forest supporters, each sporting the colours of the club and each supporter cheering loudly, was proceeding along Dale Street, where a number of gentlemen in tall hats and frock coats raised a counter-shout. Of course, this led to a lot of good-natured banter, which was at once exceedingly diverting and a good advertisement for the match. Gentleman from 'Change are, just at present, taking an hilarious interest in football matters.

These obviously well-heeled local gentlemen from the Liverpool Exchange financial district might even have attended this Everton fixture, where it was reported that 'a well-known local bookmaker' had promised local players a £5 note if they won: they did. Not that working people and the poor were excluded from involvement in the sport in the city – far from it. Some attended matches, and at least they could all *play* a form of football. The Liverpool press was soon complaining, for example, that the previously harmless 'improvised footballs of paper and rags tightly tied with cord' were now being replaced on Liverpool streets by 'stones converted into footballs'. The local urchins of Merseyside must have their sport, too.

A fine Lancashire League unbeaten run meant that Liverpool could still edge ahead of Blackpool as champions if they could just defeat Southport Central away in their last fixture. In a chaotic scene familiar to all Sunday footballers, the match was delayed by 40 minutes because no match official turned up. A local spectator was eventually persuaded to take charge, but the visitors could manage only a 1–1 draw. No matter: Blackpool also failed to win, and, on goal average (sixty-six for, nineteen against), Liverpool FC won its first title in its first season, winning seventeen out of twenty-two matches, losing three (two to Blackpool) and finishing top of the Lancashire League with thirty-six points.

There was only the small matter of the Liverpool Cup final left – which, after sweetly defeating Bootle 1–0 in the semi-final, Liverpool played out against 'a mixed team of the renowned Everton organisation' in an early example of player rotation. Everton, in fact, were also committed to playing a lucrative friendly at Renton in Scotland on the same day, so their resources were inevitably stretched. Despite training at Hoylake on a mixture of 'teetotalism, good living, skipping rope and golf', Everton's first team had already contested, and lost, the 1893 FA Cup final (0–1 to Wolves) at Fallowfield, Manchester, in chaotic circumstances. There were crowd incursions, and the press and FA dignitaries were harried from their seats by some of the estimated 60,000 present. The *Daily Post* of 1 April 1893 was justifiably scathing about the facilities offered by their near neighbours and regional city rivals, and about the hapless FA arrangements for the final: 'They should have taken precautions . . . and had something more than matchwood barricades and a handful of "dummies" in blue to protect the field and the players from invasion.' The Liverpool press was also angry – and not for the last time – about a football-induced rise in rail fares, this time from Liverpool to Manchester, and about the FA putting profit – 'a commercial affair to make a pot of money out of' – before the safety and comfort of fans. The men from Merseyside had made their point: Goodison Park would host the next FA Cup final, in 1894, for the first and last time.

The Liverpool Cup final, the first competitive Everton v. Liverpool derby, was blighted by another issue: accusations by Everton of foul play and refereeing ineptitude. How little really changes in the game. Liverpool won the cup 1–0 in a decidedly rugged affair, the goal scored by Tom Wyllie. Everton were denied a possible penalty and angrily lodged an immediate protest 'against the general incompetence of the referee'.[13] The cup was not presented because of this determined and sour response and the inquiry that followed, thus short-circuiting planned celebrations at the Sandon Hotel, with a beaming John Houlding eager to hold court. Everton lost much public support for their transparently surly attitude. 'It was rather paltry of them,' concluded the *Liverpool Review*, 'to protest against the referee in the match and so spoil the victor's chance of carrying the cup in triumph off the ground. A waggonette and four, I believe, was waiting for the winning team and cup.' The Liverpool horses would have to delay, although Everton's protest was eventually overruled and the trophy finally ended up in the Sandon Hotel after all. But this was not the story's end. Perhaps some light-fingered Evertonians could still not accept this inaugural derby defeat, because both the Lancashire League and Liverpool cups were soon stolen, with Liverpool Football Club forced to cough up £127 to replace them. It was a sad (and expensive) end to a highly promising first season of competitive football for John Houlding's new sporting concern. His ambitions for his new club continued to burn brightly.

THE FOOTBALL FEVER FINISHED IN LIVERPOOL?

Lancashire League football was a start, right enough, but Houlding and McKenna had much bigger plans. The latter 'allowed his Irish impulses to carry him away' in 1893 by applying for membership of the Second Division of the Football League.[14] In fact, the timing was just right: Rotherham Town and Newcastle United had already been elected into the Second Division, and, aiming for two sections of sixteen clubs each, the Football League had advertised for two more clubs to join. Within a few days, Liverpool, Woolwich Arsenal, Middlesbrough Ironopolis, Doncaster Rovers and Loughborough all applied, with Woolwich Arsenal joining Liverpool as the league's choices, thus including two clubs from the same city and expanding the competition into the south for the first time. This was a brave move, considering the travelling costs to London for other clubs, but it was also a vital one if the Football League was ever to be considered a truly national affair.[15] Ironopolis would get their chance of league football after all when Accrington later resigned, and when struggling Bootle FC collapsed because of financial pressures this scotched the league plan for symmetry between the two divisions: it would be a sixteen-club First Division but a fifteen-club second section for 1893–94.

Bootle FC's sad demise could only strengthen Liverpool FC locally, of course. Anfield was now the undisputed second football base in the city. The failure of local clubs even produced alarming 'THE FOOTBALL FEVER FINISHED' headlines in the Liverpool press in May, though the *Liverpool Review* used the local vernacular to reassure its readers: 'Football – it's a gran' game chiel, ye ken an. In Leverpule the people are fair gone crazy o'it.' Which, translated, meant that football had not lost its hold on the Liverpool public. The *Review* also argued that it was actually a good thing that Houlding and Everton had been at such divisive loggerheads in 1892 because the new Goodison Park was 'perfection . . . accommodation unrivalled and supreme'. The city now had two first-class football stadiums instead of just one.

Culturally, at this time, Liverpool and its surrounds were an extraordinary mix. The city's civic fathers were committed to providing a typically Victorian range of cultural exercises and excursions, including museums, galleries, lectures and the theatre, all aimed at the moral and social 'improvement' of its better-off citizens. Working people also had their leisure pursuits, of course – including sport – so it would be wrong to paint a picture of working-class life that was too bleak or dismal.[16] It was often gently philanthropic purveyors of working-class leisure, such as the brewer A.B. Walker, who also donated funds for local elite cultural provision, in this case in the shape of the splendid new Walker Art Gallery.[17]

Liverpool's streets were still routinely depicted as being populated at night by roguish young 'Dicky Sams', vagabonds, thieves and wretched drunks. The inebriated antics of late-night engine drivers and guards on the Liverpool trains caused one local letter writer to have 'trembled for his own life and that of fellow passengers'. 'Brutal Bootle' had a measly 64 police officers to cope with its widespread drunken violence and burglary. The New Year's Eve celebrations in Liverpool in the early 1890s also brought press complaints about inebriated men and women who were colourfully reported to be 'indulging in conduct from which even a Mexican nigger might have shrunk'.

The local police in Liverpool often seemed little better disposed than some of the excitable football supporters, street ruffians or drunkards they were supposedly patrolling. In May 1893, an indignant letter to the *Liverpool Review* recalled a genial Liverpool constable who offered the reader a yuletide drink. 'While struggling to pull a large bottle out of his coat-tail pocket,' the correspondent reported, 'he suddenly slipped on the frozen pavement and sat in the gutter. The bottle smashed with a loud noise, and the only remaining whisky was in the lining of his pocket.' So much, it seems, for the sobriety of the law.

Also in May that year (1893), the drink flowed in the Sandon Hotel when John Houlding, 'the lion at the evening', finally got his hands on the Lancashire League cup (albeit briefly). Liverpool Football Club meanwhile had strengthened for the winter challenges that lay ahead by signing Patrick Gordon, a right-sided forward, from Everton's reserves, Jimmy Stott, a Darlington-born goal-hungry striker from Middlesbrough who scored 14 goals in just 17 Liverpool appearances, and Scottish utility forward Davy Henderson, with whom Stott briefly formed a useful striking partnership. But most important of all turned out to be the signing of Liverpool-born Thomas 'Harry' Bradshaw from Cheshire's Northwich Victoria, a dashing left-sided attacking winger who would play 138 league and FA Cup games for the club, scoring 53 times.

After so many imported journeymen, Harry Bradshaw was the first authentic locally born hero of the Liverpool supporters. No wonder the Merseyside crowds loved him. The historian Thomas Preston has shown that between 1893 and 1914 only 10.7 per cent of Liverpool's players actually came from the Liverpool area – an average of about one local player in each Reds team. This early history puts into perspective complaints today about a Liverpool club with too few Scousers. Forty-six per cent of Reds players came from Scotland, especially from the football hotbed mining areas of Dumbartonshire. Everton recruited fewer Scots (36 per cent) and only slightly more locals (15 per cent).[18]

Signing for Liverpool also meant good prospects of a public-house tenancy for players on retirement – a favourite with veterans – because of the local influence in the brewing business of John Houlding. But there would be no pub to run for Bradshaw. Scandalously, the local man played but once for England – being callously dropped after a 6–0 demolition of Northern Ireland. Harry would score many crucial goals for his club before eventually leaving for Spurs after almost five years of fruitful service. But like many Victorian players his football career was tragically brief, his retirement non-existent: Bradshaw died of consumption in 1899, aged just 26 years.

A 2–0 debut Liverpool win at fellow Football League new boys Ironopolis was followed by the first Liverpool FC Football League match at Anfield, a 4–0 victory over Lincoln City, with the hosts famously fielding eight 'Macs'. There were plenty of Liverpool-based Scots present, boosting the home crowd, reported to be around the 5,000 mark. At the next home league match (v. Small Heath), the crowd continued to grow with late arrivals, and up to 8,000 finally saw Liverpool turn around 3–1 up and add two more second-half goals with no reply. Three matches, three wins: this league football must have looked easy for the 'Houlding satellites' as they were described locally. As the *Liverpool Review* put it on 16 September 1893, referring to match-day transport chaos as the football thrived, 'The old Anfield glories may be revived and the traffic once again goes crashing up London Road.' Liverpool remained serene and unbeaten in the league into the new year. They had lost only one of twenty-six games in total, and this a prestigious 'friendly' fixture against formidable Football League founder members Preston North End.

The city of Liverpool at this time was rapidly becoming a national centre for sport. Over one weekend in January 1894, the Rugby International Board met on Merseyside and then the management committee of the Football League convened there. 'When Liverpool [FC] gets into the First Division,' commented the *Liverpool Review*, 'we shall be even a bigger football centre than Sheffield, which is at present the only town possessing two first league clubs.' In fact, the combined gates of Liverpool and Everton were *already* larger than those combined in Sheffield. Everton's match attendances were bigger than anywhere else in England (which probably meant the world), and Liverpool's were growing fast. The city was already looking like the world capital for football and would soon host the sport's biggest club fixture of them all, the FA Cup final.

Ever alert for a bit of helpful publicity, on 18 January 1894 John Houlding hosted a dinner for his unbeaten Liverpool team and club officials 'when the harmony which exists between players, committees and president was very happily exemplified'. Liverpool FC presented its leader with a silver kettle, lamp and stand, in a near-parody of public self-promotion and congratulation. 'No wonder,' commented a clearly smitten *Liverpool Review*, 'the Liverpool Football Club carry all before them in the league when the members are privately so well in league with each other.' It was more free media blather for the club. In February, Liverpool FC showed its growing stature, if not its class, by paying fellow Second Division club Grimsby Town £100 to relocate their home FA Cup tie against Liverpool to Anfield, where a reported 'seven or eight thousand people lined the enclosure'. Town paid heavily for their greed, with a 3–0 win for Liverpool in a wind-ruined encounter, one notable for an unusual loss of temper for the generally unflappable Reds captain Andy Hannah.

Everton's brave FA Cup defeat at Stoke City came with complaints that the referee – a Mr Kingscott – could not keep pace with the game and so missed vital penalty claims within the 12-yard area, then in place across the full width of the pitch. Why not, asked the Liverpool press, forward looking as always, 'appoint a couple of sub-referees whose sole duty it shall be to watch the play . . . within each of the 12-yard lines?' One hundred and fifteen years later, in

2009, UEFA would finally take notice of Merseyside on this score, at least for Europa League matches.

At home against bottom club Northwich Victoria on 3 February 1894, a puny crowd, barely enough to populate the goal ends, turned out to see Liverpool triumph 4–1. Many more locals were watching Everton's *reserve* games. Liverpool FC, clearly, still had plenty of ground to make up, and their fans might have been bored by its poor opposition. But here at least one could detect the first signs of the legendary wit and playfulness of Anfield crowds. The club's supporters followed the goals and tried, gallantly – as they would have to do over many years to come – to create some energy and interest out of a miserably uneven encounter. According to the *Liverpool Review*, 'So one-sided was the game that it was taken quite humorously by the spectators, and the visitors had to undergo a lot of ironical comments in the way of shouts to "play up".' The report went on to describe the voluntary evacuation of the away-goal end at the interval, leaving the Liverpool goalkeeper abandoned. 'It was amazing to notice how at half-time the sightseers all emigrated, as one man, in the direction of the Northwich goal leaving McOwen, who might have played skittles on the halfway line had he so chosen.'

Things were very different when Liverpool next hosted, because the match was against Preston North End in the second round of the FA Cup, drawing an 18,000 crowd. The Anfield pitch barriers were broken down in half a dozen places, but 'very good humouredly, the crowd did not interfere with play and violate the game as a cup tie'. This general orderliness was to be the Liverpool Way over many years to come. More than £450 was taken at the turnstiles, a club record. 'Here, ladies and gentlemen,' said the *Review* grandly, 'is something significant to con over. Is the Liverpool organisation to, at last, mount the financial rudder, as they have already done in form?' The match was played in 'typical Liverpool Football Club weather', wind and rain, and contained 'some very earnest, not to say rough, play'. The crowd was described as 'quite divided' in its partisanship, leading the local press to speculate that opposing Evertonians might have been present. In fact, Everton had arranged a friendly home fixture at the same time with Sheffield United at Goodison Park to act as a spoiler for Liverpool's great day and to try to hold on to their own support. Liverpool scored early on through David Henderson and then McVean, but North End replied to make it 2–1 at the interval. The visitors 'meant serious business' after the break and soon equalised through Frank Becton, but a centre to Henderson produced the Liverpool winner: 3–2. This was a huge moment. 'Last Saturday,' said Centre in the local press later, 'Liverpool quite extinguished Everton in the public interest. It was indeed a novelty to find an overflow Anfield audience seeking refuge and entertainment at Goodison Park.' People locked out at Liverpool FC? Supporters moping over at Everton? What next?

The major local security concern in the city of Liverpool in 1894 was about the possible presence of anarchists and the danger of 'dynamiters lurking around'. But Everton's chief concern was something almost equally explosive: it was about their neighbours' rapid rise and the Reds' possible promotion and FA Cup double. Everton's play was already described locally as 'clever, scientific and fascinating' compared to the more rough-edged, prosaic approach of Liverpool. These labels would endure. But the Anfield club was certainly challenging the traditional Blue ascendancy. Missing both Henderson and Jim McBride, a 'large and enthusiastic following' from Liverpool paid two shillings from Exchange Station on a football-excursion train to the next FA Cup match. It was to no avail: in a bog at Bolton Wanderers the Reds' FA Cup run hit the buffers, with a sobering 0–3 defeat. Nevertheless, the prospects for Liverpool promotion were exciting local football followers in the city, and even the Everton board might have perked up at the promise of raised gate receipts with Liverpool FC as direct rivals the following season. The 'Linesman' welcomed the Red advance in the local press, but he did so in strangely Alan Partridge-like tones:

> Verily, Liverpool proceeds apace. It is all for the best. We can easily support two first class football organisations in Liverpool and healthy rivalry will begat better fare. Anfield at Everton, and Everton at Anfield – in First League games. Aha! Aha! Commence to save up your three-penny bits my brethren, for there are joyful things in store for us, and the prices may be raised.

Raised prices for football would certainly be an issue in the Merseyside FA Cup final year of 1894.

LIVERPOOL: FA CUP FINAL CITY

Perhaps promotion for Liverpool to the First Division would bring more efficient match-programme sales at Anfield? The local press certainly hoped so: they relied on local urchins to provide a 'Bill of Play' on match days, but complained that these young 'demons' were never on the right side of the ground. In fact, all of the city of Liverpool would need to raise its organisational game soon, because towards the end of March 1894 the city would offer all that was best in popular culture and sport in a single weekend. It was, arguably, the greatest sporting and entertainment weekend so far in the life of any provincial English city. The world-famous Grand National meeting in racing was hosted at nearby Aintree, the FA Cup final in football was played out at Goodison Park, and versions of *HMS Pinafore* and *Cinderella* ran to packed houses at the city's main theatres. Football in the city was positively booming: in six Liverpool and Everton home matches over four days during the Easter period between 23 and 26 March 1894, an unprecedented 59,000 people attended. 'These have been record times,' confirmed the Linesman. 'The city has never shown so well in the football firmament as it has during the last fortnight . . . If this kind of thing goes on Liverpool will be the greatest football centre in the kingdom.'

The city of Liverpool was a veritable kaleidoscope of colours and cultures at this time: from the 'courtly nobles, knights and dames' who mingled with 'the common herd' on Grand National day, in what was as much a social carnival as a mere race meeting;[19] to the sharp Liverpool street pedlars who showed their enterprise by knocking out exotic tortoises from flat-topped barrows; the finery and pomp of the city theatre crowds; and the loud revelry and public display of the football enthusiasts from Nottinghamshire (Notts County) and Lancashire (Bolton Wanderers) who descended on Goodison Park in 1894 for the only Merseyside FA Cup final.

Moving *out* of Liverpool, meanwhile, as if to remind observers of the city's continuing core problems of poverty and destitution in the face of all this sporting carnival and consumption, were 420 boys and 430 girls who had been 'snatched from poverty and crime by various agencies' and were now embarking from the dockside to Canada in search of better lives. The charitable John Houlding had established the Fazackerly College Homes for Children in the city, and he would later visit these young Merseyside exports in Canada, taking a large tin of Everton toffees with him to remind them of home. Charity clearly has its limits. If there were 'fewer broad acres preserved for the rich,' the *Liverpool Review* observed wisely, 'such wholesale migration might be unnecessary'.

Despite apparent local enthusiasm aplenty, Merseyside's only FA Cup final was a cruel disappointment. Two poorly supported and low-quality sides (Notts County were below Liverpool in the Second Division, and Bolton had recently been well beaten by Everton) produced a one-sided contest (4–1 to County), a gate of only 23,000 and paltry receipts of £1,300. The Liverpool press knew the game was up right away and claimed, mischievously, that nearby Manchester's advantage in this respect was that it was 'not so satiated with first-class football and consequently are not so exacting in their demands'. Ticket prices were deemed locally to be 'absurd', but even the one-shilling areas of the ground were not filled for the final. This drew local comment that football fans in the city were lamentably narrow followers of their *clubs* rather than the game at large. But the *Daily Post* probably had it about right when it observed on 7 April 1894 that it was impossible 'to tempt the people to pay an especially high fee to see the "Trotters" get thrashed by a Second Division club, as the public had pretty much made up their minds they would be'. An unbalanced FA Cup contest could not overcome local affiliation. The city of Liverpool, it seemed, had had its chance for FA Cup glory, and, in the direst of circumstances, it was deemed by the elites at the FA to have failed to deliver.

UNBEATEN – BUT ONLY JUST

Intense *local* football affinities were soon to the fore once more on Merseyside, especially at Goodison Park on 7 April 1894. On the same day, thus far unbeaten Second Division Liverpool were 0–2 down at Burslem Port Vale. This latest score was posted by a reporter in front of the press box at Goodison, to predictably loud cheers from gloating Evertonians. At that same moment, 'numerous obstreperous gamins' openly celebrated the fact that all-conquering Liverpool had apparently 'been knocked'. In fact, the Reds later recovered with goals from McVean and Matt McQueen to draw 2–2, thus saving their proud league record. 'What a grim spirit of antagonism there is even now,' concluded the *Liverpool Review*, 'between the supporters of Goodison and Anfield.' The incident had repercussions later when the winning Liverpool result in the post-season Test match (between the top Second Division and bottom First Division club to decide on the promotion/relegation issue) was *not* posted by the press at Goodison Park. Enraged Everton fans now surged to the press box and accused the reporters of cowardice – for being too afraid to put up a *positive* Liverpool scoreline. This was all too much for the Goodison correspondent from the *Liverpool Review*, who commented, 'How contemptible is the attitude which the Everton people are taking up in regard to Liverpool – an attitude so unsportsmanlike that no amount of argument and sophistry can explain it away . . . The Everton officials should remember that the hallmark of a gentleman lies in the fact that he even treats his supposed inferiors with respect.'

Today, this would seem overly alarmist, even priggish: the application of a highly moralistic middle-class tone to (mainly) working men who were clearly beginning to identify strongly with their own football clubs. In so doing, these Blues supporters were developing a predictable antipathy towards the fate of their near neighbours and rivals in a city that undoubtedly had something of a 'democratic swagger' derived from its sea trading, but in which quite extreme forms of localism were also already defining features.[20] Unbeaten Liverpool would soon join Everton in the top tier. But not before a huge scare. Facing Burslem, once more, in their final Second Division league fixture at Anfield, a clearly nervous Liverpool soon went behind to a goal scored from midfield that deceived goalkeeper McOwen – 'a terrible and most surprising shot'. Liverpool then laid siege to the Port Vale goal, but they could not score, until a 'scrimmage' occurred on the visitors' goal-line, providing 'a dangerous and unedifying' spectacle.

The scrimmage was something akin to a ruck in modern rugby but was then a staple part of association football. Eventually, both teams' players 'piled on top of each other in a struggling, kicking and also a fighting mass', the ball lying somewhere beneath them. The referee allowed this quite legal affair to continue for some two minutes, causing spectators to 'gasp in dismay'. He then blew up in despair at ever seeing the leather again, deciding on a drop ball right on the Burslem goal-line. This was simply a recipe, surely, for another ball-obscuring mass brawl, but something else occurred. The referee 'threw up the ball in the middle of the twenty-one men and after a report like a gun, into the net it went and the Liverpool record was saved'. It was the unlikely figure of Reds captain Andrew Hannah who had rescued the day, scoring his only ever goal for the club in the process. Liverpool scored another late goal, through McQue, to win the match 2–1.

It was extraordinary that no player was badly injured here, because the very real dangers of playing football at this time should not be underestimated. A correspondent to the *Liverpool Review* on 21 April 1894, for example, reported on 341 football 'accidents' during the current season, with 24 ending in death. No such list was compiled for football in Liverpool, but football mortalities were still depressingly routine affairs in Britain.

So, for the first and only time in its history, Liverpool FC would finish a season unbeaten in the Football League. Not even Bob Paisley would achieve this feat. The new league club had won every home match and had drawn just six out of twenty-eight fixtures, ending up eight points clear of second-placed Small Heath. But Liverpool still had to beat the First Division's bottom club, Newton Heath, in a one-off Test match to confirm their promotion. The contest, at Ewood Park, Blackburn, in front of 5,000 fans, was comfortable enough, with Matt McQueen 'as cool and safe as a cold-store brick building' and McLean 'practically faultless' hitting a free-kick deflected in by Pat Gordon, later added to by Bradshaw's 'low, lightning shot' for a routine 2–0 Reds win. As the *Liverpool Review* pointed out, the celebrations for this first Liverpool FC title in the Football League were suitably exuberant:

Needless to say, there were great rejoicings among the Liverpool contingent after the victory and on arriving at Tithebarn Street station the team was met by an enormously big and correspondingly enthusiastic crowd. Different players were carried shoulder high to their special conveyance and after lubrication at the Alexandra Hotel the men drove off to the Sandon, where another tremendous reception awaited them ... The team have done wonders; so, indeed, have the committee and officials of the club.

The truth was that for all their magnificent Football League record, this Liverpool team had been mainly functional and determined in the Second Division, with a well organised defence (only six goals conceded in fourteen home fixtures) and an inconsistent if resolute attack. After the Reds had impressively seen off Preston North End in the FA Cup, First Division Bolton Wanderers had quite casually crushed Liverpool in the next round. Did the club really have the necessary quality to survive higher up the embryonic football food chain? It would, as it turned out, prove to be a very difficult test indeed.

CHAPTER 2 REFERENCES

1. Physick, *Played in Liverpool*, pp. 84–7
2. Corbett, *Everton: The School of Science*
3. Kennedy and Collins, 'Community Politics in Liverpool and the Governance of Professional Football in the Late Nineteenth Century', p. 768
4. Kennedy and Collins, p. 776
5. Kennedy, 'Locality and Professional Football Club Development', p. 383
6. Kennedy and Collins, p. 788
7. Kennedy, 'Class, Ethnicity and Civic Governance', p. 847
8. Kennedy and Kennedy, 'Ambiguity, Complexity and Convergence: The Evolution of Liverpool's Irish Football Clubs'
9. Taylor, *The Leaguers*, p. 7
10. Inglis, *League Football and the Men Who Made It*, p. 25
11. Wilson, *All Change at Anfield*, p. 2
12. Kennedy, 'Locality and Professional Football Club Development', p. 384
13. Young, *Football on Merseyside*, p. 45
14. Young, *Football on Merseyside*, p. 46
15. Inglis, *League Football and the Men Who Made It*, p. 31
16. Pooley, 'Living in Liverpool: The Modern City', p. 236
17. Milne, 'Maritime Liverpool', p. 289

18. Preston, 'The Origins and Development of Association Football in the Liverpool District *c.*1879–*c.*1915', p. 125
19. Pooley, 'Living in Liverpool: The Modern City', p. 254
20. Milne, 'Maritime Liverpool', p. 308

3

TURNING ICE INTO FIRE
Tom Watson, the First Great Liverpool Manager

THE 'FOOTBALL FEVER' RETURNS TO MERSEYSIDE

With the Second Division title in the Reds bag, the much anticipated Senior Liverpool Cup 'derby' final between Liverpool and Everton of 1894 proved to be a huge let-down. According to the local press, it produced 'farcical football', with Everton 'contemptibly' fielding a combination (reserve) side and Liverpool, apparently in an angry response to their neighbours' cynicism, a team of amateurs. Weakened football teams are no modern invention. The message was already clear enough: the Football League and the national FA Cup were now becoming increasingly important trophies for these dominant local clubs. Local football was already on the long slide into relative obscurity – though even sixty years later derby games like this one in local cup competitions could still draw very large crowds on Merseyside.

According to the local press, the joyful Liverpool FC Second Division championship celebrations meant that a sporting disease was back on Merseyside:

> This city has the football fever especially violently and badly; it will have it ever so much worse in the future. And those colossal sums paid by spectators to witness a football fray of ninety minutes' duration. What does this mean?

There was much more of this sort of incendiary stuff in the Liverpool press. 'The city of Liverpool will invariably be the scene of crush, enthusiasm, excitement,' said the *Liverpool Review* in a lengthy editorial of 19 May 1894. 'In other words, of the football fever. When the two XIs of local champions meet – Whish!!! Crash!!! Bash!!! Bang!!! Hurroo!!!' Was this exuberant irony or simply proof of the early existence of tabloid styles of journalism on Merseyside? Liverpool FC, it was said, was looking for yet more new recruits, and, once again, the football kingdom of Scotland would be freely drawn upon. Moreover, football was already more important in the city even than politics. The *Review* continued on its tack:

> The fact remains, be it a sign of moral degeneration or not, that in Liverpool football and footballers are more discussed than are other games or any other class of gamester. Council and Imperial Parliament matters sink into insignificance in most companies when the great winter game is turned on tap. It may sound ironical and an exaggeration, but it is very questionable whether in political circles a change of Prime Minister is more anxiously and vehemently discussed than the transfer of some famous footballer is in football circles . . . In short, it is everywhere. And there is no use denying the fact. Liverpool, and Liverpool men, take a very forefront place where the game is concerned . . . In the future, Liverpool will prove itself to be its biggest and most financially successful centre.

In the years that followed, of course, regional rivals Manchester would have plenty to say on this last point. And the general antipathy between the two cities that would light up the next century was already plain to see during the royal opening of the Manchester Ship Canal in 1894. Liverpool people, it was reported in the city's press, could look towards 'Cottonopolis' only with 'grim humour and unconcern'. There was no use denying the fact, it was conceded on Merseyside, 'that the two cities had been at open and secret warfare for a considerable time'. These north-west rivals also shared in another rather ghoulish competition: only Salford had a higher mortality rate than Liverpool among all large towns and cities in England. There seemed to be some local agreement that 'there are probably more social sores to be seen in Liverpool than in any other city outside London'. You didn't have to look too far from Anfield for evidence. 'I have had occasion to travel along Sheil Road late at night,' a correspondent told the *Review* on 11 August 1894, 'and many are the disgusting sights I have witnessed. It is quite time that something was done to clear the neighbourhood of the drunken and abandoned creatures who infest it.'

Partly because of press reports such as these, the 'curse' of puritanism was now also at large along the Mersey, aimed at 'saving' working people and the Liverpool destitute from an early grave. There were public calls for more prohibitions in the city on the evils of betting, drink, tobacco and even dancing. This was part of a long history of Liverpool's middle classes attempting to regulate and 'purify' free entertainment and the public use of the streets in the city. Certainly, Liverpool had a national reputation for drunkenness, though the chief constable at the time stressed that Liverpool police simply *arrested* more drunks than happened elsewhere.[1]

In the face of this moral onslaught and the burgeoning social ills of the city, perhaps the only sensible answer was a radical one: to emigrate. In the 1890s, to be American was to be modern, a view reflected in Liverpool's showy transatlantic waterfront and its expansive ambitions.[2] A passage to America from Liverpool could be bought for just £2 in 1894, a sum that included the 'agent's commission, the seven days' food on board and the usual kit for steerage passengers'. Some 'Dicky Sams' took the American route to a new life, forsaking both the social and moral reformers in the city *and* the beautiful game. Those who stayed put in Liverpool awaited the city's first authentic derby match in the vertiginously dizzy atmosphere of the First Division of the Football League.

THE NEW ANFIELD – AND FIRST DIVISION BLUES

With the new season now on the horizon, Liverpool FC finally looked to extend the Anfield grandstands into some of the adjacent land owned by Joseph Orrell (brother of John). But John Houlding rejected Orrell's proposed price for the deal, and there was even brief press talk of the club touring and training in the USA and then relocating to *another* arena in the city for their first season in the top flight. It seemed as if the club was back to the sorts of problems that had plagued football at Anfield in 1892. But agreement was eventually reached with the vendor, thus ensuring new facilities and that 'Anfield will, indeed, be a Paradise compared to what it was before'.

Anticipation for the new season was now acute, with the Linesman even offering in the local press a useful glossary of football terms for potential new supporters and helpfully reporting for those who did not know that match officials were paid one guinea plus rail and cab fare per match, with optional overnight accommodation. The Everton match diary for the forthcoming season also included Liverpool's fixtures for the first time, a commercial decision, no doubt, but also a sign that the two major clubs in the city might co-exist on friendlier terms than had previously been possible. In fact, these rivals would share a match-day programme until the 1935–36 season.

An 'enormous crowd' gathered on Tuesday, 22 August 1894 to witness a pre-season practice match in the 'newly equipped and greatly improved Anfield ground'. The rudimentary pitch markings they gazed upon would be pretty unfamiliar to today's sporting eye, consisting of a centre line, two twelve-yard lines (instead of penalty boxes) and two semi-circles at either end of the pitch instead of six-yard boxes. Only in 1902 was a rectangular penalty area and a penalty spot introduced, along with six-yard boxes to replace the old semi-circles. The crowd was reported to be reluctant to leave the empty ground and instead 'stood still gazing at the imposing skeleton of the handsome new grandstand, which is now in course of construction'. Because of its imposing height and unusual length this new Main Stand, in the fawning view of the *Liverpool Review*, 'will be without doubt the greatest grandstand on any football ground in the kingdom'. Anfield could now hold up to 30,000 fans, with 3,500 under cover in the new stand and 3,500 standing in the Paddock below. It already exhibited the dimensions and grandeur of a modern sports stadium.

The best seats at Anfield would now cost 21 shillings for a season ticket, with tickets in other covered stands costing 15 shillings. An uncovered standing season ticket was 7s 6d (which was soon withdrawn). There were price reductions for older members, and 'ladies' could get season tickets for half price in the rather patronising hope that their presence at football might help to gentle the more boisterous male throng. The plan was also to reconstruct the goal-end terracing into a half-moon shape by the opening day of the new season to allow better viewing and to give the stadium an even more handsome appearance. Given a good first season at the top level, the Liverpool board also planned to replace the old (Kemlyn Road) stand with one to mirror that constructed on the Main Stand side. Alas, Liverpool Football Club would not have a good season at their first attempt at the First Division – not by a long chalk.

Why did Liverpool fail so badly in this its first season in the top flight? They ended rock bottom with twenty-two points and relegation, taking ten matches even to register their first victory and a further eight attempts for their next. Well, it was a familiar football tale: the new signings did not impress. The 5 ft 9 in. Willie McCann from Paisley Abercorn, the Scotland reserve team goalkeeper, shipped 39 goals in his 15 League outings. He stayed only eight months. Wales international full-back Abel Hughes played only one match, none in the Football League. At least David Hannah – newly arrived cousin of Andrew – managed to score in the Anfield derby in November, contributing to the point that was saved thanks to a last-minute penalty by Jimmy Ross in a 2–2 draw.

Star signing Ross, £75 from Preston North End, did much better than most, with 12 league goals in his first season and 40 goals in total in 85 Liverpool appearances. He was a tough and fiery character with an abrasive tongue and wit, a man who had scored eight of the record twenty-six goals that Preston had once put past Hyde in the FA Cup. He was also credited with some early coaching at Anfield.[3] But his arrival at Liverpool also came with complications. Jimmy's more famous footballing brother Nick died tragically at just 31 years of age, and on his death bed he begged brother Jimmy to stay loyal to Preston North End. Understandably, this plea made relations with Ross's new club rather 'strained and awkward'. Jimmy eventually settled down at Anfield, but he could not get Liverpool firing despite John Houlding telling his players, inelegantly, during the pre-season that a league title would make him 'die content and live contenteder'.

By the time the first Football League derby game in Liverpool arrived on 13 October 1894, the Reds were already in trouble at the foot of the table. The players retired to Hightown to prepare in the week before the match. The contest at Goodison Park was rough and ready, with Everton unbalanced by an early injury to Bell and Liverpool desperately trying to raise the tempo. But the Blues showed their extra class – they began the season with eight straight wins and eventually finished league runners-up. Everton managed to claim a half-time lead, a header by McInnes. Liverpool strived hard for parity in the second half but were caught on the break by Alex Latta for the crucial second goal in an eventual 0–3 defeat. The return, at Anfield a month later, was a much tighter affair and ended in stalemate. But elsewhere Liverpool's defence was too readily shipping goals – five without reply at West Bromwich, Aston Villa and Sheffield Wednesday, respectively – and the club's players were also falling like ninepins to injury and illness. Despite a mini-revival after New Year, there would be no avoiding the privations and tensions of the promotion and relegation Test match on this form and with this luck. It duly arrived after a last-day thrashing at home to Preston, by 2–5. At Ewood Park, once more, for the nerve-jangling relegation-deciding contest, not even the sending off of the Bury goalkeeper for a wild kick to the stomach of a Liverpool forward could help the Anfield men. Liverpool surrendered the Test match 0–1 – and with it their hard-won place in the First Division.

RISINGS FROM BELOW

Liverpool, still in shock, reinforced for their return to the Second Division by signing striker Fred Geary from Everton, a goalscoring inside-left Frank Becton from Preston North End to link up brilliantly with Harry Bradshaw, and two much-needed new defenders, a stylish Scottish footballing right-back Archie Goldie from Clyde and the reliable Edinburgh-born Tom Wilkie on the left. Bill Dunlop had also signed from Paisley Abercorn in January 1895, and, after a slow start punctuated by injury, he was to be the mainstay of the Liverpool defence for the next 13 years. He was unarguably the most consistent Liverpool full-back until Phil Neal took over the mantle in the 1970s. Tom Cleghorn, a fiery little left-half from Leith who was signed from Blackburn Rovers in 1896, added further energy to the left side.

But it was the £100 that Liverpool paid Leith Athletic for 20-year-old centre-forward George Allan that proved the key investment. Allan had fire in his boots and in his belly, scoring twenty-five goals in just twenty league games and three more in the vital play-off matches. Allan's antics once so upset the legendary Sheffield United goalkeeper Willie 'Fatty' Foulke that the keeper conceded a penalty by up-turning Allan and jamming the forward's head in the mud. Allan managed 56 goals in just 96 Liverpool appearances, but he tragically died from illness at just 24 years of age, his huge potential only partially fulfilled.

The Reds were Second Division champions again in 1896, this time on goal difference, with a league record 106 goals scored – runners-up Manchester City managed just 63. The 18th of February 1896 marked the club's record league win, 10–1 against hapless Rotherham Town, a match in which 'Liverpool might almost as well have won by 20 goals, so persistently did they attack and shoot'. Liverpool scored an astonishing sixty-five goals in just fourteen home matches, but still had to face a post-season mini-league of play-off matches, in which they played the two lowest-placed First Division clubs, home and away, for the right to be promoted once again.

After beating the same opponents 4–0 at Anfield, a poor 0–0 draw at Small Heath was explained locally by a lengthy rail trip for the players (which took from 1.30 p.m. to 5.15 p.m.) to this Monday evening fixture, but a crucial 2–0 home victory against West Brom in front of 20,000 fans was the key result to send the Anfield club back into the top flight. The press suggested this home scoreline had been 'arranged' because Liverpool later casually lost the away match at Albion by the same score, playing 'fancy touches' and using 'gallery tricks'. Both clubs were eventually promoted as a result. This accusation was certainly hard on George Allan, because when he scored in the first match with 'a truly memorable effort, the sphere travelling into the net at thunderbolt rate, there was a loud, long and lusty demonstration' on the Anfield terraces. The negative publicity and press concern about alleged match-fixing was enough to stir the men at the Football League to wonder just how long the controversial Test matches could survive the obvious threat of corruption. It was a routine fear around English football fixtures right up until the First World War.

LIVERPOOL, SPORT CITY – FOR MEN

The year 1896 had been an eventful one for the city of Liverpool and its environs: it marked the opening of the Anfield crematorium and the Palm House in Sefton Park, as well as the extension of the overhead railway line and the opening of the new Wirral railway. Crabs caught off the Isle of Man were reportedly becoming a 'toothsome dish' in the city, and in March 1896 Liverpool was labelled, to some acclaim – if not among local social reformers – the 'greatest beer drinking city in the United Kingdom'. Early in 1897, the electric light was used in nearby New Brighton for the first time and would soon arrive in Bootle. The period also signalled a welcome upturn in commercial and industrial activity in the city after many years of depression.

Meanwhile, brewer, football-club owner and local councillor John Houlding spoke in a conference in Glasgow in 1896 on the rather prosaic topic of 'The History of the Treatment and Disposal of City Refuse in Liverpool During the Past 50 Years'. As a young man, the pragmatic Houlding had seen the effects of the plague on his father's milk business, and he now championed better sanitation for the Merseyside poor – including ending the practice of dumping raw urban refuse into the Mersey estuary. Houlding was also carefully making his football club a local force in his adopted city: the Anfield men acquired the red-and-white municipal colours of the city of Liverpool in 1896. From 1901, the club crest incorporated the Liverpool liver bird.

But football did not hold everyone's imagination in Liverpool. In June 1896, a crowd of some 5,000 at Newsome Park watched the Union club play Everton in a baseball match, a signal of the Liverpool–USA cultural exchanges, though strangely the scorers could not agree on the final result. The year produced, too, the first mention of 'lady footballers' in the city, who were summarily dismissed by local reporters (as they were elsewhere) as 'too funny for words, merely making the game ridiculous'. These women played a match in North Wales in July under the auspices of the newly formed British Ladies Football Association. 'This being the first appearance of the new women in the football field,' commented the *Liverpool Review*, 'the visitors, the majority of whom were attired in knickerbockers and short skirts, attracted considerable attention and although there was a gate of a thousand there was no hooting.'

On 1 August, the *Review* reported, with obvious satisfaction, that the women's team had 'bust up' after its organiser had ended up in hospital with scarlet fever. Football was clearly regarded as no pastime for 'respectable' women – it might even have been organised in Liverpool by 'do-gooding' social reformers. 'Other members of the company, some fifteen in number, were practically destitute,' it was reported. 'Several of the girls receive relief from the parochial authorities and in some instances food was supplied to them by the police. What a fiasco!' Women on Merseyside would face a long struggle throughout much of the next century to be accepted as footballers, or even as active club supporters.

RED MEN

TOM WATSON, THE FIRST LIVERPOOL FC MANAGER

Finally, in 1896, there was the arrival in the city of the 'silver tongued' Tom Watson at Liverpool Football Club, 'football's first prototype of the modern football manager'.[4] On 1 August 1896, the *Liverpool Review* announced this extraordinary news:

> Mr Tom Watson, who has done such a very great deal for the Sunderland Football Club, has undertaken the secretaryship of the Liverpool Football Club. This is undeniably a good stroke on the part of the Liverpool management and it would appear that now, at any rate, the Anfield Roaders will not figure in the Test matches for a very long time.

John Houlding certainly wanted to avoid the risk of an immediate slide out of the First Division, but this was, by any measure, an audacious move. Watson was, arguably, as important in the early development of the Liverpool club as Bill Shankly and Bob Paisley were to prove to be in the post-war era. Tom Watson was born in Newcastle in 1859, the son of a skilled worker who was a supporter of the independent educational tradition. This meant that as a child Tom studied both in Newcastle and in York. Watson had no real playing career to talk of, but he became very active and influential in local football administration in the north-east in the 1880s, founding the Rosehill club in 1881. Watson then acted as honorary secretary at both the Newcastle East End and Newcastle West End clubs, where he was charged with recruiting capable Scottish professionals. By the late 1880s, some directors were beginning to realise that running a professional football club was a full-time project, requiring deep knowledge of both players and administration. It was his work with the so-called 'Team of All the Talents' at Sunderland FC that cemented Watson's reputation for innovative tactics and leadership. He had brought three league titles to the north-east, in 1892, '93 and '95.

Watson was now thinking of retirement, but he was headhunted for Liverpool by John McKenna and William Houlding, who was now Liverpool's chairman. John Houlding had moved upstairs as president and was soon to become the mayor of Liverpool. McKenna accepted that the Liverpool club now needed someone to work full-time with the players and to deal with administration on the playing side – though Everton and many other clubs continued to resist the very notion of anything approaching the modern football manager. McKenna also accepted that Liverpool should pay top money, given Watson's impressive record, so an annual salary of £300 was agreed, generally assumed to be the largest in football. Watson was also a Freemason, so he fitted in very well with the Liverpool FC hierarchy. In fact, much of Watson's own responsibilities at Liverpool were focused on financial matters at Anfield. It was unlikely he had complete autonomy in team selection, which probably only came to the manager after the arrival at Melwood of Bill Shankly late in 1959. But the local press soon described Liverpool as 'Watson's team', and he clearly exerted considerable influence in player selection, thus beginning the cult of the football manager that became such a prominent part of the Anfield tradition.

What Tom Watson provided was positive direction and cohesion in both team and financial affairs, and also a considerable flair for public relations and the constructive use of the press, especially as the game grew in its popularity and status. These approaches were very much the mark of the modern, media-friendly football manager, of course. Bill Shankly again comes to mind. As Jimmy Catton, editor of *Athletic News*, put it when reflecting about the gregarious Watson, 'No secretary contrived to be mentioned in print so often as Tom Watson of Liverpool. He loved to see his name in good type. It was a little weakness of his – and quite pardonable, for most people have their spice of vanity, although they take pains to conceal it.'[5] Despite Watson's much heralded arrival, in which he was soon reported to be 'rapidly getting things in order' whilst 'the eyes of the football world are turned in the direction of the city', the Liverpool team which consolidated its place in the First Division was pretty much the same as that which had blasted its way out of the Second Division.

But Liverpool soon showed obvious signs on the pitch of Watson's more 'scientific' influence on tactics and organisation. The impact was akin to that of the Continentals Gérard Houllier and Rafa Benítez a century later. Watson insisted, for example, that Liverpool adopted a very different approach to that of the club's last First Division campaign, notably a much stronger concentration on defence. This meant that barely an away goal was scored at Anfield in three months. Admittedly, this cautious philosophy did not always go down well with local scribes. After a dull 0–0 home draw against West Bromwich in November 1896, for example, and under the headline 'What Fans Want', the *Liverpool Review* concluded, 'This kind of thing will not raise Liverpool's status. The man who pays his sixpence and is the supporter of football wants to see goals scored. He wants something for his money and a draw, as in this case of 0–0, narks him. The motto should be "Score boys, score".' A 1–2 defeat at Goodison in early October hardly improved Watson's Anfield standing either, though the 'good humours' displayed by the Liverpool football public at the match – presumably through gritted teeth – 'were a pattern to the football world and to followers of any other sport'.

By early November 1896, after humbling Sunderland 3–0 at Anfield in mist and drizzle that the visitors thought unfit for play, a resilient but prosaic Liverpool topped the entire Football League for the first time in the club's short history. Eventually, though, it would be Liverpool's 'well organised, swift-covering and ruthless-tackling defence' that would be the key to their healthy showing, with the Reds finishing fifth to Everton's seventh and conceding only 38 goals, the same number as champions Aston Villa.[6] Despite forward George Allan's best efforts, Liverpool could only score 46 times in 30 matches. A turn-of-the-year 3–3 home draw with Villa, a match described as 'the finest at Anfield for a very long time', was atypical but also symbolic of Liverpool's obvious improvement under Watson and their capability at this level. By mid-January, Liverpool were second in the league to Villa but had played four games more. They were never really serious title contenders. Club discipline at Anfield was also occasionally challenged at this time – and was quickly re-established: three 'class' players – reputedly Wilkie, Allan and Neil – were credited with 'setting out on a bout of so-called enjoyment' a few hours before an important Lancashire Cup tie with Bolton in January. They were summarily dropped by Watson.

This was also the first season (1896–97) to offer the real possibility of an all-Merseyside FA Cup final – it would actually be delayed by almost 90 years. Liverpool reached a semi-final for the first time, meeting with Aston Villa in Sheffield, by disposing of Burton Swifts, West Bromwich and Nottingham Forest, while Everton eventually lined up in the semis against Derby County at Stoke. 'Centre Forward', writing in the *Liverpool Review*, was more than confident: 'I expect to see one, if not both, of the Liverpool clubs left in the final.' Liverpool, certainly, 'went away in dashing style' and even had two goals disallowed against Villa. But in a 'rough and tumble forcible game' a 'fluky goal' from John Cowan followed by another from a corner that should have been a goalkick put the Reds unluckily on the back foot. Villa's Charlie Athersmith finished them off with a second-half 'classic shot' for a comprehensive 0–3 Reds defeat. Everton beat County 3–2 in the other semi, thus keeping their side of the Mersey bargain, but they fell, in turn, to Villa (2–3) at Crystal Palace in a coruscating final.

The failure of the Merseyside clubs to secure major silverware (though Everton did win the Lancashire Cup) despite paying high wage bills and attracting the highest aggregate crowds in England now provoked a very early example of something sports readers in the city and elsewhere would become very familiar with: the press questioning not only of the salaries of players but also their lifestyles, status and attitudes. 'Go Straight' was an editorial in the *Liverpool Review* on 27 March 1897 that rounded on the alleged 'don't care, get-what-we-can attitude' of professional players. Already, here was barely concealed nostalgia for the old days when 'the training the men got was at their daily work with a run around the parks at night-time'. Which meant, of course, that these past players had much more commitment and enthusiasm for the game than did the pampered full-timers of the present.

'Weak' football selection committees were also criticised for their alleged kowtowing to the stars and especially for 'allowing leading players to dictate as to who shall play in a team, or to say, "If you don't play so-and-so, I *can't* do my best (which often means *won't*)."' Early footballers needed managing and motivating as much as later celebrities did. Club committees were also alleged to offer illegal financial inducements to their stars when footballers should actually be seen primarily as *workers* – as simple employees. 'This is not right. A football player, like a mechanic or a professional man, should always give his best services to his employer at the stipend mutually agreed upon.'

Here were the first real press arguments for much more discipline and control over football affairs for the likes of Liverpool's Tom Watson. When Everton lost to little Rock Ferry in the final of the Liverpool Cup in 1897, the 'richest club in the country' was urged by the Liverpool press to appoint a 'team manager' who should 'with the trainer, have full charge of the team'. Instead, the Everton board decided they knew best.

LOCAL HEROES OR IMPORTED STARS?

But a more powerful theme in the local press was the growing public debate about local versus imported players. Letters to the *Liverpool Review*, for example, suggested that the major football clubs might better look to local leagues for their new signings. They certainly provoked a strident response from Centre Forward on 22 May 1897, who argued that possibilities for success for the major Merseyside clubs in late-nineteenth-century Liverpool already depended on *rejecting* just this sort of parochialism in selection:

> I am at one with the letter writers that every effort should be made to unearth good, local men ... But to stick to local players whether they are up to form or not would ruin any club in existence ... Everton and Liverpool have built up their football following by good, scientific football. You could not fill the Everton and Liverpool teams with local players and still keep in the league, and we would soon see these two fine organisations drift to the level of minor local clubs.

As these sorts of exchanges developed and became more heated, it also became increasingly clear that there was a strong public preference, even in cosmopolitan Liverpool, for English players rather than for Scots, Irish and Welsh professionals. A press survey of the 16 teams in the First Division in October 1897 revealed that 97 out of 176 top players (55 per cent) were English. Liverpool actually had six Englishmen, Everton only two and Bolton Wanderers a bare one. 'The prevalent desire of the football public is not necessarily for purely local talent,' argued 'Goodison Park' in a letter published on 8 July 1897, 'but there is a widespread wish that more *English* players should be signed by our local clubs ... It is surely but reasonable that professional English clubs should consist, for the most part, of English players.' Another letter complained that club officials were ignoring public opinion on these matters and that certain football officials were already 'being busy on the rummage up north'.

No prizes for guessing who was rummaging. On one such trip, Liverpool's Tom Watson signed right-winger Bob Marshall from Leith Athletic, though George Allan had unaccountably moved the other way, having been sold to Celtic for just £50. His goals would be sorely missed. Watson also signed a large number of younger players as part of a new longer-term plan to develop the club. There is no evidence, however, that new president John Houlding brought back football players with him from Russia. He had recently travelled there, looking ceaselessly for ways of bettering Liverpool life, and the Liverpool FC president did offer some typically eye-catching 'hard-headed and political' lectures in the city in order to publicise his eventful trip.

LIVERPOOL BEAT THE BLUES, AT LAST!

After a jittery and winless start to the new season, in September 1897 a great moment finally arrived: Liverpool's first Football League win over rivals Everton. Thirty thousand fans – of all types – crammed into Anfield, with local supporters complaining about the lack of transport to the stadium. 'I waited nearly an hour opposite St George's Hall,' claimed one, 'and then only got a chance brake.' The *Liverpool Review* reported that, 'The spectators came from everywhere and they represented all kinds and conditions of men, youths, boys, yes, and women and girls. For hours there was intense excitement.' So great was the crowd pressure at Anfield that twice the pitch-side barriers gave way, leading to stoppages in play.

This was, indeed, a rather heated affair, producing 'blind and unreasonable partisanship' in the crowd, which only intensified after Jack Taylor gave the visitors an undeserved lead after 25 minutes. The raw-boned and stocky new Liverpool signing Daniel Cunliffe and then Joe McQue replied for the Reds before the break. From this point on, only Harry Storer's 'champion form' in the Liverpool goal kept the hosts ahead, until a Frank Becton goal finally secured the points. Brave, confident and reliable goalkeepers, with skilled feet and hands such as Storer had, were especially important at a time when keepers could wander some way from their goal and grab the ball. This victory was a marvellous moment for Houlding, McKenna and Watson, and for all Liverpool fans. But in late October it was clear that Everton were determined to have their revenge at Goodison Park. They got it, too, by 0–3, after Becton was injured early on, thus making him 'practically useless' for the rest of the match. Ten-man Liverpool were reportedly 'never in the hunt' due to rugged Everton's 'questionable tactics'.

The 1897–98 season produced consolidation but no improvement in Liverpool FC's fortunes: a modest ninth place in the league, with a long injury list and a struggle for goals. But the following 1898–99 season began to show Tom Watson's astute influence to near full effect, as Liverpool avoided injuries and began to prepare for imminent Football League successes by challenging for the league and FA Cup Double. They were destined just to fail, controversially, in each. Tom Watson had obviously been given the green light by the Liverpool committee to make new signings, because a few key players arrived in 1898, mainly again from his favoured Scottish hunting grounds. But first there was a highly unusual football signing: at right-half Rabbi Howell was the first full-blooded Romany traveller to play as a professional footballer in Britain and to be capped by England. Born in a caravan, the son of a tinker, Howell was a small and wiry half-back with good speed and stamina who had won a championship medal with Sheffield United in 1898 before leaving the club under a disciplinary cloud and moving to Liverpool for £200. He stayed at Anfield until 1901, but, like many players, his career was cut short by injury.

A new full-back, the exotically named General Stevenson, signed from Padiham near Burnley, and Hugh Morgan, a skilful and canny forward, arrived from St Mirren to bolster the Liverpool attack. From Hearts, Liverpool signed John Walker, a dribbling right-sided attacker with a penchant for long-distance shooting, and Tom Robertson, a talented and elusive left-winger, for a combined fee of £350. Both would become Scotland internationals and would be key figures in Liverpool's first championship team in 1901. Robertson and Morgan would finish top league scorers for the club in 1899 – but with a paltry ten goals apiece. But all of these new arrivals, impressive as they were, were overshadowed by the era-shaping Liverpool signing of the nineteenth century. In May 1898, a fair-haired 20-year-old Scot, Alexander Galloway Raisbeck, signed for Liverpool for £350. It was a steal.

Raisbeck was born in Dolmont, Stirlingshire, one of seven brothers, and he had worked in the mines as well as playing professionally in Scotland for Hibernian. He had helped Stoke avoid relegation in the Football League Test matches of 1898 before, inexplicably, returning north of the border. Perhaps the Potteries club could not afford the required fee to sign the Scot? Maybe family demands drew him northwards once more – Raisbeck would eventually father an impressive 14 children. Maybe the great man was just waiting for a club with the potential of Liverpool to approach him? At 5 ft 10 in., Raisbeck was tall for his day and showed quite brilliant timing in the air. His speed, aggression and precision in the tackle and in defensive recovery were legendary. He also boasted huge stores of stamina in supporting forwards and was restless in his covering for defenders. In short, he was the perfect attacking and defending centre-half, an absolutely outstanding all-rounder, possibly the best ever to play for the club over an extended period, service which brought him two league titles. He also kept his feet admirably on the ground, being a noted amateur bowler and once remarking that he would be happy to return to a collier's life if things went badly for him in football. In volume four of Gibson and Pickford's *Association Football*, published in 1908, Raisbeck was profiled, justifiably, as one of the 'Giants of the Game':

> His great forte as a half-back is a dashing, breezy versatility. He is like an intelligent automaton, fully wound up and warranted to last through the longest game on record. To watch him at play is to see a man pulsating to his finger-tips with the joy of life. Swift, rapid movement, fierce electric rushes are to him an everlasting delight. One would think that he had discovered the secret of perpetual motion. He keeps on and on and never flags.[7]

Raisbeck sacrificed Scotland caps for the sake of Liverpool matches in the club's near-Double year of 1899, and this temporary rejection of his national team might explain his miserly final tally of just eight caps (seven v. England) in an era, admittedly, of few international matches. (Alan Hansen was also poorly treated by Scotland more than 70 years later.) No English player was allowed by the rules of the Football League to resist the call-up from England.

The Liverpool team under McKenna and Watson would certainly be built around Raisbeck for much of the next decade. In an era in which the 2–3–5 formation became the dominant system of play, the centre-half was the fulcrum or pivot of the team. He had to be a multi-skilled jack of all trades, a defender and an attacker, a fierce leader as well as a creative inspiration. Not without reason did the great Austrian football writer and intellectual Willy Meisl describe the early centre-half in football as 'the most important man on the field'.[8]

LOCAL BRAGGING RIGHTS

The Football League expanded again in 1898, this time to thirty-six clubs in two leagues of eighteen, with the rising New Brighton Tower joining the group of league clubs from the Merseyside area. This league expansion actually prevented a mutiny. Raisbeck's club at the time, Stoke, and opponents Burnley had publicly stated their plan to draw their final Test match with each other to ensure that both clubs were promoted. The clubs' players spent the match kicking the ball aimlessly into the crowd. Fortunately, the two victim clubs, Newcastle United and Blackburn Rovers, were promoted anyway due to the increase in the size of the league. But it was the end of the controversial Test matches to decide promotion and relegation issues – at least for the time being.[9]

Glossop North End was one of the two clubs automatically promoted in 1899, with Glossop thus becoming the smallest town ever to be represented in the First Division – they lasted just one season. Also, Second Division Grimsby Town sensibly proposed a different-coloured shirt for goalkeepers in 1898, but their idea was rejected by the league – it would eventually be agreed 11 years later, in 1909.

Big-spending Everton were reported to have laid out a whopping £5,787 on new players in 1898–99, but it was Liverpool that started the new season with a bang, a 4–0 home rout of The Wednesday in front a reported 18,000 crowd. The *Liverpool Review* was also in good form, soon sermonising about the lot of professional players. It quoted one who allegedly said, 'When a player signs a professional form he literally sells his body and figuratively his soul.' And what of the early show by what the *Review* called 'Tom Watson's pets'? (This namecheck for the Liverpool manager was a very early admission of the new man's influence and his worth at Liverpool Football Club.) It was, the paper observed, 'faultless in every particular'. Moreover, 'It is evident that the Liverpool men are no "paper" artists this season. There is no question about their capabilities and apparently there is no doubt about their desire to try.'

For their part, Everton's average home crowds would now be overtaken for the first time by those at Aston Villa. But for big matches – for derby matches, for example – Goodison Park could still be stretched near to its limits. On 24 September 1898, 'with everybody on the tiptoe of excitement . . . the population of a large town' turned out to see Liverpool triumph at Everton 2–1 in a match that hit no great technical heights. 'A good sprinkling of blue jackets [sailors] mingled with the crowd,' reported the *Daily Post*. Proudfoot scored early on for the Blues, with the Scottish reserve utility forward Alex McCowie replying for Liverpool. The visitors got in front courtesy of a penalty awarded by the eagle-eyed referee Lewis against the uncompromising Blues full-back Walter Balmer, who had to be quietened in his protests by the Everton captain. McCowie doubled his tally from the spot. The Liverpool defence was 'the best department on the field' as Everton tried to respond but ran out of time. The 'snowy fronted stands' set against the emerald turf and the music of an 'excellent band' added to the visual and aural attractions of the occasion for local reporters. It was Goodison Park in full bloom – and stormed by the men from Liverpool Football Club.

Following this buoyant result, inconsistent Liverpool struggled to a 0–0 home draw with Notts County before embarking on a spell of three consecutive losses, including a 1–2 defeat to Burnley at Anfield. This result relegated Watson's team to the lower half of the table. Four early matches had brought Liverpool six points, followed by four more producing just one. But by December 1898 things had changed, once again, in this topsy-turvy season for the club's loyal supporters. They were offered the seasonal present of a return of five points from three away matches. By early January 1899, Liverpool had moved up to fourth place on a run of nine matches that had produced six wins and just one loss. 'Tom Watson must be a genius,' commented a relieved and impressed *Liverpool Review*. 'He can almost turn ice into fire.' Watson might have needed this trick at the home match against Stoke on 4 February. In a fierce snowstorm, during which the rolling football gathered snow, the visitors succumbed 1–0 in the kind of game 'that not only pays, but is pleasing and pretty to behold'. For their admirers, this victory in adversity meant that 'Liverpool remain the wonder and admiration of the football world'.

THE 1899 FA CUP SEMI-FINAL FIASCO

By March 1899, the Liverpool press was even able to allow itself the luxury of speculating on the possibility of the Anfield league and FA Cup Double. Liverpool now lay second in the table to Aston Villa and were preparing to play Sheffield United in the FA Cup semi-final in Nottingham. The local press priority seemed to be to bring home the FA Cup rather than the league title. Everton, after all, had already returned the league crown to the city, but the national FA Cup had never resided on Merseyside. At West Bromwich in the FA Cup quarter-finals, the Reds had ridden their luck, scoring two fortunate early goals and then hanging on for dear life. But hang on they did, defensive resolve again to the fore.

The decision to play the resulting Liverpool–Sheffield United semi-final in Nottingham, rather than at nearby Fallowfield, puzzled the Liverpool press. The Manchester venue was 'a decided sell', despite the chaos that had occurred at Everton's 1893 final. A moderate crowd of 35,000 showed up to the first encounter, a 2–2 draw. The first replay was at Burnden Park and still could not separate the teams in a 4–4 extravaganza, by which time Manchester was indeed calling. But it turned out to be a predictably unsatisfactory afternoon in the Fallowfield bowl – one of dangerous chaos and confusion.

The Fallowfield stadium was sited in a semi-rural setting and was designed to host athletics and cycling events, not major football matches. Its single stand could accommodate only 15,000 people, and the sightlines elsewhere – and stadium security – were abysmal.[10] Even before kick-off, some spectators had rushed the gates and crossed the running track, and thousands more poured onto the ground to line the touchline, many of them from Liverpool. Few could see, and barriers were smashed and piled up around the perimeter for fans to stand on. But the match kicked off, nevertheless, and Liverpool scored a goal through George Allan between two disallowed United 'goals'. Soon, the handful of policemen present were fighting to control groups of frustrated spectators, and after a short period members of the crowd invaded the pitch in front of the goals. The players and officials left the field for the first time. Police reinforcements eventually arrived, allowing the teams briefly to return at 4.53 p.m., with the intimidated and demoralised Sheffielders 'about as eager as snails'. At 5.18 p.m., referee Kingscott seemed to abandon the match, at which point, said the Liverpool press, 'the crowd goes clean off its head. Chaos develops into riot.' But by 5.22 p.m., the police had done their work, once more, and the players and officials came back on to finish the first half – which ended at close to six o'clock, some two hours after kick-off.

But that was the last any spectator saw of this doomed tie. The officials and police deemed the situation too dangerous to continue, leaving the Liverpool pressmen to rage that the Reds had been 'robbed of a goal' scored legitimately and possibly of a place in the FA Cup final. They were also concerned that gate receipts, which had exceeded £1,400, would be destined mainly for the coffers of a calamitous FA in a 'match that never was'. At least people from Liverpool could teach neighbouring Mancunians something about 'how to build football grounds, how to behave ourselves on them and how to play football, too'. But Liverpool's chance had already been stolen from them. Their stability restored, the Sheffield club came out on top in the final (third) replay, at Derby County, by the only goal. Liverpool would have to wait another 15 years to make their first FA Cup final appearance.

CHASING A FIRST LEAGUE TITLE – AND CHOKING

Back in the league, meanwhile, Everton v. Aston Villa was identified in the Liverpool press as a match that the hosts might be willing to 'throw' to ensure that their near neighbours floundered in the league race. In fact, the fixture ended honourably, at 1–1. Villa were also suspected of 'squaring' their matches against West Bromwich and Notts County, indicating the levels of suspicion around the results of top football matches at this time.

A 'rousing, exciting match . . . full of remarkable incident' between Liverpool and Newcastle United at Anfield on 3 April 1899 finished 3–2, producing 'terrific plaudits' from a reported four trainloads of visiting Geordie fans. The 23-year-old Wellingborough-born Bill Perkins made his debut in the Liverpool goal, having just signed from Luton Town. He joined Blackpool-born Jack Cox, a dribbling, sometimes over-elaborate flying winger who could play on both flanks. Cox had been signed by Watson for the title and FA Cup run-in. The winger had real talent and was something of a dietary and fitness fanatic, despite what was described darkly as an 'active' social life. The doomed George Allan, meanwhile, was injured, reducing Liverpool to ten men, and the home team went behind twice. But each time the depleted home squad responded with an equaliser before getting their noses in front to claim two vital points 'to save their championship bacon. It was a glorious game.' And it was a glorious Liverpool victory against the odds.

A 2–0 win against Blackburn Rovers meant that Liverpool, uniquely in the history of the Football League so far, would face their final league fixture at Villa Park locked at the top of the table on 43 points with their hosts. Free-scoring Villa needed only a draw to claim the title on goal average. Liverpool would end up scoring only 49 goals in 34 league matches, compared to Villa's 76. There were some other bad omens. Villa had already destroyed Liverpool by three clear goals at Anfield in October, and whilst new Reds goalkeeper Perkins had seemed deceptively 'cool' against Newcastle and Rovers, perhaps his demeanour was actually more a sign of catatonic nervousness. Local reporters on Merseyside were hopeful more than expectant, but they were sure of one thing: 'They may best us at cup winning, but the Villa people can't teach us anything about cheering.' This seemed like thinly veiled resignation before the off. Nevertheless, Tom Watson had taken his squad away to sunny St Anne's near Blackpool for a week's preparation. At 1.30 p.m. on Saturday, many of the 41,357 fans were already heading towards the Villa stadium for a 3.30 p.m. kick-off and the season's grand finale.

An eager Villa started like a train. Liverpool looked like an outfit exhausted by their season's endeavours and disappointments. After four minutes, Billy Garraty headed Villa in front, and then their experienced forward John Devey 'sent in a lightning shot which completely beat Perkins'. Soon after this dagger, Villa men Smith and Wheldon combined before the latter shot into the corner of the Liverpool net with the uncertain Perkins 'making a feeble attempt to save'. Now

Villa Park was in a state of pandemonium, and a 'bully' involving a large number of players in front of the Liverpool net eventually broke the ball to Jimmy Crabtree, who netted for number four, followed by Wheldon again for 0–5 to Villa. By half-time! Some seventy-seven years later, another famous championship-chasing Liverpool side would also turn around at Villa Park having conceded five first-half goals. But this catastrophe must have seemed to Tom Watson and Liverpool in 1899 as if their potentially wonderful season was collapsing about their ears.

At half-time, reported the *Daily Post*, the Midlands band poignantly played 'Au Revoir'. It was 'goodbye' all right for Liverpool's title dreams, and it was a disastrous end to a season of great promise, though no further goals were conceded. Even the *Liverpool Review*'s wry comment that 'we would rather have the Villa beat us than any other team because they invariably play a sportsmanlike game' rang hollow in the face of this slaughter. But Tom Watson knew that this defeat was a temporary glitch. He would return, soon enough, with a championship team of his own.

THE USES – AND ABUSES – OF VICTORIAN FOOTBALL

The next season (1899–1900), Liverpool slumped to tenth place in the league, with Villa retaining their hard-won title. Who could measure the mental and physical impact on Watson's men of what had gone before? Liverpool began the new campaign disastrously, with eight straight league defeats, a top-division record that still stands. After this awful start, so much of what followed was actually close to title form. This was the clue that things were about to go very well for Watson and his men as football became a much more civilised sport. Apeing the comments often made today about 'new' football compared with its tougher versions in the 1970s, in *The Windsor Magazine* in 1899 the great gentleman sportsman of his day C.B. Fry wrote:

> It is the barbarian in us that loves football. The game is exceedingly civilised and scientific nowadays . . . In olden days the sport was nothing but a free fight; now it is, as it were, a very refined form of the same. Indeed the game has become almost too refined. It was at its best when just entering upon its civilised stage, before there were quite so many rules and regulations.

In an editorial on 6 May 1899, the *Liverpool Review* worried at the condition of two-thirds of the football audience for the modern version of the sport – the working-class artisans, men who might be moved to spend seven and sixpence of a weekly wage of thirty shillings on a single trip to Birmingham for a football match. Is the game, 'admirable as it is, worth the time and money and thought he expends upon it?' the *Review* asked. But then there were also the positives of football – its contribution to local pride and to the lives of working people. The paper had its own quite strange and rather eclectic list of the sport's key strengths, which might have had some wider support in the city of Liverpool at this time:

> It supplies an agreeable topic for rational conversation, and it circulates money. If it dis-employs and distracts labour, it employs it and recreates it also. It encourages the instinct for manly endeavour and discourages femininity and namby-pambyism. It inculcates a respect for muscularity and places a heavy discount upon cowardice and funk. Hence, the love of football indirectly strengthens the virility of the nation and makes its masculinity a force . . . These, you will agree, are more than enough to counteract the evil that is in it.

So, football was, in this account at least, a force for improving the local economy and the masculine base of the national stock – important matters at the time of the Boer War and challenges to the British Empire – and it guarded against the supposed veiled dangers of homosexuality. This was quite a list. By 1901, a total of 339 teams and possibly in excess of 4,000 men played football in the Liverpool area, helping to reaffirm local masculinities, community identities and solidarities.[11] Football also primed the local economy, of course. On this last point, as the city of Liverpool lurched uncertainly towards the twentieth century, its sea-faring businesses were certainly doing well out of the war in South Africa: 60 vessels had been chartered for transport, with profit 'getting towards a couple of millions'. But football – and, it must be said, the Liverpool police – seemed helpless to curb the 'empty headed noodles' and the 'hordes of roughs' who were involved in the fancy dress, drunken rowdyism and other 'disgraceful scenes' that took place during the city-centre celebrations on New Year's Eve in 1899. It was noted that the presence of hundreds of inebriated young children, 'bare footed and black faced gamins', meant that 'every slum seems to have vomited its inmates into Church Street' as the new century approached. As reformers eagerly pointed out, there would be a grand total of 4,107 arrests in the city for drunkenness in 1900 to welcome in the new century.

But this sort of arch and contemptuous press coverage of the city's poor was distinctly lacking from discussions of the behaviour of local *football* crowds. Indeed, when Liverpool fans cheered distant news of Lancashire neighbour Bury's FA Cup final win during a routine 1–0 Anfield victory over Nottingham Forest in

April 1900, it was deemed locally to be a signal of 'what unselfish people we are'. There were also other signs of local self-preening. 'They want a tower in St John's Gardens as a memorial to the Liverpool war heroes,' one local newspaper letter writer remarked in June 1900. 'But why? We are all heroes in Liverpool.' However, in July 1900, the *Liverpool Courier* warned that not all local folk were made of the same right stuff. There was a new form of sharp practice reported in the city: a workman calls upon the 'lady of the house' offering coal at an absurdly low price. Two shillings is asked for, and is given, on account – the man (and his coal) disappears. Like it or not, street smartness has always been one of the necessary survival tools on the Mersey.

Football sometimes seemed almost similarly self-serving. The game's leaders used a 'cold, calm business tone' to argue in 1900, for example, against the pooling of gate receipts to help the weaker league clubs survive. 'When wages are cut down and something is done to make each team really representative of its own city,' commented the *Liverpool Review* testily, 'the Football League will be still more assured of a very long and lusty life.' Liverpool Football Club was in no mood to share its profits. Instead, Tom Watson and John McKenna put its cash towards some shrewd signings for the new campaign. A combative left-sided forward with a booming shot, Charlie Satterthwaite, arrived from Burton Swifts in November 1899 and added much needed direction, bite and aggression to the Liverpool frontline. Cheshire man and wing-half Charlie Wilson also arrived to offer the club reliability and continuity in what would be 40 years of devoted service, first as a player, then as a scout and trainer up until the Second World War. But the New Brighton Tower forward Sam Raybould was the real jewel, a key playing find for Tom Watson and a vital figure in Liverpool's title wins of 1901 and 1906. Chesterfield-born Raybould had not really set the Wirral football world alight, and he seemed like a pretty ordinary 25-year-old utility forward when he first signed for Liverpool for a hefty £250 fee in January 1900. But appearances were deceptive.

Of course, the public-school men at the FA still considered transfer fees in sport to be vulgar and 'unsportsmanlike', and they had recommended a maximum charge for the transfer of a player at this time of a puny £10. The Football League management committee effectively and sensibly ignored them.[12]

At goal-starved Liverpool, Raybould soon found his shooting boots, and eventually he would manage 128 goals in 226 appearances, including a goal at Goodison Park only 30 seconds into his derby debut. He also managed a pre-Second World War club record 31 goals in 33 league starts in 1902–03 and was a formidable replacement for Harry Bradshaw. Moustachioed and lean, Raybould was also quick and brave, a willing worker as well as a reliable goalscorer. 'When

Raybould gets the ball anywhere near the half-backs,' purred the *Liverpool Mercury*, 'there are stormy times ahead for someone.' And yet the robust Raybould could attract no support from the England selectors, despite his league-title heroics for Liverpool. But, frankly, could Tom Watson and the club's followers care less?

THE FIRST LIVERPOOL CHAMPIONSHIP, 1900–01

Tellingly, Liverpool had won nine of their last eleven league matches to end the first season concluded in the 1900s. They took off from the same place in September 1900, trouncing Blackburn Rovers 3–0 and then West Bromwich 5–0. In these victories, Raisbeck was 'ever prominent with head and feet', and the physical and spritely Satterthwaite showed 'his special penchant for being among the bruises'. Notoriously shy full-back John Robertson, meanwhile, a recent signing from Stoke, was showing 'sound defence' and thus 'ingratiated himself in the favour of the spectators'. But the big change at Anfield was the scoring of more goals: against WBA, for example, 'the visiting backs were run to a standstill' and were taunted as Liverpool's wingers 'flashed along in exhilarating style'. The new man Raybould was 'the pivot of every attack'. This was a dimension of Tom Watson's Liverpool persona that the Merseyside public had not yet seen – and it was thrilling and uplifting stuff.

Against Everton at Goodison Park in September 1900, however, it was much tougher going in a 1–1 draw, a match played in filthy conditions. It was the sort of no-quarter-given contest designed to bring the very best out of Alex Raisbeck, who dominated proceedings as 'the prominent figure in every movement whether of attack or defence'. The *Liverpool Mercury* was astonished by the Liverpool man's all-round commitment and ability, an Alan Hansen and Steven Gerrard combined. 'Now taking the ball clean from an opponent's toes, now urging on his forwards with a well judged pass, now darting to the assistance of his backs and checking many a dangerous rush. Always when danger threatened or opportunity presented itself was the light-haired Scot.' When Liverpool lost 1–2 at home to Tom Watson's old boys Sunderland on 29 September 1900, the 'fully employed' Raisbeck was 'the only one among the backs who appeared able to check the rapid rushes of the visitors', as home goalkeeper Perkins 'saved his side from utter collapse'.

The talented Wales international Maurice Parry replaced the injured Raisbeck when Liverpool beat Bolton Wanderers 2–1 in the next home league match, but the replacement inevitably paled by comparison with the great man (as any reserve would). Unlike Raisbeck, Parry 'lacked life, his passing was slow and his tackling feeble'. The bionic Satterthwaite, meanwhile, was carried off after colliding with the Wanderers keeper John Sutcliffe in scoring Liverpool's winning goal, but, typically, he recovered for the Reds' trip to Notts County. He eventually played only 21 league matches, mainly because of injury. The match in Nottingham produced a potentially shattering 0–3 loss for Liverpool, even with the mighty Raisbeck reinstated. Which all meant that the Reds stayed second in the league table behind leaders Nottingham Forest.

It was probably on 10 November 1900, in front of 18,000 fans at Anfield, that the locals really began to believe that the league crown might actually be a possibility for Tom Watson's Liverpool. The visitors that day, Aston Villa, were chasing a hat-trick of league titles, but a 5–1 Liverpool victory, based on the 'persistency and untiring effort' of the home side, destroyed the Midlands men, who eventually limped home just above the relegation slots. Tom Robertson, charging down Villa's right flank, was the pick of the home men as he 'flashed along the touchline to the corner flag' to set up three goals, including the fourth, a sumptuous volley from Raybould so that Villa keeper Billy George 'could only feel the waft of the air as the ball crashed past him'.

But Liverpool still struggled for consistency, and although in December the legendary Sheffield United heavyweight keeper Fatty Foulke 'had to save repeatedly' to help his club stay afloat at Anfield, it was enough for United to chalk up a 1–2 defeat for the Reds, despite another Satterthwaite goal. After twelve eventful matches, Liverpool had fallen back to fifth place, four points behind Forest and with four defeats already as dark stains on their record.

It was the sort of form to dim even the positive economic news on Merseyside in the new century. Plans for the world's largest warehouse had been recently drawn up for the Stanley Dock – the port of Liverpool was still booming, if facing an increasingly uncertain future. It might also have driven some of the club's supporters to the sort of blasphemy and street cursing that meant that at the Liverpool workhouse in December 1900 a censor was appointed to vet the songs being prepared by inmates for a Christmas entertainment for the nurses. Or perhaps it might have driven some Liverpool supporters to try the exotic Bavarian Münchener beer and Löwenbräu lager that was already being widely advertised in the *Liverpool Mercury*. British ale was off the menu for some; at the time, a scandal about the poisoning of beer with arsenic had resulted in prominent court cases. Meanwhile, more discerning folk in the city might even have chosen an evening out with the young Winston Churchill. The future prime minister was speaking at the city's Philharmonic Hall in November 1900 about the rights and (less probably) the wrongs of the Boer War.

In December 1900, with Alex Raisbeck once more in 'capital trim', despite being choked by a 'very disappointing exhibition of football', a single goal by Jack Cox at Anfield was enough to see off the then FA Cup holders Bury in the league. Raybould, 'clean through' in the second half, had obviously left his shooting boots elsewhere. On 22 December, the Reds, away at league leaders Nottingham Forest, held on for a 0–0 draw in front of a 10,000 crowd, although Raybould again had 'an open goal, but shot over the bar'. Towards the end of the contest, the home goal was reported to be 'hotly besieged'. This improvement in Liverpool's form was carried on into the new year, when Stoke were despatched 3–1 on a 'treacherous surface' at Anfield. Much more of this and the club's fans would be making good use of the improved tramway service in the city, which meant that people who lived in the Parliament Fields, Smithdown Road and Edge Hill areas of the city would no longer have to travel into the centre of town to get an overloaded tram back out to the Anfield stadium. Nevertheless, letters soon followed to local newspapers about the new problem of tram overcrowding caused, it was alleged, by 'poor conductoring'.

Now a real local test. 'Everything else pales into insignificance today,' trumpeted the *Liverpool Courier* on 19 January 1901. It was derby day at Anfield. But a 'terrible downpour of rain' turned the ground into a quagmire and threatened to ruin Liverpool's entire season in front of an estimated 18,000 fans. The match kicked off 15 minutes early, in fading light, just to ensure a finish. It was tough luck on those ticket-holding customers who came to the stadium on time! Jack Taylor scored for Everton after 20 minutes, and Raybould might have replied had the ball not stuck in a pool of water in conditions described as 'frightful'. Jack Cox, 'who up to this had been practically idle, pounced upon the ball like a greyhound' and scrambled in the equaliser for a 1–1 score at half-time. The sodden and muddied teams reappeared in fresh kit after the interval, and the two captains, Raisbeck and Settle, evidently discussed the possibility of abandoning the match, as did the officials. But the crowd cried, 'Play the game!' It was best not to invite a riot so play continued. Centre-half Tom Booth headed in for the visitors, and this time there was no reply: 1–2. Disaster!

Three days after this sporting 'tragedy', the whole nation would join Liverpool football fans in mourning. Queen Victoria had finally passed away. In the city of Liverpool, as elsewhere, 'sad-eyed groups packed the pavements' and 'the anguish of the community was terrible indeed'. But this public grief for royalty was actually short-lived in the city. Next morning, reported the *Liverpool Review*, with some admiration, 'the city of Liverpool went about its business pretty much as if little or nothing had happened'.

The Rugby Union and the FA reacted immediately and patriotically to the monarch's death, in the latter's case by postponing all forthcoming FA Cup ties. This irked the more pragmatic men at the Football League, because the gesture promised future fixture congestion. All league fixtures were also postponed on

2 February, the day of the old Queen's funeral. Liverpool would have no match now until their rearranged FA Cup tie with Notts County on 9 February and then a league fixture with Bolton Wanderers on 16 February: they lost both, scoring no goals. A 'display of ineptitude' was how the *Liverpool Courier* described the Reds' limp FA Cup exit. Wingers Cox and Satterthwaite, the newspaper complained later at Bolton, 'hardly seemed to understand each other'. Liverpool were now drifting to midtable oblivion and apparently out of title contention. With the passing of Queen Victoria – who had defined an astonishing era in British history – seemed to slide any fading Liverpool FC hopes of winning football silverware in 1901.

And yet there was still hope. This faltering at Bolton would be the last Liverpool league defeat of 1900–01. As a shipment of 'wild beasts' was exported out of the city by steamship from Cross's famous menagerie on Earle Street, and Dr Lasker, chess champion of the world, visited the city of Liverpool to lecture at the Central Chess Club on North John Street on the crucial question of the king's gambit, there followed a twelve-match unbeaten Football League run for Liverpool Football Club, nine of them victories. This sequence took the Anfield club from eighth place to league champions. And what looks suspiciously like what we might now call 'mind games' were not beyond the wily Liverpool manager Tom Watson. He strived to take every advantage to secure the club's first league title.

In March 1901, a letter from Watson was read out at an emergency board meeting called at Manchester City. In it the Liverpool manager denied a claim that a Reds director had said loudly before the meeting of the two clubs that all the opposition had to do was to contain the great City winger Billy Meredith. 'The rest are no good.' City duly collapsed. Was it Watson who was behind this psychological ploy? It was certainly a devastating aside, one probably designed to dissolve the morale of fragile opponents. The Liverpool manager was certainly a deep admirer of the brilliant Meredith. In 1906, when the Welshman signed for Manchester United, Watson told him, 'Why didn't you come to us; we'd have given you the docks?'[13]

Liverpool conceded just two goals in their last ten league fixtures, with ex-New Brompton full-back John Glover covering for John Robertson at right-back and the Welsh Methodist teetotaller 'Long Legs' Maurice Parry doing the same brilliantly for Wilson at half-back. John 'Sailor' Hunter filled in up front when needed for the injury-troubled Satterthwaite. Bill Perkins (in goal), Bill Goldie and winger Tom Robertson were the league title ever-presents with 34 league starts, but Dunlop, Raisbeck, Cox and Raybould all played more than 30 times, with the reliable John Walker stuck just behind on 29. The consistent form of this core of players – and avoiding injuries – was the crucial factor in this final charge for the title. Liverpool's 1901 favoured title-winning XI lined up like this:

Liverpool FC, league-title winners, 1900–01

Perkins

Robertson (J)   Dunlop

Wilson   Raisbeck   Goldie

Cox   Walker   Raybould   Satterthwaite   Robertson (T)

Narrow wins, first at challengers Sunderland and then at home against Wolves, with Satterthwaite again in the wars and hobbling, started off this title sequence, with a 'clever victory' by 2–0 in 'very greasy and treacherous' conditions at Aston Villa to follow. As we all know, momentum means a lot in football, and this Liverpool squad and their manager now seemed to have it in spades. But a 1–1 home draw against The Wednesday, following a misjudgement by Perkins of Fred Spikesley's header for the visitors, slowed down the upward surge. Raisbeck's absence in favour of the England v. Scotland clash at Crystal Palace on 30 March as Liverpool faced Newcastle United threatened more lost points. Instead, with Dunlop authoritatively assuming the captaincy, replacement Sailor Hunter came up with two vital goals in a 'businesslike' 3–0 victory. No other Liverpool players were on international duty that day: this group was a *team*, not a collection of stars. Incidentally, things got no better for Newcastle. At the club's next match – versus title-chasing Sunderland – there was rioting as locked-out angry spectators stormed the palisades. Sunderland fans pulled up the goalposts, and the police baton charged the 'rough elements' in scenes of chaotic violence reminiscent of the very earliest wild days of the Football League.

In the calmer waters of Anfield, meanwhile, on 8 April 1901 in a match that 'might possibly decide the question of the championship', Liverpool squeezed past Notts County 1–0. It was one of so many crucial narrow victories. Cox centred, Pennington fumbled and, with 15 minutes to go, Johnny-on-the-spot Raybould 'tipped the leather into the net amidst a hurricane of cheers from an intensely excited crowd'. The Reds were now five points behind leaders Sunderland but with three games in hand. The title was actually in reach.

Manchester City were next to be put to the sword at Anfield, with two goals for Robertson, while an overly exuberant Cox was 'penalised for an exhibition of rugby play' and the off-form Raybould was merely a 'broken reed' in attack. A 0–0 grind at rugged Bury followed, but then, unusually, defender Goldie scored from a 'beautiful shot' in the next home fixture against Nottingham Forest.

This after Cox's first-half opener had been 'cheered to the echo' and Forest had been conveniently reduced to ten men through injury. Winger Cox had now contributed ten crucial goals and numerous assists in the campaign.

The expectant Liverpool directors had enraged the Merseyside press – and their neighbours Everton – by resisting FA attempts to bring the 1901 FA Cup final replay between Tottenham and Sheffield United to Goodison Park on the same day as the vital Liverpool v. Forest league fixture. They claimed, not unreasonably, that staging the final across Stanley Park might have deleterious effects on the Anfield attendance. The 'cloven hoof of commercialism', the *Daily Post* called the Liverpool objections; 'mean and unpatriotic' offered the *Liverpool Review*, who saw this move as the craven actions of businessmen, not visionaries or even football enthusiasts. Had the Liverpool board acceded to the FA's request then the city of Liverpool might have seen the destination of the FA Cup and the Football League title decided on either side of Stanley Park on the *same* afternoon. The city of Liverpool might even have hosted future FA finals. As it was, the city would never again host an FA Cup final or a final replay – and Liverpool Football Club would have to grind out its first league title in the club's last match of the 1900–01 season, in the West Midlands.

For Liverpool's final league fixture, away at already relegated West Bromwich Albion in front of a miserable crowd of 2,000 at kick-off and around 4,000 at the end, 'The weather was far from favourable and greatly affected the attendance,' reported the *Daily Post*. Merseysiders continued to arrive long into the season's final match. In 1947, and again in 1976, Liverpool would return to the Black Country to win Football League titles. But surely in 1901, unmotivated, resigned and weak WBA would simply collapse in the face of the champions-elect? Nothing could be further from the truth. Liverpool were at strength, with Parry in for Wilson their only concession to injury. A win was needed to be sure to secure the title from Sunderland, but it was the hosts who began as if their very lives depended on the outcome. It was typical of the English way.

The Liverpool goal 'was kept in a perfect state of siege' in the first half, at least quelling any fears that this fixture might have been 'settled' in advance. Eventually, the visitors got a foothold, and a shot from Raybould slithered out of goalkeeper Joe Reader's grasp. John Walker was there to bundle the ball in for an entirely undeserved half-time Liverpool lead. Now it was all about the Reds digging in and seeing out time. As the minutes ticked down, 'Liverpool worked hard to the finish to maintain their great advantage,' reported the *Daily Post*. The visitors held on 'and amidst a scene of excitement and enthusiasm, they left the field champions of the league for the season 1900–01'.

It had been a stupendous final run-in by any measure: 21 points won out of a possible 24 and no defeats, even if it was a rather scruffy and nervous end. The final title-winning margin was a comfortable two points, with Liverpool winning nineteen, drawing seven and losing eight of their thirty-four matches for forty-five points. Raybould had contributed seventeen precious goals, but Alex Raisbeck had been the standout talent. The Scot had helped prevent many more goals against Liverpool at the opposite end.

'Long before 11 o'clock last night,' reported the *Daily Post* on 30 April 1901, 'a large concourse of people assembled in the Central Station' to welcome their league champions home. A fife and drum band struck up 'The Conquering Hero' as the train drew in, and disembarking players were lifted onto the shoulders of the 'many thousands' of jubilant fans present. A few ambitious admirers even tried to lift aloft the rather portly Tom Watson 'but no arms were long enough to grip his girth and no muscle strong enough to lift him up'. They had the correct man all right: 'Owd Tom' had done his stuff and was recognised locally for it. It had taken just nine short years for a declining John Houlding to finally square matters with his Everton detractors. How sweet this first league triumph must have been for all the ex-Evertonians at Anfield – Houlding and Barclay – and also for McKenna. And, of course, for the marvellous man from the north-east, Tom Watson, Liverpool Football Club's mainly forgotten first great football manager.

CHAPTER 3 REFERENCES

1. Pooley, 'Living in Liverpool: The Modern City', pp. 241 and 244
2. Milne, 'Maritime Liverpool', p. 278
3. Carter, *The Football Manager*, p. 43
4. Carter, *The Football Manager*, p. 31
5. Carter, *The Football Manager*, p. 45
6. Young, *Football on Merseyside*, p. 59
7. Quoted in Young, *Football on Merseyside*, p. 68
8. Quoted in Wilson, *Inverting the Pyramid*, p. 22
9. Inglis, *League Football and the Men Who Made It*, p. 44
10. Inglis, *Made in Manchester*, p. 62
11 Preston, 'The Origins and Development of Association Football in the Liverpool District *c.*1879 *c.*1915', p. 174
12. Inglis, *League Football and the Men Who Made It*, p. 46
13. Harding, *Football Wizard: The Story of Billy Meredith*, pp. 61–2

4

AS MANY DOWNS AS UPS
The Topsy-Turvy 1900s

POST-TITLE STRESS

'It is a pity,' wrote a scribe in the *Liverpool Review* of 31 August 1901, on the brink of another new football season, 'that the managers of Liverpool Football Club cannot be prevailed upon to provide some music to while away the time previous to the match commencing.' Talk about being ahead of its time. Roll on the era of today's Anfield stadium music man George Sephton. The newspaper wanted an ode, or even a symphony, for the new Football League champions from Liverpool. And everyone wanted to see this Liverpool team play. A letter writer to the local press, who signed himself W.H.B., was already warning about the likely 'overcrowding' of tram cars to the stadiums in the city and the 'shock' that awaited any new fan when they first experienced the dangerous enthusiasm for the sport both inside and outside Goodison Park or Anfield. 'I myself have been carried off my feet many a time for fully a hundred yards,' he reported. 'Outside the Liverpool enclosure,' he went on, 'once I was lifted up and did not alight on terra firma again until I found myself inside the ground.' He recommended more self-restraint among supporters and a queuing system for the turnstiles.

Within weeks of his letter, something rather more chilling on the same front was reported in 1901 by a Reds fan calling himself simply 'A Footballer'. Before the derby game in September at Anfield, he recounted, the pay boxes were soon closed at the Oakfield Road (Kop) end, producing a rush of fans towards the Anfield Road entrances. On the terraces at that end of the ground, it 'suddenly felt as if all the juice was going to be squeezed out of us. Word came that the entrances were being rushed and for a time we were like sardines in a box and literally panted for breath.' Accounts like this rarely made it into the press, though pretty much all 'shilling fans' would have had similar stories to tell.

Most people had anecdotes about 'almost' being injured or about being crushed or discomforted at a football match. It was remarkable that serious accidents at English football were so relatively few in number, given the size of crowds and the intensity of the 'football fever'. Stadium facilities in Britain at this time were still basic at best, and mechanisms for counting supporters into stadium areas or for ensuring their safe exit were either crude or non-existent. At least fans could still escape onto the pitch in emergencies. Eventually, though, some poor souls would surely pay the ultimate price. They did so: in Glasgow just a few months later at a Scotland v. England home international match at Ibrox in April 1902; at Burnden Park, Bolton, in 1946; and at Hillsborough in 1989. British football had often been warned, but it didn't always seem to listen.

On the pitch, and in a pattern that characterised much of the next two decades, Liverpool Football Club now slumped from title winners to midtable also-rans. Perhaps taking the players to Paris as a reward for winning the title dulled their senses for its defence? Only one win in the club's first ten league matches – including a 2–2 Anfield draw with Everton – signalled that trouble was ahead. Loss of form and especially the impact of injuries played its part. Just fifteen players had filled all but five first-team slots in the title season. Now Tom Watson was forced to call upon 24 players in a squad that between them could muster only 42 goals in 34 games, a miserable 14 goals away from home. Only Derby County scored fewer goals.

At Everton in January, it was a 0–4 drubbing for Liverpool, and it was expected the Blues would 'do' for the Reds in the first Merseyside FA Cup derby, on 25 January 1902. The *Liverpool Mercury*, forever hopeful, wondered if the tie might not 'awaken the champions from their somnolence', while the *Daily Post* complained that local rivals should simply not be drawn together at this early stage in such a prestigious competition. It suggested a novel form of regional 'seeding' to replace the 'old fashioned' open draw of the FA. This would require two hats: one containing clubs from the north and the other clubs from the south. 'This would give fair play and avoid clashing.' Predictably, the proposal fell on deaf ears in London.

The *Liverpool Courier* reported on Tom Watson's frustrations with the Liverpool injury count but also on his resolution that 'We are not giving in. The men we have are as fit as can be and they mean to play for all they are worth.' There was also an insight into the club's preparations at their Lytham FA Cup base: 'Walking, sprinting, football training and hot baths', with billiards to follow in the evening at the local Working Man's Institute. The Liverpool chairman William Houlding and the other club directors 'showed their interest in the team by paying them periodical visits'. Despite this, all was set fair for an

Everton victory. However, in 'vile' weather in front of around 25,000 huddled souls, 'the revival of Liverpool was remarkable', with the home side dominating the exchanges in a hard-fought 2–2 draw. 'If the team does as well at Goodison and shoots a bit straighter,' argued the *Daily Post*, '[Liverpool] will come out of the test all right.'

A reader wrote to the *Liverpool Courier* to complain about the behaviour of 'roughs' in the Oakfield Road area of Anfield who 'amuse themselves by playing so-called football in the open street and, moreover, are often heard to be making objectionable remarks to any of the public who happen to be passing by'. These young tyros were probably encouraged by the weather for the derby cup replay, which was much improved. After 40 minutes of sparring, home full-back Walter Balmer mis-headed a Raisbeck free-kick past the unsighted Blues keeper George Kitchen, who 'making a wild kick missed the ball, which rolled slowly into the goal'. This rather comical and welcome clanger was 'greeted wildly' by the Liverpool supporters present. After a 'rather prolonged' interval, Everton's Sam Wolstenholme deliberately handled, and from the ensuing free-kick Sailor Hunter advanced to score for the Reds with a 'beautiful long shot'. There was no reply forthcoming from a jaded Everton.

As the *Daily Post* put it, it was a result that 'staggered most people', but it was only a temporary respite for Liverpool. Southern League club Southampton – on their way to their first FA Cup final – dumped the Reds 1–4 in the next round. Liverpool lost only two more matches (twelve) than did second-placed Everton in the league in 1901–02, but they won only ten in total, fewer than any other club. A lack of penetration saw them draw 12 times, including at eventual champions Sunderland.

The signing in March 1902 of right-winger 'Graceful' Artie Goddard from Glossop promised more consistency and more attacking threat – the marvellous Goddard played more than 400 times for Liverpool, scoring 77 goals. Cox moved to the left to replace the transferred Tom Robertson, and in 1902–03 ten outfield players each mustered at least twenty-seven league appearances, a return to some of the stability of the title season. But there were two other main reasons why Liverpool climbed back up to fifth spot. The first was a change in playing philosophy, which meant a little more risk-taking and attacking football, an approach that produced more wins (17) but also more defeats (13) than in the previous season. The second was the fantastic form of Sam Raybould, 31 goals in 33 league matches and a club record 32 for the season (also netting in a 1–2 FA Cup loss to Manchester United). It was also noticeable that the early Scottish leanings of the two Merseyside clubs were now being balanced by more English influences.

PAYING FOR SUCCESS – AND KING JOHN'S CURTAIN CALL

A good example of the decline of the Scottish influence came when Liverpool and Everton played out a 0–0 draw in April 1903 – notable for Raybould's 'wild marksmanship'. The *Liverpool Review* wrote that 'at least fifteen out of the twenty-two performers were born below the Border, a truly striking observation on the present predominance of English football'. And, we might say too, a sign of the declining influence on the playing and recruitment side at Liverpool of Honest John McKenna. The Liverpool man would be a future vice chair of the players' union, and he was now also serving the Football League. McKenna had been a bitter opponent in 1900 of a new FA rule that limited the maximum weekly wage of professional footballers to £4 (£208 per year) and a plan to ban the payment of bonuses. This meant that top professional footballers were well rewarded but not excessively so; officially, they now earned wages commensurate with lower-grade professional men, about twice the wage of skilled workers and clerks and just under twice the wages of foremen and supervisors.[1]

Unofficially, the earnings of many top players – including those at Liverpool – were simply not contained by the £4-a-week wage limit. The retain-and-transfer system in England effectively tied players to their clubs and under-the-counter payments were rife. What right anyway did the FA have to interfere in the private business of Football League clubs? By 1904, the league was effectively back in control of the players' wages issue, but it refused to abolish the maximum wage and, frankly, why bother? The richer clubs had long worked out ways of rewarding players surreptitiously. The Wales star Billy Meredith would later agree that the 'secret of success' behind Manchester City's 1904 FA Cup win was that 'the club put aside the rule that no player should receive more than £4 a week'. He estimated that City had paid £654 in bonuses: 'The team delivered the goods and the club paid for the goods delivered and both sides were satisfied.'[2]

In 1906, Manchester City lost almost an entire team, including Meredith, on match-fixing charges in an investigation that also revealed that some of the club's players had been receiving at least £6 a week in wages since 1902. According to the Liverpool FC directors, the Anfield players who won the 1900–01 league title were paid even more, a basic £7 a week. With bonuses, this figure could reach £10 a week – more than double the permitted maximum.[3] The smaller league clubs, of course, were probably very thankful for the constraints on costs promised by the maximum wage, thus producing in the boardrooms of the football elite a 'silent conspiracy in which subterfuge became the accepted norm'.[4]

If it was assumed that the 0–0 result with Everton in April 1903 meant another corner had been turned for Liverpool Football Club, then a rude awakening lay ahead. Liverpool's goals dried up, and the club's confidence and defensive meanness almost completely disappeared. So too – not entirely coincidentally – did its founder and long-time leader. At 7.15 a.m. on 17 March 1902 in Cimiez in the South of France, after a lengthy illness, the remarkable John Houlding died in his 69th year. The Everton club acknowledged King John's huge role in establishing the *two* major professional football clubs in the city by flying flags at half-mast and having the Blues team wear black armbands as a sign of respect on the occasion of his passing.

Houlding's death followed hard on the heels of that of the local philanthropist and great Liverpool Liberal politician William Rathbone, who was honoured by a funeral cortège a mile long and a wreath sent by Florence Nightingale in recognition of his work on district nursing. But the great John Houlding also had his own strong claims to good local works: with the aged poor of Everton and the homeless young, for example; on improving sanitation for the least well off in the city; in the Liverpool mayoral office, fighting against the 'murderous protests' of local temperance supporters; and, of course, in establishing Merseyside professional football on both sides of Stanley Park. Many people from 'humble backgrounds', as well as the nation's football cognoscenti, attended his funeral. 'He had no pretence to inspired genius,' remarked the *Liverpool Courier*, perhaps a little too unkindly, 'but had abiding faith in diligent, painstaking work.' More importantly, in the words of the *Liverpool Mercury* on 24 March 1902, 'His place can never be filled and the Liverpool club is staggering under one of the heaviest blows it has ever received. The future of the Anfielders seems far from reassuring now that their leading spirit has passed away.'

LIVERPOOL FC AFTER JOHN HOULDING

Houlding's death and the loss of his steely influence *did* hit Liverpool FC hard. But on the pitch it was also crucial that forward Sam Raybould missed the first 19 league games in the 1903–04 season through injury and that no one stepped in to fill the resultant goals vacuum. Moreover, new defensive recruits John Chadburn and Fred Buck proved failures at Anfield, though the latter, at just 5 ft 4 in. tall, remarkably went on to play at centre-half for WBA in the 1912 FA Cup final. Like Chadburn, the locally born amateur centre-forward Syd Smith played the opening two Football League fixtures, scoring in the first and attracting good press in 'a most promising exposition of the soccer code'. But he was then unceremoniously ditched by the perfectionist Watson.

The uncomplicated but reliable Nottingham man Alf West was signed to play right-back in November 1903, but by then much of the damage had already been done – including five straight Liverpool defeats at the start of the campaign. Even Alex Raisbeck was moved to full-back as Watson sought a foothold, and a 2–2 draw with Everton in October offered some hope, though the *Daily Post* was little fooled, commenting that Liverpool 'must have played a little above their form and the probability is that they will not again this season be seen to such advantage'. These proved to be wise words. A 2–5 hammering at Stoke followed – Stoke would finish one point above Liverpool, in safety – with even the saintly Raisbeck being roundly criticised by the *Liverpool Echo* for his panicky defending. The Anfield team was now at rock bottom and praying for a signing. 'Surely,' asked a plaintive *Daily Post*, 'the resources of Mr Tom Watson and his directors are not so beggarly as they appear?'

A further run of eight matches without a win around Christmas 1903 and then another 2–5 hammering in the return derby at Everton on 1 April 1904 seemed to have all but killed off Liverpool. When a struggling Stoke, rather suspiciously (for Reds fans), won at a canter at Goodison Park of all places, the game was really up for the 1901 champions. A new signing from Sunderland for £500 in February, inside-right Robbie Robinson, offered plenty of future promise, and he began to score goals immediately he arrived towards the back end of the season. But wins at home to Bury and then at Blackburn came way too late to swing things around for Liverpool. With Everton comparatively lording it in third place, it was ignominious relegation for their near neighbours just three years after title glory – what a come down. Old rumours were now ominously reported again in the *Daily Post* in April 1904 questioning the very future of the club without its founder, predicting that if Liverpool were indeed relegated 'it would sooner or later drop out of existence as the owners of the land at Anfield intend to build on the ground . . . It would surprise nobody if the rumour was correct this time.'

Following John Houlding's death, the ownership and control issues around the club – including around the Anfield stadium – still needed to be resolved. It was a crisis not unlike the 2010 version. But Liverpool Football Club homeless? In May, the *Liverpool Review* could not resist producing the words of an imagined sporting operetta, featuring a mournful Tom Watson, who summed up the club's gloomy predicament when he supposedly sang:

> McKenna's not smiled for a week,
> He thinks we'll sail off in a sloop.
> We're all without fable,

Dressed in crepe and sable.
In the Second they've placed us
They've gone and disgraced us.
Because – and I have it on the very best authority –
We have all been drowned 'in the soup'.

'In the soup' and downbeat Liverpool Football Club may have been, but they were far from down and out. The 37-year-old goalkeeper Teddy Doig, recruited from Sunderland for 150 quid in August 1904 – still the club's oldest signing – gave the Liverpool backline the confidence it had so palpably lacked when the club had been demoted. Doig, a trained boxer, could punch a ball to the halfway line and he soon struck up a rapport with the early Kop. Given that relegation-threatened Middlesbrough paid Sunderland a record £1,000 fee for Alf Common in February 1905, it could hardly be argued that Tom Watson was trying to 'buy' the Anfield club out of their problems. 'Bee', the *Liverpool Echo*'s football correspondent, said of Watson on Owd Tom's death that, 'He had signed more cheap and good players than any secretary in the world.' It was not a bad commendation. In fact, the Liverpool manager/secretary was convinced that he had the core of a squad that was capable not only of running through the Second Division but even of challenging again in the First. Not for the first time, Watson showed his sound judgement.

Complaints abound today about the alleged chasm in playing quality between the Premier League and the Championship, but the lack of real depth in the early Football League was also very plain to see. The demoted Liverpool stormed to the Division Two title in 1905, dropping just two points in their first thirteen matches and scoring ninety-three goals in losing only three times in thirty-four matches. Twenty-year-old Bootle forward John Parkinson offered vital goalscoring support to both Raybould and Goddard: the three players scored sixty-three league goals between them, Parkinson scoring twenty in just twenty-one league appearances, including a hat-trick in an 8–1 demolition of Burslem Port Vale. The only opponent Liverpool failed to beat in the league was the also promoted Bolton Wanderers, not that the club's supporters were always convinced by the Reds' form. Against Lincoln City in January 1905, the Anfield crowd produced 'ironical cheers' and 'a continuous roar of derision' as the home players struggled to find their promotion form. Maybe fitness was the problem, because when the Reds were drawn to play First Division table-topping Everton at Anfield in the FA Cup in January 1905 eight of the home players weighed in at over 12 st., compared to only three Evertonians. Almost a century before it became commonplace to focus on such matters, an amateur statistician reported to the *Liverpool Courier* that Everton had the best of the 1–1 Cup draw on corners (7–3) and throw-ins (50–46) won. The Blues had also forced sixteen goalkicks from Liverpool, compared to taking seven of their own. Everton won the replay but were reported to have been 'distinctively lucky' to have done so.

A few weeks later, on 22 February 1905, a public meeting was held at the Carlton Hall on Eberle Street to start finally to plan the post-John Houlding era for the Liverpool club. Every season bar one since Tom Watson had been made manager, Liverpool FC had made a profit. Chairman Edwin Berry told the meeting that the club had £700 in the bank and was financially stable, but also that, 'In name it [LFC] was a limited company, but practically it was a one-man show.' Out of 3,000 existing Liverpool shares, the Houlding family held 2,000. This needed to change. The club debt to the late John Houlding was £10,000, with a further £5,000 bank overdraft guaranteed by the Houlding family. William Houlding had approached the board, said Berry, to put the club 'on a more popular basis, so that it would really belong to the people'. Houlding had agreed to give up the 2,000 family shares and to wipe out the debt if the club agreed to relieve him of the bank-loan guarantee. Other existing shareholders, it was reported, had also agreed to give up 50 per cent of the money they held in the company. It was a new beginning. A share issue was agreed for 1906 of 15,000 shares at £1 each and, supposedly, a more 'popular control' of the club with much more public accountability would be established.

Liverpool FC could now purchase the Anfield ground from Orrell and the Houlding estate. With this last point in mind, a shareholder, Fred Perry, suggested that the club consider installing a cycle track around the pitch, a move that would be supported by the National Cyclists' Union. Chillingly, Edwin Berry promised that the Liverpool board would give the matter serious consideration, but it never came about. There were no big money men behind the new Liverpool. The local businessmen of modest means who fronted the new share issue were: William Houlding; John McKenna; Alexander Nisbet, a relieving officer; John Ramsey, a bookkeeper; John Dermott, a tobacconist; William Evans, a cashier; and Albert Edwin Berry, a solicitor's clerk. Relatively little of this assumed 'spread of control' to put the club in the hands of local people was actually in evidence in the years that followed, as the club's board quickly established a lasting dominance in share ownership. Football supporters who were dubious about the role of football club directors might have been amused by article number 45 of the Liverpool FC 1906 Memorandum of Association, which read, 'If any member is a lunatic or idiot he may vote by his committee or other legal curator.' Football club directors and shareholders as lunatics – surely not? The new Liverpool board had already assembled plans to redevelop the ground, given some reasonable stability on the field – which meant, minimally, staying in the First Division.

CHAMPIONS AGAIN

The formation of FIFA in 1904, a new international body for the administration of football, spoke eloquently enough of football's widening global horizons. But the home countries generally kept their distance from the new body in case it diminished the influence in world football of the British. An expansive Liverpool FC had at least voted for the domestic growth of the Football League in 1905, from thirty-six clubs to two divisions comprising forty clubs. This produced 38 league fixtures, although most top clubs also still played lucrative friendly fixtures and local and regional cup matches, bringing the total fixture load for the elite up to around 60 or even 70 matches in a season.

This minor expansion in the league programme also helped to air differences of opinion about the Football League's real ambitions and future status: was it to remain a largely regional competition for selected members, or did it have true national aspirations?[5] Woolwich Arsenal was the only southern club in the First Division, having been promoted there in 1904, though the strong performances of both Tottenham Hotspur and Southampton in the FA Cup had shown the obvious and growing strength of the rival Southern League. Major structural changes lay ahead.

The game itself was also changing, becoming less brutal and slightly more 'scientific', with systems of passing play now replacing aspects of the more traditional 'kick and rush' tactics. Tackling was still central, of course, and the brawny British shoulder charge was certainly not outlawed. But the charge was now permissible only if it was deemed to be neither 'violent nor dangerous'. England international William Bassett wrote in 1906 of the new flexible approaches to playing the game that 'the one-style team is not the successful team . . . if forwards cannot adapt themselves to all conditions they are not likely to be permanently successful'.[6] Liverpool would have to look to their mettle.

They began their return to First Division football with the veteran Doig in goal, but in October 1905 Tom Watson invested £340 in what would later become Chesterfield's factory for goalkeepers by signing Sam Hardy for the task. This was a brilliant piece of managerial business – Hardy was a magnificent keeper – and Watson was seldom beaten to the transfer punch. Later, a telegram about a Reds transfer target sent from a Liverpool scout to Watson went astray. It landed instead in the lap of the press, and the player was lost to Leicester Fosse. The next day, Watson changed the Liverpool telegraphic address to the distinctive 'goalkeeper' in order to rule out any more costly communication mishaps.

'Safe and Steady' Sam Hardy became the England goalkeeper from 1907, collecting 21 caps, and he displayed 'a rare, quiet competence', becoming an imposing fixture in the Liverpool defence for the next seven seasons.[7] Watson was pressed so rapidly and so decisively into the transfer market because Liverpool lost five of their first eight matches back in the top flight, conceding twenty goals in the process, including a 2–4 defeat at Goodison and a 0–5 humiliation at Aston Villa. The *Daily Post* certainly had it right when reviewing the Reds' defensive inadequacies during the events of a 'bewildering rapidity' at Goodison Park, where 'the multitude who on Saturday, by their numbers and enthusiasm, demonstrated the amazing influence which football exercises over the British peoples'. On the early condition of Liverpool FC, it opined that, 'West might work like a Trojan and Raisbeck be as ubiquitous as a sprite, but with a disheartened custodian [Doig] and full-back [reserve Murray] the game was up.' In stepped new signing Sam Hardy, and Liverpool never looked back.

Reds forward John Parkinson had broken his wrist in the opening match against Woolwich Arsenal, and he would play only nine times in the league. But with the rock-solid Hardy now on board, only 26 goals were conceded in the 30 Liverpool league matches that followed. Chester-born centre-forward Joe Hewitt had signed for Watson from Bolton Wanderers back in January 1904 for £150, but now he got his chance with an extended run alongside Sam Raybould and ended up top scorer with 23 goals. He supplied his entire life to Liverpool Football Club. After playing 164 times for Liverpool, scoring 71 goals, Hewitt later served the club as a coach, club steward and even press-box attendant over a 60-year period. From Stoke, Watson filched hard-working left-half Jimmy Bradley in September 1905, and the new man played 31 times in the league in the 1905–06 title season and 185 times in all for Liverpool, another typically astute signing. From 21 October 1905, when they played Nottingham Forest, Liverpool took 20 points from the next 22 on offer, and they were chasing the title rather than fighting relegation, as had been initially feared. The typical Liverpool XI in 1905–06, in 2–3–5 formation, was this one:

Liverpool FC, league title-winners, 1905–06

Hardy

Dunlop   West

Parry   Raisbeck   Bradley

Goddard   Robinson   Hewitt   Raybould   Cox

Of these players, Dunlop, Raisbeck, Parry, Raybould and Cox were all men who had survived from the 1900–01 title campaign. Cox had almost left Liverpool for Fulham, only to be forced to stay at Anfield, fortuitously, on a technicality following the late intervention of the FA. Of the dual title winners, arguably Dunlop, Raisbeck and Raybould all have a good case for consideration for inclusion in the club's greatest team of all time. Goddard was also a fantastic servant, and even the occasionally inconsistent Cox was considered 'the fastest left-winger playing today'.

The grey-haired Dunlop, a 'powerful punter' with great stamina, had made his debut in 1895 and ended up playing at the club for 15 seasons. Dunlop was a real leader, Watson's cohering figure in the 1905–06 Reds dressing-room, and he was a fair musician who would entertain the Liverpool players when they were away from home preparing for major cup ties. In his benefit-match programme in 1906, it was said that 'there was never one who, year in year out, has given such wholehearted service as Dunlop has to Liverpool'. It was a fitting tribute to a totally committed club man.

By December 1905, when Notts County were hosted at Anfield, according to the *Football Echo*, Tom Watson's work was apparent to all. 'The attitude from start to finish was excellent . . . The Reds were engaged in a very pretty attack which showed off the scientific methods of the Liverpool front line to perfection.' Liverpool were top of the table with a 2–0 victory, and they rarely looked like conceding their advantage. In March 1906, it was Middlesbrough's turn to suffer at Anfield, clouted 6–1, with local reserve forward 'lively Jack [Carlin] of Wavertree' helping himself to two goals. According to the by now near-poetic *Liverpool Echo*, this was a performance of 'such dash, such virile shooting, feeding and racing' that 'the Reds were in excelsis'. Not to be outdone on the poetry front, the *Daily Post* said more simply, 'The Reds were standing on velvet.' What could stop this title charge?

Actually, a 0–3 league defeat next up at Notts County came as quite a jarring shock to the Liverpool system. There was little poetry, and not even too much pretty prose, here. But a stirring 2–1 win at title rivals Preston North End, with utility man Tom Chorlton grabbing a priceless goal, put Liverpool back on track for two forthcoming derby matches: one in an FA Cup semi-final at Villa Park on 31 March, the other in a league meeting at Anfield on Good Friday. Liverpool had certainly been favoured by good fortune in the FA Cup draw, comfortably beating Leicester Fosse, Barnsley, Brentford and Southampton all at home, conceding only one goal and thus avoiding any First Division Football League opposition. Now here was another opportunity for the Reds to strike for a possible league and FA Cup Double. Everton, on the other hand, had been uncompetitive in the league and so could focus strongly on the cup.

Because of its inclusiveness and history, the FA Cup was still seen in 1906 as more of a national 'championship' than was the Football League. But injuries kept key men Cox and Raybould out of the Liverpool line-up, and the first real signs of tiredness had also started to show in the Anfield ranks. Two Everton goals within two minutes in the second half settled it. The second, from Hardman, drifted in past a 'fascinated' (transfixed) Hardy and resulted from the keeper dropping the initial strike, having 'kept out a dozen worse shots'. A goalkeeper, alas, is always remembered for the key mistakes, not his great saves. 'There was more excitement and sensation merged into ninety seconds,' said the *Daily Post*, 'than the whole ninety minutes. It was all over with the Reds then.'

Liverpool sought some revenge for this grave FA Cup disappointment in the vital league derby fixture on 13 April, and with Everton fans keenly anticipating the FA Cup final, a much larger than normal holiday crowd of 33,000 turned up for the contest, some of whom forced the gates and spilled onto the pitch. 'The referee and officials had great trouble in placing the encroaching crowd,' reported the *Daily Post*, 'so that the touchline and corner flags were clear enough to proceed with the game.' This excited supporter disruption went on throughout the match, and as Everton advanced in the first half 'Hardy, who was impeded by some of the spectators, emerged from his charge to clutch the leather from Young'. Sam Hardy was usually unflappable, immovable, but the intruding spectators, who now assembled in 'deep ranks' along the touchlines, had definitely ruined his concentration. He dropped the ball again following this easy save, with Everton's Jack Taylor on hand to net the gift. This error gave the Blues an undeserved – and a crowd-assisted – half-time lead.

It took fully 25 minutes even to get the game restarted because of further 'difficulties' with the crowd, but in one of Liverpool's 'hot attacks' in the second half Taylor fouled Parkinson in the penalty area, and Alf West converted from the spot 'amidst terrific acclamation'. Rival spectators now held their breath and struggled to keep each other off the field of play. Liverpool continued to press, but there would be no more goals – or pitch invasions. It was probably fortunate that things remained even at one-all so that all spectators could return home peaceably, honour satisfied on both sides. As a result of the shared spoils, Liverpool were still top, and a confident Everton now faced fancied Newcastle United in the FA Cup final. Local 'Dicky Sams' were beginning to think of Merseyside football glory once more: a league and FA Cup Double, different clubs, one city, one big party.

At bottom club Wolves on 14 April 1906, the hosts put up a 'capital fight' against the prospective champions Liverpool, but in a 'rough and tumble' scrappy match 'class and training told its inevitable tale'. With the injured Raybould and Cox now out for the season, goals by Hewitt and Goddard sealed the Reds' win. But it was nearer the Liverpool goal that the victory was really forged. 'The half-back line showed splendid confidence in their own ability,' judged the *Daily Post*. 'Neither Raisbeck, Parry nor Bradley ever for a moment lost their heads.' Nor had they done so for most of the campaign.

In the penultimate round of fixtures, Liverpool lost away to Bolton Wanderers, 2–3, with the last ten minutes 'almost painful as each side attacked in turn'. But it was of no matter. The pressure of the chase also told on the Anfield club's closest challengers, Preston North End, who lost 0–2 at Sunderland on the same day and thus conceded the title to Liverpool. When the sheepishly defeated but triumphant Anfield men arrived back at Exchange Station at nine o'clock that night, they were met by 'several hundreds of enthusiasts who cheered the players lustily and escorted them to their waggonette'. Ordinary travellers were reported to have joined in the celebrations when it was reported to them that the league champions were back in town. Inevitably, the Sandon Hotel waited for a party that continued long into the misty Merseyside night.

A HOUSE DIVIDED AGAINST ITSELF

In reviewing Liverpool FC's extraordinary recent history, the *Football Echo* of 17 April 1906 referred delicately and quixotically in a 'comment' column to Tom Watson's relegation year as a 'quaint experience'. It was a nice touch. But the author also had no doubt that the Liverpool manager 'has worked indefatigably all the time, and to a large extent the success now achieved may be ascribed to the excellent spirit which he contrives to infuse into the team'. It was true that the Watson 'of the iron nerves' had not gone in for signing star players or for recruiting an over-large squad that might risk festering discontent. Liverpool FC were a very tightly knit group: most of the players lived very close to the Anfield stadium, between Breckfield Road and Oakfield Road. Raisbeck lived at 16 Elsie Road, Parry and Dunlop on Arkles Road. Sam Raybould lived on Lyon Road, James Bradley on Thirlmere Road and Arthur Goddard on Walton Breck Road.

Words of praise were also saved for club trainer Bill Connell and even the Anfield groundsman. The wily Connell was soon featured in the local press endorsing 'Zam-buk', a skin cure for cuts and bruises. The *Echo* trusted that ticket prices would not be increased next season 'when the new ground, which is to be started within a week, is in readiness'. Typically, club chairman Councillor Edwin Berry commented that the Liverpool club was looking to sign only 'class men' (not simply class *players*), and it was noted that Liverpool 'have fewer players on their list than any other club in the First Division'. Maybe this was part of their success? The *Liverpool Echo* further pointed out that in 1905–06 'every position has been filled by a tryer, and there are not more than three outfield brilliants [by which it meant Raisbeck, Bradley and Dunlop]. It is collectively that the Reds were superior to opponents.' This was indeed a championship win in the typical Liverpool Way.

This left only the ritual of a title celebration for Liverpool and their supporters to see out at home against Sheffield United (a valedictory 3–1 win) in a now largely redundant fixture that was scheduled, nevertheless, for the same kick-off time and day as the FA Cup final at Crystal Palace. Significantly, when news of Everton's FA Cup-winning goal finally reached Anfield, 'This was the signal for tumultuous cheering, which did not subside for several minutes.' Unlike some of their Blue rivals, Liverpool supporters seemed genuinely pleased at their neighbours' – and the city's – success. The crowd that welcomed the Everton party back to Lime Street later that night was reportedly 'immensely good-humoured, and partisans of both Liverpool and Everton clubs shared alike in the enthusiasm'. At the civic reception that followed for Everton at Central Station, Liverpool FC directors were present to hear the lord mayor say that the city was in a position no other had experienced and that 'at least half [only half?] of the male citizens of Liverpool were sympathisers with the game of football'. He argued that there was no ill-feeling in the rival camps and 'trusted for years to come there might be a good feeling between the two clubs and that they might work together in harmony and good fellowship'.

It was a nice idea, this cosy football bond, one born out of a moment of near-unique twin football success for the city. But it was unlikely to last, and no fan of either club was liable to apologise too much for that. As a correspondent to the *Evening Express* put it on 26 April 1906, perhaps just a little *too* bleakly:

> Actually, healthy rivalry cannot but have a beneficial influence, but I fear that generous, kindly rivalry is sadly lacking in the ranks of our local clubs. The partisanship is bigoted: too many of each club's supporters are utterly intolerant of the other club's merits; each set of followers are carping critics of the other side. In short . . . we are a house divided, against itself.

For the *Daily Post*, a combination of 'stout hearts, good constitutions and a determination to overcome difficulties' had aided Liverpool in surviving their horrendous start to 1905–06, although this sounded perhaps more like the making of a resolute mountaineering club rather than that of a champion football team.

It was certainly some achievement to come back from the foothill depths of 1904. Two titles in two seasons: from Second Division champions to champions of the Football League in a matter of months. Indeed, it had been a tumultuous six years for the club and for Tom Watson: league champions in 1901; twelfth; fifth; relegated; champions of Division Two; and league champions again in 1906. 'Roller coaster' seems a modest description. In a speech at the first AGM of the 'new' Liverpool FC in June 1906, Watson (to loud laughter) twinkled that the club 'had always been [one] of ups and downs'. He trusted that 'they had finished with the latter, and that upwards was their future motion'. There followed a loud crescendo of applause.

Today, of course, few top manager–coaches would have survived the shock of a mid-period demotion and still be in office to make this kind of cheeky little observation. But this was a different age, and this Liverpool board believed in their manager, who, in turn, believed in his players. In any case, there were few authentic football managers in the game in 1906 and, while crowds harangued players and referees, there was certainly no media-induced sacking culture to identify and harass them. Average gates at Liverpool in 1905–06 at 17,736 exceeded those at neighbours Everton (15,920) for the first time, though receipts at Everton still beat those at Liverpool. The total balance available at Anfield in June 1906 amounted to a very healthy £3,360. The champions had (officially at least) paid their players £4,440, less than Everton's £5,270, and wages made up about 35 per cent of gate-receipts income – happy days indeed. With the promise that the new Anfield stadium would be 'considerably altered and improved' and would be 'one of the best equipped in England' by September 1906, good times surely lay ahead again for Liverpool Football Club. You think?

THE END OF A STADIUM ERA

Before the remodelling of Anfield in 1906, the Liverpool stadium was made up, like most others of the time, of irregular timber crush barriers, unterraced earth and ash slopes, and very basic iron and timber flat-stand roofs covering wooden bench seats. There was, as yet, no complete outer wall to offer either definition or convincing security. The chimneys of John Houlding's Stanley House home could clearly be seen from the uncovered Kop as they jutted out over the modest Anfield Road covered terrace.[8] This was no haven of early modern comfort or prestige, and it was hardly a fitting home for the 1906 Football League champions.

Not that the situation for local football in Liverpool was much better. In 1908, the city had a maximum of 81 football pitches for use by local clubs compared to 360 in Manchester. This situation led to local campaigns to better resource the woeful participation side of the sport on Merseyside.[9] But the early years of the new century would produce something of a revolution in building design, technology and engineering. Iron was replaced by precision-made standardised steel for stanchions, stairways and beams, for example, and also, crucially, reinforced concrete was used to replace the sometimes unstable fire-risk wooden structures in buildings, including football grounds.[10]

As professional football expanded at an astonishing rate in British cities, so the new club owners sought ways of increasing stadium capacity and improving customer comfort, and also of maximising returns on their investment. The brilliant young Scottish engineer Archibald Leitch was a revolutionary figure in stadium design. But he had the horrifying experience of attending the Scotland v. England match at Ibrox Park in 1902 when the 'flimsy and insubstantial' wooden stands he had designed collapsed before his eyes. Twenty-six people were killed and five hundred and sixteen injured. Scotland fans, oblivious to the scale of the disaster – there was no public address system in operation – chaired off a home hero, the future Liverpool recruit Teddy Doig. The devastated goalkeeper was clearly in tears.[11] Unsurprisingly, Leitch was emotionally drained by these events, but he was also determined to use the new advances in technology and materials to build bigger and safer stands at British football grounds. He moved the family home to Blundellsands, just north of Liverpool, in 1909, having worked with both the Liverpool and Everton clubs in the redesign of two of the premier football grounds in England.

On 25 August 1906, the *Liverpool Echo* provided an enticing glimpse of what would be the new Anfield, designed by the precocious 31-year-old Leitch, with its walled-in 'fancy brick setting', large exit gates on all four sides, raised pitch (by five feet) and its extended 'elevated terrace consisting of 132 tiers of steps, which will afford space for something like 20,000 spectators'. Only the Anfield Road end would survive unaltered. This new development constituted an extraordinary vision of the new, modern era of British sport. The original plans laid out in June 1906 had also included a roof over the Spion Kop, newly named by sports editor of the *Liverpool Echo* Ernest Edwards. But this cover would not be added until 1928 and by a different architect, local man Joseph Watson Cabre. The topmast of the SS *Great Eastern*, one of the world's first iron ships, had been salvaged when the ship was broken up, and it was floated up the Mersey. It was then hauled by horse to the Anfield ground, where it had first been raised inside the corner of the Oakfield Road outer wall in 1891, presumably to signal the city's connection with the sea and seafaring.[12] The new stadium incorporated the mast, and it remains outside the Kop to this day.

'The entire scheme [of 1906–07],' the *Echo* continued, 'is modelled on a new departure from what football grounds are generally supposed to be and when completed will provide ample space for about 60,000 visitors.' This improbable projected figure seemed astonishing. It dwarfed the official Anfield capacity in 1905 and, crucially, was larger than that at Goodison Park. The jewel of the Leitch plan was to resite the then current main stand (opened in 1894) to the Kemlyn Road side of the ground and replace it with a completely new structure, combining a seated area with a standing paddock in front. It was Leitch's first football stand made in reinforced concrete, and it was lauded by building-design experts for its 'elastic strength' and 'durability'. It was probably the first of its kind in Britain. The curved gable of the new main stand would be the characteristic Leitch signature for Anfield until it was replaced by a much more functional and ugly flat roof in 1970.

Impressed and alarmed in equal measure by the imposing Anfield redevelopment, in 1908 neighbours Everton hired Leitch to rebuild their own new main stand to keep pace with their rivals across Stanley Park. A journalist duly described the new 80-ft-high Goodison Park monster edifice as the 'Mauretania Stand', after the world's largest ship.[13]

Sadly, the league champions Liverpool could not match in their performances the obvious grandeur of their new surroundings. Perhaps the players missed the greater intimacy and hostility of the old stadium? Whatever the reasons, after a scrambled first-day home win against relegation candidates Stoke, there followed two draws and five consecutive defeats in the league for Liverpool, including a 1–2 home loss against Everton. Third from bottom with four points from eight matches, the *Liverpool Courier* deemed that 'drastic action' would have to be taken to resurrect a campaign that so far had brought 'no credit to an organisation with the strength and resources of Liverpool'. Problems clearly lay at both ends of the pitch: up front 'chance after chance was thrown away', while at the back an unusually uncertain Sam Hardy 'shared . . . the demoralisation of his colleagues. He is not altogether blameless.' With a small squad, serious injuries to Dunlop, West and Parry all contributed to growing defensive uncertainty, while in the forwards Joe Hewitt lost both fitness and form, and no one came in to replace his vital goals. Left-sided attacker Bill McPherson, signed for £200 from St Mirren in August 1906, eventually contributed a useful ten goals in twenty-eight league games.

By the middle of October 1906, with a trip to Bury in the offing, the local scribes concluded, not unreasonably, that Liverpool's form had been 'atrociously disappointing'. The directors (no mention of Tom Watson here) took a 'strong step' by leaving out Cox from the forwards, and the tide turned for the champions with a 3–1 win, which showed some of the 'dash and spirit' previously lacking. Gone was the current pattern of possession and pressure without the finish, and in its place was the penetration of old, with Raybould weighing in with two familiar goals. The next eight matches brought six Liverpool wins and just two defeats, and included a 6–1 home mauling of Preston and a 'perfect farce' of a 5–1 Anfield victory against an eight-man Notts County. The visitors had left-back Jack Montgomery ordered off for flooring Raybould and two men carried off.

Liverpool had now climbed to seventh place, six points behind leaders Everton. By the time the squad took to their Christmas quarters in Southport, facing three games in five days, hopes were even high of another title challenge. But instead it was five goal-less Liverpool performances that followed, four of them defeats, and a slide down to 14th place. 'Unless some revolutionary alteration is seen,' said the *Liverpool Courier* after a January 1907 0–2 reverse at Blackburn, 'the team is certain to drop still lower and further besmirch the reputation of league champions.' New man McPherson 'was unable to do the right thing at the critical moment', while some truly great Liverpool players of this era were now obviously in decline. 'Bradley was the best of a very moderate trio of halves, and Raisbeck the worst . . . an accurate pass was rarely seen among the whole team.'

After this drought, there were goals galore at the Sunderland v. Liverpool fixture on 19 January 1907, ten of them, in an amazing 5–5 draw. But Liverpool had been 4–1 up at half-time, succumbing later to some very dubious offside and penalty decisions by a poor replacement referee that let the 'kick and rush' Wearsiders back into the match. Later, in March at Aston Villa, another referee, a Mr Mason, was delayed by rail problems, as was the Liverpool left-back Tom Chorlton. The match at Villa Park was delayed by some 15 minutes, with an obviously embarrassed Chorlton taking the pitch only after the late start in a sorry 0–4 Liverpool defeat. With Liverpool ejected from the FA Cup by eventual winners The Wednesday, some pride was at least salvaged for the Reds in a scrappy 0–0 draw with Everton at Goodison Park. But only one win in the last eight league fixtures (and this against relegated Derby County) meant an unceremonious slide down to a final 15th position. 'It is doubtful that such a disastrous month as April has ever been experienced,' opined the Liverpool press.

The local post-mortems pointed to injury and loss of form as the key factors in the slump, which meant that 'the team had to be constantly reshuffled, fore and aft'. West and Dunlop were sorely missed. The latter's replacement, Percy Saul, signed from Plymouth Argyle, was 'erratic' before eventually finding his feet. This chopping and changing was the exact opposite of the approach in the title year, when the same reliable Liverpool team seemed to play match after match. But the crucial figure here was really Raisbeck, who had shown poor form at the start and had missed matches later through injury. The *Daily Post* on 29 April 1907 was troubled:

> Raisbeck is beyond comparison. Raisbeck has been for years the Liver's lucky star – a great, outstanding personality, not only in his team but in the football firmament . . . Without Alex Raisbeck Liverpool would have to be born again, so to speak. That the redoubtable half-back may regain health and strength during the recess is the earnest prayer of everyone. It is, however, probably a subject which will cause the executive most serious deliberation.

In September 1907, the *Liverpool Echo* noted Raisbeck's absence from the Liverpool line-up once more, 'as one never likes to even contemplate what might happen in his absence'. This was no serious injury: Raisbeck was suffering from a rather strong dose of diarrhoea. But he would play only twenty-three league fixtures for two goals in 1907–08, with defender Dunlop restricted to just two appearances. The inestimable Raybould had also now been sold to Sunderland, with Joe Hewitt taking over the main striker duties and scoring a decent 21 league goals – no one else got into double figures. Inside-forward Charlie Hewitt joined from Spurs for £75 in August, which was one year later than he had hoped. His Anfield career was short enough – just 16 matches. Hewitt had joined what was once a great team that was now winding down, it seemed – one shored up, but not improved, by bit-part signings like his own.

'HURRAH FOR THE REDS'

The *Liverpool Echo* on 7 September 1907 came up with a different and novel explanation of Liverpool's sudden fall from grace – a *lack* of Scots: only one, McPherson, had played in a recent match. 'This is a transformation indeed,' said the *Echo* wryly, 'but one unattended with success.'

One Liverpool fan, a W. Seddon from Tuebrook, even came up with a rallying song, 'Hurrah for the Reds', which appeared in the press on 31 August 1907, aimed to rouse the team and the club's fans. Were Liverpool fans already singing collectively at matches? Certainly, Manchester City supporters were singing odes to their favourites, especially Billy Meredith. And supporters 'borrowed' songs and catchphrases from the music hall at this time – Sheffield United fans sang the drinking song 'The Rowdy, Dowdy Boys', for example.[14] It seems likely that the strong 'performance' culture and oral tradition on Merseyside would have produced early local versions of their own songs at football, though the evidence is actually quite scarce. In an FA Cup replay at Barnsley in 1914, the *Liverpool Echo* reported that Reds supporters had 'transposed the song of 1906 and made it "Aye, Aye, Lacey scored the goals".' So singing does seem to have been going on in sections of the home crowd at Anfield at around this time. Mr Seddon's early 'masterpiece' certainly hints at a great oral tradition around support for the Reds, one that is still evident more than a century later. It went:

Hurrah for the boys to play the game
Hurrah for the Reds
Hurrah for the boys, there's none can tame
Hurrah for the Reds
There's Hewitt and Mac to lead the attack
With Hardy to hold the fort, boys
There's Goddard and Cox and Raisbeck the fox
And more to the good old sorts, boys
Hurrah! Hurrah! Hurrah! Hurrah!
Hurrah for the Reds.

This typically stirring anthem might even have been behind an early 2–0 home win against Blackburn Rovers in September, in which the referee was 'as blind as justice', according to the *Football Echo*, for disallowing a 'lovely, perfect' home goal by Joe Hewitt. The Rovers were themselves encouraged 'by some Blackburn choristers on the Spion Kop'.

In November, the *Echo* claimed that it was quite justified to complain about the class of football recently served up by Liverpool, which had been 'of the poorest description', and even a 6–0 home rout of Notts County had served up first-half fare that was full of 'wild tackling, totally inaccurate passing and dreary football'. These were high standards indeed. Fortunately, Joe Hewitt was 'in rare trim', dishing up a hat-trick past visiting keeper Albert Iremonger. Liverpool were now sixth after 12 matches, a 4–2 victory at Everton comfortably on board. But the Reds were already nine points behind early leaders Manchester United. Inconsistency was the only reliable here, and by an early kick-off on Christmas Day the Reds were on the slide once more, losing 1–4 at home to newly arrived Chelsea.

After this latest defeat came a signal about the precarious economics of the sport and the lowly status and power of professional players. Rather than return home to their families, the Liverpool squad, astonishingly, was required by the club's board to travel immediately to play Woolwich Arsenal at distant Plumstead in a Boxing Day *friendly* match (2–2). Presumably, this trip was agreed simply for a cut of the gate. The Reds caught a train to London at 4.05 p.m. on Christmas Day, 1907, after the home thrashing by Chelsea. One can only imagine the atmosphere in the team's carriage. The *Echo* duly noted that 'more than one of the players objected to this unnecessary addition to an ordinarily long programme'. But there was no comeback – these employees simply did their job.

What was the highlight of the rest of this forgettable season? What about Liverpool seven, runaway league-leaders Manchester United four on Wednesday, 25 March 1908? 'Eleven goals for sixpence!' the *Echo* crowed about an evening fixture for which 'atrocious weather' limited the crowd to fewer than 10,000 souls. 'Yesterday the Redbreasts were brilliant,' wrote a local scribe – although this particular moniker for Liverpool FC had no possible hope of catching on. Ted Doig, temporarily back in the Liverpool goal for Sam Hardy, had a poor time of it, but his teammates revelled in the heavy going. Joe Hewitt, Bill McPherson and Robbie Robinson shared the goals as Liverpool climbed to seventh in the table. Alas, it would get no better. Indeed, by the time Aston Villa had inflicted a 1–5 hammering in April, in a tight league Liverpool were just three points off the relegation places. Ronald Orr, a chunky, small and direct Scotland international inside-left, had made his reputation at recent champions Newcastle United, and Liverpool now snapped him up in April 1908 for £350 as an insurance against the drop. He was good value, too, scoring against Villa and claiming a total of five vital goals in his seven appearances as the season leaked away. Praising the uncomplicated new signing, the *Echo* asked, rhetorically, in closing, 'Do we not overestimate the value of dribbling and rather undercut the praise for good, hard, well-directed shots?' Stylish play or results by any means? The debate would continue.

ANFIELD TROUBLE – ON AND OFF THE PITCH

Orr's admirable 20 goals in 33 league matches could not save the following 1908–09 season from being another mediocre campaign for the Reds, topped off by a 2–3 second-round home defeat in the FA Cup to lowly Norwich City. The failures to beat Everton at Anfield were also now beginning to stack up; a 0–1 loss in October meant no Reds victory in the Merseyside derby so far that century. But in the spring and summer of 1909 much larger issues were on the horizon – the possible further expansion of the Football League and potential players' industrial action. In March 1909, the Southern League suggested an amalgamation with the

Football League in order to produce a 60-club national league, comprising the current First Division and two Second Divisions, north and south. The Football League (which already housed six 'southern' clubs) rejected the proposal, partly, it was argued, because some league officials feared that it was beginning to lose its provincial character and spirit and to assume 'too much of a London complexion'.[15] It was only after the First World War that the idea of a league competition for football really chimed fully with wider cultural, social and economic developments in Britain around the concept of the 'national'.

Despite the historically strong links between drink and football, the game at this time was also put forward by its supporters as a boon to the temperance movement. An FA official argued that in Liverpool dock workers tended to 'rush home from work and hand over their wages before going to the match' whereas in the summer months there was a tendency for them to 'spend their money before they reached home', often in a pub.[16]

On the players' front, the Football League continued to oppose the FA's rule 31, which prohibited the payments of bonuses to players. But the FA retorted that dangling money to induce players to win matches was degrading and confirmed the view that business had overtaken the sport. It was a classic stand-off between the league professionals and the FA amateurs. The new players' union, led by representatives of the 1908 league champions, the already glamorous Manchester United, sought protection and strength in this dispute by affiliating with the Federation of Trade Unions in 1909. This move so appalled both the FA and the Football League at a time when strikes and riots were becoming a common feature of industrial Britain that they promptly withdrew their recognition from the players' union. Far from backing down, however, the players threatened to strike, only withdrawing at the eleventh hour as clubs assembled squads of amateurs ready to fulfil fixtures. A number of top Liverpool players even refused to re-sign their contracts. Public support for the players – and the union members' resolution – began to fade. In April 1910, the rule on the payment of bonuses was finally amended, but rule 30, restricting the maximum wage to £4, remained. What clubs wanted to pay their players in bonuses was now down to them, and professionals could still not initiate their own transfer. In effect, the clubs still held all the cards.[17]

The following season (1909–10) produced storm damage to the Anfield Road stand, which cost some £1,500 to renovate. Manchester United were about to unveil their own 80,000 capacity Edwardian 'super stadium' at Old Trafford in 1910, and so the stadium advances on Merseyside would soon be overshadowed by their regional rivals. On the field, Liverpool were a highly creditable second in the league, losing out to a superior Aston Villa, with 78 goals scored. It was important that the Reds upped their game, according to a journalist for the *Cricket and Football Field* on 5 June 1909, because 'spectators nowadays will pay only for the best article'. This improved league performance more than counteracted a 0–2 first-round FA Cup exit at Bristol City.

Tom Watson was slowly rebuilding, breaking up the 1906 Liverpool championship team. Both West and Dunlop were effectively gone, and in 1909 Watson brought in half-back James 'Head Up' Harrop from Rotherham as a possible future replacement for the incomparable Raisbeck. Harrop matched Raisbeck in his intelligence, if not in his all-round game. The Liverpool legend was eventually sold to Partick Thistle in June 1909 for £500, but he would return later to give further service to the club.

The highly capable Harrop stayed at Liverpool for four years before moving on to star for Aston Villa in the 1913 FA Cup final. The feisty Scot John McDonald replaced Cox on the left-wing and offered high-quality crosses at pace. His compatriot, inside-right Jimmy Stewart, signed from Motherwell, produced 18 goals in 37 league matches in his first influential season. But the main reason for the Liverpool league revival was the form of a local man, Bootle-born centre-forward Jack Parkinson, who had made his debut at the club back in 1903. Parkinson had since struggled with injury, but he now grabbed his chance with both feet. Eight times he scored more than two goals in a league match in 1909–10, including four in a 7–3 Anfield drubbing of Nottingham Forest in April. Parkinson and Orr scored the goals that satisfyingly beat league-champions elect Aston Villa at Anfield on 30 April 1910, the closing day of the season, but it was too little, too late to affect the title outcome.

The Villa match also publicly revealed the very real hooligan potential of the Liverpool crowd, especially if it was aroused by perceived unfairness on the pitch. From the evidence we have, football crowds at this time seem to have been made up mainly of slightly older male sections of the 'respectable' working class, though there were younger fans, female supporters and also some middle-class followers, too, especially in the Anfield seats. Hooliganism at football at this time typically involved low-level incivilities, such as pouring beer on rivals, running onto the pitch 'for a laugh', pelting the visiting mascot with fruit or peel, gambling, jostling, and general rowdiness on streets and in local bars.[18] But these latest incidents in and around Anfield for the visit of Villa were of a rather different order. Their source was injury to the Liverpool goalkeeper Sam Hardy, who dislocated his wrist after an ugly collision with the long-serving Villa centre-forward Harry Hampton.

Hampton was a man who, due to his 'dashing propensities', according to the local press, already had an 'unenviable reputation' in the city. This meant that the England international enjoyed putting himself about on the pitch. Reds fans started 'booing, hooting and yelling' for Hampton to be sent off, and referee Ibbotson threatened to halt the match. Liverpool captain Artie Goddard appealed to the crowd, 'owing to a stone thrown from the spectators striking [Villa forward Joe] Bache above the eye, necessitating the attention of the trainer'. When matters eventually calmed down, Goddard went in the home goal, and Robbie Robinson 'worked himself to a standstill' in order to secure a famous Liverpool victory. But then the fun really started, as the *Evening Express* of 2 May 1910 reported:

> At the end of the match the brake conveying the Villa players to the city was followed by a yelling crowd of youths and boys who pelted the occupants for some considerable distance. The brake was stopped and one or two of the ringleaders marked out. There was some sharp scuffling and Hunter, one of the Villa players who had accompanied the team to Liverpool, received a severe blow to the face. In a few seconds the police arrived on the scene.

Fights such as this between visiting players and local spectators were unusual, but the *Evening Express* also noted the recent 'disgraceful barracking' at Anfield of the injured Notts County full-back Bert Morley. Missiles had also been thrown by the Liverpool crowd at the Sheffield defender Bob Bensen. It was agreed that this sort of incident 'is getting the Anfield ground an unenviable reputation'. In reply, a correspondent calling himself 'Anfielder' showed little remorse, assuring the *Evening Express* that Liverpool supporters would not settle for the 'laxity of certain referees' in ignoring illegal tripping.

There seems to have been no FA action taken as a result of these street assaults – the main incidents took place away from the ground, after all. But they marked out the real risks sometimes posed to visiting players and officials at Liverpool and elsewhere when locals were roused by perceived wrongdoing. Ironically, rival fans might have been rather less at risk at this time.

SEE-SAW LIVERPOOL

At the club's AGM in June 1910, the Liverpool board reflected on the union 'agitation' of the previous summer and reported that the club was 'in a healthier position, so far as feelings between directors and players were concerned, than for years'. It was also announced that 'an appeal for money to meet the demands of summer wages met with a generous response'. Fans would have to dip into their pockets once more. Total income was £12,931, and income over expenditure stood at a healthy £4,435, with average home attendances up from 17,660 to 21,620 (thus overtaking Everton once again). The chairman remarked that the quality of the football seen at Anfield during the season had been 'most creditable', adding that 'those who had witnessed the memorable match against Newcastle United would never forget it'.

It is strange that matches between Liverpool and Newcastle should crop up as items of note over the next 100 years. But this meeting, on 4 December 1909, was a rare classic. 'One of the most remarkable games in the history of the league,' argued the *Liverpool Courier*, 'and certainly the most sensational that has been witnessed in Liverpool.' Albert Shepherd had scored four times before half-time for the then league champions Newcastle, who led 2–5 at the break. But the visitors were 'simply overwhelmed' in the second half. Goals from Parkinson and Orr revived Liverpool. 'When Orr equalised from a scrimmage the crowd nearly went frantic with delight. Newcastle were absolutely outplayed.' Goddard headed the late winner for a quite breathless 6–5 home win – and there could well have been more goals.

After this brief promise and excitement, the years leading up to the First World War were eventful ones for the city, if very disappointing ones indeed for Liverpool Football Club. League finishes of 13th, 17th (saved from possible relegation in 1911–12 only by a late run of four victories in the last six matches), 12th, 16th and then 14th in 1914–15 were hardly what the Anfield board and the Liverpool public had expected, especially after pushing Villa so close to the title in 1910. Until 1913–14, neither were there lengthy FA Cup runs for Liverpool to offer its supporters compensation for lack of success in the league.

Meanwhile, in the city of Liverpool, as in other great British cities, unemployment and claims for better wages and working conditions for working people continued to ravage communities and dull the senses as national strikes were now threatened and public disorder erupted. Even as the new 'skyscraper' Royal Liver Building was regally unveiled on the Merseyside seafront in August 1911, strikes by local dockers and other transport workers in Liverpool brought the British Army onto the streets of Merseyside to keep order. Eighty thousand people turned out in Lime Street to demonstrate, and the Riot Act was read as crowds refused to disperse. Word spread: the *New York Times* on 17 August reported that bread supplies in Liverpool were almost exhausted and that soldiers now bivouacked at Edge Hill had been ordered not to shoot over the heads of rioters but to aim their guns at 'apparent ringleaders' of the mob. Two unarmed local men were shot dead as crowds attacked vans conveying striker prisoners to Walton Prison. Liverpool streets around the Vauxhall and Scotland Road areas, always simmering with tribal enmities and the privations of poverty, suddenly came to the boil, too, hinting at the underlying tensions in the city.

After this tumult eventually subsided, the effects of growing unemployment in the city lived on. 'The reading room adjoining the museum in William Brown Street is not a cheerful place to visit,' reported the *Evening Express* on 3 May 1912. 'There is a suggestion there of slowly dying hope. Persons of all ages are to be found there, from boys who dream of the world of work as a pleasant land . . . to old men, grey, haggard and disillusioned.' More uplifting perhaps was the sight of the construction, early in 1913, of the extraordinary white Palace of Industries building on the Edge Lane Hall Estate for the Liverpool Exhibition of that year. In 1906, the Street Betting Act had outlawed betting on public streets in Britain, but gambling was as rife in Liverpool as it was in all major British cities, and arrests were frequently made of people who were attempting to organise coupons for football betting, either on the street or out of their own homes. It seemed to many commentators as if the legislation revealed a class bias by effectively criminalising popular working-class leisure. It offered 'one law for the rich and another for the poor'.[19]

Meanwhile, the laws of football continued in their own refinement. In 1912, goalkeepers were reined in to handling inside the penalty area only, and in 1913 defending players were required to retreat ten yards from free-kicks. On 12 May 1912, the players of Swindon Town FC spent the evening at the Empire Theatre and the Adelphi in Liverpool before sailing on the SS *Ortega* the next day for an eight-match tour of Argentina. Football was increasingly an international sport, one that the English professed to both spread and dominate. The Merseyside press reminded its readers accordingly that cosmopolitan Everton Football Club had already played 22 times abroad and had yet to be beaten.

At the Liverpool FC AGM in May 1912, a brave shareholder complained that results for the club had actually been better in 1906 when less money had been spent on signing players. Chairman John McKenna replied that he thought the directors could hardly be blamed for spending *more* money on players today than six years ago. Another shareholder argued that there should be 'less experiments with veteran players' while yet another asked why Harrop, Hardy and John McDonald had all not been re-signed, to which the chairman replied that owing to what had happened last season – when Sam Hardy had apparently refused to move to the area – Liverpool 'were going to insist in future that their players should reside in the district'. The chairman now asked, rather defensively, whether any supporter in the meeting could point to a club with *more* honours after such a short history. One shareholder responded sharply, and to loud laughter, 'Has any club had a more see-saw existence than what the Liverpool club has had?'

What exactly was wrong with Liverpool Football Club during this period? Its 'old failing', according to the *Evening Express* in 1913, was not converting chances. 'Liverpool's forwards should know that goals count,' it argued, helpfully. 'A good motto for forwards: Get Goals!' As a remedy, the Wexford-born Ireland international left-winger Bill Lacey was signed from Everton in February 1912 in a swap deal the Blues would live to regret. Lacey added pep and goals to Liverpool for the next 12 years. And yet it was long-term, mainly *defensive*, recruitment for the new era that continued apace, a Tom Watson policy that would herald much better days for the club soon after the war.

In September 1910, Bolton-born right-back and future Liverpool and England captain Ephraim Longworth made his debut for Liverpool, the first of 490 consistently excellent appearances in peacetime and at war for the club. On 31 May 1912, the *Evening Express* reported that a Bootle-born full-back or wing-half, Walter Wadsworth, had also signed professionally, having 'last season assisted Ormskirk with distinction'. The fearless 'Big Waddy' would prove a crucial figure and local leader in the dual championship-winning team of the 1920s. Scottish left-sided defender and dead-ball specialist Donald McKinlay signed in 1910 from a local club in Glasgow, an inspired Watson discovery this one, a man who went on to give Liverpool 19 years of near-unblemished service.

With Longworth and Wadsworth, McKinlay became the club's new defensive shield in the early interwar years. Finally, on New Year's Day 1913, those Liverpool supporters who had stilled their hangovers sufficiently to travel to Newcastle would have seen the first glimpse, in a 0–0 draw, of the final defensive cog for the new Liverpool of the 1920s. Guarding the visitors' goal that day was a young goalkeeper who would become a legend, the brusque and brilliant Irishman Elisha Scott. It was reported later that young Scott had an injured (possibly broken) arm but chose to play this match nevertheless. Newcastle United instantly offered Liverpool £1,000 for the goalkeeper. The offer was turned down. In goal, at least, the Reds' future could reliably take care of itself.

But back in the present, Liverpool's star had sunk low enough for the team to be accused in a letter to the *Fulham Times* in March 1913 by the Fulham and Woolwich Arsenal director H.G. Norris of lacking the necessary 'desire' when losing at home to relegation-threatened Chelsea. In short, Norris sniffed a fix. New Liverpool club captain Ephraim Longworth responded with indignation. In a rare interview given in the *Evening Express* on 5 April, he expressed his disquiet that Norris should have 'led the man in the street to infer that the

Liverpool players deliberately lay down and allowed the other side to win . . . There is not an atom of truth in the suggestion.' The FA and Football League inquiry that followed could also find no proof, even if there were certainly plenty of poor performances by Liverpool that season to choose from – an aggregate league loss to Sunderland by two goals to twelve, for example.

THE GREAT LIVERPOOL FOOTBALL SWINDLE

Just two years later, on a rain-soaked Manchester afternoon on 2 April 1915, Liverpool players incontrovertibly *did* help to fix a match, a sensational 0–2 defeat at Manchester United, which, this time, threatened to send Chelsea down. The ensuing inquiry resulted in four Liverpool players, Jackie Sheldon, Tommy Miller, Bob Pursell and the wonderfully named tough-tackling Scottish half-back Tom Fairfoul being suspended. But the post-war expansion of the league to 22 clubs meant Chelsea escaped the relegation places after all. The suspensions for the Liverpool players were eventually lifted soon after the end of hostilities. With no summer wages in the offing because of the war, the players involved from both sides had bet heavily on a 0–2 result, and once this score had been reached – and to the consternation of the sodden crowd – the co-conspirators began to kick the ball into the stands. Jackie Sheldon missed a penalty and another Liverpool forward was bawled out by a teammate when he almost scored near the final whistle.

This was 'undoubtedly the worst scandal to afflict the league in its twenty-seven seasons', and it perpetuated rumours about payment for strange results, especially given the wage restraints on players.[20] But Liverpool FC and its followers could, at least, reflect on the club's first FA Cup final appearance, in 1914, after more than 20 years of trying. And most people's concern was now focused on the much greater, and much more deadly, 'game' that now lay ahead.

CHAPTER 4 REFERENCES

1. Taylor, *The Leaguers*, p. 115
2. Harding, *Football Wizard*, p. 97
3. Taylor, *The Leaguers*, p. 102
4. Inglis, *League Football and the Men Who Made It*, p. 54
5. Taylor, *The Leaguers*, pp. 10–11
6. Taylor, *The Association Game*, p. 89
7. Young, *Football on Merseyside*, p. 79
8. Physick, *Played in Liverpool*, p. 54

9. Preston, 'The Origins and Development of Association Football in the Liverpool District *c.*1879–*c.*1915', p. 187

10. Inglis, *Engineering Archie*, p. 34

11. Inglis, *Engineering Archie*, pp. 21 and 23

12. Inglis, *Engineering Archie*, p. 89

13. Physick, *Played in Liverpool*, p. 55

14. Taylor, *The Association Game*, p. 95

15. Taylor, *The Leaguers*, p. 14

16. Tischler, *Footballers and Businessmen*, pp. 134–5

17. Inglis, *League Football and the Men Who Made It*, pp. 73–4

18. Russell, *Football and the English*, p. 62

19. Chinn, *Better Betting with a Decent Feller*, p. 203

20. Inglis, *League Football and the Men Who Made It*, p. 96

5

THE FIRST FA CUP FINAL
1914 at the Palace, and Then War

THE ROAD TO THE 1914 FA CUP FINAL

The FA Cup final had its brief visits in the nineteenth century to the north – to both Manchester and Liverpool – and then a stopover at Old Trafford for the 1915 'wartime' final. But from 1895 right up until 2001, when it moved briefly to Wales, the FA Cup final found its resting place in London, despite its many northern critics. Early sports historians commented approvingly when the final returned to Crystal Palace in 1895. 'It is good that the Cup Final is played in the great Metropolis again, for however much our cynical provincial friends may effect to despise "Lunnun" and Cockneyism, there is no denying that London is the place for a great sporting battle.'[1] Certainly, going down to London in the spring was a popular trip for the football 'hordes' and alleged sporting 'barbarians' from the north and the Midlands. For once a year, at least, they could look ahead to teaching their so-called betters from down south a thing or two about 'footy', supporter styles and having a rollicking good time.

But Crystal Palace was a rather strange place to host the FA Cup final, its last, in 1914. The Palace was no less than a Victorian pleasure garden in the suburb of Sydenham that housed an inadequate pitch and pretty terrible viewing facilities for spectators. It was overlooked by an odd array of sights and amusements, including the glass structure of the Crystal Palace itself and also the forbidding 'Switchback' fairground ride. This seemed more like a venue for a sunny family day out with the children than one set up to host the world's premier football club fixture to the satisfaction of its mainly cloth-capped and beer-fed visiting partisans from the provinces. After the war, in 1920, the final would move briefly to Stamford Bridge before English football had a stadium suitable for staging its major club occasion. And even in 1923, *managing* the game's premier event at the new Empire Stadium at Wembley initially proved quite beyond England's football authorities.

In the context of English national life, the FA Cup final manages to combine several important messages at the same time: about sport and male working-class culture; about a shared national ritual in a familiar calendar of sporting events; and about a constitutional link between sport, the British people and the royal family.[2] The 1914 FA Cup final was the first one truly to signal the increasing respectability of the English game and also the new nationwide reach of professional football. The King, George V, would attend the final for the first time. This public royal sanction for association football, the people's game, even led *The Times* to conclude on 27 April 1914 that perhaps the old divides between amateurs and professionals, between the humble sixpenny or 'bob' terrace supporters and the 'toffs' in the stands, could finally be laid to rest:

> Professional football of the best kind is no longer regarded as a spectacle only suited for the proletariat . . . The fact that the King himself has attended a Cup Tie and shown a keen interest in its vicissitudes . . . will, let us hope, put an end to the old snobbish notion that true-blue sportsmen ought to ignore games played by those who cannot afford to play without being paid for their services.[3]

What *The Times* did not yet know, of course, was that all these ingrained class and social divisions – and more – would soon be dragged up again by the national and local press when the Football League refused to halt the league programme as war began to engulf Europe later that same year. But Liverpool's quest in 1914 was to capture the FA Cup at last, and the Reds' journey to the final began, inauspiciously enough, on a heavily sanded Anfield pitch in January against a determined and rugged Barnsley, the 1912 FA Cup winners. The Yorkshire club fielded seven of their cup-final heroes, and it showed. Although Lacey squeezed a long shot under the napping Jack Cooper in the Barnsley goal before half-time, the visitors more than deserved their equaliser, a George Travers shot that rattled in off the underside of the crossbar. 'Liverpool were fortunate to draw,' concluded the *Liverpool Echo*, which now feared the worst in the replay.

At Barnsley, Travers soon kicked Robert Pursell, the cultured Liverpool left-back who had been recruited from Queen's Park in 1911, 'and a fighting pose was adopted by both players'. Referee Bamlett stepped in to show that he was like this contest – hard. All FA Cup finalists, it is said, need luck en route to the final. Liverpool had theirs here – in boatloads. The 800 Liverpudlians who had made the trip to south Yorkshire saw their keeper Kenny Campbell assailed by 'beefy shots' from all sides, but he remained defiant, and when Lacey again sent Cooper diving the wrong way in the 89th minute it was clear that it was Liverpool's day.

A home draw against distant and mysterious Gillingham was Liverpool's reward. A 'genuine crush' occurred before the match at a windy Anfield, which saw the Kemlyn Road stand full and closed long before the start, causing a 'grievance' among visiting fans, who, the *Echo* remarked sniffily, 'did not seem used to finding their way around in a big crowd'. Forget the patronising treatment; it took the home team more than eighty minutes to break through the Gills' defence, and then Lacey and Robert Ferguson, a stylish Scottish half-back who had been signed two years before from Third Lanark, both struck to end the debate.

For the third-round trip to West Ham on 21 February 1914, according to the *Football Echo*, there were a few flighty overnight Reds in tow – Liverpool were 'followed at midnight' in their trip to London 'by a fairly large crowd of supporters'. After heavy rain, the Boleyn Ground pitch was a mudheap, having only a few patches of green at each corner flag. The visiting pressmen also wondered at the extremely tight walling-in of the East End ground because, for a forward player with some pace, 'a collision with a cement wall is not inviting'. Tom Miller, a physically robust centre-forward recruit from Hamilton Accies in 1912, scored the Liverpool goal immediately after the half in a tough 1–1 draw that was full of good football, especially given the conditions. The *Echo* noted, in passing, that both West Ham and Burnley were now 'shilling gates', but it reassured its readers that Liverpool understood well the harsh economics of the Merseyside area, that they had had 'wonderfully generous support from the city throughout the season and will not dream of raising the prices of admission'. Here was a hostage to fortune if ever there was one.

How would people in work and school in Liverpool attend the daytime midweek rematch? The *Echo* had some streetwise doggerel to explain exactly how these tricksters might excuse their way to Anfield, part of which read:

> There'll be grandmothers to bury,
> At the Anfield Cemetree [sic]
> And lots of sudden illnesses,
> Next Wednesday at three.
> There'll be reams of lies on paper
> Special Spion Copper Crammers
> There'll be lots of French leave taken
> For the fun'ral of the Hammers

A crowd of some 43,729 eventually squeezed into Anfield, and thousands were turned away by officials who 'wisely decided they could not take any risks'. The capacity of a pre-war football ground was something of a movable feast and clearly down to local interpretation. Many matches played to audiences that were well under – or over – the official limit, depending on the willingness of club officials and the crowd to allow more customers to be squeezed onto the terraces. The *Liverpool Echo* commented that supporters could also move to all parts of the ground, meaning that the take up of space was highly uneven. 'The Spion Kop in some parts is crowded and in other parts could stand more spectators.' One thing was clear: such was the appetite for the game in Liverpool in 1914, as the *Echo* averred, 'The schoolboy nowadays is not au fait if he does not have a complete knowledge of football matters.' Liverpool cruised this cup reunion by 5–1, and the packed Anfield stadium played its part – and not for the last time – because, for the *Echo*'s correspondent, 'The surroundings had some of the Hammers upset. Spion Kop's thickly populated crowd frowned down upon the visitors and they have previously had no frown like it.'

Crowd frowns or no frowns, promise or no promise, FA Cup ticket prices were not frozen at Anfield. Dream again – this is business. For the fourth-round home tie with Queens Park Rangers on 7 March, prices *were* raised and some local supporters threatened a boycott. But how often do fans ever vote with their feet? In the event, the Kop was closed at 2.20 p.m. for a 4 p.m. kick-off, and the large crowd was in beered-up, boisterous form, judging by the oranges playfully used as missiles before the start. Liverpool had met 'curious clubs' in its FA Cup run so far, agreed the *Liverpool Echo* – it meant, of course, mainly feeble southern non-Football League clubs – but 'nothing weaker has been tackled than Queens Park Rangers'. The visitors first tried the physical stuff and then resorted to the 'one-back' offside trap, but nothing worked for them. The 5 ft 6 in. tricky winger John 'Jackie' Sheldon had been bought by Tom Watson from Manchester United in November 1913, and it was he and centre-forward Tommy Miller who got the goals here in a 2–1 win. This was the height of their Liverpool careers: within 14 months both men would be banned after the Manchester United 'fix' fiasco.

Twenty-eighth of March 1914: a London FA Cup semi-final for Liverpool and also the university boat race. The *Echo* pressmen thought that the japes of the Oxbridge student spectators compared very poorly with the dignified demeanour of northern and Midlands football fans in London for the match: 'Their hustling and mad-brained tricks were a disgrace to civilisation and the top-hat brigade.' The cup experts and holders Aston Villa were overwhelming favourites to win through at White Hart Lane. Villa even had the esteemed ex-Red Sam Hardy in goal, a man who had left Anfield back in May 1913. The London press certainly gave Liverpool no chance at all, and Tom Watson was so enraged by this slur that he delivered a 'storming speech' to his men that they should show the football public that this Liverpool side was, indeed, 'on the man'. A 2–0 scoreline for the Merseysiders registered an underdogs' glorious triumph. 'The surprise of the season,' as one national newspaper put it. The 'big-timbered' Liverpool unit was slow to get started, but it soon moved into gear. And it was not one of Hardy's 'safe and steady' afternoons. Instead, he needlessly conceded the corner from which Glaswegian forward Jimmy Nicholl scored the first of his two goals of the afternoon for Liverpool. Like many other players, Nicholl's short football career at Anfield was effectively ended in 1915 by the war. Bill Lacey, especially, tormented and teased his old comrade Hardy for the remainder of the contest, which Liverpool dominated.

When news of Nicholl's goals and Liverpool's win eventually filtered through to the reserves' Central League match being played on the same afternoon at Anfield, it was reported that 'scenes unprecedented in the history of the club were witnessed between players and spectators alike'. Joy was unconfined as the match was stopped dead and players and people in the crowd gleefully hugged each other. Back in London, the victorious Liverpool players had no time even to put on their coats and collars before pouring excitedly into taxis bound for Euston to catch the last non-stop train to Liverpool. At Lime Street, they were exhausted but ebullient as the club's supporters and players mingled and contemplated something quite unique in Liverpool Football Club's short history: an FA Cup final appearance at last.

THE KING'S BIDDING

'We are authorised by the Earl of Derby,' reported the *Daily Post* solemnly on 18 April 1914, 'to state definitely that the King has signified he will be present at the final contest for the Football Association Cup at the Crystal Palace.' Excitement gripped Merseyside, though it was also made clear that, in these troubled times, the monarch might not even be able to stay to present the cup and medals. Tom Watson would be there, of course. And he also had a novel idea to satisfy those supporters who could not make the trip for this first royal 'Lancashire final', which would pit Liverpool against Burnley. Why not replay the match later, in Liverpool, for charity? So, arrangements were made for Burnley to visit Merseyside to play soon after the final and for the FA Cup to be paraded at Anfield, regardless of who had won it. From today's perspective, it seems like an extraordinary suggestion.

Did such a strange proposition mean that Tom Watson was worried, or was he super-confident? He was certainly concerned about a knee injury to his steadying captain, the Derbyshire born half-back Harry Lowe, who had made his debut for Liverpool back in 1911. According to the *Liverpool Echo*, the club trainer Bill Connell 'doesn't get full publicity when the deeds of Liverpool are mentioned. He has his men in perfect trim and gets the last ounce of energy out of them.' Connell was optimistic (he was paid to be), and he told the *Post* that a specialist had ensured that Lowe 'will be certain to play'. On the very eve of the match, it was reported in the city that Lowe 'has improved wonderfully, and is expected to be quite fit'. Was this pre-match bravado, or possibly even time-honoured football subterfuge? In fact, like Bob Paisley in 1950, the Reds skipper Lowe would miss the 1914 FA Cup final – he was replaced by Bob Ferguson. This late change might well have swayed the outcome by a fine margin towards Burnley. Liverpool's opponents had been promoted into the First Division only in 1913 and had finished 12th to Liverpool's 16th in 1914, so compared to Aston Villa they were no FA Cup or league giants. After their semi-final showing, Liverpool, at odds of 4–6, were widely expected to win this London meeting.

Unusually, Liverpool chose to base their FA Cup final players' camp down south, in Chingford, while Burnley remained closeted up north, in Lytham. Light training only was the order of the day for the Liverpool squad, including 'sprinting and ball punching', while the Reds players were reported to have 'spent a lot of time on the golf links'. The Liverpool outfield men had had no practice at all with a football during their entire week in Essex, save for a few 'accidental' minutes on Thursday afternoon 'when a ball came in their way as they were going for a stroll in the forest'. Even under the visionary Tom Watson, the team was expected to benefit most from rest and starvation of collective practice with a ball. It was the way of the times and the way of the English, a people who were generally dismissive of too much practice and coaching, the preserve of Continentals. Bill Connell had replied with a world-weary shake of the head to the *Liverpool Echo* scribe of 24 April 1914 who thought that ball practice was 'the one essential in the course of training prior to an important cup tie'. The inscrutable Connell reminded the Liverpool press that:

When the boys beat the Villa they had not seen a ball for a week. Their football was good enough, eh? They relish the sight of the ball on the Saturday, and they have had such a hard time latterly that it is necessary to take measures to get their full stamina. A team of men like I have under my control do not want training in the full sense of the word. They simply want to keep the muscles lissom and the wind and limb sound. The course of training this week will be simple . . . For the moment, 'ball lost' is the order.

The Liverpool players would be expected, magically, to click into gear, hungrily find their best game and invent their own tactics as the match developed. Tom Watson had special words of praise in the build-up for young McKinlay and full-back Sam Speakman, a local man, both of whom were 'reserves who did not grumble and were as delighted as the rest of the team as if they had played in the ties'. These were true Liverpool club men, McKinlay especially – he would go on to epitomise the very heart of Liverpool Football Club after the war. Watson would tell his players that Burnley were 'a good sporting side and if they won the day he would be the first to heartily congratulate them'. But there was no doubt that he expected Liverpool to win the 1914 FA Cup.

The Reds would certainly not want for support at the Palace: on Friday evening alone, 12 special trains carried Liverpudlians down for the final, and an estimated 170 special trains in total would reach the metropolis, ferrying the majority of the 'below par' 72,778 crowd to their destination. Thomas Cook & Son confirmed that all previous records had been broken concerning the number of passengers who had made arrangements to travel to London from Liverpool. Some fans would, clearly, do whatever it took to make the journey, even if they lived outside the city and struggled for cash. William Hatton, a shed-man from Wigan, for example, ended up in court on 22 April 1914 for stealing copper and brass from a railway shed. His defence was that his £1-a-week earnings were not a living wage and that he had 'arranged a trip to London for next Saturday's English cup final and . . . having paid his fare found that he would have no money left to spend when he got to London'. The bench was not made up of football supporters: Hatton was fined ten shillings and costs were imposed.

The 'travelling village' from Merseyside, as the *Liverpool Echo* described it, was argued to scotch the views of those predicting that the meeting of two Lancashire clubs 'would not create a great deal of enthusiasm'. A reporter for the *London Evening News* commented later that this meeting did not strike the imagination of the ordinary football fan and that 'I cannot remember any final that has created so little interest, except possibly in Lancashire'. It was seen as two modest, midtable northern clubs playing in the game's southern showpiece.

Many of the earliest travellers from Liverpool were reported to have been working all night, so they planned to catch some sleep on the train. Portraits of the Liverpool team and players were stuck to carriages that were sometimes crammed with groups of 15 or 16 supporters who did not want to be separated. The *Echo* produced souvenir cardboard hats for supporters which said 'Cap them in the Cup'. Some fans came with facsimiles of the cup stitched to their coats, while others brought sandwiches loyally wrapped in red-and-white paper. They had also packed 'not a few well-filled bottles'.

The *Daily Post* of 25 April 1914 also described the 'pandemonium' around Lime Street station on the Friday evening as supporters departed and reported that a popular souvenir for the trip was a black-edged card grimly headed 'In Memory of Burnley', which contained a verse of triumphant doggerel on the demise of the East Lancastrians and how Liverpool had:

> Rushed them and pushed them, until they were sore,
> And beat them all hollow, as they'd oft done before.

Was all this crowing too early? On the chaotic station platforms:

> Red button bouquets, red hats, red jackets and red flags besprinkled the crowd, and as if these were not enough to show how the wind was blowing in regards to the prospects of the match, corncrake rattles were rung with hideous sound. Shouts of 'Liverpool forever!' were heartily endorsed and passed around. It was very seldom that the name of Burnley was mentioned.

In London on the day of the final, according to the *Echo*, 'the Lancastrian was the predominant personality: "John Willie" was everywhere' and the 'best of good fellowship' prevailed when bleary-eyed rival supporters passed each other in the West End to the general astonishment of the 'solemn Londoner'. Hundreds of 'four-in-hand' brakes carried visitors through the London streets, and a fleet of about two hundred motorised omnibuses was chartered to take supporters sightseeing. But these enthusiastic northern excursionists had some act to follow. An extraordinary crowd in excess of 120,000 had seen Aston Villa play Sunderland in the 1913 final at Crystal Palace, many of them having no view at all of the pitch. Perhaps the FA authorities were basing their match preparations on this latter figure, because the *Daily Post* carried details of the food that would be set aside to feed the masses from Lancashire at the Palace. The FA seemed to assume that every single spectator would dine lavishly at the final. Compared to today's stodgy fast-food football diet of pies, sausage rolls and burgers, this seems like a feast. The 1914 FA Cup final football menu included:

75 rumps of beef	30,000 rolls and butter
80 loins of mutton	75,000 slices of bread & butter
250 fowls	25,000 buns & scones
150 hams	1,500 dozen bottles of minerals
12,000 sandwiches	48,000 slices of cake
2,500 veal and ham pies	6,000 pastries
1,000 dozen bottles of beer	2,000 gallons of beer

The men from the north also exercised a characteristic determination not to be taken for a ride by the 'sophistication' of the capital. Even in 1914, the notion that London and the FA might try to exploit its guests seemed well founded for those who visited from the provinces. Spectators had to pay a shilling for admittance to the Palace pleasure grounds, for example, before gaining access, at an additional cost, to the football stadium. Most visitors grumbled at this double whammy, effectively a London football 'tax'. But then they conceded later that a once-in-a-lifetime sight of the famous glass monument might have been worth the extra money after all.[4] Following all this paraphernalia and exhausting build-up, the match itself was a huge disappointment, at least to the people from Merseyside. Liverpool lined up, without the injured Harry Lowe, in familiar 2–3–5 formation:

Liverpool FC, FA Cup final team, v. Burnley, 1914

Campbell

Longworth   Pursell

Fairfoul   Ferguson   McKinlay

Sheldon   Metcalf   Miller   Lacey   Nicholl

The versatile Wearsider Arthur Metcalf had joined Liverpool from Newcastle United for £150 in May 1912, and he had been top scorer for the club in season 1912–13. But injury then intervened, and he played only ten league matches, mainly at inside-right, in the 1913–14 season. He was preferred in the cup final to another north-easterner, but a less consistent goalscorer, Bill Banks.

On a warm afternoon, there was pre-match entertainment from the bands of the Irish Guards and the First Liverpool Regiment in front of a 'perspiring crowd'. The First Liverpool Regiment, based in Aldershot, had volunteered to play before the final, and all members of the regiment wore the Liverpool team favours on their sticks and in their caps, which was, according to the *Liverpool Echo*, 'quite unique in the history of the British Army'.

'WHAT A BERNARD SHAW SHAME!'

The *Daily Post* focus in its match report in 'perfect Palace weather' was on a popular Reds theme: 'Cleverness without finish counts for nothing.' Liverpool had plenty of the play all right, but Miller 'muddled several chances' as the Merseysiders pressed right up until half-time to break the deadlock, when Tom Watson could get to work once more. As the players rested and anticipated the second half at the sweltering Palace, back at Dingle Park, where South Liverpool were entertaining Tranmere Rovers in front of 18,130, a spectator prankster changed the local scoreboard to show Liverpool to be leading Burnley 2–0 at half-time. This news caused some of the crowd to throw their hats and walking sticks in the air and even to perform somersaults along the touchline. Only later did they realise the cruel hoax, and when the real state of affairs was announced 'an audible murmur of disappointment ensued'.

After half-time, Burnley began to have more of the ball and soon scored the crucial and only goal in a move that was 'bewilderingly sudden'. A throw-in on the right was crossed to inside-left Teddy Hodgson, who trapped the ball and flicked it gently to ex-England and Everton forward Bert Freeman. Freeman was undoubtedly a class act, a man who had scored 61 times in just 88 appearances for the Blues. No doubt he enjoyed flashing this volley past Liverpool's Kenny Campbell, 'who did not even see the ball'. At Goodison Park, where Everton and Liverpool's reserves were clashing, cheers and cries of 'Good old Burnley' and 'Good old Freeman!' rang out from the home sections when the score was announced. A Liverpool man wrote later to the *Echo* to point out that Evertonians had not long ago barracked the same Freeman and to complain about this 'disgraceful display of partisanship'. (What else did he expect?) It was a great cup-final goal, no question, and the Reds were stunned. But they later rallied and 'the last moments of the struggle were all in favour of Liverpool'. But a 'chance shot' from Donald McKinlay missed its target, and it was all over.

The *Daily Post* man was apparently close enough to events to report that the King had said a sympathetic 'hard luck' to the 'blushing Scotsman', the Liverpool captain Ferguson, as he picked up his loser's medal. In a later editorial, the *Post* rehearsed the greeting of the terrible news of the Reds defeat on the streets of Liverpool when a local 'urchin' was reported to have responded to an *Echo* newsboy's comments on the scoreline with the extravagantly despondent (and rather educated) outburst, 'What a Bernard Shaw shame!' One thousand supporters turned out to welcome the Liverpool party home on the Monday, but there was little time to commiserate – the Liverpool players had to rush directly to Anfield, where they were playing Sheffield United that very evening in their final league fixture. What was planned as a huge celebration turned, instead, into a sullen 2–1 victory. There was still no FA Cup for Liverpool.

When the FA Cup trophy eventually *did* come to Anfield on 29 April, for the Theatrical Gala charity match against Burnley that had earlier been agreed by Tom Watson, hundreds of boys poured over the front of the Kop at the end of the match to get a better look at the silverware. In their enthusiasm, they knocked over an Anfield salesboy who was carrying cigarettes, chocolates and cakes in a basket for sale to supporters. They pounced. When the poor seller emerged from under the ensuing scrum, his basket – like Liverpool's trophy cabinet – was pitifully empty.

Looking ahead to the summer and to the awful prospects of war, the *Post* sagely suggested that, 'A nation which wastes time over football is likely to last longer and do more enduring work in the world than a nation in arms.' These were wise words, indeed. But the English game was about to face one of its biggest battles yet.

'PLAY UP, PLAY UP AND PLAY THE GAME?'

English football's so-called 'crisis season' of wartime football in 1914–15 has been described as one of the most damaging in the sport's history.[5] Lacking guidance from the British government, the outbreak of the Great War on 4 August 1914 meant that the whole of British sport faced difficult decisions about if and how to proceed. Broadly speaking, amateur sport halted its activities immediately in order to face the enemy square-on. But, with its wider responsibilities to its employees and customers, professional sport tried to continue. Inevitably, these different routes attracted strong comment, especially along the lines that the sports professionals were essentially in conflict with both patriotic and properly sporting values. Class prejudice was also strongly in play here, especially given football's roots in the working-class, urban communities of the great industrial cities and towns of the north and the Midlands. The Footballer Battalion was eventually formed in December 1914, as national press coverage of football became more and more hostile. But this move looked, to many, like a mere public relations exercise, and by March 1915 it was reported that just 122 out of 1,800 professional players had come forward to join the military.[6]

In August 1914, the Football League management committee, with a strong 'over by Christmas' mentality in play, was preparing for the new season almost as if life was proceeding as normal in Britain and the rest of Europe. With no national conscription in force, in September the men from the league were close to publicly describing football as some kind of 'magical potion' that would act as an 'antidote' to war. The management committee even claimed it would be a 'national calamity' if league football was curtailed.[7] A reader's letter to the *Daily Post* on 3 September 1914 commented, acidly, that until he had read the league's manifesto, 'I had no idea . . . that these matches would stir up the patriotic spirit.' The British public seemed not quite so sure, as gates fell by more than 50 per cent, and the Football League instigated reductions on players' wages and a central fund to which all clubs contributed to try to keep the financially worst-affected members afloat.

In Liverpool, club chairman John McKenna, who was also president of the Football League, announced that the club's players had agreed to contribute 2.5 per cent of their wages to the War Fund for the rest of the war, and Will Cuff, the Everton secretary, promised that equipment would be secured to allow rifle practice during the club's training sessions. McKenna was, without doubt, a brilliant advocate for Liverpool and the league. 'He talked like an American,' said one player of an earlier dispute. 'He quoted figures, income, expenditure, gates and liabilities that simply floored those who imagined the clubs were rolling in wealth.' Honest John was, indeed, a master servant of the management and economics of the sport and of his local club, and although both loved and feared equally he had few airs and graces: he lived modestly in a terraced house in Anfield even when he was chair of Liverpool and president of the league. A fierce opponent of gambling on sport, his brusque exterior and straight-talking demeanour masked an even temperament and a man who was happy to mix with all classes of people. Making arrangements for wartime league football in the face of national criticism was not likely to ruffle him. Remarkably, he remained president of the Football League until the day of his death on 22 March 1936, when he was 81 years old.[8]

Tom Watson was also squarely behind wartime football. He reassured the local press on Merseyside in September 1914 that 'our boys have been anxious that they should be trained from a military point of view, and they and we welcome the league's decision [to carry on playing and ensure players train for national service]. We shall soon have the league's views carried into fact.'

Meanwhile, the amateur Liverpool Rugby Football Club (and the RFU) had adopted a demonstrably different stance. A Mr E. Roper from Liverpool RFC told the *Daily Post* proudly on 1 September 1914 that 'between fifty and sixty of the club's players . . . had joined the forces, and there was not a player left'. This revelation made footballers look like war-dodgers. Judging at least from the letters to the *Daily Post*, public opinion in Liverpool towards football's stance – and thus to the local clubs – was hostile enough. 'Is it not

The men who made Liverpool Football Club. Clockwise from top left: John Houlding, early Everton man and Liverpool FC founder; John McKenna, Irish stalwart of Liverpool FC and of the Football League; Joe McQue, a scorer in Liverpool's first-ever Football League match in September 1893; and Tom Watson (with hat, and with Reds goalkeeper Sam Hardy and defender Tom Chorlton), peerless architect of the first two league-championship wins in 1901 and 1906.

A rare view of the 1914 FA Cup final at Crystal Palace. Even the presence of the King could not save Liverpool from defeat and a 51-year wait for cup success.

The historic Liverpool squad that won back-to-back league titles in 1922 and 1923. Trainer Bill McConnell is in the middle row (far left) with manager Davie Ashcroft front left and secretary George Patterson front right. The fearsome Jock McNab is to the left of the goalkeepers and the hunched genius winger Bill Lacey shows off his sharp centre-parting (front row left).

WADSWORTH, Liverpool

A Reds collector's item featuring Bootle-born Walter Wadsworth. Wadsworth, who flattened a bandsman at Sheffield in 1923, was a feared opponent in Liverpool's 1920s championship teams.

A hot ticket: a menu card for the Liverpool championship dinner at the Midland Adelphi, 1923. It would get even hotter: Liverpool FC now faced 24 long years without winning a major trophy.

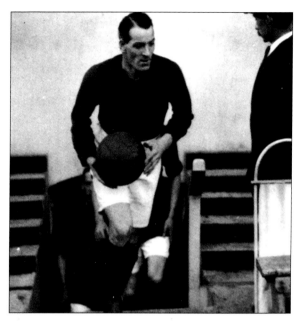

Donald McKinlay, brilliant Reds captain and loyal servant for two decades from his signing in January 1910, a man who cared more about playing for his beloved Liverpool than winning caps for Scotland.

Harry 'Smiler' Chambers, later chased by the taxman, provided the goals for Liverpool's title-winning teams of 1922 and '23.

H. CHAMBERS
LIVERPOOL

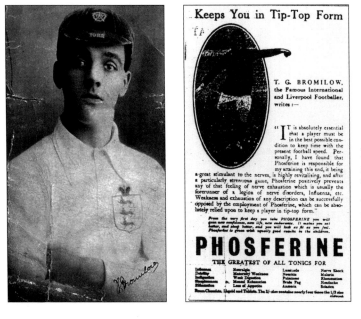

England international
and Liverpool captain
Tommy Bromilow,
the midfield brains
behind the
championship sides
of 1922 and '23 and
also a tonic advertiser
– a nice little earner
back in the early '20s.

South African forward Gordon Hodgson
wowed the Kop from 1925 and he
became a mainstay of the inconsistent
inter-war Liverpool teams.

The incomparable Elisha Scott, an authentic
Kop hero of the 1920s and '30s, a man who
often preferred to talk to the Liverpool crowd
rather than his own defenders.

enough to make one despair of his race?' blustered one correspondent. 'Apart from withdrawing the services of scores of trained athletes, it encourages thousands of supporters to withhold their own.' Another letter accused the league of the 'prostitution of a noble sport' and suggested that entirely new leagues be formed of players aged between 16 and 19 and of those under 16, and that the government should 'commandeer . . . playing grounds for drilling purposes, preferably for artillery regiments'.

Football followers in the city were rather more supportive of their clubs. When a poor Liverpool side lost 0–5 at home to Everton on 3 October 1914, for example, the crowd was well over 30,000 and was 'in high spirits and its colour scheme was deeply tinged with patches of khaki'. Lord Derby – a local dignitary and Tory football supporter, and a man who had survived a devastating political put-down from Lloyd George that 'like a cushion, he always bore the impression of the last man who sat on him' – now came up with the novel idea of a 'census' of the crowd at football in Liverpool, ostensibly in order to demonstrate the potential contribution to the war that could be made by the Merseyside football audience. Survey cards were handed out to the players and supporters at the Liverpool v. Manchester United 1914 Boxing Day 1–1 draw.

The Liverpool FC minute books for the time show that the club was committed to pay half the wages of any player who joined up under Lord Derby's scheme. The *Liverpool Echo* of 29 December 1914 reported that out of a healthy crowd of 27,015 at Anfield, 1,453 were soldiers and 3,044 boys, and that elsewhere the custom of free admission for soldiers had reduced receipts at some clubs by a reported 80 per cent. 'Maybe football clubs will have to ask these sporty soldiers to assist them in the late months of the season,' argued the *Echo*, 'by paying half-price for admission.' The ravages of war were soon apparent: when Liverpool played Preston at Anfield on 22 October 1917, out of a crowd of 15,422 some 3,345 (22 per cent) were soldiers, including 1,769 who were wounded.

Lord Derby was probably better at running his various estates than he was at doing research. Out of 16,000 census cards distributed at the match, only 1,034 were returned by men, but they made interesting reading nevertheless. From the replies, 308 supporters were too young, too old or married and so were ineligible to enlist; 144 were in the type of work that prevented them from enlisting; 335 were unfit; 31 were already enlisted; 10 were unsigned. This meant that there were around 206 supporters present who were eligible to enlist. Extrapolated to the whole crowd and allowing for a sprinkling of female fans, this could mean around 5,000 potential recruits – who, instead, said the critics, were watching football.

On 23 April 1915, the council of the FA finally announced a formal suspension of all football for the next season, a decision that meant that 1915 league champions Everton would end up holding the title for the next five years. Strangely, the Blues would also win the last league title before the Second World War, in 1939. In July 1915, the Football League finally suspended the league competition, but the management committee agreed to come up with a regional form of the sport so that there might be football played throughout the country to maintain national morale.

REGIONAL FOOTBALL AND THE BLIGHT OF WAR

Perhaps it was a sign of the sheer cultural and economic power of the sport on Merseyside that the *Liverpool Echo* on 20 July 1915 felt able to heartily endorse the league's determination to allow the game to carry on in a new, reduced format, with expenses only allowed for players who trained sparingly, on Tuesday and Thursday nights. Local firms that offered players employment were given complimentary tickets in return. In other northern football heartlands, such as Blackburn, Newcastle, Sunderland and Middlesbrough, and in many of the Midlands' strongholds, it had been decided not to play football during the war. 'They are entitled to their opinion and their stand. We respect people who have theory,' argued the *Echo,* tartly. 'But, sirs, the backbone of the army is what may be termed "football inclined", and I say emphatically that we ought to play football for their sakes, if for no other.' John McKenna, on behalf of both Liverpool FC and the Football League, said, 'We feel we owe a duty to the game and to those who perforce must stay at home.' The city of Liverpool was determined to play on and buck the trend elsewhere.

Money was certainly tight in the war years. In August 1915, the Liverpool club doctor was offered only half his fee from the previous year, and Bovril halved their payment to the club for exclusive rights to sell sweetmeats inside Anfield. Also in line with general cuts, the Liverpool minute books reported that 'it was decided that Mrs Lilly's offer of eight shillings for washing and repairing players' clothes be accepted'. The minutes also show how all major financial decisions at this time – on policing, admission charges, advertising and match programme rights – were made in direct consultation with neighbours Everton. When Liverpool told the Goodison board in August 1915 that they now planned for the 'non-issue of intoxicants in the boardroom' as an economic measure, the resident Everton Methodists received the news with 'distinct pleasure' and said that such moves would be 'strongly supported' across Stanley Park.

Liverpool FC received many requests for financial assistance at this time, including a begging note from ex-keeper Joe McQue, who was sent a 'nice letter' in reply stating, sorry, the club could not help. A letter received at Anfield in December 1915 asked for 'comforts' for an ex-player Harold Fitzpatrick, who was now a prisoner of war. The chairman instructed that 'two parcels of groceries be purchased from Coopers at about 10–6d each'. One was sent immediately, the other held back 'in case Fitzpatrick is heard of again'.

In February 1916, the Anfield stands were insured against air attack, and in September of that year the still-banned Jackie Sheldon asked if he could attend the Reds home match v. Burnley. He was admitted free as a wounded soldier but was told sternly by the Liverpool board that 'he must not go near the dressing-rooms'. He did better, at least, than local 'lady footballers' who were raising money for the war effort. They asked for the loan of a room at Anfield in December 1917 – and were, of course, refused.

The regionalised football competition that was played in the war years was often chaotic – Liverpool were late arriving for the club's first match, for the fourteen-club Lancashire Section Principal fixture, at Bolton – but the core of the Reds' league squad remained. And there was even a decisive home win at last (4–1) to celebrate against a depleted Everton, in November 1915. A ten-match supplementary tournament filled in the months of April and March 1916, though, inevitably, crowds fell substantially compared to the league average of 24,315 who had watched Liverpool in the 1913–14 season. Later, restrictions on transport and fuel also added to the problems of completing wartime fixtures.

THE PASSING OF OWD TOM

In all this confusion and disturbance brought by war, perhaps it was in some ways a blessing that the great Sunderland and Liverpool football man Tom Watson was spared the cannibalising of the Football League format and the teams that played in it. On 5 May 1915, the much loved Owd Tom died suddenly of pneumonia and pleurisy. His death came barely a week after he had been attending a South Liverpool v. Liverpool match and had complained to friends about 'feeling odd'. The Liverpool board wrote later to Tom's wife of the 'irreparable loss' they had sustained by Watson's death, which was overshadowed somewhat by news of the sinking of the Liverpool-registered SS *Lusitania* on her maiden voyage and the anti-German rioting and vandalism in the city involving 'wreckers and looters' from Seaforth to Garston that followed. This meant that all Germans and Austrians were soon advised to leave the city. But it was still very clear, even through this haze of war-induced violence and hatred in Liverpool, that, as the *Football Express* put it with some understatement, 'the football world has lost one of its ornaments'.

Watson, undoubtedly, was, as the *Echo* described him, 'perhaps the most popular figure in the association code of professional football', a man who had 'no enemies' but had a genius for signing good players at low cost. He had not only guided Liverpool to league titles and promotions, but he was also intensely affable, and he had had an unusually wide vision for the sport in an age when the English football establishment was unsure about how to respond to the spread of football around the world. 'Bluff, hearty, jovial, fond of a joke, could tell one in spasms, and was always prepared to listen to one,' mused the *Liverpool Echo* on his death. The *Liverpool Express* reasoned that the late manager had the capacity to attract recruits to the Liverpool club by the power of his sheer geniality, although trips to sign favoured players did not always work quite as planned. Watson enjoyed telling a story of a scouting trip to Scotland that led to the Liverpool party following the player concerned to the dynamite factory where he worked, only for them to be chased by navvies armed with the company's products. They thought the intruders were employer's agents.

'During the summer season, Mr Watson was in the habit of spending his holiday abroad,' recalled the *Echo*, 'and he had a distinct influence in popularising the game on the Continent.' In fact, Watson had just planned a trip to the USA to assess football there. He was also a regular church-attender and a keen local bowls man, typically acting for a spell as the president of the Liverpool Bowling Association. But what had made Watson so unique in football was his huge network of trusted contacts in the game, which aided so much in his famed 'talent tracing'. As one newspaper put it, 'Tom, as a manager, must have had the record for signing on men he had never seen.' Watson also had an assured capacity to bend the press to his will. 'Bee', the *Echo* football writer, recalled that Watson had insisted to him that newspapers should always 'encourage' football and had argued that it was difficult to convince the press that the game was not 'the blackguardly thing some supposedly good folk believe it to be'.

At his funeral at the Anfield Cemetery, paid for by the club, hundreds of supporters and the English and Scottish football world turned out in large numbers to pay their respects, including all the Liverpool club directors: Messrs John McKenna, John Asbury, W.R. Williams, A. Worgan, R.L. Martindale, T. Crompton, E.A. Bainbridge and W.C. Briggs. There were rather narrow limits to the club's generosity, however: it was reluctant to contribute towards the cost of a headstone for Watson's grave. There were more than one hundred wreaths at the funeral, which 'represented all the leading football associations', and seven former Liverpool players, including Alex Raisbeck and goalkeeper Ted Doig, as well as the great Liverpool trainer William Connell, acted as pall-bearers. The sport – and the city of Liverpool – agreed that it had lost one of its early greats.

LEARNING TO FLY

Football during the war continued without Tom Watson, and with no new Liverpool football manager to replace him. It would be five years before a 'football man' would step into the role. Because of the general economic problems in the game, each club was now required to pay 20 per cent of its wartime gate money to the visitors, a practice that was unimaginable before 1914 but now became the economic mainstay of English football for almost 70 years. Wartime matches were reduced to 80 minutes in length, but the minimum cost of admission was actually increased, from sixpence to ninepence, following the introduction by government of an entertainment tax in October 1917 – it would cost Liverpool FC some 37 precious shillings to repaint the headstones advertising the new prices at Anfield. In January 1918, there was more ground expense as the Liverpool board decided to move the official club entrance, from Walton Breck Road to Anfield Road.

In these straitened times, flexibility was the watchword. The nearby Southport club, for example, was allowed by the Football League to rename itself Southport Vulcan because of its support from a local factory, thus becoming still the only club in the history of the Football League to have an overtly commercial name.[9] In 1919, Leeds City were expelled from the Football League for violating wartime regulations and withholding information regarding the payment of players, and the league management committee actually sanctioned proposals from the owner of Huddersfield Town, Hilton Crowther, to move his club to play at the now defunct Leeds stadium, unless fans in Huddersfield could raise the necessary funds to buy Crowther out. They did so, thus ensuring that Town did not become, in 1919, England's first professional 'franchise' football club.

In March 1919, Arsenal were also gerrymandered into the First Division of the Football League ahead of other, more deserving cases, allegedly because of the friendship between Liverpool's John McKenna and Arsenal's powerful chairman Sir Henry Norris. Money and power talked, and the London club became the first and only Football League club to gain such a promotion for reasons other than merit – they have never been relegated since. These were very extraordinary football times indeed.

When Liverpool Football Club eventually resumed its 42-match league football programme in August 1919, the Reds voted for the southern challengers

Chelsea and Arsenal to make up the new numbers in the enlarged First Division. The city of Liverpool, meanwhile – like London and parts of South Wales – had been badly scarred by 'race' riots in the summer, with the *Liverpool Echo* on 6 June 1919 unsympathetically describing the erupting local black communities in the city as 'distinct foreign colonies' and their separateness from the mainstream as 'partly a check against the pollution of a healthy community by undesirables'. *The Times* of 10 June 1919 reported that a large body of police requisitioned by the city authorities to quell disturbances on Merseyside soon got into their stride: 'Whenever a negro was seen he was chased and, if caught, severely beaten . . .' The next day the south end of the city was in turmoil, 'the streets filled with thousands of excited people'. According to the *New York Times* on 4 August 1919, the city was given over to more disorder, consecutive nights of 'riot and pillage' in the face of strikes and local food shortages. Troops were drafted in as the local police went on strike and mobs gathered in Scotland Road and raided stores on London Road. Local children continued their work after dark. Other rioters targeted beer-bottling plants in Tariff Street and Love Lane and were confronted by armed soldiers who shot some of the offenders. The routine treatment of the city's poor and of Liverpool's long-standing ethnic-minority communities was finally beginning to come home to roost.

Compared to this kind of serious social and economic unrest, football in the city had a veritably easy ride. True, Liverpool FC still had no manager, but what it did have was the core of a potentially great team, built mainly by the late Tom Watson. The capable Kenny Campbell was still in goal, even though he had asked for a transfer back to Scotland in 1915. But Elisha Scott, the young Irishman recruited by Watson for free from Belfast, was now getting rave reviews in the Liverpool reserves. At the club AGM in June 1915, Scott was mentioned by name by John McKenna as the player whose performances had rescued Liverpool's season. The backs were the impressive Donald McKinlay and Ephraim Longworth, and also included in their reserve ranks was the skilful, but slight, St Helens-born right-back Tom Lucas. The half-backs included the improving Bootle enforcer Walter Wadsworth – whose winger brother Harold had also joined the club – and a very talented left-sided link player from Liverpool, the brilliant Tom Bromilow, a man who had been invalided out of the army because of septic poisoning.

Jock McNab, a raw, young tough-tackling Scot, also began to make small waves at Liverpool in 1920 – he would do plenty more later. In the forwards, there was Bill Lacey and the rehabilitated right-winger Jackie Sheldon, Preston-born marksman Dick Forshaw and a versatile and reliable – if sometimes injury-prone – forward, Harry Lewis, a Birkenhead-born inside-forward who had scored freely for Liverpool in the war years. Harry 'Smiler' Chambers, a trained shipworker who had spent his war service in Ireland playing as a guest for Distillery FC and Glentoran, was now back with Liverpool and determined to make a name for himself as a goalscoring centre-forward. Most of these men would be key figures in taking Liverpool Football Club back to the very top of the Football League in the early 1920s, even as social division, depression and hardship wracked the city.

Before the 1919–20 season began, Eph Longworth, the Liverpool captain, unusually gave a long interview with the *Echo* on the issue of the working lives of professional footballers. This came about mainly because players had typically worked during the war and then had played football on Saturdays. This made some critics doubt the need for full-time professional football players at all. Longworth argued that in this period of climbing post-war unemployment, most footballers had decided, patriotically, that 'it would not be playing the game to stay on in our positions'. He also pointed out that wartime football had meant less competitive play and much less travelling – all this would change again as 'the pace of play in the coming season will be swifter than for four years'. Matching playing professionally with working in industry during the week would inevitably take its toll on a man's strength and was an idea, Longworth suggested, that came from people 'who have never spent more than an afternoon at a training ground'. It was a spirited and articulate defence of his profession.

Even with players becoming full-time once again and increasing their pre-war wages by 50 per cent, the new season was not entirely without its teething problems, as the nation and its people struggled to recover from the privations of war. All club expenditure had to be accounted for: Liverpool had a cash balance of just £175. Director Tom Crompton was even required to report to a full board meeting in October 1919 that he had successfully purchased a set of new balls for the club billiard room. The occupational status of professional players was hardly improved by the war. In September, Liverpool's footballers asked the board for two complimentary tickets for each home match. The Anfield hierarchy barely blinked in formally regretting that this request 'could not be agreed'. The Liverpool minute books also show that in June 1919 the club paid Sunderland a fee of £100 to move their fixture at Anfield from 26 April to Christmas Day. But generally the war habit of playing the same club home and away on consecutive weeks was maintained by the Football League.

Liverpool's home midweek fixture with Arsenal on 1 September 1919, in front of a poor crowd, was much delayed because of the late arrival of the referee, which meant the match 'was finished in semi-darkness'. When Liverpool later visited Chelsea in October a breakdown on the tube meant that many people were still pouring into Stamford Bridge well after kick-off. In the same month, the *Football Echo* commented that travel even within Lancashire was prohibitive.

'The inaccessibility of Burnley from Liverpool is proverbial,' the newspaper observed. 'Today's journey, its stoppings and changes, showed that improvements in the matter of railway facilities is still far to seek.'

Liverpool had started the new era slowly and the club had had an especially disappointing October and November. But they battled to an encouraging 0–0 draw at Goodison just before Christmas. The return fixture at Anfield on 27 December was a red-letter day in the club's history – the first Football League victory over the old enemy at Anfield since the previous century – since 1899 to be precise.

By now football had begun slowly to recapture the imagination of an increasingly enthusiastic and demonstrative Merseyside public, one that was desperately attempting to escape the recent traumas of conflict. A massive crowd of 49,662 gathered at Anfield to witness a famous 3–1 derby home win. The *Liverpool Echo* noticed a change in the match atmosphere and in the character of the local football crowd, warning, 'There was a need for more crush-barriers [at Anfield], more effective barriers and many more police, together with some honourable stewards . . . The wonder was the game was finished, for the crowds at the corners swung inward to the playing space as soon as ever there was an exciting piece of play in the vicinity.' The main home excitement centred on the utter solidity of Longworth at the back against the 'very big men' at forward for Everton and two goals from Tom Miller that followed an early score from Harry Lewis.

In a news feature headlined 'Is Football a Lost Art?', the *Evening Express* on 24 January 1920 also detected an alleged new post-war hedonistic focus among football supporters in the city, in the sort of complaint that might have easily been heard 80 years later:

> One only has to mingle with the crowd and listen to their comments to realise that it is the excitement rather than the finer points of the game which are generally appreciated . . . [It is] fair to admit that the pace at which matches are now played has never been surpassed . . . The old-fashioned dribbling, finessing forward of 20 years ago is a very rare type today. The impression left in an old stager's mind is that in modern football, particularly in forward play, everything has been sacrificed to speed.

Also sensing change, the dean of Durham argued in the press that 'association football has been pretty well ruined by the betting upon it', but an ex-international player, the Reverend Kenneth Hunt, saw only changes for the good, arguing that post-war football 'has replaced tendencies that were far more vicious. It was the greatest challenge to the public house on Saturday afternoons. Football provided for the masses the recreation and excitement they obviously needed.'

How exactly were players recruited to conjure up this excitement produced every week at Liverpool FC? Well, the decision-making Liverpool board meetings at this time had a very simple structure. They were weekly and dominated by numerous reports from members of the public, scouts and Liverpool directors on prospective players. Club officials could, seemingly, be dispatched to the distant south coast, Scotland or Ireland on the flimsiest basis of a letter of recommendation about a player from a scout, supporter or onlooker. In December 1919, ex-player Matt McQueen joined the Liverpool board – it required special FA permission for an ex-player to join these gentleman ranks – and he at least offered some recent practical expertise in player assessment and recruitment. There were stock phrases used by Liverpool directors at this time to describe watched players: 'worth another look'; 'will not suit us'; 'on the small side'; 'showed much promise'; 'club would not part'; 'could not recommend him'. There seemed little discernible structure to these scouting visits and most were to local non-league clubs where Liverpool clearly hoped to pick up bargains, largely at random.

On many occasions, scouting trips proved to be so much wasted time. Communication difficulties made precision rather difficult. Fancied players were injured or omitted from teams, or matches were simply moved to other venues without notice. In October 1920, for example, Matt McQueen and a director travelled to watch a player at Atherton only to find that the fixture they planned to watch was being played at far-away Darwen. Liverpool board meetings also dealt, variously, with: the medical needs of players; fixture changes; financial and stadium matters; letters from the FA and other bodies and individuals; requests for charity fixtures or for use of the club stadium; and pleas for donations. They invariably ended with the naming by the board of the selected first team and reserve teams for the forthcoming club fixtures. These selections were then boldly written out in the minute books. If the board meeting was held before the busy Christmas or Easter holiday periods, complete teams might be chosen and written down in advance for *three* first-team Liverpool matches, irrespective of player form or the opposition. In the absence of a dedicated team manager, only injuries or illness could lead to late omissions and last-minute call-ups.

NEW BEGINNINGS

On New Year's Day 1920, Archibald Salvidge, the arch-Conservative leader of Liverpool City Council, spoke publicly of the urgent need for local renewal in the city, because 'Liverpool is engaged upon problems of reconstruction, which are colossal'. The government committee appointed to assess the health of British men in the wake of the First World War reported on the condition of 66,000 men from Liverpool and remarked on the high levels of TB in the city and the poor physique among 18 to 20 year olds. Some local males were described as 'old men at 38'. The *Evening Express* argued that the city of Liverpool was too old-fashioned, much behind 'Cottonopolis' (Manchester), and that people in the city were 'stodgy and slow and too conservative'. This might have been partly why, in February 1920, in an extraordinary development, the blue-chip retail giants Harrods finally ditched well-advanced plans to open up a proposed nine-storey £750,000 Liverpool store in Church Street because of disagreements with Liverpool City Council. The proposed investment duly disappeared, so a huge post-war branding and retail commercial opportunity, which would have had an impact on the city for decades to come, was lost.

In the arena of popular leisure, the Liverpool Parks and Gardens Committee now agreed to allow an experiment with evening dancing in Stanley Park during the summer months. But on the streets the struggle for popular leisure was never-ending. In 'an apparently new departure by the police', two youths were hauled in front of the Liverpool stipendiary magistrate in January 1920, charged with the offence of playing football in the street. 'It seems a remarkable thing,' argued the perplexed magistrate, 'that boys should be arrested for playing football.' Later in the same month, Henry Ainsworth, a fitter, was fined £61 for printing football coupons and dispersing them in the city. The FA thanked the Liverpool magistrates for suppressing this 'menace to the game'. Meanwhile, a young Manchester entrepreneur called John Moores and his partners were experimenting with a new football pools business that would help shape the Liverpool economy and the national public consumption of football for the next 50 years.

A winning sequence for Liverpool FC in January and February 1920 followed the December defeat of Everton, and it pleased new Reds manager, the Irishman David 'Little Dave' Ashworth, an ex-referee and coach, just five feet tall, who had been recruited in June 1919 by the Liverpool board as a safe pair of hands from Stockport County. Ashworth was no Tom Watson, but he shared Owd Tom's love of humour and tall tales – he was a 'great teller of Lancashire dialect stories'. He also liked to relieve the tedium of long railway journeys for pressmen and players with his dry wit. But Ashworth was a bundle of nerves during matches, claiming never to have seen a penalty kick taken in his entire career as a manager for fear of its outcome.

He would soon be opposed in the city by Harry Makepeace, Everton's first secretary–manager. The *Evening Express* commented on 10 August 1921 on this new trend in city football towards younger player–coaches and managers, which, it argued, would mean that quality young players would now find it easier to make their way inside the local clubs: 'Too often a young player of promise is picked up by the league team and because he does not develop with sufficient speed he is allowed to go. Now, when a youth shows skills, he will be encouraged and helped to master the game by the club coach.' Was this modernisation at last?

For the visit of Liverpool to Luton Town in the FA Cup in January 1920, 'the big railway fare prevented the visitors from having a large contingent with them', reported the *Evening Express*, 'but the mascot was in evidence in a variegated suit, dancing to his heart's content and well, too'. Later, at Bolton, 'the [Liverpool] mascot was again in full bloom'. But was the Reds mascot present, one wonders, when on 26 February 1920 the future Anfield great Elisha Scott finally made his post-war Liverpool reappearance? We can only guess. Scott's restart with Liverpool came after an injury and an operation, and at Notts County in a 0–1 defeat Scott had no chance with the County winner. But when Harold Hill got in a useful shot in the second half, the *Football Echo* reported, prophetically, that 'the Irishman caught it like a master'. By 9 March, perhaps sensing what the future held for him, the loyal Kenny Campbell asked again to be placed on the transfer list in order to be able to return to Scotland. Scott was immediately promoted to the Liverpool first team. By 3 April 1920, a 3–0 demolition of Derby County, Liverpool were yet to concede a single league goal at home that year.

A fourth-round 1–2 away FA Cup defeat in March to eventual finalists Huddersfield Town did not dampen club spirits. The build-up to the tie in the *Evening Express* also revealed details of the physical make-up of this emerging Liverpool team. Only two players, the departing Campbell and Walter Wadsworth, reached 5 ft 11 in. in height and everyone else was below 5 ft 9½ in., including Lucas, Sheldon and Harold Wadsworth, who all measured around the diminutive 5 ft 6 in. mark. Only one player, the chunky 5 ft 9 in. Irishman Bill Lacey, weighed in at over 12 st. This was no powerhouse of a football team, even for the 1920s. Nor was entertainment always guaranteed from them. When Liverpool struggled past lowly Sheffield Wednesday at Anfield on 10 March 1920 by a 1–0 score, in characteristically humorous style the 'home crowd became so fed up that they started shouting for the Wednesday'. These Reds supporters might have given thanks that they were not Chelsea followers: the London club defender Jack Harrow sportingly missed a penalty kick *on purpose* in March 1920 when he agreed with his Notts County opponents that their alleged handling offence was accidental.

Jackie Sheldon badly broke his leg near the end of the campaign, but Liverpool finished off a highly promising effort by overtaking Sunderland

into fourth place after a 1–0 last-match victory at Roker Park. This was
the first season when Liverpool's John McKenna, on behalf of the Football
League, began the tradition of presenting the league-championship trophy
to the winners on the field – it was to prove just in time for his beloved
Liverpool Football Club to benefit from the new arrangements. The *Liverpool
Courier* astutely identified some of the core strengths of this emerging post-
war Liverpool side:

> Undoubtedly, Scott, Longworth and McKinlay won the game. Scott made
> good saves when only good ones would prevent a goal, but the backs were
> brilliant...both tackled with confidence and judgement and kicked perfectly.
> In the middle, W. Wadsworth was a very effective power ... Only a leader
> who uses his brains would have headed [the] goal, as did Chambers.

Consolidation followed around this strong group of players in 1920–21, another
Liverpool finish of fourth in the league behind champions Burnley – but ahead of
Everton in seventh place – and a dull second-round FA Cup defeat at Newcastle
United. Liverpool conceded fewer goals (35) than anyone in the First Division
and did not concede a penalty throughout the entire season. But only Smiler
Chambers and a fast and brainy centre-forward signing from the north-east,
Dick Johnson, made any real impression on the scoring charts. Liverpool were
slowly building their strength and consistency from the back, and it was about
to pay off handsomely.

Also paying off was pressure from the players' union for a wage increase
for its members. Attendances and the cost of living were rising after the
war, but even the union must have been surprised when, in March 1920, the
maximum wage was doubled by the league management committee, to £9 a
week, and made payable over the whole 52 weeks, not 39 weeks and training
weeks as before. The Football League also expanded from 44 to 66 clubs by
incorporating the Southern League as a new Third Division, before adding
another 20 clubs in 1921–22 to form regionalised third divisions, North and
South, and including Southport, Tranmere Rovers and Wigan Borough from
Merseyside and the surrounding area. Now, for the first time, the Football
League could really claim, as the FA Cup had done before it, that it was a
premier football competition and a truly *national* one.

These had been difficult years. The debate about whether to play in the war
had been a damaging one for football, although in Liverpool public opposition
had been more muted. Tom Watson had been lost, but the Reds were rebuilding
on the back of his excellent work and had a new manager. It did not know it

yet, but Liverpool Football Club was preparing to be the first club since The Wednesday in 1902–04 to win back-to-back Football League championships. More importantly, Liverpool FC would be the first truly *national* Football League champions of England.

CHAPTER 5 REFERENCES

1. Quoted in Hill, 'Rite of Spring', p. 87
2. Whannel, *Fields in Vision*, p. 3
3. Hill, 'Rite of Spring', pp. 91–2
4. Hill, 'Rite of Spring', p. 104
5. Taylor, *The Association Game*, p. 119
6. Taylor, *The Association Game*, p. 120
7. Inglis, *League Football and the Men Who Made It*, p. 93
8. Inglis, *League Football and the Men Who Made It*, pp. 80–2
9. Inglis, *League Football and the Men Who Made It*, p. 98

6

THE ROARING TWENTIES
Liverpool Back on the Title Trail

THE LAST STAND OF HONEST JOHN McKENNA

For what would prove to be a memorable 1921–22 season, there were more changes afoot at Anfield. The entire playing area was returfed and a concrete wall was built to replace the old wooden palings around the pitch. Fortunately, Anfield was not as tight a location as the local press had claimed the Boleyn Ground at West Ham to be. In fact, a passage down each side of the ground measuring 8 ft wide and 5 ft at each end was added to the site, which tacked on between 5,000 and 7,000 new places to the existing stadium capacity. Moreover, 'ambitious ground improvements have already been projected', promised the *Evening Express*.

The Liverpool ground was beginning to catch up with developments elsewhere, not least those just across Stanley Park. But the Liverpool club could still do much more to improve its rudimentary stadium management and also perhaps its public relations. Early in 1922, a merchant, Robert McCulloch of Wavertree, sought court proceedings to sue the club for three shillings after he paid for two seats that were no longer available on his admission to the stadium. This was no occasional mishap before reliable numbered seating was established: the court heard that 'many other claims are pending'.

But there was a real bombshell to hit Liverpool before the start of this momentous season. It was the summer resignation from the Liverpool board of 'the sheet anchor of the club', John McKenna, after 29 and a half years' unbroken service. McKenna resigned at the Liverpool AGM in the summer of 1921, ostensibly because the club's major shareholders had decided to vote off the board ex-Liverpool favourite Matt McQueen, who had been McKenna's own nomination to the Liverpool administration 18 months before. McKenna had clearly had enough of this sort of malarkey at club level and he had plenty already on his plate as president of the league. The Liverpool shareholders, McKenna complained, 'seem to have quite failed to recognise the ability and genuine hard work done by these men on behalf of the club. I am certainly not going to be a party to it.'

McQueen would soon return to the Reds board, but this was a sad end to relations between McKenna and the club, especially since Liverpool also announced at the same AGM just the sort of progressive and money-saving policy the Irishman favoured – the running of a Liverpool third team or 'A' team for amateurs and local young professionals which would play at Sutton Lance Lane, Wavertree, managed by chief scout Charlie Wilson. This was aimed at 'fostering talent, which undoubtedly abounds in this area'. As the *Daily Post* reported it on 6 July 1921:

> The club had taken this step with the object of nursing young players. Present transfer fees were prohibitive and they [the Liverpool board] did not feel justified in spending large sums in acquiring players who might, or might not, prove successful.

In fact, the high transfer spending of Sunderland in the new season would provoke much wider discussion in the game about limiting the number of transfers, perhaps to one major signing per club, per season.

This innovative new Liverpool scheme might have been just made to attract talented local players, such as the Michael Owen-like waif John Hallows, a 15-year-old Chester-born 8 st. orphan who was much in the local sports news. He was described by the Liverpool press as 'the finest centre forward for his age in the country'. Hallows, reportedly a potential 'gold mine', had scored three hundred goals in just three years of junior football in the area – but he would not make it into the Liverpool system at Wavertree. Instead, Hallows played briefly for West Bromwich Albion and then turned out 164 times for Bradford City in the 1930s, scoring a tidy 74 goals. Nevertheless, this type of planned prudence in producing local young players was exactly typical of the new Liverpool FC approach that had been developing under the wily Tom Watson. The club was not – and never would be – about 'buying' success, despite Watson and John McKenna's early raids on Scotland for playing talent.

SEEING OUT THE BAD TIMES?

On 21 August 1921, the Liverpool minute books report that, 'It was decided that the duties of the manager be to have the full charge of all players and trainers on the books of the club and that all matters appertaining to the players be under his control.' Here was a clear statement of managerial status and duties but one which stopped short of the key issue – selecting the Liverpool team.

One promising player who was disappointed not to be offered a contract by Liverpool in 1921–22 was the talented amateur Ted Ray. Instead, Ray did what most Liverpudlians do for free: make people laugh. He went on to become a nationally known professional comedian and performer. Ray very probably made much more in earnings than did the professional football players he had so wanted to emulate. A First Division manager at this time revealed that top players at his club earned, on average, around £6 5s a week in 1921–22. The First Division clubs would have to find a reported £531,208 in first-team wages for the 613 First Division players employed.

With this new local focus from Liverpool FC, it was also widely hoped at this time that the *economic* situation in the city – and even relations between Protestant and Irish Catholic communities on Merseyside – might be changing, too. Liverpool's Orangeism had penetrated the civic culture of the city more than in any other city in Britain, including Glasgow.[1] But unlike in Glasgow, it had made relatively little impact on the support for, or the 'meaning' of, the two major football clubs, despite Liverpool FC's Protestant roots. Both clubs supported similar charities, and both Liverpool and Everton signed players irrespective of their religious background. This might well have been partly because of the unusual origins of the clubs and the fact that neither served a specific geographical area of the city, thus guarding against the sort of territorial tribalism in football seen elsewhere. Liverpool FC's early Orange administration might have caused it to be labelled the city's Protestant club and Everton's earlier north Liverpool base might have contributed to its soft identification as the Catholics' team in the city, but for most people on Merseyside these descriptions were simply that – labels. People in the same families often supported different clubs – and do today – irrespective of creed or religious affiliation.

If the city of Liverpool and its surrounding area was suffering from the impact of national recession, then it was also trying characteristically hard to show that it might just party through the bad times. In July 1921, for example, applications were made to build *seven* new cinemas in and around the city centre, with Liverpool FC director Edwin Berry behind the proposed 1,700-seat giant £200,000 Rialto development at the corner of Upper Parliament Street. But ultimately these were difficult days for this sort of popular leisure expansion, and within six months Arthur Williams, the managing director of a number of Liverpool picture houses, was asserting that 'the cinema, like many other trades, is going through a very bad time'.

In sport, a summer baseball match between England and Wales on Stanley Park in 1921 attracted a crowd of 4,000, and a fierce debate now took off in the Liverpool press about the local demand for Sunday sport in the city's parks. Some letter writers described Liverpool on Sundays as 'old fashioned' or even 'the city of the dead'.

The core identity of the city was also under attack, because in a controversial lecture delivered locally Robert Gladstone argued that the Liverpool liver bird was actually a grossly misleading copy of the seal granted to the city by King John and that it should really be an eagle. 'The corporate seal of the city is an atrocity,' he went on, with apparently little care for local sensibilities. 'Its design is ludicrous and its motto gibberish.' His view was clear enough.

THE FA'S KNIFE IN WOMEN'S FOOTBALL

A crowd of 9,000 people attended a match involving the famous Dick, Kerr's women's football team in Southport in August 1921. Perhaps because of its popularity, on 5 December the women's game was effectively banned by the FA due to alleged 'irregularities' in managing funds raised by women's charity matches during the war. In Liverpool, the FA decision provoked a strong response. A furious Mr Cecil Kent wrote to the *Evening Express*: 'Why have the FA got their knife into girls' football? . . . Are their feet heavier on the turf than men's?' A Mr J.H. Harrison, who ran Suggs' Amazons, a women's works team from Liverpool that had planned to play a Boxing Day game in Bootle, argued, 'Surely this is for the players to decide. The girls merely play against each other on equal terms, and if they think it is a suitable game to play that ought to settle it.'

Liverpool would clearly not give up women's football so easily, and a well-attended women's 'international' match was staged after the ban, at the Stanley Athletics Ground, Fairfield, in March 1922. It was refereed by Everton defender Dickie Downs and was fought out between England (Dick, Kerr's) and France (Olympique de Paris). The teams were hosted before the fixture at a lavish dance in the Adelphi ballroom by the mayor and mayoress of Liverpool. But this women's contest drew little support from the Merseyside press. An *Evening Express* editorial on 30 March 1922 argued, 'Nothing more likely to injure the dignity of womanhood could be devised. Nothing less likely to inculcate a respect for femininity among boys and youths could be imagined.'

The vehemence of general male opposition to women footballers should not surprise. After all, football had been developed as a tough and physically exacting working-class diversion in cities such as Liverpool. Football was a male retreat from the constraints of home and, in the 1920s, a refuge from an increasingly uncertain future for men.[2] Older women now had the vote, and a speech in Wallasey in the early 1920s by a Miss S. Midgley argued that it was as 'humanly natural' for women to desire wealth as it was for men. Maude Roydea from the Victorian Women's Settlement in Liverpool even suggested in a lecture that ambitious young girls were already asking why they needed husbands at all and why should they not have children outside marriage.

In short, the post-war world – including the world of sport – was transforming fast. Many Liverpool men were threatened by the pace and direction of change. 'Backlash' letters to the local press were all too common, such as the one from 'Elkay' suggesting a night-time curfew on women in Liverpool. Or 'Strap-hanger' to the *Evening Express* in January 1922, who argued that women workers should be required to show a special pass on Liverpool trams. For Merseyside men, seemingly under attack from all sides, the prospect of women taking over their beloved football was probably just a step too far.

BUILDING FOR THE LEAGUE TITLE

The 1921 census revealed Liverpool's population to stand at an impressive 803,118, an increase of 6.5 per cent. Liverpool and Everton were attracting around 70,000 people on average every fortnight to football in the city, even when times were hard, so demand for football was clearly still very high. Everton actually *raised* seat season-ticket prices in 1921, from 35 shillings to £2 10s, and George Patterson, Liverpool's secretary, used the local press to inform Liverpool club members in August that their tickets should now be collected from the Anfield office 'without delay as the number is limited'. Meanwhile, Sunderland, Liverpool's first opponents in the new season, announced that it would *not* be issuing season tickets at all this term because of fears about the effects of the recession on attendances.

'Liver', the football writer of the *Evening Express*, travelled to see Liverpool lose 0–3 in front of 40,000 fans at Roker Park, and, surveying the streets of Wearside, he announced himself to be 'greatly impressed by the large number of men who were apparently idle . . . They did not appear to have any work to do.' He really need only look on his own doorstep: 5,000 men demonstrated outside the Liverpool town hall for the right to work in September 1921. In October, unemployed protesters in the city outside St George's Hall fled with their leader Robert Tissyman into the Walker Art Gallery, where they were locked in and then roundly beaten by the Liverpool police. The Liverpool unemployed in the 1920s proposed boycotting both local pubs and football matches at this time as a form of protest about the lack of work locally, thus suggesting that at least some of the jobless might still have been attending matches at Anfield and Goodison. But there was also little doubt that the rise of minimum entrance from sixpence to ninepence in 1917 and then to one shilling after the war probably meant that regular attendance at football was beyond their means and even that of some skilled workers.[3]

Writing to the *Evening Express* in 1921, a Mr D.C. Williams from Smithdown Road had a futuristic answer to Liverpool's growing unemployment problem: employ idle men on public works to dig a road tunnel under the Mersey. It was just a thought – but it would have to wait. Instead, work would begin in the autumn of 1922, offering employment for some, on a 27-mile £3-million arterial road linking Liverpool to Manchester.

Away from these sorts of social and political tensions, Liverpool Football Club's playing ranks were bolstered for the new campaign by the emergence from local football in Garston of forward Danny Shone, a short and stocky left-footed player with real promise, who soon won Red hearts by scoring his first goal for the club against local rivals Everton. St Helens-born right-half and England cap John Bamber also started against Sunderland, but he would soon lose his place, briefly, to Seaforth man Frank Checkland, who gave way, in turn, to the gritty fighter and Scottish midfield enforcer Jock McNab. Cyril Gilhespy, an outside-right bought from Sunderland, also briefly made a splash. But the most important new man at Anfield was certainly outside-left Fred Hopkin, signed from Manchester United for a hefty £2,800 fee in May 1921.

The balding Hopkin was no manic goalscorer – only 12 goals in 360 appearances – but when he finally broke his Liverpool goal duck at Anfield after 70 matches, against Bolton Wanderers in March 1923, amidst the excitement a fire broke out in the Anfield Road stand, reportedly because some straw had been ignited by a discarded cigarette butt. The *Liverpool Echo* reported that the fire brigade could be heard 'hacking away at the goal-stand' as the match continued and smoke blinded the visiting goalkeeper. Hopkin was hard-working and quick, and he provided plenty of ammunition for men who knew better where the goal was, characteristically dropping on his right knee and looking for suitable targets when crossing the ball.

The *Echo* had praised the 'courage' of the Liverpool directors for fielding the 'enthusiastic and ever ready' local man Shone at Sunderland, but the 0–3 reverse in the north-east was an early shock. That the future England international Sunderland's Charles Buchan congratulated Elisha Scott on his 'thrilling saves' in the besieged Liverpool goal was a nice touch, and Hopkin shone on his debut in his left-side forward combination with Chambers. It emerged later that Tom Watson had almost brought the brilliant Buchan to Liverpool back in 1910, after agreeing a fee of £750 with the Leyton club. But by the time the cautious Liverpool directors had agreed to pay this sum, the price for Buchan had risen to £1,000 in a seller's market. Despite Liverpool's best efforts to scrape the money together, Sunderland stepped in first to clinch the deal. It would not be the only time a Liverpool manager would be frustrated by his board – almost 90 years later Rafa Benítez would have similar complaints. Certainly Liverpool's slide after 1906 might well have been arrested by Buchan's arrival, but the history of the game is chock full of these ifs and buts.

Bizarrely, the *Liverpool Echo* blamed the shot-shy display from the Liverpool forwards at Roker on their training on the spongy, lush new Anfield turf, where 'the ball drags a lot when driven'. In the return, Liverpool won 2–1, relying heavily on goals from Wales international Billy Matthews and Dick Forshaw, and, again, on Elisha Scott to save brilliantly from a goal-bound Buchan header. Liverpool would not lose again in the league until 26 November, at Middlesbrough, winning seven and drawing seven (all by 1–1) of the next fourteen matches. It all seemed a little 'safety first', but manager Ashworth's approach was effective, and by the time of the first derby match on 5 November 1921 Liverpool's 'rock-like' defence had conceded only 11 league goals in total. Both matches against Everton were tough 1–1 draws, though after the Goodison stalemate the *Evening Express* reasoned, 'I think the most biased Evertonian will admit that Liverpool were the cleverer eleven.' In the return at Anfield, Tommy Bromilow starred – 'England has no finer,' argued the *Echo* – and the irrepressible Elisha was reported to be in 'jubilant mood'.

Was there a little football bias about in the city of Liverpool? Each of the major clubs had their own press correspondent and point scoring was common in the daily sporting press. But a letter from a 'common spectator' to the *Evening Express* on 17 November 1921 complained about the 'Blue spectacled' football reporting in the local press and also, caustically, about the high-handed criticism from reporters that standing football supporters were blocking the scribes' view of the match:

> As to spectators, including myself, who pay our money to see the match getting in the way of our noble pressmen, we will have to see about getting the mounted police to guard the press box and also hire a band to play them into their seats. How would my critic like to fight to work each morning?

RED MEN

Liverpool finally threw off their shackles for all to see in a 4–0 home defeat of Middlesbrough in November, where Bromilow, according to the *Echo*, was 'again the star half-back of the day. He accomplishes everything by pure skill.' Danny Shone also won plaudits for a hat-trick and a 'capital game throughout', and in the return the following week the forward had a goal unluckily disallowed for offside, with Liverpool already 1–0 up. The visitors slid from a likely win to a 1–3 defeat but then set off on another 15-match unbeaten run in the Football League until the middle of March 1922.

In December, as Liverpool rode high and clear at the top of the league table, neighbours Everton languished at fourth-bottom and were reported to be 'worse off than at almost any period in the club's history'. As Everton struggled, even Liverpool's reserves were attracting attention from other clubs. The deposed Ephraim Longworth's request for a transfer was refused, and England half-back John Bamber was reported to have drawn a bid from an unnamed club of a very tempting £7,000. The Reds had no need to sell, and the retain-and-transfer arrangements meant that Bamber could not choose to leave. He stayed, to play an important back-up role in the Liverpool FC league-title successes that followed.

'THIS INTENSE SOLIDARITY' – THE 1921–22 LEAGUE CHAMPIONSHIP

Into the new year in 1922, even the generally supportive *Evening Express* admitted that Liverpool had been 'lucky' to take a point at Newcastle United on 2 January, relying inevitably on 'some wonderful saves by Scott'. The home pressure was obviously intense: the contrary Liverpool goalkeeper was sternly warned twice by the referee for time-wasting. 'But,' said the *Evening Express*, 'I would ask what team does anything of note in a tournament like the league without enjoying some luck?' It was a fair point.

After a drawn FA Cup tie at Sunderland that was 'full of hair-raising situations', influenza ran through the Roker side that came to Anfield for the replay in front of a record midweek crowd of more than 46,000. This type of sickness was no trifling matter: 25 people died from influenza in Liverpool in January 1922 alone. On the left-wing, Hopkin was irrepressible for Liverpool, 'beating man after man' before setting up Forshaw in a 5–0 demolition. The Liverpool crowd laughed contentedly as the tiny Harry Lewis marked the imposing Buchan, 'a case of the long and short of it'. Lord Derby visited the Reds dressing-room after the game to congratulate the bubbling hosts, who were now starting to believe that this really could be their year.

With Tom Lucas strongly challenging the unsettled Eph Longworth for the right-back slot and often replacing him, the England man suddenly resigned as Liverpool captain. The directors quickly appointed Donald McKinlay in his place. A letter from 'RPW' from Dingle to the *Evening Express* on 18 January 1922 highlighted some of the local concerns among Reds supporters about morale in the squad, even with Liverpool comfortably heading the league table from Burnley. He wanted Longworth restored to the team to 'stop rumours of discontent', and he wondered 'if it is a record for league leaders to have such a poor total in the goals-for column'. Liverpool had lost only two matches, but in seventeen out of twenty-five league games thus far Liverpool had scored only one goal or fewer. 'Having watched every home game this season,' the writer continued, 'I would like to ask the directors are they making the best use of the talent at their disposal.' RPW wanted, as a minimum, full-back Donald McKinlay's dead-ball expertise moved up into the forwards: 'We "specs" roar for Mac whenever a free-kick is to be taken near the opponents' goal.' This appeared to be a rather radical suggestion. Liverpool seemed to be close to winning the league title, but were they winning over their own supporters?

There might have been too much caution and even a little disharmony in the Liverpool ranks, but this paled into near-insignificance when compared to the growing unrest at a rapidly fading Everton. The Blues were dumped 0–6 at home in the FA Cup by Second Division Crystal Palace and would eventually slump to 20th in the First Division. When Aston Villa were hosted by the Blues in January 1922, Everton players Sam Chedgzoy amd Stan Fazackerley complained bitterly at half-time about the barracking they had received from their *own* supporters. Fazackerley, a £4,000 buy, was later suspended by the Everton directors for 'disobedience to orders'. By contrast with this shambles, when Liverpool's players attended the Liverpool Stadium for boxing entertainment in January before the club's forthcoming home FA Cup tie against West Bromwich Albion they enjoyed a 'big rally' from local sports fans.

This public adulation proved to be of little help: Liverpool lost 0–1 to WBA in front of 49,332, who paid £3,050. The result was attributed by the *Evening Express* on 30 January to 'the lack of a first-class centre-forward' at the club. Two local brothers who were unlikely to be moved by this shock Liverpool loss were James and Robert Yates. They were otherwise engaged, arrested for stealing a Singer car from outside the Anfield stadium during play. Liver, however, saw some time-honoured consolation in the Reds defeat when he admitted, 'The double is definitely off. Perhaps, after all, it is as well. I don't expect the directors to agree with me in that, but competition is so keen nowadays that it is well nigh impossible to win the cup and head the league in the same season.' Liverpool were four points clear of Burnley in the league, but no team had done the Double since Aston Villa in 1897, in the first decade of the Football League. It was generally agreed that talent was so evenly spread in the game, and that the league programme was so penal, that winning both trophies was beyond even the strongest outfit.

Meanwhile, in early February 1922 police teams from Bootle and Chester played a charity football match at Hawthorne Road for the benefit of Liverpool's unemployed, with Walter Wadsworth, Dick Johnson and reserve Liverpool goalkeeper Frank Mitchell acting as the officials. It was a small sign at least of local football solidarity with those in dire need. What else could the clubs do? In Barrow, where the unemployed had been allowed to attend football matches free of charge, near-riots had broken out.[4] Frustration and anger was also routinely spilling out now into local football, in what has been described as the 'crisis' of 1919 to 1922, which saw the local game purportedly blighted by an upsurge in 'free fights', betting and bad language.[5] The FA gave regular warnings around this time about alleged 'rough' play and poor discipline in local football. When Bootle St James and Bootle Rovers met on the North Recreation Ground in February 1922 – in a case that was becoming familiar in and around the city – John Nolan, a supporter acting as a linesman, assaulted the referee Ernest Ellis and ended up in court. The chair of the bench commented, 'It was very essential in the interests of the sport that it should be carried on in an honourable manner. It was a most disgraceful thing to assault a referee.' Ill-discipline seemed rife, but public facilities were at least expanding for local football in Liverpool at this time, from 154 corporation pitches in 1921 to 172 by 1930.[6]

Back in the rather more tightly controlled professional football ranks, title-chasing Liverpool won 2–0 in the league at a snowy Birmingham, with two goals from Smiler Chambers. When Chambers scored his late second goal after a run of 'spirit and dash' by Longworth, who was replacing Donald McKinlay, it was the first occasion in the campaign that the Reds had scored more than one goal away from home. The *Evening Express* began to wonder at these comparative riches and if Liverpool supporters were 'inclined at the moment to get ready for jubilation'. This was even with 15 games left – including both meetings with main rivals Burnley. David Ashworth, Liverpool's manager, now had to work hard to keep the club on track by denying potentially destabilising rumours that regional foes Manchester United were trying to sign two of the club's reserves. This news came out just as Falkirk in Scotland paid a record fee of £5,000 to West Ham for England international forward Syd Puddefoot – talent was moving north, not always coming south. Despite Everton's free-spending reputation, ten players in the club's A team in the Liverpool County Cup semi-final were actually locally born.

With a free Saturday on 18 February 1922, and having been reportedly 'inundated with offers to play', the Liverpool directors 'very wisely', according to a Liverpool newspaper, resisted the temptation to arrange a friendly fixture. It was agreed that 'first team men should take advantage of the holiday'. Liverpool's England internationals – John Bamber and Tommy Bromilow among them – would get a further rest because the proposed France v. England fixture was cancelled, highlighting deep schisms in the new international football order. The still-amateur French association had objected to England's plans to field professionals in their ranks. At least the England men would get their chance to play eventually. By contrast, the Liverpool minute books show that the Anfield board routinely turned down requests from Ireland for the release of the players Lacey and Scott as 'impossible'. These men missed international caps as a result.

It was the clear-thinking Liverpool chairman Walter R. Williams who was behind the unusually commendable Reds restraint not to arrange additional fixtures to fill in free weekends. He had first been elected to the chair in 1919, and he would later be followed into the Liverpool chairman's seat by his son Samuel, thus confirming the family ethos at the club first established under the Houldings. Williams was presently recovering from illness, which gave a chance for the *Evening Express* on 10 February to reflect favourably on his role and the general good work and good sense of the current Liverpool board:

> The Liverpool club is directed by a body of gentlemen who work smoothly and amicably together. Mr Williams holds the reins with rare tact and judgment and much of the present season's success is due to the chairman's wise guidance on all affairs appertaining to the welfare of the club. Mr Williams is never happier than when his team is doing well.

And Liverpool continued to do well. Another narrow home win (1–0) against Birmingham in a poor display on a hard and slippery pitch in which even the saintly Scott 'made the crowd hold its breath' when he dropped the ball stretched Liverpool's lead to five points. 'JC', a reporter in the Manchester-based *Sporting Chronicle*, pointed out the most admirable – if not exactly the most exciting – decidedly *British Isles* features of the Liverpool title assault:

> Look at Liverpool's record and it will be seen that in 13 matches – nearly 50 per cent – they have not forfeited a goal at all. Since December 3rd they have lost four goals in 12 matches . . . It is this guardianship of the goal, this intense solidarity, which discourages opponents and wearies them. But there in Elisha Scott stands the most complete and the surest keeper of the day.

[Liverpool have] a pan-Britannic defence, including England [Longworth], Ireland [Scott], Scotland [McKinlay] and Wales [Parry], almost the best of the four nations. I am not forgetting Bromilow the artistic tapper; Wadsworth the worker; and McNab, the big Scottish bustling intervener. But the stalwarts of the four nations come to final grips. Not even by implication do I intend to detract from the craftsmanship of Lacey, the dash of Hopkin, the thrustfulness of Forshaw and the calculation of Chambers, but it is the pan-Britannic guard which so often decides the issue.

This is a very astute summary of the team but also of some of the traditional Liverpool Football Club British strengths – much of the same combination of complementary Celtic and Anglo qualities would be discussed in the press and by fans over the next 80-odd years. The strongest Reds formation for this title-winning season, in classic 2–3–5 formation, looked like this:

Liverpool FC, league-title winners, 1921–22

		Scott		
	Longworth (or Lucas)		McKinlay	
	McNab	Wadsworth	Bromilow	
Lacey	Forshaw	Lewis	Chambers	Hopkin

The obvious positives here were the solidity and security of the Liverpool back three, the sheer power and consistency of the half-backs, the trickery and work ethic of the wide players, plus Bromilow's organisation, intellect and creativity in the centre, and the goals of the bow-legged Chambers. The only real weakness was at centre-forward, where neither Lewis nor the Garston youngster Danny Shone truly convinced. Elisha Scott was, unquestionably, the greatest goalkeeper of his day, probably the best of all keepers before the Second World War. He was a perfectionist, routinely berating his defenders for their failings, and his later duels with Everton's Dixie Dean would become the stuff of legend as the 1920s rolled on. But just one description, taken from the season, shows Scott's real worth to the 1921–22 Liverpool team. It is not from a spectacular win, not a dazzling show or even from a crucial fixture. It is taken instead from a crucial, ground-out 0–0 draw at Blackburn Rovers in March 1922.

Liverpool were collectively off colour at Blackburn, no question. They had Gilhespy and the Welshman George Beadles filling in for Lacey and Lewis, and it was not working out. But Scott simply refused to buckle behind this general incoherence, as press accounts from the time confirmed. 'Elisha Scott saved some remarkably fine shots,' said Liver for the *Evening Express*. 'The Irish keeper was cool and collected throughout and at the finish had never turned a hair. His display gave one the impression that no matter what the rest of the side did, he would not fail.' This was typical Scott, irascibly succeeding individually when the collective threatened to break down. The return at Anfield showed another side of his sheer bloody-mindedness. This time he led the exasperated Blackburn forward Johnny McIntyre a merry dance, which ended with 'Scott circling round and round bouncing the ball with McIntyre after him' and his beloved Kop, of course, in gales of laughter.

Ephraim Longworth, the 'prince' of full-backs, right from his Liverpool debut in October 1910, had been noted for his 'raking stride' and for his unshowy excellence in both tackling and distribution. His kiss-curl hairstyle belied his reliability and toughness and also his leadership qualities, which were recognised by his selection as captain of both Liverpool and England. Longworth formed a formidable defensive partnership with Donald McKinlay, another leader, who won two caps for Scotland in 1912 but deserved more. McKinlay would play centre-half and all the left-sided positions in his 19 years at the club, and he ended up scoring 34 priceless goals, as if to show his game was not all about impenetrable defence. These great men were hardly glamorous figures: the Scot had his false teeth broken at a match in Blackpool in 1923, and he had to apply to the club for them to be repaired. Wadsworth and McNab were both hard nuts at half-back – the latter, especially, could be relied upon to 'leave a foot in' when it was needed. The Bootle man Wadsworth was also a ruthlessly committed tackler who liked to fly the ball forward quickly and was a dead-ball specialist of some repute. He was also a man who could be notoriously abrasive with his own supporters as well as the opposition. He often brusquely rejected requests for autographs, and in December 1923 Wadsworth assaulted a bandsman after a match in Sheffield but was excused by the Liverpool board because of the 'great provocation' he had endured.

Wadsworth and McNab left much of the fancy half-back work to Tommy Bromilow, the slim passing genius and the brains of this Liverpool title team. Here was a complete master of the true arts of half-back play, a man who, unlike his combative midfield partners, scorned physical contact and was also a true sportsman, the first choice of many good judges for any match to be played without need of a referee.[7] With the goal-shy Hopkin and the dark-haired Irishman Lacey forcing things wide and serving up chances for Chambers and Forshaw, this was a new Liverpool team fit to challenge the Reds title winners of 16 years before. When Liverpool destroyed Arsenal 4–0 in February, with a Forshaw hat-trick, it was Hopkin who did the real damage. 'He controls the ball like a juggler and his dribbles are a delight to witness.' Tellingly, too, according to the *Evening Express* – and like almost every one of this Liverpool team – he was also 'not frightened to give or take a hefty charge'.

WINNING UGLY IN THE HOME STRETCH

In early March 1922, Liverpool became 'more than ever the capital of Wales', or so crowed the local press when England took on the Principality (the Rose v. the Leek) at Anfield, with Bromilow and Chambers both in the England party. Then, on 18 March 1922, a real Football League shock: a Liverpool home defeat, 0–2 to Bolton Wanderers. There was serious mitigation, however: Chambers, Bromilow and Lacey were all selected to play for the Football League against the Scottish League on the same day, so it was a much weakened Anfield unit that fell prey to its first league defeat since 26 November.

How odd was this? Here were the prospective league champions potentially undone by the selections and scheduling of their *own* league body. It seemed like a bizarre state of affairs indeed. Only at a conference held in Liverpool on 7 January 1931 between the national associations and the Football League would real progress finally be made on the staging of international and representative matches that clashed with league fixtures. But more bad news was to follow for Liverpool sympathisers in 1922: an immediate 0–1 defeat at relegation-threatened Arsenal. Tellingly, the match ball was replaced right after its drunken flight path took Baker's surprise shot wobbling past Elisha Scott. 'Have Liverpool started on the toboggan?' asked a worried *Liverpool Courier*.

Calm was briefly restored, however, with a 3–1 Liverpool win at Bolton, while Burnley lost at Cardiff. Spurs were now lurking in the wings. Liverpool were prepared to fight and to win ugly if necessary, as they had been all season. The home favourite Vizard was 'incapacitated' by McNab in the first half, and the Scot was then 'heckled by the crowd throughout the game'. Or more accurately he was heckled for his remaining time on the pitch, because the sometimes brutal McNab was eventually sent off for tangling again with the already stricken Vizard.

These results stretched Liverpool's lead to six points once more. By 6 April, the lead was seven points with a match in hand. It might be needed after Liverpool, without Tommy Bromilow (who was on England duty), slumped 0–4 at Oldham. But the Reds were all but home and dry with a 1–1 draw at closest rivals Burnley on 14 April – the otherwise magical Bromilow even missed a penalty. A 5–1 Liverpool home win against Cardiff City followed on 15 April, including a hat-trick for Smiler Chambers and an extraordinary swerving cross-shot by Bromilow. Two footballs were lost in the Liverpool stands during this latest procession, and while the arrival of a third was awaited a wag in the home crowd threw on a small rubber ball, creating 'hilarious laughter' off and on the field. Everton shareholders, meanwhile, were not smiling: they were busy circulating venal letters claiming that the Goodison board had spent £30,000 on transfers and had done little more than make the club a 'laughing stock'.

The crucial Liverpool home league fixture with Burnley now loomed on 17 April 1922 – three vital matches would be played in four days, all teams simultaneously selected in advance and handwritten in the minute books by the Liverpool board. Anfield was crammed for the visit of Burnley. 'It was necessary at various points in the ground,' reported the *Evening Express*, 'for the spectators nearest the wall to climb over and there was quite a ring of enthusiasts on the grass around the pitch.' Played in bright sunshine on a holiday Monday afternoon, the affair was end to end, with both Scott and Burnley's Dawson called upon to make early saves. Then Lacey passed to Chambers, who neatly tricked the Burnley defence and 'shot the ball like lightning into the far bottom corner of the net', beating Dawson comfortably. Liverpool continued to play 'storming football' and were good value for a 1–0 lead at the half. In the second period, Scott twice saved brilliantly from visiting forward Bob Kelly but could not stop George Richardson from equalising. The home crowd audibly gasped at this setback, and with the match leaking away, and Lewis struggling with a suspected face fracture from a flying boot, it looked as if Liverpool would have to wait at least another week to claim the title.

But up stepped the reinstated Ephraim Longworth, defensive master, now goal-maker. 'He suddenly took it into his head to retain possession and dribble down the field,' wrote the *Evening Express*, as if the England man had briefly lost his mind. 'Veering into the centre he looked for a likely opening. The full-back was brought down, however, and as he lay on the ground he managed to push the ball to Forshaw.' Seventy-eight minutes had passed.

The willowy Dick Forshaw was consistency personified. A man picked up for free in 1919 on one of the club's erratic scouting missions, he would be the only player to play in all eighty-four league matches in the two Liverpool championship seasons in the early 1920s, scoring a priceless thirty-six goals. He would go on to win another league title with Everton in 1928, the first player to win titles with both of the top Merseyside clubs. Here he picked up the loose ball and carefully placed it past the exposed Dawson. Both he and the prostrate Longworth were then 'promptly mobbed by their colleagues'. With

Oldham Athletic beating Spurs, no one could now catch Liverpool with three matches still to play.

To the victors, they say, come the spoils. Not necessarily in football. It might not surprise people to know that while 1922 champions Liverpool earned £32,852 in receipts for winning the title, ninth-placed Chelsea made more: £34,043. But commercial opportunities were becoming more available to the top football players in the 1920s, though not quite advertising the sort of luxury items we see today. Tommy Bromilow soon appeared in the pages of the Liverpool press, for example, advertising Phosperine, a well-known cure-all for chronic exhaustion and everything else, from sleeplessness to malaria. 'Today,' Tommy and his advisers told the great British public, 'football calls for a greater amount of physical exertion than ever on account of the marked increase in the speed of the game and the extension of the league programme.' He was right, of course. And Tommy's own exquisite sporting skills stretched much wider than to football: in July, playing in local cricket for Bootle Extras, he scored 131 blissful runs against Wavertree CC.

With the football pressure now released, Liverpool lost to both Cardiff and at home to West Bromwich Albion, with the Kop barracking Albion's ex-Everton man Stanley Davies and potentially tarnishing, according to the local press, the fact that 'Liverpool crowds have in the past gained the reputation of being very fair'. But Albion were beaten away 4–1 in the final league fixture, so Liverpool racked up fifty-seven points, six clear of Tottenham and eight ahead of Burnley. Everton hung on to their First Division place, just above relegated Bradford City and Manchester United. Forshaw and Hopkin had played every league game for the Reds in the 1921–22 season, and Bromilow had missed only due to international call-ups. Liverpool had used 22 players in all but had relied on a core of 14 and, crucially, had suffered no major injuries. Only Middlesbrough had called on fewer players. If truth be told, the championship had been nailed on well before Christmas, won on the basis of defensive strength, teamwork and goalkeeping magnificence.

The Charity Shield match with FA Cup-winners Huddersfield Town was played on 10 May 1922 at Old Trafford, and 'in a match that had not been advertised as it might have been' around 8,000, mainly Liverpool, supporters turned up to see the championship trophy presented to the club by the familiar figure of John McKenna. How bittersweet this must have seemed to the man who had done so much to help build the Liverpool club. How ironic, too, that the very early birth pangs of the football video replay suggested that Town might not even have been worthy FA Cup winners to play in this match. The Topical Film Company had filmed the 1922 final and, in a special showing for journalists, had slowed the pictures down sufficiently to show that 'in the cold, impartial record of the film camera' in the crucial penalty incident that decided the match there was 'little doubt' that both Hamilton of Preston and Smith of Huddersfield were at least a yard *outside* the penalty area. It would be more than 40 years, of course, before slow-motion replays were common in the English game. More than 80 years after this first controversy, the game is still debating the proper use of video technology.

David Ashworth and trainer Bill Connell, as well as the Liverpool players, received medals, and John McKenna's presentation speech at Old Trafford was barely audible over the 'hubbub' made by the club's supporters. Club chairman Walter Williams said in reply that he hoped that Liverpool would now win the elusive FA Cup another season. Typically, too, every key member of staff from Anfield, from the assistant groundsman and helpers to the chairman, participated in the presentation. 'No one was forgotten, and it was a kindly thought on the part of the directors to see that they all shared in the triumph.'

When the Liverpool players reached Exchange Station on their 'joy ride' from Manchester at around 10.30 p.m., there was a big crowd to meet the team. The Everton Terrace Boys Band turned out to welcome the players, and captain McKinlay could not avoid the revellers. 'Donald tried to walk to the "chara",' reported the *Evening Express*, 'but he was picked up and carried in triumph out of the station. One trembles to think what would have happened had last night's match decided the championship.' The players retired for their celebrations, as they had done back in 1906, to the late John Houlding's Sandon Hotel. Looking ahead, they might have had one thought in their minds: could winning the elusive FA Cup in 1923 be any more difficult than trying to retain the Football League title?

CHAPTER 6 REFERENCES

1. Belchem and MacRaild, 'Cosmopolitan Liverpool', p. 327
2. Holt, *Sport and the British*
3. Taylor, *The Association Game*, pp. 137–8
4. Inglis, *The Football League and the Men Who Made It*, p. 126
5. Fishwick, *English Football and Society*, p. 19
6. Taylor, *The Association Game*, p. 128
7. Young, *Football on Merseyside*, p. 105

7

'WHERE'S LIVERPOOL?'
'Top of the League!'

CIVILISING THE GLOBE THROUGH FOOTBALL

The Liverpool players' 'reward' for winning the 1922 league title was a summer tour to stifling Italy – to play their erstwhile title rivals Burnley! The Liverpool board accepted a £100 payment and all expenses paid by their hosts to make the trip. Players were given a royal ten shillings expenses a day. The two clubs even travelled together to Stresa and stayed in the same hotel, with their exhibition match planned for the city of Milan. Making money was behind the venture, no doubt. Tom Bromilow wrote a column for the Merseyside press, informing the Liverpool public about the unusual events and sights from abroad. Little reached Britain about the development of football on the Continent, of course, so this was all entirely new and exotic material for the Merseyside sporting public to chew over. It made grim reading.

In 'terrific heat', and with buckets of water scattered around the pitch to aid with rehydration, the match in Milan (which was won 0–1 by Burnley) was frequently reduced to walking pace, and 'a certain section of the spectators showed their disapproval by some hooting and booing'. This surprised the visiting players, especially since an estimated 25 per cent of the 10,000, mainly Italian, crowd was female. Bromilow was not much impressed by the 'typical' Italian spectator, though it was hard to know whether the local reaction to English football was a result of cultural difference, the effects of the heat or simply poor British technique. 'What an excitable people these Italians are!' said a bemused and disapproving Bromilow. 'Whenever a possible chance presented itself and the shooter failed, he was greeted by a combination of howls of derision or disappointment . . . The players took no notice.'

A week later, on 6 June 1922, when Liverpool played a combined Italian team from Tuscany and Ligne in a 2–2 draw, cultural differences were to the fore once more. The match teetered on the very brink of disintegration after an Italian was barged and fell heavily, breaking an arm in the process. Things immediately kicked off. Never, said Bromilow, had he played in a match in which the opposition had shown 'such recklessness and disregard for the rules. I have never played in such a game wherein so much hacking, kicking and pushing was tolerated. In fact, the home side indulged in everything except biting. They would not play the game properly, nor would they allow us to.' This was a common English complaint of the time and later, of course – 'foreigners' who did not really know the game or its standards or who failed to match up to the physical challenges of the British. These sorts of accounts and experiences would colour the football relationship between Britain and other Europeans for many decades to come. As respected northern football commentator W. Leslie Unsworth told *Evening Express* readers on 17 June 1922, these football trips abroad were no beano, no joy, for English teams. They were undertaken only out of a sense of national duty. 'Foreigners focus on the science, tactics and niceties,' he wrote, 'but they still have a great deal to learn in the matter of showing the sporting spirit. We need more visits to "educate" the Continentals.' It was the British leading the way, once more.

These deep-seated ideas and prejudices about 'foreigners' and their unsuitability for football were unquestioningly reinforced by a series of fictional football stories carried in the Liverpool *Evening Express* at this time. In one, published on 21 October 1922, entitled 'Team of All Nations', an ex-British serviceman called Sam formed a football club to try to bring people of the world together in post-war harmony. Inevitably, his plans were doomed to failure. The team was made up of unreliable Swedes and Egyptians, and a Spanish goalkeeper who 'you could smell a mile [off]' and who pulled a knife when dropped from the team. Also involved was Mass Tull Dixon, a 'coal-black coon' on the wing who was psychologically destroyed when teammates smashed his banjo. Finally, an effeminate French player, Hyacinth Bourget – 'he has some flower' – ridiculously challenged a love rival to a duel. What was the moral of this mess, drawn out for the Liverpool readers of the *Evening Express*? That 'football's essentially a game for Britishers. These foreigners ain't got the right temperament.'

WORLD IN MOTION

Elsewhere in the summer of 1922, the Liverpool press was reporting on an exciting but unstable world. The violent blackmailing and robbing antics of British racecourse gangs fascinated the popular press closer to home. So, too, did the news from the Postmaster General that it was 'quite possible' that every village in Britain with more than 2,000 people would presently have a telephone call office. Sir Henry Norman, vice-president of the Wireless Society, reported that all homes would soon have receiving sets and that the city of Liverpool was especially well placed as it was near a designated broadcast command centre.

Not that too many Liverpool *voices* were ever likely to be heard on the new wireless. They had that unmistakeable nasal combination of English, Irish, American and Welsh influences that was a mile from received English. Could the Liverpool dialect be described at all as Lancastrian, asked the *Evening Express* on 10 May 1922? 'Not Liverpool. Liverpool is everything BUT Lancastrian . . . The Liverpool twang must remain outside the pale. It is distinctive, indescribable and absolutely un-Lancashire. Liverpool is altogether *too* cosmopolitan.'

The closure of the famous Reynold's Waxworks in Lime Street now signalled the end of an era in the city. Nine out of ten visitors to Liverpool had attended the gory attractions of the waxworks in its heyday, but it had long fallen out of public favour. Instead, 40,000 £1 shares were offered for sale to local people in the new futuristic 1,500-seat Sefton Picturedrome, which was to be built to the south of the city centre. Meanwhile, the Midland Adelphi hotel proudly announced 'dances for every evening of the week during the season' and it was reported that 'large, eager crowds have been present each evening'.

The really big news story in the area, however, was a much more troubling one. It was about the new port extension at Southampton, which directly challenged Liverpool's supremacy in port cargo and distribution, having already stripped the declining Merseyside port of much of its major passenger transport custom by sea. A spokesman for the White Star Line offered reassuring words on Merseyside about the city's 'favourable' geographical position for cargo work, but there were also plenty of stern warnings about the apathetic and conservative Mersey docks and Harbour Board and the risks for Liverpool of poor and declining facilities if she should 'tarry on the road to progress'. The dangers were clear enough, and they were accentuated by the news that Manchester was soon to open a new air terminal, offering daily flights to London and Continental connections to Paris, Amsterdam and Berlin. Too much of the employment in Liverpool derived from trade through the port. The city had fallen behind in many ways and would fall still further – the halcyon days of the Merseyside docks were already over.

It was enough to drive locals to drink – and other drugs. A 'Mrs E' told the *Liverpool Courier* that recently on Church Street she had noticed an unfolded piece of blue paper lying on the pavement with the word 'COCAINE' printed on it twice in black ink. There seemed little subterfuge here. In nearby New Brighton, however, the locals were at a peak of excitement about something rather more wholesome and certainly less addictive: they were preparing to stage the World Cycling Championships of 1922 between 28 and 29 July. Adding to this sense that the Merseyside area was a world centre for *sport* and not just football in the 1920s was the fact that leading Liverpool swimmers gave exhibitions for the public at the local baths in Garston in south Liverpool in 1922. Among them was multiple record-breaker Hilda James, one of the four Garston swimmers who had made up most of the team of six swimmers who had competed for Great Britain in the 1920 Olympic Games in Antwerp. As the *Liverpool Courier* proudly reported, Garston – and only 15 years after the local baths were completed – was now 'world famous in swimming'.

TITLE CELEBRATIONS – AND 'GOING IN' FOR THE FA CUP

Back out of the pool and into the shark-infested waters of professional football, Blackburn Rovers proposed a sensible move back to 'random' rather than the back-to-back fixtures favoured in the Football League in order to increase variety and reduce 'needle' between players. But the proposal was turned down by the league management committee. The FA was soon complaining about 'rough' play in league matches in 1922–23, precisely because clubs were meeting again instantly in competitive combat. The Scottish FA suggested a new offside law: a 25-yard line across the pitch beyond which no forward could be offside. This was designed to counter the 'three-defender' law that currently operated and that had helped make Liverpool so solid defensively. Again, it was turned down, though this debate about offside would not disappear.

Liverpool FC announced a £30,609 credit balance for the 1921–22 season. Players' wages and bonuses reached £12,477, about one-quarter of total income. Entertainment tax creamed off almost £10,000, and Anfield season tickets, it was announced, would retail for £2 10s to watch the English champions next season. They would not want for takers.

At a special dinner attended by 276 shareholders and held by the Liverpool club at the Midland Adelphi hotel in June to celebrate the title win, 14 members of the 1905–06 team who were invited to attend turned up. The great Alex Raisbeck and his colleagues challenged the current Liverpool title-winning squad to a match – at tug of war! Raisbeck reiterated the now familiar Liverpool mantra that the club should now 'go in for the cup'. Three of the 1906 squad – Alf West, James Bradley and Sam Raybould – were 'owing to the present trade depression, faring none too well', and the Liverpool board voted to give £50 to each of them to aid their recovery. It was a nice touch, but it also smacked perhaps too much of charity. It was certainly not a gesture that would solve the difficulties of three of the club's best servants, with almost five hundred and fifty Liverpool games between them. 'The directors' action, I am certain,' said 'Cri' of the *Evening Express*, 'will be approved by all supporters of the Reds, while it is an incentive to players and clubs of today.' The truth was that very few football clubs cared much for their old warriors, no matter what their campaign medals might be.

The 1922 Liverpool title-winning players were all presented at this event with a gold watch – a traditional employer's gift to his willing workers. Chairman Walter Williams agreed that the players 'were gentlemen on and off the field. A happier and more united family all round, directors, players and staff, could not be found anywhere.' Liverpool Football Club in this period did seem a particularly unified ship, especially compared to strife-torn Everton. Williams also spoke out against the Football League's reduction in players' wages – to £8 per week maximum – and against large transfer fees, arguing that paying £4,000 for a player would be a worse policy than 'signing players they believed would fit into their present condition'. In reply to his chairman's words, club captain Donald McKinlay said, modestly, that speech-making was no game of his. But he expressed gratitude for the 'generous and sporting way' in which the directors had met the players. He then mentioned the main aim for the new season: 'We will do our utmost to win the English cup.'

'THEY COULD WIN ANYTHING'

Some of the extra income derived from the Liverpool championship win of 1922 was ploughed back into the club to further improve the Anfield ground. Concrete walls and steps were built at the back of the Kop, costing £4,500, and plans were announced for a revolutionary new triple-decker stand, a so-called 'hat-trick' stand, for the Anfield Road end, with the club 'deciding that as they cannot extend they must build up'. It was innovative but overly ambitious, and the stand was never constructed. But a new boys' pen *was* added, to the right of the press box on the Kemlyn Road side, to be entered from the Anfield Road end of the stadium. The enclosure was formidable, running half the length of the stand and built to accommodate some 4,000 boys. It seems almost unimaginable today, reflecting both a determination to tap into young support and early concerns about youthful misbehaviour. It was surrounded by iron-spiked railings to dissuade any younger supporters from trying to join the general crowd. It would later be much reduced in size and relocated to the Spion Kop. The club's plan was clearly to reduce nuisance and pitch encroachment, as well as recruit more, younger supporters, so the Liverpool directors put out a clear message through the local press that 'they would be glad if all boys who attend the game would make for this enclosure'. Was football really such a bad thing for a boy's education? The *Liverpool Courier* joked lightheartedly on the issue of 'how football crips the young':

TEACHER: Can you do arithmetic?
BOY: Yes, sir.
TEACHER: What's 2 and 6?
BOY: Half-a-crown.
TEACHER: Where's Liverpool?
BOY: Top of the league!

Liverpool manager David Ashworth was also hopeful of more first-team success, and why not? 'We ought to have a very good season,' he reasoned. 'There is perfect harmony from the boardroom to the dressing-room and that goes a long way.' He also had forward Dick Johnson back from a serious knee injury to add a little more substance to the Liverpool attack, and all the key members of the title team remained fit and well. Why not another championship, then, or even a run in the 'pimpernel' FA Cup, as the chairman had described it? Johnson certainly started well in a 5–2 season opener against Arsenal: two goals in the first five minutes and a hat-trick overall in front of 40,062 of the faithful. Arsenal's defence was 'in a tangle dealing with Liverpool's long passing and the triangular work of the Reds'.

But at bogey ground Roker Park – where Liverpool had played and lost in that stadium's opening match back in 1902 – there was another defeat, in gruelling circumstances. Under leaden skies, with a heavy ball and with darkness approaching, the referee decided there was no time for half-time, so the teams did not leave the field at all. In December 1922, a match between Blackburn and Stoke was abandoned with four minutes to go because of darkness. The satirical magazine *Punch* had noted that on the opening day of the league campaign, the press complained about players kissing a goalscorer. 'It is noticed, too, that nobody ever kisses the referee.' Not here, not today. In the gloom and on sodden turf, a heroic Elisha Scott saved again and again – playing against Charles Buchan always sparked the Ulsterman's interest. Scott produced one 'masterpiece' save from a drive by Jock Paterson. But the home centre-forward would not be denied, and the visitors left pointless, with a single goal against. At Arsenal, soon after, it was another wet, 'horrible' day for football, with no goals in open play and Liverpool's Walter Wadsworth conceding the deciding penalty kick – and another loss.

It had been a poor start for the champions Liverpool, no doubt about it. But a Wednesday evening return meeting with Sunderland in dry conditions at Anfield produced a 5–1 home win and sparked a run of seven wins in eight matches, enough to get Ashworth's men back to the top. 'It is a tribute to the efficiency of W. Connell, the Anfield trainer, that the Reds invariably outstay and outpace the opposition in the second half,' commented the *Liverpool Courier*. It was true that Liverpool often scored in the second half, and Chambers, Forshaw and Johnson were all in the goals against Sunderland. Everton were then downed twice in one week (there *were* attractions, after all, to these back-to-back fixtures). Liverpool had only won four out of twenty-two games against Everton at Anfield since the great split of 1892, but, according to the *Courier*, 'the days have gone by when the old jibe was that Liverpool only had to see a Blue shirt to be mesmerised into inactivity'.

The paper was right. This time all the mesmerising was done by Liverpool in the club's fourth five-goal haul in just nine league matches, with only one defeat, 0–2 at old adversaries Burnley. In East Lancashire, 'Bromilow was not up to his usual standard', and Elisha Scott, for once, missed a cross, leaving Weaver an easy finish. After the match, it was revealed in the *Liverpool Echo* that Scott, Johnson and Wadsworth had all received letters offering a £10 bribe to lose to Burnley. These 'honest players' had 'instantly' reported the matter to the Liverpool committee. Scott was also later asked to 'let his side down' at a match at Newcastle. 'Only a lunatic,' counselled the *Evening Express*, 'would take such an attempt seriously.'

Everton FC had already hit the big screen in 1922: footage of their home match against Newcastle United had been advertised as the *Evening Courier* film on show at various times at the Scala cinema in the city and on at the Futurist later in the week. This seems like a precursor to the Sky TV pub offerings 80 years later, but who would want to watch it? At Anfield against Everton, more than 50,000 fans paid record receipts of £3,200 to see Williams put Everton ahead by half-time, but Bill Connell's fitness regime soon had Liverpool roaring back. With his shirt outside his shorts, the urchin McNab was outstanding, including a trademark 'unnecessarily heavy foul on Hart which drew a stern warning from referee Andrews'. The veteran Everton goalkeeper Tommy Fern had a bleak time of it, at fault with at least two of the five goals that followed, including a hat-trick from the uncontainable Chambers. 'Longworth,' said the *Liverpool Echo*, 'was a study in enterprise. He was ceaseless in his work, he was everlasting in his sure punts and he had ideas of marching forward, like a king going forth to war.' It seemed like last season all over again, Liverpool already top and Everton struggling among the paupers at the bottom.

But tragedy also struck at this match, because Charles Newman, a forty-six-year-old butcher and father of five, fell and was killed on leaving the Kop, after hitting his head on one of the new concrete steps. A collection for the dead man was held at the next Liverpool home match, raising £94 7s for his family. Liverpool director Edwin Berry reported that inasmuch as Newman 'was not in very affluent circumstances', the club would also bear all the expenses of the fan's funeral. Was there any assumption of guilt in play here? Another director and head of the Liverpool FC grounds committee, Walter Cartwright, was instructed by the board to take up the matter with the club's insurers 'in case of any claim made for compensation', and he was soon inviting in the local press to show them the installation at Anfield of 17 new crush barriers around the ground. The unfortunate Mr Newman missed Liverpool winning 1–0 at Goodison Park, with his team having resorted to shameless time-wasting following Johnson's early goal and injuries to Lacey and Chambers. The Reds repeatedly hoofed the ball into the mainly Everton crowd. Lacey was 'almost useless' in the second half, but he stayed on the field, thus aggravating an injury that would keep him out of the next 12 league matches. Sportingly, Everton also held a collection for the deceased man Newman, which realised £26, and two Liverpool directors contributed £10 each to make, with fan subscriptions, a total of £158 for his widowed family. It was another sign of the close relations between the Liverpool clubs, and between supporters and the clubs in the city.

As the 1922 autumn British general election rumbled along in the background, and as Mussolini announced in Italy that the Fascist military command had assumed the direction of affairs at the recent Milan location for Liverpool FC's 1922 summer tour, the Anfield club, with the willing Gilhespy replacing Lacey at right-wing, continued to collect victories and points in domestic competition. Not even a 0–3 reverse at Cardiff in October could move them from the top of the table. This was a pathetic Liverpool show in South Wales, one that produced just one visitor's corner and provoked an acid poem, allegedly from the pen of a furious Elisha Scott:

> Twinkle, twinkle little star
> How I wonder what you are
> Wheel 'em in and wheel 'em out
> Cardiff three, Liverpool nowt.

Also in October, the Football League introduced forms for use by clubs to assess the performance of referees: they would be put to good use over time. Research at the time suggested that English players now dominated the top Football League clubs: in the First Division one hundred and eighty-two players were English, forty-three Scottish, ten Irish and just seven Welsh.

The experiences of ex-Everton star Joe Clennell, who played for Cardiff but still lived in Liverpool, also brought to mind more recent cases of very affluent professional players as potential crime victims. Clennell's Liverpool house was burgled while he was playing football and while both his wife and his servant were out of the home. Clearly, top footballers in the 1920s could lead pretty well-appointed lives, even if this meant they combined their football with other work. Liverpool's Walter Wadsworth, for example, had apparently blossomed as a manufacturer of superfine wax polish. It seems that the residences of some football players were obvious and easy targets for local criminals from quite early on and that some top players often lived some way away from the site of the club to which they had been transferred.

A 4–2 Liverpool victory at Tottenham in November 1922 had a Spurs director commenting that if the Liverpool team could keep up this standard of play 'they could win anything' and the *Evening Express* drooling over a brilliant Liverpool second-half spell 'when they would surely have beaten any opponents in the world'. The return match was much less impressive, a dull 0–0 draw that meant that 'suddenly the little boys who shout "1–2–3–4" do not look as debonair as usual'. But even vocal young Liverpool partisans like these were likely to show their respects at this time for the requirements of Remembrance Sunday. The Great War had been over only four years, and a press reporter recorded Liverpool local football's impressive response to the salute for the war dead. A morning match was in heated progress on the White Star Athletic Ground in Wavertree on the due date. But at the signal for the minute's silence at precisely 11 a.m., the players stopped rigid on the pitch in the middle of an attack and all the spectators immediately removed their hats and dipped their heads. Football had learned a lot since the controversy of 1914.

TITLE GIANTS OR A BUNCH OF 'ROUGH HOUSES'?

When Liverpool beat Aston Villa 3–0, also in November, Villa's own 'bad boy', England half-back enforcer Frank Moss, reportedly 'went about the field giving the Liverpool players a fearfully good time'. Unsurprisingly, the return match at Villa the next week had 'rather too much red light about it'. Liverpool won 1–0, moving two points clear at the top, but it was a crude affair, a 'too robust game', claimed the *Liverpool Courier*, with too much 'man before the ball at Villa Park'. A 'hack' by Moss on Chambers 'made the latter momentarily lose his head . . . Hopkin grabbed him.' The formidable Walter Wadsworth got into the bad books of the crowd 'by his heavy work and restless kicking . . . Wadsworth was too reckless in his interventions and must need to curb himself in this direction.'

McNab and Wadsworth could match anybody if things got rough in midfield. Only a miraculous late save by Scott from a 'headlong dive' kept Liverpool ahead after Chambers had scored just before half-time.

This contest at Villa was just the kind of wild tussle that later led Everton's Dixie Dean to describe the Liverpool team of this period as 'no more than a bunch of rough houses'. He probably had a point, but the truth was also rather more complex than that. The Liverpool teams of the early 1920s could certainly play – Bromilow, Hopkin and Forshaw were all refined footballers. The great Charles Buchan had also said of Walter Wadsworth that he was the most difficult half-back proposition the England forward had ever faced: 'You never know what he's going to do next. He's so unorthodox and seems to "get there" without disclosing his intentions.' But Liverpool could also mix it compared to the 'prettier' approach of Everton and others – they were formidable at 'practising a resolute cohesion', as one commentator delicately put it, when they needed to.[1] This sort of toughness and sheer will to win was the basis of dual league champions. But was the sporting ethos fast disappearing from English football? Was all this alleged aggression and ruthlessness, and also the money at the top end of football, ruining *all* levels of the sport?

This seems to have been a constant media theme of the day, what with champions Liverpool getting into ugly scrapes, FA Cup tickets for the 1923 final at the new Empire Stadium announced to be priced from a hefty five shillings and Hull City keeper Billy Mercer bloodying a fan's face by hurling a stone into the crowd at Barnsley.[2] A junior local club in Liverpool, Earle FC, even wrote in its own magazine, *Goalpost,* that 'referees are constantly being booed and are the object of many an unsportsmanlike and unnecessary remark'. Nationally, the *Daily Herald* argued, 'Ninety-nine spectators out of a hundred go to a football match, not so much to see a sporting game as to see their team win by hook or crook . . . the truth of the matter is when money comes in, sport goes out.' But Cri, the local Liverpool football reporter for the *Evening Express,* replied evenly and sensibly that this view that football was sliding into anarchy was actually 'tosh'. He contended that professional players in the city were 'sportsmen to their fingertips' and that 'league soccer is not a money-making business. It takes most clubs all their time to meet their obligations.' Liverpool Football Club also had another league title to win.

CHASING ANOTHER DOUBLE – BUT LOSING A MANAGER!

The night before Liverpool won 1–0 at Newcastle in December 1922, the visiting players and journalists went to see a Charlie Chaplin-style comedian perform in a theatre revue built around a gormless character called 'Dick Johnson'. The Liverpool man of the same name was 'unmercifully ragged' by his teammates the next day – but he played well enough and saw Chambers athletically volley the winning goal from his high pass. In the return match, a shock 0–1 defeat, the Newcastle forward Tommy McDonald, a Scot, won a chase with Ephraim Longworth to a penny thrown from the Anfield stands. The visitor kept it 'firmly clasped in his left hand until the conclusion of the game'. He then handed it to a United director who had it gilded and made into a brooch for his wife, engraved with the date and score of Liverpool's first home loss of the season. But it had started life as just a penny.

Liverpool, shaken but not stirred, now faced three matches over Christmas 1922 in just four days: Forest (away) on Saturday, 23 December; Oldham (away) on 25 December; and Oldham (home) on Boxing Day. When a letter writer complained to the *Evening Express* about Christmas Day football, Cri pointed out that these were pretty much the only games that shopkeepers and assistants and other similar workers could actually attend. The debate about Christmas football was thus ended before it had really begun – at least for now.

There now followed a real bolt from the blue: Liverpool FC, via secretary George Patterson, announced that the club manager David Ashworth would be 'released from his engagement' with Liverpool, 'which does not expire for a few months yet so he can take up duties as the manager of the Oldham Athletic club'. In short, in the very middle of an already thunderous season, Ashworth was asking to leave prospective league champions Liverpool for a relegation fight in Oldham – which he would ultimately lose. There was no mystery here, 'no friction whatsoever' between Ashworth and the Liverpool board, though the Liverpool FC minutes of 28 December 1922 show a rather cold approach to the whole business: 'All moneys, keys, etc., belonging to the club to be returned to the secretary before leaving.' The Stockport man's wife and daughter were both invalids, and Ashworth simply wanted to live in the family home in Stockport rather than in digs in Liverpool, as he had been doing. Oldham were willing to pay very well to recruit their man. But the Liverpool press pointed out that Ashworth had been in charge of a 'ready-made team' at Anfield so he had had 'no necessity to join in the feverish search for players which makes the lives of so many managers a burden to them'. The Liverpool manager was giving up a lot.

Ashworth was no builder of a side or of a specific ethos in the manner of a Tom Watson, and his departure also probably signalled the extent to which the Liverpool directors had assumed, once again, direct selection responsibilities following Watson's death. But this shock departure was still a blow, and it would surely affect the Liverpool players, who had to play Ashworth's new club Oldham *twice* over the coming days! In fact, Liverpool won both matches, thus effectively sending Athletic down before their new manager had even arrived to take charge. On 26 December, it was Elisha Scott's turn for a benefit match – although the Irishman would play at Liverpool for another 12 years. As always, the club asked for volunteers to act as collectors with buckets. The papers reported that 'a fine collection is taken'.

The effects of Ashworth's departure on Liverpool were immediately apparent – with Dick Johnson injured, the adventurous Jock McNab volunteered to play at centre-forward on Boxing Day in an 'extraordinary experiment'. McNab even tried a 'pantomime somersault' to try to reach a wild Hopkin cross. The Liverpool directors were thinking outside the box, all right. But the Reds were four points clear of Sunderland going into the new year, and an advert was promptly placed for a new Liverpool manager in the *Athletic News* and the *Sporting Chronicle*, applications to 10 Cook Street by 15 January. Unusually, the Liverpool directors at their board meeting of 28 December put on record their appreciation of the 'splendid performances' of the Liverpool team during the holiday matches. Meanwhile, Little Davie Ashworth would have few chances at Oldham to enjoy what he really liked about the game: three-goal leads, so 'then he can puff on his pipe – from which he is seldom separated – in peaceful tranquillity'.

Liverpool's FA Cup campaign without David Ashworth would begin at home against Arsenal. The Londoners prepared in brine baths in Southend while Liverpool retired to Rhyl for some bracing Welsh sea air. Arsenal played Dr Jimmy Patterson, an amateur, on the wing in a dour 0–0 draw at Anfield, but at Highbury Liverpool turned it on in a 4–1 replay win. In a high comedy moment, the home keeper Robson was chased by a stray dog while carrying the ball and then kicked the ball straight to Johnson – who scored. As did 'Sharkey' Chambers – a strange new moniker, this one, for the Reds forward. Elisha Scott hotly disputed a penalty awarded against him for punching the bustling Turnbull on the back at a corner, but Scott saved the kick anyway. Ephraim Longworth had cleverly packed the Liverpool players along the line of the penalty area immediately behind the kicker to offer abusive comment and to restrict his run-up. The FA took note and eventually (in 1937) introduced the restraining arc on the penalty area to offer proper clearance for spot-kickers. It remains the last official change to pitch markings.

In unfamiliar stripes and back in the league at Middlesbrough later in January 1923, Liverpool's Jock McNab took 'strange exception' to his pen picture in the Boro programme, which had been provided by a Liverpool journalist. It had described the midfield man as an 'unspeakable Scot. Stutters when talking and is hard to follow by word or deed for, indeed, he is dashing and the best shot of the lot, though half-back.' Liverpool chairman Walter Williams lodged an official complaint, though much worse could have – and had – been said about the fierce McNab outside the city. Liverpool won 2–0, with home keeper Williamson to blame for Chambers' low shot finding the net. Liverpool had now taken 22 out of the last 26 league points and looked unstoppable in the title race. The usual question was now raised: could this actually be the year for an FA Cup and league Double at Anfield?

CHAMPIONS AGAIN – BUT FRUSTRATED IN THE CUP

As neighbours Everton tried to spend their way out of a crisis with a £10,000 transfer spree, so nearby Chester FC held a fans' crisis meeting early in 1923 as the club's overdraft doubled in the face of falling crowds. The latest Liverpool beneficiary, meanwhile, was the captain Donald McKinlay, a true and loyal leader who was 'no martinet' but instead was happy to listen to the opinions of other players and to 'see that justice is done'. McKinlay was no public speaker either, and he had few interests outside the game except his family. 'Ask him about his little girl,' the *Evening Express* suggested, 'and Mac will wax quite eloquent.' Asked about the possibility that he might play for Scotland again, McKinlay replied with the sort of direct assurance and fortitude that has marked out the Liverpool club's best servants for more than 100 years. On 25 January 1923, he told the *Evening Express*, 'Red is my colour. I'll play for Liverpool as long as they will have me. I don't want to play for anybody else and when I pull off the red shirt for the last time I expect I will finish with football, at any rate as a player.' Jamie Carragher had his role models to follow: the magnificent McKinlay was true to his word, playing his last-ever Football League match – for Liverpool against Aston Villa – on 1 September 1928. The defender was part of a Liverpool team that was more solid, more reassuringly predictable, than even the 1922 equivalent. It read, pretty much on a weekly basis, in its traditional 2–3–5 formation:

Liverpool FC, league-title winners, 1922–23

Scott

Longworth   McKinlay

McNab   Wadsworth   Bromilow

Lacey   Forshaw   Johnson   Chambers   Hopkin

Only Lacey (twelve missing league matches from October to December 1922, mainly replaced by Gilhespy) and Wadsworth (five matches missed in March 1923) would suffer anything like an extended run of absence for injury during the season. The form of Longworth had seen off Lucas at full-back, and Dick Johnson had made the previously problematic centre-forward position his own.

This consistency of selection, the experience gained from the previous season's success and the relative absence of injury would all contribute considerably to Liverpool maintaining the league title in 1923. But could they win the cup? Drawn to play at Wolves in the FA Cup on 3 February, Bill Connell had the Liverpool players away at Rhyl, once more, kitted out in flat caps, collars and with golf clubs on the local course. The *Evening Express* praised the psychological work of the Reds trainer, who fully 'understands human nature as applied to football' because 'though his velvet glove may conceal the proverbial iron fist, Bill never needs it'. Who says modern methods were not used in the past? The modest Connell, for his part, praised his players' 'great spirit of unselfishness and cheery optimism'. Managerless Liverpool now sent club secretary George Patterson to Bradford to sign cover for Tommy Bromilow and the great Elisha. The Liverpool man came back with Algernon Wilkinson for goalkeeper and utility man David Pratt. Sadly, the wonderfully named keeper would never play for Liverpool before being sold to Blackpool – Scott could never be dropped or rested. But the ex-Celtic man Pratt became a useful Reds squad player in the years that followed.

Liverpool FC – and the club's fans – were quite outstanding in a 2–0 win at Molineux. 'The Anfield club has followers the like of which most clubs would be proud of,' said the *Liverpool Echo*. 'They are loyal to the core, and their vocal efforts would put some army camps to shame. There was a vocalian company behind me at Molineux, and their chants were stunning the natives.' This latest FA Cup win was a 'fine stroll', according to the *Evening Express*, and 'a great day out ended up with a fight out of Lime Street, where another enthusiastic crowd gave the players a strenuous welcome home'. Liverpool were also in 'invincible form' at home to West Brom, where a 2–0 league victory courtesy of goals by Forshaw and Johnson could easily have been 22 but for the display of the veteran visiting keeper Hubert Pearson. A win pocketed, the Liverpool directors even went into the away dressing-room to congratulate the Albion man after the game. A Midlands letter writer to the *Liverpool Echo* compared Liverpool to Preston North End in their prime, gushing that 'Liverpool were simply great'.

Clear in the league as title holders, dominant in the FA Cup, a wonderful team ethic and everybody fit and playing to their maximum: it was not a bad outfit for an incoming manager to take over. Matt McQueen and two other ex-Liverpool players were reputed to be in the final three for the job, and it was McQueen who was chosen, some consolation for his humiliation at the hands of the Liverpool shareholders back in 1921. McQueen had refereed after his playing career had ended, up until the First World War, and had then been co-opted onto the Liverpool board in 1919. He still lived in Anfield, and despite his inexperience in this sort of job he was well known and trusted by the Liverpool board, who admired his understated qualities of leadership and integrity and his intimate knowledge of the club. He frequently scouted players for Liverpool and was brought in as manager essentially as a line of communication and a buffer between the board and the dressing-room. Not that McQueen did much shouting himself, because when the *Evening Express* went to interview the new man the reporter had to overcome McQueen's obvious diffidence – it was the first press interview Liverpool's new young manager had ever given in his life. What was the difference between today's Liverpool and the great teams McQueen had played in almost 30 years before at Anfield? On this point there was no hesitation. Any previous Liverpool goalkeeper, said McQueen with real feeling, 'was not anything like as clever as Scott'.

Sheffield United at home in the FA Cup in round three looked like an invitation for Liverpool and Matt McQueen to progress gently towards possible Double glory. Would their new manager inspire a great Reds performance? Instead, he brought crashing disaster, a 1–2 defeat in front of 51,859 spectators crammed into Anfield. Chambers' early goal was never enough as Liverpool spluttered and finally capitulated to their moderate guests – who also later thumped the Reds 1–4 in the league at Bramall Lane just to show that this was no fluke result. This shuddering FA Cup setback at least meant that it would not be Liverpool and its supporters who would be caught up in the crowd fiasco that symbolised the chaotic first Wembley FA Cup final in 1923. And despite back-to-back 0–1 losses in March, to Blackburn Rovers and Manchester City, Liverpool's league form continued mainly to hold up.

A sequence of five straight league draws in a crowded April after the hammering at Sheffield might be taken as a sign of a nervy Liverpool finish, or else a tired stumble by some struggling veterans up the home straight. Perhaps the team was missing Ashworth's guiding hand? But it could also be reasonably read as a dip in form and a loss of edge due to the lack of any really threatening pressure from below. There was no credible title challenge from Sunderland or Huddersfield Town, or from any of the other chasers, including Everton, who had now clambered up to fifth place. When Liverpool drew 1–1 at home to Huddersfield on 21 April, Chambers equalising a quickly taken Town free-kick, Sunderland's same-day loss at Burnley simply confirmed what had been apparent since Christmas: that Liverpool would easily retain the Football League title, this time with two games to spare and ultimately by a crushing six points.

There was just one more party piece for the rather spoiled Liverpool crowd to enjoy before the season's end – a beaming Bill Lacey excelling in goal and keeping an Anfield clean sheet in a 1–0 home victory, with Chambers scoring against the already relegated Stoke. Elisha Scott had picked up a thigh injury in front of John McKenna, representing the Football League. When the trophy and medals were presented, according to the *Liverpool Echo*, McKenna said that the Anfield club was noted, above all, for consistency and that given the 'strenuous character of today's games there could be no doubt that Liverpool's performance stood high above anything else that had occurred'. Most of the cheering crowd heard little of this praise. Nor did they hear the ebullient Walter Wadsworth say to McKenna, 'See you again next year, sir!' The modest Matt McQueen absented himself so he would not receive the manager's medal that was really not of his deserving. He had tinkered admirably little with the winning formula he had been bequeathed, and he was mainly directed in his management duties by the Liverpool board.

Walter Wadsworth, with an eloquent little speech in his best Bootle accent, presented the Liverpool backs and former captain and current captain, Longworth and McKinlay, with a miniature cup on behalf of the players and staff as a tribute to their service, leadership and sheer playing quality. It was a touching moment and typical of the respect players in the Liverpool squad held for each other. The club got permission from the Football League to give presents to the players to the value of £25 each – about three weeks' wages. Chambers had contributed 22 league goals in 39 appearances and Forshaw 19 in 42, but it was in conceding only 31 times in 42 fixtures and losing only once at home that the championship was really won.

'There were mounted police outside to ensure there was no Wembley nonsense,' said a scathing *Liverpool Echo* in its conclusion to the day's events. The newspaper was reflecting, of course, on the recent farce at the white-horse Wembley final. Altogether 'it was a memorable day in the history of the club'. Double league champions: it sounded wonderful. Where next for Liverpool – and indeed for English football? Change, as always, was lurking just around the corner.

CHAPTER 7 REFERENCES

1. Young, *Football on Merseyside*, p. 106
2. Huggins and Williams, *Sport and the English*, p. 18

8

THEY SHALL BE OUR TEACHERS
The First Internationalisation
of Liverpool FC

LADY LUCK – AND A NEW FOOTBALL AGE

The kind of luck needed to win consecutive league championships in an age in which money was much less the key divider between football clubs than it has since become is unlikely to last long. So it was with Liverpool Football Club under its new manager Matt McQueen. Indeed, McQueen's own personal luck was also to turn bad, painfully and cruelly so. Injuries beset the Anfield club on and off the field in 1923–24, as if in payback for the relatively clean bills of health for the title-winning seasons before. Added to this, McQueen and the Liverpool directors could not quite bring in the high-quality replacements that had been common currency when Tom Watson had been at the club. Some key Liverpool players of this period were now ageing, but why try to fix what ain't broke? Bill Shankly faced the same question almost 50 years later. This eventually meant a problem for the high-tempo, aggressive game built around the traditional 2–3–5 formation initially perfected by Watson that had brought Liverpool so much recent success. In 1923, Ephraim Longworth was approaching 36 years of age, Donald McKinlay was 32, Billy Lacey 34 and Walter Wadsworth 33. 'Can the Liverpool veterans rise again to a new challenge?' the *Liverpool Courier* asked, hinting strongly that it already feared it knew the answer.

This kind of continuity and loyalty at least meant that Liverpool could hang on to their values and vaunted team spirit, so that when the club reached the Lancashire Cup final later in the new season the club invited all its staff to attend, plus ex-manager Davie Ashworth, and also insisted on presenting a full benefit cheque of £650 to the departing Harry Lewis. As the local press agreed, 'Such little acts of forethought speak well for the camaraderie of the team and officials.' But the game was also moving on, finally ridding itself of the shackles of the First World War, even if a major global economic depression was brewing. Manchester City, for example, had opened a vast stadium at Maine Road with new creature comforts, reportedly capable of holding an astonishing 90,000 people. Football spectators were beginning to demand much more for their shilling. New, more 'scientific' tactical advances were also slowly emerging on the pitch, despite the continued British focus on aggression and physicality. Ironically, these developments abroad were actually led by an Englishman, Jimmy Hogan. The deep-thinking Hogan had, briefly, returned from football coaching on the Continent to live in Liverpool after the war, and he worked as a dispatch foreman for Walker's Tobacco. Sadly, his huge talents were not sought out by Anfield. Hogan's futuristic visions of preparation and coaching, and of new systems of play, were little supported among any of the hardened working-class professionals or football-club directors in England. But his early teachings on the importance of technique and tactics, using chalk on a blackboard, heavily influenced the so-called *Wunderteam* of Austria and helped produce the 'Danubian School' of football that radicalised the traditional Scottish passing style and would lead the rest of Europe into modern approaches to football play.[1]

Not that the English football hierarchy was much impressed at all with the Continental game. Writing in the *Football Echo* on 18 December 1924, the Football League's powerful Charles Sutcliffe, an ardent anti-European and a man known variously in the English game as either 'the brains of football' or the 'football dictator', told the people of Liverpool how little he thought of the Continentals from Belgium whom he had just seen play limply against an English team.[2] 'I have no desire,' said Sutcliffe, 'to see another game with Continentals in this country.' FA secretary Stanley Rous confirmed later that in the English football hierarchy well into the 1930s, 'There was a sense of natural superiority, a smug feeling that all was right in our enclosed world and others had nothing to teach us.'[3] The English still had a lot to learn about developing their international ties through sport.

The new, more subtle approaches to the game were led in the 1920s and 1930s by the extraordinary Herbert Chapman, the educated son of a Yorkshire miner and ex-bare-knuckle fighter. Chapman was only a moderate player, but he did show an early knack for the spectacular – and for predicting the future – by playing in bright yellow football boots.[4] Huddersfield Town, under Chapman, won the FA Cup in 1922 and then three league titles in a row following Liverpool's Double, from 1924 to 1926, two of them under the Yorkshireman.

Following on from the strides made by Liverpool's Tom Watson, Chapman was probably the first British football manager to have complete control over the entire running of a football club. He also revolutionised player preparation and football tactics, though few British managers were actually able to follow his lead in the 1920s. When Huddersfield beat Liverpool 1–3 at Leeds Road on 10 November 1923, their style and the result was widely interpreted by the British press as a crucial shift in the balance of football power in England. The move was from the physicality and strength of the Anfield title-winners to the altogether faster and more skilful approach of the Yorkshire club.[5] Within a year, Bee in the *Liverpool Echo* was commenting on Liverpool football (with admirable partisanship *and* honesty) that 'we have become slothful, stereotyped, rutty in our thought and manner of play'.

English football as a whole certainly needed change. On 22 November 1924, a female correspondent to the *Football Echo* signing herself 'Play the Game' complained about the negativity of the current offside law in football (*three* defenders required between forwards and the goal). Teams playing the so-called 'one back' tactic – thus continually catching forwards offside – had meant that 'games are simply ruined from a spectators' point of view'. When the home football associations, via the International Board at FIFA in 1925, amended the offside law to just *two* defenders, a flood of goals initially resulted in league football. But the new law change also led directly to more strategic defensive tactics: the 'third back' or the W–M formation. This change made the traditional centre-half much more of a defensive player rather than the versatile half-back do-everything pivot, such as Liverpool's Alex Raisbeck.

LEFT-BEHIND LIVERPOOL?

Chapman joined Arsenal in 1925, and by the early 1930s his new counter-attacking W–M formation was fully established. Full-backs now marked wingers, rather than the inside-forwards: wing-halves watched the inside-forwards, rather than opposing wingers; centre-halves played deeper and marked the centre-forward rather than acting as a team pivot; and inside-forwards dropped deeper, too, rather than supporting the centre-forward. In funnelling back and allowing opponents to 'come on' to Arsenal and then striking them on the break, Chapman, according to the *Daily Mail*, had become the modern controller of a football machine, 'the first manager who set out methodically to organise the winning of matches'.[6]

Following the Chapman revolution on and off the pitch in England, the clubs from the south would now pose much more of a threat between the wars to the commanding traditional giants of the north and the Midlands. Was Liverpool Football Club simply falling behind at this seminal moment in the sport's development, lacking both foresight and, especially, tactical and managerial innovation? It looked like it, because initially the club persisted with 2–3–5, though, more simply, Liverpool also lacked a reliable forward to build on the good work of Harry Chambers in the early 1920s.

In the first season after the change in the offside law (1925–26), Liverpool scored more goals (63 up to 70), but the goals-against column also moved up, from 55 to 63. Champions Huddersfield Town scored 92 goals and fifth-placed Sheffield United a thumping 102. Even relegated Manchester City scored 89. But Everton's new star forward Dixie Dean was the man to plunder goals in this more open era, scoring by some estimates a staggering century of goals in all competitions *on his own* in season 1927–28, when the Blues won the league title. Sixteenth-placed Liverpool scored 84 league goals in total.

At Anfield there was little obvious adaptation to the new era. But long-term injuries to key figures – especially among the forwards – undoubtedly hit Liverpool hard in the mid-1920s, and they also affected the form of other players who had been so vital in bringing title success to Anfield. The cultured Forshaw, for example, had contributed nineteen crucial goals in 1922–23, but he could now manage only five in thirty-nine appearances in 1923–24. Even Harry Chambers was reduced to just thirteen goals in thirty league appearances, and *all* of Johnson's goals disappeared in 1923–24 – he made only two league appearances because of injury.

IN THE GRIP OF A CLERICAL TYRANNY

All this change was still ahead when in the summer of 1923 the Liverpool directors held an unusual board meeting on the train from Merseyside to Llandudno on 3 August and decided on an early version of corporate ticketing for the new league champions. Two complimentary season tickets were allocated to: the Bank of Liverpool; the Royal Liver Company; the chief constable and his deputy; and HM Customs and Excise. Even the Reds players – double league champions after all – were finally allocated two complimentary tickets for each home match. By 1929, there would be the first authentic steps towards identifiable corporate hospitality at Anfield. 'Mr Cherry is appointed as steward in the refreshment room,' the Liverpool minute book entry reads, 'and a commissionaire [is to] be engaged at the entrance to ensure that no one is admitted without refreshment tickets.' Keep the riff-raff at bay. Later, the Reds chairman Walter Cartwright might have welcomed ticket-only access, because in October 1929, while returning by train from another Reds defeat at Leicester City, a travelling companion – presumably a fellow director – made a 'serious allegation' concerning his integrity. After an apology was given, Cartwright cooled down and was given a vote of confidence by the board. But his Liverpool team was already struggling.

In the city, meanwhile, in the early 1920s, a 'beautiful and vastly improved' Clayton Square shopping precinct, 'a magnificent pile of buildings', was promised by the Liverpool Estates Committee as part of continuing modernisation. This was in line with a policy, reported in the *Evening Express*, to make Liverpool 'a more attractive city to visit, a greater centre for shopping and amusement, a cheerier, more cosmopolitan sort of a place than ever'. It could have been the 2008 Capital of Culture talking.

In 1923, three young Manchester entrepreneurs led by John Moores were experimenting with distributing football pools coupons outside Merseyside football grounds. They had borrowed the idea from Birmingham, where the pools business had failed. Their Littlewoods football betting business would eventually provide thousands of jobs for Liverpool women.

Betting was frowned upon locally in the 1920s, not least because the patently 'dull' city of Liverpool was still held in the iron claw of religion. It was also no closer to getting Sunday sport for working people. In July 1923, Liverpool City Council turned down, by 60 votes to 25, another motion to allow the playing of Sunday sport in the city's parks. Alderman Austin Harewood described Liverpool as being 'in the grip of clerical tyranny'. Perhaps the Merseyside clerics were simply underestimating the positive power of football. In 1923, the *Evening Express* reported that a Bradford man, Percy Bottomley, who had lost his capacity for speech after being blown up in Germany in the Great War, suddenly found his voice again during a local football match in the city. He blurted out, 'Leave it, it's mine!'

ACCIDENTS WILL HAPPEN?

The Liverpool Football Club players were rather less hamstrung by tradition and restraint than were the city's authorities. Three of them – Dick Johnson, Harry Chambers and the reserve Welsh full-back Ted Parry – only narrowly missed serious injury as the new season began when the motorcycle sidecar they were riding in was hit head-on by a car. Early road transport had its risks. This was not the only – or the worst – Liverpool FC traffic mishap of the new campaign. In November 1923, half-back Jock McNab suffered serious facial injuries requiring 17 stitches when he hit the windscreen of the taxi cab he was travelling in when it collided with a car after midnight. His injuries kept him out for 12 league matches. Life could be dangerous for footballers in the 1920s. Later in the same year, Tommy Ball, the Aston Villa centre-half, was tragically shot dead by his neighbour and landlord in Perry Barr after an on-street argument. Liverpool played Villa soon afterwards in an eerie atmosphere at Villa Park in which both sides wore black crêpe armbands.

When Liverpool opened the new campaign against West Bromwich Albion on 25 August, they 'failed to show the sparkle' of the previous season, and worse, Dick Johnson, a key figure, broke down with a serious knee injury. Patchy form followed, though Johnson's replacement Jimmy Walsh showed up well, ending as top scorer with 16 goals. The visit of the prime minister and Lord Derby to Anfield on 3 November could produce only a 1–1 draw with Chapman's rising Huddersfield Town, and Liverpool had already settled into the midtable obscurity from which they would never escape. Matt McQueen and the Liverpool directors' response was hardly earth-shattering: they signed Joe Keetley, a 23-year-old forward from Third Division Accrington Stanley. Keetley managed two goals in his nine starts, but the Reds were soon in a goal drought. In nine league matches across November and December 1923, Liverpool managed only five goals, with five straight losses.

By this stage, Johnson, Lacey, Longworth and Bromilow had all been missing for lengthy spells due to injury, and only five of the Liverpool title-winning team contested a turgid 0–0 draw at Villa Park in November. The Liverpool press accused Villa of having the 'most partisan of all supporters' and of being schooled missile-throwers. Elisha Scott was a past expert at riling the Villa faithful. Here, the Liverpool goalkeeper was 'subject to a great deal of vituperation and was nearly hit by something thrown by one of the crowd'. In December, Sheffield United warned their own fans about bad behaviour after a Liverpool player (probably Walter Wadsworth) was 'grossly insulted as he walked off the playing pitch' at Bramall Lane. But Liverpool's real problems were *on* the field. On 27 December 1923, after a defeat at Newcastle United, a *Liverpool Courier* headline – also reflecting the rise of new harsher media values and reporting style – read, simply, 'Liverpool going from bad to worse'.

Things could not get much worse, certainly not for the unfortunate Matt McQueen. While scouting for players in Sheffield, the Liverpool manager was hit by a car, suffering serious leg injuries in the collision. What was it with the Liverpool staff and road accidents all of a sudden? By February 1924, septic poisoning had set in, and the great Liverpool player and manager had to have a leg amputated. The club paid McQueen's medical bills amounting to £100 2s 6d. Already knowing his fate, McQueen bravely and jauntily wrote to Cri at the *Evening Express* on the subject of Liverpool's improving form. 'I say old chap, the Reds are doing all right now, eh?' This voice sounded more like a country squire than that of the Liverpool boss. McQueen promised that 'if everything goes on with my "baby" as desired', he hoped to meet the Reds players at the FA Cup final at Wembley in April. Neither Matt McQueen nor Liverpool Football Club would make it to Wembley intact. Worse, Liverpool was now without many of its best players *and* its stricken manager.

On 8 January 1924, the *Evening Express* reported that Liverpool FC was on the brink of a full-scale crisis. 'With manager Matt McQueen in hospital and more than a full side in the hands of the doctor, chairman Mr W.R. Williams, his fellow directors and secretary George Patterson are at their wits end to know what to do for the best.' Did the best it could do involve signing Hector Lawson from Rangers? Lawson was the Scotland understudy of Alan Morton, the renowned middle-class, teetotal international wing genius. Lawson was snapped up on the uncertain premise that anyone capable of stepping in for Morton must himself be a very good player. Sadly, Lawson was not.

'BOUNDLESS AND UNENDING INSPIRATION'

Hope flickered eternal in the FA Cup, especially after Liverpool dispatched Bradford City at Anfield and then turned over cup holders Bolton Wanderers on 2 February 1924 in a 4–1 away upset that bore all the hallmarks of a club heading for Wembley. Five football-special trains had departed Liverpool for Bolton, but still hundreds of Reds fans were left disappointed and stranded at Exchange Station. Walsh was the obvious Liverpool hero on the day, with a superb hat-trick, but it was McNab who was 'the talk of the match'. Bolton's Jimmy Seddon (who later coached at Liverpool) was injured and off the field for most of the second half. Serious match injury shaped so many crucial football encounters before substitutions were sanctioned.

A big crowd waited to greet the Liverpool squad at Exchange Station, but the players cleverly 'escaped' the throng into a party at the Exchange Hotel, also attended by John McKenna. Honest John wanted so much for *his* Liverpool to lift the FA Cup. Chairman Williams spoke warmly of the loyalty shown by players during these difficult times, and Donald McKinlay mumbled some thanks before saying, 'I reserve the rest of this speech until the return from Wembley.' Belief was already growing.

Why not? With injured players returning, and form and results picking up, the omens seemed better for Liverpool. Being drawn away to Southampton in late February 1924 did not deter hundreds of Reds fans from catching the quarter-past-midnight train on Friday evening, to arrive at 7.30 a.m. on the south coast for the day's festivities. Liverpool might have been a little windy about the tie, because directors Cartwright and Troop complained in advance to the FA about seats being 'too close' to the goal-line at one end of the ground. A tight 0–0 draw included the usual 'miraculous' save from Scott, this time to keep out forward Art Dominy.

At Anfield, for the Wednesday-afternoon replay, local workplaces must have been short-staffed, because thousands of locals were left locked outside, and 'enthusiasts' in the corners of the ground climbed the concrete walls to sit around the pitch. There was the first report at Anfield of what the *Evening Express* described as the 'rather dangerous' practice of supporters passing children over their heads to the front of the crowd. The Southampton mascot, clad in red and white, amused the locals with his wild dancing, while Liverpool supporters inflated hundreds of red balloons in an early show of FA Cup football carnival. One visiting supporter, squeezing in late, comically caught his coat in a closing entrance gate and missed the entire first half as a result. In a match of 'accidents', which had both Donald McKinlay and Southampton's Fred Titmuss hospitalised with head injuries, Liverpool's ten men beat off the Saints 2–0 in a scrappy encounter. It was 'poor football', admitted half-back Tommy Bromilow unapologetically later, 'but both sides were upset by the accidents'.

The Liverpool minute books reveal that a Mr Kay was given permission by the club in February 1924 to produce a booklet about its history, with 750 copies to be given to the club free of charge. Was it ever produced? Also, Liverpool and Everton agreed to play a historic exhibition game as part of the celebrations at the new Wembley Stadium in 1924, with the clubs sharing 50 per cent of the receipts. It would have been a Merseyside coup, but the proposed match was cancelled at the last minute because of the poor state of the Wembley pitch. 'If there was a greater and larger spirit in Liverpool than in other towns,' commented Member of Parliament T.P. O'Connor during the festivities at Wembley, 'it was largely because Liverpool was always in touch with the boundless and unending inspiration of the rolling ocean. The sea was really the mother of Liverpool . . . It was the great cosmopolitan site of banter and exchange, and through it passed the production of every land.' The mythologies of the city of Liverpool and the deep origins of its unique character clearly ran very deep.

DREAMS DASHED

The rather maligned borough of Bootle began to rise to the challenge of poor facilities for local football when on 4 September 1924 the *Daily Post* reported that the local authorities had bought from the Earl of Sefton, for £7,416, a 30-acre site near Captain's Lane to be developed along the lines of Stanley Park and to include 20 football pitches. It was indeed, as the local chairman of the parks committee put it, the 'cheapest bargain Bootle has ever made'. For the best part of the next 50 years, these 'pleasure fields', as they became known locally, would serve Bootle football enthusiasts. But the men in Bootle were the lucky ones. Early in 1925, following the FA ban on women's clubs, the *Football Echo* reported, 'Lady football teams have, by now, hardly got a kick left in them.' Meanwhile, the emergency committee of the Liverpool County FA reported that offending local footballers increasingly refused to give their real names to officials and that its 'duties in dealing with players sent off the field are as onerous as ever, and if the proceedings of this committee were ever published, it would be an eye-opener to the general public'. Harsh times in local football.

Snowstorms gripped much of Britain by the time the 1924 FA Cup quarter-finals approached on 4 March, but not in Saltburn on the north-east coast, where elderly Liverpool director Edward Bainbridge was, as usual, travelling with the Liverpool players and officials as they prepared, using the hydro-baths of a local hotel, for their crunch FA Cup meeting with Newcastle United. The simple committee structure of the largely self-selecting Liverpool board at this time divided up responsibilities for its various directors between ground issues, finance, the playing side, etc. Chairman Williams and directors Cartwright, Crompton, Wood and Troop all travelled up from Exchange Station on Friday afternoon to finalise the Liverpool team, with Mr Astbury indisposed and Richard Martindale looking after the Liverpool reserve side. The Martindales were to become another of the great Liverpool Football Club supporting families, with Richard briefly becoming the club chairman in 1924. His son Robert Lawson Martindale was co-opted onto the board in 1931.

Some Liverpool supporters also left a freezing Merseyside for the north-east in high spirits and lively red-and-white fancy dress, the best wishes of comedian George Robey (playing at the Olympic Theatre in the city) ringing in their ears. The Red half of Merseyside was buzzing with Wembley anticipation, convinced it was their time. But it was all so much hot air, because, according to the *Evening Express*, 'Liverpool never approached within a mile of their proper form' in a drab 0–1 defeat. As the visitors slumped, Jock McNab, typically, began using 'robust methods' to try to quell outside-left Stan Seymour, drawing the anger of the locals and also a stone from the crowd, which hit him on the back of the head. The deciding goal (whisper it very quietly) was an Elisha Scott mistake. A McDonald header from 12 yards out bounced awkwardly at the goalkeeper, who could only flap jerkily at it with his left arm, scooping the ball high into the net. It would be Newcastle United, not Liverpool, who would go on to win the 1924 FA Cup. With this latest cup exit, the Reds' season was all but over, despite just one defeat in the last 11 league matches, for a respectable finish in 12th position.

A LONG TIME COMING

It must be difficult for modern football fans to contemplate that a club such as Liverpool could play 16 seasons and go fully 24 years without winning a major title or even reaching the final of a national competition. And yet that was the situation that faced the club from the mid-1920s to the late 1940s. The FA Cup seemed perpetually out of reach, with only a run to the sixth round in 1932 offering any sort of real promise for a second final appearance. The FA Cup is notoriously quixotic, of course, with club officials and supporters often complaining about the vagaries of the draw. This Liverpool team could hardly claim ill-fortune, however: from 1929 to 1934, for example, the Reds were knocked out of the FA Cup five times after having been drawn at home in the tie. 'Considering the city of Liverpool has been in football since its infancy,' wrote Ephraim Longworth in his regular column in the *Football Echo* on 2 January 1925, 'the fact that we [Everton and Liverpool] have won the cup but once is a standing disgrace to us.' The failure of Liverpool FC in the FA Cup in the period leading up to the Second World War can probably best be explained by three things:

1. Self-induced anxiety
2. The decline in the club's own high standards, especially in forward play
3. The relative rise of the strength of the game in the south and particularly *outside* of its traditional early strongholds.

Between 1925 and 1939, Liverpool lost in the cup no fewer than eight times to clubs from outside the main northern and Midlands centres, including twice to Cardiff City (1928 and 1930) and twice to Arsenal (1927 and 1936). There were also defeats to Southampton (1925), Fulham (1926), Chelsea (1932) and even to lowly Second Division Norwich City in a third-round embarrassment in January 1937. This was now truly a national game and a national competition.

In the Football League, the picture was barely brighter, with only two top-five finishes for Liverpool (fourth in 1925 and fifth in 1929) and three brushes close to relegation (eighteenth in 1934, nineteenth in 1936 and eighteenth again in 1937). By the mid-1930s, some Liverpool supporters were beginning to blame the club's general approach to the new systems of play as the prime reason for its poor performances. After a crushing 2–9 loss to Newcastle United in January 1934, for example, 'Red Hot' wrote to the *Liverpool Echo* to say he was 'disgusted with their play of forwards [half-backs]. If it is orders to play that type of football, then the sooner they forget the W-formation the better.'

'Springbok', from Wallasey, noted that after an hour the score at St James's Park stood at 2–2, and he argued that:

> It is obvious . . . that Liverpool exaggerate the W-formation . . . It means the inside men become extra half-backs; that it leaves only three forwards in attack. The inside men have too much work: they are compelled to defend and attack. The result is generally a pronounced falling off in the second half: they tire. No wonder Liverpool are suffering from a preponderance of injuries. The inside men have double the work to do.

The Reds had difficulties adapting to the new offside law and new playing styles. Meanwhile, neighbours Everton seemed to have few such problems. Being inspired, initially, by the Birkenhead-born bombshell Bill Dean, the Blues mocked Liverpool's mediocrity by winning three interwar league titles, in 1928, 1932 and 1939, and one FA Cup, in 1933. Most Evertonians would probably accept their club's shock relegation for one season in 1930 – scoring 80 goals but conceding 92 – in return for these triumphs. Certainly, most Liverpool supporters, one suspects, would have done so.

THE (SOUTH) AFRICAN INVASION

The Liverpool minute books for the mid-1920s show that the club's directors were working feverishly to sign players, and they were even adopting a more 'scientific' approach to player recruitment and preparation. On 29 December 1925, for example, 'the manager was instructed to keep a book with the heights, weights and ages of all players, amateurs and professionals'. This looked like progress of sorts, and it echoed work at Melwood later under Bill Shankly. In September 1929, the club even purchased an Electrical Massage Machine from Good Bros for £30 to quicken up player recovery. The Liverpool directors and scouts travelled ceaselessly, scouring for cheap talent, though the board decided that the north of England, Scotland and Ireland were the best areas to pick up Liverpool players – the club had no southern scout at all until the mid-1930s. They did pick up occasional bargains: the wily Matt McQueen talked Aberdeen down from £4,500 to £1,750 for ace centre-half James Jackson, for example. A young S. Matthews in Stoke City reserves was also watched and noted but was never the subject of a bid. Liverpool did sign centre-forward Sam English from Rangers for a weighty £8,000 in 1933, not realising how mentally blighted the Northern Irishman had been by his fatal on-pitch collision with the Celtic keeper John Thomson two years earlier. But Liverpool also missed out on many star players – goalkeeper Frank Swift and genius inside-forwards Patsy Gallagher and Alex James were examples – because the Anfield board simply refused to pay substantial transfer fees, or else the player concerned refused to come because of the uncompetitive rewards on offer.

Both Walter Wadsworth and Harry Chambers now had serious income-tax problems and wanted transfers away from Anfield, as the club agreed in 1925 to buy a 'parking ground for motors immediately behind the new stand'. Many players – like most fans, of course – could barely afford their taxes, never mind buy a car. By 1931, soil was used to replace the cinder border behind the goalmouths at Anfield to reduce incidents of missile-throwing, and major boxing matches were now being staged at the stadium for a suitable fee. The footballing Brazilians of Botafogo wanted to come to play Liverpool in 1932 – but asked for £350, too much cash – and the club settled instead for a sequence of exhibition home fixtures against top Viennese clubs. These were all early signs of the modern football world approaching. As, indeed, was a letter sent to Elisha Scott reported in the minute books on 27 January 1927. A local bookmaker contacted Scott saying that he stood to lose £6,000 if Liverpool beat Derby County. He offered the Ulsterman £50 to ensure Liverpool lost by two goals. The fixer promised to meet Scott at Lime Street Station to pay up, wearing a trilby, spats, white scarf and red rosette for identification. He ended his note with a warning: 'Do as I say Elisha and don't let me down, for God's sake.' Liverpool beat County 3–2 and the police turned up at Lime Street, but there was no sign of Scott's correspondent.

On 1 October 1924, Liverpool had turned out a strong mix of first-teamers and reserves to play a touring amateur representative team from white South Africa. On paper it looked like a gentle training exercise for Liverpool – it was anything but. The Africans won 2–5 in a blistering exhibition of technique and movement, 'one of the most enjoyable games ever witnessed on the ground'. The *Daily Post* saw the drubbing as 'a lesson for English players', an exciting alternative to dominant British approaches, which still required that the ball be passed slowly within the team and then to the wingers, who tried to outwit the opposing half-back before crossing. The South Africans played a much more direct and central game, one sprinkled with the 'back-heel touch' and an approach of 'simple methods of passing and by the upwards pass'. For Bee in the *Liverpool Echo*, the South Africans were nothing less than a revelation. 'We must learn our lesson afresh,' he advised. 'They shall be our teachers.'

Bee made much of the way in which the visitors, by 'taking the ball as it comes, moving it to right or left', had speeded up the game. They accepted passes first time without trapping or 'deadening' the ball, as was the traditional

British way. The *Daily Post* reasoned that this unusual style was due to the 'hard pitches' in South Africa but anticipated that supporters in England might reject this fast, more direct, approach to football. 'Perhaps English crowds are the barrier; they so like to see a ball worked and to see a player become tricky.' The *Post* also noted the athleticism and maturity of the South Africans compared to Liverpool players, despite the relative youth of the visitors. 'The goalkeeper, a tall and keen fellow who has reach, anticipation and a safe pair of hands, is only 20, but he looks more like 35. The inside right is only 19, but plays like a seasoned professional.' These 'mystery' players were the Transvaal men, and future Liverpool signings, Arthur Riley and Gordon Hodgson.

At the Adelphi Hotel reception held after the match, John McKenna for the Football League highlighted the beneficial effects that English teams touring South Africa had had on African football, though the final tour record in Britain was actually very patchy: played twenty-five matches, won ten, lost fifteen. But the Liverpool board had seen enough – perhaps the best – of the touring party, and by December 1924 had made groundbreaking offers to three players. According to the *Cape Argus*, 'They regard Riley as the most promising goalkeeper in England, Brunton as one of the best backs now playing football, and Hodgson as the best inside-right in the country.' It was the physicality, as well as the cleverness and pace, of the South Africans that really attracted the Liverpool directors – and their cheapness. The distinction drawn in British law between the colonial and the foreigner was helpful. As the former, the South Africans were British subjects who were free to enter and settle in the home country.[7] Brunton never made it to Liverpool, but both Riley and Hodgson signed – for just £90 travelling and hotel expenses, and no transfer fees, of course – and once this English-speaking Empire route was effectively opened up, so were scouting networks and more South Africans followed between the wars to the familiar and welcoming territory of Anfield Road.

By the early 1930s, 'Liverpool were qualifying for some kind of record by their trade with South Africa', with at least six South Africans on the club's books by the start of the 1933–34 season and sometimes only two Englishmen, talented Bootle-born goalscoring winger Alf Hanson and Newcastle-born full-back Jack Tennant, in the side.[8] These African recruits would include Lance Carr, a Johannesburg-born left-wing flyer who later moved to Bristol City, and Harman van der Berg, another outside-left. Liverpool's sudden internationalism was startling, and these South Africans soon knew that they had come to a truly football-mad place. A social survey conducted in Liverpool in 1934 found that 15,000 to 20,000 adult males now played the game 'fairly regularly' in the city alone.[9]

This early batch of 'foreign' signings in the 1920s and early 1930s was actually a fantastic piece of business for the club. The big and powerful, if rather ungainly, Hodgson (241 goals in 377 appearances) was the main forward spark for Liverpool and the club's regular top scorer for much of the next decade. On making his first-team debut against Manchester City in February 1926, the very muscular Hodgson impressed. He was comfortable at either inside-right or centre-forward and authentically two-footed in a period – and in a culture – in which this remained an unusual trait. But a local scribe commented that 'a little more speed . . . would send up his stock a great deal'. Hodgson established a partnership of 'perfect understanding' between 1927 and 1929 with the Gillingham-born winger and ex-dockyard worker Dick Edmed, a man who later scored for Bolton *against* Liverpool in May 1932 in a terrible 1–8 Reds humiliation.

The Liverpool minute books show that in April 1926 Hodgson was allowed to return to South Africa and that he was 'very doubtful' of ever returning to Liverpool because of family problems. But Hodgson *did* come back, and by October 1928, when he scored three goals in a 4–4 draw at Highbury, the *Evening Express* was able to sum up the forward's strengths: 'He may appear clumsy, but he makes the fullest use of his 13 st. weight in bullying the opposing defence. His height is a distinct advantage in intercepting centres from the wing with his head and he is most deadly in his shooting with either foot.' After the South African had ploughed through a hapless Burnley defence in an 8–0 drubbing at Anfield over the Christmas period in 1928, the *Evening Express* even argued that 'Hodgson is becoming almost as much a hero as Dixie Dean as a thrustful leader of attack . . . The demoralisation of the Burnley backs was largely due to the relentless bustling tactics of the Liverpool leader.' Typically South African, Hodgson was also a broad-shouldered cricketer of some note for Lancashire CCC, but he eventually won three caps at football for England, his adopted country. In 1930–31, Hodgson would need every inch of those broad shoulders for his football work, scoring a then record 36 league goals in a rather ordinary Liverpool side.

Hodgson was joined at Anfield in 1933 from Germiston Calies by Berry 'Nivvy' Nieuwenhuys, a tall, loping right-winger with deceptive pace and a fierce right-foot shot who made 260 Liverpool appearances over 14 years, including 15 in the 1946–47 championship season. 'Nivvy' had penetration and directness, and, like wingers today, he enjoyed using his strength and height in the air at the back post against smaller full-backs. He could also work back, thus showing the novel demands on wingers in the new W–M era of the 1930s. He effectively sealed his relationship with Kopites in his first full match, in September 1933, by scoring at Anfield in a 3–2 derby win over Everton. 'It was an uncommon home debut,' enthused the *Liverpool Echo*, 'because he got a goal, gave [made] a goal and not only introduced new methods to the public, but also showed that he could lend a "surprise item" by falling back and taking the ball from an unsuspecting Everton forward.' It was a perfect start for the South African.

Goalkeeper Arthur Riley, a pragmatic, brave and reliable number one, had been signed, of course, as cover and the long-term replacement for the ageing Elisha Scott. When he filled in for the injured Scott at Leicester in October 1927, the *Daily Post* wrote, 'Riley, in any other side, would be the senior goalkeeper and Liverpool are fortunate to have such a deputy for Scott. He made some remarkable saves.' Riley actually seemed to have displaced the wonderful Ulsterman by the late 1920s, before losing his own form in 1931 and allowing the 37-year-old Scott back into the side. Riley was also briefly challenged for his place in the Liverpool goal in the mid-1930s by the Durham-born Alf Hobson and also the Cape Town man Dirk Kemp, another Anfield recruit from Africa. In these turbulent years of transition for defenders and for Liverpool Football Club, it is true that the unfortunate Riley often faced a barrage from the opposition. These included a 1–6 last-day thumping at Old Trafford in May 1928; an embarrassing 0–6 home defeat by Sunderland in April 1930; a 0–7 loss at West Ham in September 1930 – though the *Evening Express* insisted that 'it was doubtful if he had a chance to save any of them' – and a 1–8 mauling at Bolton Wanderers in May 1932, after which the *Liverpool Echo* correspondent reported, 'I have never seen [Liverpool] play worse . . . Goals came like hailstones; it took all my time to keep tally with them.'

In September 1934, when Arsenal repeated this 1–8 dose, the *Echo* wrote, 'Riley's was a sickening job. There is not the slightest charge against him.' Finally, in November of the same year, the final straw: Liverpool lost 0–8 to bottom club Huddersfield Town when 'Riley kept the game from a cricket score'. This era was clearly a time for forwards and for goals – and no goalkeeper was entirely safe from its effects. When Liverpool were humiliated 2–9 by Newcastle United on New Year's Day in 1934, it was the ailing hero Elisha Scott who was in goal, rather than Riley. The Ulsterman, improbably, gave 'a display of heroic proportions', according to the devoted *Liverpool Echo*. Despite these various beatings, 338 Liverpool appearances in goal confirmed the original judgement of the directors and the Liverpool manager made back in 1924 that in the young Arthur Riley Liverpool had secured a fitting heir – albeit from an unexpected quarter – to the great Elisha.

THE COMFORT OF STRANGERS ON THE COVERED KOP

By 1928, many of the core members of the Liverpool championship side were either already gone or were now well on their way out of Anfield. Dick Forshaw was perhaps the most spectacular departure, in March 1927, because he not only joined local rivals Everton, but he also scored on his debut for the Blues and then – a real dagger this to the heart of any Reds fan – he won a league championship medal in his first full season at Goodison Park in 1928. Ephraim Longworth, especially, had been a remarkable leader and servant to the Liverpool club, but it was perhaps a sign of their stretched loyalty to favoured players – and of Liverpool's current travails – that Ephraim continued to play in the First Division when well past his best. In his final appearance for Liverpool, a 0–2 defeat by Birmingham on 27 April 1928, the *Daily Post* remarked that it was 'only natural that he was beaten for speed'.

On 15 February of that year, another local favourite, manager Matt McQueen, had finally given in to his health problems and resigned. The Liverpool board reasoned that *they* could continue selecting the team and recruiting players, and that the club secretary George Patterson could easily pick up the rest of the managerial tasks, thus saving on salary costs. Patterson kept the secretary–manager job until 1936. It was another sign of a lack of focus and the penny-pinching at the club, and that Liverpool had failed to see the importance of what had been recently happening in the era of Herbert Chapman on the coaching and management side of the game. In 1928, there was also a major restructuring of the Anfield training staff: Bill Connell retired but continued to scout for Liverpool; and Charlie Wilson took over as trainer, with Ephraim Longworth and Joe Hewitt as his assistants. All three men had played for Liverpool.

In 1932, Maurice Parry, another ex-player, was briefly appointed as 'coach' at Anfield – a barely heard-of role – but he lasted only a year. The board decided it needed no coach, instead instructing the Reds training staff that 'more ball practice be given to the players' while the trainers awaited the arrival of a 'ball board'. Robert Lawson Martindale was the director who seemed keenest on modernising the playing side of the club, registering his frustrations at the slow pace of change and conferring with the people at the Adelphi Hotel gym in February 1933 before fitting out Anfield with a rowing machine, wall bars and a weightlifting bench. Off the pitch, in the mid-1930s the entire Liverpool club was administered by one full-time salaried staff member, George Patterson, one man on a weekly wage, J.C. Rouse (the secretary's assistant), and a lowly clerk, Mrs Hilda Riley, who was paid £2 per week. It was a 'corner shop' arrangement.

On the occasion of the official opening of the new £38,000 Joseph Watson Cabre-designed roof over the 28,000-capacity Spion Kop at Anfield for the home match v. Bury on 25 August 1928, VIP guest John McKenna congratulated the Liverpool board on providing more covered accommodation than any other club in the Football League. But he also offered a word of advice to the Liverpool directors: 'Stay your hands in the matter of further improvements of the ground and devote your finances, energy and intelligence to creating a *team* worthy of its splendid ground accommodation.' Was anyone listening?

The Crosby-based Watson had been a surprise choice for the Kop project – he worked mostly on private houses and religious restorations. The new construction was the largest such structure in England, measuring 425 ft wide and 80 ft high, but its new roof could not disguise the dangerously poor terrace design and the limited circulation routes on the Kop, which would mean routine injuries for fans and give rise to the time-honoured tradition of some male Kopites being forced to urinate where they stood at half-time.[10] From the start, the covered Kop was a highly social space – chanting and also betting among its members were soon established. The Kop catered mainly for male, working-class supporters, with the 'toffs' or the 'mobs', as some Kopites called them, located in the stands and the Paddock.[11] Nevertheless, the *Liverpool Echo* made much of this supposed new luxury in spectator provision, which included roof glazing that was 'wire-woven, to protect the spectators from broken glass if someone raised the roof shouting "goal"'.

Such opulence – and it was added to by the grand erection of a franchise tea stall on the Kop in September 1929. 'To be in keeping with the glorious new stand,' the *Echo* continued, with an eye on gentrification and the young confection-sellers who paraded their wares inside Anfield, 'they might put gold knobs on the goalposts and the chocolate boys should have their hair water-waved and scented.'The match programme for the Bury fixture carried an artist's impression of a proposed new double-decker stand at the Anfield Road end of the ground, which carried the distinctive criss-cross balcony design of Archibald Leitch. But the playing success at Anfield said to be needed to raise the funds for the new development never came.[12]

As a Football League man, McKenna might have been expected to stress prudence, structures and planning over signing new players and a thirst for immediate success. But then McKenna was no ordinary Football League official, at least not as far as Liverpool Football Club was concerned. When he was club secretary at Anfield, he recalled he had but a shed for his office. 'Those people who pay their shilling to go on the Spion Kop,' said the new Liverpool chairman Mr T. (Tom) Crompton at the grand opening in 1928, 'have really been the backbone of the club. Wet or fine they have loyally filled their places and it has given great satisfaction to the directors to now make them as comfortable as possible with every protection against inclement weather.' McKenna responded, in turn, 'No one knows better than I do that we cannot live in the past, but I think that the past should at least be an inspiration for the future.'

The *Liverpool Echo* reporter also ruminated on the contradictions of the opening of this wonderful new structure, which implied that everything in the Anfield garden was lovely, while angry voices rang out from the Kop claiming, 'So-and-so, you are a **** twister!' 'There are times,' the *Echo* continued, '[when players] catch sight of the culprit and would like to take the law into their own hands – and also the culprit's neck!' In fact, there would be many occasions under this grand new roof when Liverpool supporters would run out of patience with their often ragged team. But only twice in this troubled period, in 1935–36 and 1937–38, did Liverpool lose more than five league matches at home – the Kop was obviously a factor in this, and it would be for decades to come. But the Reds frequently struggled to win more than five matches *away* in a season, managing only two away victories in the near-calamitous 1935–36 season. After the undreamed-of success of consecutive league titles in the early 1920s, it had been a troubling period in this part of the footballing district of Liverpool 4. Worse was to follow. The Liverpool fans had their newly covered Kop at last, but they were about to lose a local folk hero, and arguably the club's greatest-ever player.

CHAPTER 8 REFERENCES

1. Wilson, *Inverting the Pyramid*, pp. 25–9
2. Inglis, *The Football League and the Men Who Made It*, p. 110
3. Rous, *Football Worlds*, p. 90
4. Carter, *The Football Manager*, p. 50
5. Page, *Herbert Chapman*, pp. 126–7
6. Wilson, *Inverting the Pyramid*, p. 51
7. Taylor, *The Leaguers*, p. 234
8. Young, *Football on Merseyside*, pp. 130–1
9. Jones, *The Social Survey of Merseyside*, p. 291
10. Physick, *Played in Liverpool*, p. 58
11. Kelly, *The Kop*, p. 16
12. Inglis, *The Football Grounds of Great Britain*, p. 210

9

LISHA! LISHA!
Elisha Scott and the Liverpool Kop

THE SCOTT AND DEAN SHOW

As Liverpool Football Club struggled collectively after 1923, the aura around the club's remaining great individual talent, the Irish goalkeeper Elisha Scott, continued to grow stronger, even when most of the 93 league goals that Liverpool conceded in 1931–32 were put past the great man. This mythologising accelerated as Scott's duels with Everton's Dixie Dean offered an alternative focus for a generation of Liverpool supporters who were now pretty much starved of FA Cup and league-championship prospects. These two great rivals were made for each other, and they were undoubtedly good for football business in the city at a time when, frankly, Liverpool were struggling to be even vaguely competitive with the near neighbours. Mr Justice Charles at the assizes in Liverpool was a football man and a great admirer of Elisha Scott's goalkeeping. When they met, according to a *Liverpool Echo* story in 1934, the exchange was typical of the rather taciturn and obtuse Scott, and also of his disregard for fripperies or even praise:

Said Judge Charles, 'I think it is very wonderful the way you keep goal.'
'Och,' said Scott, 'I'll be better a year from today.'
'How do you make that out?' asked the judge.
'More experience, see; more experience, see,' said Scott.

Bill Dean did not lack confidence or experience. He scored nine times against Scott in their eight derby meetings, and few forwards had a better record against the Ulsterman. Not that Elisha Scott – a man with his very own Kopite chant of 'Lisha, Lisha' – was intimidated by Dean, or by anyone else. Not even when Dixie sent the Liverpool keeper a tube of aspirin and a warning note to his

Wallasey home before every derby game. In reply, Elisha good-naturedly taunted the Everton forward in the tunnel before each derby meeting with, 'You'll get none today, you black-haired bastard.'[1] A journalist of the day famously described Elisha Scott as having 'the eye of an eagle and the swift movement of a panther', and the pugnacious and lethal Dean agreed that Scott was 'the greatest goalkeeper I have ever seen'.

When Liverpool first scouted Scott as a teenager, the report came back that he was 'as raw as meat', but he already had both presence and courage. Dixie highlighted the biggest strength of the Liverpool man to be less his shot-stopping capacities than his early preparation and fearless 'point-blank charge' to meet a forward head-on. A determined and fearless moving goalkeeper, even at a modest 5 ft 9 in., was a threat in the corner of the eye of any forward. The Liverpool keeper was 'never still', reasoned the Everton icon Dean. 'As soon as the attack against him crosses the halfway line, watch Scott jump.' Another journalist commented, 'To the end he could leap to the high ones like the magnificent human stag he was.' On 19 September 1931, Dean did finally manage to get his Anfield hat-trick with Elisha in goal. It was scored in a deadly nine-minute spell in a 1–3 Liverpool defeat. The Everton man then cheekily bowed three times in front of the foaming Kop and, predictably, received a volley of 'choice language' in reply. Elisha Scott was in a rage.

By this time Elisha, the younger brother of another Irish international goalkeeper, William Scott, had become especially well known, as the *Liverpool Echo* put it later, for his 'sallies with the crowd, his looks of despair at some forwards – or his own side – his shrill cry "rate" [meaning "right"] can never be forgotten by followers of the club'. Scott very willingly and very publicly *communed* with the Liverpool supporters, said the *Echo*. 'They have heard him; he holds conference with them; he chats and back-chats; they hear his opinion about positions and positional play. He was built in with the Kop!'

By now, this vast standing terrace had already established its own highly distinctive identity. Its members furiously thrashed rattles adorned with club colours, abused the carriers of the pitch-side blackboards that noted team changes, bawled wildly at referees and rival players, and lustily sang along with the brass-band players before matches. 'Yes, We Have No Bananas' was an early Kop favourite. The terrace had few airs and graces. Jean McDonald, as a 12 year old, was, unusually, taken by her father to the Kop in the mid-1930s, when, 'There were no ladies' toilets or anything like that.'

Scott loved the earthy male humour and the bawdy irreverence of the Kop. During home matches, he was usually furious with the Liverpool defender Jimmy 'Parson' Jackson, a former Clyde shipyard worker, a church elder and devout Christian, who had studied Greek and philosophy at Cambridge University and would be ordained a Presbyterian minister in 1933. In August 1947, Jim Jackson, now a reverend and a Liverpool man through and through, would officiate at the funeral of the former Liverpool chairman W.H. (Bill) McConnell.

Jackson was the son of a professional footballer, but by no stretch was he an obviously 'typical' British professional. He was certainly a mile away from the brusque Scott in both background and temperament. Jackson was a scrupulously fair, intelligent, big-hearted, determined and versatile defender, a Liverpool captain who played 224 times for the club, usually at either right full-back or centre-half. The largely working-class, strongly Irish-flavoured Kop sided unconditionally with its heroic and volatile – and often expletive-ridden – Irish goalkeeper. The club centre-half, by way of contrast, represented brushed-up, staid authority. Jackson would go on to have many an even-handed tussle with Dixie Dean in his long and honourable Liverpool career, but few would be as painful as Dean's hat-trick match at Anfield in 1931. Jackson's chief crime was that he was the man who had allowed Bill Dean to humiliate Elisha in front of his own people – and in fewer than ten excruciating minutes.

The abrasive Scott (like his friends on the Kop) thought that Jackson was far too gentlemanly with opposing forwards and that he should have tried more to 'rough up' Dean. He bawled this out in no uncertain terms in front of the Kop. The sensitive Jackson was distraught and shocked by the goalkeeper's industrial language, confiding in an amused Bill Dean, 'William, I never want to play in front of *that* man again.' Ironically, Dixie, the Liverpool goalkeeper's most-feared opponent, seemed more Elisha Scott's personal cup of tea than were his own defenders. After derby games, regardless of the outcome, the two great internationals would retire to the Lisbon pub in Victoria Street, where they could discuss the outcome. As the world raged around them, the notoriously penny-pinching Scott would be hunched quietly over a bottle of Guinness with Dean nursing a pint of bitter, oblivious to all except their own professional friendship forged in the intense heat of battle. Both men, tough as old boots, would be amused to learn that today the Lisbon is firmly on the Merseyside gay-and-lesbian pub circuit.

FOOTBALL – AND FA CUP – DEPRESSION

In January 1932, the Merseyside clubs were drawn together in the FA Cup third round at Goodison Park, the first FA Cup derby since 1911. The *Industrial Survey* of 1932 predicted that 'a vast problem of unemployment would weigh upon Merseyside for many years', and throughout the 1930s unemployment in the area remained above 18 per cent, double the national average.[2] So this FA Cup meeting was an effervescent local tonic to dispel some of the gathering industrial gloom.

Everton were favourites, and the Liverpool team contained only Elisha as a survivor from the great years of the 1920s. But the visitors still had some reputable performers – and were reassuringly chock-full of Scottish men. Scott's place in goal was now increasingly challenged by Arthur Riley. Jim Jackson played at the back, and Gordon Hodgson was the key Liverpool man up front. Willie Steel, an intelligent Scottish full-back, replaced the more attack-minded Runcorn man Robert Done on the left side, and it was he who accompanied Jackson and fellow countryman 'Tiny' Tom Bradshaw, a strapping 6 ft centre-half in the Liverpool backline. Bradshaw had played in the 'Wembley Wizards' Scotland team that had thrashed England 5–1 in 1928, but, perversely, this had proved to be his only cap. He had been signed by Liverpool for £8,000 from Bury in 1930 and eventually clocked up some 291 Liverpool performances.

At right-half, Tom Morrison, another Scot, made over two hundred and fifty appearances for Liverpool but won no senior trophies and scored only four goals for the club – a consistent rather than a dynamic contributor in a fallow Liverpool period. Something similar could probably be said of the superior Scotland international at left-half, Jimmy McDougall, a man who skippered his country twice and, like Ray Kennedy many years after him, was originally a forward who was converted by the club to a left-sided midfield player. Between 1928 and 1937, the stocky and cultured McDougall was consistently first choice at Liverpool, making 338 league starts in total. Another Scot, Danny McRorie, played against Everton on the right-wing, having temporarily replaced the more established Lancastrian favourite Harry Barton, who switched to centre-forward alongside Hodgson. At inside-forward was yet another Scottish recruit, the bald-headed utility forward David Wright, who was standing in for the injured Archie McPherson, a clever but rather goal-shy inside-left. Completing the line-up at outside left, and along with 'Tiny' Bradshaw the only ever-present for Liverpool in the 1931–32 season, was Chester-born Gordon Gunson, a precision crosser and the man who scored the crucial equalising goal against Everton that helped keep Liverpool in the FA Cup.

In the new W–M formation, the still-unnumbered 1932 Liverpool FA Cup side lined up like this:

Liverpool FC v. Everton, FA Cup round three, 9 January 1932

Scott

Jackson   Bradshaw   Steel

Morrison   McDougall

Hodgson   Wright

McRorie   Barton   Gunson

Football attendances had been hit hard in the city by a combination of the economic downturn and inconsistent form, especially from Liverpool. In 1927–28, the Reds averaged just a fraction under 30,000 for league matches compared to champions Everton's 37,461. In Everton's single season in Division Two, in 1930–31, Liverpool's average crowds just bettered those at Goodison, with both clubs touching a little over 26,000. But by 1931–32, at the height of economic depression, Liverpool's average crowds, for a tenth-place league finish, had slumped to a post-war low of 22,742, with crowds at champions Everton up again, to 35,451. In the years leading up to the Second World War, only in 1933–34 did Liverpool's average attendances top those at Everton, although little divided the teams in terms of league performance at this time, until Everton won the league title again in 1939.

During this period of severe economic difficulty, people who could not afford to attend at Anfield would simply stand outside the ground to savour the atmosphere and, on hearing a roar inside, would chant 'Who scored?', awaiting the inevitable reply.[3] When the Pilgrim Trust reported on unemployment in Liverpool in 1938, it noted that unemployed men who could not afford the shilling entrance fee used to turn up on Saturday afternoons just to watch the crowds going to the match.[4] On 9 January 1932, the *Evening Express* captured well the real sense of occasion and the symbolic importance generated by the FA Cup meeting between the Merseyside clubs, especially in the midst of so much local economic uncertainty and poverty. Three policemen were reported to be on the roof of the Goodison Road stand to monitor the heaving crowds. Many people in the city clearly still had money to spend on association football and its various, gaudy paraphernalia, as the local press reported:

> Rattles swung vigorously kept their owners warm, while all kinds of Red and Blue favours were being sold by vendors who met with a ready sale. These favours ranged from red and blue roses to celluloid dolls dressed in red and blue, names of star players being stamped on them. The crowds

were boisterously cheerful. 'All seats now guaranteed' was one catch-phrase they shouted. Some of the fans wore blue or red bowlers and sashes of similar colours.

There was a great demand for hot tea and coffee which was supplied by the shops in the vicinity . . . By 1 p.m., thousands of spectators were already in the ground but still they came. Crowded tramcars arrived every few minutes, while motor-cars, taxi-cabs and omnibuses set down hundreds more. A strong force of foot and mounted police marshalled the crowds. They were happy crowds. What was a bump or a push on a day like this?

Evertonians were happier still when after just 15 seconds of the contest the talismanic Dean scored against a strange-looking Liverpool 'in their somewhat vermilion-coloured shirts'. The Liverpool captain Bradshaw had been a doubt all week, with doctors attending his pleurisy, and it was his misunderstanding with Morrison that let 'the Blue Devil' Dean in to beat Elisha Scott with a left-footed shot via the inside of the near post. But the Reds defender gathered his men about him in heroic fashion, aided, of course, by 'Parson' Jackson and the astonishing Reds keeper Scott. Gunson got Liverpool's first-half equaliser after the ball broke to him following a rather aimless free-kick taken by the fouled McRorie. Now came the turning point. 'With the score at 1–1,' reported the *Evening Express*, 'Dean delivered one of his best headers. It looked all over a goal, but Scott, who had advanced from his goal, clutched at the ball with the keenness and quickness of a cat and held it.' How many times had Scott saved Liverpool? With 15 minutes left and Everton increasingly nervous and under pressure, Gunson and Wright combined to release Hodgson, whose 'task was easy and pleasurable for a man of his size'. The South African shrugged off two defenders to score robustly past Ted Sagar in the Everton goal. 'Never was a scorer so pounced upon by his own men,' reported the *Evening Express*. The scenes that followed were 'fifteen minutes of full-blooded cup-tie enthusiasm', but Liverpool survived intact. At the final whistle, 'roars nearly wrecked the roof of the stand'.

After the match, Everton captain Dixie Dean graciously crossed to the celebrations at Anfield to personally congratulate Scott and Liverpool in a short speech in which he also thanked the Reds for 'beating some of the best clubs in the league' that season, so aiding Everton's latest (and ultimately successful) league-title challenge.

Could it be the FA Cup *at last* for Liverpool? How many times had their supporters had similar hopes? The lord mayor and lady mayoress followed the Reds to Second Division Chesterfield in round four, where ground attendance records were broken and red balloons and rattles were much in evidence. It proved to be Harry Barton's match. The makeshift Reds centre-forward was 'like a greyhound out of the leash'. By half-time, Liverpool led 3–0, all three goals scored by the Liverpool flyer who simply had too much pace for Chesterfield's lumbering defenders. He scored a fourth, too, in a 4–2 stroll for the visitors. Next season it would get even better for Barton, a hat-trick from the wing in a 7–4 Anfield derby extravaganza against Everton.

A home tie against First Division Grimsby Town was Liverpool's – and Barton's – reward, but it proved a tense battle. Town played 'splendid football', according to the *Daily Post*. The Reds needed encouragement – 'in this case the crowd unmistakably carried the victory to the home side, after a struggle by Grimsby against fate and her curious tricks'. It was the Kop to the rescue once again. When Gunson hurtled in to head the winner from a cross by Wright and ended up standing enmeshed in the back of the Kop goal, 'it created a crush in the Spion Kop and many injuries for those caught in the jam'. Cup-cursed Liverpool were in the FA Cup quarter-finals once again, this time to face a moderate Chelsea at home.

The eyes of the British sporting public were on Anfield – or at least they *could* have been: Liverpool refused permission for 'cinematographic photos' to be taken of the contest. Both Paramount Pictures and British Movietone wanted to film but for no fee. Liverpool FC simply locked the cameras out. The Merseyside sporting press was at yet another pitch of FA Cup excitement, but it was all to no avail once more. Chelsea's Hughie Gallagher was just too cute at centre-forward for the towering Bradshaw, the latter colliding with Chelsea's Harry Miller and cutting an eyebrow as Gallagher pounced on a cross 'in the last breath of the first half' for the crucial first goal. Liverpool then panicked, its 'wild, erratic attack' crying out for more composure in a frenetic second half. But Chelsea scored again on the break, and Liverpool's best opportunity to win the FA Cup before the Second World War would intervene had gone. This was also effectively Elisha Scott's last chance of FA Cup glory. Everton would win the FA Cup in 1933, beating Manchester City 3–0 in the final.

ELISHA SCOTT'S 'MATCHLESS' KOP

After the lame 1932 FA Cup exit to Chelsea, the much-abused Liverpool shareholders seemed finally to be shamed into some action. Clause 66 of the Articles of Association of 1906 allowed the Liverpool directors to replace any retiring or deceased director with someone of their own choosing. The board was a self-selecting members' club. Uniquely, 83 disgruntled Reds shareholders now called for an extraordinary general meeting to demand that new Liverpool directors must be elected at an AGM. One shareholder, Tom Sayle, also demanded that each of his colleagues receive a copy of the Articles of Association and the name and number of shares held by each shareholder. The board decided it could not entertain this final request and voted to 'pledge ourselves individually and collectively to use all our power' to re-elect retiring board members. But from then on, at least the election and re-election of Liverpool board members would be done in public in front of shareholders – although the process was still very tightly controlled by the existing board.

Also in 1932, the *Liverpool Echo* sent the fearless Bee onto the Spion Kop – it seems Everton had no equivalent terrace spectacle to scrutinise – in order to gauge local sentiment and assess the knowledge and varied make-up of these partisan Reds supporters who had such a strong affinity with their cultish Irish goalkeeper. Bee's mission produced one of the first early pieces of journalistic anthropology on football fans. It offered real insights into the inner life of one of the great pre-war football terraces. The account was presented rather as investigative journalists in the city had earlier penetrated local gangs or else explored desperate communities pierced by poverty and disease. 'I climbed the steps of the Kop,' the piece began, apprehensively, but then:

> Here was loyalty, here was belief; here was a trusting nature; they cursed the directors for having missed the Cup boat; they had commentaries on all phases of play, players, press and from their unequalled view they reckoned they saw things that the people in other parts of the ground could not hope to see. Yes, the Kop is the home of the loyalists.
>
> Two women were there, one in chocolate brown and another daring to wear a blue hat, a tricky thing of beret design, but the colour scheme did not seem to be quite inviting, as she was in the Anfield ground. Two swarthy sons of Ireland came beside me. They had come to see the MA of goalkeepers, Elisha Scott. One wore a black velvet beret and a film face that suggested a Valentino. He was plainly of Basque extraction and was silent as the grave . . .
>
> Where I had expected slashing attacks on players, I found praise and kindness. The kind way they talked of the players astonished me. True, Liverpool were playing better, but these were embittered partisans who could hardly forgive a Cup defeat. They were an object lesson to me . . . Their sportsmanship was a great feature; their language was fit and proper, and they treated the players encouragingly and in a sporting manner. Anfield's all right if they can keep this man at their back. They have tantalised him, he says, by some of their movements, but he's loyal to the core and he goes on talking his matches, debating his matches. This spectator is matchless.

This sort of approving media coverage only added, of course, to the early mystique and reputation of this great football beast. Watching football from here was no longer about simply taking one's place on just any goal-end terrace, a man lost in the crowd. The Kop itself was a performer, a football forcing ground with a membership of tens of thousands and a disarmingly fearsome goalkeeper as its spiritual leader. The Liverpool defence had Elisha Scott, and behind Scott there was the priceless Kop. How could the club be in such a slump with these unique assets?

In 1932, J.G. Hickling, the secretary of Huddersfield Town, argued that with 7.30 p.m. kick-offs under lights, the game could easily 'double the followers of football', with club bank overdrafts becoming a thing of the past.[5] But both the FA and the Football League were dubious in a climate of economic downturn, and, like most innovations in the English game, it would take another 20 years for this one to really catch on.

Meanwhile, despite the Kop's obvious intelligence, loyalty and support at this time, Liverpool continued to struggle horribly. At the end of the 1932–33 season, there was a player clear-out at Anfield, with 16 professionals placed on the transfer list. The totemic Scott even wrote to the club's directors saying that he was considering retirement – he had been complaining about pay, had been slack in training and Arthur Riley was back in the Liverpool goal. In the league in 1933–34, it was a disaster, with Liverpool at one stage going thirteen games without a win and looking certainties for the drop. It was Gordon Hodgson (who else?) who came to the rescue in March 1934, scoring a hat-trick against Middlesbrough in a 6–2 win and all four goals against Birmingham in a 4–1 victory. The South African forward was beyond value for Liverpool now, and Harry Hibbs, the England goalkeeper, described Hodgson as 'the greatest shooter he had ever known'.

But things were still in the balance when the Reds – without Elisha Scott – visited Hillsborough on 21 April, even though the home club 'looked upon Liverpool with a friendly eye'. Liverpool were slaughtered by Wednesday's football, but the home team could not get a lead that would stick. At 1–1, replacement keeper Arthur Riley suddenly came into the picture. 'He had not had his fingernails cut or he would not have stopped a ball from crossing the line,' said the *Echo* reporter. 'That save will always remain in my mind as the save that kept Liverpool from the Second Division.' This moment possibly changed the course of a club's entire history. Bootle-born Alf Hanson (unfortunately christened Adolph) then scored Liverpool's improbable winner with a 'cross-grained drive' to keep the Red Men just about afloat for another season. Saved from the drop by Elisha Scott's replacement and a man called Adolph. What next lay in store in the 1930s, in this 'morbid age', for Liverpool Football Club?

FACING THE UNTHINKABLE – ELISHA SCOTT LEAVES LIVERPOOL

The royal opening of the Mersey tunnel in 1934 symbolised the slow upturn in the economic fortunes of the city of Liverpool. The tunnel was fundamental to improving local transport links for a new generation of businesses that might bring a wider range of much-needed employment to the Merseyside area. But the diversification of Liverpool industries over the next decade should not be exaggerated. The Liverpool University-based social scientist David Caradog Jones argued in 1934 that the industrial landscape of Liverpool 'was very easily sketched', and this remained the case for many years to follow.[6] On 16 January 1934, the Liverpool Football Club directors decided they should each have a special card granting permission for their entrance to the car park from Anfield Road. Club officials would now have more and more special privileges to mark them out from ordinary spectators.

These new arrangements might have been a red-letter day for the club's directors, but the date 18 April 1934 was certainly more important for most Liverpool football supporters. The Merseyside press announced what many Reds fans probably thought was unthinkable: that Elisha Scott, fast approaching his 40th birthday, was 'not wanted' by Liverpool and that he must look for another club. Even given Scott's advanced age, it is difficult to think of a more contentious proposed transfer in the entire history of Liverpool Football Club. This moment certainly compares with Bill Shankly's shock retirement announcement 40 years later. In 1928, Everton had first asked about Scott but were rebuffed. In January 1930, the Liverpool minute books show that the club had actually secretly accepted an offer from Everton of £5,000 for the keeper. As luck would have it, the Ulsterman injured an ankle and the proposed deal was called off, thus avoiding a local earthquake. But four years later this parting of the ways looked like the real thing – and Everton were involved once again. The *Echo* saw this development as a 'shock' to the supporters on the Kop, who were losing both 'an institution' and one of their own. But it also reasoned that supporters should not go 'off the deep end' in their opinions about the break in a long chain. This breach with the past had to come sooner or later. The *Echo* might have saved its breath. A reader's letter of 19 April 1934 signed 'Red' was typical of the local response:

> To say that the action of the Liverpool directors in relation to Elisha Scott is a bombshell with violence to his countless admirers in this city is to put it very mildly. Not only is it a knockout blow to the team but what is even more important, the *coup de grâce* delivered by the directors to the most loyal and wholehearted band of supporters to be found wherever the game is played.

I submit they have alienated that great-hearted crowd who have cheered and 'gagged' their best beloved star and idol during all these years.

Another emotional letter writer, who signed his missive 'Disgusted' and had it published on 24 April, saw the whole process as demeaning, both to the club and to a great servant who was still needed:

To think, the one and only Elisha should have to submit to the indignity of a transfer is unthinkable, especially as it is being proved week in and week out where the weakness is. He is the world's best. The 'owld man' could do for me if he came out and played in goal on crutches.

Some of this was just rhetoric, a product of frustration. Scott's brilliant career with Liverpool stretched back to before the First World War, and he was the last link to the 1920s championship years, but he was now also well past his best. What really hurt was the idea that this Liverpool icon, possibly the club's greatest-ever footballer, would now be sold on by the Liverpool board, just like *any other player* might be.

These sorts of feelings intensified when it was mischievously intimated that *Everton* might be the club interested in signing Scott. In fact, the Ulsterman wrote two letters to Bee of the *Liverpool Echo* on this matter, the first saying, 'I think the loyal Anfielders are upsetting the directors more than you and me. If you know of any Second or Third Division club wanting a goalkeeper, I am prepared to go to them.' The second took a very different tack: it stated that discussions had been ongoing and that Scott had actually been prepared to sign for Everton that afternoon for £250, 'but, unfortunately, there is a hitch. I don't know what for.' The Liverpool board had stepped in as a flood of letters from the club's supporters made their views clear: letting the great Elisha go was one thing but letting him go to Everton was tantamount to writing a collective suicide note. That deal was off. Instead, Scott eventually returned to Ireland as player–manager for Belfast Celtic, winning the Irish league championship seven times between 1935 and 1941.

Because he was injured, Elisha missed the season's closing fixture at Anfield against Manchester City, but a microphone was set up in the Main Stand for his goodbyes. It was a poor crowd, the stadium barely one-third full. Was this a protest from Liverpool supporters against the board? The Liverpool chairman Walter Cartwright, another from the Liverpool 'family' of administrators and who was followed into the role later by his son Harold in the late 1960s, told the crowd that the club would honour the full share of Scott's accrued benefit.

'Scott has taken the view that football is a young man's game,' he continued, 'and it was his own desire to make room for a younger man.' The Kop then howled its unhappiness when a young supporter broke the spell by running onto the pitch to get a better view of matters. The intensely private and obviously emotional Scott then spoke in his distinctive Belfast growl. 'We have always been the best of friends and shall always remain so. I have finished with English association football. Last, but not least, my friends of the Kop. I cannot thank them sufficiently. They have inspired me. God bless you all.' A generation of working-class men had grown up with this stooped, wiry figure guarding the Liverpool goal in front of them, risking life and limb. And now it was all over. Many hardened men were in tears. It was, indeed, the end of an era.

The brilliant Elisha Scott was never forgotten by those Liverpool supporters who had grown up with him on the Kop during his 468-match Liverpool career. When the great goalkeeper died some 25 years later, in 1959, floods of letters reached the offices of the *Liverpool Echo*, all packed with memories of Scott and of his unique relationship with the Liverpool fans. Where was such togetherness now, they asked? One recalled a popular local story about a complete stranger who had stopped Scott and launched into a long conversation outside Anfield in the 1930s. Eventually, a perplexed Elisha asked the man, 'Do I know you?', to which his new friend indignantly replied, 'You ought to. I threw the ball back to you from the Kop last Saturday!' Billy Liddell and later Kenny Dalglish would both become great Liverpool idols, but, arguably, neither would have the affinity with ordinary Liverpool fans once enjoyed by the incomparable Elisha Scott.

SURVIVING THE POST-ELISHA ERA

With a new bunch of recruits, Liverpool tried to turn things around in the post-Elisha Scott period. The Liverpool minute books tell us that in 1934 the Reds board resolved that 'In all future cases of players being secured for a transfer fee an independent medical certificate and birth certificate be obtained'. Too many players in the past had been found later to have lied about their age and their fitness. These new Liverpool men included two full-backs to try to stem the flood of goals flushing past Arthur Riley. The elegant, sweet-passing Stoke-born England right-back and captain Tom Cooper was signed from Derby County for £7,500 in December 1934. He followed in another England man, the cultured left-back Ernie Blenkinsop, who had come from Sheffield Wednesday for a £5,000 fee in March. Here, it seemed at last, was a full-back pairing with the potential to replace the great Longworth and McKinlay partnership of the 1920s.

Bob Savage, a tall and strong right-half, stepped up from the Liverpool reserves, and Cheshire-born Fred Howe came in from little Hyde United to bolster a forward line that, apart from Hodgson, had lacked presence and devil for years. When Liverpool memorably thumped an injury-hit Everton 6–0 in the league in September 1935, with the largely one-footed Howe scoring four times, the *Liverpool Echo* exhorted, 'Let us encourage Howe and believe he is the centre we have so long looked for. We have stared into the past 25 years for a leader.' A week later, Liverpool lost 0–6 at Manchester City but then put seven goals past Grimsby Town. Who could manage this contrary team?

Despite the best efforts of Howe and the South Africans, Carr and Nieuwenhuys, there was to be no Liverpool renaissance in the late 1930s. The exhausted Gordon Hodgson was sold to Aston Villa in January 1936 for £3,000. Goals conceded by Liverpool were reduced, but just 17 league goals scored away from home in 1935–36 told its own sorry story. And while Liverpool and some of the other northern giants of the past struggled in the 1930s, so Arsenal began to fly the flag for professional football in the south of England, bolstering traditional north-south antipathies and adding fuel to suggestions that southern successes on the field of play increasingly reflected material inequalities off it.[7]

Arsenal were also the national darlings of the new age of broadcasting about football, but Liverpool FC would continue to be one of a number of league clubs who would be staunchly opposed to live broadcasting or to allowing newsreel companies ground access. But in other ways club communications were improving. In 1935–36, for example, Liverpool FC produced its own one-penny, red-fronted match programme for the first time, finally breaking away from the weekly black-and-white effort that had been jointly issued with Everton. By 1938, the programme price had doubled to twopence, but there were also cover photos and lively features for the committed to enjoy. The club's minute books reveal that by March 1939 a home crowd of 18,380 produced programme sales of 2,805 – about one in six fans bought one. By 1950, the club was pressed to issue warnings about supporters buying 'pirate' programmes on sale outside the ground (early fanzines?) as official sales rose to 25,000 before the post-war paper shortage in 1951 halved the print run.

A promising if fragile young Liverpool-born inside-forward called Jack Balmer now began to get a few first-team starts, and he impressed good judges, as did the versatile future England international Phil Taylor, who was bought in from Bristol Rovers for £5,000 in March 1936. We would hear more about these two men later. Notable, too, was the signing from Manchester City for £8,000 of a stylish young Scottish half-back called Matt Busby. Busby was a converted inside-forward who lacked the pace to play higher up the field, but he was technically excellent and a cultured thinker and distributor, a true leader at half-back. Like so many players, Busby's playing career would be severely curtailed by the war. The Liverpool board agreed that it had paid an 'extremely high figure' for the half-back but that it had acted wisely and had 'laid something in for the future' of the club.

John McKenna, the remaining original founder of Liverpool FC, finally died on 22 March 1936 in Walton Hospital, Liverpool, aged almost 82. He had devoted his entire life to football. In his last few years, the strictly anti-gambling McKenna had seen tensions grow between the Football League and the Liverpool-based Pools Promoters Association. The pools companies relied on access to league fixtures for their business, which now attracted an estimated six or seven million punters. But the Football League management committee was still morally opposed to any sort of match betting. In February 1936, the crunch finally came, and the Football League refused to confirm the weekend's fixtures. Chaos ensued, with confused football supporters, and even parliament, siding with the pools companies. Eventually, the league backed down, deriding claims from John Moores of Liverpool's Littlewoods Pools that league representatives *had* talked about demanding 'exorbitant' amounts of money in possible payment for exclusive access to fixture lists at an earlier meeting. In the end, the public outcome was that the Football League refused to accept any payment from the PPA for sole use of the fixtures, and the pools companies continued to make their huge profits. In effect, it was like football throwing cash away.

MANAGING THE COUNTDOWN TO WAR IN A CAR WITHOUT PETROL

On 14 July 1936, the Liverpool board advertised for a football manager who might better understand the emerging modern game. Fifty-two applications were received. The club recruited, from Southampton, George Kay on £600 per annum and a £250 bonus for finishing first or second in the league. He brought with him trainer Albert Shelley. The Liverpool board even resolved to build a manager's office for the first time, erected by Tyson and Co. for £63 in 1936. However, the issue of a new 'boss' was typically discussed at the 1936 Liverpool AGM *not* in terms of the importance of bringing in an experienced and influential football manager, but of releasing George Patterson from his residual management duties 'because the value of secretarial work was growing enormously'. The main question from the AGM floor revealed how little the manager's post was valued by shareholders: would the appointment of a new manager involve the payment of an extra salary?

The Manchester-born Kay had spent most of his playing career with West Ham United, and he had captained the Hammers in the first Wembley FA Cup final, in 1923. Kay certainly knew the game, and he was sympathetic to players, even if it was difficult to describe him as a 'tracksuit manager'. Kay insisted on always wearing a collar and tie, in order to identify with the board and club officials above rather than with the dressing-room below. This may explain why he favoured 'left-wing' politics but also sent his two sons to Winchester public school. But Kay was a good talker and motivator, and he could get close to professional players. Matt Busby, for example, was greatly influenced by Kay and the way he managed to treat his players at Liverpool with loyalty and consideration, compared to the brutality of the regime Busby had experienced at Manchester City. Busby also saw how the pressures of the job eventually got to Kay, who was often seen 'shouting, beseeching – wringing his hands, holding his head in apparent anguish, and making an excellent attempt to head and kick every ball in the match' from the trainer's bench.[8]

George Kay had more to say on transfers and tactics on the pitch, and perhaps he also had a little more luck than some previous Liverpool managers had, because it was Kay who sat in the manager's chair at Anfield in the summer of 1938 when the club made its best signing for almost 30 years – and for no fee. A slight 16-year-old winger called Liddell scrawled his signature on the dotted line as an amateur. On 17 March 1939, he signed professional forms on £3 a week in the Liverpool A team. Here was a future Reds hero to take over the mantle from the departed Elisha Scott.

The son of a Scottish miner, Liddell had played both rugby and football at school, and he had considered careers in both the ministry and in accounting while playing soccer for Lochgelly Violet for 2s 6d expenses. When Partick Thistle fatally hesitated over taking Liddell, it was Matt Busby who rang George Kay suggesting that Liverpool take a look at the boy.

Soon after, Liverpool's Scottish scout Johnny Dougary visited the Liddell home with an offer. 'Willie, how would you like to live in Liverpool?' Chairman Bill McConnell and George Kay then visited and offered Liddell's parents two assurances: they would provide 'homely' accommodation for young Liddell, and their son would be able to continue his studies for accountancy. The deal was done. 'Willie' would live with the widow of Ted Doig, the ex-Liverpool and Scotland goalkeeper. Liddell recalled later how the very different characters of the two men who came to Scotland – men who each had an intense love of Liverpool Football Club – did the necessary convincing. 'Mr McConnell, quick and volatile, Mr Kay, inclined to introspection and slower to make up his mind, made a wonderful pair, the one the ideal foil for the other.' The inspiring, fast-talking local man McConnell especially impressed Liddell with his rags-to-riches story of a Liverpool-crazy youngster, shirt hanging out his pants and holes in his shoes, blagging his way into Anfield as a boy. After many years at sea, McConnell eventually became the proprietor of restaurants and dockside canteens in the city before becoming a director and then the chairman of the football club he loved. Manager George Kay impressed the caring Liddell in a rather different way:

> If ever a man gave his life for a club George Kay did so for Liverpool. He had no other thought but the good of Liverpool during his waking hours, and also during many of his nights. He told me often of the time he had lain in bed, unable to sleep, pondering over the manifold problems that beset every manager, but which can be a curse to the overly-sensitive or excessively conscientious ones.[9]

As football writer Percy Young put it in relation to the Billy Liddell capture by Liverpool, 'One man does not make a team, but one outstanding personality can do much to fix the positive image of a team.'[10] Liddell would define the post-war era for Liverpool, but in an early A-team game at Blackburn in 1939 he suffered a 'badly injured knee' in a horrible collision with concrete posts sited too close to the pitch. The Reds board heaved a huge sigh of relief as their new prospect slowly recovered. Reflecting the traditional relations between a club board and players at that time – but also the essential decency of Liddell as both a man and an employee – in 1960 Tom Williams, chairman of Liverpool, said about the Scot, 'Whatever he has been asked to do he has done willingly and with good grace, content with the knowledge that even if it was occasionally not just what he would have preferred, it was for the good of Liverpool Football Club, which has always been his primary aim.'[11] Billy Liddell was a wonderful servant for Liverpool Football Club and the club's best post-war footballer for at least three decades.

Despite this crucial signing, George Kay would have his work cut out. Liverpool's form continued to oscillate alarmingly. After a three-goal loss to Second Division Norwich City in the FA Cup third round in January 1937, it was too much for many. Later in 1937, Kay tried to sell arguably the club's best players, Phil Taylor and Matt Busby, to raise funds for transfers. A letter from 'Paddock Mug' to the *Liverpool Echo* called on the entire board to resign and asked why Liverpool had spent thousands of pounds on full-backs when 'the pace of modern football was beginning to tell its tale' and 'when forwards were the urgent need'. Another letter writer, who signed off as 'No Work, No Pay', asked if the new Liverpool manager was 'restricted from purchasing much needed players', which would be like 'expecting a chauffeur to drive a car without petrol'. He wondered why the club's players were not sacked, because they were 'not worth their wages'. Players on the maximum wage at this time would have earned £386 per annum, about double a skilled worker's or a clerk's salary.[12] Yet another Merseyside letter writer argued that 'they [the board] have done nothing right' at Liverpool for some time and that Anfield Road lacked 'discipline'. It was a Liverpool Football Club low point, no doubt about it.

Bizarrely, Liverpool began their FA Cup campaign of 1938 in highly unusual red-and-white hoops against Crystal Palace, and in February 1938, after yet another FA Cup capitulation, this time at home to Huddersfield Town, the *Evening Express* reported on innovative plans among a group of Reds fans who wanted public feedback on an idea for the formation of a Liverpool Football Supporters Club. Meanwhile, Fred 'Bullet' Rogers, a tidy, blond Cheshire-born centre-half or right-half, played thirty times in the 1938–39 season, with young Balmer and the increasingly impressive Matt Busby being the two ever-presents in the Liverpool team.

'Prospects are brighter than for a long time,' commented the *Echo* in May 1938 about Liverpool's supposed recent progress. This was more in hope than expectation. Albert Shelley had replaced the ailing Charlie Wilson, and he, the manager and a number of directors even attended an FA training course in Leeds in 1938 as the new approach to coaching in England slowly began to take hold in the ranks of professionals. The message from club chairman Will Harrop in the first match programme of 1938–39 was an idealistic call for supporter patience: 'We cannot command success . . . Never forget the players are not machines and they are not machine-made, and to err is human, to forgive divine.' But when, on 1 October, the Merseyside clubs met for the Goodison derby, won by Everton 1–2, it was a sense of denial about the possibility of war that was very much in the air: a special performance of the national anthem took place to mark the return of Prime Minister Chamberlain from Munich. English club footballers touring Germany were among the few who could see a nation gearing up for war. At least Liverpool managed to drag themselves up to a respectable 11th-place finish in this final league table before the conflict began in 1939. But they had to look a long way upwards to see neighbours and rivals Everton, reigning supreme as champions again.

On 6 May 1939, the 'international situation', as it was now euphemistically called in the press, was said by the *Echo* not to interfere with Liverpool's post-season plans to tour Sweden. But the Liverpool club became the first in Britain to announce that all its players, the manager George Kay and assistant secretary Jack Rouse were to join the Territorial Army as a unit: 'A grand example to the remainder of the football world.' Albert Shelley had to treat the players' feet for blisters after route marches in ill-fitting army boots.[13] These seemed like strangely mixed messages from Anfield as the country now prepared for war.

RED MEN

The band struck up 'Auld Lang Syne' on 6 May 1939 as Manchester United and Liverpool players left the field at a final league match of 'intense dullness', according to the *Daily Post*. 'It would certainly be a hardening off process,' said the *Echo*, not wholly convincingly, in assessing the forthcoming TA military training period for the Liverpool players. 'They would certainly be 100 per cent fit for the start of the new season – if any!' Of course, at this precise moment no one could say exactly when the world's oldest football league might restart. Or, indeed, exactly *which* Liverpool Football Club it would be that arose again from the ashes of war.

CHAPTER 9 REFERENCES

1. Keith, *Dixie Dean: The Inside Story of a Football Icon*
2. Belchem, 'Celebrating Liverpool', p. 38
3. Liversedge, *Liverpool, We Love You!*, p. 22
4. Mason, 'The Blues and the Reds', p. 20
5. Taylor, *The Leaguers*, p. 259
6. Milne, 'Maritime Liverpool', pp. 264 and 270
7. Russell, *Looking North*, p. 255
8. Carter, *The Football Manager*, pp. 71 and 79
9. Liddell, *My Soccer Story*, pp. 28–9
10. Young, *Football on Merseyside*, p. 131
11. Liddell, *My Soccer Story*, p. 9
12. Taylor, *The Leaguers*, p. 115
13. Rippon, *Gas Masks for Goal Posts*, p. 9

10

FOOTBALL LIFE DURING WARTIME
Surviving the Conflict and Emerging Stronger

WAR STOPS PLAY

At the AGM of the Football League in 1939, the main agenda items were, to say the least, varied. Elliptical goalposts were made standard at all Football League grounds, though they would keep square posts for many years in parts of Scotland. It was also made compulsory that players wore numbers – though when Liverpool played Walsall in the FA Cup in January 1947 the Third Division Midlands men were recklessly numberless (Reds player Bob Paisley was also kicked by a fan when leaving the field). The league had finally caught up with some of the pre-war ideas of Herbert Chapman. But much more substantive problems now loomed in the sport. Professional players would get numbers on more than their shirts in 1939 – they would also be on their call-up cards.[1] When war was finally declared on 3 September 1939 and the assembly of large crowds was banned by the Home Office, the Football League remembered the painful controversy of 1914 and this time went immediately onto a war footing. They dusted down the arrangements for regional competition that had been formulated during the First World War.

There had been time for just three normal league fixtures in the 1939–40 campaign, with the 19-year-old Liverpool-born Cyril Done, an uncomplicated and direct forward presence, reportedly putting 'pep' into Liverpool's attack by scoring his first Football League goal in a closing 1–0 win against Chelsea at Anfield. Many of the Liverpool players in the forces had been on military duty until the early hours of that Saturday morning, and the band at the match played 'old time' war songs, with the teams coming out to the winsome strains of 'It's a Long Way to Tipperary'. At the end, Liverpool stood fourth in the embryonic league table for 1939–40 – who could have guessed what was going to happen in the rest of the season? Then, Britain's foes in Europe called 'time' on Football League action. For how long, no one knew.

The players' union agreed that in matches played for charity during the war their members would play without remuneration, and on 16 September 1939 the *Evening Express* reported that the local police authorities had given permission for the Merseyside clubs to play in a 'sectional competition'. All players' contracts were cancelled, although, crucially, clubs still held the registration of players and crowds were initially restricted to 15,000. It was agreed that the players be paid 30 shillings a match, raised to £2 in 1943. The players' union claimed it was a licence for clubs to profiteer.

Liverpool warmed up for the new challenge with friendly matches against Chester and Blackburn Rovers. The trip to Ewood Park was typically eventful for the time. Five Liverpool players made it to Ormskirk Station and were then joined at 2.10 p.m. by George Kay and Jack Rouse. Liverpool director Ronnie Williams went on ahead to Blackburn in his car to tell Rovers that the visitors would be late. But his vehicle broke down. Other Liverpool players eventually arrived from military duty and the match kicked off, considerably delayed. Wartime football would often be a chaotic affair. Apparently unaffected, Liverpool won 5–0 at Rovers – and the score could easily have been doubled.

When the regional football competitions began, they were deemed a success, attracting not far short of 200,000 spectators on the first weekend. But this was still less than one-third of normal gates. Anfield crowds fell dramatically if the opposition was weak, but the story was the same elsewhere. Twelve clubs, including Liverpool, lined up in the strangely titled Western Division, and just fewer than 5,000 supporters, sprinkled with khaki, saw a broadly familiar Liverpool line-up defeat Stockport County 3–0 at Anfield in the first fixture. Despite the reduction in competitive football, the vigilant Football League still found plenty of vital things to do, of course. Liverpool FC were fined in 1939–40, for example, for admitting juveniles for fourpence, instead of the minimum charge of sixpence. It was something short of a hanging offence in the circumstances.

The careers of a whole generation of football players and staff were hugely affected by the war. By June 1940, Liverpool announced it could no longer pay salaries to its staff, and manager George Kay was placed on £4 per week with a week's notice. He was given a cash float of £50 for 'emergencies'. Bob Paisley, a dour but highly productive left wing-half who had been recruited from Bishop Auckland, impressed in pre-war Liverpool trials, and he played 32 times for Liverpool in the early years of the war. But from 1941, Paisley was abroad with the British Army, making his return to play for Liverpool only in September

1945. Meanwhile, George 'Stonewall' Jackson, the Everton full-back, played for both of the major Merseyside clubs, including, during emergencies, as a goalkeeper. He once played in goal for wartime Liverpool against Everton in a 3–1 Reds win, an example that shows both the flexibility necessary for wartime football and also the essential lack of competitive edge now involved, even in local derbies. Small clubs crammed with guest players routinely beat the game's giants. Young talent still shone through, however. In March 1940, manager George Kay described Liverpool's 18-year-old trainee chartered accountant Billy Liddell as 'the best thing that has come out of Scotland in the past ten years'. The coltish Tom Finney, England's equivalent of Liddell, also made his senior debut for Preston, at Anfield in August 1940, against a Liverpool team that boasted a star guest, Stan Cullis, at centre-half.

Several Liverpool players were promoted in the forces even before the fighting began. The South African goalkeepers Arthur Riley and Dirk Kemp, for example, were made sergeants in the 9th King's Liverpool Battalion. Tom Cooper, Willie Fagan, left-back Bernard Ramsden and the tall and elegant Reds left-half Tom Bush were promoted to lance corporals. Billy Liddell joined the RAF as a navigator and ended up serving in Canada, Bob Paisley became a desert gunner in the Royal Artillery, while Phil Taylor and Jackie Balmer were learning to drive tanks and Willie Fagan became a trench mortar expert.[2] Later, full-back Ted Spicer, a lieutenant in the marines, was promoted to captain after capturing a German NCO who turned out to be a football international!

Among those who were initially employed in reserved occupations, Berry Nieuwenhuys managed to find work on nights as a driller on Merseyside, mainly so he could continue to play golf during the day. 'Nivvy' had an interesting war. He had his jaw broken while guesting as a player in January 1943. As an RAF flight-sergeant, he was later decorated for his work with the Czech Fight Squadron. Then the wily South African captain of Liverpool was suspended for life (later rescinded) by the Football League for asking other clubs for more than the regulation £2 fee for wartime appearances. Liverpool had six players decorated for war service, including a Military Cross for the amateur Len Carney.

CELEBRITY FOOTBALL FOR WAR HEROES

The limits of the regulation football training and pre-war preparation of players in England was soon revealed by the fact that as the game settled down in the war years it was widely considered to be of better quality and to be at least a yard faster than its pre-war counterpart. The extra fitness showed in those players who were now marched and generally exercised on a daily basis in the Armed

Forces. But great sportsmen are also not immune from the very real dangers of war. Tragically, the stylish Reds full-back and regimental policeman Tom Cooper lost his life on 25 June 1940 when his motorcycle was in a head-on collision with a bus near Aldeburgh. He was the only Liverpool FC fatality during the conflict. Only Crystal Palace and Wolves contributed more than the 76 players in total from Liverpool FC who gave wartime service.

As the war dragged on, players turned out for their clubs whenever possible, but it all depended on where they were stationed and whether they could get leave. They could play for other clubs within a reasonable distance, with the consent of the club that held their registration. But this system was open to abuse, with star guests often replacing other willing players at the last minute. In February 1942, for example, the brilliant Irish international Peter Doherty travelled to Blackpool to watch Liverpool play, and he casually called into the Reds dressing-room before the match to chat with friends. He was immediately asked by George Kay to turn out for Liverpool, with Leeds United's George Ainsley cruelly being told to step down.

Clubs could also seemingly track down international footballers, even in camps of thousands of men. A youthful Bill Shankly later recalled being approached by Norwich City, and he played under the false name 'Newman' for the Canaries in January 1943, scoring twice in an 8–4 win against an army XI in front of 484 people.[3] But it was clearly a risk to have valuable professional players turning out for local clubs in uncertain conditions. Cyril Done, Matt Busby, Phil Taylor and Jack Balmer all played for the same works team to keep themselves fit and all suffered serious knocks. Liverpool's prize asset, Billy Liddell, stepped into a pothole on a pitch at Bridgnorth in 1943 and suffered serious injury just above the ankle. The damage might have ended Liddell's league career before it had even begun.

Liverpool finally gave in to the broadcasters when the BBC agreed to pay five guineas to cover the second half of the Liverpool v. Blackpool match on 14 February 1942 – the Reds lost 1–3. But, as the Liverpool minute books tell us, 11 years later it was conservative Liverpool FC who proposed a resolution to the Football League 'deploring the action of the FA in granting permission for the televising of the whole of the FA Cup final on 2 May 1953'.

Another way of trying to get wartime crowds interested in 'big name' recruits as guest players was to sign up unlikely star names from other sports. In 1944, Liverpool Football Club registered the world heavyweight boxing champion Joe Louis, then aged 30, but manager George Kay seemed reluctant to select the fighter to add punch to the Reds attack. As the *Evening Express* pointed out in October 1939, in wartime football 'names will still count in the matter of players, but not so much in the matter of clubs'. But, to be fair, there was plenty going on to deter even the most determined football fan from attending wartime football matches: air-raids, for example, often caused long delays to kick-offs, especially if some players were also ARP (air-raid protection) wardens who then had to report for duty.

Amazingly, the Liverpool football ground avoided suffering major war damage, though the strategically important city of Liverpool suffered substantially in the Blitz. Much of the national focus on the bravery of the British people, however, largely ignored Liverpool and other provincial cities (causing some resentment in the north) and homed in on London instead. But many Liverpudlians responded to the privations of war with typical innovation and energetic creativity. Almost anything – including, it was rumoured, Spitfire parts – could be found offered for sale in pubs in the city, and as the war and its misery progressed it became clear that 'the whole of Liverpool was beginning to feed and clothe itself on the black market'.[4] Football was also important in raising the national morale, especially after the initial shock of war slowly began to diminish. A letter to the *Evening Express* on 4 January 1940 commented, for example, that football in Liverpool was 'spirited and skilful to a high degree' and that 'football is a valuable asset to the home front and deserves the support of all lovers of our characteristically British game'. A survey by Mass Observation in 1940 found that 65 per cent of pre-war football supporters were not attending matches because of a variety of wartime reasons, but by 1945 the sport's followers were beginning to flood back to matches in Liverpool and elsewhere around the country.[5]

PLAYING FOR BRITAIN

In front of generally very modest crowds, Liverpool finished second to Stoke City in the 12-club Western Division in 1939–40. The really exciting news from the Reds camp was that on New Year's Day 1940 the 17-year-old Billy Liddell made his debut at Anfield against Crewe Alexandra and scored after just three minutes, a low header from a Nieuwenhuys cross in a 7–3 victory. When Liverpool won by the same score at Manchester City a week later, the *Evening Express* correspondent noted the outstanding 'brilliance' of the 'amazingly cool' Liddell and thought the Scotsman was 'the most promising young winger I have seen in years'. Here was potential already being realised. 'He is becoming two-footed and . . . uses his brains and has complete control over the ball,' enthused the *Express*. 'He had a direct hand in five of the Liverpool goals.'

The fact that the young Liddell seemed comfortable with either foot was entirely unusual in the English game in 1939 – as, indeed, it is today. Once, at

Preston North End, the winger lined up for a free-kick with his right foot but at the last moment the wind blew the ball across to his left. Without hesitating or changing stride, he struck the ball with his left instead, and it thundered past the bemused keeper. How could you stop him? In 1942, Liddell scored on his enthralling Scotland debut in a 5–4 win over England, and by 1943 the *Evening Express* was already describing Liddell as 'irresistible'. In September 1945, when Liverpool beat Everton 2–1 at Anfield, the Reds' fast, long-passing style overcame Everton's more intricate short-pass build-up, and the newspaper was simply in awe of the Scotsman. Liddell was 'unpredictable, like a flash of lightning, and the essence of versatility. Liddell . . . has everything.' The winger had destroyed Everton, scoring the first goal and terrorising the visitors' defence. 'Liddell,' said the *Express* with just the slightest trace of hyperbole, 'is one of the greatest, if not *the* greatest, all-round forwards in football.'

In 1946, Billy Liddell's immense talents were recognised internationally when he was selected to play in a Great Britain v. FIFA match at Hampden Park to celebrate the re-entry of the home countries into FIFA after the war and to raise money for the ailing international football body. The Great Britain forward line of Stanley Matthews, Wilf Mannion, Tommy Lawton, Billy Steel and Liddell is still argued by many good judges to be the greatest array of British forward talent ever assembled on these shores.[6] A crowd of 135,000 watched as the British XI thrashed FIFA's select 6–1, thus probably perpetuating the mistaken view in these islands that Britain was, inevitably, best at football and that it was great wingers rather than the tactical advances being made elsewhere that would really shape the modern game.[7]

In 1940–41, Liverpool played in the extended Northern Regional section, which listed the standings by percentage of 36 northern clubs that had played between 16 and 38 matches each, including local and national cup fixtures. Liverpool finished a mediocre 16th in a highly volatile competition, which produced results as varied as a 9–1 Reds win over neighbours Chester and a 6–4 victory over New Brighton, as well as two heavy defeats at the hands of Preston North End. Everton were played six times by Liverpool in the season to lift crowds, producing only one Liverpool win and four defeats. For the next three seasons, the Northern section was divided into two competitions for different numbers of clubs. These were staged, broadly speaking, before and after Christmas.

Liverpool actually finished top of the second Northern section in 1942–43, having ended up second to Blackpool in the first section. After beating Bolton Wanderers 4–0 at a one-quarter-full Anfield on 1 May 1943, the *Evening Express* congratulated the club on a 'really brilliant season' in which, even with these modest crowds, Liverpool had commanded 'a support as good as any – and better than most'. It credited everyone at the club, from chairman Robert Lawson Martindale down to each member of the ground staff. Manager George Kay was also praised as being a man who had taken on extra tasks and 'has had his finger on the pulse throughout the season . . . handling both managerial and secretarial duties with an amazing energy and conscientiousness'. In the two-legged Lancashire Cup final that followed – played for the prize of four saving certificates for each winner and two for every losing player – Manchester United won easily at Anfield in the first leg. This left Liverpool with a 1–3 deficit to make up at Maine Road. Jack Balmer scored a brave hat-trick in Manchester, but it could only produce an honourable 3–3 draw for Liverpool in the leg and thus no Lancashire Cup or savings-certificate extravaganza.

A SQUAD FIT FOR PURPOSE?

After the war, football gradually began to shake itself into recovery mode. In July 1945, less than three months after VE Day, Liverpool became the first senior English club to play on German soil after the hostilities, in two matches against British Forces teams. The Reds returned with a smart set of new red shirts, reputedly made of material previously used to make Nazi flags. In 1945–46, the Football League staged its transitional return to a forty-two-match programme in the shape of northern and southern versions of the league, with 'only' six guest players allowed. Liverpool, apparently returning to its moderate performances before the war, finished a disappointing 11th. The 1939 league champions Everton were threatening ominously once again, finishing second to Sheffield United. A version of the FA Cup returned, too, played over two legs, with the Reds easing past Chester in the third round. But then, with 5,000 Liverpool supporters travelling to Bolton in the next round, including in dozens of corporation double-decker buses, the visitors dominated the match but collapsed 0–5. Without the unavailable Liddell for the second leg, the Reds clawed two goals back, but that was all.

Bob Paisley, out of uniform at last, played 25 times in the transitional league in this rehearsal for real football combat the following season, and Fagan, Liddell and Jack Balmer combined well at forward to score 56 out of Liverpool's 80 league goals. Something important was clearly developing at Anfield. 'Beyond a shadow of a doubt,' concluded the *Evening Express* in August 1943, 'the war break has not impaired their abilities.' Young players were coming through strongly, gaining useful experience without the usual pressures brought by titles and relegation, large and demanding crowds, and the sheer treadmill of a normal league campaign. The backbone of a quietly impressive post-war Liverpool side was beginning to emerge at Anfield, out of the confusion and unfulfilled promise of the late 1920s and the 1930s.

Ideas about 'new beginnings', thus connecting with the prevailing national post-war sentiment of reform in Britain, were also prominent at the offices of the Football League in 1945. What about a British League or a new League Cup competition, members of the management committee were asked? Both were turned down. Everton (and others) wanted the FA Cup to be played over two legs from then on. But this money-spinning idea, designed to protect the larger clubs from early cup embarrassments, was again rejected. Radical proposals to modernise football, for example by having four up and four down in the league, were also put to the management committee. These notions especially incensed Ronnie Williams from ever-watchful Liverpool FC, who replied sternly, 'What was wrong with football [before the war]? Were the public dissatisfied?'[8]

Liverpool's regular and most impressive performers during the regional competitions in the Second World War included the very competent north-east goalkeeper Alf Hobson. Winger Berry Nieuwenhuys was still a fixture and he had been joined by future Wales international full-back Ray Lambert, a laid-back but highly consistent defender who would make 341 senior appearances for Liverpool. Club captain Willie Fagan and wing-half Phil Taylor, plus Liverpool-born right-half George Kaye and the emerging young forward talents of Jackie Balmer, Billy Liddell and Cyril Done were also prominent. Done scored an impressive 122 goals in just 103 wartime appearances from 1941 to 1944 before a broken leg cracked this rich spell. There was also an imposing and intelligent young centre-half from Liverpool, Laurie Hughes, who was beginning to make his mark. Though regularly troubled by injury himself, 'Big Lol' was a consistent and football-playing defender who would go on to parade his skills at international level for England in their ill-fated World Cup campaign in Brazil in 1950. He figured in all matches there, including the infamous 0–1 England defeat to the USA, which probably cost him his international career. Among this group of war 'veterans', the core of a new Liverpool title-winning team was slowly beginning to crystallise.

PLAYERS WANTED – MUST HAVE CHAMPIONSHIP POTENTIAL

There were still a few problem positions to attend to in order to produce the new Liverpool XI. The club even advertised for players: 'Particulars of age, height, weight and clubs played for (mark envelope "Trial") to be sent to George Kay,

Liverpool 4.'⁹ The South Africans Riley and Kemp were no longer options in goal, for example, and Alf Hobson would soon drift down to South Liverpool. So Cyril Sidlow was recruited by George Kay for £4,000 in February 1946 from Wolverhampton Wanderers. Sidlow's career had barely got off the ground at Molineux before war had intervened. But this Wales international was a good shot-stopper, and he was one of the few goalkeepers who had begun to explore throwing the ball out to half-backs and defenders as a more accurate means of holding onto possession. Just in his 30s, Sidlow was a generally mature and stabilising figure at the back, making a good combination with the emerging young centre-half Hughes.

At right-back the very spritely and tough Scottish defender Jim Harley, a war hero, stepped in to replace the much mourned Tom Cooper, and he briefly picked up his nascent pre-war partnership with Yorkshire-born left-back Barney Ramsden. When Stoke City hosted a sprint competition for £100 at the Victoria Ground in August 1944, the lightning ex-commando Harley – who had won the famous Powderhall Sprint as an 18 year old – took part. The elegant and cerebral Phil Taylor had taken over from Matt Busby, who was now finished with Liverpool at right-half. The brilliant Scot Busby might well have stayed much longer at Anfield, and he could even have changed the course of football history if Liverpool had made more positive noises about his possible management prospects there. Instead, Liverpool stuck with George Kay and offered Busby a five-year coaching contract. But Manchester United stepped in with a management job, and Busby took his chance at Old Trafford. It clearly riled the Liverpool board that Busby chose to leave the club, because an invitation for him to play in a farewell exhibition/benefit match was later withdrawn.

That pugnacious half-back Bob Paisley (very much part of Liverpool's glorious future, of course) was finally back from his foreign manoeuvres to play on the Liverpool left. The reinstated 'Nivvy' shared the right-wing slot with the clever Blackpool-born Harry Eastham, and they now partnered the prodigious Jack Balmer at inside-right. Balmer was a great cross-field passer, a man of real talent, but he split Liverpool supporters because of his deep reluctance to tackle. Balmer's footballing uncles had sensibly warned him to protect his ankles for his future health. Cyril Done and Willie Fagan shared duties at inside-left, with the precocious Billy Liddell outside. Bill Jones, a reliable and versatile defender, and Eddie Spicer, a tough-tackling full-back, made up the main Liverpool squad. Which left the crucial centre-forward berth to fill – it had been a problem position for Liverpool for the past 20 years. The Reds looked to the north for their man. They were not disappointed.

RED MEN

KING ALBERT

The powerful and speedy red-haired twenty-seven-year-old Geordie centre-forward Albert Stubbins, a former shipyard draughtsman, had had a good war – twenty-nine wartime hat-tricks and five-goal hauls on five occasions. This man could score goals for fun. Jock Dodds, from Blackpool and later of Everton, was one of the few British forwards to score more wartime goals. Stubbins was powerful and fiercely quick but also 'dainty', unpredictable and exciting, hardly attributes that had characterised recent Liverpool centre-forwards. Stubbins could bring a ball under control immediately from any height, and he could bind together a forward line and bring other players into the game.

Ironically, Stubbins had no real intention of leaving his native Newcastle United. In fact, he had grand plans to open a business there after he stopped playing, and his family was well settled in the north-east. That is until *both* of the Merseyside clubs came up with their record offer for him of £12,500 in September 1946. Stubbins was, famously, watching a film in the Northumberland Street News Theatre when a message flashed across the screen that he was to report to St James's Park right away. He loped off in his size-11 shoes to find that United had accepted the offer: no wonder the post-war Newcastle struggled so hopelessly to win league titles. Albert would need to keep hold of his formidable football boots: in the post-war gloom, professional players struggled to get a pair that fitted, and Bob Paisley even played in boots of different sizes.[10]

So, all that needed to be decided by Stubbins was *which* Merseyside club to join. With no official differential in wages to worry about, on the face of it this selection might have seemed fairly obvious. Everton, after all, were 1939 league champions and had won the FA Cup in recent memory. All Liverpool's league successes were more than 20 years ago, and the Anfield men had *never* won the FA Cup, the holy grail at Newcastle. But because he had made no plans to move and had had little time to think, and perhaps because he feared causing offence by being seen to make a choice, Stubbins tossed a coin to decide which club to speak to first. It came down in Liverpool's favour. It was the most important coin toss in the club's history – at least until Liverpool's European escapades began in the 1960s. The silver-tongued Liverpool chairman Billy McConnell probably convinced Stubbins to come to Anfield by offering him a club house – much sought after following the war – and assuring him that he could live in Newcastle later to look after his business interests. There would be ructions about this in time. But for now Liverpool had paid out big money and had its goalscoring centre-forward at last.

The war had turned football upside down, but it had survived. Even the Littlewoods Pools company (based in Liverpool) had offered up its premises and turned its hand to printing call-up papers and the production of parachutes and barrage balloons during the conflict.[11] It could now hope to get back to employing women checkers in the city and making a tiny number of winners reasonably rich while making vast profits. But for millions of people, sitting checking the pools coupon on a Saturday evening would also signal a return to some kind of normality.

One player who was probably looking forward to the resumption of serious sporting rivalries at last, with a smile of satisfaction that was likely to be rather wider even than those of his Liverpool colleagues, was full-back Jim Harley. He had been sent off in the very last official league fixture played in the 1939–40 season, versus Chelsea at Anfield. Would the game's guardians catch up with him six years on? He need have no fears. Not even the normally nitpicking FA was willing to carry a suspension over this sort of period. So Harley was free to start the new campaign with a clean slate. He would play only four matches before injury cut him down and would finish with seventeen league appearances in total. But he played a significant part, nevertheless, in what would prove to be one of Liverpool Football Club's greatest-ever seasons.

CHAPTER 10 REFERENCES

1. Inglis, *The Football League and the Men Who Made It*, p. 165
2. Rollin, *Soccer at War*, pp. 15–16
3. Rollin, *Soccer at War*, pp. 45–6
4. Rollin, *Soccer at War*, p. xi
5. Belchem, 'Celebrating Liverpool', p. 44
6. Rous, *Football Worlds*, p. 96
7. Wilson, *Inverting the Pyramid*, p. 86
8. Inglis, *The Football League and the Men Who Made It*, p. 169
9. Taw, *Football's War and Peace*, p. 52
10. Taw, *Football's War and Peace*, p. 61
11. Reed, *Football and Fortunes*, p. 20

11

1946–47, CHAMPIONS AGAIN
George Kay and the Willie and Albert Show

DANGEROUS GROUNDS AND ARMCHAIR FANS

For most people, the return of league football to England in August 1946 signalled the return to aspects of what passed for normal life after the war. But times also remained incredibly hard. The Liverpool-based football-pools business had continued at a lower level during the war years, but it was now back to full throttle: between ten and fourteen million people did the pools in Britain in the 1940s, and by 1950 Liverpool employed around 18,400 people in the industry, 17,000 of them women. In this sense, football engaged with almost every British household in some way. But many of these small-time pools gamblers were probably just too poor to be among the one million weekly football spectators who would now attend Football League matches as the game moved towards its post-war peak.[1]

And there were plenty of desperately poor people about on Merseyside. In January 1947, for example, the *Evening Express* reported that, with coal rations exhausted and the 'big freeze' of that year really starting to bite, families in Bootle 'are burning books, rags, old wooden toys and bicycle tyres in an attempt to provide warmth and heat for cooking purposes'. Power cuts were a norm in 1947 as the fuel crisis deepened. No wonder a writer who had left the city six years before told the *Express* that Liverpool looked 'drab and dismal, a gloomy, dusty film seems to have grown over the streets'.

Gangs of teenage 'desperados', aged from ten to fifteen years, were routinely rounded up for appearances in Liverpool courts at this time, usually charged with petty gas meter break-ins or else bouts of shoplifting. Meanwhile, on Boxing Day night 1947 three Liverpool men broke into the safe at Anfield Road hoping to steal £4,000 in match receipts from the fixture against Stoke

– but they found just £72 instead. New post-war concerns now regularly expressed in the Liverpool press included that of troublesome 'youth', while in 1947 Birkenhead 'teen-age' girls (another new idea) were offered 'expert tuition in charm' by the local youth-welfare service, including in dress sense, hairstyling and deportment. Even in these grim times, a new world for the young was already coming.

The minimum admission charge for football in the war years had been increased to 1s 6d, but with a reduction in Entertainment Tax this was reduced again to 1s 3d – though superior standing areas kept the 1s 6d charge. The maximum wage for players was increased from £9 to £10 – though only 5 per cent of professionals actually received the maximum, despite the post-war boom in gates. A motion to the league management committee in February 1947 that players' wages be further increased to £12 was supported by only six clubs, one of which was Liverpool. Liverpool's average home gate in the last full season before the war was 31,422, but in 1946–47, as the club fought for the Football League title even in these hard times, it would rise to 45,732, eclipsing Everton by almost 5,000 per home match. Only Newcastle United had larger average crowds in the Football League, though for some time it looked like fixtures would not be completed due to the foul weather and a government ban on midweek football to save energy and to guard against absenteeism. In March 1947, James Fay, the players' union secretary, even suggested playing games in midweek behind closed doors to get matches completed. Instead, Football League fixtures would bleed into high summer in the most unimaginable of circumstances.

With large, enthusiastic football crowds would also come the need for greater regulation and improved facilities to meet the new demand, though such lessons seemed difficult to learn. In March 1946, 33 people were crushed and killed at Burnden Park in the type of stadium disaster that had actually threatened throughout the entire history of the English game. Admirably, the Liverpool press called for instant change: a new licensing regime for sports grounds; capacities of sports stadiums to be assessed, section by section; and for ticket-only matches to be introduced. As the *Evening Express* aptly put it on 11 March 1946, even after six years of daily sacrifice in war 'the thought that men and women should be suffocated and trampled to death in the atmosphere of sport is distressing beyond words'. People in Liverpool, of course, would have these words come back to haunt them more than 40 years later.

But throughout the late 1940s and early 1950s there would be a succession of 'near misses' at Anfield and elsewhere, when sometimes hundreds of people were injured on the terraces or else were forced to leave the stadium – sometimes well before kick-off – because of the risk of excessive crushing. Hundreds climbed in over the outer wall of the Kop. In December 1946, when Liverpool played Wolves, for example, the *Football Echo* reported:

> There was some ominous swaying of the crowd in the corner between the Spion Kop and the Main Stand, and just after the second goal the police and ambulance-men helped out about 30 spectators onto the cinder track and shepherded them down the players' exit. One or two of the more elderly ones had to be supported.

In October 1948, a 'constant stream' of supporters left before the Liverpool v. Middlesbrough match 'and there were a number of stretcher cases'. Goalkeeper Cyril Sidlow remembered a Christmas Day fixture in 1950 during which streams of people were led onto the Anfield track – including a young woman carrying a baby in her arms.[2]

On 31 December 1949, a Mr O'Gorman from Amity Street in the city wrote to the *Football Echo* to register a public protest after 200 or 300 fans out of 58,757 had elected to get out of Anfield before the match kicked off against Chelsea 'rather than risk injury of excessive crushing'. He wrote, 'Hundreds inside had to fight their way out . . . The condition at the Kemlyn Road corner of the ground made another Bolton Wanderers disaster imminent.' A club record 61,905 crowd was ruthlessly shoehorned into Anfield for a fourth-round FA Cup tie against Wolves in February 1952. The message was simple enough: clubs would do pretty much anything to satisfy demand, and football grounds in England remained occasionally unstable, potentially dangerous places as a consequence. Anfield was no exception from any other venue in that respect. No comment came from the club about this, or any other such complaint, beyond a general plea that supporters in the ground should close up spaces on the centre of terraces and let latecomers in to ensure safety and good order. It was a case of negligence without punishment.

Despite such concerns, the growth of television as a popular medium in the early 1950s helped in 'nationalising' the sport of football and to spread its influence. Liverpool would finally reach the FA Cup final again in 1950, but perhaps the 1948 final between Manchester United and Blackpool signalled the birth of the modern game for fans. Ticket touts reportedly asked for – and got – 20 times the cover price for tickets as northern supporters poured into London in what would become a familiar annual scalping ritual. But it was the television coverage of the 1953 'Stanley Matthews' final, in which Blackpool recovered to beat Bolton Wanderers 4–3, that is often regarded as the key moment when the 'traditional' English game moved into the new media era. The nation now increasingly gathered collectively in their millions around the 'telly' every May to watch the FA Cup final as part of a great national ritual that confirmed the 'national community' of British people and their families, as well as the symbolic closure of yet another winter season of sport.

Television, radio and the expansion of the sporting press would also help people keep more 'connected' with their local clubs, especially as working-class communities were dispersed from around the old city centres to 'overspill' housing estates because of the damage inflicted by war. It was estimated that 148,000 people in Liverpool fitted this 'overspill' category, and they were dispersed throughout the 1940s, '50s and '60s, some of them first into 3,500 new 'pre-fabs' in and around the city, and then to an outer ring of city-corporation housing estates in Kirkby, Halewood, Huyton and Speke. The growth rate of these outer estates was incredible: the first house in Kirkby was built in 1952, but by 1965 some 52,000 people lived in the area.[3] Travelling by tramcar or walking to home matches at Anfield, as many people had done before the war, would increasingly no longer be an option in this new era of post-war urban redevelopment and cultural change in which the private motorcar would all too soon become king.

FUELLING FOR THE FOOTBALL LEAGUE

'Tomorrow,' wrote the *Liverpool Echo* on 30 August 1946, 'sees the start in England and Wales of what promises to be the biggest boom season soccer has ever known.' The war years had produced, according to this account, only 'ersatz soccer', but here was the real thing once again in all its gory glory. The *Daily Post* – messing about with its figures slightly – predicted 'the greatest season in its sixty-year history' for English league football. Some people in the game wanted promotion and relegation to be suspended for two or three seasons while clubs 'settled down' again following the strains and disruptions of the previous six years. But the Football League pointed out that all clubs were in the same boat, and what had the 42-game transition season been about if not getting the clubs attuned to the new demands?

George Kay cleverly took his team out of 'ration city' Liverpool to North America in the pre-season, mainly to get some high-quality food into his players. In 1945, the Liverpool chairman Billy McConnell had been on a Ministry of Food mission to the USA to study catering, and he knew very well the value of good nourishment to athletes. The Reds players put on an average of half a stone during the trip, with Liverpool averaging seven goals a game in a ten-match unbeaten tour. But it was not all plain sailing. 'Played under lights and the ground rough and poor,' George Kay wrote in a telegram about the match against Falls River FC. 'Lights not effective in the night game: spectators a bad lot.' Liverpool were hosted by Branch Rickey, president of the Brooklyn Dodgers, who seemed willing to offer British footballers £20 to £25 per week to join the new American Professional Soccer League.[4] Although the players still looked like scrawny scarecrows when the Reds eventually won the league title in 1947, both the chairman and the Liverpool manager would highlight the 'good food our boys had in America' as a key reason for the club's immediate success. Who says attention to diet for footballers was an invention of the 1990s?

Cheekily, on their return from North America Liverpool made an offer straight off for Everton's unsettled England international Joe Mercer, just to stir the local pot. Mercer was at serious odds with Everton manager Theo Kelly about his injury problems, and he had asked for a transfer. There was no believing for a moment at Anfield that the Goodison club would sell an England captain to their near neighbours and keenest rivals. Liverpool's enquiry might even have been a bit of tit for tat for the Elisha Scott affair back in 1934. In any event, Mercer eventually joined Arsenal for £7,000, but his connections with Liverpool Football Club did not stop there. Mercer continued to live in Hoylake, and he trained at Anfield during the week, travelling down to London at weekends for Arsenal home matches. This arrangement of having players from other clubs training with rivals was not unusual, and the Mercer situation continued right up to the 1950 FA Cup final meeting – between Liverpool and Arsenal.

THE WILLIE AND ALBERT SHOW

Liverpool began the first post-war league season slowly but steadily as the team, without Billy Liddell, who was still with the RAF, scored a last-minute winning goal by Len Carney, the little-used 31-year-old ex-local amateur, and claimed both points at Sheffield United. But a confidence-draining home loss to Middlesbrough followed, with Laurie Hughes scoring a classic own-goal header. The new post-war impatience of football supporters was already apparent as 'a hurriedly called meeting of Liverpool fans . . . assembled outside the club's offices . . . with the object of calling upon the directors to make quick team changes'.[5]

It was the Anfield clash with a strong Chelsea side on 7 September that showed the real potential of this new Liverpool team. Charlie Ashcroft, an England B international, deputised for Sidlow in goal, but it was no coincidence that Bob Paisley and Billy Liddell both made their post-war debuts on Liverpool's left side, Liddell offering searing pace and goal threat backed up by Paisley's tenacious tackling and precocious long throw-ins. Bob Paisley was a committed and aggressive player, often using the shoulder charge to barge opponents off the play so that his more skilful centre-half Lol Hughes could pick up the ball unmolested and send Liverpool off on another attack. These three players – Hughes, Paisley and Liddell – complemented each other perfectly down the Liverpool left. The Chelsea match ended up as a 7–4 home win, but, as the *Evening Express* reported, it could have been many, many more for Liverpool, who led 6–0 on 50 minutes and whose forwards 'made the Chelsea defence look absolutely inept on occasion'. Liddell (2), Fagan (2) and Balmer all scored, as did Bill Jones, a long-serving 'play anywhere' squad man who appeared twice for England and got two goals here as a forward. He would move back into a more defensive role later in the campaign. Jones also proved his intelligence and adaptability when he returned to work for the club in the 1960s as a scout.

The Reds' new star signing, centre-forward Albert Stubbins, was a hard man to second-guess. He was reported 'missing' by the *Daily Post* when he failed to meet Liverpool club staff off a 10 p.m. train from Newcastle on 13 September 1946. Had he decided to join manager Theo Kelly at Everton after all? Waiting journalists, manager George Kay and the Liverpool captain Willie Fagan all searched the train compartments with amused press hounds, but eventually they tracked the elusive Stubbins down to the Hanover Street Hotel. Liverpool had booked a room there for their new man, and not expecting a reception committee and little recognised on Merseyside he had simply slipped off the train and into the night. The centre-forward would soon learn about the intensity of interest in the game and its stars in the city of Liverpool. Stubbins brought more than a touch of glamour to the city. Assailed by autograph hunters, he was later taken by the Liverpool party to the Adelphi Hotel, where he stayed the night and where 'he answered a battery of questions with all the composure of a Hollywood film star'.

Stubbins missed the trip to Manchester United, where Liverpool were painfully reacquainted with Matt Busby in a 0–5 win for the home side. There was other mitigation. Sidlow was still out, Liddell again missed, awaiting demobilisation, and Jim Harley was soon a passenger, seriously injuring his left leg, which meant he would miss much of the season. The *Evening Express* complained in January 1947 that three key Liverpool players – Liddell, Sidlow (still not demobilised either) and Hughes – were effectively still part-timers and that this was affecting the Reds' early cohesion. Notwithstanding these handicaps, Liverpool were, it was agreed, 'completely outclassed and outplayed' by this 'devastating' United outfit. Better was to come at Bolton, with Liddell back and Stubbins on debut in a 3–1 win. 'This is the best forward line I have ever played in,' said the grateful new Liverpool centre-forward to the club's blushing chairman Billy McConnell immediately after the match. 'I am only sorry I could not give you more than one goal.' Scoring on debut and still apologising? It was music to any director's ears. And it was also exactly the type of goal the club had signed Albert Stubbins to score: a head-on from Nieuwenhuys, and the centre-forward latching on and shrugging off two defenders before driving the ball right-footed past Wanderers keeper Stan Hanson.

The *Daily Post* marked the debut qualities of Stubbins as 'good timing, a long stride and an almost nonchalant style', but it also asked that if Stubbins was worth his huge fee then what price Cyril Sidlow, 'who makes victories possible'? It was a point well made, especially as goalkeepers' transfer fees would remain resolutely below those of top forwards in England for decades to come. In this new sporting world, sports journalists now even got the occasional interview out of players after matches to spice up their copy. Not that there was too much controversy here. 'Thanks,' said the new man Stubbins evenly to congratulations from waiting local press men. 'But I promise you I'll do better.' The red-headed Albert already seemed far too good to be true.

But if Albert Stubbins was to deliver some of the extra goals that Liverpool needed – eventually he would score 83 in 178 matches for the club – it was the Presbyterian Scot Billy Liddell who provided the essential speed, guile and bite down the left side that marked out this Liverpool team as exceptional. On occasion, the 24-year-old was simply unplayable – but Everton were alert to his tricks for the Anfield 0–0 derby meeting of 21 September that followed. With Phil Taylor playing 'delicious football' in the middle of the field, Liverpool chairman McConnell said he thought it was the best local derby game he had seen for some time, though most supporters saw a different match. The *Daily Post* used the convenient imagery of war to suggest that some of the younger players on both sides were 'shell-shocked by the atmosphere, the pace and the urge to play a hero's part'. The truth was that two well-marshalled defences and the 'snappy, non-stop worker' on Liverpool's left, Bob Paisley, had easily managed the attacking threat from both units in a frenzied 0–0 encounter. Although Stubbins had failed to score, and might even have been feeling the weight of his great fee in his feet, he also produced many 'bright things'. The Liverpool supporters, so the local press commented, 'will always be glad to have his relief from the drab, stereotyped methods common to so many of our players'. In short, this draw was a disappointment but no disaster.

'LUCKY' LIVERPOOL

Berry Nieuwenhuys was now approaching 35 years of age, and in a newish, young Liverpool team he was beginning to look a little like yesterday's man, short of real pace and guile, certainly compared to Liddell and Stubbins. He was a player who signified the disappointing pre-war Liverpool past, one laced with too many so-so South African imports, rather than a possibly brighter post-war, mainly British, future.

Supporters noticed his decline: time catches up with even the greatest of footballers, especially when fans have been starved of entertainment for six long years. They were certainly much harsher and quicker now in their judgements. 'Spectators at Anfield,' reported the *Daily Post* on 30 September 1946, talking about the treatment of Nivvy, 'have a bad habit of verbally marking a man and they trouble a player by reason of their alleged humour.' The tall winger got his own back on the Anfield knockers by scoring a header from a Liddell corner against Leeds United in a 2–0 Liverpool canter in the autumn sunshine. But one good week would not be enough: Nivvy was replaced in the next game by Harry Eastham, a sometimes overcomplicated but popular wing-man from Blackpool. Jack Balmer scored the other goal, Albert Stubbins missing a penalty, his first blot.

These were really complaints from Reds supporters in a time of relative plenty, rather than those signifying potential famine. It was a fact confirmed by the 6–1 Liverpool tanning of Grimsby Town that followed in Cleethorpes. Billy Liddell ran half the length of the field 'at lightning speed' to add to Stubbins's opening goal, and then the second-half flood gates opened, with all the key Liverpool forward men of this campaign – Stubbins, Liddell, Balmer and Willie Fagan – getting goals. Balmer was clearly offside but sensibly netted before checking. 'The referee,' reported the *Liverpool Echo*, 'bore the brunt of the Grimsby barracking.' The Reds were up to fourth place after this rout. 'The best thing Liverpool have done all season,' was the *Daily Post's* smug verdict. The Liverpool managerial 'brains trust' then had a late-night discussion about tactics with journalists in a Redcar hotel before the 2–2 draw at Middlesbrough – it was truncated by a local resident's complaints about loud voices in the night. Perhaps this interruption meant they had only had time to talk about the *first* half, because Billy Liddell put Liverpool two goals up by the break, only for the Boro to reply with second-half goals from Fenton and Dews. 'I was thankful when the final whistle blew,' confessed the home manager David Jack. But it was still only one point for Liverpool in a contest they had all but wrapped up after forty-five minutes.

Stubbins missed the home match against Charlton, allowing Cyril Done a start at centre-forward – and a goal – in a 1–1 draw in front of 51,127 spectators. Sam Bartram allowed Done's header from a Lambert cross to squirm over the goal-line. In the second half, even the switch of Fagan and Liddell to allow the Liverpool star to roam more effectively from his restricting left-wing channel could not pin back a gallant Charlton. The key man for the visitors was their on-field leader Don Welsh, who scored an excellent equalising header after 58 minutes. Welsh would resurface at Anfield five years later as George Kay's replacement in the management seat, but here he was stealing a valuable point rather than the Liverpool manager's job. Cyril Done held his place for the visit to Huddersfield on 9 October, replacing the injured Willie Fagan, who was out for three months with a strained Achilles tendon. Billy Liddell missed out because of international duty, his stand-in being an able reserve, the South African Bob Priday. The ex-Southport man Ray Minshull made his debut by replacing Wales's Sidlow in goal. He was 'absolutely faultless'. But the real star turn was Cyril Done, with a 'brilliant' hat-trick, scored after Town had taken the lead. Balmer took over penalty duties from Albert Stubbins, but he also missed from the spot before scoring in open play. It was Liverpool's fourth goal in a commanding performance. The win was set up by the doughty Bob Paisley, 'the best intermediate on view', according to the *Evening Express*. It was a show of Anfield strength in depth on a potentially difficult day. 'Lucky Liverpool,' argued the *Express*, 'to have such excellent reserves to take the places on international days.' It was either luck or else good management.

STUBBINS FINDS HIS HOME SCORING BOOTS

Albert Stubbins – all £12,500 of him – had still not scored at Anfield, so the winning goal he produced against relegation-bound Brentford on 26 October 1946 was a relief as well as a guarantee of two hard-won points. Billy Liddell sped up the Liverpool left and crossed low to Stubbins, who beat the stubborn Brentford goalkeeper Joe Crozier low down in the left-hand corner after 50 minutes. The Liverpool man was given a 'tumultuous cheer' by the locals. But although the Reds were supported by 'trainloads of fans, including a contingent of schoolboys' next up at Blackburn Rovers, they had to settle for a goal-less draw in East Lancashire. Billy Liddell was at last playing for the club again as a civilian. Liverpool now lay in third place, two points behind early leaders Blackpool. Manager George Kay, a thinker and a boss who cared about the well-being of his players, announced he would be taking his squad to Buxton around the fixture with Derby County on 16 November for some country air and relaxation. This was designed 'to help tone them up for the hectic holiday rush and the FA Cup ties ahead'. It was good management and a sensible strategy in a long season. It would also pay handsome dividends.

The experienced Jack Balmer sometimes lacked the commitment and confidence that a full England cap might have brought, so George Kay and the players made him Liverpool's captain in the home game against Portsmouth to give him a boost. More good management – and it worked. The inside-forward would stay captain. Against Portsmouth, he scored a hat-trick in a 3–0 win and then set off on an astonishing record league run of scoring ten goals in three matches, while scoring in six consecutive league games. At Derby on 16 November, it was all four in a 4–1 win, including 'one of the best goals he is ever likely to get', according to the *Liverpool Echo*, drifting to the right past four defenders and then cutting back his shot into the left-hand corner. Harry Eastham did a 'Matthews trick' in dribbling to make the fourth so adeptly that another Balmer hat-trick in the 4–2 home win over Arsenal on 23 November was no longer a surprise. Balmer scored from a penalty before Arsenal responded to lead 1–2. But Billy Liddell (who else?) dragged Liverpool back into the contest with a 'scintillating run', before flicking off the outside of his right boot to Balmer, who instantly finished in the top corner.

The *Football Echo* compared the wild Anfield celebrations at this equaliser to those at Everton when Dean had scored his stunning 60th goal back in 1928. 'Rarely has an Anfield goal given so much joy. Liddell's part was as great as that of the scorer.' When Balmer got his third goal – and a Football League record three hat-tricks in consecutive matches – it produced 'the biggest cheer Anfield has ever known in its long history'. Stubbins wrapped up the scoring before some post-war professionalism from the home team, of a kind that might well have pleased the wily Elisha Scott from a generation before, annoyed local scribes. 'It was a great pity,' opined the rather pious *Echo*, 'that Liverpool employed time-wasting tactics right at the finish, putting a blemish on the match. Arsenal were trying and playing right to the end.'

Perhaps these were the early signs of a new approach to playing league football, one more directed at winning matches, come what may, rather than just entertaining. Supporters certainly seemed more demanding, quicker to condemn. But Liverpool supporters could say they had both good football and points: twenty-seven goals in ten games, seven wins, no losses and top of the table. The test would come at close challengers Blackpool on 30 November, when 'thousands of followers of Anfield made the trip by car, coach and train. Favours and rattles and whistles added to the atmosphere.' Blackpool led through a stunning volley from McIntosh, but Balmer equalised on 35 minutes, his low, slow shot from the right-corner of the penalty area bobbling gently onto the left-hand post – and in. Jimmy Blair scored again for Blackpool, and the game seemed up when Stan Mortensen flicked in the third from close range on 87 minutes. But Cyril Done scored right from the restart, setting up a frantic finish in which Liddell 'flashed the ball inches wide of the post amidst tremendous excitement'.

It was a 2–3 loss, but Liverpool were still joint top with Wolves on 24 points. The Wanderers just happened to be the next visitors to Anfield.

The Liverpool team against Wolves was the standard one in a very loose version of the W–M formation, with Harley and Fagan both injured. With the exception of the versatile Bill Jones – who would fill in brilliantly later for both Lol Hughes and Barney Ramsden – and the fading Berry Nieuwenhuys, this was, broadly speaking, the team that would win the 1946–47 league championship for Liverpool. It was a highly competent Liverpool side rather than a truly great one, one lit up by Billy Liddell on the left. There was no one of the quality of Alex Raisbeck or Elisha Scott, nor full-backs to match Dunlop, Longworth or McKinlay from earlier Liverpool eras. There was no star wing-half or inside-forward schemer of the Tommy Bromilow type from the early 1920s, either. Neither Balmer nor Done were really classic inside-forwards in the W–M tradition. Phil Taylor certainly had a touch of class at half-back, and Bob Paisley did have something of the Bill Goldie about him from 1901 or even the bite of Jock McNab from 1923 – but without the Scot's occasional indiscipline. This pair complemented each other well.

Liverpool FC, league-title winners, v. Wolves, 7 December 1946

Sidlow

Lambert   Hughes   Ramsden

Taylor   Paisley

Balmer   Done

Eastham   Stubbins   Liddell

Albert Stubbins had much of Sam Raybould's instinct for goal in the early Liverpool title teams, and Jack Balmer was undoubtedly a very clever player, some argue one of Liverpool's best ever despite his obvious lack of bravery. These were quality forwards, no doubt about it, but not quite Liverpool's greatest. Lol Hughes had some of Walter Wadsworth's defensive presence and comfort on the ball. But there was no one on Liverpool's problematic right flank in 1947 to match, say, a Jack Cox from 1901 or a Bill Lacey from 1922. Instead, much of this Liverpool team's creative threat came from down the left, where the dynamic Billy Liddell would often push inside if he was getting isolated on Liverpool's left-wing.

Some of this relative weakness in the 1947 side was about to be highlighted. Liverpool could do little to promote their 1947 league title cause against Wolves at Anfield because, frankly, it was a horror show: a home thrashing by their closest rivals in front of 52,512 people, most of whom had expected something quite different. It was the sort of 1–5 home defeat, in fact, that had manager George Kay tossing and turning in his bed, looking too hard and too long for solutions, damaging his brittle health. The Wallasey-born Dennis Westcott, formerly of New Brighton, a rapid centre-forward who scored goals at every club he played for, got four for Wolves, all of them in the first half. Liverpool crumpled to a side for whom forwards Pye and Hancocks were constant threats to a nervous home defence. Hughes and Sidlow were on different wavelengths for once, as long balls straight up the middle accounted for three goals. Mullen scored a fifth after a slip by the Liverpool centre-half, who had a truly miserable day. A late Jack Balmer penalty was all the deflated Reds could manage in reply.

RESILIENCE NEEDED – NOT YET FOUND

After two crushing defeats, one week later things looked different again in the fog and then driving rain at Sunderland on 14 December, in a 4–1 Reds win. Scorer Nieuwenhuys was back to add some experience and stability on the right, and Bill Jones was in for Ramsden. 'Liverpool back to their best,' was the *Football Echo*'s verdict, with the adaptable Jones 'a complete success' at the back and 'the wing-halves in brilliant form'. At home against Aston Villa on 21 December 1946, fog intervened again, delaying the arrival of the visitors until ten minutes before kick-off. The disorientated Midlanders then faced a heavily sanded pitch and icy, bare patches for a repeat 4–1 home result, with Paisley 'playing brilliantly' and Balmer (2), Stubbins and Nieuwenhuys all on the scoresheet, as they had been in the north-east. Liverpool now trailed Wolves by two points. But it would have seemed to George Kay and the Anfield board that they had survived a rocky spell and were back on track as the Christmas fixtures approached. How wrong could they be? Five defeats in the next six matches – that's how wrong.

The first of these losses came at Stoke City on Christmas Day – what a rotten way to spend the holidays. Tom Bush, a strapping centre-half who had been at Liverpool since 1933, got a rare start for the injured Hughes. Bush was blackly lucky, because he witnessed a masterclass. Stanley Matthews utterly outshone Liddell, his centres providing Steele with two goals, one in each half. Stubbins scored a header with eight minutes to go, but it was only a consolation. The next day, Boxing Day, the same men met at a different venue. But Matthews brought his tricks again, even more of them and more dastardly ones. 'A slimly built, wasp-waisted, wan-looking winger stole the show,' said the *Daily Post*.

'When they walked off, Stanley Matthews' kit was cleaner than any, although he had done twice as much with half as little effort.'

'Go to him!'

'Tackle him!'

'Don't be frightened of him!'

This was the crazy advice reportedly hurled down from the Liverpool terraces, but 'Matthews was the complete footballer in this game', no less than a 'football mesmerist'. To commit yourself against Matthews on this sort of day was to risk ridicule, no matter what the crowd bawled for. Fans who saw it never forgot this exhibition. Matthews in the clear on the deputising Minshull lobbed the goalkeeper exquisitely but onto the crossbar, and Steele missed a gaping net from the rebound. But one great player and dollops of good football cannot alone guarantee success. You also need luck. The prosaic Nieuwenhuys in comparison had already headed Liverpool in front (something as mundane as heading was below Matthews), and with five minutes remaining the otherwise anonymous Stubbins sealed a thoroughly undeserved Liverpool win with a left-foot shot.

Good managers are not fooled by wins such as this one: they prepare for the worst, and it was coming. Four Liverpool league defeats in a row followed, broken only by a 5–2 thumping of Walsall in the third round of the FA Cup and a 2–0 win over Grimsby in round four. For Liverpool's training preparation for the Walsall match, the *Evening Express* reported that the 'shooting box in the old car park was kept busy', while for the visit of the Mariners the presidents of both the Italian and French football federations were present at Anfield. Who were they spying on? The *Daily Post*, meanwhile, reported that the huge post-war crowds (and shamefully poor player wages) had reduced Liverpool's £28,000 overdraft to virtually nil, and another 50,961 hopefuls contributed to the cause when they came to see Sheffield United escape with the points from Anfield. The unfortunate Ray Lambert handled for a penalty and then diverted a Nightingale shot past Minshull, thus sandwiching a Stubbins equaliser. Chelsea, inspired by Tommy Lawton, then defeated Liverpool 1–3 at Stamford Bridge, and when Lol Hughes was injured off at home in a rough encounter with Bolton Wanderers the writing was on the wall for yet another Reds defeat, this time by 0–3. 'If there were a sliding tackle championship,' commented the Wanderers acidly, 'Liverpool would win it.'[6]

The late-January 1947 headlines in the Liverpool press were 'Warmer in the Antarctic' and 'All Britain Shivering in Coldest January Spell for Many Years'. People were skating on all the park lakes in the city. The corridors of Anfield were certainly trembling. So it was a snow-covered Goodison Park that hosted a quiet and sporting derby encounter, woken only by Everton's Wainwright heading past Sidlow in the 58th minute. It was a bleak Liverpool house, indeed.

INTO THE BLEAK MIDWINTER

Liverpool were now down to fourth place in the league, five points behind leaders Wolves. And worse news was that there was also something of a national sentiment building behind Wolves for the title in 1947. The great England half-back Stan Cullis was planning to retire, his prime playing years stolen by the war, and this was his last chance for some silverware after the disappointment of the 1939 FA Cup final Wolves lost to Portsmouth. Liverpool still had to play Wanderers again, of course, but the meeting would be at Molineux.

The roots of the Reds' problems were clear enough. The young defender Hughes had begun to lose his nerve, and Jack Balmer had gone off the boil. Fagan and Cyril Done had been missing through injury, and Liddell had lost some form over the holidays. The half-backs were struggling to compensate. Were Liverpool tired, despite all that rest and early good food? At Leeds United, where the ball dragged in the snow and there were drifts on the wings on a near-unplayable pitch, Willie Fagan was back and created a goal for Stubbins, the one Liverpool man who had kept on scoring during the crisis, even though the local press now saw him as 'more a creator of chances than a taker'. But an equaliser from Grainger 'sent the 25,000 spectators joyful, as if it had been a cup final goal'. No matter: red-headed Albert delivered again on 85 minutes. Liverpool were back on the league rails.

Was there no ridding of this snow? The winter of 1947 was as severe as anyone could remember, and some clubs resorted to using former prisoners of war to help clear snow from their pitches.[7] Liverpool beat Derby County at home 1–0 with a welcome goal from a limping Jack Balmer in frosty conditions in the FA Cup. For the first time, a standing area of Anfield, the paddock, was made all-ticket for this match after a belated safety campaign by the local press. The same tactic might soon be tried for Liverpool's younger fans, it seemed. 'The club asks the lads of the boys pen to keep their orange peel to themselves,' warned the *Evening Express* on 7 February, 'or else other arrangements will be made for boys in future.' Complaints had already been made in the local press about booing and cries of 'Send him off' from these 'young hooligans'.

Only the one-inch cushion of snow on an iron-hard Anfield pitch allowed Liverpool v. Grimsby Town (5–0) to take place in the league on 12 February 1947. No snowballs were reported, but there were plenty of good signs here. Liddell was back on song, creating goals from powerful runs and accurate crosses. Cyril

Done scored a hat-trick as a result, and Willie Fagan continued his comeback from injury with two goals. The pressure on Jackie Balmer to score was thus relieved, and he could begin to relax back into his best form. This was the theory. 'The great mystery at Anfield,' admitted the *Football Echo* on 22 February 1947, 'was how Huddersfield could take the ball up to goal so frequently . . . and still fail to score.' On the usual icy, slippery pitch, Liverpool at last made use of Bob Paisley's unusually powerful throws. Paisley's long delivery persuaded Cyril Done beyond the Town defence in this match, and the big man unselfishly passed to Stubbins, who evaded the slithering visiting defenders to score the only goal. 'This was Huddersfield's most unlucky day,' said the Liverpool press. But don't good teams make their own luck?

Two hard-fought 2–1 Liverpool wins followed in the league – against Blackburn Rovers at home and in desperate blizzard conditions at Portsmouth away – and Liverpool had clawed their way back up to second place in the table with eleven games still to go. But they were still four points behind Wolves, and Blackpool, Stoke City and Manchester United were also challenging. What a title fight!

However, for the Merseyside press it was still the FA Cup that had all the romance. This was the competition that really grabbed the public's attention. Another home FA Cup draw, which brought Birmingham City to Anfield in the sixth round, had begun to get the city buzzing again about Liverpool Football Club's 'missing' FA Cup. Such was the local interest, the Liverpool directors decided to make this meeting the first-ever all-ticket league or FA Cup match on Merseyside, with the ground capacity limited to 51,911. It took a while for Reds supporters to get used to the idea: most ticket applications by telephone came from the crew of ships who would be in port when the match took place. One optimistic letter from a ship asked for '500 tickets for the Kemlyn Road Stand'. Chairman Billy McConnell warned supporters to check on the source of their tickets because counterfeiters were at work in the city, and on the day of the match an *Evening Express* reporter was offered a pound for a five-shilling ticket.

Because of transport problems, not all of the 12,000 ticketed Birmingham fans arrived in Liverpool to join in their chant of 'One, two, three, four, five', but the match will always be remembered for a remarkable goal from hat-trick man Albert Stubbins, a near-horizontal diving header in the 66th minute on bone-hard ground, scored from a fiercely driven Billy Liddell free-kick. Bob Paisley was also knocked unconscious when competing for a header, and he moved briefly to the right wing to replace Willie Fagan to clear his head. The Liverpool players secured their £8 FA Cup win bonus when Balmer added to the Stubbins three, for a comfortable 4–1 victory.

MORE FA CUP MISERY

Prospective league champions Liverpool were drawn against Second Division Burnley in the 1947 FA Cup semi-final. Burnley had conceded just seven goals in twenty-eight matches but this looked a sure-fire route to Liverpool's second final and, surely, its first and long overdue FA Cup win. And it was quite a sporting weekend, because on its first Saturday run 300,000 people watched the 100–1 shot Caughoo win the Grand National at Aintree by 20 lengths. But the FA Cup meeting at Ewood Park would prove a bizarre affair. How would people reach the match? There were no football-special trains allowed by government, and restrictions on transport and fuel were severe. Many Burnley fans resigned themselves to *walking* the 14 miles to Blackburn, while in Liverpool 'bicycles were hastily overhauled by hundreds . . . and the "one-made-for-two" was a common sight in Blackburn'. Some Liverpool supporters were forced to travel to Lancashire a day in advance and spent the night wandering the Lancashire town's streets until first light. 'From dawn onwards,' reported the *Evening Express*, '[these men] made the streets of Blackburn ring with incessant chatter and the inevitable clamour and whistles.' Counterfeiters made detection easy for once – they had misspelled 'competition' on their fake tickets.

These devoted travellers and explorers then faced a largely open, overcrowded stadium so that 'the pouring rain forced spectators to use handkerchiefs and newspapers for head covering'. Many were carried out injured or exhausted. It must have tried the keenest of supporters, this gruelling test of their devotion. The 'reward' for the 52,700 crowd was a suitably damp squib 0–0 draw, with Liverpool's Ray Lambert the 'immaculate defender' on the pitch and Burnley's negative game plan working, with tough defenders Woodruff and Atwell assigned to try to quell the spirits of Billy Liddell. Comedian Robb Wilton led Liverpool's post-match reception, but there was really nothing to smile about. The Reds were now edgy and facing a trip to Maine Road on 12 April to resolve this troublesome matter.

Before that there was league business to attend to. Liverpool squared up to three matches in four days over Easter, and Paisley (ankle), Jones (groin), Liddell (thigh), Stubbins (leg bruising) and Harley (thigh) were all doubtful for the visit to Preston. Lacking at centre-half, George Kay might possibly have turned to the Dutch giant Jan van Albert, who had turned up in Liverpool to much hoo-ha in order to appear in a 'freaks' review at the Shakespeare Theatre. But, fortunately, Laurie Hughes was back from injury and the Scot Tom McLeod, an army man, made his debut at centre-forward in a much changed Liverpool team that dogged it out for what would prove to be a crucial 0–0 draw. The next day, against Blackpool at Anfield, George Kay made *nine* changes – Rafa Benítez did not invent rotation. But despite leading 2–0, Liverpool eventually went down to the odd goal in five and were now fully five points behind Blackpool and four adrift of Wolves with only eight league games left. The Reds were now a 100–1 shot for the title, according to the *Daily Post*. It looked like the end of the league challenge and that everything would have to hang on the FA Cup. But against Preston at home on 8 April Liverpool dug into their reserves and won 3–0. Bill Shankly missed a penalty for Preston after Liverpool captain Jackie Balmer tipped off Minshull that the kick would go to the goalkeeper's left – it did.

A few players had made a case for inclusion in the Liverpool FA Cup replay team – Eddie Spicer and Laurie Hughes among them – but the Liverpool directors stuck with the XI who had played at Ewood Park, with Fagan on the right wing, Harley at right-back and Jones at centre-half. Hopes were high on Merseyside. So much so that three twelve-year-old members of a juvenile gang ended up in a Liverpool court on 10 April after stealing food from Islington shops and running away from home. In the letter they left for their parents, they said they were headed for London 'so they will be there for the cup final'. Alas, Liverpool Football Club would not be. With so little time to complete any replay, the Burnley directors agreed to play an extra *hour* if it were needed to split the clubs, but the Liverpool board refused. Were they confident, or afraid?

Burnley set out to defend and frustrate Liverpool from the outset, and it proved a successful ploy. The crucial goal came on 80 minutes, the usually reliable Sidlow missing a punch from a corner and Harrison driving home the loose ball for Burnley. This felt like the final FA Cup blow, especially for the now terminally ill childhood Reds fan, Liverpool club chairman Billy McConnell. The day also got a little worse for 42-year-old James Haughey of Epsom Street, Liverpool, who was later arrested for being drunk and disorderly in the city, saying, 'I had a few drinks when Liverpool lost.' He was fined by a possibly Everton-leaning magistrate. Little Burnley had foiled Liverpool in the latter stages of the FA Cup for the second time.

RUNNING ON EMPTY

On the day they should have been playing in the FA Cup final, 26 April 1947, Liverpool Football Club were instead grinding out a 2–1 league win at Aston Villa, with goals from Willie Fagan and the 25-year-old ex-Prescot Cables right-winger Bill Watkinson, who would replace the injured Cyril Done in the last six league matches of the season. Results had favoured Liverpool in the league, so that when Albert Stubbins scored the single goal from a Liddell cross to beat the blue-shirted Manchester United at Anfield on 3 May local press headlines predictably declared 'Stubbins' Goal Worth 4 Points'. For the *Football Echo*, 'there was more than a shade of spike and spirit' about this contest. The league table now read:

TEAM	PLAYED	POINTS
Wolves	37	53
Manchester United	39	51
Stoke City	37	50
Liverpool	38	50

A Stubbins hat-trick in a 3–1 win followed at FA Cup-winners Charlton Athletic, keeping Liverpool in the hunt. Painfully, two of the girl Dagenham Pipers had paraded the FA Cup before the start at the Valley so that the Liverpool players and supporters could get a look. While title rivals Stoke City chose this strange moment to agree to the transfer of Stanley Matthews to Blackpool, the Liverpool board tried to make their intentions clear by agreeing a record fee of £15,000 for Morton's Scotland international forward Billy Steel. Predictably, negotiations broke down with the player before a scraped 1–1 Reds draw at lowly Brentford. 'Paisley's tackling was deadly,' according to the *Football Echo*, '[but] Liverpool did not show the necessary devil.'

Liverpool were now left with two tricky away fixtures to complete their season, at depleted Arsenal and Wolves. Bob Paisley would miss both with a knee-ligament strain. The Reds were level with Stoke City on fifty-three points and were just one point behind Wolves and Manchester United. Any one of these four clubs could still win the title. Liverpool's brave 2–1 win at Arsenal ensured the trip to Molineux would at least be meaningful. Liverpool were now two points ahead of Stoke, and one ahead of Wolves and United. George Kay – who, incredibly, missed some closing Reds matches to scout players – had moved Bill Jones forward to replace Fagan in the last ten minutes at Highbury, and two Liverpool goals had resulted. It was a masterstroke. But with Stoke City having two games left and a superior goal difference to Liverpool – and not due to complete fixtures until 14 June – even a Liverpool win at Wolves on 31 May would not yet decide matters.

On 2 June, in the week of the Epsom Derby, the *Daily Post* commented, not unreasonably, that 'football in June seems out of place'. The *Liverpool Echo* reported, 'The Reds produced speed, stamina and classic football to sweep Wolves off their pedestal at Molineux.' In the blistering summer sun – 91 degrees in the shade, with the officials refereeing in white tops, no blazers and soft shoes

– Wolves 'had four scoring chances to Liverpool's one'. But it was a 'picture goal' by Jackie Balmer and a brilliant dash half the length of the field by Albert Stubbins for the second that won the day in a famous 2–1 Liverpool win. A tearful Stan Cullis was inconsolable later, but there could be no Liverpool celebrations yet. A win by Stoke City at Bramall Lane in two weeks' time would still scupper everything. After all their hard work – seven wins and one draw in the last eight league matches, five of them away from home – Liverpool Football Club would win the 1947 Football League title only by waiting.

There were no Anfield officials in Sheffield on 14 June 1947 to ensure fair play. After all, Liverpool were playing a delayed Liverpool Senior Cup final against Everton at Anfield on the same summer evening. One Reds player had to be smuggled into Anfield that evening to avoid the police, who had questions to ask about alleged tax evasion.[8] In Sheffield, it was a story highly typical of English football and the resolute British football professional. Sheffield United had nothing to play for, except pride and a £2 bonus, and yet they battled like demons in a deluge that threatened to swamp the pitch. Stoke City, searching for their first league title, simply could not cope on the shifting, unstable surface. Their hopes, according to the Stoke *Evening Sentinel* on 16 June, 'crashed on the rock-like defence of Sheffield United'.

The news of Stoke's eventual 1–2 defeat, delivered over the PA by director George Richards, was greeted with scenes of extraordinary joy back at Anfield, where supporters watching the Reds pound Everton invaded the pitch in wild celebration. Later, Sir Francis Joseph, president of Stoke City, said that it might be strange to some people abroad that a country in crisis, so short of coal and short of production, should focus so intently nevertheless on a mere football match. But this devotion to sport was essential to the 'British character'. Had not Drake completed his game of bowls with the sails of the Armada in sight before setting off to rout the Spanish?

To commemorate this dramatic title win, the Easton Press published a pamphlet entitled *The Sport's Spectator's Story of Liverpool Football Club* for 1s 6d. As a tilt at the club's history so far and a summary of the current players' strengths, this publication had its moments – and its faults. It noted that others depicted this 1947 Liverpool as the 'Crazy Gang' – an inconsistent mix of the very good and the very bad. Albert Stubbins was described as being 'very tall, very gentle', Bob Paisley as having a 'riotous tackle' and Willie Fagan as having 'a nonchalance that makes his work stand out'. Bill Jones, it argued, 'could be the best back in the world'.

It had certainly been an extraordinary season, the final poignant act of which was for the ailing Billy McConnell to leave the Radium Institute, where he had been a patient for five weeks, to collect the championship trophy from the offices of the Football League and transport it respectfully to Anfield in an open-topped taxi. It was a life-long dream of his to hold the Football League trophy for his club. Later, Liverpool FC cancelled a proposed 400-person championship celebration dinner scheduled for 8 August, because on 7 August 1947 the former butcher's boy and Liverpool supporter, and a director since 1929, died at the age of 59. It was a cruel moment for his family and the club, but there was a smile in Billy McConnell's heart.

Several thousand people attended McConnell's funeral at the Anfield cemetery, where he would join Tom Watson and many other Liverpool greats in rest. He had done his duty for his club and for his people – the Liverpool supporters. When fellow Reds director and ex-chairman Walter Cartwright died in October 1947, after 27 years' service, the much reduced Liverpool match programme was printed in black, not the now familiar red, as a mark of respect. Now a new generation would have to pick up the Anfield reins to face the challenges which surely lay ahead.

CHAPTER 11 REFERENCES

1. Fishwick, *English Football and Society*, p. 122
2. Taylor and Ward, *Three Sides of the Mersey*, p. 66
3. Murden, 'City of Change and Challenge', p. 396
4. Taw, *Football's War and Peace*, p. 72
5. Taw, *Football's War and Peace*, p. 93
6. Taw, *Football's War and Peace*, p. 171
7. Inglis, *The Football League and the Men Who Made It*, p. 178
8. Taw, *Football's War and Peace*, p. 221

12

THE ALMOST SEASONS
The Double Frustration of 1950

POST-TITLE BLUES

You have to be a very special football team indeed to follow on a league title win and then show exactly the same levels of commitment, endurance and skill necessary to do it all again just a couple of months later, when all your key rivals – and others besides – begin again from exactly the same place you do. The psychological strength required alone is enormous. So it was tough for Liverpool to maintain the same emotional levels, especially after the amazingly draining and late end to season 1946–47 and also the early death of their popular and influential club chairman. It must have been harder still when only 11 players in a tight group of 16 who had made a major contribution to winning the league title received a championship medal. This strict policy on medals was an example of Football League parsimony to the nth degree. Incredibly, Spicer, Done, Nieuwenhuys, Ramsden and Eastham all missed out. Barney Ramsden, especially, had played 23 times in the league in the title season, but the full-back had also upset the Liverpool board by saying he wanted to leave for the USA and get married there. The Liverpool directors simply turned down his request, but he left in May 1947 anyway. He was out of the team (and the medals). The Reds started the new season slowly, and came with a rush at the end of it, but 11th position was no satisfying follow-up for a club that had been so close to winning the league and cup Double in 1947.

What is it they say in football and life about standing still meaning that you are actually moving backwards? George Kay had certainly moved things on in the title year by pursuing his keen interest in player diet and by holding 'tactics talks' with his players before matches. There was little of this going on before the war. Kay was, according to the late Bill McConnell, 'the greatest manager in football' and player Cyril Done later described him as 'the Shankly of his day', though Kay actually had little of the Scot's confidence and charisma. Was the English game slowly waking up to innovations elsewhere at last? England finally had a national team coach in Walter Winterbottom, but, discussing tactics, 'Pilot' in the *Evening Express* admitted that some people in English football still 'try to dismiss these talks as so much rubbish'.

So maybe Liverpool under the kindly but usually unsmiling George Kay had a measurable advantage here. In December 1949, Kay attributed the post-war Liverpool success to the 'willing cooperation of all players in pre-match practical workouts and theoretical discussion and to their excellent coordination of tactics on the field of play'. Others had different views, pointing to the strength and knowledge of the experienced Liverpool backroom staff of Albert Shelley, Ephraim Longworth and Jimmy Seddon – the last named had played for the Bolton team that had beaten Kay's West Ham in the 1923 FA Cup final. Kay stayed in his office, chain-smoking, during much of the week, surfacing only at weekends, so he left much of the daily work at Anfield to his trusted coaches and trainers.

All this talk about tactics and theory was still rather foreign to English football. In fact, the Liverpool trainer Albert Shelley thought that football in the 1920s was as good and as fast as English football in the 1940s, and that training and coaching methods in the two periods were not hugely different. He had support from Eph Longworth, still on the Liverpool ground staff and 'for his years the fittest man I have ever seen', according to Albert Stubbins. The latter wrote later in the *Football Echo* about the real differences between Liverpool and elsewhere in the 1940s. 'Although coaching is much more in evidence than it was in 1939, I have met several first-class players who think that if a man is a natural player he doesn't need coaching.' Players at Liverpool were probably getting more coaching and certainly more tactics now than at most other English clubs, though that was still saying very little compared to some developments in football abroad.[1] George Kay probably had a little more autonomy in team affairs than most other football managers of his day, but he still had to submit his team suggestions for discussion and revision by the Liverpool board at its weekly meeting. He was not his own man.

A NEW POST-WAR LIVERPOOL?

Another north-west football club, Blackpool FC, with the saintly Stanley Matthews now in their ranks, was not about to stand still either. In the summer of 1947, the Tangerines promised to build a 'Wembley of the North', a stadium capable of holding a startling 150,000 people, because 'Lancashire is the home of football'. Of course, no northern ground could ever really rival the allure of Wembley. And what other events might be held there to make it pay its way? The so-called northern Wembley remained a dream.

Nor was the city of Liverpool easily accepting that its best years were now in the past. Firebrand local Labour MP Bessie Braddock, for example, kept the city in the national news headlines by irreverently 'dancing a jig' on the floor of the House of Commons during an evening debate and ending up exhausted in Winston Churchill's chair. A town-planning exhibition in Radiant House, Liverpool, in the summer of 1947 promised that the post-war 'new' Liverpool would share some of Mrs Braddock's brio by becoming more like a pre-war Paris or Berlin in its activities, architecture and design. Sure, the Blitz had destroyed 6,500 houses, 1,500 commercial buildings and 400 factories/works in the city, but this destruction offered a 'great opportunity' for social and design experimentation and innovation. Lewis's department store, it was announced, was to be restored on Ranelagh Street at a cost of £1.2 million, and Blackler's store was also to be rebuilt and modernised. Here was a start for the new Liverpool. The war was not a gloomy trough in the city's fortunes, as some people seemed to believe. But the city of Liverpool's economic future, and also its core thinking about approaches to popular culture and working-class leisure, would really have to change – and change fast – to make this sort of ambitious vision work, even in part.

A public vote among local electors in Liverpool in 1947 had finally swayed the reluctant Liverpool City Council on the vexatious issue, locally, of allowing Sunday cinema. But in August – and even after the Archbishop of York had said publicly in July that he saw 'no harm in playing amateur football on a Sunday' – Thomas Parry, a mill worker from Timpson Street in Liverpool, was actually fined by magistrates for playing a pick-up game of football on a Sunday on the Lower Breck Road recreation ground. The Liverpool religious protagonists were still at large in the city, it seemed, and mainly in charge. Youth workers in Liverpool and Birkenhead were also concerned about the capacity of the local authorities to deliver in the new era on 'boom' sports such as football. Where would the budding Liddells and Balmers *play* their early football in the city? They claimed that 'more than a thousand' Liverpool boys would be denied the opportunity to play organised football in the late 1940s because of a post-war shortage of pitches and facilities in the area.

There were other key post-war shortages afoot and also some notable changes of habit in the city. Huyton MP Harold Wilson, the president of the Board of Trade, for example, controversially said that there were still barefoot children in Liverpool streets in 1950, while the County Licensing sessions noted that since the war 'it is now usual for men to take their wives out for a drink'. A census of licensed premises in Liverpool found that one local pub had one thousand customers crammed inside because of a shortfall in the number of suitable venues in the city. Barefoot children crushed by poverty and wandering around outside overcrowded Merseyside pubs? It could have been Victorian Liverpool all over again.

While the Everton team manager Theo Kelly said that he wanted his club's supporters to look to the past and revive the traditional Everton nickname 'The Toffees', Liverpool Football Club's new chairman Ronnie Williams also wanted change, but of a very different kind. Liverpool had had real problems allocating tickets throughout the FA Cup run of the previous season. Demand always outstripped supply, and safety problems at Anfield pointed in the direction of more all-ticket affairs in future. Some Liverpool directors probably secretly dreaded reaching a major final because of the potential problems of coping with local ticket demand – shades of Athens 2007. Williams called on the league management committee to lobby the FA for a rise in the number of tickets allocated to the FA Cup finalists. Here was a popular move for all football supporters but not for football administrators – there was no seconder for the Liverpool motion. Williams and Liverpool were met, instead, by bland assurances that the league would 'review' the situation, but nothing much changed.

The players' maximum wage was finally raised to £12 in the winter (£10 in summer), though there were still no simple answers (nor questions asked) about exactly *where* all the money in the sport was going. It was not being spent on players' wages or on stadiums, that was for sure. Billy Liddell still worked in his accountancy firm, including on Saturday mornings before home matches before catching the number 26 tram with Liverpool supporters up to Anfield. He also supplemented his football pay by doing some reporting for the BBC's new *Sports Report* programme. Liddell had a key to the local BBC office in the city and was instructed to catch a tram and let himself in on a Saturday evening to deliver his material 'in the event of anything newsworthy occurring at Liverpool's matches at Anfield'. It seemed a pretty wide brief.[2]

As football crowds continued to grow, so did the number of clubs now trying to get into the Football League. Twenty-seven applied for four possible places in 1947, including South Liverpool and the interestingly named Annfield Plain (from Wearside). But because this was the first season after the war, the league decided to keep all existing clubs on board, without even taking a vote. So there would be only one Anfield, and only one Liverpool, in the Football League after all.

LIVERPOOL FC ON THE SLIDE

Berry Nieuwenhuys was now finished at Anfield, effectively signalling the end of that era of the Liverpool South Africans, but everyone else stayed, with Bill Watkinson holding his place on the right and the post-war 'Holy Trinity' of Balmer, Stubbins and Liddell all starting the early league matches in 1947–48. But Liverpool struggled to score goals and won only three of their first twelve league matches – though one of these was a 3–0 canter at Goodison Park in September. By Christmas, this inconsistency had already ruled out a title challenge. By the end of January 1948, relegation looked more likely: the Reds went five matches without a goal and took just one point from seven games. When they lost 0–3 to Burnley in a violent rainstorm on 17 January 1948, even the lack of a change strip was blamed for their capitulation. Burnley had exchanged their sopping wet outfits for dry and warm shirts at half-time. Jackie Balmer reported that the Liverpool players 'could not move' because of the sheer wet, cold clamour of their sodden cotton shirts. They had no change strip. Anfield attention turned, urgently, to acquiring more clothing coupons – and ideally, of course, the FA Cup.

After comfortably defeating Nottingham Forest at Anfield, Liverpool were drawn away in the cup against Manchester United in the fourth round. But United still had no use of the bombed-out Old Trafford after a long period of homelessness. The tie was switched to Goodison Park, where forged tickets and boys and men climbing the stadium walls kept the local police honest. Tens of thousands were locked outside. A Merseyside record crowd of 74,721 (many more sneaked in) saw Liverpool slide irresistibly to a 0–3 deficit at half-time and out of the FA Cup. So, when Everton played at home in the FA Cup (v. Wolves) on 31 January 1948, Liverpool played at Anfield in the league (v. Portsmouth) in an unusual case of a Merseyside football-fixture clash. This double booking was generally to be avoided, not only because of logistical problems for the police, but also because of the grounded suspicion in the city that a large number of people still attended *both* clubs' home matches. The evidence on this occasion seemed quite strong, if not entirely conclusive. Everton drew a gate of 72,579, while Liverpool could attract only 23,097 to another 0–3 disaster. Liverpool were certainly on a poor league run, and in dire form, but their previous home-match attendance (without a similar Everton distraction) had been a very respectable 48,665. The question raised here was: could as many as 20,000 people in the city be regular watchers of *both* Everton and Liverpool?

With a choice of local matches, it certainly looked as if quite a large number of football supporters in the city might well have been not so highly committed to a specific club at all. They might have opted, instead, for the better-quality contest on the day. But an Everton shareholders' meeting in November 1949 suggested something rather different: a voice from the floor argued that Reds followers were routinely coming across to Goodison Park when Liverpool were away to jeer the struggling home favourites in blue. No one had made the same suggestion about Everton fans coming to Liverpool for the same purpose. Liverpool letter writers to the *Liverpool Echo* insisted that this was an aberrant handful and that most Liverpool supporters 'were sorry to see Everton in their present plight'. But there might well have been plenty of 'overlap' at this time between membership of the Liverpool and Everton crowds. At least at Anfield any new supporters would now have some decent information and entertainment to rely upon: the Automatic Telephone Company agreed to install loudspeaker equipment at Anfield for £300 for season 1948–49. With their club sliding down the Football League table, the Liverpool directors reportedly offered Newcastle United £18,000 for the clown prince himself, Len Shackleton, but the forward rejected the move to stay in the north-east, eventually joining Sunderland for £19,000.

Instead, Bevin Boy Kevin Baron (Bevin Boys were wartime mining conscripts) occasionally figured for Liverpool at inside-forward, but it took until 6 March 1948 for his club's first league win of the year to come, with the Reds hovering uneasily in nineteenth place in the First Division table. The victims were Huddersfield Town, downed by four Albert Stubbins goals and an impressive debut by left-winger Ken Brierley, a £7,000 purchase from Oldham, with Billy Liddell shunted over to the right-wing to make way. Stubbins had received a threatening letter before the meeting with Town warning him his leg would be broken if he went near the visitors' goal. Typically, it merely made him more determined than ever to score – but where would he get *four* legs to break? It would get better still for Brierley, grabbing a goal in a 4–0 drubbing of Everton at Anfield in the 80th league derby in April, as Liverpool finally raised their game to finish with eight wins in the last eleven league games and just one loss, to Aston Villa.

ALBERT DOCKS

In August 1948, an outbreak of interracial rioting near the Rialto Cinema and on Upper Parliament Street in the south end of the city stunned Liverpool, as it had done in the past and as it would do again in much more spectacular fashion some 33 years later. Sixty people ended up in court on this occasion, most of them 'coloureds', as the local press insisted on calling black Liverpudlians. The tensions here, on the surface at least, seemed to be about local 'turf wars' between young white and black men. But the defence also challenged the role of the Liverpool constabulary in these incidents, claiming that 'the defendants were badly knocked around by the police'.

Racism and systematic exclusion and absence underlined these outbursts from Liverpool's long-standing (and long-suffering) black population: in education, employment, law and order, leisure, and sport. Why should football be any different? Black Liverpool faces were almost entirely absent in roles inside the two major football clubs (and everywhere else in England). Despite the recent (white) South African connection, neither Liverpool nor Everton had yet signed a black player or had a black member of staff. There were few signs either that black spectators had yet made a visible place for themselves inside the supporter cultures of either Liverpool Football Club or Everton. Would they have been welcomed if they had?

As this court case continued in the Liverpool press, it was a different type of absence that caught the eye of the local sporting public. Liverpool's star signing Albert Stubbins had failed to report back to training and had not re-signed for Liverpool, as every footballer had to do annually. This was almost unheard of. It transpired that Stubbins was tending to his business affairs in Newcastle, and he claimed that the late Liverpool chairman Billy McConnell had agreed that the centre-forward could live and train in the north-east in order to manage his businesses while still playing on Merseyside. The new board said no, so Stubbins then asked for a transfer. Again the board said no and offered to help the forward find a sweets and tobacconist business on Merseyside. Liverpool held Stubbins's registration, so he could not play for another club, but nor was he playing for Liverpool. He was replaced by the underrated Liverpool-born Les Shannon, who later had a successful career as a wing-half at Burnley.

This was a state of impasse that lasted until mid-October 1948, when the Liverpool directors agreed to purchase the house Stubbins had bought in the north-east and that their record signing could now live in Newcastle and that he should train at Gateshead FC. When Stubbins played in a warm-up in the Central League, a reported 20,000 turned up to welcome back the prodigal son. His first-team reappearance at Anfield on 23 October, 13 games in, seemingly added about 15,000 supporters to the gate to see the Reds crush Middlesbrough 4–0. Although Liverpool Football Club had a policy that its players should live in or near the city, most Reds supporters and much of the press on Merseyside seemed to side with Stubbins in the dispute, though Liverpool supporters might also have been sore at the Reds board about a rise in stand ticket prices at Anfield, from 2s 9d to 3s and 3s 6d.

Albert never recovered his earlier Liverpool form, almost certainly because he spent so little preparation time with his teammates. By 1951, Liverpool were trying to offload him to Middlesbrough, but Stubbins refused to leave, and the remainder of his career was frittered away. Stubbins was intelligent, respectful and well liked locally, and he had a thoughtful regular column in the *Football Echo*. He was no typical troublemaker or disruptive, pointing out that all his conversations with the club on this matter 'have been conducted without the slightest acrimony'. He was also well aware of the special bond that existed between the players and supporters at Anfield. 'Liverpool players are important in one respect,' he told *Echo* readers on 13 November 1948. 'We don't receive poison-pen letters which occasionally drop in on clubs in other parts of the country. They are a cowardly form of attack on players who usually don't mind honest criticism.' The affair was a painful lesson for the Liverpool board.

It was easy to see why the club had eventually been forced to accede to Stubbins. Without their forward pivot, Liverpool's goals had almost completely dried up: just four in a nine-match spell before the great man's return. But even with Stubbins back in harness, and with Jimmy Payne, a crowd-pleasing Bootle-born right-winger, emerging to offer guile and threat on the touchline as the putative 'Merseyside Matthews', Liverpool could find no consistency or real goalscoring potency. Indeed, many Liverpool supporters thought that the gentlemanly Stubbins never regained his original spark for the club because of this interlude and that he was kept on by the Liverpool board way beyond his peak or original commitment to the club as Liverpool began to slide towards relegation trouble.

Captain Jack Balmer ended up as top scorer with just 14 goals from 42 league matches, with Cyril Done weighing in with 11. 'Stork' in the *Liverpool Echo* identified another problem – Liverpool, he suggested, was becoming a long-ball team. 'More construction is needed in the half-back line – the lifeblood of a successful football team. Pumping the ball up the middle and chasing it will not do.' To be fair, Stubbins was plagued by injury after his late start to the season – perhaps this was due to his lack of pre-season preparation and the quality of his training at Gateshead? It was difficult to imagine that either George Kay or Albert Shelley were happy with the situation as Liverpool's season petered out to a midtable finish and elimination from the FA Cup by Wolves.

THE MODERN WAY

In the summer of 1949, full-back Tom Liddell – brother of Billy – joined Liverpool from Lochore Welfare in Scotland. Sadly, the brothers were never to play together for the club. Tom would certainly struggle to better Ray Lambert, 'a sure kicker of any sort of ball' and Liverpool's youngest-ever schoolboy signing at 13 and a half – at least before modern football academies began to trawl around for kids young enough to watch TV cartoon shows. But in 1949, Liverpool were beginning to refine their approach to recruiting young local players. 'Prior to the war,' opined the *Liverpool Echo*, 'much lip-service was paid to the nursery system.' Now things were getting much more serious, as transfer fees were rapidly rising (Everton had recently offered a staggering £25,000 for England man Wilf Mannion).

In August, the Liverpool club held public trials at the Anfield nursery ground in Prescot. But in contrast to the 'open house' approach of before the war, when literally anyone could turn up and have a trial, triallists were now confined to 'youths who have been vetted by the club's official scouts or recommended by friends of the club who have seen them in action'. This was a more rational selection process, one designed better to sift the wheat from the chaff and to establish a constant process of assessment of young players in local leagues and in the seven hundred and fifty amateur football clubs that the Liverpool County FA said existed within twenty miles of Liverpool town hall.

Other clubs were also starting to be more 'scientific' in their general approach, for example in their assessment of the opposition. 'Ranger' from the *Football Echo* noted that Bolton officials came to Anfield in 1949 to watch Liverpool play before the clubs met in a league fixture. 'Once upon a time,' he confirmed, 'this sort of preliminary investigation used to be reserved solely for cup-tie opponents.' No more. Some football clubs were now beginning to take opponents into account in planning their playing strategy. Liverpool were also beginning to play around a little with player numbering and positioning, many years before it became de rigueur. Much of this caper centred around the role of Billy Liddell, who was regularly switching now between centre-forward, right-wing and left-wing to offer the team some spark. But generally he wore the number 11 shirt wherever he played. Cyril Done recalled later how much confusion this sowed in opposition ranks when England captain Billy Wright of Wolves tried to work out before an FA Cup tie exactly why Done (9) was playing on the left-wing while Liddell (11) lined up in the middle. Who was Wright to mark?[3]

Other, perhaps less welcome, signs of the more 'modern' vision of the post-war game now came in the shape of some early product marketing around the Merseyside clubs. Unofficial Everton and Liverpool ties in club colours could now be purchased locally (price 7s 6d). More interesting was the brief appearance of the *Echo Magazine* and in it the connections already being drawn between football and sex. Here, as early as 20 August 1949, actress Virginia Mayo, 'owner of Hollywood's loveliest legs', was pictured in a bikini alongside a hastily sketched-in football and set of goalposts. The actress was 'fit and raring to go when the kick-off sounds' trilled the *Echo* commentary, heralding decades of similarly cheesy money shots to welcome every new league season in the tabloids in England. It was the type of local feature that was actually the precursor to *The Sun*'s later page-three dolly 'fan' of the 1970s and beyond.

Another noticeable post-war media development was the increasing local press intrusion into the family lives of star footballers. In September 1949, for example, the *Echo* began, briefly, to carry a regular feature on star local football players at home with their wives and children. This was an entirely new departure, and its main focus was on the 'ordinariness' and the wholesome nature of footballer family life. Cyril Sidlow was one of the first to figure from Liverpool, snapped with his children Rita and David as he was undertaking some woodwork as a hobby at home. Bob Paisley later featured, seen around the piano and also studying his books for his physiotherapy qualification. Billy Liddell's wife and new-born twin boys were covered later in the press at the christening of the new arrivals. These were hardly provocative or overly glamorous player profiles, but they were the very early signs of the British media's – and the British public's – increasing fascination with the lives of top footballers away from the playing field, an interest that would eventually coalesce – much later, of course – into a focus on football players as fully fledged local and national celebrities.

THE INTERNATIONAL ORDER – AND LIVERPOOL'S 'KICK AND RUSH' MERCHANTS

As the new football campaign got underway in England, Liverpool's Albert Stubbins was soon bemoaning not only the dearth of young British football talent, but 'the shortage of good old-fashioned steaks' as the sort of fuel needed to build up the stamina of young players. George Kay liked to take the Liverpool players to Birkdale, north of the city, before home matches for sea air, rest and good food. The Liverpool sporting press was also looking ahead to the World Cup finals in 1950, where England would be competing for the first time. This growing 'internationalisation' of the game had already been reflected in the city in 1948 in an audacious (and unsuccessful) bid by Italy's Roma to sign the brilliant Everton centre-half Tommy 'T.G.' Jones and in 1949 by the visit to Liverpool of a team of barefooted Nigerians to play at South Liverpool under floodlights. In 1950, there was the arrival of the 'tip-tapping style' of AIK from Sweden in a guest match at Anfield. Liverpool FC were also invited by the Colombian government and that country's top clubs to tour the South American country in the summer of 1950, but the trip was eventually called off after FIFA objected that the major clubs in Colombia had broken away from the national federation and were thus operating as a rebel league.

Although Liverpool had experienced lights on their North American tours, floodlights were still not permitted in the Football League and few people in Liverpool – or Britain – seemed to see them as part of the future of the sport. Certainly, Liverpool were way behind a number of other English professional clubs in seeing the potential of floodlit play, first trying out lights in a friendly at Watford in November 1954 and even refusing to play Accrington Stanley competitively under lights in the event of an FA Cup replay as late as January 1956. The visiting Nigerians, it was argued archly by the *Liverpool Echo*, would obviously be advantaged by playing under lights because 'their natural vision tends to be sharper than ours in the shades of night'. A gathering of 13,007 at Holly Park saw a 2–2 contest that brought 'almost unceasing gasps of amazement from the crowd at the Nigerians' speed or powerful barefoot shooting'. Their frightening pace, reported the *Echo*, 'by comparison would make some of our senior players resemble rheumaticky old cab-horses'.

The Swedes from AIK visiting Anfield were notable for something rather different: compared to English teams they made hardly any 'full-blooded clearances'. Players and coaches from around Britain came to watch this fixture. Few people in Liverpool would have seen top Continental footballers close up like this, of course, and the Swedes showed a very modern face of football, the importance of which would only really register with Bob Paisley and his staff at Anfield more than 25 years later: they *kept* the ball rather than simply hoof it out of defence. 'They made practically every pass with the inside of the foot,' commented the startled *Echo*, 'and they were remarkably accurate in all they did. When the full-backs or wing-halves found the way blocked to making good use of the ball in a forward direction, they were not above turning around and started a passing move towards their *own* goals.' These were strange tactics indeed to British eyes in the 1940s.

These were international football visits to the city in the late 1940s that highlighted real differences elsewhere, but did they point to obvious British failings? The Swedes thought that the forthcoming World Cup finals were more important than club football, while Everton manager Cliff Britton was sure that many English players 'do not train half as hard, or as seriously, as Continental sides'. But passing *backwards*? And likening British players to knackered old cab-horses? This kind of criticism must have seemed a little harsh in the autumn of 1949, because with Eddie Spicer in at left-back and Willie Fagan returned, and with Payne and Baron now fixtures on the Liverpool right, the Reds made a solid start to the new season – six draws and two wins in the first eight matches – which then blossomed into a fantastic nineteen-match unbeaten run, a modern league record at that time for the twenty-two-club First Division, beaten only by Leeds United in 1973–74. At Arsenal in September 1949 in a 2–1 win, Liddell and Stubbins simply tore the Gunners apart. 'Liverpool were so much on top,' said the almost disbelieving *Liverpool Echo*, 'that they indulged in all manner of artistries.' When woeful Everton, by contrast, lost 0–7 at Portsmouth at around the same time in front of the bemused comedian Arthur Askey, the Liverpool funnyman remarked, 'If you see a body thrown on the pitch, it's mine.'

With Everton's current travails and Liverpool's wonderful form, October 1949 must have seemed to the *Football Echo* like the ideal time to start a letters page for supporters' comments 'in response to numerous requests'. It soon disappeared again, but the early months of the postbag were sure to have been dominated by gripes from Goodison Park – Everton still seemed like the senior Merseyside club in terms of its coverage in the local press. But it was an open enough forum to capture complaints from a 13-year-old Bootle schoolboy that the boys' pen at Anfield was already a jungle in which 'the older boys bully the younger ones and push their way to the front'. There were also claims from Liverpool fans that the club's traditional style of play had been misrepresented and maligned by their opponents. The *Echo* agreed, arguing on 12 November 1949 that to label this current successful Liverpool side as 'kick and rush merchants' was a harsh judgement. 'Liverpool's speedy and direct methods of play demand just as much science, accuracy and skill as the close-passing moves of sides who prefer the more old-fashioned type of game.' Liverpool, the *Echo* argued, was actually playing a faster, more modern style of football compared to the failing, more laborious methods from across Stanley Park. It was a new angle on a very old and crude Merseyside debate about supposed Anfield graft and perspiration versus Goodison Park craft and inspiration.

After Liverpool had thumped Manchester City 4–0 on 5 November 1949, with Liddell, Brierley and Baron all scoring, *Echo* letter writer 'Red Well-Wisher' highlighted what many people in the city already clearly saw as the unremittingly positive media focus on regional rivals Manchester United. This was almost a decade before the Munich disaster would make United a focus for national sentimental attachment and some 30 years before relations between United and Liverpool fans deteriorated dramatically, for largely the same reasons. 'If there is a better team playing at the moment I have not seen it,' Well-Wisher wrote of Liverpool's current form, 'and I have seen the darlings of the press, Manchester United, who can do no wrong apparently.' Media darlings or not, by the end of November 1949 Liverpool were three points clear of Busby's United.

Even after losing 2–3 at Huddersfield on 10 December, thus finally ending the record unbeaten league run, the Reds were still clear at the top. Not that this was much to get the Liverpool press too excited, not with the FA Cup coming around again and with Liverpool Football Club still searching for its first FA Cup triumph.

THAT FATEFUL FA CUP, AGAIN . . .

In the FA Cup third round, Liverpool drew 0–0 at old rivals Blackburn Rovers on a 'sheet of mud' at Ewood Park before defeating Rovers 2–1 at Anfield in a Wednesday-afternoon replay in front of 52,221 supporters. No wonder government and local businesses were so ambivalent about football – were *all* these supporters really granted time off work to watch this fixture? Five thousand people had applied for the two thousand seats on sale for Anfield after season-ticket holders, shareholders and visitors had all had their slices of the total 7,400 seats on offer. Perhaps more seats would have been a good idea, because five minutes before kick-off people were being led out of the paddock again for fear of being crushed. For those who stayed, goals by Payne and Fagan – the latter looking suspiciously offside – replied to Edds' volley 'at lightning speed' for Rovers.

This win lined up a fourth-round home meeting with Third Division South club Exeter City. The visitors from Devon took the plaudits for a 'terrier show', punctured only by Kevin Baron's scrambled goal on 44 minutes. Three more goals in the last ten minutes – one for Smart for Exeter – settled a 3–1 win in which all the breaks went Liverpool's way. An Exeter fan wrote later to the *Liverpool Echo* with thanks on a 'happy day and a clean game', but he also pointed to the 'novelty' of a city that still had working trams – the very cheek of it.

Almost 60 years ahead of his time, the FA chairman Brook Hirst suggested in February 1950 that FA Cup semi-finals be played at Wembley, a proposal that brought only contempt from Ranger in the Merseyside press: 'London is not the hub of the football universe.' The idea was discreetly dropped. A record 27,833 crowd saw Liverpool scrape through round five, 2–1 at Third Division North's Stockport County. As usual, the lower-level club looked to pack in as many supporters as humanly possible for a mouth-watering, money-making tie such as this one. Partly as a result, a fence collapsed during the first half, which had Reds supporters spilling onto the touchline. But it also confirmed that 'there were likely to be a few more spectators [inside], for some people had climbed a wall into the ground so had got in "on the nod"'. A Liverpool supporter wrote later to the *Echo* that he was 'disgusted' at the County arrangements and that 'fully 3,000' paying customers inside had been unable to see the game. Fifteen minutes after kick-off, local police let out hundreds of paying spectators who simply had no hope of getting any sight of the pitch.

Ranger argued later for standing season tickets to help sort out ticket allocations and ground regulations for cup ties such as this one as the best way to avoid another Bolton tragedy. One male supporter in Liverpool wrote, 'Women are a contributing factor to overcrowding,' but he also pointed out, gallantly, that 'they are entitled to go to see the Reds or the Blues'. The overwhelming popularity of football was clear, but clubs were poorly regulated and barely accountable. With little in the way of organised supporters' campaigning, club officials seemed to care little about this type of spectator maltreatment, and there were no complaints for Stockport from the Anfield boardroom. These early departing Reds fans were at least spared a frantic Liverpool performance in which everybody, bar the referee, agreed that Phil Taylor had brought down veteran Scotland international Alex Herd from behind for a nailed-on home penalty, not given. This was before Willie Fagan scrambled the ball past goalkeeper Bowles on 57 minutes following a Liddell cross. Rain had now turned the pitch into a bog and the ball into a sodden cannonball – Arsenal had recently returned from Brazil with a waterproof laceless football, but a drowning England was not yet ready for this type of space-age technology. With 20 minutes left, Albert Stubbins showed his class at last: a run from halfway was finished decisively by him after his first attempt rebounded back off the Stockport keeper. Herd scored a late consolation for brave County, who frankly deserved more.

'Although the Cup is Liverpool's main objective,' reported the *Liverpool Echo* on 15 February 1950, 'they have a great chance of winning the championship.' The league title was definitely treated as a secondary goal, but a 2–1 Liverpool league home win against ten-man West Bromwich Albion, courtesy of keeper Sanders effectively punching into his own net with three minutes remaining, kept the Reds on top. 'If Liverpool's luck continues as it has recently,' commented the tongue-in-cheek local press, 'they will be a good bet to win the league title, the cup, the Grand National, the boat race and the Statue of Liberty from America.' But luck deserted Liverpool at Middlesbrough with a crashing 1–4 defeat that allowed Manchester United to go top by goal difference. Blackpool's visit to Anfield on 4 March in the sixth round of the FA Cup did not promise goals on this scale: the Tangerines had conceded only 23 in 23 league games. But the absence of the injured Stanley Matthews added somewhat to home confidence, and the Liverpool programme 'hoped' that the community singing before the match, conducted by invitation by Wembley's Mr Philpott, 'will not affect the Spion Kop's roar'.

Visiting Blackpool supporters – the Atomic Boys – joined in the fun by bringing a live duck painted tangerine as their mascot, which was described later by Liverpool supporters as 'the funniest turn since silent picture days'. But it failed to stop Willie Fagan scoring, following a 19th-minute corner, with 'a cute and most deliberate right-foot effort', the ball being gently passed into the opposition net. Within six minutes, though, Laurie Hughes had handled at the other end, and Sidlow could only palm Stan Mortensen's penalty into the side of the Liverpool net. At this stage, 'Blackpool's shots so far outnumbered Liverpool's, by ten to one.' But the Reds held on, with a draw looking the likeliest outcome until, with nine minutes left, Jimmy Payne hared up the left wing. Instead of crossing, the clever Payne delayed and carefully passed the ball inside to the lurking Billy Liddell, who 'slewed it with his right foot beyond the dismayed Farm'. As Kopites celebrated, there followed more FA Cup cheer. 'Roars and cheers greeted the news, which spread like lightning around Anfield, that Everton too had won [2–1 at Derby County].' So much, then, for those who still argued that Reds fans wanted to see the Blues damned.

THE GREAT MERSEYSIDE FA CUP SEMI-FINAL – AND TROUBLE IN MANCHESTER

Could it actually be a Merseyside FA Cup final at last, fifty-eight years after the great 1892 split that produced two intense rivals out of one seed? Sadly, the FA showed no sense of history, drawing the Liverpool clubs to meet in a Maine Road semi-final – and on Grand National weekend to boot! The owners of the Aintree course, the Topham family, appealed to the FA to change the match date but to no avail. With Arsenal playing Chelsea in the other contest, it was the first time in almost eighty years of FA Cup action that two clubs from the same city were competing against each other in both semi-finals. An exodus to Manchester was promised from Merseyside – 400 motor coaches and 30 football-special trains were booked for travel. Some people – including relatives of the players – spent most of one day queuing for train tickets simply to get to Manchester. But how was Liverpool FC to sell these prized match tickets?

Despite objections from residents, some 60,000 Merseyside supporters queued outside the respective stadiums for their chance, some staying out overnight to make sure they got a ticket. As the ticket offices opened, supporters on both sides of Stanley Park panicked and one hundred spectators were injured in the ensuing stampedes, with six of them hospitalised. Tension and tempers were definitely rising on Merseyside as the great football conflict approached. In the days before the match, the Fitzsimmons brothers from Spellow Lane, Edward and Michael, were accused of assaulting a George Kelly from the city after the latter had made a 'jocular remark' about the Liverpool v. Everton semi-final. This incident wasn't that funny: the unfortunate Kelly risked losing an eye from his injuries.

Everton went to Buxton for three days' relaxation and light training before the match, but Liverpool stayed at home until Friday before leaving for Alderley Edge in Cheshire. 'Match of the Century for Merseyside Folk' was how the *Football Echo* headlined the meeting on 25 March 1950. Future Blues manager Harry Catterick would play for Everton, but would Bob Paisley play for Liverpool? With the versatile Bill Jones showing solid form at both half-back and in defence, there was a broad hint in the local press that even a fully functioning Paisley might not now be in the optimum Liverpool FA Cup team. 'Most of their followers feel that had [Laurie] Hughes been fit and Jones available to cross to left-half,' said the *Echo*, 'the side would have gained in strength.' As it turned out, Hughes was unfit with a cracked little toe, so Paisley played – and scored – in a match that the Reds dominated in the spring sunshine, forcing fifteen corners to relegation-threatened Everton's five.

After 30 minutes, Everton keeper Burnett punched a Payne cross only as far as the advancing Paisley, who lobbed the ball back into the danger area. Billy Liddell jumped cannily with Burnett and the distracted Blues full-backs, but none of them made contact as Paisley's hopeful punt leaked into the Everton net. At first, the local pressmen assumed that Liddell had got the final touch, but it was Paisley's goal, aided by Billy's quick thinking. Now Baron especially but also Jimmy Payne continued to stretch their opponents on the Everton left, and Liverpool's half-backs – the stylish Phil Taylor, the terrier Paisley and the ice-cool Jones – made a nice balance and controlled proceedings. Everton's Eddie Wainwright prevented a corner on 62 minutes, though it looked as if it might have crossed the goal-line. Better for him that it had, because in saving the kick he inadvertently fed the ball to Liddell. Bad move. Billy could smell his Wembley day out, and he scored low at the far post from an acute angle – 2–0 to Liverpool. Liddell also hit a post late on in a comfortable Reds victory in which Cyril Sidlow 'has never earned his money so easily'.

Off the pitch in Manchester, things, clearly, hadn't been quite so easy or so orderly, even in this so-called 'Golden Age' of generally good behaviour from English football spectators. A reduced crowd limit made possible by ticketing had prevented excessive crushing, but outside Maine Road it had been a very 'lively' afternoon. A letter in the *Football Echo* from 'Fairplay' of Kenyon Road, Liverpool, for example, a man who said he was no 'crank' and that he enjoyed himself 'among the lads of the Kop' as well as 'under the clock at Goodison', described the kind of eventful trip to Maine Road that could have occurred at any time in the ensuing 30 years, and beyond:

> I was ashamed of being a native of Liverpool. At one time there were three fights going on around me, among so-called sportsmen. Later, I saw two youths knocking the stuffing out of one another and on going to the bus station saw the sorry spectacle of a Manchester bus conductor with a black eye, caused through one of our 'supporters'. On the journey into town some youths were bragging about what they had 'pinched' . . . and were using obscene language . . . I do hope those folk who are going to Wembley behave in a reasonable manner.

But this was no time to anticipate Wembley. Liverpool now had *seven* vital league games to play before the final – and they also had to make special training arrangements for the captain of their FA Cup final opponents Arsenal. Local man Joe Mercer was currently training at Anfield. Move him out? Not a bit of it. Liverpool simply asked Mercer to train in the afternoon, and they provided the Arsenal half-back with a goalkeeper for shooting practice and an outfield player to help with his ball work. These were different times, indeed – politely helping out your direct cup-final enemies seemed perfectly reasonable. Three consecutive Liverpool league wins – against Manchester City, Charlton Athletic and Burnley – revived the Reds' title hopes, as the club now wrestled with methods of allocating the 12,000 FA Cup final tickets without inducing the sort of chaos and injuries that had characterised the semi-final distribution.

Rather than risk more queuing and mayhem, Liverpool asked supporters who wanted a ticket to send in a plain postcard containing just their name and address. A public draw would then be made for the three-shilling Wembley tickets. The scope for trickery was obviously considerable here: there were no limits on how many postcards supporters could submit, or indeed on who might send them in. An avalanche was expected, and an astonishing 170,000 cards were reported to have arrived at Anfield. This scheme made methods used for European Cup final ticket allocation for Athens 57 years later seem entirely plausible by comparison. To rule out accusations of possible foul play in the postcard selection, the club even recruited two blind boys from Birkenhead and Belle Vale to make the draw. Most people, of course, missed out via this route and tried others, no matter how desperate. In nearby Colwyn Bay, for example, Gordon Jones's tobacconist shop was swamped with North Wales Reds enthusiasts after one of his female customers heard the proprietor talk about the 'cup final' tickets he had for sale and then spread the word. Jones was actually talking about the Cookson Cup final, between Colwyn Bay and Colwyn Boro. He was fortunate to escape intact from the angry and confused scenes that followed.

BACK TO THE LEAGUE

The condensed run of Easter fixtures started to take its toll on a Liverpool club now chasing the league title and FA Cup Double again. A tired and bedraggled side faced the holiday match at Newcastle without Paisley (thigh), Lambert (groin), Balmer (knee) and Sidlow (sciatica). At 0–2 on Tyneside, a concussed Albert Stubbins was helped off by Albert Shelley after a heavy collision, and Liverpool collapsed to a 1–5 defeat. But they were still third in the table and only one point off leaders Sunderland with four games left to play, though one of these remaining matches was carelessly blown in a 0–1 home loss to Burnley. Missile-throwing in this match by frustrated locals led to an FA admonishment and warning notices being posted at Anfield. But other clubs at the top were also losing, so everything was still possible.

Arsenal, meanwhile, had no such worries. They were busy giving a trial to a completely new FA Cup final strip in their league matches: gold, white shorts and gold socks. Both clubs had to change for the final under FA rules, so Liverpool decided on white shirts and black shorts, wearing the club badge for the first time. Not that this was a useful option against Fulham, who drew 1–1 at Anfield, with Billy Liddell missing on international duty. With two league games left, Liverpool were now one point behind new leaders Portsmouth, but other clubs were in contention and results now needed to go Liverpool's way for any title attempt to work out. The next league match was Portsmouth v. Liverpool on 22 April, and it still had the ring of a possible 1950 league-championship decider.

The bluff George Kay managed to persuade the FA to allow him to take his Liverpool players to Wembley en route to the Portsmouth match, just over one week before the cup final. This was unprecedented stuff, with Cyril Sidlow quipping that the final should be easy pickings for the respective goalkeepers – there were no goalposts up at the Empire Stadium as the Liverpool party got a feeling for their future surroundings. But was this Wembley trip also a distraction before a potentially crucial league match? Was it another sign of the absolute priority Kay and the Anfield board now placed on winning the elusive FA Cup?

At Portsmouth, Kay wanted Liverpool to try out their FA Cup final kit (another distraction?) but he discovered after arriving on the south coast that Liverpool could not play at Wembley in their usual red-and-white socks. The

FA had meant that the *entire* kit must be changed for the final. Liverpool had travelled south with their white kit but with no change of socks, and Kay wanted this to be an authentic rehearsal for the following week, so he sent Albert Shelley off to a sports outfitters in Portsmouth. The trainer returned with the only set of football stockings he could find: blue-and-white hooped ones. Liverpool wore them at Fratton Park and would thus play their first FA Cup final for 36 years sporting the colours of their closest rivals. Did this seem like bad karma at all?

Minshull was a late replacement for the struggling Sidlow (thigh muscle) at Portsmouth, and Paisley and Payne were both out, but Laurie Hughes was fit – which was potentially bad news for Paisley, even if he recovered for the FA Cup final. Lambert and Albert Stubbins were OK to start in a tightly contested and tense first half, which ended goal-less, even though the pace of Portsmouth's wingers was troubling the visiting full-backs. On 52 minutes, Albert Stubbins scored for Liverpool, a shot from a centre by Liddell. Was the impossible actually possible after all? This dream lasted ten minutes, by which time Reid had equalised with a header from a cross from Harris. Liverpool's main hope Billy Liddell looked exhausted now, 'a shadow of his normal dynamic self', and Liverpool had no reliable forward outlet as the pressure began to pile on their defence. Finally it told. With nine minutes left, Froggatt headed the Portsmouth winner from Scoular's precise cross. Defeat at home against Huddersfield Town in the final, meaningless, league fixture would follow and took Liverpool down to eighth place in a tightly packed final table. But this finish hid the real story of this valiant Liverpool 'Double' campaign, which remained alive almost until the final fixtures of the season.

THE SHAMBLES OF WEMBLEY 1950

After scoring a semi-final goal against Everton, Bob Paisley was left out of the 1950 Liverpool FA Cup final team. But it was no real surprise locally, certainly not to the *Echo*'s Ranger, for whom Paisley was 'the obvious twelfth man' if all other contenders were fit. Bob had played 23 league fixtures in a season troubled by injury; Bill Jones had played 26 games, admittedly many at centre-half, but Jones was also more mobile and certainly a more flexible half-back at that stage than Paisley. The rest of the Liverpool cup-final team pretty much picked itself – the ageing Jack Balmer was now well behind Kevin Baron in George Kay's eyes, and Cyril Done had played only 14 league games. Everyone in the side selected by Kay for Wembley had played more times in the league than the distraught Paisley had managed in the season.

For the kindly George Kay, this sort of tough decision contributed to the stress the manager habitually suffered, and he was taken ill before the final. He turned up at Wembley pasty-faced and drawn on what should have been one of the greatest days in his managerial career. Paisley's omission was a sad personal footnote to a generally distressing Liverpool experience, and he said graciously later that facing up to missing the biggest game in his career steeled him as a manager to making difficult selection decisions of his own.[4] Bob Paisley certainly thought seriously about leaving Liverpool in 1950 after missing out at Wembley. But his omission was probably not quite the injustice it was obviously felt to be by his family and some supporters. And Bob Paisley would be remembered for becoming a truly great Liverpool football manager more than he would for having been a very capable and unconditionally loyal Liverpool footballer.

Arsenal, capably managed by Tom Whittaker, pinned their Wembley hopes mainly on experience, fielding one of the oldest teams ever to play in a Wembley final thus far: George Swindin in goal, Wally Barnes, the Compton brothers and Joe Mercer were all highly seasoned professional footballers. The Arsenal team averaged 31 years of age and had eventually finished sixth in the league, above Liverpool, although they had spent almost the entire campaign in their wake. The heavy pitch and unseasonably cool conditions would suit the veteran Gunners, who were in form, as they would be able to play the final at a pace that suited both their style and make-up.

Before the war, the TV viewing figures for FA Cup finals were no higher than 10,000 to 12,000 people, but by 1950 the number of licensed sets had risen to 386,750, meaning that this was probably the first FA Cup final to be seen on British television by an audience of more than 1 million people.[5] For the first time, people who had not actually attended the match could hold an informed opinion on its incidents and outcomes.

The post-war fashion was to treat the FA Cup final as 'just another match', so Liverpool eschewed any special training regime for Wembley, and although George Kay valued tactics he didn't want his players, as he put it, to be 'cluttered up with a mess of theoretical ideas' that might make them seize up on the day. Accordingly, the Liverpool party travelled to Oaklands Park, Weybridge, for the last 48 hours before the match. But their arrangements were not quite as watertight as they might have wished. The hotel they had chosen was unusually crowded – who was making the bookings here? – and trainer Arthur Shelley and Reds inside-forward Kevin Baron found themselves bumped onto camp beds in the hotel ballroom, 'the only place where beds could be fitted up for them'. Young Baron would therefore play in the biggest game of his young life having slept the night before in a public space on a put-up bed alongside the club trainer. It seemed more like Sunday-league stuff than thought-out preparations for a historic Liverpool FA Cup final appearance.

Liverpool FC, FA Cup final team, v. Arsenal, 29 April 1950

Sidlow

Lambert Hughes Spicer

Taylor Jones

Baron Fagan

Payne Stubbins Liddell

Proud Arthur Shelley's spirits were certainly not dampened, either by the heavy London showers or by his own pre-final sleeping arrangements – he turned out for his day of a lifetime as Liverpool trainer in a striking, if rather slightly incongruous, outfit of red shirt and trousers and a cream linen jacket. The wives and relatives of players dressed in their own finery who had opted for uncovered seats to be closer to the action would rue the decision – it poured with rain, making the whole day an even more miserable affair for the defeated masses from the English north-west. The 5.50 a.m. Saturday train from Lime Street had transported probably the youngest fan on the whole trip from Merseyside, almost three-year-old Eric Stubbins, who carried a pair of clogs and a red teddy bear hoping, no doubt, that his dad might do the trick for Liverpool and for these people around him who were breaking out beer at breakfast time. The press on Merseyside carried pictures of the semi-official Liverpool mascot in London, James Phillips of Speke Road Gardens, dressed in all-red and hoisting a bell, while ticket touts were out in force: three-shilling tickets were fetching forty shillings on the capital's streets and top seats were going for £10 or more. But it was not only hard cash that was changing hands 'down south' in a still austere Britain in which the north was especially badly hit. The *Evening Express* reported that there was more than money on offer for tickets. 'In one café a black marketeer produced a box of American nylons. At a coffee stall another opened a suitcase full of bottles of scotch.' If only Reds fans had known what was in store for them, such treasures might even have been tempting.

Before the match, as the massed bands played and the community singing rang around Wembley Stadium, a Liverpool supporter dressed in white shirt and red shorts evaded the 500 stewards on duty and raced onto the middle of the pitch, shook hands with the Wembley conductor and then, typically, briefly conducted the crowd himself. The Liverpool supporters stirred, glad of a diversion from the soaking most of them were enduring. Meanwhile, inside the bowels of Wembley Stadium, players from both sides were retching with nerves in the bathrooms. Liverpool's Billy Liddell, a religious man and later a lay preacher, was sitting in the toilet for another reason. He was saying a prayer to help him get through the match and to ask for the safety of all the participants, a ritual he had performed before every major football match in which he had played since he was 16 years of age.

The rain and the lush thickness of the Wembley grass meant that Arsenal's footballer of the year and Anfield lodger Joe Mercer had to spin the coin twice to get it to lie flat for the choice of ends and kick-off to be decided. These players had seen so little grass on a football pitch for months, and now they had this greasy carpet to master. Mercer shook Phil Taylor's hand warmly and looked directly into the Liverpool man's eyes. Here was a player he had spent comradely years with on many a cold and dank training day at Anfield, not anticipating for a moment that they might actually meet here in deadly opposition in the most important club match of all in English football. Now they must put all friendship aside, like good professionals.

FINAL DESPAIR

In the opening exchanges, the players of both sides slithered around on the shiny green surface, but it took Joe Mercer's Arsenal only 17 minutes to settle down and to take the lead, a knife to Liverpool's nervous heart. A corner was only half-cleared by the Liverpool defence, to be returned instantly by Logie for the unmarked Reg Lewis to swivel and score from about ten yards. On the flanks, Liverpool were being buffeted and dominated, with Payne out of the game and the Reds' key danger man Liddell struggling on the sodden turf but also getting a pre-meditated roughing-up from the rugged Scottish half-back Alex Forbes. Loud Liverpool boos attached to Forbes whenever he got possession or hacked at Liddell, but the Liverpool man got little protection from Bedfordshire referee Henry Pearce, an official who reportedly changed his whistle every six weeks. He showed little sign of using it judiciously here. The Arsenal veterans coldly and professionally 'played' the referee and continued to dish it out to Liverpool's creative players, meaning it was difficult for the Reds to get any meaningful foothold in the contest before half-time.

For a period just after the interval, Liverpool actually pressed forward with some belief and purpose, and Payne finally came to life with a header to force a 'wonder save' from George Swindin in the Arsenal goal. Billy Liddell then embarked on a mazy run to beat three defenders, but he was squeezed out before he could shoot. This was much better; a Liverpool equaliser was potentially in sight. Moreover, a team that comes from behind often has the necessary momentum to accelerate past their shocked and doubt-ridden rivals to victory. But after 62 minutes, a clinching second goal arrived for Arsenal, Cox to the free man Lewis once again and another clinical finish. Liverpool could not come back from this deficit, not in these conditions and not against this sort of experience and confident resolve.

So a man who knew Anfield and its staff very well would climb, after all, to the royal box to pick up the 1950 FA Cup. But it would not be a Liverpool player, and his shirt would be a sweat-plastered golden yellow, rather than a rain-splattered Liver-birded white. The next morning, Arsenal captain Joe Mercer knocked on the door of the hotel room of Albert Stubbins to commiserate with his friend – and to play on the floor with his young son Eric. It was typical of Mercer to care like this for his fellow professional. This was a scene from a more sporting era, and it was a memory that stuck with the curiously detached Stubbins rather more than the match itself.[6]

On the Sunday after the final, the Liverpool party went to Brighton to relax before returning to Merseyside on the Monday afternoon. Liverpool's defeated return to the north was a hugely emotional occasion. Even hardened hacks seemed visibly moved by the bond expressed between the club and its supporters in such times of loss. 'All the way from Lime Street Station to Anfield,' reported the *Liverpool Echo*, 'cheering crowds up to ten deep lined the route and made one's ears ring with their cheers, rattles, bells and what-nots.'

The players went to Anfield, where a junior match was in play, to be rapturously received by the 30,000 crowd present. A further 20,000 people had gathered in Town Hall Square to reassert their ties with the club and its players in a season that had come so close to producing a near-unique achievement, but which had now been reduced to so much ashes. 'I doubt whether any club in the country can possibly possess such a fine bunch of supporters as Liverpool,' said the *Echo* proudly. 'No wonder Hitler's hordes couldn't break the spirit of Merseyside, in spite of all their efforts.'

This might have seemed like so much hyperbole, but it was only nine years or so since Liverpool had been blitzed, and the war remained a powerful and painful memory. But it was also a cohering one for almost every adult in the city. The language and idioms of war and football are also near-constant cellmates in English football parlance, even today. English football professionals are often ranked by their performance in the trenches, which can apply either to a muddied foreign football field or else to the bloodied ditches of France and Belgium. These are the brave warriors, the comrades upon whom you must rely for your profession or your life, the troops of both sport and war. The *Echo* was quite within its rights to draw upon other images of community suffering and mutual support to explain this emotional bond.

Despite their ultimate failures, this post-war group of Liverpool players had shown their mettle by winning a league title and also coming close to the Double *twice* in four years – in 1947 and in 1950. But their collective time was now coming to an end, and George Kay, his managerial successors and the Anfield board would have to build a new Liverpool, albeit on these sturdy foundations. But their attempts to do so would attract some sharp local criticism and the sorts of metaphors that are of a kind also connected to times of war: lions led by donkeys was one of the suggestions made. As football historian Neil Carter has argued, at this time in the English game 'boardrooms were riddled with complacency and characterised by staleness and immobility, with shares generally passed on to relatives and friends'.[7] This image of a lack of dynamism fitted the 1950s Liverpool Football Club perfectly, and its supporters would have to wait a while for inspiring new leaders to emerge. The football people of the city who had assembled to cheer and weep, simultaneously, in Town Hall Square in May 1950 did not yet know it, but some very difficult and perplexing years lay ahead for Liverpool Football Club in the next painful decade.

CHAPTER 12 REFERENCES

1. Wilson, *Inverting the Pyramid*
2. Keith, *Billy Liddell*, p. 104
3. Taylor and Ward, *Three Sides of the Mersey*
4. Keith, *Bob Paisley*, p. 47
5. Inglis, *League Football and the Men Who Made It*, p. 184
6. Taylor and Ward, *Three Sides of the Mersey*, p. 85
7. Carter, *The Football Manager*, p. 82

13

THE ROCKY ROAD TO GLENBUCK
The Bleak 1950s

MEN WITHOUT MASTERS: THE PASSING OF GEORGE KAY

Did Liverpool Football Club enter the new decade on a high after almost achieving the FA Cup and league Double? Initially, the signs were good. Reds players Bob Paisley, Cyril Done and goalkeeper Ray Minshull even appeared as authentic football celebrities on a 'spontaneous and unrehearsed' Radio Luxembourg quiz-panel show against local rivals Manchester United in December 1950. Surely this confident Liverpool team was on an upwards spiral? But no. Actually, Liverpool Football Club was on a severe downslope: it had an ageing team, a spent and ailing manager, and a lacklustre board that displayed no real ambition and drive. Within four years of appearing at Wembley in 1950, the club was relegated.

Losing its chairman Billy McConnell through illness in 1947 had certainly robbed Liverpool of one of its most dynamic and forward-looking figures on the board, and losing the services of its manager George Kay through illness in 1951 further damaged the crucial infrastructure and the deep football know-how that had existed inside the club since the mid-1930s. Key players had also declined or left the club, or else retired in the normal process of team renewal. Albert Stubbins faded very badly from his marvellous years in the 1940s, and crucial men from all core segments of the team – Sidlow, Fagan and Balmer, to name but three – would all soon be gone and would not be effectively replaced.

Only one man saw out much of the decade with the sort of commitment, loyalty, quality and sheer will to win that had symbolised the great Liverpool teams of the past. For 11 full seasons after the war, and save for international duty or injury, Billy Liddell's name was pretty much the first on any Liverpool team sheet, irrespective of manager, board shenanigans or fixture. His number and position might have changed over time but never his passion, honesty and focus for his only football club. Certainly, playing in the Second Division was no shame or hindrance to Liddell, just as long as he could pull on the red shirt of Liverpool. No other club ever seriously attempted to wrench him from Anfield, such was the strength of his allegiance and the manner in which he virtually defined the Liverpool club on the pitch for two decades. Only an Alex Raisbeck or an Elisha Scott could have done the same. Indeed, these three football players were the unquestionable greats from the pre-Bill Shankly Liverpool – from the league championship teams of the early 1900s, the 1920s and the 1940s, respectively. They would also walk, unassisted, into any team selected from those who have represented the Liverpool club. (Sadly, by 1954 five of the great Liverpool team of the 1920s – Chambers, Wadsworth, Lucas, McNab and Johnson – were all dead.) One championship medal and a single loser's medal in the FA Cup was barely reward for Liddell for the routine but extravagant brilliance he showed selflessly for Liverpool in his then record 534 appearances for the club.

In January 1951, Liverpool manager George Kay finally retired due to illness after 15 years at Anfield. He had been in hospital for some time, suffering from stress and nervous exhaustion caused by the job. He died on 19 April 1954 as the club he loved was also ailing and falling into the Second Division of the Football League. There was little side or polish to the man, who was a good friend to his players, a very human confidant for them almost as much as a boss. He was someone who found it painful to make hard but necessary decisions about their futures. Worst of all, every important football match for Liverpool was a war of nerves for him. He would frequently start games relatively detached in the grandstand but then would end up on the touchline, pacing out meaningless yardage, making every tackle or pass and wringing his hands with tension. As the *Liverpool Echo* put it about Kay on his death, 'Bitter irony that he should lose his zest for living, and finally his life, through strain and worry imposed by his association with the game he loved.'

The Liverpool board continued, without fuss or a manager, for five months while Kay was in hospital, connecting with the players via Albert Shelley. But in January 1951, Kay told the board from his hospital bed that he 'felt he would never be able to return to his duties', and out of more than 40 applicants (including a young Bill Shankly) in March 1951 Liverpool finally appointed the ex-Charlton Athletic forward Don Welsh to the role. Welsh had been manager at the Third Division South's Brighton and Hove Albion, without exactly pulling up any trees, but he had also played for Liverpool at centre-forward as a guest player during the war, scoring 42 goals in 41 appearances. The Liverpool board knew and trusted him. He was also young enough (just forty) to offer a good link between the boardroom and the Liverpool players, and he was seen as something of a tracksuit moderniser, but not one who was too headstrong or had too many of his own ideas. And, best of all for these cautious, parsimonious Liverpool directors, he was cheap.

The thinking inside Anfield was that Welsh could learn how to manage a top football club by relying on the wisdom and experience of the Liverpool board. As the *Liverpool Echo* supportively put it, 'If two heads are better than one, then nine directors and a manager must be better still.' It was a view, certainly. Welsh believed in the typical English virtues of strength and power, and he was something of an upbeat, extrovert joker and athlete, a man who liked to get up in fancy dress and to walk on his hands in hotels and the dressing-room, challenging others to do the same. He made training more interesting, with much more ball work and different exercises, so this much was an advance on what had gone before.[1] Liverpool also appointed a qualified physiotherapist to work on the players' fitness for the first time.

When the Liverpool chairman George Richards welcomed Welsh and introduced him to the Liverpool players, he left the new man and the squad in no doubt as to exactly why he had been brought to Anfield. 'Mr Welsh's career as a player entitles him to your confidence,' he told the staff, 'and I trust that in the not-too-distant future he will lead you to Wembley.' It was the FA Cup again.

REBUILDING – TOWARDS RELEGATION

With Albert Stubbins now generally out of sorts or else injured much of the time and Jackie Balmer in decline, in the new Don Welsh era Liverpool plainly and urgently needed to recruit quality goalscoring forwards to support Billy Liddell in this crucial exercise. The demand that young players do national service in the forces at this time offered a further complication in signing younger men. Lowly Sheffield Wednesday splashed out a world-record £34,500 on Jackie Sewell in 1951 – and were promptly relegated. Liverpool's record purchase remained the distant £12,500 spent on the suddenly unproductive Stubbins. The Liverpool club had been involved in more than a dozen major transfer negotiations for forwards since 1946, pretty much all of which had mysteriously fallen flat. What was going on here? Was the Liverpool board deliberately aiming impossibly high at unfeasible targets – Shackleton, Mannion, Steel, Hagan among them – merely to give the impression locally that they were trying hard to make big-money signings? This was one prominent theory. Another was that the board was unwilling to meet the substantial fees demanded by clubs. The Liverpool minute books suggest the Anfield transfer strategy was that Liverpool directors typically asked rival directors what was the lowest figure they would accept for a player – and then offer substantially below that figure as a bargaining stance. Unsurprisingly, this was seldom a successful tactic.

The club often trotted out the line about its responsibilities to shareholders as well as supporters, and the Liverpool board seemed quite unwilling to speculate in order to accumulate. Another theory was that the board would not offer the necessary 'extras' required to sign top players in those days. Because of the constraints of the maximum wage and the black-market hangover from the war, the transfer system was widely assumed to be bent. Maybe the strait-laced men from Anfield just refused to play ball with players and clubs on this score? When Don Welsh was accused by the FA in December 1954 of offering a £100 inducement to the Droylsden centre-half Lomas to sign for Liverpool, rather than take it in their stride the Anfield board was shocked and appalled by the accusation. As the *Liverpool Echo* put it, 'Liverpool are determined not to take part in any "under the counter" business.'

The Liverpool board had regularly tried to assure the club's supporters that it would only sign the right men at the right price. Chairman George Richards, for example, said, 'The search for good players still goes on. The board are prepared to pay top price for men of proven ability when they are available for transfer.' But the local press became increasingly dubious: 'That age-old formula has been trotted out so many times now that folk are becoming rather cynical about the effort to sign new players of experience.' But the Liverpool board was also generally cosseted from hostile public opinion, even when the team was playing below what was expected or required. The Merseyside press was largely friendly and supportive, and the club's supporters had a tradition – unlike at Everton – of near-unquestioning loyalty to the Liverpool board, manager and players. More importantly perhaps, the Liverpool club directors had a vice-like control over the club's shares. These men held overlapping duties and responsibilities in local businesses, public office and in high levels of local politics, invariably in the Liverpool Conservatives. They ran a very tight ship indeed, one that brooked little or no internal dissent or external opposition.

This last point meant that since the Liverpool shareholders mini 'revolt' of 1932, there were seldom difficult or 'unharmonious' Liverpool AGMs or even contested director elections at Anfield, as there frequently were over at Goodison Park. When a Liverpool club servant was deemed to have 'fallen out' with other key board members – perhaps after an unusually high level of trading in shares, as happened in 1955 to ex-chairman and director for 24 years Ronnie Williams – the unfortunate man who opposed the usual consensus was simply frozen out with minimum fuss or discussion. 'An odd question or two has been asked from time to time, usually in apologetic tones,' recalled the *Liverpool Echo* of the typical Anfield AGMs of the time, 'but rarely has anything approaching a spanner been thrown into the works.' Indeed, it was difficult to remember a single emergency general meeting successfully called by any group of shareholders in the entire history of the Liverpool club thus far. The nature of share ownership there, as well as the ingrained culture of the club, simply prohibited such a potentially dynamic move from taking place.

In July 1953, for example, after a quite awful season in which Liverpool had finished seventeenth in the league and had lost in the third round of the FA Cup to little Gateshead, there was barely a whimper at the AGM. The *Liverpool Echo* reported, 'Many a church choir meeting has produced greater dissension and more bitterness than Liverpool's annual gathering of shareholders.' For once, the board was divided on who should replace the deceased director R.K. Milne, but the most that club chairman George Richards could bring himself to say on the matter was that the board was 'not undivided'. As Ranger put it:

> Altogether, this was another 'All pals together' meeting, without a dissenting voice, apart from the gentleman who doubted the genuineness of the board's unanimity. There was not even a question about the prospects for next season, which was rather surprising. Nobody felt bold enough to insert a discordant note into the happy and cheerful atmosphere.

Seldom did the Liverpool directors come to an AGM in any way publicly split or disunited because 'domestic affairs, team problems, and any other matters on which there has not been unanimity . . . have always been kept private, which is right and proper'. This was the much vaunted and historic 'Liverpool Way' in action, of course, an approach to directing the club that could be traced right back to the autocratic rule of John Houlding and that ran through the 1920s and 1930s. Don't do your dirty washing in public. But it also must have been immensely frustrating to some Reds supporters in the 1950s to have so little response to how the club was performing, and it made the club's directors almost completely unaccountable – except, of course, to themselves. Only very occasionally did the directors' veil slip, slightly, as it did at the 1954 post-relegation 62nd Liverpool AGM, when a shareholder called Parker asked whether potential opponents to the election of Harold Cartwright and Chief Inspector J.W. Morris to the Liverpool board had been dissuaded from standing by the club chairman Alderman Will Harrop. The chairman was alleged to have told them, 'You have no chance. If you withdraw now, you might have a chance next year.' This was typically the way in which contested elections were avoided. Harrop, of course, was affronted and vehemently denied the charge, and the meeting moved quickly on (Parker himself was later quietened because he was soon elected to the board). Someone then enquired about Albert Stubbins, who was said still to be registered with Liverpool. The directors responded, evenly, that the man who had won the league title for the Reds in 1947 would 'never play for the club again'. It was business as usual.

A GLOBAL GAME, BUT A LOCAL CRISIS

Club director T.V. Williams, who had joined the board in 1948, was a man with a little more vision than other directors. It was Williams who decided that Liverpool now needed its own training ground, and he orchestrated the purchase of land in West Derby for the purpose, bought from a local school. But beyond building a new boundary wall, the Liverpool board was unwilling to spend much cash on the new facilities at Melwood. Williams was also the key figure in appointing Bob Paisley as second-team trainer and budding physiotherapist when the rugged wing-half retired at the end of the relegation season in 1954. Paisley could instinctively judge a footballer's body as easily as many working-class men from Durham could weigh up racing animals – dogs, horses or pigeons.[2] The kindly but shrewd ex-Manchester City man Joe Fagan followed Paisley onto the Liverpool backroom staff in 1958.

Liverpool's slide into football obscurity was masked somewhat by Everton's own relegation in 1951, but by 1952 the writing was probably already on the wall for the Reds. Liverpool went 23 weeks – from 13 October 1951 to 22 March 1952 (10 matches) – between home league wins. Some old-stagers were still doing their stuff – Liddell, of course, and Bill Jones had been in 'scintillating form' in defence, while Ray Lambert continued to be 'a tower of strength' at full-back. Reserve goalkeeper Charlie Ashcroft had finally been given his chance, but he did not always convince. However, when the Yorkshireman Russell Crossley replaced him in goal in 1953, Spurs' full-back Alf Ramsey scored over the new goalkeeper's head from a free-kick near the halfway line. Injuries to other stalwarts such as Paisley (wrist), Hughes (ligaments) and Taylor (cartilage) were serious disruptions as Liverpool limped to a final 11th-place finish. By April 1952, Jack Balmer had been offered an Anfield coaching job, Cyril Done had been released, and Sidlow and Fagan were on the transfer list. In May 1952, Liverpool met Everton in a 'thrill-packed' Liverpool Senior Cup final – a competitive derby game at least – won for Liverpool by a goal from Welshman Mervyn Jones, a man so small that Bob Paisley had once asked him in a team-photograph group whether he could see over the football he was carrying.

The Liverpool board finally bought to try to plug the goals gap up front by bringing in the bruising Sammy Smyth, a 27-year-old Northern Ireland international from Stoke City, for £12,000. It wasn't exactly the 'statement' signing that Reds supporters had been calling for, and Smyth had been signed only after the 1953 FA Cup deadline because fog had interrupted plans for the Liverpool directors to meet with the player. But the new man's goals in three crucial league matches won in February 1953 helped save the club from relegation. His forced omission from the third-round FA Cup tie at lowly Gateshead, and the fact that the Liverpool board could find no place for Stubbins, which, for the *Daily Post*, 'surprises few', was probably decisive. Liverpool slipped miserably out of the Cup, 0–1, in dense fog and on a typical early FA Cup pitch that was 'almost the consistency of plasticine'.

Later in 1953, national hero Stanley Matthews won his FA Cup-winner's medal at last with Blackpool, a new young queen took her place on the British throne and, appropriately, *women's* football was poking its head above the parapet once more in the Merseyside area. At the Tower Ground, New Brighton, in July, for example, Manchester Corinthians played Dynamo Women of Cheshire in a charity game. Later, Preston's Dick, Kerr's took on a London Select at the Stanley Track in Prescot Road in aid of Liverpool City RLFC. Women footballers had not simply disappeared since 1921 after all. Local Sunday footballers in the city might as well have disappeared: they were still locked out of Liverpool parks. 'One would almost think they were engaging in crime instead of healthy sport,' complained a correspondent to the *Liverpool Echo* in July 1953. People in the city who had been relocated to the 'salubrious and well-planned' outer Merseyside estates of Kirkby and Speke were rather happier with their lot, according to the *Echo*. They were finding 'a whole new joy in their surroundings and the pure air saves no end of cleaning'. This optimistic message rather simplified – and probably misrepresented – the real experiences of many of those who had been yanked out of tightly bound city neighbourhoods and plonked miles away in areas with no shops and little in the way of infrastructure.

In Durban, South Africa, meanwhile, a Liverpool and Everton football social club was set up for expats – an astonishing 18 Scousers turned up for the first meeting. A Liverpool-born singer, Lita Roza, had a number-one British hit in March 1953 with the unlikely '(How Much Is) That Doggie in the Window?', and stylish 'zoot suits' made their first appearance in the American-obsessed city of Liverpool, as some young people began to earn decent wages at last following the austerity years after the war. Robert Lawson Martindale, Liverpool FC director and chairman of the Liverpool magistrates, was soon talking in court in 1953 about 'gang warfare' and 'knife gangs' in parts of the city that would continue to exhibit the same sorts of tribal problems more than 50 years later. He was one of four justices of the peace on the Liverpool board, which was still dominated, of course, by Conservatives and Freemasons, but also by local men with a strong sense of civic duty. Certainly, Liverpool FC continued to exhibit a reasonable sense of public community responsibility and attachment. The annual pre-season first team versus reserves practice match in the 1950s, for example, regularly produced between £600 and £800 in receipts for distribution between 30 or more local charities. Also, between 20 April and 9 May 1953 Anfield staged a staggering 16 local community, schools and charities football matches and finals, all virtually free of charge. But not everyone could be taken on board. In March 1955, for example, the application by a Mr Lott of Aigburth Road to be admitted to matches in his invalid carriage was refused – facilities at Anfield simply did not permit disabled access of this kind.

Robert Lawson Martindale valued both public service and responsibility, and it was he who urged the Liverpool board to cut its own cloth in February 1953. He issued a list of alleged director excesses, including quaffing champagne, high lunch bills and poorly monitored expenses. Predictably, the board threw out most of his suggestions, but at least it ended the tradition of holding Liverpool board meetings over a groaning lunch at the Adelphi Hotel. They would now take place at Anfield or at a director's workplace.

George Band, from Bebington on the Wirral, would have had little time for this sort of high living: this local man looked after the radio equipment and food supplies on the Sir John Hunt-led expedition that famously conquered Mount Everest in 1953. George briefly became something of a local hero on Merseyside, and, in the 1950s, for a man who was not a footballer or an embryonic pop star this was quite a trick. The year 1953 certainly felt like a good one to be British again – but not, perhaps, to be either a Liverpool or an Everton football supporter.

GOING DOWN, AT HOME AND ABROAD

Liverpool embarked on a marathon six-week tour of the USA in the summer of 1953, which seemed to drain them fatally for the new campaign. After losing 0–4 at Newcastle in September, Ranger said sternly, 'It is a rather sad story I have to tell, but the time is now for true criticism and Liverpool at the moment do not promise any great things for the future.' How true this would turn out to be. Gloom hung over the entire Anfield area. During training in the car park in November 1953, a Mrs Morris of 35 Lothair Road was hit by a stray football and had her false teeth broken – the club had to fork out £22 to repair them.

Actually, incurring injury was one of the very few ways that females could get any sort of payment out of Liverpool, because there were few real employment opportunities at Anfield for women in the early 1950s. Even when the club advertised for a shorthand typist in February 1954, the club minute books show that the board insisted that the word 'male' was firmly and prominently inserted in the ad to put off any unwanted applicants.

As Everton started to tear up the Second Division at last, Liverpool meekly propped up the First. A 0–6 defeat at Charlton saw 'Liverpool in the depths', according to the *Daily Post*. There were rays of hope, nevertheless. Centre-forward Louis Bimpson from Rainford was something of a raw reincarnation of Cyril Done, and he scored all four goals as Liverpool saw off Burnley at Anfield in September to end a run of eight league matches without a win. Correspondent Leslie Edwards in the *Daily Post* still saw a downside to the victory. 'I can imagine no more frightful place for the light-fingered than this huge terrace mound,' he said of the Kop. 'Rabid and highly elated supporters might almost be sledge-hammered without knowing it.' But there would be only three more Liverpool league wins for the Anfield faithful (and local pickpockets) to celebrate before the middle of March 1954, when it was already too late to avoid the drop. 'Have they signed him yet?' the *Post* suggested was the question on all Liverpool lips in October 1953 as the club sought a transfer saviour. 'Too many players have grown old too quickly. Do not players want to come to Anfield, or have the club been slow moving?'

The truth was that the Liverpool board did not want to spend anything approaching big money, and the new Reds manager Don Welsh had neither the personality nor the independence or experience to press for new blood of sufficient quality. John Atyeo, a £20,000, 6-ft, 21-year-old centre-forward from Third Division Bristol City, was briefly a target, but even he escaped the Anfield net. He might have baulked at Liverpool's doomed position at the bottom of the table. Atyeo burned brightly very briefly and then disappeared without trace. By December 1953, Eddie Spicer had badly broken his leg and retired from the game, and even Liverpool's 16-year-old mascot David Goodman was in hospital – he missed an incredible 5–2 Reds victory over cup-holders Blackpool at Anfield, in a run of one league win in nineteen games. It was 'the turn-up to beat all turn-ups', the press reported. Or maybe not . . .

On the national football stage, on 24 November 1953 Ranger, speaking confidently of the forthcoming international match between England and Hungary at Wembley, said, 'It is an old English custom to belittle our own skill and magnify that of the opposition. Maybe it springs from our own innate modesty.' Or maybe the English just had a lot to be modest about. This was typical national hubris, and over the next few days Ranger, like many others in the British press and inside the English game, would have to eat plates of humble pie – with cream on it. England lost for the first time at Wembley, savaged 3–6 by the kind of sheer skill, pace and movement that English football supporters and players had rarely seen. Ranger now recalled the Englishman Jimmy Hogan's coaching work with the Hungarians – the Magyars had learned everything from us, after all – before suggesting that the FA should finance their own squad of full-time players rather than periodically 'loan' them from clubs. 'Professional football' in England, he argued on 26 November 1953, 'has degenerated into a lazy and indolent life for all but the few really conscientious players.' Suddenly English football seemed outmoded and inept. 'The unpalatable fact is that 50 per cent of players have neglected the need to master their craft from A–Z. For years a lot of paltry and aimless stuff has been put before the long-suffering spectator in the guise of first-class football.'

It was hardly surprising that the general technical quality of the English game had suffered. While the Continentals were already talking about 'science', tactics and variety in player preparation, the English approach to training was still incredibly basic, drawing largely on the brutal fitness regimes learned in the forces during the war. It was aimed at producing stamina and strength for the long slog ahead more than at developing ball skills. Training at Liverpool was a case in point. Monday was the day off training, while Tuesday was spent at Melwood on exercises and perhaps with a brief practice match. Wednesday and Thursday were usually Anfield days, spent endlessly lapping the pitch under the eagle eyes of Albert Shelley and Jimmy Seddon, while on Friday the players were back at Melwood in spikes for some sprinting and speed work. If it rained, the players would slog up the covered terraces or else they would do some basic gym work. There were still very few practical or creative activities undertaken with a football in training, and nothing at all on set-pieces.[3] The Liverpool directors routinely reported to board meetings on the hundreds of players they scouted by referring mainly to their size, physique and weight of kick. These were among the reasons why the top English clubs were also vulnerable to FA Cup defeats by the lower orders. There was little technical or tactical advantage higher up the English football food chain that had been generated by superior coaching.

The English would never really learn the full lesson of 1953. Decades later, managers of English clubs were still doubting what we could learn from football cultures abroad. And there could be no doubt that 'paltry and aimless' was a good description of Liverpool's current form. The Reds eventually called on 31 of their large group of 44 professional players for the 1953–54 league campaign, a sure sign of trouble ahead. Among these, however, was a skilful, balding

Liverpool-born inside-forward called Jimmy Melia, a man who never quite won over the whole Liverpool crowd but who would be a key figure in eventually dragging the club back into the big time. The 23-year-old Geoff Twentyman, a rangy and intelligent half-back or centre-half, a leader and briefly the Liverpool captain, joined for £10,000 from Carlisle United in December 1953. He would return to the club in the late 1960s as a coach and scout under Bill Shankly. Alan A'Court, a sparky Prescot-born left-winger with a fierce shot, now began to figure, and he would prove an undoubted star in a weak Liverpool team, playing three times for England in the World Cup finals in 1958, while his club was still rooted in the Second Division. A'Court actually stayed long enough at Anfield to play in Liverpool's first-ever tie in Europe, against KR Reykjavik in 1964. Forward John Evans and a 'dainty and stylish' full-back Frank Lock signed jointly from Charlton Athletic in December 1953 in a Liverpool spending spree totalling £12,500. The Reds even went to bitter rivals Manchester United to sign another full-back, Tom McNulty, for £7,000, but it was money poorly spent. These latter signings made a less than long-lasting impression – Liverpool continued to slump.

Early in 1954, things finally began to overheat among the club's long-suffering supporters. On 2 January, a Reds fan got onto the pitch at Anfield and wrestled with the Bootle-born Bolton Wanderers goalkeeper Hansen at the Anfield Road end after a goalmouth melee towards the end of a 1–2 defeat. The player suffered a split lip in the assault, and a section of the crowd stayed behind outside the ground afterwards to carry on the argument, as Hansen was slipped out by the back door. Imagine the hoo-ha this sort of thing would produce today!

An older supporter, John Roberts from the Isle of Man, wrote to the *Daily Post* on 6 January summing up what many Reds supporters probably thought about the current Liverpool:

> When they last went into Division Two it was because they lacked money. Today they must be fairly well off. I think the way the club has been run in the past couple of years has been scandalous. To start this season without a single decent signing to replace the old faithfuls was shocking and an insult to their most loyal supporters.

By 1 March 1954, when Liverpool went down 1–2 at Aston Villa, even Billy Liddell had lost heart and the scoring touch, supplying only six league goals in the season. The *Daily Post* reported that Liverpool officials 'profess themselves surprised that the press and their followers have been so kind; that the criticism of the side has been so tempered'. Well they might.

By 5 March, Liverpool were reported to have circulated to all clubs that they were prepared to receive offers for players in all positions. (Did they mean Liddell, too?) It looked like a closing-down sale. Still, 'the crowd was full of encouragement' and a remarkable 46,074 turned up for the 'must-win' home match against Huddersfield Town – which was lost 1–3. 'Of all the games Liverpool have played over the past 50 years,' said the *Daily Post* glumly, 'this one rates as the heaviest of black borders.' Nine league games were left, but Liverpool were already effectively stranded, ending half a century in the top division, even though four of their nine league wins that season came in April. This run included a victory at Maine Road, their first away win in 24 attempts. George Kay passed away just as the First Division last rites were also being read for Liverpool Football Club. 'In a hydrogen-bomb age,' mused Leslie Edwards wisely in the *Daily Post*, 'should we really worry too much about the prospects of no First Division club in the city next year?' He had no need to worry too much, at least not about football: Everton were already on the up escalator and moving out of the second rank, even as Liverpool crashed down.

SECOND DIVISION WOES – AND A RECORD LEAGUE DEFEAT

Don Welsh was now at the end of his first three-year contract, with an unimpressive record, but he was instantly reappointed. After all, he was doing the Liverpool board's bidding without complaint. He told his directors, not unreasonably, 'We have too many players growing old together.'

Things got only a little better at the lower level. By the end of December 1954, Liverpool already had ten away defeats and no away wins at all in the Second Division. After 20 matches, they had 20 points and were just midway. In one comic moment, Liverpool beat Middlesbrough 3–1 in front of just 26,749 at Anfield on 4 December. When the Reds were awarded a penalty, Boro keeper Rolly Ugolini left his goal for the penalty spot to ask Billy Liddell if he wanted a bet on whether he would score. The Kop hooted. Billy growled that the keeper could have any money on it he wanted – and scored.

English clubs were now starting to acquire lights, awaiting a relaxation of league regulations. Liverpool finally got theirs in the autumn of 1957 at a cut-down price of £12,000. On 10 December 1954, meanwhile, the *Liverpool Echo* previewed the club's forthcoming league visit to Birmingham City with the businesslike headline 'Liverpool Visit Birmingham in Search of Elusive Away Win'. Were they joking?

Ken Rudham, Liverpool's third South African goalkeeper, had now pushed his way in front of Ashcroft, and Lock and Ray Lambert had teamed up at full-back. Brian Jackson, a southerner ex-schoolboy international who had been brought in from Leyton Orient, was now playing on the right wing with the Bishop Auckland amateur George Wilkinson behind him at right-half, taking advantage of the fall of the 1947 trio of Taylor, Jones and Paisley. He accompanied the long-serving Laurie Hughes and also Geoff Twentyman at half-back. Eric Anderson, a Manchester-born lightweight inside-forward, offered what help he could to Evans and Liddell. Future international Alan A'Court patrolled the left-wing.

This was the uncertain XI that travelled apparently with some hope to Birmingham. In the event, Liverpool lost 1–9 at St Andrews on 11 December 1954, the club's record league defeat. The explanation offered – though it seems grossly unprofessional – was that Liverpool staff had misread the frost-bound Birmingham pitch and so players wore the wrong boots in the Midlands. Nothing at all was said about the scale of the defeat in the Liverpool minute books or the need to change policy. Perhaps the defeat never happened? Amazingly, most Liverpool supporters seemed resigned, rather than angry, at this capitulation, though there was some public angst on Merseyside at this latest humiliation. As 'Fed Up' told the *Football Echo* on 18 December 1954:

> Liverpool's debacle at Birmingham calls for a full inquiry. They are going from bad to worse, and I fear for the future. Don't ask us to keep on cheering, we haven't the heart. They have no reserves of any promise.

The Liverpool directors made their own point by saying (apparently without irony) that 'the result should not be taken too much at face value'. In fact, they decided to field the same 11 players in the next league fixture, against Doncaster Rovers. This match was also lost, but by only 1–4, so this was obviously an improvement. After Birmingham, a supporter had asked the teetotaller Billy Liddell why he had had 'one over the eight' on Saturday, and Liddell also heard of Reds supporters who went to bed on hearing the result and stayed there all day Sunday. During a Merseyside v. Birmingham amateur boxing match at Byrne Avenue Baths a few days later, a count of nine against a Birmingham fighter brought from a wag in the audience the observation, 'There's nine back for Liverpool!' This was black humour of the most desperate kind, because this was surely Liverpool Football Club at its lowest twentieth-century ebb. When the Reds played Ipswich Town at home on Christmas Day 1954, only 24,073 bothered to turn up, suggesting both public disillusionment in Liverpool and changing social habits. Christmas Day was increasingly a family day to be spent at home, not freezing and despondent at a football match. It would finally disappear as a day for football in England in 1958.

As if to add insult to injury, Liverpool were drawn to play Everton at Goodison Park in the FA Cup on 29 January 1955. It looked like more certain gloom for Anfield. Few could have predicted the outcome, a remarkable 4–0 win for Liverpool. The unexpected victory came after the Reds sprung Everton's offside trap following a helpful telephone call to Anfield from a supporter who had noticed that the Blues always advanced up-field at free-kicks to play their opponents offside. Notably, it had taken the unsolicited advice of an observant Kopite to get the Reds to consider any kind of set-piece practice, and it paid off in spades here. Everton collapsed in the match after being so brutally exposed. Sadly, Huddersfield Town had no such foibles or weaknesses and comfortably beat Liverpool next round up. A 2–2 draw when hosting Birmingham in the league at Anfield in May 1955 restored a little more lost respect. But a chaotic 1–6 Reds defeat to promotion-chasing Rotherham in the season's last league match showed just how much there was still to do to get Liverpool Football Club out of the Second Division.

FROM THE DEPTHS OF DESPAIR

In the summer of 1955, two men who would see the club into a brighter future, T.V. Williams and Sydney Reakes, began to assert themselves much more prominently on the Liverpool board. They hinted at a change of policy and direction for the club at last. Tom Williams, a former postman, had been a keen supporter of Liverpool all his life, and he had watched the club from the Kop as a young man. Williams was a long-standing shareholder who had been approached earlier to be a club director He had decided then to focus on his growing cotton-broking business but was now retired and in his late 60s. He did not lack energy or ambition. It was Williams who would provide the historic link between McKenna and John Houlding and Bill Shankly, as Liverpool Football Club finally threw off its 1950s gloom.

In February 1956, on the death of Will Harrop (another man who had been unchallenged as a director of the club for 30 years), Williams would become Liverpool FC chairman for a period of crucial transformations. But before all that, Liverpool had a contest in the annual director elections for once. When Harrop was asked by a Reds shareholder why this had happened, he replied, to general surprise, 'It was felt that the possibility of a change of directors on the board might do the club good.' Finally, the closed shop was opening. Clifford Hill, another director, said that he was willing to forego the directors' box to watch the A or B teams, or even the Liverpool youth team, if it would help build up the first team. This seemed like revolutionary stuff, though it actually turned out to be more like evolution.

Tom Williams argued that in offering his leadership, Harrop had sacrificed 'football's greatest honour' – the possible presidency of the Football League – for the sake of Liverpool FC, and he added this warning: 'Four years ago the writing was on the wall . . . If there is a member of this club, from the chairman down to the youngest ground boy, who does not pull his weight then we will sweep him out of the way. We mean to keep it that way.' For the sometimes slapstick Liverpool manager Don Welsh this kind of language must have sounded either like a declaration of war or else an assurance that he would now be given the financial ammunition he had previously lacked – although Will Harrop confirmed, wearily, that the club had no intention of paying 'fantastic' prices for 'ordinary' players. It seemed unlikely, in any case, that Welsh was in a position to demand big-money signings from his employers. In fact, his comments on the general failings of Liverpool players sound eerily like the sort of thing that all drowning football managers dredge up to say in mitigation today. 'Players are money conscious instead of playing conscious,' he told the Liverpool board in 1955. 'There are so many interests provided for them now that they do not practise as much as boys used to a generation or two ago.' But he was not talking here about a stocky and pugnacious little Liverpool-born left-back Ronnie Moran, who was now pushing himself into the Liverpool first team and who struck such a level of consistency and resilience that he would miss only six matches in five seasons beginning with 1955–56.

With Moran shoring up the Liverpool left side and the club's league shirt now carrying the distinctive liver-bird club badge for the first time – most clubs would wait until the 1960s or '70s to adopt club crests on their shirts – Don Welsh managed to get the Reds back into promotion contention again in 1955–56, with a 7–0 home win against fancied Fulham the highlight. The Reds made it up to third place in the table. But for the local press Liverpool – like their manager – generally 'lacked subtlety and craft', and two losses against Doncaster Rovers (again!) in March and April 1956 probably finished off their chances – and also finished off Welsh.

Liverpool Football Club was a very large and well-supported enterprise in Division Two in the 1950s, and the size – and occasionally the behaviour – of their travelling support, with little to cheer on the field, sometimes threatened to overwhelm local police forces. The visits to Doncaster were obviously among a number of lively away affairs at this time. Rovers fielded future stand-up comedian Charlie Williams at centre-half, one of the few black players in the

English game in the 1950s. A letter to the *Liverpool Echo* from James Corish from Doncaster on 4 April complained of Liverpool racism, claiming that Williams had been 'reviled by a loud voice snug in the crowd; this being coupled with the colour of the player's skin'. A knife was reportedly thrown at the Doncaster keeper from the visitors' end, and local letter writers to the *Echo* were generally alarmed about the actions of 'filthy-mouthed, beer swillers' from the city and worried that 'several Liverpool fans [were] ready to fight – literally – over their team'. Another letter, this time from 'Ever Red', a Liverpool fan, reported on 'the element of sheer, savage hooliganism among some of our supporters'. It was a warning.

Two years later, in March 1958, when Liverpool lost 1–2 in the sixth round of the FA Cup at Blackburn, there were much more serious and widespread disturbances. Shop windows were smashed, goods stolen and police officers attacked before and after the match. The police used truncheons to deal with troublemakers, and eighteen Liverpool men eventually appeared in court, with four sent to prison, after what one local commentator described as 'the worst case of hooliganism I have ever seen in Blackburn'. Much of this kind of thing was the result of sheer frustration, of course, but it also seemed to echo wider developments in youth culture in Liverpool and elsewhere at this time. Drinking and public-violence offences began to soar in the city and around Britain in the late 1950s. In June 1956, for example, a 'teddy boy brawl' occurred in a Wallasey cinema, and on 11 June Bootle was said to have 'declared war on teddy boys' after a very large street fight in Strand Road ended up with a rack of local offenders in court. The message seemed to be that post-war British life was rapidly changing and that English football was not immune to some of its more difficult consequences.

On 4 May 1956, the inevitable happened. The *Liverpool Echo* reported that Don Welsh had finally resigned, noting, 'During his period at Anfield he has not had a free hand with the selection of the team and this, no doubt, is one of the reasons for his recent unhappiness with the club.' Welsh had no more to offer. 'As everybody knows,' he told the press, 'team selection at Liverpool has always been a board affair and there we have not always regarded things in the same light.' In an era in which other clubs were now giving rather more responsibility and independence to their managers, the Liverpool board was clutching inertly to its historic right as employers and owners to have the final say. Tellingly, there were no traditional messages of thanks to the outgoing manager in the Liverpool minute books. When discussing a new incumbent, Billy Liddell was mentioned, of course, but Welsh's replacement indicated that little would actually change. Phil Taylor was a well-liked ex-player who was now a coach at the club.

But the board described his appointment as that of a mere 'liaison man' in the dressing-room. Taylor became the acting Liverpool manager on a wage of £18 per week – a saving of £12 a week on Welsh. The club's board, it was announced, reserved the power to have 'the final say in all matters of importance affecting the success and well-being of the club'. It was not a formula that was likely to succeed in either the short or the longer term.

But some things did change: a 'shooting box' was bought for Melwood for £140, and a short-wave therapy machine was purchased for £400 to treat players' injuries. A four-yard-wide cinder track was also laid out at Melwood to aid with speed training. Taylor had undoubtedly had an impact. New, solid players also arrived at Anfield, but all within Liverpool's strict budgetary regime – and none with a schemer's flair or a goalscorer's golden touch. Right-back John Molyneux moved across from Chester for £4,500, for example, and he was a consistent presence in the Liverpool defence for the next six years. Dick White, a versatile defender who could play full-back or centre-half, came in from Scunthorpe for £8,000 in November 1955 and would eventually play a key role in dragging the Reds out of Division Two. Tommy Younger, a chunky Scotland international keeper, joined from Hibernian in June 1956 for £9,000, and the hard-tackling, fierce-shooting England right-half Johnny Wheeler came in from Bolton Wanderers for the same price.

These last two players were the first sizable signings of the new Taylor era but not much had really changed at the club. Liverpool remained competitive in the Second Division, but team selection still seemed too haphazard and overly cautious to guarantee promotion. In a vital match against Leicester City in February 1957, for example, the *Daily Post* pointed out that Liverpool had fielded three centre-halves – White, Twentyman and Hughes – and lost. Later that month, on a snow-bound Anfield pitch in the FA Cup against Manchester City, Billy Liddell famously 'scored' an equalising 'goal', but just after the referee had blown for time. In the ensuing confusion, many spectators left the tie sure it had been drawn. The occasion certainly made a big impression on one young Kopite that day: the Anfield-born youngster Tommy Smith dreamed on the terraces that his time would eventually come – as indeed it would – at Liverpool Football Club.

As Liverpool struggled to get out of the English second tier, the game around them was now evolving fast, and they were in danger of falling irreparably behind. In April 1957, a 'slow and listless' Liverpool played 'almost entirely without fire and fight' and lost limply 0–3 at Sheffield United, thus condemning the Merseyside club to yet another season among the also-rans. Tellingly, in the same week the English title holders, Manchester United under Matt Busby, were playing in a newish competition, the European Cup, against the Spanish champions Real Madrid. The great Welshman John Charles was also leaving Britain to sign for the Italians from Juventus for a fee of £10,000. Leslie Edwards in the *Daily Post* railed against this embryonic British player drain and the 'pittance' that even top English players were still paid – £17 was now the maximum wage – compared to their Continental equivalents. This meant that in England 'technicians of the highest class [were] set to work with labourers with the proviso that they should receive labourer's pay'.

In August 1957, the Liverpool players briefly made their own point about the criminally low earnings of English professionals by refusing to pose for pre-season photographs unless they were paid for doing so. But they were soon brought into line again as humble employees rather than the sporting stars some of them were. Leslie Edwards, nodding vigorously at Anfield, also called for a new charter for football managers in English football, saying, 'If a manager contracts to manage, he should be given absolute authority over the team, leaving directors to direct.' No one was listening. But at least Phil Taylor had now been confirmed as the permanent Liverpool manager, for what it was worth.

The last tram operating in Liverpool, the 293 from Pier Head to Bowring Park, made its final journey at 5.55 p.m. on 14 September 1957. The city was finally moving to a new, modern and flexible bus service to meet the anticipated needs of 1960s commuters. There were few signs that the same forward-looking processes of modernisation might soon waken Liverpool Football Club from what appeared to be its interminable post-war slumbers. However, something *was* about to happen at Anfield that would actually change the entire history and direction of the club. But first there was just a little more pain to endure.

SLOW TRAIN COMING – FROM WORCESTER

Modernisation and change in any domain brings risk and the unmetered threat of the unknown. So it was that in February 1958, in a terrible accident at Munich Airport, the guts were wrenched out of a great young Manchester United team challenging in Europe. These were British pioneers who threatened to dominate European club football. Eight players died. As the crowds slopped through the slush-sodden streets of Liverpool 4 to the Second Division Liverpool v. Charlton match on 10 February, according to the *Daily Post*, 'Men's minds were still very much on the Munich tragedy, and the hush that descended on this so boisterous ground when the black armbanded players lined up for the two minutes' silence was almost uncanny.' Liverpool Football Club even offered United the services of two Anfield players to help tide the Old Trafford club over the next few months, a neighbourly lesson from the past for the present.

The long shadow cast by Munich lifted only very slowly from the English game, in what was to prove another generally disappointing season for Liverpool. Chairman T.V. Williams told the Liverpool shareholders that 'the Liverpool Football Club was his sole concern and his whole life', but he had little solace to offer supporters regarding the club's fourth-place finish in the second tier of the Football League. Accordingly, the 1958 Liverpool AGM was typically heavily stage-managed and characterised by a feeling of 'philosophic resignation' – it was over in just 45 unrewarding minutes. Williams also sent an open letter to club shareholders and fans defending the club's (lack of) spending policy and reminding them of the responsibility that the board had to shareholders as well as supporters. It cut little ice, locally. 'Success breeds success, as Wolves and [Manchester] United have proved,' pointed out a Mr A. Mercer in a letter to the *Football Echo*. 'It is high time this great city of ours came out of the wilderness.'

The signing of Jimmy Harrower, a stylish inside-forward bought from Hibernian for £11,000, had at least given the Reds midfield a little more craft – if no more pace – but Liverpool made their, by now usual, unpredictable and inconsistent start to the new league season, playing 'bash-ball' in an opening 3–3 home draw with Grimsby Town and losing 1–2 at Sunderland, with a local young winger Johnny Morrissey getting a rare outing. Significantly, the Reds still relied on the ageing and slowing Billy Liddell for league goals, but Jimmy Melia now weighed in with 21 in 39 matches to lead the field for once. A 0–5 thrashing at Bill Shankly's Huddersfield Town on 4 October 1958 was probably the siren call for Phil Taylor. Some of the Liverpool directors knew and liked the tyro Scot Shankly, and they had noted how he had completely turned around Town, bringing in and improving young future internationals such as Ray Wilson and Denis Law without lashing out on large transfers. In August 1957, Huddersfield had drawn 1–1 at Anfield but should have won, their 'solid, smooth-looking and young' team comparing favourably with a very stodgy Liverpool. Back at Leeds Road, the men from Yorkshire had now quite wrecked the Reds, who were a goal down within a minute and never recovered. After ten matches, Liverpool under Phil Taylor were midtable and going nowhere. The Liverpool board even held a secret emergency meeting after the Terriers' rout, deciding that the club needed more discipline and more experienced coaching support to firm up the current lax Liverpool regime – and, possibly, another new team manager.

After the Huddersfield debacle, a run of eight straight league wins in December and January 1959 actually carried Liverpool up the table to second place, and this might even have saved the beleaguered Liverpool manager his job if it were not for the events of 15 January 1959, the most notorious in the club's, so far unfulfilled, FA Cup history. As the Soviet Union launched the first human being into space, gales and icy storms lashed the English north-west at the start of 1959. The desperate weather welcomed to Liverpool the tough Scotsman Reuben Bennett as the club's new chief coach. Liverpool had actually wanted to appoint Bill Nicholson to the job, but Nicholson had since accepted the team manager's job at Spurs. So the Reds turned to Bennett, who was claimed to be the best coach in Scotland. The Scot had been a sergeant major and physical-training instructor during the war and had been a goalkeeper with Hull City, Queen of the South and Dundee until 1950, then trained and managed Ayr United. Deciding that management wasn't his bag, Bennett had returned to coaching, at Motherwell and Third Lanark, before throwing in his lot with Liverpool.

Tommy Younger described Bennett as 'a quiet unassuming fellow with no regard for publicity'. This reticence was one reason why Bennett had given up on his early football-management ambitions. He was known as a 'believer in a strict training schedule obeyed to the letter', and Bennett became famous with later Liverpool players for his near-deranged hard-man insistence that training grazes could best be cleaned with Brillo Pads and that rubbing a kipper on bruises had its own special medicinal qualities. Albert Shelley would now take care of the treatment room and stores, and Bob Paisley would become the first-team trainer in his place. Phil Taylor's role in coaching and training was much reduced as a result of these changes. He was not consulted on the Shelley demotion or the Bennett appointment, and the move was a clear comment by the Liverpool board on his struggling regime and its supposed failings.

The signs were probably bad when the Liverpool FC Supporters Club premises were broken into early in the new year in 1959. The thieves, obvious music lovers, took a radiogram as well as cash and spirits. But the FA Cup was soon around again to lift local hopes, and 66–1 cup long shots Liverpool were confident, even when they were drawn, banana skin-like, to play away to Worcester City of the north-west section of the Southern League. Where *was* this place? City were already cup giant-killers that season over Millwall. But the Reds were confident, even though Billy Liddell was injured and would be missing his first FA Cup tie for Liverpool since he'd turned professional. Phil Taylor and the board had been brave enough to drop the slowing Liddell for the first time during this current campaign, though the decision had gone down badly with many of the club's frustrated supporters.

Worcester skipper and ex-Manchester City captain Roy Paul and his manager Bill Thompson had watched Liverpool, and they claimed to have identified weaknesses that their own team could exploit. But there seemed little doubt that the major advantage the non-leaguers would have over their league opponents was the very poor state of the sloping George's Lane pitch. 'It is in a mess,' said Thompson, happily. The pitch, according to the *Liverpool Echo*, was 'like iron, a bare, brown board of a surface'. Terrible pitches were part of the folklore of the FA Cup, of course, the graveyard of the elite. A late bid to thaw this icy slab of earth for the due date of 8 January failed, under the wary eyes of manager Taylor and his assistant Bob Paisley, with many of the 4,000 travelling Liverpool fans already on their way down to the south-west. Here at least was a little breathing space.

The match was rescheduled for a Thursday afternoon, and Worcester officials and volunteers spread eleven and a half tons of salt on the pitch to guard it against frost and, no doubt, to try to get the contest on while the weather was as filthy and inhospitable as possible. Certainly, the snow, fog and freezing conditions all around the West Midlands area made it look quite impossible to stage a football match. Only referee Leslie Tirebuck – and the entire Worcester City staff, of course – thought that the rutted, grassless, horribly salted pitch was playable. In short, this was a major football accident waiting to happen, in front of 17,000 gawping ambulance-chasing spectators.

The home team played the dreadful pitch perfectly, banging long balls forward with no pretence at all of trying to play any sort of constructive passing football. By contrast, Liverpool 'tried to play too much football', according to the *Echo*. The more direct approach of the hosts immediately unsettled the visiting defence, which panicked into giving away a goal after just nine minutes. A long ball from Gosling spooked Molyneux, who misplaced his backpass beyond the immobile Younger. A tottering Dick White then tried to retrieve the situation but succeeded only in directing the ball into the path of Skuse, who scored into an empty net. It was all the encouragement the hosts and their supporters needed. At 0–1 at half-time, the Liverpool players were already carrying plenty of cuts and bruises, and Twentyman was struggling with a more serious leg injury. Phil Taylor looked drawn and helpless. It was not the happiest of Reds dressing-rooms.

But help was at hand. Worcester's part-time players now began to get just a little afraid of actually *beating* this historic Football League club. So Liverpool began to make some second-half chances, which Melia and A'Court lamentably missed, while Twentyman hit the Worcester crossbar. Then, with just ten minutes left, another 'amazing combination of mistakes' in Liverpool's defence brought about a second home goal, the killer blow. Both Melia and White had chances to clear before Knowles got away for Worcester on the right wing and crossed low and hard. The retreating White – in the middle of a nightmare, clearly – trying to clear behind, could only blast the ball high into his own net over the helpless Younger. A controversial Liverpool penalty, which Twentyman converted, set up a storming finish that almost had the lot: premature pitch invasions, missile-throwing, constant whistling and a bundle of near-misses – but no more goals. Liverpool were out of the FA Cup, overturned in a town that had never – and probably would never – host a Football League club. It was a very difficult message to swallow.

BEWARE THE MAN FROM GLENBUCK

'A small fire is put out by the wind but a great fire only grows greater'

Anonymous

Phil Taylor was already effectively a dead man walking when the passing away of Elisha Scott in June 1959 reminded all older Liverpool supporters of some of the great title years and the many impressive Liverpool teams of the past. Bert Slater was the latest Liverpool goalkeeper, recruited from Falkirk, with Tommy Younger going in the opposite direction in June 1959. Slater was agile but small for a goalkeeper, and not since Scott himself and Cyril Sidlow just after the war had the club really had a goalkeeper to give confidence to the rest of the Liverpool defence. It again simply showed up the value of the great Elisha and what Liverpool supporters were missing compared to the club's greatest days.

The Liverpool board ritually reported an annual profit (of £3,178) in the summer of 1959 and said that it had offered 'an open cheque for the best player in Britain [generally assumed, in fact, to be £40,000 for Middlesbrough's Brian Clough] but his club would not accept it'. But even the local press was now running out of patience. 'Despite the oft reported statement that Liverpool will not baulk at paying top prices for top players, there is still no action.'

The club was rather luckier in their local scouting activities. And this really was luck rather than the result of some coordinated recruitment strategy laid out by Liverpool Football Club. The ex-Reds defender and club scout Bill Jones was casually watching a local football match in Cheshire when he spotted an outstanding 20-year-old goalscoring forward who had strength and incredible shooting power, a raw talent who had somehow evaded the usual networks of the professional clubs. He immediately put Liverpool onto the case, and the young man concerned signed professional forms at Anfield in July 1959. Occasionally, these good solid football professionals are late developers or else they are initially missed by scouts because they have fears about their lack of speed, poor character or dubious physical attributes. But this case was rather like those inert and incompetent book publishers who would foolishly fail to see the magic of Harry Potter. Jones had struck real gold. He had uncovered a hidden gem, a deadly, hard-running and dedicated forward and a future World Cup-winner, no less. Bill Jones had discovered, for his old football club, the selfless and brilliant Roger Hunt.

Hunt seemed like a natural. He immediately adapted to the tough environment of professional football, and he scored four times in his first five senior outings for Liverpool, from September 1959. Here was the type of goalscorer the Liverpool board had spoken about for so long, and he had arrived – as they had always dreamed he would – free of charge. How ironic for manager Phil Taylor that he would have so little time to work with Hunt and to benefit from the buckets of goals he would score for Liverpool. Because despite his new young star's contribution, when a listless Liverpool drew 1–1 with Portsmouth at Anfield on 24 October 1959 in front of a paltry crowd of 21,075 they were already nine points behind Second Division leaders Aston Villa.

On 28 October 1959, two letters to the *Liverpool Echo* summed up local feelings. Mr K. Dickenson from Belper Street, Liverpool 19, wrote, 'The blunders made by the board in the past have put the team in a dangerous position. A drop to the Third Division is a real possibility. We followers of Liverpool have never had it so bad.' A Mr G. Unwin of Kingsthorne Road, Liverpool 24, agreed, saying, 'Never in the history of the club have their local supporters' spirits and enthusiasm been at such a low ebb. We see no optimism or hope for the future in the present team.' This was bleak stuff, indeed, even for the darkest Liverpool years of the 1930s.

Fortunately, Everton were hardly tearing up the First Division, either. So how do you cheer up your most despondent supporters in times of need? How do you get the local crowd behind you once again? Easy: you sign up the iconic hero of your bitterest local rivals.

The mop-haired, erratic and occasionally terrific 29-year-old Blues centre-forward Dave Hickson had publicly reported himself to be 'not in love with playing for Everton any more', having been dropped by his manager Johnny Carey just once too often. Evertonians howled with disappointment and anger. Hickson wanted to stay in the city, so Liverpool Football Club stepped in, and after some soul-searching and haggling – and to the horror of most Evertonians – Hickson signed for the Reds for that magic figure of the then unofficial Liverpool transfer limit of around £12,000. Liverpool supporters were triumphant. An expectant 49,981 – a 20,000 crowd 'bonus' – turned up to see Hickson trash the Second Division leaders Aston Villa with two goals in his debut in a 2–1 Liverpool win. To rub in this neighbourly larceny, Kopites called Hickson 'the Red Dean' at

Anfield and put it about that thousands of Evertonians had followed their new man across Stanley Park to Liverpool. This felt much better. But the mercurial Hickson was inconsistent, and he had no magic wand, so when Liverpool lost 2–4 at modest Lincoln City in November the letters and grumbling began anew, increasing the pressure on Taylor and the Liverpool board once again. Liverpool had won only six out of seventeen league matches. In the Empire Theatre in Liverpool, comedian Arthur Askey described his new show in November 1959 as 'this indescribable and varied act'. It could easily be applied to the manager's job at Anfield. Change had to come. On 18 November 1959, the *Liverpool Echo* announced what many people had expected to happen since the backroom appointment of Reuben Bennett: Phil Taylor had resigned as the manager of Liverpool Football Club.

Despite all Taylor's problems, this seemed like a strange time to press him to leave his post, especially with both Hickson and Hunt so recently brought on board. Taylor informed the local press that it was the strain of the job that had finally told on him, that he was 'very tired at times' and that 'I have never tried to cause anyone any trouble, and I must say few have caused me concern'. It was the usual apologetic tone from a man who had been uncomplaining but who had never been given the full power of his own office. The Liverpool board announced that they would be interviewing candidates and that applications should be sent to the club's registered office, because stamped letters might alert the press to the locations of those who applied. The board seemed paranoid about the press and the possibility that the club's business might be discussed prematurely in public. But Huddersfield's Bill Shankly was already the man they had in mind. They might well have said as much to Taylor to get the old Liverpool servant to go amicably.

Shankly had first been contacted by the board when Liverpool had appointed Don Welsh back in 1951. But he would not accept the Liverpool directors picking the team, so he was rejected as a candidate. The board now wanted – and got – the Huddersfield manager, not because of Bill Shankly's independence or charisma, but rather because the Scot was beginning to develop the sort of managerial reputation the Liverpool board liked: he was a man known for capably running and reviving football clubs on shoestring budgets.[4] Growing media criticism of football directors was also paving the way for the independent modern football manager.

Always a man for making bold entrances, Shankly introduced himself to the Liverpool players by strutting into the Anfield dressing-room like the American gangsters he loved to imitate and saying, 'Some of you boys have been here too long.'[5] It was a challenging rather than a consensual start, but actually his bark was much worse than his bite and very little changed very quickly at Liverpool on the personnel front. Indeed, Tom Leishman, a long-striding left-half replacement for Geoff Twentyman, who had left to become player–manager at Ballymena United, was signed for £9,000 from St Mirren by T.V. Williams and Syd Reakes between the resignation of Taylor and the appointment of Shankly. The Liverpool board was clearly not going to give up on its powers to sign and transfer players that easily. This new relationship between an ambitious, charismatic, media-friendly young firebrand of a manager and a Liverpool board that some felt was still mired in the attitudes and values of the past would be something worth watching. Liverpool Football Club was about to be awakened from an often desperate nine-year slumber.

CHAPTER 13 REFERENCES

1. Taylor and Ward, *Three Sides of the Mersey*, p. 92
2. Keith, *Bob Paisley*, p. 69
3. A'Court, *My Life in Football*, p. 16
4. Carter, *The Football Manager*, p. 88
5. A'Court, *My Life in Football*, p. 70

14

BILL SHANKLY AND THE NEW LIVERPOOL

Or How the Liverpool Board Finally Learned How to Spend Money

'AMONG FOLKS OF MY OWN KIND'

Right from the start, Bill Shankly's brand of exuberant west-of-Scotland popular socialism and collective ambition and the rather penny-pinching, cautious individualism of the English high Conservatives in the Liverpool boardroom were a potentially toxic mix. But the new manager actually liked the Liverpool chairman Tom Williams, and rather than seek out confrontation Shankly, initially at least, simply sought to establish a very different identity for himself inside Liverpool to the 'employee' or 'servant' tag that had been hung like a millstone round the neck of both Welsh and Taylor and many before them. For one thing, Shankly had chosen to have no contract for his £2,500-per-annum position, saying confidently, 'If I cannot do the job, it is up to the people who employ me to do as they wish.' Here was an audacious and principled stand right from the start. For another, Shankly wanted the freedom to manage, precisely the arrangement denied to the men who had gone before him. The Liverpool board swallowed hard, but it would have to get used to this new direction. Shankly especially wanted to establish a sense of personal ownership of the Liverpool project, mainly in two ways: first, through his sheer devotion to the club, its supporters and to the sport – few men *lived* football as Bill Shankly did, few dedicated themselves so totally to the game to the exclusion of family and friends; and, second, by his very practical determination to improve the basic infrastructure of the Anfield stadium and the Liverpool training ground.

When Shankly filled in forms at hotels and elsewhere that asked for details of his place of residence, he often wrote 'Anfield' in the space provided. It felt to him like he lived in the football stadium he had now adopted. Accordingly, he soon started to deal with the Liverpool ground as if it was his own home, a place that 40,000 or more personal and valued friends might be expected to visit every fortnight. So it had to be kept properly spruced up and habitable. He got the Liverpool directors to pay for a pipeline to ensure all the toilets in the ground could be flushed and the pitch could be watered, and he soon had the apprentices and the Liverpool ground staff busy painting walls, staircases and crush barriers. He and Bob Paisley were often discovered by the Liverpool directors – he probably engineered the meetings – late at night inside Anfield painting the toilets or passageways. Paisley even built the dugouts at Liverpool when the traditional box for the brass band sited under the main stand was no longer needed.[1] All this was part of the contract that Shankly felt he had made with the working-class people of Liverpool: to offer them better facilities at the club, facilities that had been allowed to diminish because the Liverpool board had refused to spend on players or regular upgrades.

Another way in which the new manager tried to keep his bargain with local people was to involve them more inside the club by rebuilding the strong bond that used to exist between the club staff and local supporters when Tom Watson and the late Elisha Scott were all-powerful at Liverpool. In many ways, Shankly's presence and style began to epitomise the sort of intimacy that Scott had once engendered with Kopites.

Although the *Liverpool Echo* initially described him, insanely, as 'not a man with the gift of the gab', Shankly actually communicated his enthusiasm and commitment for Liverpool Football Club very well through the local press, which had been starved of decent copy on this score during the troubled recent regimes. Shankly was built for the television age. But he also wanted to maintain the grounded links between players and 'ordinary' people in the city, something that would risk strain with the lifting of the maximum wage in 1961. This was one of the reasons why Shankly liked to invite in local workers, such as Liverpool's dustbin-men, to play football matches against his young apprentices. This was more than simple practice. The message was that no one should be outside the scope of the club and that no player should ever get beyond his station in relation to the people who funded their careers – the manual workers of the city of Liverpool. 'I knew that, by and large, the people who produced that [Kop] roar were men just like myself who lived for the game of football and to whom football was their abiding passion,' Shankly said later. 'I knew that no matter what trials lay ahead I would be at home among folks of my own kind.' He had mixed with passionate Liverpudlians at boxing promotions in the city. Shankly knew about the sheer desire and sporting potential in Liverpool.

Shankly was depicted, cartoonishly, in the local press as a 'sergeant-major with the human touch', the kind of manager who made 'wild claims' about some of his players: he said that Denis Law was 'the best thing on two feet', for example. This was part of the new manager's famed motivational technique, which he later used to 'big up' his Liverpool players and rubbish the opposition, no matter their status. He used to tell his hard men at Liverpool, his leaders on the pitch, 'Don't take any shit from anyone,' and he warned the Scots who came to the club – and he brought in many – never to soften up and never to lose their working-class Scottish accents. He wanted his imports to be proud and impervious to temptations in a city reawakening with the hum of pop culture and youth consumption.

Shankly was suspicious of the new coaching regimes then being established at the FA in the wake of the country's international failings. Simple methods, talent and practice were what really mattered: pass to the nearest red shirt and move for the next pass. This might sound like typical mulish British opposition to modernisation. But the Scot was no simple traditionalist, no blind flag-waver for the British way above all others. As the *Liverpool Echo* put it on 15 December 1959, Shankly's approach would be a real eye-opener to those Liverpool supporters who had been raised on an outmoded and now mundane diet of rough-and-ready British playing styles:

> Shankly is a disciple of the game as played by the Continentals. The man out of possession, he believes, is just as important as the man with the ball at his feet. Continental football is not the lazy man's way of playing soccer. Shankly will aim at incisive forward moves by which Continentals streak through a defence, when it is closed up by British standards. He will make his players learn to kill the ball and move it all in the same action, even when it is hit at them hard and maybe awkwardly; he will make them practise complete mastery of the ball; he will ensure that whatever else they may not learn, it won't be the fundamentals of good soccer.

Notwithstanding the weird journalistic double negative used here, this was quite an agenda, but one pretty clearly stated. It was also an ambitious programme for a club that was still locked in the middle of the English Second Division. In line with Continental standards of professionalism, Shankly suggested flying his team to long-distance away games, such as at Plymouth, and he liked to have modern technology in the treatment room for work on his injured players, even if none of the Liverpool staff seemed quite sure how to use it. Some of this approach could also be applied in new Melwood training regimes, which prioritised much more ball work, the playing of small-sided games and five-a-sides, and the use of punitive training boards arranged into a square to build up control, passing accuracy and stamina.

It had its effects, this new regime. Club captain Ronnie Moran said Liverpool would have soared out of the Second Division much earlier with Shankly involved. He said he learned more in the first three months of Shankly at Liverpool than he had in the previous seven years. New signings were also astonished at the fitness levels demanded under Shankly, Reuben Bennett, Bob Paisley and Joe Fagan. 'No team will field fitter men,' promised Shankly. 'They will all go flat out for 90 minutes.' They did.

Bill Shankly's first competitive match in charge of Liverpool was at home to Cardiff City on 19 December 1959, and 27,291 came to see it – the new manager obviously paled as a crowd draw compared to ex-Everton man Dave Hickson. Shankly desisted from picking the Reds team, leaving that to Bob Paisley. But when right-back John Molyneux cried off with boils on the shin, it was Shankly who decided that the current reserve full-back – the young Welshman Alan Jones – be promoted automatically into the first team. The inexperienced debutant was rinsed in a 0–4 defeat. A 0–3 loss at Charlton immediately followed. But then Shankly found his feet, with six wins and two draws from the next eight league fixtures. A poor run in March 1960 killed off any possible promotion hopes, including a 4–4 draw with Aston Villa after Liverpool had led by four goals – fitness again. A striker strangely called Linnecor then scored a hat-trick in a 1–3 Anfield defeat by Lincoln City (making it an unlikely league double over Liverpool for the Imps). The *Liverpool Echo* reported on the sadness in this match of seeing Billy Liddell 'once the lion of Anfield . . . left out in the cold so often as a player whose active days are numbered'. It was almost as if the great man Liddell had to sign off as a Liverpool player before the new era for the club could begin under the man from Glenbuck.

LIFE AFTER LIDDELL

The demise, finally, of the 1940s and '50s home-based Liverpool hero Liddell – a man whose whole career had been based on modest wages and just two days' training a week to fit in with his accountancy work – corresponded almost exactly with the 1960s consumption boom, the rise of televised sport in Britain, the lifting of the maximum wage and the start of the emergence of football players as authentic sex symbols and televised national celebrities. Liddell's last Liverpool game, for example, would come only a couple of years before the debut of George Best at Manchester United, but the two men looked decades apart in terms of their respective styles and their attitudes to the sport and life. The world was changing again – and fast. The FA even sanctioned Sunday league football at last in 1960, and the Football League Cup was added to the professional football roster in England in the same year. In 1960, too, the city of Liverpool was also announced as one of the host cities for the 1966 World Cup finals.

In the Liverpool press, meanwhile, flashy advertising for home goods and services – cars, televisions, twin-tub washing machines, bank loans, hi-fidelity music systems, 'luxury' underwear – now challenged news stories for space. In November 1960, the first bona fide pop acts started playing at a little-known Liverpool nightclub called the Cavern.[2] Soon its local products would stun the world. An upstart supermarket company called Tesco made a £2-million takeover bid for John Irwin and Sons grocery stores in the north-west, American-style skyscraper blocks appeared on Merseyside, and more were planned. This was the modern world.

By April 1960, still in his first season and with promotion no longer an issue, Bill Shankly could begin to experiment with some of the young talent he was beginning to scrutinise at the club. He had watched plenty of reserve and A- and B-team football already at Liverpool, and now he wanted to throw some youngsters into the first team to see if they could swim. Liverpool-born left-back Gerry Byrne's career was one of those that was hugely affected by the new manager's arrival. Byrne had been transfer-listed and unwanted under Phil Taylor, but now he was in the Liverpool first team under Shankly, heading for league and FA Cup medals and eventually a place in the 1966 England World Cup squad. So, too, was the just 18-year-old right-winger Ian Callaghan from Caryl Gardens, Liverpool, who was also en route to a record 857 appearances for Liverpool Football Club. Callaghan played brilliantly and received a standing ovation on his debut, a 4–0 Anfield walloping of Bristol Rovers.

The stocky Liverpool-born wing-half Bobby Campbell was also getting his chance, though he would later make his name in the game more as a football manager than he ever would as a player. In June, Shankly managed to wring a record £13,000 out of the Liverpool board to buy Kevin Lewis, a 19-year-old right-sided goalscoring winger/forward from Sheffield United, and then in August 1960 he brought in Gordon Milne, another record at £16,000, a polished and tough little right-half who joined from Preston North End. Shankly had been a neighbour of the Milnes, a football family, and he had watched this kid grow up to become a 'right-living, right-thinking boy. He neither smokes nor drinks.' Here, already, were the beginnings of the new Liverpool.

RED MEN

At the suddenly interesting 1960 Liverpool AGM, Bill Shankly 'played a blinder', according to the *Liverpool Echo*. The new manager said that he felt he had the full support of the board and that he thought a 'new chapter had begun at Anfield'. He called on the supporters and shareholders to 'forget the past . . . all the hard luck stories. I am sure success will come much sooner than some people anticipate.' No one had ever heard a Liverpool manager talk like this at an AGM, at least not since Tom Watson before the First World War. There was real applause at the boldness and style of the manager's delivery. Here was a Liverpool boss, at last, who was definitely his own man. Maybe this was real change, a new future? There would still be ructions, of course, especially when the Liverpool board tried to buy and sell players, thus provoking Shankly to threaten to resign on a number of occasions. But things did seem to be changing at Anfield. Even the Reds supporters had a voice of sorts now at the Liverpool high table: a Solly Isenwater spoke from the floor for the newly formed Liverpool Shareholders Association, though he raised only minor issues: ticket prices for OAPs and had Liverpool by any chance bought a copy of the film of Real Madrid's extraordinary 7–3 destruction of Eintracht Frankfurt in the 1960 European Cup final at Hampden Park?

To puncture this excitement just a little, Liverpool reported a loss of £4,918 due to a fall in attendances that was attributed to wider social and cultural processes connected to rising car ownership and televised sport. Football was now part of the 'entertainment business', and there had even been talk in football circles in 1960 of a possible British 'super league', while television coverage of floodlit English and European football was now a very live and present issue. Liverpool's average home gate had held up pretty well for a club in the Second Division, in the light of all of this, at 30,269. But even in the relegation season of 1953–54, First Division home gates at Anfield had averaged 40,488, which meant a 25 per cent fall in crowds over six years. English football as a whole had been losing supporters, year on year, but everyone at Anfield knew that a promotion campaign and a return to First Division football would bring some of the crowds back to Liverpool. Could this enthusiastic young Scot, a man who liked boxing, hard-man American cinema heroes and wilfully short holidays up the north coast in Southport and Blackpool, really work the oracle?

It wouldn't happen right away. Billy Liddell's final competitive match for Liverpool was at centre-forward in a 0–1 home defeat against Southampton on 31 August 1960, when the great man was clearly 'out of touch'. It looked as if Shankly might even have given Billy this final competitive league game at home to say goodbye to the Anfield crowd. The new manager admired Liddell as a great Scotland international, and he was not beyond a touch of sentiment in deserving cases. But without Liddell, who would offer Liverpool a spark? When a labouring Reds side beat Scunthorpe at home 3–2 on 18 September, it was a 'lifeless, uninspiring, untidy display', and there was slow handclapping on the Kop. A crowd of 38,789 then turned out on a filthy Liverpool night to salute Liddell in his testimonial match, launched by a magnificent 16-page *Liverpool Echo* souvenir in which Danny Blanchflower best described the Scot as 'a wonderful, stirring, awesome force, liable to erupt at any moment'. The club would never see his like again.

With Billy now celebrated and gone, and after a poor start in the league, Liverpool went on a 14-match unbeaten run to take them up to second place behind Sheffield United at Christmas, until a 0–1 defeat at Rotherham on 28 December broke the spell, with police climbing into the crowd at the end 'to deal with a fight between rival supporters'. When Liverpool lost at home 3–4 to Middlesbrough on 2 January 1961, with a brilliant Brian Clough scoring twice, police ended up patrolling the goal areas after the visiting goalkeeper Appleby had been struck in the face by a coin thrown from the crowd. Liverpool's crowd problems had not disappeared.

Sunderland had just too much know-how for the Reds in the FA Cup a few weeks later, and it would prove another near-miss in the league for Liverpool, confirmed when Norwich City downed Shankly's men 1–2 at Carrow Road on 17 April 1961. Liverpool finished third again, behind Ipswich Town and Sheffield United. But things were finally taking shape. Byrne, Lewis and Hunt were all now established in the Liverpool first XI, and Milne and Callaghan were gradually being eased into first-team football. This was real progress, a talented young player base already established. Bert Slater in goal and Dick White at centre-half both played 42 matches, and John Molyneux played 39 at right-back, but 58 goals conceded were too many advantages lost for the Liverpool coaches and manager to endure. Dave Hickson scored a respectable 16 goals in 33 matches, but he lacked the real pace and cleverness needed to help open up rival defences in the modern era. Bill Shankly had much still to do to get his squad in the sort of shape he wanted.

GOODBYE, CRUEL WORLD

'In my opinion, Liverpool can, and will, be one of the leading 12 clubs in the country.' This was Bill Shankly talking in 1960 at the Liverpool Football Club AGM. What was he thinking of? Today, this kind of claim would seem ludicrously unambitious coming out of Anfield. But in the early 1960s, these words, thunderously spoken in that characteristic west-of-Scotland growl, at least offered Reds fans a brighter football future. Here was some hope, at last, of a release from the icy wastes of a barren decade. They believed in Bill Shankly, and he fed upon their energy and hope. So did club captain Ronnie Moran, to whom Shankly had cleverly written a long letter explaining his approach to management before even coming to Anfield. The President of the Hungarian FA, Sandor Barcs, seemed less sure about the talents of British football managers. He had scoffed at club training in England in August 1960, saying that many British coaches 'still seem to be living in the age of your dear old Stephenson, who invented the steam engine'.

Liverpool Football Club had certainly seemed to be locked in the Dark Ages during their post-war slide. They had been conservative, unimaginative and rigid, both on and off the pitch. It was a team poorly led, cheaply recruited and badly selected by the club's directors. Training facilities at Liverpool were abject. This was quite unlike the set-up at dashing and successful Manchester United, where its brilliant, recovering young manager Matt Busby had already been in charge for more than a decade. Liverpool had been stuck in the outdated training doldrums, shamed in their shambolic training ground and its holed and ragged austerity training kit, under the 'nice' but deferential and undemanding Phil Taylor and his predecessors. But here was real change. The new Melwood coaching team – Reuben Bennett as head coach, Bob Paisley as first-team trainer and Joe Fagan as reserves trainer – was hard-nosed, but it was also young and dynamic and full of imaginative work and new ideas. It just needed a whirlwind, a catalyst such as Bill Shankly, to galvanise and release them from the clutches of the inert Liverpool board. And now he had arrived.

Reuben Bennett was the fitness man. He pounded out merciless laps at Melwood with the players, building up their reserves of strength and mocking the freezing cold weather. Joe Fagan had been recommended to Liverpool by Harry Catterick, who was then manager at Rochdale, and Bill Shankly had once tried to sign him as a player for Grimsby Town. He was kindly, a listener, but also a very sharp football man and a good coach. But Bob Paisley was to be the key backroom character. Bob had grown up at Anfield, of course, and had studied physiotherapy towards the end of his playing career. The Liverpool directors got him informal access into Merseyside hospitals so that he could study the mechanics of the human body close up. He was one of the few trainers in the Football League in the 1950s to have any kind of medical training, a major step-up from Albert Shelley's shambolic cursing and cold-water-bucket treatments. Paisley even managed to get the club to buy some of the latest heat and sonic equipment for the treatment of muscle injuries. It was a little like bringing the vestiges of science to bear on otherwise primitive communities.

The first of these machines was known enigmatically at Anfield simply as 'the Electric'. Many injured players were so reluctant to try it out that Paisley was happy to trial it on the pet dogs of people passing by Anfield.[3] Suspicion of being consigned to the Anfield treatment room and its supposed barbaric practices would survive well into the 1980s.[4] Paisley had some of the same communitarian, northern-village, working-class values of his new manager, if little of Shankly's communication skills and chutzpah. Paisley often compared the physiology and mental make-up of top football players to thoroughbred racehorses. He thought they had a common athletic 'edginess', and Bob became very well known among the players for his intuitive capacity to diagnose injuries from simply watching them stand or walk, much as he would sum up the runners in the paddock for the 5.15 race at nearby Haydock Park. Great footballers implicitly trusted their bodies and their careers to him, and Liverpool developed a deserved reputation as a club whose footballers simply did not get injured – or at least hid their injuries well.

Paisley was no great talker or motivator – Shankly did all of that stuff. Frankly, Bob's musings were near-incomprehensible to most. And he was no trusted counsellor for the players – this was Joe Fagan's job. But Bob did have to keep the impact of the local nightlife on Liverpool's players in check, a generally uneven contest. And he even had to paint out the white Adidas stripes on the players' boots – no English club yet had endorsements with any kit manufacturers. But most of all Bob was a dispassionate and quietly brilliant assessor of footballers, focusing on their mental and physical make-up equally, making sure that Liverpool Football Club recruited men who were courageous winners as well as having a physique that was up to the brutal task of playing large numbers of high-tempo, intensive British football matches. Players could only show their worth to Liverpool if they were out on the pitch. Famously, Shankly believed that footballers who were injured were being disloyal to him and to Liverpool Football Club, and he found little time to sympathise or even to talk with them. 'Good players don't get injured,' he liked to say.[5] Indeed, it is generally assumed that Liverpool had fewer injuries than most other clubs at this time, in part because players had real difficulty in telling Shankly, face to face, that they were incapacitated. Better to play on in pain and hold your place than to have to tell the man from Glenbuck that your body had let him – and Liverpool Football Club and its fans – down.

This kind of backroom collective expertise – the core of the later famous Liverpool 'boot room', of course – was a more than useful legacy for the relatively inexperienced Bill Shankly to inherit. It was one offered up to him by the much criticised Liverpool directors. He had to concede that Tom Williams and his colleagues had at least chosen the club's backroom staff incredibly well, even if they were often hopeless at selecting and signing players. Shankly reported in the local press that, in time, he and his coaching team had 'reorganised the whole training system' at Melwood. First, gone were the rag-arsed training outfits. Were these professional footballers or tramps? 'Every phase and detail was planned,' said Shankly, 'so we could move swiftly from one function to another.' After about a year spent eyeing things up, checking on all the club's players and facilities, 'everything changed', said the young Roger Hunt. 'Suddenly, everyone seemed to be walking about with a new sense of purpose.'[6] Alan A'Court noticed a sea change, too, but only after Shankly had carefully sized up the job. 'In no time at all, both Anfield and Melwood were buzzing with an electric atmosphere. It was rather as if you were on board a powerful new racing car and he had just switched on the engine.'[7]

Gone was the disorganisation and easy-going atmosphere at Liverpool training. Notes were taken and kept on the effectiveness of different training routines, and players were graded and trained in groups because, as Shankly put it, 'different players require different exercises and quantity of training'. No eating facilities were built at Melwood, because Shankly wanted his players to cool down on the coach journey back to Anfield before they ate. These daily coach trips also helped to bolster banter and team spirit. This was mainly informal but actually very advanced football thinking in England for the time, the sort of detailed preparation designed to help the Liverpool coaches 'size up the requirements of individuals to reach and retain peak fitness'. There was not a sign of Stephenson's *Rocket* steam engine in sight.

Shankly's approach to playing the game was best described by the phrase 'continuous movement'. It came from his old Huddersfield boss Andy Beattie, who had stressed the importance of instant control and moving the ball quickly. The emphasis was on organised fluidity within a team structure: players being constantly available for the next pass and having the highest possible levels of fitness. Shankly was not interested at all in set-pieces; he thought they were static and ugly and too dependent on luck and players' instincts. So Liverpool never practised them. When the team did try out something for free-kicks in a match situation, it invariably ended up in chaos. Shankly was keen on psychology and tactics but not on how the coaching men from the FA taught mental preparation and the new theories of the game and its systems. He barely lasted a couple of sessions on FA coaching courses at Lilleshall. He hated the new technocratic language of football, of 'overlapping full-backs' and the 'penetrative through-ball'.[8]

Liverpool FC in transition: the 1928–29 squad. Gordon Hodgson and Jimmy McDougall (either side of Elisha Scott) were key figures. The intemperate little master Scott and defender James 'Parson' Jackson (three from left, front row) were not always on the same wavelength in Liverpool's creaky back line into the 1930s.

The globalising game: an urbane-looking Liverpool squad in transit for the tour to Sweden in 1939 under George Kay (far left). Matt Busby is sixth from left, just behind the blond Tom Cooper, who would be a fatality of the war. Strange football times beckoned during the conflict.

A young – and decidedly Goth-looking – Bob Paisley gets stuck in on the Anfield car park just after the war.

Walking off the effects of war: Liverpool players troop around Anfield during a less-than-strenuous 1940s training session.

'Film star' post-war centre-forward Albert Stubbins tracks his son, Eric. The toddler also travelled to Wembley in 1950 and was comforted by winning captain (and Anfield interloper) Joe Mercer.

Billy Liddell greets the locals on Liverpool's title-preparing 1946 summer tour of the USA. The Reds only went stateside to get some decent food – and it did the trick.

Willie Fagan (in the suit), Albert Stubbins (centre), a rather dubious-looking Billy Liddell, and the ailing Reds chairman Billy McConnell (far left) finally claim the league-championship trophy of 1947. The title came only after a lengthy wait to see off Stoke City's challenge.

Jackie Balmer, Liverpool's captain just after the war, enters the fray under the ever-watchful eye of the bizzies. Not everyone's hero, perhaps, Balmer was undoubtedly a great Liverpool post-war goalscorer under manager George Kay.

All quiffed up and somewhere to go, the stylish new Liverpool begins to take shape.
Manager Bill Shankly (rear) amongst his men before a Reds training session in 1962.

The FA Cup at last, after 73
hard years of trying. The 1965
triumph (2–1) over Leeds
United is celebrated by the
Liverpool players – with
pints of milk and a fag.

The Reds off to conquer Europe
in 1965 – but Bill Shankly was
duped by Helenio Herrera
and Inter Milan.

Bill Shankly says his long goodbyes in 1974. His was no easy passing for Liverpool, but his apprentice Bob Paisley took over the mantle and won three European Cups.

Jimmy Case and Phil Neal get some serious kissing action on the 1977 European Cup, in Rome, the start of a run of European successes under Bob Paisley and then Joe Fagan.

Over land and sea: Liverpool fans in full bloom at the European Cup final, Wembley, 1978. Following the Reds in Europe during the 1970s and '80s became an alternative 'career' route for many in the city.

The healing after Hillsborough: Liverpool drew 0–0 at Goodison to get restarted and then beat Everton 3–2 in an emotional first all-Merseyside FA Cup final in 1989. A tragic year – and for much more than just football.

Liverpool Football Club greats, past and present: the extraordinary Billy Liddell meets the brilliant Kenny Dalglish.

The new global Liverpool. But could Steven Gerrard, Fernando Torres, Dirk Kuyt and others finally deliver that elusive Premier League title? (© Getty Images).

Magnetic discs representing opponents would be theatrically swept off a metal pitch-board in team meetings at Melwood, the Liverpool manager aping frustration that he could find nothing positive at all to say about these pitiful rivals or that he was wasting his time even trying. The tenor and style of his own football team talks he attributed to his early coal-mining experiences, which had taught him that brashness or humour could relax men for the physical and dangerous task at hand. Many of the players in the Liverpool dressing-room came from the same, northern manual working-class roots as the people from Glenbuck.[9]

A pre-match tactical session at Liverpool properly evoked the comradeship and cod-democracy of the past: football matches in England were peacetime battles to be won by skill, fortitude and brave hearts – and through trust in your own ability and in your teammates. Toughness was central to all this: poor or uncommitted opponents had 'a heart as big as a caraway seed'. Whenever his own football 'hard men' were growing cocky or showing weakness, Shankly would simply throw photographs of real-life American gangsters onto the dressing-room table, saying that *these* guys had it really tough – they could be shot for making mistakes.[10] There was little room for fancy tactics or any consciously planned strategy. In 1962, Shankly told the *Liverpool Echo*:

> It is not my function to stand in front of a blackboard haranguing the lads. A tactical session is more like a good discussion group in the Forces, with me as the officer leading it . . . I start the ball rolling, but anybody who has anything to say knows that he is expected to say it.

The Second World War had been over for some 17 years, but its influence – in the wartime training and fitness regimes established for young men and the uplifting spirit and camaraderie ingrained in the Forces and that could still be experienced in national service – was hugely formative for Bill Shankly and Bob Paisley and for other football men of their generation. Its impact and memories lingered long as a contributing feature of coaching in the British game. Even in the brash and brand-new 1960s, most young footballers in England still had to complete their two years in the Forces before they could commit themselves entirely to their professional clubs. But who could say what a football future might hold without the threat or the remnants of war?

There were certainly some free-thinkers on the subject still around at Anfield. 'Nothing is more certain than in time we shall see a European league established,' confided Billy Liddell in his newly published autobiography. 'In another decade or so, rail and coach travel will be as outmoded as stage-coaches are today.'[11]

This sort of visionary 'blue sky' thinking was clearly not always exactly right on the button: players never did travel to European fixtures in helicopters that disembarked them inside the stadium as the saintly Billy had predicted. But the retiring Liddell had certainly seen part of the future. Within four years, Liverpool Football Club under Bill Shankly would be travelling to Iceland to begin a rollicking adventure with Europe's football elite that would last for much of the next four decades. It would eventually bring five European Cups and other European baubles back to Anfield. Few people in the early 1960s – except perhaps Bill Shankly himself – could have predicted that. But first he would have to convince the notoriously frugal Liverpool board to start spending big money. As it turned out, he would receive help to deal with this once-intractable problem from a rather unexpected source.

HEY, BIG SPENDERS

Bill Shankly and his staff now had to drag the Reds out of the English Second Division – and the Liverpool board, kicking and screaming, out of its transfer-fee torpor. Littlewoods Pools man and Eccles-born Blues supporter John Moores had taken over as chairman at stumbling Everton in 1960, promising to pump big money into the Goodison club. Moores was true to his word, and after appointing Harry Catterick as manager in 1961 Everton won their first post-war league title in 1963, mainly on the back of the new chairman's free-spending. But the Moores family also held shares in Liverpool Football Club, and John Moores was a bridge partner of the Reds chairman T.V. Williams. Moores gently chided Williams about Liverpool's parsimonious transfer spending. He thought the Anfield club had to show a little more initiative and willingness to take risks in its transfer dealings if it wanted to progress.

John Moores decided to place his own nominee, Eric Sawyer, on the Liverpool board. The shrewd Sawyer was in charge of accounts at Littlewoods, and he became the financial director at Liverpool in 1961, with a mandate from Moores to start loosening up the Anfield purse strings. John Moores was no commercial mug. He was a man of expansive vision and some daring who told the *Football Echo* in December 1960 that he had even tried to bring the Hungarian master Ferenc Puskás to Everton in the 1950s but had faced opposition to his plans from the conservatives at the FA, the Football League and the Home Office. The lifting of the maximum wage in 1961 and the challenges from the players' union to the retain-and-transfer system that would finally succeed in 1963 promised more movement of top British players to football clubs that were free-spending, ambitious and progressive. Everton would buy more than their fair share of stars in this new age for football. But Moores wanted to see both of the major football clubs in the city of Liverpool become successful and competitive in this new television and marketised era for the game. After all, the turnstiles at the Glasgow clubs Rangers and Celtic, and at City and United in Manchester, rattled best when these bitter local rivals were both winning and snapping at each other's heels. In a period of dramatically falling gates in England, having Liverpool FC near-dormant in the Second Division and apparently refusing to pay top dollar for top talent was simply bad for football business in Merseyside. This was felt even across Stanley Park at the Football League champions-elect from Goodison Park. Something had to change.

The modern Liverpool FC transfer revolution finally began in the spring of 1961, some 15 long years after the title-winning capture of Albert Stubbins from under Everton's nose in 1946. Sawyer and Moores were right behind the new Anfield buying policy, helping to steer it through. Before the transfer deadline, Liverpool had again offered £40,000, plus a £10,000 promotion bonus this time, to Middlesbrough to sign star centre-forward Brian Clough. But the bid was again rejected; Clough would move to Sunderland. Frustrated, Bill Shankly then spotted a small item in the Scottish sports press early in May 1961. The story said that Motherwell's young Scotland international Ian St John was being made available for transfer. He blinked. St John was a deep-lying centre-forward who positively bristled with intelligence, youthful aggression and energy. He was a man Shankly had been tracking for close on two years in the hope that one day he would become available. The Motherwell forward might be better even than Brian Clough – and he was a Scot.

But signing Ian St John for Liverpool would cost. The manager first phoned up the Motherwell secretary to ensure this was no set-up. He then collected Syd Reakes and Tom Williams to check that his own club was in big-spending mode. He wanted no sticking points on money, though Shankly actually had no experience of big-money signings before coming to Liverpool. The biggest transfer deal he had been involved in elsewhere was for just £4,000. The trio then drove in Reakes's Rolls-Royce to watch St John play against Hamilton Academical that same evening, sweeping into Fir Park like land-grabbers. At half-time, the clubs' respective directors went into negotiations, and just after midnight a deal was struck. Charlie Mitten, the manager of Newcastle United, had been sniffing around the Scottish centre-forward, but he turned up too late to start an auction. Ian St John and his wife Betsy, meanwhile, sat outside the boardroom whispering like nervous patients in a surgery waiting room.

The young Scot did not finally agree to sign for Liverpool before the couple had been driven to Merseyside and shown a club house under construction in 'salubrious' Maghull, where they might live in comfort with their new baby. The areas of Maghull and West Derby were regarded as close enough to Melwood for players to make it into training, even without a car. Seeing what the club had planned was enough. The St Johns were living in a pokey flat in Motherwell, and the £1,000 signing-on bonus Liverpool had promised to pay him would buy a new Vauxhall and some furniture. The Anfield board had finally learned to bend the rules a little.

Although a full international, St John was still playing part-time football in Scotland, and while Liverpool was a Second Division club it was one that had big plans – and a fast-talking, utterly charismatic Scottish manager who wouldn't take no for an answer. St John also knew and admired Reuben Bennett from his Motherwell days, so Liverpool Football Club seemed something like a home from home to him.

This signing was a sea change in Liverpool's post-war fortunes and particularly the club's intent. Above all, the brash, young Ian St John symbolised the arrival of the 1960s at Anfield. He had the swagger and the confidence to challenge authority, and the irreverent youthful style that underpinned wider social changes in Britain, and which would soon produce a wonderful surge of working-class musical creativity in the city. On the pitch, St John produced real verve and invention – and the sheer devil that had been missing from the Liverpool team for a decade or more. Off it, he was at the forefront of many of the illicit adventures involving the club's players in the new fleshpots and nightclubs at home and abroad. Bob Paisley would soon be on his case.

Not that his new club was offering St John anything like the wages now reportedly available elsewhere. Unlike at some other clubs, where selected international players were immediately moved from £20 to £100 a week after the lifting of maximum wage, Bill Shankly wanted all of his players to be locked onto the same basic wage in order to maintain a common purpose and a sense of natural justice – it was a nod to his strong belief that 'team spirit was a form of socialism'. Shankly had picked up his political ideas, and the importance of local togetherness and a sense of community, from his early years in the village of Glenbuck, and especially from the effects on local people of the privations of the General Strike (when Shankly was just 12 years of age).[12] Keeping all players' wages level was also a way of keeping costs down, of course, and of making more money available to him for transfers. Wages paid to players by Liverpool rose to £35,595 in 1961–62 compared to £29,635 the previous season, suggesting that players' salaries at Anfield rose by around 17 per cent in the first season of the lifting of the maximum wage, hardly the catastrophe some clubs might have feared at a time when the wages of manual workers were also rising.

The brash and ambitious Ian St John was rather less politically minded than Shankly, and he told the local press on signing for Liverpool, 'I like money. Who doesn't?' In fact, the Saint later reported that, depressed by his low early wages, he had once been involved in negotiations to fix a match for cash in Scotland but the deal was called off. He now happily accepted the new arrangements at Anfield and its crude equality principle.[13]

So, at the very moment that the USA was sending its first man into space, Liverpool Football Club also seemed to be sailing into orbit. 'Boy, what a ride!' the Yankee spaceman Alan Shepard told the world's press in blaring front-page headlines that week. It could easily have been Bill Shankly enthusing to his new signing and his prospective Kop worshippers about the glorious Liverpool future he was now planning for them all. Shankly had more than doubled the club's previous transfer record by getting the Liverpool board to spend £37,500 on a little-known Scottish steel-mill worker. Eric Sawyer had clinched the deal by telling those fellow Anfield directors who wavered, 'I don't see, if we have real ambition, how we can afford not to do it.' This was precisely the sort of 'spend to accumulate' philosophy that the club seemed to have been resisting for much of the 1950s. Sawyer was willing to back Bill Shankly's judgement all the way.

The league fixtures were already done, but on 8 May 1961 Liverpool faced Everton in the Liverpool Senior Cup final, and St John made his debut. A crowd of 51,669 turned up to watch a thrilling and bruising encounter. According to the *Daily Post*, 'Some of the tackling was out of this world and certainly well out of the rule books.' It was a good test. The new Liverpool man was up against Brian Labone, a player who was fast emerging as one of England's toughest and best young centre-halves. St John confused and then terrorised him, completing a hat-trick in the last minute of a hugely promising 3–4 Liverpool defeat. Shankly at least had something positive to take to the 1961 Liverpool AGM, where he blamed the accumulated tension of seven years of trying for the latest Liverpool promotion failure. 'What a tonic it was to see him [St John] play against Everton in the Senior Cup,' Shankly said, sparkling at the memory of his new man's debut. He knew promotion was now in reach.

But the members of the Liverpool Supporters Association who were present at the AGM displayed an unusual 'underlying annoyance', arguing that the Liverpool board had, as normal, acted too little, too late, and that it should be condemned for its inaction and latest promotion failure. For once, the usually unflappable Tom Williams lost his temper. He rose to his feet and bellowed, 'Rubbish!', claiming that the Anfield directors had travelled hundreds of miles in the season to look for new players. He was agitated and angry, especially having been pressed by Eric Sawyer so recently to lay out a cool £37,500 for a new untried centre-forward. A Mr Adler then jumped up from the floor and shouted that this was no way for the chair to talk to the club's shareholders, and he called for a vote of no confidence in Williams. This was real drama.

Meanwhile, Bill Shankly looked on, both intrigued and impressed: these supporters had guts as well as loyalty. It was the first real sign of a direct challenge by the club's followers to the Liverpool board, but Adler could get no seconder for his resolution. The meeting eventually calmed down, with Williams, Syd Reakes and Clifford Hill all being re-elected unopposed. The storm had quickly blown over, but it was probably the most exciting – and the most disharmonious – AGM in the entire history of the club as a limited company so far. At last something was brewing at Liverpool Football Club.

HEADING FOR PROMOTION

Bill Shankly now had the front-end and the middle of his new team pretty much sorted out. Ian St John would be the perfect foil for Roger Hunt, a man to link up defence and attack, but also a centre-forward who would score his share of goals. The Saint had once scored a hat-trick in 150 seconds in Scotland. But the deep-lying St John would not deprive Hunt of the vital penalty-area oxygen – the space – the inside-right needed to complete his own deadly work. Kevin Lewis or the young Ian Callaghan would deliver the bullets from the right wing, and the England international Alan A'Court was a more than reliable provider on the left. In midfield, Jimmy Melia was clever and consistent, a goalscoring, balding little general, and Gordon Milne would grow into his work on the right. The experienced, long-striding Tommy Leishman would be the defensive anchor, balancing on the left side for Milne's inexperience.

At the back, the Reds full-backs Gerry Byrne and Ronnie Moran were rugged and solid enough – Byrne was not allowed to tackle in the training five-a-sides on Fridays at Melwood because he was just too brutal and people were liable to get injured. But the Liverpool defence still lacked a pivot and a leader, a real physical presence. The young Jack Charlton was an early target. Shankly had also tried to tap up Leicester City's Scotland captain Frank McLintock for the role, even dragging him out of the club banquet on the night City lost to Spurs in the 1961 FA Cup final. McLintock declined, joining Arsenal instead. Bill Shankly typically rubbished the Scot for his audacity – and stupidity – and he turned his attention to Scotland once again, carrying with him Eric Sawyer's best wishes and the once little-seen chequebook of Liverpool Football Club.

Ron Yeats was from Aberdeen, but he was a Rangers fan. In junior football at 14 years of age he had been converted to centre-half from left wing-half, and the growth spurt that followed confirmed him as a left-sided defensive stopper rather than the sort of guy who stepped out from the back, as an Alex Raisbeck might or as Alan Hansen was to do brilliantly a decade later for Liverpool. Yeats had happily worked on shifts as a slaughterman from 15 years of age, and he enjoyed the toughness and the camaraderie of the job – it certainly paid more than part-time professional football ever did in Scotland. When he signed for Dundee United in 1957, he typically went to work at 2.30 a.m. on Saturday mornings, clocked off at 11 a.m., grabbed a few hours' sleep and then played football. After just twenty-eight United appearances, Yeats went on to do two years' National Service in the Royal Army Service Corps, including captaining the British Army football team in a match against Liverpool. Bill Shankly took note.

But when Shankly and his directors first travelled to Dundee to discuss a deal for the huge centre-half, they were greeted with what the manager later called an 'arctic reception'. But they persisted, and when his club recalled Yeats to Edinburgh in July 1961, saying that a 'big' English club wanted to sign him, the centre-half dreamed, naturally, about Manchester United, Arsenal or Spurs. He knew nothing about Second Division Liverpool or their slightly deranged Scottish manager. But his managers at Dundee United had always been grimy and insecure, only just above the shop-floor culture of the Tannadice dressing-room. By contrast, Liverpool's Bill Shankly had the glossy, almost corporate or even film-star air of a man really going places. Here was a man who had his red ties specially made for him in Germany. Shankly made a big first impression on Ron Yeats when they first met:

> I always remember this: he was a lovely dresser: lovely suit and tie, and white, white teeth. That really impressed me. And then he's walking round me, I can hear him at the back of me and he says, 'Jesus Christ, son, you must be about seven feet tall!' And when he comes back to the front, I said, 'No, I'm only six foot two,' and he said, 'That's near enough fucking seven foot to me!' I thought, there and then, I *like* this man.[14]

Shankly talked up the Hollywood looks and especially the sheer size of Ron Yeats into the defining feature of his new £30,000 signing by inviting journalists to marvel at the supposed immense scale of his 23-year-old centre-half. It was psychology, of course, more than anything else. Yes, 6 ft 2 in. was big, but it was hardly super-giant class. Yeats was also broad and powerful, but there were plenty of other big men in the English game, and the Scot's scoring record for a big centre-half was actually quite unimpressive. Nor was he a great shouter or a natural organiser on the pitch – he was deceptively quiet and reserved, a rather gentle man. But Shankly wanted opponents to *feel* that this guy was huge, a colossus; he wanted them to fear Yeats for his physique and his alleged bullying temperament before they even saw him lining up against them. Generally, it worked. Ron Yeats certainly made people sit up and take notice. Liverpool director Syd Reakes was so excited about the signing of 'Big Rowdy' that he insisted on doing all the driving himself back from Edinburgh with no stops, not even for a cup of tea.

Now Shankly had his new side – Byrne, Milne, St John, Hunt and Yeats were the core – and he was almost completely in charge of it. At last, some 47 years after the death of Tom Watson, probably the last man to have some real freedom in team selection at Anfield, Liverpool's directors would talk, from now on, mainly about the stadium and the club's finances and not about Liverpool's players or the team set-up. There would be no more weekly submitting of the proposed line-up to the board for its approval and changes. Molyneux was out, and Dick White was immediately moved by Shankly from centre-half to right-back. With Byrne, Yeats and Tommy Leishman also regularly in the Liverpool team, this was now a physically imposing but mobile new defensive shield. The age of the Reds' first-team squad had also been reduced radically from that under Phil Taylor in 1959 – Byrne, Yeats, Milne, Hunt, St John, Lewis and Callaghan were all in their early 20s or younger. In the Liverpool reserves, there already appeared the names of Tommy Lawrence, Chris Lawler, Alf Arrowsmith, Gordon Wallace and Tommy Smith. They were talented and hungry, all these men, and they also had skill and toughness. It was as if the modern game had suddenly arrived at Anfield in the boardroom, on the training ground and on the pitch all at the same moment. A combination of shrewd buying, the fruits of the club's youth policy and a lucky break in spotting Roger Hunt in local non-league football had produced a team and a club that no longer looked at home in Division Two of the Football League.

The truth of it is that Liverpool Football Club completely routed the clubs in the Second Division in season 1961–62. It was a profoundly unfair contest, almost embarrassingly easy right from the start. The *Daily Post* said that the new post-maximum-wage era would mean that 'it will be no use for managers to ask civil servants and teachers and engine drivers in the ground to be patient. They've been patient long enough, thank you.' There was little need for patience at Anfield. After a crushing 3–0 defeat of fancied Sunderland in August 1961, the local press reported that 'football was reborn at Anfield last night' and ran headlines reading 'Liverpool's Finest Team for Many Years'. A 5–0 pounding of Leeds United followed, with a first Roger Hunt hat-trick, some 71 matches into his Liverpool career. Hunt would score three more league hat-tricks in that season alone – the signing of Ian St John had released him to ransack defences with goals. The Merseyside press reported that the presence of Ron Yeats had 'bolstered the defence almost beyond belief' and that St John was 'an artist . . . full of ambition'. In honour of the new forward, the Kop had begun to sing its first real modern song in anger: 'When the Saints Go Marching In', adapted later to 'When the Reds Go Marching In'.

By the end of November 1961, there were only two Liverpool league defeats to report, at Middlesbrough and Derby County. No team would win at Anfield during the season, and only three took league points there, though it would take two goals in the last two minutes to save the home record against Charlton Athletic on 30 April. Liverpool were now unbeaten in the league at home since 31 December 1960, a real fortress. Even the club's reserve and B teams were unbeaten at home. The Reds were already clear, destined for promotion, despite the hiccup of two consecutive losses in Yorkshire over Christmas, to the Uniteds from Leeds and Rotherham, respectively.

But Shankly wanted more. In March 1962, Everton and Liverpool both bought new Lancashire-based goalkeepers in the same week, Liverpool signing Jim Furnell from Burnley for £18,000 and Everton splashing out even bigger money on the erratic but entertaining Gordon West from Blackpool. Furnell, as it turned out, was just keeping the gloves warm for the young Tommy Lawrence, who was growing up in the club's reserves. Liverpool conceded only one goal in three tough FA Cup meetings with Preston North End in February 1962, but it was the *only* goal, scored by a dashing left-winger called Peter Thompson. Bill Shankly was impressed.

Bert Slater had conceded only 27 goals in 29 league matches, but Shankly had decided, ruthlessly, that his keeper was just too small to really dominate his penalty area, and the Burnley reserve Furnell went straight into the Liverpool first team. With Ian Callaghan now in for Kevin Lewis on the right wing and Ronnie Moran filling in for Dick White at full-back (Gerry Byrne had moved across to right-back), the 'new' Liverpool was now in full bloom, and this was beginning to look increasingly like a group of players who would not only win promotion as champions, but could actually achieve something in the First Division, too. And then – who knows?

Liverpool FC, Second Division champions, 1961–62

		Furnell		
	Byrne	Yeats	Moran	
	Milne		Leishman	
Callaghan	Hunt	St John	Melia	A'Court

With seven games left and five points clear, and with one game in hand over nearest chasers Leyton Orient, it looked like a clear run-in, a formality. Roger Hunt had already smashed Gordon Hodgson's 36-goal league-scoring record in a season for the club – he would eventually end up with 41 goals in 41 appearances – and he had just scored on his full England debut, against Austria. Later, 'Sir Roger' was presented with (and he valued) a canteen of cutlery by the Liverpool Supporters Club for his achievements. But 'real life' then took a hand, once again, when a deadly smallpox outbreak in South Wales meant that Liverpool's fixture at Swansea was postponed in early April. This meant that promotion was finally clinched only on 21 April 1962 in a constant downpour against Southampton at Anfield, with two goals from the returning Kevin Lewis, who was filling in at centre-forward for the occasionally hotheaded and currently suspended Ian St John. The Saint had typically sneaked into the ground to watch proceedings, even though the FA ban barred him from Anfield.

There were still five league fixtures left – including the entire Easter programme – but Liverpool's promotion had been an open secret almost since the early exchanges. Liverpool would end up eight points clear of Orient and, tantalisingly, on ninety-nine league goals scored. The Southampton team gallantly made a rather sodden and bedraggled guard of honour for Liverpool as the teams left the field, and one soaked pitch-invader plonked a red-and-white hat and a kiss on a bemused Ron Yeats's head. Tom Williams and Bill Shankly both tried to make speeches from the Main Stand, but the Liverpool PA system was so poor and the supporters so excited that no one could hear them. The players got showered while the Kop repeatedly chanted, 'We want the Reds.' The players even tried to do a lap of honour in mufti, but it lasted about 20 yards before they were mobbed and forced back into the players' tunnel. The fans had to feast, instead, on dressing-room photographs in the next day's newspapers, showing the players and staff drinking champagne out of crockery mugs: a nice touch this one, the sporting artisans getting just a little taste of the high life. At the front of the shot, a proud Bill Shankly was beaming.

When the Second Division trophy was finally presented at Anfield after the lucky home win against Charlton Athletic, in the crowd was a list of past Reds greats, including Fred Hopkin, Eph Longworth, Bill Jones and Jim McDougall. Six-year-old Reds mascot Leslie McCann was also present, as he had been at all Liverpool's matches, home and away, that season. But pride of place went to the 80-year-old Joe Hewitt, a man who had served the Liverpool club for more than 60 years. As Ron Yeats held the trophy aloft, Joe had a discernible tear in his eye. The old warrior's hand tightened around a small object that he had carried carefully in his pocket that day: it was his 1905–06 Liverpool league-championship medal.

It had been 12 long years since Liverpool had last appeared at Wembley and 15 since the last Liverpool league title, in 1947. But all that achievement seemed like it was from quite a different age. This, after all, was the 1960s, a period in which attacks on the 'old order' in Britain came from all directions, including comics, television and politics, as well as from sport.[15] Even Billy Liddell and his ilk already seemed consigned to Anfield history, alongside Joe Hewitt and all the other Liverpool greats. The message from Bill Shankly and his team was that there would be no more Liverpool gloom in the second rank of the English game. All that darkness was over. The club had sleepwalked into this dreadful slump, led, largely, by its own directors. It had taken a stimulus from local rivals Everton to refloat the Liverpool vessel. Now the Reds had the wind in their sails again and an ambitious manager for whom nothing seemed out of reach. 'A trip to Wembley,' hazarded Leslie Edwards in the *Liverpool Echo*. 'That is the next mission, I would think, on Shankly's list of priorities.' It would take Shankly three more years to achieve that elusive Liverpool FA Cup target – and we all know that a lot can happen in football in three years.

CHAPTER 14 REFERENCES

1. Smith, *Anfield Iron*, pp. 30–1
2. Leigh, *The Cavern*, p. 86
3. A'Court, *Alan A'Court: My Life in Football*, p. 84
4. Kennedy and Williams, *Kennedy's Way*
5. Taylor and Ward, *Three Sides of the Mersey*, p. 96
6. Ponting and Hale, *Sir Roger*, p. 19
7. A'Court, *Alan A'Court: My Life in Football*, p. 70
8. Taylor and Ward, *Three Sides of the Mersey*, p. 97
9. Bale, *The Shankly Legacy*, p. 70
10. Taylor and Ward, *Three Sides of the Mersey*, pp. 99–100
11. Liddell, *My Soccer Story*, p. 16
12. Bowler, *Shanks*, pp. 8–9
13. St John, *The Saint*, p. 62
14. Quoted in Williams, *The Liverpool Way*, p. 100
15. Sandbrook, *Never Had It So Good*, p. 567

15

EE-AYE-ADDIO, THE FA CUP AT LAST!
Liverpool FC at Wembley
and in Europe

LOST AND FATALLY ADRIFT

On 24 April 1962, spoiling the Liverpool Second Division promotion party somewhat, local thieves on Merseyside returned to check out a familiar target. Safe-blowers stole £4,000 of match takings from a safe sited in the Anfield office of the then Liverpool FC club secretary Jimmy McInnes. These persistent crooks had finally got a decent result out of Liverpool Football Club, and the conscientious McInnes felt the loss personally, as if it was somehow his responsibility. It was typical of the man. The diminutive Scot had played 51 times at left-half for Liverpool after signing from Third Lanark in March 1938. In line with the club's 'family' policy of recruiting ex-players, he had joined the administrative staff at Anfield after the war. McInnes would have seen the chaos around distributing FA Cup tickets in 1950. He had been club secretary since 1955 and had seen his responsibilities grow. He was a kindly, undemonstrative man, a university graduate who dealt with his duties quietly but efficiently. In the backwaters of the English Second Division, with few sell-outs or all-ticket events to deal with, the role of a club secretary promised a reasonably uneventful life. Not so in the top flight.

But in the next three years under Bill Shankly, Liverpool Football Club rocketed from being a marginal outpost rooted in the domestic second tier to being one of Europe's major football clubs with top players and a celebrity manager. This happened in a city that had suddenly become a magnet for global attention for both its music and its football. The Liverpool club probably underestimated the strain placed on its backroom staff by some of these rapid changes. As we have already seen, the club also had an unfortunate reputation for penny-pinching in some of its policies and appointments, and in its provision of administrative support. Even its top players were earning no more than £35 per week as a basic wage as the club began to win league titles and the FA Cup and compete in Europe from the mid-1960s.[1] Cost-cutting was an established part of the club's identity.

In the middle of 1965, these pressures would already have become acute: Liverpool played in the European Cup semi-final for the first time and in the FA Cup final within a matter of days, so the demands on ticketing and other connected matters in these pre-computer days would have been quite out of proportion to anything the club had previously dealt with. The pressures behind the scenes were intense. His wife, Joan, said later that McInnes had been 'worried and overworked for a long time'. He worked 12-hour days and often stayed all night at the ground on a camp bed. He had 'months and months' of backlog of work to get through. The precise circumstances of what happened next are unclear, beyond the fact that McInnes and his small staff were stretched enormously – ironically, by Liverpool's sudden, extraordinary success. This is what everyone in the club had been striving for since the war. But it is the backroom staff that typically bears the brunt of supporters' anxieties, expectations, complaints and demands in these times of plenty. What we do know is that on 5 May 1965, four days after Liverpool had finally managed to win the FA Cup after seventy-three years of gut-wrenching trying, a distressed and exhausted Jimmy McInnes walked to the silent darkness at the back of the Spion Kop and under a hut at the Archway turnstile hanged himself. He was just 52 years of age. It was, to put it glibly, a very tragic end to an unprecedentedly glorious period of Liverpool Football Club success.

MOVE ON UP

With promotion assured back in 1962, and Bill Shankly acting as both bold figurehead and club cheerleader, Liverpool's average league crowds jumped in the 1961–62 season from 29,608 to 39,237, just below Everton's seasonal average of 41,432. This was actually Liverpool's largest average crowd figure since 1953–54 – the club's last season in the First Division. But the general football-crowd trend in England was still decidedly downwards. More than 41 million paying customers in the post-war peak season of 1949–50 had dwindled to just under 28 million in 1961–62. Four and a half million football supporters had been lost to English club football even since 1960. European club football and concerns about rising hooliganism were already part of this wider picture.

A conservative and hidebound Football League was another – that there was no need for the sport to modernise or change appeared to be its position. This seemed an extraordinary stand to take, especially considering what was happening to youth culture and general patterns of consumption in Britain, not least in the city of Liverpool itself. The Cavern, in the city centre, had been a jazz music venue since 1957, and the poet Adrian Henri thought that the Liverpool of the late 1950s was a site for exotica, which 'seemed to me like Paris in the 1920s'.[2] But 1962 was the year that Liverpool really started to become a national and then international centre for pop music, with the Cavern as its beating heart. The Beatles emerged to national prominence, to be followed by a shoal of Liverpool music acts, and the Cavern even offered the decadence of lunchtime beat-music concerts in 1962 for those 'hip' enough to get access. The 'Fab Four', of course, were regular early performers, allegedly clocking up 275 Cavern appearances alone in the early 1960s.[3] The city itself also seemed to be in relatively resurgent form, with the docks enjoying a temporary revival in international trade, though the still overwhelming dependence of the local economy on the fortunes of the port continued to make Liverpool vulnerable 'both to the structural decline of its service and manufacturing specialisms and to downturns in international trade'.[4]

A Football League survey in April 1962 identified some of these themes of rising incomes and growing consumer choice in accounting for the relative decline of active football-club support. The report highlighted greater prosperity but also uncomfortable league grounds and defensive football, as well as pressures from women for their husbands and boyfriends to spend more time with them and their children on Saturdays as the key reasons for falling attendances. Pop music offered a leisure outlet for young men and women away from their parents that had very different things to offer from standing on open terraces in the rain. But Joan Kennedy of Anzio Road in Huyton resented the underlying assumption here that women had no place at football in Liverpool or elsewhere. She wrote angrily to the *Echo* on the matter on 27 April 1962, criticising the sport for its chauvinist attitudes:

> Women don't like to be left out, as they feel they are when their husbands and boyfriends go off alone or with their pals to football matches. Why not encourage the girls and women to go along and watch, instead of discouraging them . . . Girls can be just as enthusiastic as men about football.

In June 1962, the *Liverpool Echo* reported on a new local enlightenment. 'It seems there is sufficient interest to form a Liverpool ladies football team in the city.' But it was a false alarm. In fact, it would take almost another 30 years for football in England to really take the role of women in the game seriously, either as players or spectators. By that time (in the early 1990s), near-terminally damaged finances, hooliganism and terrible stadium disasters – with Liverpool supporters as both perpetrators and victims – had finally forced the sport's hand to modernise, with satellite television now increasingly pulling football's purse strings. But a series of official reports on restructuring football in England in the 1960s had been rejected by the heads-in-the-sand Football League. The English game would continue to plough its traditional furrow, even as crowds tumbled. The single international triumph for the England national team – at Wembley in the World Cup final of 1966 – masked many deeper problems that were festering in English football at this time, both on and off the pitch.

None of these issues troubled Liverpool FC in 1962, of course. The club and its supporters simply contemplated life back among the sport's elite. Some football clubs, ill-resourced and small, just manage to scrape into the top flight and see a year in the spotlight as a bonus before sliding back into obscurity. It happened to Second Division runners-up Leyton Orient, promoted behind Liverpool. Some clubs go up on the back of an already ageing side that is past its peak – achieving promotion is the very apex of their ambitions. Still others lose their best players or their manager to other clubs *because* of promotion. Others spend wildly once promotion is achieved. None of these cases applied to Liverpool in 1962. Bill Shankly had built a new young team at a big club with a large and enthusiastic fan base. He now had a supportive board that was not quite so afraid to spend big money, and his ambition was to win the FA Cup (as soon as possible), the league title and, ideally, the European Cup.

As a starter, he won a local bauble when Liverpool beat Everton 1–0 in the Liverpool Senior Cup in May 1962, with a 30-yard 'missile' free-kick from Ronnie Moran deciding matters. All wins against Everton were valuable, and Shankly would never, ever lack for confidence or for a memorable one-liner aimed at the Goodison Park club. When World Cup-winner Alan Ball signed for Everton in 1966, the Liverpool manager phoned him up to welcome him to the city. 'Congratulations, son,' said Shankly. 'You'll be playing *near* a great side.'

At the celebratory Liverpool AGM that followed in 1962, chairman Tom Williams warned the club's occasionally disorderly young supporters about their behaviour, saying, 'Do not let yourself be carried away by the excitement of the moment.' He might have better addressed his remarks to his occasionally excitable Scottish manager. An iridescent Bill Shankly sparkled with a story about the 'cauldron' Anfield had now become and about how, not being the coolest of people himself, he had recently been paid a wonderful compliment by a visiting manager. This rival boss was, in contrast with Shankly's animation, calm 'almost to the point of contrition'. Shankly paused for maximum effect now, eyeing up his Liverpool AGM audience. What *had* the rival boss said to him? Shankly continued his story, reporting that the visiting man had nodded toward the Kop before growling to the agitated Shankly, 'You're worse than those people on the terraces.' The Liverpool manager beamed with pride at the memory of the moment as his audience laughed approvingly. The Scot, as he liked to say, was among his own people.

But the Liverpool board was not yet completely cowed by their manager. They moved the winger Johnny Morrissey on to neighbours Everton for £10,000 in August 1962 – and to a league title, of course – behind the manager's back. Shankly was furious and had to be persuaded not to walk out. The board finally agreed to do no more deals without the manager's approval, and there were no other major arrivals or departures at Anfield when the Reds returned to the top level. This inaction might have been a mistake. Liverpool's proud undefeated home league record could not even survive the club's first match back in the First Division, a 1–2 home defeat to Blackpool. In fact, there were four Liverpool defeats in the first seven top-level matches, though a 2–2 draw at Everton in September steadied any shredding Anfield nerves.

The step-up had already proved too much for wing-half Tommy Leishman, who was now dropped and later sold back to Scotland for a small profit in January 1963. In came a silky left-sided wing-half from Glasgow Rangers for £20,000. Willie Stevenson was a brilliant passer, if a sometimes reluctant tackler, a man who was just about holding up the great Jim Baxter at Ibrox, so he was keen on joining the Liverpool project. But Willie 'Stevo' did not lack in confidence. Like Graeme Souness, who would follow him later into Liverpool's midfield, Stevenson had more than a touch of the grand stylist about him, preferring cognac and snappy, expensive suits to beer and the knitwear favoured by the 'peasants' in the Liverpool squad. When Peter Thompson arrived to play on the Liverpool left, Stevenson told him, 'Just stay out on the wing and I'll supply you with everything. In fact, I'll make you an international if you're good enough.' It was a long way from Billy Liddell, but the famed Liverpool dressing-room banter of the modern period had already begun.

Stevenson's arrival on Merseyside coincided with the promotion of the Lancastrian–Scotsman goalkeeper Tommy Lawrence to replace Jim Furnell. The stocky and awkward Lawrence hardly fitted the photofit of a modern keeper: he was neither tall nor particularly agile. He was even known affectionately by Liverpool fans as 'the flying pig'. But he was brave, solid and reliable, and he also had some of Elisha Scott's alert reading of the game. Lawrence was quickly off his line whenever he spotted danger, confidently sweeping up anything that got behind his defenders, even straying out of his penalty area to deal with local alarms. He could use his feet as ably as most outfield players, and he helped to revolutionise the traditional goalkeeping role because of the way he knitted his job in with those of his outfield men. Reds defender Tommy Smith, not a man to impress easily, thought Lawrence was probably the greatest goalkeeper in the world in the middle of his time at Liverpool. Enough said.

The winter of 1962–63 was a particularly bad one, the worst since 1947, with Liverpool occasionally training on the dog track at Lower Breck Road because of frozen pitches at both Melwood and Anfield. But these new men, Lawrence and Stevenson, made an almost immediate difference to results, with Liverpool setting off on a nine-match winning streak in the league in November 1962, conceding only five goals in the process. Shankly was in ebullient mood, telling the national press in November 1963:

> There are a lot of very ordinary sides in the First Division and Liverpool were far from ordinary when they came into it. Now the penny has dropped, there is no reason why they shouldn't keep on doing well. They might do even better if so many of their opponents were not obsessed with negative soccer.[5]

This winning league run was ended only by bogey side Leicester City on 2 March. Leicester also later saw off the Reds in an FA Cup semi-final at Hillsborough in 1963 and were described by football historian Percy Young as having played 'the most imaginative football seen in a cup tie for years'. Imaginatively dull, perhaps: Liverpool had more than thirty attempts on goal compared to City's three. It was a match that echoed the one-sided 1947 semi-final Liverpool defeat to Burnley, and it only confirmed Shankly's fears about defensive football. England goalkeeper Gordon Banks resisted everything Liverpool threw at him that day, as City parked the bus and banked on snatching the vital single goal and then holding on. It worked and reduced a distraught Ian St John to tears.

In the league, meanwhile, champions-elect Everton also shut up shop in a 0–0 draw at Anfield in April 1963, as Liverpool briefly threatened a title challenge following a 5–2 Easter thumping of Spurs. But three days later, in the rematch at White Hart Lane, came a result more reminiscent of the roller-coaster 1930s than the Bill Shankly years. Liverpool were crushed 2–7, a slippery Jimmy Greaves scoring four times. This reverse seemed to sap the young team's resolve, as the Reds rapidly slipped out of contention, with only one win secured in the last nine league matches. As the season dribbled away, Shankly experimented with Gordon Wallace, a young Scottish forward, Alan Jones, a Welsh schoolboy international right-back, and Bobby Thompson, another Scottish defender who Shankly had brought in from Partick Thistle for £7,000. None would have a future at Anfield. The robust and quiffed Manchester-born forward Alf Arrowsmith would promise to do much more until injury cruelly struck him down in August 1964.

SILENT KNIGHT

But the emerging new Liverpool star for the future, briefly seen at this time, was a young, technically gifted centre-half and England-schoolboys captain called Chris Lawler. For his first Liverpool match, deputising for Ron Yeats against West Brom in March 1963, Lawler took two buses to get to the ground. When he got off at Arkles Lane, he was bemused by how few people were milling around the stadium. He suddenly realised that the Liverpool crowd was already safely inside, awaiting his debut.[6] The quiet and considered Lawler was initially frustrated by the lack of first-team opportunities behind Ron Yeats, and he even asked Shankly for a transfer, before becoming a regular at full-back in the 1964–65 FA Cup-winning season. This confronting of the Liverpool manager took some courage. Lawler's footballing skills were unusual for a tall defender, and so was his scoring record of 61 goals in 549 Liverpool appearances. His clever footwork and his predatory strikes at corners and from headers on diagonals for Liverpool attacks would rescue his manager and teammates from many a prickly situation.

Eighth place in the First Division was a respectable finish in 1963, but it hurt that Everton were champions, and Shankly knew that he was so close to producing a title-winning side. Kevin Lewis's Liverpool career was now effectively over, because Ian Callaghan was established on the right wing, and 29-year-old Alan A'Court's football world was also about to shatter when the Liverpool board sanctioned a £37,000 bid for Preston's outrageously talented left-winger Peter Thompson in August 1963. The slowing A'Court was immediately relegated to the Central League team, playing in front of a few hundred anoraks as Thompson played all 42 matches in the 1963–64 title season. There was no room for sentiment here, and, like most players of the time lacking an agent or anyone to advise him on a future move, the international A'Court simply languished in the reserves as his career dribbled away. He eventually left for Tranmere Rovers.

Meanwhile, the new man Thompson thrilled his manager, who saw him as a modern, if occasionally over-elaborate, version of Tom Finney. The Liverpool crowd also fell in love with Thompson's trickery and his sinewy runs and crosses. He was the perfect balance for the more direct and hard-running Ian Callaghan on the Liverpool right. What a pair of wide players. 'Cally' could run night and day. With Arrowsmith available to cover for injury in the forward positions and the ghostly Lawler ready to do the same defensively, Shankly knew that if he could steer clear of injuries his squad was capable of challenging for the title in 1963–64. And so it proved. He also had the setting for success. In 1963, the old Kemlyn Road stand was demolished to be replaced by a cantilevered new structure seating 6,700 spectators at the incredible cost of £350,000. Liverpool Football Club was going places.

THE LEAGUE TITLE – AND INTO EUROPE

The real signal that Bill Shankly was finally where he wanted to be, with the squad and board he craved and with real prospects of winning the sport's biggest prizes, was that in August 1963 he finally signed a contract at Liverpool for the first time. The agreement was for five years. He told the *Daily Post*, 'I suppose it is the modern trend to have agreements such as this, and I have simply fallen into line.' It was well known that ambitious Nottingham Forest had been making overtures to the contract-free Shankly, so the Liverpool board, not unreasonably, wanted to tie their man down. The move also offered some greater general stability to the club and more security to the Liverpool boss. Shankly had begun to identify strongly with the Liverpool people – and they with him.

The Liverpool and Everton football clubs were both riding high after some years in the wilderness, and the city's musical success had brought the world's press to Merseyside. The Beatles' many imitators and protégés in the city meant that on 3 October 1963 the BBC screened a nationwide documentary called *The Mersey Sound* and that for a fifty-one-week period, between April 1963 and May 1964, there would be a recording by a Liverpool artist at number one in the national pop charts. With a new Labour government soon to be formed and headed by ambitious local MP Harold Wilson, it felt like Liverpool was at the very centre of a radical shift in generational and class politics and was the key place for popular culture in Britain – and perhaps the world. It was exciting to be a part of this shimmering Liverpool cultural scene, which was now very different from the rather austere provincial backwater the city had sometimes appeared to be just a decade earlier.

Bill Shankly was a Labour man, of course, but he was no great lover of glamour or pop music. Instead, the Scot preferred a quiet game of cards or else ballads by Jim Reeves, Tom Jones and Ray Charles to going out or to listening to the racket produced by Liverpool's pop groups. But Shankly also recognised and enjoyed the energy of the city and its people and the public focus they now attracted. His players regularly mixed socially with local pop stars, and some of them had begun to exude some of their confidence. Shankly was well attuned to the demands of the 'performance culture' favoured by the city's emerging stars in music, comedy and football. He was something of a comic performer himself. It was no surprise to him that the BBC's first match on its new Saturday night BBC2 TV football highlights show *Match of the Day*, on 22 August 1964, was screened from Liverpool – where else? Only 75,000 armchair viewers watched on TV as the Reds beat Arsenal 3–2, but it was a start. The club's younger fans were singing Beatles and Gerry and the Pacemakers pop songs on the Kop, thus defining the new links between the three key modern cultural domains of youth, football and music.

Shankly had no desire at all to produce a glamorous team, of course. This was not his way, and football was too important to be showy. Anyway, Manchester United along the East Lancs Road were already dominating in the razzle-dazzle stakes. No, why leave the city of Liverpool when you had built a young team and when signs of regeneration and well-being were all around and everyone else seemed so desperate to move there? Bill Shankly signed his new contract and prepared for his assault on the league title.

The Liverpool league-championship win of 1963–64 was eventually almost as definitive, almost as predictable, as the Second Division triumph had proved to be in 1962. But it did not start that way. In August 1963, Liverpool lost consecutive home matches to Nottingham Forest and Blackpool, and then lost at home again to West Ham United in mid-September. What had happened to the so-called Anfield fortress? By the time Everton visited Anfield on 28 September 1963, the Reds had accumulated just nine points from nine league matches, but two Ian Callaghan goals were enough to see off the champions from Goodison and to kick-start Liverpool's season. Not that Leicester City could be shaken off – another 0–1 home defeat followed to the East Midlanders. But a string of league wins, and a 6–1 Boxing Day home trouncing of Stoke City, revived Liverpool's title hopes. Liverpool would eventually lose eleven league matches, but they drew only five, thus securing a relatively high number of league wins at twenty-six. Losing the derby return to Everton 1–3 in February seemed like a painful blip rather than a defining moment, and by the time Liverpool lined up against Second Division strugglers Swansea Town at home in the sixth round of the FA Cup on 29 February 1964, having already dumped Arsenal in the fifth round, it even felt like a Liverpool league and cup Double might be possible once again. It was daft – and possibly distracting – thinking.

Every team has its FA Cup day, and this was Swansea's. Their goalkeeper, Republic of Ireland international Noel Dwyer, had an inspired match – and bucketfuls of luck. When he dived the wrong way under the Liverpool siege, the ball simply hit his legs or else the post or the bar, or a loitering, absent-minded defender saved him. When Ronnie Moran stepped up to take a Liverpool penalty kick, it was almost ordained that he would miss. And he did. Liverpool could do little else to avoid the 1–2 defeat that resulted, arguably the club's second-most humiliating FA Cup exit after Worcester City in 1959. But at least it meant that the league could now be the sole focus.

Relegation-threatened Ipswich Town paid for the Swansea debacle with a 6–0 thrashing at Anfield. The goal-snatching rocker Alf Arrowsmith, who was replacing the injured Jimmy Melia, was prominent, scoring two of the goals. His contribution would prove vital in the title run-in: 15 league goals in 20 appearances. It also signalled the end at Anfield for the little midfield general Melia, as Shankly now sought more of a power game – and more defensive cover – from the central areas.

The 1964 league title was decided – as many had been before – during the crowded Easter programme. In nine days, between 27 March and 4 April 1964, Liverpool defeated title-challengers Tottenham Hotspur twice, bogey side Leicester City at Filbert Street and eventual league runners-up Manchester United 3–0 at Anfield, scoring eleven goals in this period and conceding only two in the process. Roger Hunt scored a brilliant hat-trick at White Hart Lane in a 3–1 win, and his combination with the burly Arrowsmith gave Liverpool an attacking edge they had previously lacked. No one could match this burst of points-collecting. A comprehensive 3–0 win away at Burnley on 14 April 1964 set up the home match against Arsenal as a potential title decider, with a further three fixtures still outstanding. Roger Hunt had an ankle injury, but he kept it from Shankly and played in what turned out to be the key fixture. Had George Eastham scored a penalty to equalise St John's early goal, the result might have been different. But Liverpool stormed away instead, Peter Thompson scoring two goals in a 5–0 rout. From 7 March, Liverpool had scored twenty-seven goals in nine breathtaking league matches, conceding only three. They were worthy champions.

Winning football matches, rather than settling for draws, had been the key to the Liverpool triumph. Six players – Lawrence, Milne, Hunt, St John and Thompson – had played forty league games or more. The Liverpool-born Phil Ferns had spent most of his Liverpool career since September 1957 playing second-team football, but he had filled in capably for both full-backs and for Willie Stevenson, playing 18 league matches and claiming an unlikely league-championship medal. Roger Hunt and Ian St John between them had scored 52 of Liverpool's 92 goals. Liverpool lost two and drew one of the 'dead' fixtures they had left – the club's players have never shied away from celebration – so their final points tally was fifty-seven, four clear of Manchester United. The margin could have been much greater.

Virtually this entire 1960s Liverpool side had now been raised or bought by Bill Shankly, and the following season would offer two main targets: an extended run in the European Cup – Liverpool's first season in Europe – and a real tilt at the FA Cup. His team was young and hungry for success, but the Liverpool squad was small and lacking in experience in key areas. Arrowsmith's critical injury and Gordon Wallace's failings left a hole at inside-left. The slim Scot Bobby Graham threatened to fill it after scoring a hat-trick on his league debut against Aston Villa in September 1964, but he seemed fragile and inconsistent and never quite gained Bill Shankly's trust.

Geoff Strong, a versatile forward from Arsenal who could also play in midfield and defence, was brought in for £40,000 in November, and his arrival hinted at Shankly and Bob Paisley's thinking. Perhaps one of the inside-forward berths should involve a much more defensive role than had previously been supposed? Liverpool's full-backs were caught up in marking wingers – most clubs played two wide players – and for all Ron Yeats's dominance in the air, he could be caught on the ground by a fleet-footed forward, especially on his weaker right side. One was likely to come across more skilful and more intelligent forwards in Europe. Maybe asking Strong – or someone like him – to play more defensively from the inside-forward position might allow more cover and pace across and behind the Liverpool defence? It could also mean skilful attacking full-backs, such as the emerging Chris Lawler, could get forward much more effectively. Detailing four players to defend most of the time was not necessarily a defensive move if it released your full-backs with width and your wing-halves to do more attacking. This was the theory of it.

But everything had to be proved out on the pitch, not in the boot room. Liverpool struggled to defend their league title: eight defeats and only four victories in the first fifteen matches in 1964–65 told the story. This run included a humiliating 0–4 home reverse to Everton. The club's focus was elsewhere – on the Continent, to be precise. The Reds were late into Europe compared with some of their English rivals, and it was difficult to balance priorities at home and abroad, even though the European Cup was played in an unseeded straight-knockout format. The Liverpool European adventure finally began with a 5–0 win in Iceland, part of an 11–1 aggregate walkover against little KR Reykjavik in September.

There followed a much stiffer task against the Belgian champions Anderlecht, who included in their number the prodigious inside-forward Paul van Himst, arguably Europe's best young player. Before the home leg, Shankly came up with not one but two innovations. First, that Liverpool would wear an all-red strip for Europe from then on, ditching their white shorts and red-and-white socks. Psychologists have long argued that the colour red offers a positive advantage to its wearers. Why not all red? Long before the kit manufacturers began to see profit in producing exclusive European kits, and rather as Reds supporters did when they came back from Europe with stylish new gear, this strip would also signal a new chapter in Liverpool's development as a fully European club. Second, Shankly wanted to get his defensive, tough young tyro Tommy Smith into the Liverpool team, perhaps to shadow the dangerous van Himst.

Shankly was worried about the technical ability and the pace of the Belgians against a possibly exposed Ron Yeats. The number 10 shirt was available, but he wanted to try Smith out in the new defensive position he had discussed, alongside the Scottish centre-half. Shankly consulted Yeats and St John – an unusual practice in itself – and then opted to field Smith as his number 10. His new role and his strange numbering was as confusing to the Liverpool public as Billy Liddell's role had been playing centre-forward while wearing the number 11 shirt in the 1950s. But the Liverpool formation was also different, much more of a 4–3–3 system, with Smith defending, St John dropping deep to work with Milne, and Stevenson and the wingers supporting Roger Hunt. If Liverpool got on top, St John played further forward in a 4–2–4.

The new system worked perfectly against the Belgians at Anfield, with Liverpool strolling the first leg, winning 3–0. A relaxed Ron Yeats even got on the scoresheet. In Belgium for the second leg, Liverpool sat back and risked being overrun, but Tommy Lawrence was inspired in goal, and Roger Hunt even stole a winner in injury time to clinch the match and the tie.

With the fearsome Tommy Smith now firmly in the Liverpool first team and quickly acting like a veteran, Liverpool's league form picked up. But Manchester United were already stretching away at the top, so the cup competitions became the key Reds targets in 1965. West Bromwich Albion away in the third round of the FA Cup was a tough enough assignment without Ron Yeats picking up the ball in the penalty area after he heard a whistle, only to see the referee pointing to the spot for handball. Bobby Cram missed the kick, sparking Liverpool to a 2–1 win. The Reds were even luckier at home in round four against the bottom Fourth Division club Stockport County, grinding out a horrible 1–1 draw courtesy only of a last-second goal-line clearance by Gerry Byrne. Almost uniquely, Shankly had missed the match on a European Cup spying mission in Germany. When a customs officer told him the score on his return to England, the Scot assumed the official was mad.

As if trying to make good – and also recalling the horrors of Worcester City – Shankly now came up with some 'magic' footwear for the replay, which was fought out on a frozen and rutted pitch. These rubber-soled, cleated boots (possibly picked up while he was abroad in Germany) allowed Roger Hunt to score two goals to see Liverpool through the replay. Ian Callaghan was the unlikely hero at Bolton Wanderers in round five, with a late headed winner in a very hard-fought 1–0 victory. Only really dedicated Reds can recall Cally headers for Liverpool. The FA Cup was in sniffing range once again, but how often had this been said about Liverpool in the previous 70 years?

Before all this, Liverpool faced the Germans from FC Cologne – nicknamed 'the Billy Goats' – in Europe. In two classic European meetings, the Reds held Cologne scoreless in West Germany on 10 February 1965 and then waited until 17 March for the return – a Liverpool blizzard had ruled out an earlier meeting – but could not break through the visitors' defence at Anfield. Without penalties to turn to, a third match in neutral Rotterdam in front of almost 48,000 mainly locals saw Liverpool take a 2–0 lead before the Germans replied with two goals of their own. Extra time produced no more returns. These two clubs could not be separated on the pitch in over three hundred minutes of football, and UEFA apparently preferred the toss of a disc over any kind of test of football acumen to resolve this epic contest. It seemed like a farce, a gross dereliction of duty, but the clubs were stuck with it. As had happened at the 1950 FA Cup final, the first toss agonisingly came up stuck in the mud and indecisive. But it was Liverpool who 'won' through when the disc was re-tossed and eventually came up 'red'.

As the players celebrated, Bill Shankly shook his head and quietly walked over to the Cologne bench to commiserate with his opponents. He told the opposing coaches that this was no way to decide such a hard-fought and evenly balanced European Cup tie played over a 42-day period and that there was no real honour for his own club in proceeding in such fashion. Shankly himself would be on the losing side of a coin toss in September 1968, when Athletic Bilbao went forward in the European Fairs Cup at Liverpool's expense. Inter Milan now lay waiting in the European Cup semi-final.

Liverpool were also still alive in the FA Cup, having held old adversaries Leicester City at Filbert Street in round six and winning through at Anfield with a lone Roger Hunt left-footed goal on 72 minutes, following a run and cutback by the dynamic Ian Callaghan. Hunt's low shot, sweetly hit in a very even contest, followed the striker as he wheeled back to the centre spot, such was the ferocity with which it rebounded from the goal stanchion. All this meant that, three days after playing an emotionally and physically draining European Cup extra-time match in Holland, Liverpool now faced a young and talented Chelsea FC in the FA Cup semi-final at a muddy Villa Park. The London club was managed by the flamboyant and outspoken Tommy Docherty, another potential headache.

Shankly and Paisley were certainly concerned about the impact of Rotterdam on their team, and they also wanted to unsettle Chelsea with new tactics if they could. Tommy Docherty had definitely surprised the Liverpool management by inviting Ron Yeats and Ian St John round to the Chelsea man's Dutch hotel room right after the Cologne match for a few late-night beers. Enraged, Shankly and Reuben Bennett managed to track the party down and ordered the Liverpool men back to the official party before laying into 'the Doc'. It was ostensibly an innocent affair, based around Docherty's Scottish links and his supposed access to spare FA Cup final tickets, the holy grail for players. But drinking abroad with the opposing club manager a few days before an FA Cup semi-final? And being offered cup-final tickets by him? Well, the press would have a field day today, and the meeting was seen in some quarters as being a prima facie case of bringing the game into disrepute. You could see their point.

After flying direct to their Birmingham base and ordering a couple of days of almost complete rest, the Liverpool coaching staff decided to advise the players to temper their typical, all-action style and try to play more conservatively, easing their way into the contest before trying to pick Chelsea off. This might conserve Liverpool's energy levels, but it was a strange way indeed to approach an FA Cup semi-final, which tended to be the most 'British' of all football contests, one played at a frightening pace on a usually worn or muddy surface. And Shankly had already, typically, spiked his own players by producing in the Liverpool dressing-room just before the match a copy of Chelsea's presumptuous FA Cup final brochure. He might even have printed it himself. This sort of contempt for his players deserved, nay demanded, a response, he told his team. In any case, with warriors such as defenders Eddie McCreadie and Ron 'Chopper' Harris in the Chelsea ranks and Tommy Smith and Gerry Byrne lining up for Liverpool, this was never likely to be a quiet or a restrained affair. In English FA Cup semi-finals, even the most talented sides have to 'earn' the right to play, which invariably means sticking your foot in and establishing dominance and respect.

After a little over an hour of just this sort of sparring, stopping a few inches short of out-and-out violence, one of the real creatives in the match, Liverpool's Peter Thompson, made the decisive play. Willie Stevenson and Thompson had their usual grinding relationship on Liverpool's left side: Stevo wanted more help defensively from Thompson and the ball delivered more quickly from the flank; Thommo chided Stevenson for lacking the pace to offer more support in attack. They were constantly at each other. It was exactly the same sort of left-sided griping that would later characterise the fractious partnership between Alan and Ray Kennedy under Bob Paisley. What was it about these Reds left-footers? Shanks loved Thompson, but even he criticised the winger occasionally for not getting the ball into the box early so that Hunt and St John could take advantage of a defence not yet set. And what about coming inside and shooting now and again? Thompson had a fierce shot in both feet, but he seemed so consumed with humiliating his full-back and dancing down the line that he seldom went for goal himself. But today he did so, cutting inside for once, to near the angle of the six-yard box and firing past a startled Peter Bonetti. The Red half of Villa Park, still steaming from the rain and the heat generated by thousands of alcohol-enhanced bodies, erupted. When Ian St John cleverly 'bought' a penalty from the furious Ron Harris on 79 minutes, the only other surprise was that it was Willie Stevenson who silently grabbed the ball and took the kick. No one disputed it, even though it was the only penalty the Scot ever took for Liverpool, a moment of supreme confidence and willingness to take responsibility. (Remember Steve Nicol in Rome in 1984? A less happy memory.) All's well that ends well. Liverpool Football Club were through to their third FA Cup final in 73 years of trying.

WONDERFUL, WONDERFUL WEMBLEY

Liverpool now stumbled to the end of their league programme with four consecutive defeats in April and just one goal scored. Chelsea had their revenge, of sorts, in a 0–4 reverse for Liverpool at Stamford Bridge, with Gordon Milne crucially picking up an injury that would rule him out of the rest of the campaign. In the club's last league fixture, at already-relegated Wolves (which Liverpool won 3–1), Wallasey-born forward John Sealey played and scored in his only ever game for Liverpool, in an unrecognisable Reds team that also included one-match-wonders defender Tom Lowry and England schoolboy international wing-half Alan Hignett. It was one of the very few occasions that Shankly ever rested or rotated players in an era when the FA came down hard on clubs that failed to field their strongest team in all fixtures. He had some cause: Liverpool had played a remarkable ten league matches in April 1965. The Reds eventually finished a respectable and exhausted seventh in the league, but a mile behind champions Manchester United and second-placed Leeds United, who they now faced in the club's third FA Cup final.

By 1965, the city of Liverpool's brief but ecstatic reign as world 'Beat City' was probably already over. The Beatles had left the city for good, and the UK was now swamped by original US musical imports and increasingly challenged by the rise of hippy culture in San Francisco and elsewhere.[7] But it still felt wonderful to be a Liverpudlian in the mid-1960s, and the links made between local pop culture and football glory were everywhere to be seen in the city in the build-up to the 1965 final – even though, ironically, relatively few pop stars from Merseyside at this time had any sort of real allegiance to either the Liverpool or Everton football clubs.[8] Bill Shankly was even on BBC radio's *Desert Island Discs* in the week of the final, and he chose many of his and the Kop's – and all Liverpool's – favourite songs. It was great build-up work, and it added to the manager's aura. The programme was played on the bus on the way to Wembley, to the mock groans of the players. The manager also arranged for a second bus to follow immediately behind the first, just in case the Reds' vehicle broke down.

For fans and players, Liverpool's European football adventure had also added a splash of colour to a generally black-and-white domestic football landscape. Incredibly, to modern sensibilities at least, the FA Cup final of 1965 would be pretty much the only chance for anybody inside or outside the city who was not an active fan to see this Liverpool team play 'live'. There was little live broadcasting of European football yet, save if an English side reached the final of a club competition. So the FA Cup final remained a very special event, one marked by supporters in the Red half of the city by the ritual dressing of houses with home-made rosettes and favours, and souvenir pictures from the *Echo*, stocking up with bottles of beer and drawing the curtains in mid-afternoon in order better to lock out the world for a few hours and to filter the shades of a grey Wembley day on a small black-and-white TV screen. Only 12,000 Liverpool supporters would get tickets for the final; Liverpool's average home attendance in 1964–65 was over 41,000. Wembley seats and terrace places were reserved by the FA, instead, for the worthy but non-partisan staff and volunteers of County FAs drawn from around the country. In short, fanatical football supporters, the lifeblood of the game, were still generally treated by the administrators of the sport like so much rubbish and mere terrace-fodder.

Before the match, Frankie Vaughan and Jimmy Tarbuck were both in the Liverpool dressing-room, keeping the players relaxed. Ron Yeats was very confident Liverpool would win: he had spent weeks practising what he was going to say to the Queen. Nessie Shankly sat excitedly in the stands; it was her first-ever Liverpool match. Shankly gave the players a rousing pre-match speech about being willing to 'die' for the supporters, perhaps sensing some tiredness, but, frankly, the 1965 FA Cup final was pretty unremarkable – except, of course, for the result.

Liverpool FC, FA Cup-winning team, 1965

Lawrence

Lawler   Smith   Yeats   Byrne

Strong   Stevenson

Callaghan   Hunt   St John   Thompson

Leeds United were on the rise, a tough, talented and cynical team under manager Don Revie, orchestrated by Bobby Collins, Billy Bremner and Johnny Giles in midfield and held together at the back by Jack Charlton and Norman Hunter, an almost mirror-match for Yeats and Tommy Smith at Liverpool. Leeds also had a left-winger, the black South African Albert Johanneson, who offered some of the pace and trickery of a Peter Thompson. Liverpool missed the injured Gordon Milne, Geoff Strong filling in at right-half in the new flexible 4–2–4 formation.

Maybe the two teams just cancelled each other out at Wembley? Neither club had yet to win the FA Cup – meaning additional pressure – and Liverpool's recent programme had been torrid. Both teams played conservatively, in Liverpool's case a little more justifiably because after just three minutes full-back Gerry Byrne broke a collarbone in a collision with the hard little Collins. Injury jinxes were not at all unusual at Wembley, and the stricken team invariably ended up defeated. This fact was not lost on Bill Shankly. The obvious thing – the compassionate and the losing thing – to do now was to bring the defender off or else strap him up and move him to the left-wing for nuisance value only. But Byrne was tough enough, and he could still run reasonably freely, albeit holding his arm across his chest. Johnny Giles was no conventional right-winger, and Shankly reasoned – drawing on an example from his own playing days with Andy Beattie – that if Byrne soldiered on in defence sheltered by Stevenson, the best player on the field, then Don Revie and the Leeds players might not even notice his weakness.

None of the other Liverpool players knew about the injury until half-time. Reuben Bennett spent the whole match with his eyes glued on Byrne, nervously chain-smoking on the Liverpool bench. He and Gordon Milne sheltered from the rain by draping training tops over their heads like a couple of troubled nuns. They need not have worried. The Leeds coaches missed a trick and made no attempt to play on the damaged Liverpool left side. In a very tight contest, it was the sheer bravery of Gerry Byrne that probably won the first FA Cup for Liverpool. Bill Shankly certainly thought so. He said later that the man who was all but transferred out of Anfield in the late 1950s 'should have had all the medals to himself'.[9]

After a dull, goal-less 90 minutes, incredibly it was the overlapping, injured Byrne who got to the Leeds byline to pull a low cross back early in extra time, cutting out both Sprake and Charlton but finding a stooping Roger Hunt, who headed unerringly in. This score was surely enough to win what was proving to be an arduous battle. But within eight minutes, Leeds were level, an unsaveable snapshot from Bremner. This was not in the script. But back came Liverpool, Callaghan sprinting down the right, this time to cross for St John to head in spectacularly. There was no coming back from this place. Leeds United were spent, and it was no disgrace to lose this contest. This was a truly exceptional Liverpool team, after all, one that would sweep to the league title again in 1965–66 using only fourteen players, and two of those would play only four matches between them.

After all his rehearsals, Ron Yeats forgot his speech for the Queen. Instead, the monarch said, 'It looked hard,' to which the exhausted Scot answered simply, 'It was.' The winners' photographs later captured the sport in its traditional guise and yet already in transition: the Liverpool players, still in their red shirts, dutifully filling the FA Cup with milk as part of some sponsor's agreement, while a hollow-cheeked Geoff Strong slyly cupped a dressing-room cigarette. Bill Shankly reflected later on the public perception of this Liverpool side and how they were still undervalued in some quarters:

> Because of our fitness and the pressure we put upon the opposition, the teams we built came to be called 'Powerhouse'. We were strong, that's true, but we didn't get the credit we deserved for the skill in the team . . . People said we were mechanical though 'methodical' would have been a better word. At least we knew what we were doing. They said we were predictable. Well, I think anybody who is unpredictable is a waste of time. Being predictable is not too bad . . . Our players worked for each other, not for individual honours, and by working unselfishly they still won the glory of being selected for international matches. Everyone at the ground worked for a common cause. The manager trusted the players and the players trusted the manager.[10]

There was Shankly's native socialism, once again, and it reached downwards into the club's supporters. The celebrations in Liverpool when the FA Cup was finally brought back to Anfield dwarfed anything seen in the history of the club – of any English club. An estimated 250,000 people turned out to cheer and sing Beatles songs and 'You'll Never Walk Alone' and to see their heroes parade the FA Cup. The trophy had only once been seen inside Anfield, and that was more than 50 years before. It had been brought there, of course, by Burnley in 1914 for a charity match after Liverpool had lost to the East Lancashire club in the final. But now it was Liverpool's to parade by right. And all those great players from the past who had tried so hard to bring the FA Cup back to the city for Liverpool – Raisbeck, Raybould and Cox from the 1900s; Longworth, McKinlay and Lacey from 1914; Scott, Bromilow and Chambers from the 1920s; Liddell, Stubbins and Balmer from 1947 – they were all equally honoured now. They could all rest, contented at last. Liverpool Football Club had finally reached their historic goal. After so many ifs and near misses, after so many hard-luck stories and broken promises, after so much disappointment, Liverpool Football Club had finally won the FA Cup.

LOCKED OUT IN MILAN

And maybe the Liverpool story in the year of 1965 should have ended right there, with the club's first FA Cup win. It would have made a natural and wonderful conclusion to an epic journey that spanned almost three-quarters of a century. But there was still a place in the European Cup final to play for in a semi-final against the mighty Internazionale of Milan. Sadly, this contest left a terrible taste in the mouth after the glories of Wembley. Inter were managed by the Argentinian Helenio Herrera, 'Il Mago' (the wizard), the man who claimed to have invented the modern version of the defensive sweeper system *catenaccio*. Herrera had been something of a shadowy figure from the start: he allegedly changed the date on his birth certificate in Buenos Aires. He was an authoritarian boss who insisted on controlling everything a football manager could possibly control, including, ideally, the match officials. He was accused by some Italian players of running their entire lives and experimenting with pills with his junior squads, and it was constantly suggested in Italy and elsewhere that he habitually rigged big matches, including a European Cup semi-final against Borussia Dortmund in 1964.[11] He was certainly as much a cod psychologist as Bill Shankly, who called Herrera, simply, 'a remarkable little fellow, a cut-throat man who wanted to win'. He underestimated the South American.

At Anfield on Wednesday, 4 May 1965 for the first leg, Shankly insisted that Inter take the field first, which they did to a monumental howl from the Kop of such volume and vehemence that it almost blew the visitors back inside the Main Stand. He then instructed his wounded warriors Milne and Byrne to parade the newly won FA Cup around the ground to further stoke the crowd. Anfield was now at boiling point. The Reds emerged into a swirling torrent of emotion, and they tore into their opponents. The Italians simply could not compete with the energy and pace of Liverpool. Hunt scored an early stunning volley from Callaghan's cross, but Mazzola equalised after ten minutes, following a slip by Yeats. And yet Inter seemed troubled by Liverpool's attacking frenzy, something they had never faced in Italy.

The second Liverpool goal, from Ian Callaghan, came from a complex set-piece move the Reds had practised in training. When St John scored the third goal with no further Italian reply, Bill Shankly was convinced that he now had a decisive lead to take to Italy, though today the away goal scored by Inter would be regarded as a precious cargo to take back home. Nevertheless, many Reds supporters regard this 3–1 victory as the team's greatest-ever display and the club's most atmospheric home night.

Herrera said magnanimously later that Inter had been beaten before but never so comprehensively *defeated* as they had been that evening. Shankly could see his rival was shaken, and he was even alleged to have cheekily asked Herrera for tips on Liverpool's likely final opponents, the Portuguese side Benfica. Sympathetic Italian journalists smiled at this, but they remained unconvinced. Even if Liverpool could outplay Inter again, they warned the Liverpool camp starkly, 'You will never be allowed to win.' Of course, they were right.

Near Lake Como, before the second leg, the Liverpool players were kept awake in their hotel by church bells and rowdy locals, but it was on the field, in front of 76,000 witnesses, where things seriously began to fall apart. Inter's lazy midfield genius Mario Corso started things rolling, scoring directly from a controversial free-kick, which Liverpool claimed was signalled as indirect, after just eight minutes. It was the start the Italians needed and the one Liverpool had feared. And within a minute, Liverpool's entire night's work and more at Anfield was wiped out after Joaquín Peiró illegally stole the ball out of Tommy Lawrence's hands as he prepared to kick it downfield and scored the second. This was a circus goal, not even allowed in parks football. Incredibly, the Spanish referee Ortiz de Mendibil allowed both goals to stand. Liverpool were shattered, bowed by this perceived injustice.

Fachetti's goal in the second half, Inter's third, was a brilliant irrelevance. De Mendibil was later implicated in the European match-fixing scandal reported in the *Sunday Times* in 1974, but Inter Milan escaped any punishment or even any serious investigation concerning the outcome of the tie. As Italian journalists had known it would be, the outcome of the match had been shaped by Inter's darkest desires. The proceedings were an affront to Bill Shankly and his innate sense of fairness. He was desperate to win football matches, but not like this. Liverpool's hard-headed, socialist muse had been frustrated by the arch dictator and South American football manipulator Herrera.

The great Scottish manager would have his European successes with Liverpool, but to his considerable frustration he would never win the European Cup – or even come this close again. The trophy, instead, was to become the property of another great Liverpool Football Club manager, one who was already being schooled in the sometimes devious ways of the European football hierarchy by sitting quietly on the Liverpool bench alongside the Glenbuck master. Although it seemed unimaginable at the time, the boot-room apprentice Bob Paisley would rule football in the grainy 1970s even more decisively than Bill Shankly had shaped the game in the 1960s.

CHAPTER 15 REFERENCES

1. St John, *The Saint*, p. 121
2. Du Noyer, *Liverpool Wondrous Place*, p. 101
3. Leigh, *The Cavern*, p. 117
4. Murden, 'City of Change and Challenge', p. 405
5. Keith, *Shanks for the Memory*, pp. 127–8
6. Young, *Football on Merseyside*, p. 168
7. Du Noyer, *Liverpool Wondrous Place*, p. 96
8. Williams and Hopkins, *The Miracle of Istanbul*, chapter 8, pp. 191–6
9. Shankly, *Shankly*, p. 102
10. Shankly, *Shankly*, pp. 103–4
11. Wilson, *Inverting the Pyramid*, p. 188

16

NOTHING BUT BLUE SKIES
Bob Paisley in Charge at Anfield

BILL SHANKLY'S GAP YEARS

Winning the 1965 FA Cup was the end of a grand quest at Liverpool Football Club, a moment of closure on a fabulous story that had started with John Houlding and John McKenna when they established the club out of their struggle with the Everton board back in 1892. Winning the cup had become the club's obsession ever since the first Liverpool Football League title had been claimed in 1901. The early 1960s also signalled the start of the modern history of Liverpool Football Club, the precursor to a period of near-constant success in the 1970s and 1980s that is still unique in the history of English football. Seventy-three years without a senior cup win of any kind was followed by a period of seventeen years when the club barely went a season without claiming knockout silverware. In the mid-1960s, the Liverpool club arguably had the best manager and the best backroom staff in the English game. It also had a seasoned group of players who were talented and still ambitious, a stadium that was both feared and respected at home and abroad, and supporters who were feted around the globe.

By now, the great Liverpool Kop, suddenly influenced by pop culture, had become something of a celebrated international institution, with documentary film-makers from around the world patiently queuing to crawl pretentiously over its rituals as anthropologists might examine distant and strange tribes. John Morgan from BBC's *Panorama* had proclaimed the Kop in 1964 to be 'as rich and mystifying a popular culture as any South Sea Island'. Local Liverpool football hooligans – often hidden by the international tributes flowing out for the choirs of Anfield – would soon be moving from the Kop's tumbling ranks to the Anfield Road end in pursuit of more satisfying action closer to rival supporters. The writer Arthur Hopcraft described the Kop, brilliantly and affectionately, in 1968 as a 'soft-sided crane grab' that dangled its members for minutes on end and a 'monstrous, odorous national pet' that it would be a cruel act of denial to kill off.[1] Despite the changes wrought by youth culture and new supporter styles, the Kop was essentially still the terrace that had bonded so powerfully with Elisha Scott in the 1930s. It had another 26 memorable years to breathe its friendly fire at opponents as a standing conference on the quality and commitment demanded of Liverpool Football Club on the field.

The Kop's spiritual leader Bill Shankly, meanwhile, was to add another FA Cup and two more league championships to his Liverpool roster, as well as blazing the trail in Europe. But progress would be uneven for the great Liverpool impresario. In England in World Cup year 1966, when Portuguese, Brazilians, Hungarians, North Koreans, Russians and West Germans all came to play football in the city of Liverpool, Shankly's own team stormed, virtually unopposed, to another league championship. Remarkably, nine Liverpool players completed forty or more league appearances in the season, with only injuries to right-half Gordon Milne threatening the Reds' shape and serene progress. In the 1966 European Cup-Winners' Cup, Liverpool overcame the Italians from Juventus and, on a drink-fuelled semi-final night that had Scots in disorder on the Anfield Road end, the Celtic side that would win the European Cup in 1967. The Reds would now face the West Germans from Borussia Dortmund in the final on a wet Thursday night at a one-third-filled Hampden Park.

This was quite possibly the most competitive year in the entire history of this rather unloved European tournament, and it is the only notable competition entered by the Liverpool club at home and abroad that it failed to win at some stage (later FIFA inventions for television, such as the Club World Championship, need not detain us here). Dortmund were formidable opponents, no doubt about it. The German side contained a core of the players who would face England in the World Cup final at Wembley in three months' time. One of them, the dynamic blond forward Sigi Held, scored the opening goal on a quite filthy Glasgow night. The Liverpool equaliser, scored by the struggling Roger Hunt, came from a cross after Peter Thompson had run the ball over the byline, undetected by the linesman or referee. But, unfazed by this setback, the Germans would not be denied, and in extra time Libuda floated a brilliant 35-yard lob over the stranded Tommy Lawrence to win the trophy for the men from the Ruhr.

This unexpected defeat in the club's first European final seemed likely to be a blip in what would surely be a procession of titles and cups for Shankly and his team. But instead it announced a mini-drought: no Liverpool trophy for seven years. What happened to the Liverpool machine, to Shankly's indomitable trailblazing? A number of factors probably collided here. First, both of the major

Manchester clubs and also Leeds United noticeably upped their game in the late 1960s (United won the European Cup in 1968), and Everton and Arsenal also had spells of real excellence that brought league titles to both and a Double for the Londoners in 1971. Arsenal beat a transitional Liverpool side in extra time to win the FA Cup. The First Division was competitive again. Second, Roger Hunt's bountiful years as a world-class striker – and his partnership with Ian St John – were coming to an end. Liverpool's goals began to dry up as a result. Most clubs would struggle to replace this quantity of goals, and Liverpool were no exception – it was no easy task to replace a man of his quality. Third, some of the players brought in by Shankly and his contacts to score goals and freshen up the team were simply substandard. Ex-Red Geoff Twentyman (and his distinctive trilby hat) had returned to Anfield in 1967 as the club's chief scout, and it took him time to hit his straps. Despite the spending binge sanctioned by chairman T.V. Williams in the late 1950s, Shankly knew that he would have to shop around for young talent once again. 'Liverpool successful by the cheapest possible way,' as he put it. It seemed like a return to the old unsuccessful ways of the past.

Local journalist Simon Hughes later wrote a book based on Twentyman's scouting diaries, which lists the key things the new man looked for in prospective Liverpool players. The first was a 'clean kick'. As Twentyman put it, 'I've never looked twice at any prospect who couldn't kick the ball properly.' Next was passing ability, followed by pace and attitude, and then craft and brains.[2] This was the complete package. His first recommendation to Shankly to stop the scoring rot at Anfield had all of these qualities. He was the free-scoring forward Francis Lee from Bolton Wanderers. Lee might have made all the difference, but the little man was never signed by Liverpool, probably because of his price in an auction. Instead, Lee inspired Manchester City to European and Football League titles, while Liverpool went into a mini-slump. Bobby Graham, Tony Hateley, Alun Evans, Jack Whitham and Phil Boersma were all tried up front and all failed to replace Sir Roger or to ignite Liverpool.

The final reason for this mini black hole in Shankly's time at the club was the manager's excessive loyalty to his players. His signature names of the early 1960s, St John, Yeats, Thompson and Hunt, were still in the Liverpool first team as the 1970s arrived. A turning point of sorts was reached on 21 February 1970 when Liverpool lost 0–1 at lowly Second Division Watford on a muddied heap in the sixth round of the FA Cup. This campaign was no 'slump' season – the Reds eventually finished second in the league to Leeds United in 1970. But Shankly had targeted winning the FA Cup to get his team moving once again, and he had finally run out of patience. Lawrence, Yeats, St John and Thompson were all dropped – Hunt had already been discarded. Only the winger Thompson survived to make any kind of impact in the season that followed.

St John had also been omitted earlier in the season, and he took his exclusion especially badly. His manager had been unable to face probably his favourite player with the news that his time at Anfield was finally coming to a close. The Saint knew he was on his way out for sure when Liverpool's assistant secretary Bill Barlow doled out a scraggy club turkey to him at Christmas, gleefully telling the Scot that the plump birds were being saved for 'first-teamers only'. St John left to play in South Africa, spitting feathers.[3] The 'family' club could also ruthlessly punish those who had once been its nearest and dearest.

REBUILDING – FOR RETIREMENT

With the great 1960s Liverpool side at last disbanding, and with the help of his scouts and advisers, Bill Shankly set about building his second dominant Liverpool team. In came the talented but impetuous 20-year-old Larry Lloyd to replace Yeats. Roger Hunt noted astutely that Lloyd's willingness to bring the ball forward on his strong left foot added to the confidence and forward momentum of this new Liverpool.[4] Alec Lindsay, a deceptively talented but ungainly ex-pig farmer left-back from Bury, displaced Geoff Strong, and Alun Evans, an inconsistent 19-year-old striker from Wolves, replaced Hunt. The awkward but effective lighthouse and cod poet John Toshack also joined from Cardiff City for a tidy £111,000 in November 1970, and he went on to form vital scoring partnerships for Liverpool over the next eight years. Steve Heighway and Brian Hall were also recruited, two amateur forwards and university graduates who had initial problems convincing hard men such as Tommy Smith that they cared just as much about winning professional football matches as he and all Liverpool supporters did. Heighway was cerebral, coltish, long-striding and direct; Hall was earnest, busy and combative. Both would offer Liverpool service after their successful playing careers were over. The latter inadvertently entertained the Liverpool dressing-room and his manager by turning up for training at Melwood wearing the conductor's outfit he wore while earning some extra cash as a student working on the Lancashire buses.

Soon after these arrivals, a scrawny and dodgy-permed young Kirkby kid with bird's legs called Phil Thompson started putting his hand up to be selected in and around the Liverpool defence. He would become a key figure in the new era, a modern, ultra-moaning version of Tommy Smith. A European Cup defeat to a cultured, quick-passing Red Star Belgrade in November 1973 convinced the Liverpool coaching staff that the days of the British-style stopper centre-half

NOTHING BUT BLUE SKIES

were finally over. Larry Lloyd had been the bridge. Footballing centre-backs, men who could read the game, keep the ball and pass it, would now be required in the modern era, especially in order to progress in European club competitions.

Surprisingly perhaps, the Liverpool manager's only real concession to his beloved Scotland during this period of rapid change was the recruitment, in July 1972 from Nottingham Forest, of the high-stepping midfielder Peter Cormack, who added class and goals to this department – and also a Scottish voice to the Liverpool dressing-room. Cormack bravely (foolishly?) stepped in at Melwood one morning when Tommy Smith and new man Lloyd locked horns in a typical training-session ritual testing of the balls of the new recruit. The intervening Scot came out worst.

All these men played their part, but Bill Shankly constructed his new vision for Liverpool around three other key signings, all of them Englishmen, all of them bargains. The Liverpool scouting network really earned its corn here. Barrow-born left-sided defender Emlyn Hughes first attracted the attention of the Liverpool scouts in Blackpool's reserve team, and Bill Shankly was especially impressed by the physical presence, sheer competitiveness and cold-eyed nerve of the youngster. He even offered £25,000 for Hughes straight after his Blackpool first-team debut. It was rejected. Later, Shankly watched Hughes as he fronted up to a hostile crowd and intimidation from Chelsea players and their manager Tommy Docherty in a violent FA Cup tie in which Peter Osgood broke his leg tangling with the young defender. The Liverpool boss had seen enough. In March 1967, he agreed to pay £65,000 for the full-back. That night, and driving atrociously as usual, Shankly famously scolded a traffic police officer who stopped his car whilst the manager was ferrying his new signing back to Merseyside. What was he doing, this doltish plod, asked Shankly? Did he not know he was holding up a 'future captain of England'? The sheepish Emlyn Hughes was just 19 years old.

Initially, Hughes replaced the graceful Scot Willie Stevenson on the left side of Liverpool's midfield. His leadership, confidence, boyish enthusiasm and immense power made him an instant crowd favourite at Anfield – and a truly great Liverpool player. For his arm-flapping, head-down, all-action running style, the amused Liverpool crowd affectionately christened Hughes 'Crazy Horse', a label that stuck throughout his career. With this young tyro at its heart, Shankly's Liverpool won the league title again in 1973 (the first of four at Liverpool for Hughes), beating Arsenal and Leeds United to the punch. The club also won the UEFA Cup in the same year, the first time in Liverpool's history that two major trophies were claimed in the same season. Hughes was later successfully converted to centre-back to counter the pace and cleverness of European forwards. Under Bob Paisley, and with the club now tightening its grip domestically and abroad, Hughes won more league titles, in 1976, 1977 and 1979. Under Hughes's inspiring captaincy, Liverpool also won the UEFA Cup again, in 1976, and consecutive European Cups in 1977 and 1978. These achievements, and a personal Footballer of the Year award in 1977, were the crowning moments of Hughes's glittering football career at Anfield.

But, for all his qualities, the effervescent 'Yosser' could also show just too much brass neck on occasions for the barrack-room Liverpool squad. He thought a lot of himself in a team with plenty of competing talents and some egos. The self-promoting Hughes urged Bill Shankly to replace the then Reds captain Tommy Smith with someone younger – the doting Shanks took note. Tommy Smith was incandescent with rage. So, in 1974 it was Emlyn Hughes, not the loyal and abrasive Smith, who hoisted the FA Cup for Liverpool after the 3–0 Wembley rout of a limp Newcastle United. It was to prove to be Bill Shankly's last great Liverpool FC occasion, and Smith never forgave the manager, or Hughes, for this act of personal treachery. Occasionally, when they played together later in Liverpool's defence, the two men refused to communicate directly – Hughes asked centre-half Larry Lloyd to 'tell that fat bastard to pass the ball'. Smith could also be heard congratulating under his breath any opponent who had managed to lamp his defender colleague. The message was that great teams seldom get along in *all* departments.

Skegness-born 18-year-old goalkeeper Ray Clemence was bought by Shankly, just after Hughes arrived, from Scunthorpe United for a paltry figure of around £18,000 in June 1967. Shankly watched Clemence more than any other player before signing him. It was a major scouting coup and one of Shankly's best-ever signings for Liverpool Football Club. Clemence was working at his summer job, hiring out deckchairs on Skeggy beach, when word first came through that Liverpool and Bill Shankly were interested in signing him. Even as a young man, Clemence was self-possessed, a smart guy, and he was unsure that he really wanted to swap first-team football in the Third Division for a couple of seasons (or maybe more) playing in front of one man and his dog in the Liverpool reserves. But Shankly was undeterred, and he poured it on, telling the young keeper that Tommy Lawrence was an elderly 30 years of age and on his way out of Anfield (Lawrence was actually 27 and in his prime for a goalkeeper). Shankly assured Clemence that he would very soon be between the Liverpool posts, possibly playing in European finals for the recent European Cup-Winners' Cup finalists. In fact, the new man would have to wait two and a half years to make his senior Liverpool debut, after the Watford FA Cup debacle. There was no discussion at all about salary when Clemence agreed to sign. Shanks simply told him he would be 'well looked after'. For the Liverpool manager, all this young keeper needed to think about now was that he would be playing for the greatest football club in the world.

Clemence was agile and supple but not huge for a goalkeeper – he was under 6 ft tall and under 13 st. But he was an excellent decision-maker and a good and very vocal defensive organiser, a man who demanded – and usually got – excellence from his back four. His concentration levels were immense, something that was vitally important. The Liverpool goalkeeper had to stay 'in the game' even when he was getting little real match action as the Reds in the 1970s started to dominate their rivals. He usually came off the pitch mentally drained, even if Liverpool had played almost the entire match in their opponents' half. His sweeping behind the backline (he starred as an outfielder in training) and his distribution from hand or foot were first class, and he hardly seemed to make any mistakes – or to get injured. For eleven Liverpool seasons, from August 1970 until May 1981, Clemence missed only six league matches and ended up with six hundred and sixty-five major domestic and European appearances for the club. In 1978–79, he helped the team achieve the greatest defensive record in forty-two-game Football League history – Liverpool conceded just sixteen league goals, only four of them at Anfield. Clemence was also a bubbly character in the Reds dressing-room, a very positive and intelligent influence, attributes that aided him in becoming the England goalkeeping coach after he retired as a player.

The third key Shankly signing for this period was, of course, the forward Kevin Keegan. This future international and honed national sporting product – a precursor of the Michael Owen England figure – also came from Scunthorpe United, in May 1971 for around £33,000. The Liverpool manager later described the deal, proudly, as 'robbery with violence'. Keegan was recommended to Shankly by his old mentor Andy Beattie, whom Shanks now employed as part of Geoff Twentyman's scouting network. Beattie had been tracking Keegan for 18 months and was bemused that no other club had even registered an interest in him after 124 Scunthorpe appearances. Had he missed something? Absurdly, some good judges thought Keegan lacked courage. As soon as Bob Paisley saw him, he told Shanks to start preparing to woo this new talent. Other suitors eventually stirred, but Keegan signed just as Liverpool were about to lose the 1971 FA Cup final to Arsenal.

The new recruit went with the Liverpool party to Wembley and was personally devastated by the defeat. Fagan, Paisley and Shankly raised collective eyebrows. This was some commitment already to the Liverpool cause. Not that the signing made a big splash – Keegan's first Liverpool wages were little better than those he had been on at little Scunthorpe. Bill Shankly had given Keegan the 'move to a big club like Liverpool and the money will follow' speech he had worked on with Ray Clemence, and the youngster had lapped it up. But this was no deception on the Liverpool manager's part, no politician's spin or wind-up. Shankly passionately believed that his younger players should properly appreciate their rise up the ranks, and he needed to know that they were playing from the heart for Liverpool Football Club, not for their pay cheques. He need have no fears about Keegan. The two men actually became very close, Shankly as a kind of father figure and mentor to this rapidly uncoiling ball of football energy, as he had once been to the young Tommy Smith.

Although he was lacking a little in natural ability compared to other top forwards, and initially short on confidence, in the late summer of 1971 Keegan was first to everything in training at Melwood and impossible to track or predict; experienced Liverpool defenders were being given the run-around by a kid they had never even heard of. He was a demon to impress, with terrific acceleration, and he was incredibly fit and vibrantly enthusiastic, another Emlyn Hughes. Shankly was worried about a shortage of goals and pace in the Liverpool side – his forward recruits were not delivering – so he promoted Keegan directly into the Liverpool first team in August 1971. This was virtually unheard of: a raw recruit from the English Fourth Division being thrown in without any of the detailed Anfield grooming and reserve-team apprenticeship. It looked like desperation, and the manager certainly needed a boost. Keegan was crying out for a chance, and he did not disappoint. Again, like Michael Owen, his sheer naive exuberance seemed to unhinge even experienced defenders. Keegan simply never gave up. He teamed up instantly with the tall Welshman John Toshack and was to become the attacking fulcrum of the Liverpool team for the next six years, replacing at last the successful Hunt and Ian St John forward partnership of the 1960s. Keegan starred in the club's second FA Cup win, in 1974, and in the first European Cup triumph under Bob Paisley, in Rome in 1977. He also became one of the first British players in the modern period to have an agent and was the first to leave the Liverpool club to develop his career elsewhere – with Hamburg. It was a very early marker of where the European trade for footballers might eventually end up.

TOO LONG GONE

With these key signings in place, and Bill Shankly apparently in his pomp again and marked for a long stay and more trophies at Liverpool, new man John Smith (as chairman) and Peter Robinson (as all-seeing club secretary) gradually became the new driving boardroom and administrative forces around the club in the 1970s and beyond. For 17 years, between 1973 and 1990, Liverpool's 'dapper businessman chairman' Smith, a brewery sales director and deputy chairman of an electronics firm, and also chairman of the Sports Council between 1985 and 1989, ran the club not just as the traditional Liverpool 'family' concern but also as a tight and cohesive administrative and business unit. Gone for good (or so we thought) was the era of lack of leadership and focus and the endless chairman re-elections of the 1950s. Smith and his board, with Robinson close at hand, worked hard on raising the necessary cash for player recruitment to try to keep the club among Europe's elite. They also worked diligently on the important modernisation of the Liverpool stadium. The new Main Stand, seating 8,600 and with 2,150 standing in the paddock below, and a modern floodlighting system were officially opened on 10 March 1973, during the club's eighth championship season. All seemed set fair for the next great Liverpool advance.

And it duly came, with the league title won again in 1973 and the club's first European trophy, the newly named UEFA Cup, won by narrowly defeating Borussia Mönchengladbach 3–2 on aggregate over two legs in May. Inspired by Keegan, Liverpool had demolished the West Germans 3–0 in the first leg at Anfield, but not before a washout first attempt at the fixture was abandoned, leading Shankly to change his original selection and bring in John Toshack to terrorise the German defence in the air. Liverpool were truly outclassed and pummelled in the return, only just holding on to the 0–2 scoreline that won the trophy for their manager and the Liverpool hordes.

Liverpool FC, UEFA Cup-winners, 1973

Clemence

Lawler   Smith   Lloyd   Lindsay

Callaghan   Cormack   Hughes   Heighway

Keegan   Toshack

But frustration would follow for Shankly in the European Cup against Red Star Belgrade in the autumn of 1973, and the Liverpool manager so wanted revenge for his 1965 humiliation in Milan. Would it ever come? Not now, because almost without warning, the great man Shankly, the Glenbuck visionary, resigned on 12 July 1974. The glorious 12th it was not. But why go now? He was only 61 years of age, not old at all for a football manager. His new side, playing a flexible 4–4–2, had recently won in Europe and had clinically dismantled Newcastle in the 1974 FA Cup final, practising just the sort of football he had always preached: passing, movement and power combined. Liverpool supporters had even invaded the Wembley pitch to kiss his feet. Why throw all this away, with players he had developed, such as Hughes, Keegan, Clemence, Thompson, Hall and Heighway, still young and hungry? There are many theories about his Liverpool departure but very few clear answers.

Shankly had certainly dragged Liverpool into the modern era. He was made for the new age of television sport, and he had established the right of the club's manager actually to manage at Anfield without undue interference from the board. His identity was now interwoven with that of the club. The story hit so hard in Liverpool that people on the street either refused to believe it or simply gawped at the news – they just couldn't take it in. This was because Shankly had also become part of the city's mythology; he was so much more to local citizens than a mere football manager. His values and principles extended well beyond the dressing-room. It is not too much to suggest that Shankly had become something of a modern local exemplar of a kind of lived socialism. Many ordinary people had memories of him in this respect: looking for unemployed supporters outside grounds where Liverpool played to offer them match tickets; paying the train fares to away matches of down-at-heel Reds fans; attending, unannounced, the funerals of committed Liverpool supporters whom he barely knew; or even helping to carry the weekday shopping of elderly people in West Derby Village.[5] Again, images of the great Elisha Scott come to mind, in terms of feelings of attachment to and identification with local people. Indeed, Tom Watson, Elisha Scott and Shankly form a chain of continuity in this respect. Shankly would also frequently turn up unannounced at supporters' birthday parties or social events on Saturday evenings with one proviso only: that he had to be home in time to watch *Match of the Day* on TV. This was no ordinary modern football boss. When he told his players he was going to retire, the impact was so enormous that his captain Emlyn Hughes openly sobbed – much to Tommy Smith's disgust.

It is true that Shankly was something of a serial resigner. He often offered his resignation to the Liverpool board at the season's end, depressed by impending inactivity and seemingly needing confirmation that he was still valued and wanted at the club for another season. Until then, the club's directors and staff had always easily talked him out of leaving, and this summer role play had grown into something of an annual ritual. But now his backroom staff at Anfield had grown in stature – the famed Liverpool boot room had European experience and a collective voice that was separate and different from Shankly's own. If the Scot really did want to go this time, it was not quite the disaster it might once have seemed. His assistant Bob Paisley could conceivably step up, ably supported by a coterie of hardened professionals, which now included Ronnie Moran, on the Reds coaching staff. And not everyone in the Liverpool boardroom appreciated their manager's open disdain for the doings of football-club directors. Some of them would not be so sad that their attention-grabbing manager was on his way. Not that loyalty counted for much: Peter Robinson intimated soon after Shankly had departed that if Bob Paisley failed to win a trophy or to keep Liverpool in football's elite in his first season, the club would very probably be looking for a new manager again. This was business.

Bill Shankly had been under the media spotlight at Liverpool for 15 years, and the intense pressure of constant performing had also begun to tell. He once described football management as 'a soul-destroying job' and rightly rated the most important quality of a manager as being 'the natural ability to pick a player'. Its lack would unseat many pretenders who followed him. He was no simple romantic. 'Managing a football club is like drowning,' he once told Tommy Smith. 'Sublimely peaceful and pleasant once the struggle is over.'⁶ Shankly knew that his utter devotion to the game had been hard on his family, and especially on his long-suffering wife Nessie. All those away trips and deathly scouting nights away from home.

He probably really did think for an instant that he should spend more time with the other people in his life who loved him unconditionally. But it also looked as if he was deeply uneasy with his decision to retire from the game almost as soon as his resignation was reluctantly accepted. Often, a difficult life-changing choice once taken produces a sense of profound relief, a weight lifted from one's shoulders. There was very little evidence of that here. There was only confusion and regret. Significantly, Shankly had named no successor, and he looked as if he missed football and his day-to-day involvement at the club right from the very moment he left it. Had he expected the Liverpool directors to do even more to try to keep him? Had he wanted a public uprising to demand that he take charge again? He later wrote, 'It was never my intention to have a complete break with Liverpool.' But no new manager could have survived easily at Anfield with the ghost of Bill Shankly loitering in the background. And there seemed little realistic prospect of the Glenbuck socialist being invited to join the still very conservative Liverpool board. That would have been a recipe for disaster.

THE MANAGER OF THE MILLENNIUM

A terrible decision had now been made. Although Liverpool Football Club owed a huge debt to Bill Shankly, it also had to move on, to get behind the new manager Bob Paisley. The club was bigger and more important than anyone, and the old boss could not be allowed to haunt the Reds training ground – it had to be all or nothing. All of this caused misunderstanding, unhappiness and tension. There were accusations that Liverpool FC had dealt badly with its great modern leader. Shankly himself seemed bitter, and he clearly felt rejected by his old club. He even suggested that Everton was warmer towards him now than was the Anfield hierarchy, and Evertonians certainly enjoyed propagating the myth later that the Liverpool club and its supporters had soon 'forgotten' Shankly's contribution.[7] They ought to check out the Kop today and look for similar Harry Catterick flags at Goodison Park.

The truth was much more banal: the Liverpool club had not pushed Bill Shankly out, far from it. But once his decision was confirmed, the matter had simply been dealt with as ruthlessly and as professionally as Shankly himself had often dealt with great footballers who had passed their peak of usefulness to Liverpool Football Club. It might have seemed callous, but, as always in football, the future was all that mattered now.

Partly because of all this shock, sadness and uncertainty, Bob Paisley began his managerial regime at Liverpool as probably the most reluctant Liverpool incumbent since George Patterson had been pressed to take over back in the 1930s. His choice as Shankly's successor was both inspired and unusual in the English game: assistants did not naturally become managers when their bosses departed. He told his players, 'I don't particularly want the job, but someone's got to do it.' It was hardly Churchillian rhetoric, no rallying call to arms. But then Bob was no public orator. He led by example and by sound decision-making, rather than by fine words or native psychology as Bill Shankly might have done.

Few of the players could understand Bob's north-east mutterings anyway – about 'doins' and 'what's its' and 'jag down there' – but they respected him. 'Bob was great at not giving players problems,' as Alan Kennedy later put it, rather backhandedly.[8] In other words, he kept things simple and trusted his players. And plenty of things were in Bob Paisley's favour. He knew the club and its staff inside out, and the players and coaches were all behind him. Most football managers take over a club because the last man has been sacked and left the business in a mess. Nothing could be further from the truth: Liverpool were riding high with a good young core of players. Shankly had just added to it by buying the bulky and disillusioned forward Ray Kennedy from Arsenal for £180,000, a player Paisley later converted into a mobile and brilliant goalscoring left-sided midfielder, although Kennedy was ultimately a man dogged by demons and illness. Bill Shankly had left Liverpool Football Club in fine fettle.

Paisley also made some astute early signings of his own, directed by Twentyman and the Liverpool scouts. In October 1974, he recruited a versatile, authentically two-footed defender from Northampton Town called Phil Neal for £66,000, initially to replace Alec Lindsay on the left but eventually to substitute for Chris Lawler on the right. It was a bargain. Joey Jones, a raw young leg-biting Welshman, would come in a year later from Wrexham to briefly hold sway on Liverpool's left side. The 23-year-old Neal was like a top golfer, according to Twentyman: he was able to chip, drive and weight a ball perfectly, and on both flanks.[9] He was simply the most consistent and most reliable outfield player in Liverpool's history. In ten seasons – four hundred and twenty league matches – between August 1975 and May 1985, Neal missed precisely one league match for Liverpool, an injury incurred in a meeting at Manchester United in September 1983. Neal is the only Liverpool player to win four European Cups, and he played in five finals, while also winning eight league championships. He became the ever-present defensive rock of the Bob Paisley era, a wonderful servant, without doubt one of the club's greatest-ever players.

In, too, came Terry McDermott, an expat from Kirkby, a 'Duracell' midfield player who had somehow ended up at Bury and then in the north-east at Newcastle United. Many thought Paisley had wrongly spent £175,000 on Terry Mac in November 1974 when the Scouser initially struggled to get into Liverpool's team. But the new man later came to the fore with his ceaseless running and brilliant goals, and all this with a 'reluctant' attitude to training and weirdly obtuse match-day preparations. Terry Mac liked a drink – many of the Liverpool squad did – he ate all the wrong things and he also liked watching the horse racing in the players' lounge until 2.40 p.m. on match days, then dragging on his kit and tumbling out onto the pitch like any Sunday-league footballer might. The Liverpool coaching staff accepted his idiosyncrasies, as long as he continued to produce where it mattered: on the pitch. For six great seasons he did.

Paisley and his boot-room men, ex-reserve team player Roy Evans, Reuben Bennett, Joe Fagan and Ronnie Moran, spent a year settling in, and, despite Peter Robinson's warning, they were allowed their time. There were no trophies in this first season, but second place in the league in 1974–75 was just enough to keep the Liverpool board off his case. The directors (for once) knew what they were doing. The title returned to Anfield in 1975–76, and so too did the UEFA Cup, Liverpool seeing off both Real Sociedad and Barcelona from Spain before overcoming Club Brugge KV in a hard-fought two-legged final.

By now, a tough-tackling young midfielder by the name of Jimmy Case had signed from South Liverpool and was making waves among Liverpool's opposition – and sometimes in local bars and clubs, too, with his chief partner in crime the unpredictable Ray Kennedy. A flame-haired, sometimes chaotic, local attacker called David Fairclough was also trying to force his way past Keegan and Toshack into the Liverpool team. He was, more usually, making an impact as a substitute. Fairclough's chances of making a real splash at Anfield diminished still further when the hard-working England and ex-Everton centre-forward David Johnson was brought in by Paisley from Ipswich Town in August 1976. With Clemence securely in goal and Hughes by now partnering Phil Thompson or Tommy Smith in the middle of a more mobile Liverpool defence, Jones and Neal at full-back, and Case, McDermott and Kennedy all established in midfield with the evergreen Ian Callaghan – an astonishing survivor from the 1959–60 season – Bob Paisley's first Liverpool team had begun to take some shape. The flyer Heighway or Johnson accompanied Keegan up front. In just three years, Paisley had built on the Shankly legacy and produced a new, more flexible side. He would now manage to do what even his great mentor had been denied in Milan in 1965: win the European Cup.

WE'RE ON OUR WAY TO ROMA

The path for Liverpool to the 1977 European Cup final may look simple enough compared to today's marathon: Crusaders, Trabzonspor and FC Zurich (in the semi-final) were all comfortably put to the sword. But the campaign really took off in the quarter-finals, when Liverpool were drawn to play the French champions St Etienne, who had been cruelly and unjustly beaten in the 1976 final by Bayern Munich. This was a real test. After losing 0–1 in France, Liverpool faced an uphill task at Anfield when Bathenay equalised Kevin Keegan's early goal with an unstoppable long-range drive. Now two goals were needed – a situation calling out for heroes. Ray Kennedy had already scored a second goal for Liverpool in a pulsating match of high quality played in a frenzied atmosphere before substitute David Fairclough was summoned, once again, to replace the ineffective Toshack. Liverpool players marvelled at the Bionic Carrot's capacity to score goals from the substitutes' bench. But Fairclough was less sure this was a blessing. He hated the super-sub label – he wanted to start in the team. Now, put clear on the left of the French defence, he scored the crucial goal with six minutes remaining as the home crowd went wild. It was a coming of age of Liverpool in the major European competition, a memorable occasion but also a signal of intent. This was now an experienced and hardened European unit, real contenders for the top European club crown.

FC Zurich were casually brushed aside in the semi-final, but before the Rome final could be contemplated there was another league title to wrap up, with three nervy (or was it boredom?) draws in May closing the final gap ahead of Manchester City to just one point. Liverpool also survived in the FA Cup, playing in a luckily drawn semi-final to Everton at Maine Road before demolishing the Blues 3–0 in the replay. This meant that, four days before playing the biggest match in the entire history of the club, Liverpool would meet Manchester United at Wembley in the small matter of the FA Cup final. There had been no season for any English club like this one, and none to test the marital status, pockets and employment records of the club's mainly working-class supporters in quite this fashion. Plenty of Liverpudlians set off to Wembley and then carried on going to Italy – why bother driving back north? Even the Liverpool Treble seasons that followed in 1984 and then 2001 lacked the intensity of this climax. Who could catch their breath? And in the end it proved just too much for the players. In a scrappy match, United prevailed 1–2 at Wembley. The Reds now had to lift themselves for their European Cup final chance at last. Once again, the Germans from Borussia Mönchengladbach lay in wait. It proved to be an unforgettable occasion.

The 1977 European Cup final is probably mostly recalled for Kevin Keegan's headline contest with the West German international defender Berti Vogts, or Tommy Smith's bullet-headed second goal (later remembered, to no great fuss in Liverpool, by a father-of-three Scouser on a reality TV show as simply 'the greatest moment of my life'), or Phil Neal's nerveless penalty conversion to finally clinch the 3–1 win. But for those who were there, this was also a fantastic cultural experience for the people of Liverpool, one to match and then easily surpass the 1914, 1950 and 1965 great supporter flows from the city to London for FA Cup finals. Small knots of Liverpool fans had travelled with the club around Europe, but this was the first great epic European journey for a mass of Liverpool supporters – an estimated 25,000 travelled to Rome, using every conceivable route and form of transport, every possible excuse for missing work (think back to all those midweek Reds cup replays in the 1930s) and every means of raising cash for the trip. Merseyside pawnbrokers and moneylenders were even better-used than usual for a few weeks in May 1977.

Liverpool FC, European Cup-winning team, v. Borussia Mönchengladbach, 25 May 1977

Clemence

Neal   Smith   Hughes   Jones

Case   Callaghan   McDermott   Kennedy

Keegan   Heighway

This was the era before cheap flights, so these supporters were no sophisticated and experienced adventurers. Nor were they members of the sort of well-padded, mixed-sex global contingents that later followed the Reds to big finals abroad. This was a pasty-white crowd of mainly working men, pretty much all of them from the city. Many of them afforded this arduous journey about the level of preparation and respect typically demanded for an overnight stop in south London or for a football visit to Bristol in the distant south-west. Plenty of people from Liverpool (including the author) made a gruelling five-day round trip by coach to be there, with no overnight stops. Other young 'scallies' set out for this adventure in vans and by train with only the clothes on their backs, a little (British) cash in their pockets, a plastic bag full of sandwiches and possibly an apple (a vain nod, this last provision, to the importance of dental hygiene).[10] Most of these supporters got to Rome and into the Olympic Stadium and had the time of their lives in the process. But hundreds of Reds got there and then slumped in the city or even outside the ground, the worse for drink, ticketless or simply exhausted and confused by the whole process of being abroad and making it to this distant, glorious place. It was a fantastic Liverpool affair.

The Liverpool anthem for this great trek was more lyrical and inventive even than the 1965 Liverpool FA Cup final songs and the chants that had so charmed the British media or indeed any of those that had been popular in the city in earlier periods of the football fever. To the tune of 'Arrivederci Roma', the following rang out from every bus, boat, plane and van that carried Reds southwards across Europe:

> We're on our way to Roma
> On the 25th of May
> All the Kopites will be singing
> Vatican bells they will be ringing
> Liverpool songs we will be singing
> When we win the European Cup

The extraordinary party in Rome after the 1977 final involved Reds supporters and the players together. These groups were still broadly drawn from the same stock, drank (and got drunk) in the same pubs, had pretty much similar lifestyles and diets, and footballers had not yet moved into the sort of wage brackets that later had them sealed off behind tinted-windowed cars the size of small armoured trucks. But this was also the period for the emergence of new terrace rivalries about clothes and attitude in English football support, initially out of the north-west. There had been signs of this at the FA Cup final against United

– young Scousers had effeminate wedge haircuts and wore straight jeans, cords and Adidas trainers rather than the home-made punk or disco styles, or the flares that had gone before.[11] After Rome 1977, a flood of foreign sports gear started piling into Merseyside from similar trips, the more obscure, expensive and exclusive the better. Suddenly, the act of wearing sports clothing and trainers in the city was no longer just about sport. These new outfits were all signs of class distinction: about 'hardness', style, capacious consumption, club loyalty in following the Reds to far-flung locales and bringing parts of the world back to the great seaport of Liverpool in time-honoured fashion. This gear was also useful to flaunt in the face of less-favoured, more domesticated, rival football supporters. Who the fuck are *you*?

Eventually, discussions of the nuances of supporter style would make the pages of music and football fanzines in Liverpool – Pete Hooton's *The End* was positively forensic in sniffing out terrace fakers and Merseyside woollybacks – as well as fashion magazines and colour supplements. Supporters' styles even became the subject of PhD theses. It was the time of the casuals and the well-turned-out mob, and for seven years, at least, this sort of performance culture at football at home and especially abroad was hugely enjoyable, frequently anarchic, and occasionally dangerous and violent fun for those involved – and for others. And then, after Brussels in 1985, when Liverpool played in their fifth, disastrous, European Cup final, the whole business of travel for football abroad became something quite different.

PAISLEY'S LIVERPOOL: TAKE THREE SCOTS

With the club's first European Cup now safe on Bob Paisley's mantelpiece, Kevin Keegan immediately left Liverpool Football Club for Germany. The old football sage from County Durham barely blinked. Bill Shankly had built his first great Reds team around three Scots – Yeats, St John and Stevenson – and his second around three key Englishmen. Now Paisley looked to the north again to construct his new post-Keegan Liverpool. Again, he brought in three brilliant, highly intelligent Scots, a crafty intellectual balance for Paisley's native, intuitive football mind. These were men who would rule the Liverpool dressing-room, run his team on the field when tactical adjustments were needed and also lead from the front if the Reds needed to scrap. It would be the last time the English would drain Scotland for some of the world's best football talent, because the Scottish game would now dry up in the face of cultural change and global competition. It was also the end of a great tradition on Merseyside for recruiting groups of 'Scottish professors', one that had stretched back over a century and had been central in establishing Liverpool as a football club more than 80 years before.

A slightly gawky young Scottish midfielder called Alan Hansen had attended trials at Liverpool as a 15 year old in the summer of 1970. He had been rejected. Hansen's laid-back attitude and lack of pace had not impressed the Liverpool coaches, showing just how capricious the process of finding real football talent can be. The Scot was much brighter than most young players (and probably the club's coaches), and he wasn't even sure that he wanted to be a professional footballer at all. He was well educated, enjoyed golf more and got very nervous before big matches, despite looking outwardly calm. He had other options. Nevertheless, Hansen signed professional forms for Partick Thistle in December 1973, and as he grew taller his manager Bertie Auld insisted he play centre-back, a position Hansen hated. Hansen kept on pushing up from the back into midfield at Partick, and this combination of positional dexterity, defensive assurance and ball-playing invention eventually attracted English interest. Most club scouts thought that the Scot was too weak and took too many liberties to play in England. But Geoff Twentyman, for Liverpool, wanted defenders who could play at home but also in Europe, where opposing forwards needed to be outwitted more than bludgeoned into submission. Not that he was overly impressed with Hansen. 'Gives the impression,' he wrote in his scouting diaries, 'that if faced with quick forwards would struggle.' Nevertheless, in May 1977 Liverpool invested £100,000 in the 21 year old – it was a steal. Hansen filled out physically and became stronger mentally. In his defensive ability, intelligent game-reading and comfort on the ball, Hansen was arguably the best defender the club had recruited in 70 years. Hansen played 618 times for Liverpool, strolling to a first European Cup-winner's medal at Wembley in 1978 and then replacing Emlyn Hughes for good in the Liverpool team in the 1978–79 season. His calm, unflustered defending meant that for the next 13 years, if Hansen was fit, he was in the Liverpool side, no question. He often played when he was not. He was part of the on-pitch Scottish brains trust that effectively ran each section of the successful Liverpool team for Bob Paisley and his coaches until the mid-1980s.

In the midfield department, the Scot who ran things for the new Paisley generation was a haughty natural leader, a football aristocrat and a superb technician. Graeme Souness was signed from Middlesbrough for £352,000 in January 1978. The Edinburgh-born Souness had a very flaky disciplinary record as a youngster – he had trouble controlling his natural aggression and his overwhelming cockiness. But under Paisley and his coaches he managed to rein things in, combining some of Ian St John's irreverent brio and cleverness with the uncompromising toughness of the soon-to-depart Tommy Smith. He forged these potentially toxic qualities into a stocky frame that lacked a bit of pace but wanted little for self-belief and skill, and that had an utterly ruthless will-to-win mentality. Politically, Souness represented the antithesis of Bill Shankly's native socialism – the idealism of the 1960s would soon give way to the brute greed and selfishness of the 1980s in Britain. The Liverpool midfield man had a taste for money, champagne and beautiful women, and he had little time for the collectivism espoused by the west-coast Scots. But on the pitch and at the training ground, the two football men would have made a great partnership.

Souness openly mocked lesser rival players, and he soon assumed Tommy Smith's alpha-male role of 'testing' new Liverpool recruits on the Melwood training ground. His demanding standards could also be cruelly punishing in match situations, especially for his less-talented teammates. For many years, he taunted left-back Alan Kennedy, who had been brought in by Paisley from Newcastle United in August 1978 for a record fee – Souness derided the defender for his lack of style and precision. Souness's leadership, his passing and his imperious game management were his real strengths. But also right up there was his cynical determination to get the job done for his club when others might have wavered. He would do most things to win. In 1984, in a European Cup home semi-final first leg against a dangerous Dinamo Bucharest, a frustrated Souness assaulted the Romanian captain Movila, who suffered a broken jaw as a result. Liverpool struggled home 1–0. The visitors were outraged and promised bloody revenge in the second leg. The local police even seemed to be in on the act, and other Liverpool players were clearly affected by this Eastern European threat. But the unflustered Souness was quite beyond intimidation, and he fearlessly governed the match as boots flew, Liverpool winning 2–1.

This sort of trial by fire was good preparation for the final in Rome in 1984, where the home club AS Roma were eventually beaten on penalties. Fittingly, the Liverpool captain who lifted the trophy was a jauntily moustachioed and beaming Graeme Souness, a man peerlessly leading his club through all-comers once again. Always ambitious and hungry for new experiences – and for big pay days – the Liverpool captain departed to play in Italy soon after, but he would return later to Anfield in much more difficult times.

Up front, the final brilliant Scot of the Paisley era was someone many good judges argue is the club's greatest-ever player. He certainly rivals Alex Raisbeck, Elisha Scott and Billy Liddell, who would all have good claims to the title. The Glasgow-born striker Kenny Dalglish left Celtic for Liverpool as a 26 year old in August 1977 for a record fee between British clubs of £440,000. Dalglish had already won four Scottish league titles and four Scottish Cups, a fact often forgotten amidst the acclaim about the flood of cups and titles and the European honours he amassed while at Liverpool as both a player and a manager. His departure from Scotland and his later successes at Anfield even helped forge powerful links between the Liverpool and Celtic clubs, connections that were movingly visible after the Hillsborough disaster in 1989, when Dalglish was the stricken Liverpool club's manager.

Like Alan Hansen, Dalglish had once been a teenage triallist at Anfield (in August 1966), but his unremarkable physique and lack of speed counted against him for the demanding Liverpool coaches under Bill Shankly. By the time he returned to Anfield 11 years later to fill the number-7 shirt vacated by Kevin Keegan, he had developed into the complete European forward. He was collected and deadly in front of goal yet unmatched in his selfless work around the pitch for his teammates. His ego-free passing and his determination to keep the ball and play the game simply was straight from the Shankly and Paisley textbook, and his will to win was enormous. All this meant that Dalglish had more self-confidence than Hansen, but he lacked some of the taunting bravado and disrespect for opponents of Souness. When Bob Paisley had looked at his most vulnerable as the Liverpool boss – when his touchstone forward Keegan left for Germany – available and ready to sign for Liverpool Football Club was a player right in the Keegan mould but someone who was an even *better* player than Bill Shankly's adopted forward 'son'. Was this good fortune or simply great football management? Whatever the answer, Dalglish improved more modest players simply by bringing them into the game and flooding them with confidence. There was no greater sight for Liverpool supporters than the way this private and shy man's boyish, blond features lit up with unconstrained delight after he had scored or helped fashion a Liverpool goal in his 515 outings for the club. And there would be plenty of occasions to admire that smile.

Dalglish was also a magnificent reader of the game, near-flawless in his capacity to hold the ball up using his fantastic balance, awareness and lower-body power. Wise coaches spotted a real strength: the Scot had a 'big arse', and he used it brilliantly to make both time and space. He could then concentrate on threading through exquisitely weighted and invariably sublimely timed passes to his strike partner, in later years the nerveless and gauche Welshman Ian Rush. There have been few, if any, British players in the history of the game who have been more complete or more courageous. And who in Britain has ever better 'seen' a football pitch – the various angles and outlets it offered – than Kenny Dalglish? He seemed to be two, or even three, passes ahead of most opponents, making up for his half-yard lack of pace.

Moreover, when Liverpool Football Club was at its lowest ebb after the tragedy at the Heysel Stadium in 1985, banned from European club football and with its supporters unfairly reviled around Europe, it was Dalglish who stepped up as player–manager to pilot Liverpool to the club's only league and FA Cup Double, in 1985–86. He also offered incredible dignity and leadership in 1989 when the Hillsborough tragedy struck. Along with a select group of others – John Houlding and John McKenna, Tom Watson, Alex Raisbeck, Elisha Scott, George Kay, Billy Liddell, Bill Shankly, Bob Paisley, T.V. Williams, John Smith and Peter Robinson – Kenny Dalglish has claims to be remembered as one of the greatest servants and architects of the Liverpool club, both off and on the pitch. He is one of the modern proselytisers of the Liverpool tradition and mythology. He is, in short, a truly great Liverpool football man.

Once these key signings were in place, the merciless Liverpool dressing-room banter and vaunted team spirit were orchestrated around these three imperious Scottish lairds. They had willing followers: Liverpool-born Jimmy Case and stick-like defender Phil Thompson were talented and fearless competitors, a crucial ingredient in the subtle chemistry necessary to produce a great side. Bob Paisley and his men retained the European Cup in 1978, defeating old rivals Club Brugge KV at Wembley, with Dalglish scoring a delightful winning goal. At home, only Brian Clough, the Shankly-like young manager at Nottingham Forest, occasionally got the better of Bob and Liverpool.

This new Paisley team then produced arguably the greatest-ever season by a club in 42-game Football League history. In 1978–79, Liverpool won the league title at a canter, conceding only 16 goals and winning 30 matches. Included was a 7–0 virtuoso Anfield thrashing of a Spurs team containing two recent Argentinian World Cup winners. Apart from the Shankly men, Ray Clemence in goal and Steve Heighway occasionally in attack, this was now Bob Paisley's team, one completely revamped in five years from the side he had inherited. Four players – Clemence, Neal, Ray Kennedy and Dalglish – played all forty-two league matches in 1978–79; Souness missed just one.

Liverpool FC, league-title winners, 1978–79

		Clemence		
Neal	Thompson	Hansen	A. Kennedy
Case	McDermott	Souness	R. Kennedy
	Dalglish	Johnson/Heighway	

When the nerdy Welsh teenager Ian Rush arrived to play his part, from Chester in May 1980, it eventually solved the problem of who was the best striking partner for Dalglish. The poorly dressed and fragile Rush initially failed to fit in at Anfield: he struggled to score in the reserves and was the butt of the savage Liverpool dressing-room piss-takes from the Scottish mafia.[12] He looked like a hick from the North Wales sticks, and Rush soon wanted to leave Liverpool Football Club and these bastard big-heads who were running the club's social and drinking cultures and ruining his life. Maybe Paisley was wrong about the Welshman's talent and his mental strength after all? But once Rush got settled and started to shoot back at the Anfield comedians, it positively rained goals for him at Liverpool, with Dalglish as the main provider. Rush had little grace or style on the pitch, either, but this hardly mattered. His pace and clinical finishing were breathtaking, and he was also now a willing member of the Reds' formidable drinking cliques. When Liverpool played in midweek at Middlesbrough in May 1980, another league championship already won, most of the players had been out celebrating in a local pub on the afternoon before the match.

With these two Celts in harness, a recent Anfield striking tradition was continued – Hunt and St John in the 1960s, Keegan and Toshack in the 1970s, Dalglish and Rush in the 1980s – and Liverpool Football Club now seemed likely to be as unstoppable in the 1980s as they had been for most of the 1960s and 1970s. But although success on the field would continue, things off it would not be quite so simple.

JUST FOLLOWING BOB

To prepare for the new decade, there were changes afoot at Anfield. Despite Liverpool's successes under Shankly and then Paisley, the economics of the sport were already changing in a way that made it impossible to fund European and domestic success largely on the basis of income from normal football activities. In 1980, the Main Stand paddock at Anfield was seated, and in 1982 seats were placed in the home area of the Anfield Road end. These improvements resulted in a new ground capacity of 45,600 and scope to raise more admissions cash but with little provision at all for corporate customers – now standard at the larger European clubs. As stadium guru Simon Inglis pointed out, 'Anfield was still lagging behind other leading clubs in terms of executive boxes and was still often too small to cope with demand.'[13] A more visionary, a more expansive, club board might have remedied this situation during the good times, but Liverpool was caught in a positive cycle of playing success, and the board understandably wanted to invest its resources on the pitch. Britain's top players wanted to come to the club, and Liverpool's supporters would probably have opposed spending on facilities for a business class as an affront to the club's established traditions and its relationship with its core customers. Why change direction when things were going so well? In the long term, of course, this relative lack of investment in the commercial infrastructure of the club was probably a mistake.

Not that Anfield stood still on the commercial side. In July 1979, Liverpool became the first major British football club to attract shirt sponsorship, a £100,000 deal with the Japanese electronics firm Hitachi, the sixth-largest manufacturing company in the world. While still a player, Bob Paisley had predicted that footballers would become human advertising hoardings and earn huge salaries – it looked like this was coming. Liverpool certainly needed the cash. The club's turnover in 1978–79 was £2.4 million, but profits were a miserly £71,000, an accounting situation that Reds chairman John Smith described as 'absurd'. A local journalist reported around this time that Liverpool FC was 'virtually bankrupt'. The first-team squad was dragged abroad to play money-raising friendly matches whenever an opportunity presented itself, even in the middle of a taxing set of league fixtures.

Smith had some tough messages to get across about the finances of the club and the game at large. 'While we are very successful in football terms,' he told the *Liverpool Echo*, 'in economic terms we are broke. Clubs like Liverpool cannot exist on the money coming through the turnstiles alone. Costs are going up all the time. Wages are high – and rightly so – and we have to use every avenue to increase our income.' Football League secretary Alan Hardaker warned that English football at the turn of a new decade was in danger of 'bleeding to death'. Sport would have to change to survive was the message here, while Liverpool FC's main concern – and certainly that of its supporters – was that everything should remain the same.

Another European Cup followed for Paisley and his team in 1981, in a rather forgettable final against a tepid Real Madrid in Paris settled by a single goal from Alan Kennedy. In typical style, the players left the official celebrations and took the trophy around the Paris nightspots for more drink-fuelled fun. The club's supporters were also on a mission. They were greeted by water cannons and riot police, and some of them did not exactly cover themselves in glory, ignoring bar bills, raiding local stores and stealing tickets from alarmed Spaniards as well as from local touts. Plenty of Liverpudlians got in without tickets, an early and serious warning to UEFA that was ignored because no terrible disaster ensued. Things were going seriously wrong on the Continent concerning visits from English fans, but because there was no mass brawling

– at least not involving Liverpool supporters – no one in the VIP zones was picking up the messages about growing danger at these showpiece finals.

Soon after this latest triumph, the South African-born eccentric Zimbabwe goalkeeper Bruce Grobbelaar replaced the departing Ray Clemence in Liverpool's goal, thus reviving memories of Liverpool's South African recruitment policies of the 1920s and 1930s, but also pointing ahead to the future globalisation of the sport in England. He would play 628 games for the club and was also the focus, later, of a major match-fixing accusation. Craig Johnston, a perky if rather disorganised South African-born winger raised in Australia, also arrived in 1981 from Middlesbrough. Johnston was a prodigious worker, if a poor crosser, but he helped the club lift five First Division titles in the 1980s, and he played admirably in the Liverpool European Cup-winning team of 1984. He retired at 27 years of age to turn his cluttered mind to matters other than football. Both of these international players arrived with Liverpool FC at the very height of its post-war powers, clawing in league and European titles, and even dominating the domestic League Cup competition.

Reduced to mere statistics, Bob Paisley's record in major competitions over his nine years as Liverpool manager still looks outrageous. It comprises three European Cups, six league titles, one UEFA Cup and three League Cups. Only the FA Cup escaped him. He had that one losing final, in 1977 against Manchester United, when Liverpool might have been excused for being consumed by their forthcoming first European Cup final. It was the only one of eleven visits to Wembley as a manager or assistant with Liverpool that saw Paisley end up on the losing side. Liverpool under Paisley also established a then record sequence of 85 home matches without defeat in all competitions between January 1978 and January 1981. As a manager, he had matched – many would argue, surpassed – the achievements of Bill Shankly, though there would be no knighthood for Shankly or for Bob Paisley as there would be later for others when football became gentrified and politically more significant. When he finally left the club that he had served so loyally since before the war, Paisley simply returned to his carpet slippers and TV horse racing in his modest Liverpool home. He had no airs or graces and no ambitions beyond serving the club and its followers. When he finally handed over the managerial reins to his assistant Joe Fagan in the summer of 1983, Liverpool Football Club were league-title holders and League Cup winners, after having beaten Manchester United 2–1 in the Wembley final. As Bill Shankly had done nine years earlier, Bob Paisley had not only produced an astonishingly successful Liverpool team, he had handed something impressive and stable on to his immediate successor.

Two versatile defenders, the silky smooth Mark Lawrenson, signed from Brighton for £900,000 in August 1981, and Steve Nicol, a supremely consistent purchase from Ayr United in the same year, had been recruited by Paisley to add to Liverpool's all-round defensive strength. The attacking and alarmingly tough Irishman Ronnie Whelan had also stepped up from the Reds reserves, alongside a bustling and bossy little Liverpool-born midfielder, Sammy Lee. All of these men became long-serving international-quality recruits to the Liverpool cause.

As it had often seemed for Paisley – deceptively so – it sometimes appeared as if the new manager Joe Fagan simply had to pick the 11 men for the Liverpool team in the 1983–84 season and then let them play. Fagan certainly seemed relaxed and at ease in his new role. Sometimes the players seemed to be organising things for themselves, with the staff rubber-stamping their regal progress. This transforming Liverpool side was both experienced and hungry for more success. And what a first season it was for Fagan – a European Cup win in Rome, the first Merseyside Wembley final in the 1984 League Cup – though it would take a Maine Road replay and a Graeme Souness goal for Liverpool to see off Everton – and another Liverpool league title: *three* unprecedented trophies in one season. Could it possibly get any better at Anfield? As it turned out, the answer was emphatically no – not for the city of Liverpool, not for Liverpool Football Club, not for English football.

INTO THE DARKNESS

With a neo-liberal Conservative government now in power in Britain from 1979, stressing the bleak doctrine of market forces, and with the port of Liverpool haemorrhaging global influence and jobs with few signs of local regeneration, the city and its people struggled for a foothold in the new world order. But having experienced the good times in the 1960s, the new generation of resourceful and expectant young people in the city were in no mood now to accept the 'no future' mantra played back to them from London in the 1970s and 1980s. Some rebelled, during the violent 1981 street disturbances in Toxteth or via the work of Militant politics, which took hold in the Liverpool City Council; others took the music option by forming pop and rock bands and living on the dole or sampling the good life; still others decided to have their own adventures by setting off to see the world by following Liverpool Football Club across Europe and living off the land to fund their trips.

In this dark economic period for the city, the anti-Thatcher Alan Bleasdale TV drama *Boys from the Blackstuff*, shown in 1982 but which the writer began in 1978 during the Callaghan Labour administration, featured Liverpool footballers, including Sammy Lee and, ironically, the right-leaning Graeme Souness. In some ways, it was possibly the club's most 'political' statement since the gentle nod to the 1930s' unemployed and the 1960s' 'socialism' years of Bill Shankly. Bleasdale's darkly humorous TV series *Scully* in 1984 also showcased members of the Liverpool squad, especially Kenny Dalglish, and it had as its central theme the view that only football could offer an escape for young men in the city. Liverpool could boast a glorious past but for many it now faced a depressingly empty future.

There were some obvious rewards and real potential costs involved in taking the European football adventures route out of this local inertia. These included the petty (and some more serious) thieving and 'free' train travel often involved in these outings; the occasional disorder and fighting that took place – though fans of some other English clubs at this time were much more disorderly than Liverpool fans – and the counterfeiting and the mass 'bunking in' that sometimes threatened fan safety inside grounds on European trips.[14] It also seemed more than mere coincidence that while the Liverpool trip to the 1981 European Cup final had been a pretty chaotic and disorderly affair, young inner-city black Liverpudlians, echoing events in the city in 1919 and 1948, were involved in their own street uprisings later that summer. In fact, young working-class men from all ethnic backgrounds in Liverpool wanted rather more from their lives than what was currently on offer from the powers that be.

Local-born forward Howard Gayle had actually become the first black man to play for the club in the same year, 1981 – he had performed heroically for a depleted Liverpool in the European Cup semi-final against Bayern Munich. Was this the long-awaited breakthrough, the vital new connection between football and the city's estranged black communities that would break down some of the old divisions? In fact, Gayle would make only five first-team appearances in the seven years he was registered with Liverpool, being frequently frustrated by the culture of the club and by Paisley and the Liverpool staff's lack of comprehension about the importance of this courageous black Scouser's background. Liverpool Football Club seemed, in Gayle's eyes, determined to make invisible his proud racial heritage.[15] The Reds coaches just wanted to talk football. It was, arguably, an old Liverpool story of exclusion and division, albeit in new sporting clothes.

Howard Gayle was no longer in the Liverpool first-team picture (or anywhere near it) as Joe Fagan prepared for his first European Cup final as Liverpool manager in 1984. His team was assured and confident, even though the opposition were local favourites AS Roma.

Liverpool FC, European Cup-winning team, v. AS Roma, 1984

Grobbelaar

Neal	Lawrenson	Hansen	A. Kennedy
	Johnston	Lee	Souness	Whelan
		Rush	Dalglish	

This was a tense, tactical affair, the Italians seemingly nervous in front of their own supporters on such a major European football occasion. A 1–1 draw resulted, Liverpool taking the lead through Phil Neal before holding on for a penalty shoot-out after an equaliser from Pruzzo. Fagan had done little preparation for this outcome – though it must have looked like a distinct possibility. He probably thought – as many coaches in England still do – that penalty shoot-outs were a lottery and barely worth practising for. In the brief session he had organised in training for penalties, few players took it seriously and most had missed the target. Now everything rested on the penalty spot. Fagan selected his five penalty-takers on the pitch from those who showed willingness or were too slow to scurry away, and then decided the order. But young substitute Steve Nicol grabbed the ball and, ignoring his manager's and teammates' pleas, strode off to take Liverpool's first penalty. He missed, spectacularly. No problem: Neal, Souness and Rush all scored for Liverpool, while Grobbelaar's strange wobbly-legged antics induced two nervy Italian misses. Alan Kennedy had scored in open play in Paris to win the 1981 trophy for his club, but the left-back could barely have expected a repeat show. However, he had been chosen for the final Liverpool penalty. He closed his eyes, shot low and goalkeeper Tancredi dived the opposite way.

The players' night's work was over, but for the Liverpool supporters in Rome things would now take an alarming and dangerous turn. Italian knife gangs lay in wait in the dark grounds outside the Olympic Stadium, with the Rome police typically inert and inept. The Italian way in these matters is to attack the legs and buttocks with blades and to throw bottles and bricks indiscriminately. It was a dangerous chicken run, a horrible gauntlet that ensnared the inexperienced, as well as the streetwise and those willing and able to fight back. The hospital cases that resulted – it was remarkable no visiting fan was killed – meant that there would be a bounty to be paid next time Liverpool Football Club met Italians in Europe. So when the Reds reached the European Cup final again, in 1985 in Brussels, this time against the northern Italians from Juventus, it was clear that for this event to go off smoothly and safely it would require a well-appointed stadium, good and efficient policing, and a sensible approach from all of the club's supporters. Sadly – and fatally – it turned out that something was badly lacking in all three of these departments. Liverpool's great 20-year run in Europe, stretching back to 1965, was about to come to an abrupt and unimaginable end.

CHAPTER 16 REFERENCES

1. Hopcraft, *The Football Man*, p. 189
2. Hughes, *Secret Diary of a Liverpool Scout*, p. 6
3. St John, *The Saint*, p. 204
4. Lloyd, *Larry Lloyd: Hard Man, Hard Game*, p. 62
5. Gill, *The Real Bill Shankly*, pp. 124–5
6. Smith, *Anfield Iron*, pp. 278–9
7. Corbett, 'Shankly: Forgotten Man'
8. Kennedy and Williams, *Kennedy's Way*, p. 102
9. Hughes, *Secret Diary of a Liverpool Scout*, p. 179
10. Kirby, 'Rome, 1977', p. 27
11. Hewison, *The Liverpool Boys Are in Town*, p. 13
12. Williams, 'Ian Rush', pp. 173–4
13. Inglis, *Football Grounds of Britain*, p. 220
14. Allt, *The Boys from the Mersey*
15. Hill, *Out of His Skin*

17

AT THE DARK END OF THE STREET
Heysel and Hillsborough

SLIDING INTO CHAOS: THE HEYSEL DISASTER

In the depths of a national economic depression that was affecting Merseyside especially harshly, the Liverpool Football Club playing project was also perceptively starting to slide in 1985. The great enforcer Souness had gone and Kenny Dalglish was coming towards the end of his brilliant service for the club as a player. Ian Rush would soon leave for an unfulfilling stay in Italy. Their replacements were simply not of this stature – who could be? Paul Walsh, unusually for Liverpool a southerner, was an average forward only, signed from Luton Town, a man who flitted in and out of games but had little of Dalglish's assurance, guile and intelligence. John Wark, a loping goalscoring Scottish midfielder from Ipswich Town, had something of the Ray Kennedy about him without ever reaching those classy heights, and Kevin McDonald, another Scot and a left-sided ball-carrier bought from Leicester City, was a one-paced workhorse who occasionally showed flashes of something close to exceptional.

The only really exciting capture at this time was a Dane, Jan Mølby, an Ajax graduate who joined in 1984 and who stayed for 12 years and 260 appearances. Foreign players were still something of a novelty in the English game, and big Jan was something else again. Mølby, a central midfielder, had mobility problems from the outset – he would fit perfectly into the Liverpool dressing-room drinking club – but no one could doubt his exquisite touch, technique and luscious passing ability. His weight of pass was near-faultless, but his weight was a real problem. Mølby was astounded at how little Liverpool worked on tactics. He asked the coaches at Melwood how he should play and fit into the Liverpool system. They looked at him blankly and shrugged, saying just do what you did at Ajax. Mølby had much of what Graeme Souness had, except, crucially, athleticism and that unquenchable Scottish desire and willingness to turn to strategic violence when it was needed in Liverpool's cause. The Dane had real quality, but Mølby could not manage a potentially anarchic English football match as Souness once could.

Liverpool were eclipsed by a rising Everton in the league in 1984–85 and lost in a replay to Manchester United after an utterly poisonous atmosphere in an FA Cup semi-final in April. The English game was run through with nasty hooliganism, but a real spectator darkness revealed itself here as rival supporters exchanged obscenities and missiles and fought running battles outside Goodison Park. Few Reds supporters present could remember quite this level of bile and disorder, even at this combustible contest. Thankfully, the rounds of the European Cup in 1984–85 produced little of this sort of frenzied hatred (or competition) as Liverpool sauntered through to another final, dispensing with opponents from Poland, Portugal, Austria and Greece on the way. This was not Europe's elite: the Greeks from Panathinaikos were casually dismissed by a 5–0 aggregate in the semi-finals. But the formidable Italian champions Juventus now lay waiting in the final, in the Heysel Stadium in Brussels.

There were probably three reasons to be surprised (as well as appalled) at the terrible events that occurred in Brussels on the evening of 29 May 1985. First, that it had taken so long for what was happening in and around English football supporters abroad in the 1980s to produce a tragedy, and possibly fatalities, on this scale. There was a toxic combination already in play here: just too much drink; English and local mobs in xenophobic disharmony; idiotic and sometimes cowardly Continental policing; ticketless supporters determined to see it through; inept UEFA decisions and responses; and poor stadium security. These had all threatened on many occasions to produce a stadium disaster like this one. And now it had finally and tragically been delivered, live on international television.

The second surprise was that it was *Liverpool* supporters who were the key figures involved. After all, Reds fans had travelled extensively on the Continent for 20 years, and there had been plenty of minor dust-ups since with local lads, shopkeepers and bar owners around Europe. As people's lives in the city were getting harder, with joblessness booming, things had also been getting noticeably wilder, more desperate, at finals and major football matches, a fact evidenced in different ways by events in Paris in 1981, Rome in 1984 and Goodison Park against United in 1985. Something bad was probably on its way, and there was the usual routine disorder and thieving going on in Brussels on the afternoon of the match. But – and it is a small defence only – Liverpool supporters had expressly not been involved as instigators in any of the kind of major hooligan incidents on the Continent that had been provoked by other English supporters elsewhere.

Indeed, the hooligan credo for Liverpool abroad had its own highly distinctive features. It was based largely around street style, robbing, ticketless travel and ground access, and, yes, fighting, but usually when it was unavoidable and almost always small scale and away from the ground. There was no Liverpool record abroad for provoking major disturbances, mass combat with the local police or stadium wrecking. The Liverpool hooligan tradition – and one certainly existed – was largely instrumental rather than expressive. Exceptions might be made for clashes with Manchester United but few others. No one, not even among the club's most aggressive followers, was remotely interested in establishing Liverpool Football Club's international hooligan credentials through this or any other kind of major 'incident' abroad. This was one reason why local people in the city reacted so vehemently later to media suggestions that Liverpool and its people were somehow brand leaders in this sort of sporting barbarity. Nothing, in fact, could have been further from the truth.

The third reason to be surprised was that UEFA had seemingly learned so very little in almost 20 years about football supporters from Liverpool, because ticket security and the condition of the Heysel Stadium were shambolic. What were the organisers expecting for this contest: a crowd of sober, unexcited and uncommitted athletics fans? There were no recognisable turnstiles in some places, and parts of the stadium outer barriers were easily dismantled. Well before the disaster happened, the hapless Belgian police had already lost control. Like it or not, to a bevvied-up ticketless Scouser's eyes these ridiculous arrangements were actually an insult – as well as an open invitation. They were just asking to be abused, and abused they roundly were. Reds supporters poured in over turnstiles as ticket checks began to disappear. Who was really to blame here: those desperate, passionate and ticketless Reds supporters for possibly endangering their own lives and those of everyone else present? Certainly. But if you know that stadium security might be a problem, you do not produce the exact opposite of an effective strategy. You do not choose a truly terrible venue and the worst possible administrators of it for Europe's most important club fixture and simply hope that everything turns out all right. UEFA were supremely culpable for what happened next, along with the Liverpool fans involved and the inept Belgian authorities. UEFA would also be culpable again 22 years later in 2007 in Athens, though Liverpool supporters, more than any other, should surely also have learned their own lessons by then about the sanctity of stadium safety.

The details of what happened are these: Italian supporters, mainly from Belgium, had bought tickets to a supposed 'neutral' terrace, sector Z, next to an area housing Liverpool fans and separated from them only by what looked like chicken wire and a handful of police. The Liverpool sections, boosted by the ticketless, were fuller than this area, which seemed to Reds fans to be far from neutral: it housed Italians, seemingly in the Liverpool end. Some anger about the treatment of Reds in Roma the previous year might have fed resentment on this score. Before the match, missiles were exchanged and then Liverpool fans began dismantling the fence that divided these sections. This was followed, from around 7.20 p.m., by a 'charge' towards the Italians through the by-now ragged fences as Reds fans started pouring through.

The Italian supporters in sector Z – many of them 'family' fans – now panicked and rushed to their right, towards an exit away from the red invasion and trouble, as Liverpool supporters hugged in triumph at claiming this Italian territory for their own.[1] And in banal terms, the whole thing had been an enactment of typical English territorial rites at a football ground, the kind of incident that is usually sorted by the British police before ever reaching this stage. But here the mass movement in a confined space of terrified Italians caused a wall at the side of the terrace to collapse under the weight of their alarm. Thirty-nine supporters were crushed or suffocated to death, thirty-two of them Italian, but only two from the city of Turin itself.

The Liverpool players were sheltered in their dressing-room only yards away from this unfolding horror. They had heard the terrible rumble of the collapsing wall and the screams of panic outside. Alan Kennedy, who was in Brussels but not in the Liverpool playing squad, was now charged with going out to see what had happened and with relaying the awful news back to the dressing-room. He saw lifeless bodies and very angry and distressed Italians. He feared for his own safety. Back with the Liverpool players, he talked vaguely about 'crowd trouble'. Some players wanted to know what had happened, others wanted to stay completely focused on one of the biggest football occasions of their lives.[2] They all knew something very serious had occurred but, frankly, hooliganism was part of the cultural fabric of the English game. A few players – Bruce Grobbelaar among them – claimed to have realised the enormity of what had happened and expressly did not want to play. In the end, they all had to do their job.

The Liverpool supporters in the crowd had seen the disturbances and the ensuing panic, and the kick-off delay told them something pretty extreme had happened. But many had no idea that people had been killed in the disturbances.[3] Amazingly, the match eventually took place, 'for safety reasons', kicking off at 9.40 p.m. The Belgian police feared anger and frustration would turn to more violence between the rival fans if the match was abandoned. Perhaps more amazingly still, although television executives knew about the fatalities, the TV coverage continued in a near-funereal atmosphere. When Juventus eventually scored the winning goal from a penalty that was erroneously – or generously – given, the scorer, the current UEFA president Michel Platini, was widely criticised in Italy for the 'bad taste' of his wild celebrations.[4] He claimed not to have known people had been killed. Later, the Italian internationals Paolo Rossi and Marco Tardelli blamed the 'confusion and chaos' of the evening for the Italians' misjudged joyous response. It was Juve's first European Cup win in the worst possible circumstances.[5] But in truth all the Italian team and their officials celebrated in the same way. After the trophy was presented in the privacy of the Juventus changing-room, the players even came out to do a lap of honour, and some 50,000 Juve followers in Turin celebrated the win until the early hours of the morning.

Back in Liverpool, some returning Reds supporters crassly blamed the police and the Belgian authorities for the deaths, and any shame that was felt very soon gave way to anger and counter-accusations from club chairman John Smith and others about who was really involved in the trouble. But no convincing evidence was ever presented that there was some kind of right-wing infiltration of the Liverpool contingent, and no case was made along these lines by the official inquiry that followed. It seemed instead that a relatively minor case of drunken hooliganism (by English standards at least) had been allowed to escalate out of control in a stadium and with a police force that were simply not fit for purpose. But at home, the British press turned on the city and on the English game with a barely concealed mixture of venom and glee. Merseysiders were uniformly vilified. Later ingenuous accusations from Evertonians about Liverpool hooliganism abroad were especially distasteful.[6] In fact, later publications by Everton's so-called 'top lads' revealed – to no great surprise – that the Blues had pretty much exactly the same sort of rabble-rousers and hard-cases adventuring abroad as those who practised it from across Stanley Park.[7] Hooliganism in the 1980s was not a Liverpool Football Club problem, it was an *English* problem.

Twenty-seven supporter arrests (60 per cent from Liverpool) were eventually made on manslaughter charges, and after a trial in Belgium in 1989 fourteen Liverpool followers were given three-year convictions for involuntary manslaughter. Most of them were from the city. The UEFA secretary-general Hans Bangerter was rightly found guilty of negligence, and gendarme captain Johan Mahieu and the secretary of the Belgian FA Albert Roosens were charged with manslaughter and 'massacre' – each were given six-month suspended sentences. The Belgian government collapsed in July 1985 when the interior minister refused to resign over the affair. Recognising that serious spectator disorder was a general problem involving English supporters abroad, all English clubs were now banned from

European competition for an indeterminate period – including the 1985 league champions Everton. The English game was in shame.

But perhaps what was really shameful here was the treatment of the Heysel dead and their families. Neither Juventus nor Liverpool seemed to want to focus on their needs or their memory. Most of the dead were not from Turin, so mourning and solidarity there was distressingly limited. Juventus immediately displayed the European Cup, despite relatives of the dead saying that the trophy was stained with blood. Liverpool Football Club seemed unable or unwilling to take at least some responsibility for the disaster, and there were no proper memorials set up at either club's stadium. Nor was there serious discussion about compensation or even public regret for what had happened. Only when Liverpool finally played Juventus again in the European Cup in 2005 was culpability finally publicly accepted on Merseyside. Juve ultras at the match at Anfield unsurprisingly turned their backs on the Kop's belated apologetic mosaic. Here was some closure of sorts at least on a highly damaging and disreputable episode in the club's wonderful history.

KING KENNY TO THE RESCUE

Liverpool FC and its followers were now the official pariahs of European football. But not only was the city reviled internationally for its supposed depravity and poor spectator behaviour, the local job market was plummeting and Merseyside was rapidly de-populating, too: between 1971 and 1985 employment in the city fell by some 33 per cent. As one local commentator put it at the time, 'Liverpool looks to be the Jarrow of the 1980s.'[8]

As the recession kicked in hard and hooliganism thrived in England, so football crowds in the city and elsewhere fell. Once-mighty Everton averaged below 20,000 in 1983–84, and even Treble-winning Liverpool could only manage an average of just under 32,000 in the same season, including a league gate of just 20,746 against Watford on 1 February 1984. In Liverpool's case at least, this fall in crowd numbers was partly down to ennui; the club's supporters were becoming blasé about winning titles. Who was to challenge Liverpool's domestic dominance? In fact, in the aftermath of Heysel the club's crowds actually improved in 1985–86, even as they fell elsewhere in England. Some Reds supporters certainly stopped attending because of their revulsion at what had happened in Brussels, but it was also as if many local people had found another struggle. They were determined to get behind the embattled club again and reaffirm its traditionally positive bonds with the communities of Merseyside. A group of local Reds fans also started a new national supporter body, the

Football Supporters Association, to give supporters a stronger collective voice in the sport and to raise the public profile of non-hooligan fans. It was the start of the fightback on the terraces and in the stands against the press and the European and English football establishment.

As Liverpool FC tried to rebuild on the pitch in these very difficult circumstances, bravely and with great dignity Kenny Dalglish took over as player–manager, leaning on Bob Paisley for advice and the much mythologised Liverpool boot room for his philosophy: give the opposition very little and get as much out of them as you can. Dalglish turned to the Joe Fagan signing Jan Mølby as the player he might shape his new team around. The rotund Mølby was hardly built for the typical high-tempo exchanges of the English game, but what he lacked in mobility he more than made up for in technique. His penalty-taking was also near-faultless. Dalglish brought in Scouser Steve McMahon, a hard-tackling midfielder, from Aston Villa to offer balance and support for Mølby, Kevin McDonald and Ronnie Whelan in Liverpool's midfield. Jim Beglin, a one-paced but reliable Irishman, had also replaced Alan Kennedy at left-back by this time, and the gangly Gary Gillespie was brought in as centre-back cover from Coventry City. Alan Hansen, for one, was sceptical about the new squad; he had been part of great Liverpool teams in the recent past, and he thought this group was miles off a championship outfit. It lacked depth and some quality, but the combination worked as Liverpool set off on a run that would produce 34 points from the last 36 on offer. Fittingly, it was Dalglish himself who scored the goal at Stamford Bridge that won the 1986 league title for Liverpool, over runners-up Everton. And in a memorable first all-Merseyside FA Cup final in 1986, after falling a goal behind a Jan Mølby-inspired Liverpool stormed back to win 3–1. Everton's bogeyman Ian Rush scored twice to seal his club's first league and FA Cup Double. It was a fantastic response on the pitch to desperate adversity and ill-judged policy off it.

Liverpool FC, FA Cup-winning team, 1986

Grobbelaar

Nicol   Hansen   Lawrenson   Beglin

Johnston   Mølby   Whelan   McDonald

Dalglish   Rush

Gillespie, the ex-Oxford United midfielder Ray Houghton and Scouse striker John Aldridge would now all figure strongly in the 'new' Liverpool being reconstructed by Dalglish. Aldridge, especially, was delighted by his new dressing-room drinking partners, but he was also a first-class finisher, a man who had fought his way up the football food chain. But the two key new Dalglish recruits here were the England international forwards John Barnes and Peter Beardsley. The arrival of the middle-class, Jamaican-born Barnes from Watford for £900,000 in June 1987, the first regular black first-teamer at the club, stirred predictable emotions – and some racist hostility – in the city. But his wing-play was sublime. He had the strength, touch and pace to defeat almost all defences, allied to a thunderous shot and wonderful crossing ability. Barnes was the most direct and effective goalscoring winger at Liverpool since Billy Liddell, and he became almost as popular with the new generation of the club's support as the Scot had been in the 1950s. His popularity only increased on Merseyside when he was criticised for his disappointing shows for England. His general acceptance and celebration at Anfield signalled some progress at least on the historic racial exclusivity at the club.

Peter Beardsley's qualities were rather more prosaic but no less effective. Beardsley lacked the reliable technique and strength of Barnes, but he was boyishly enthusiastic, inventive and hard-working, almost in equal measure. Together, he and the ex-Watford man, allied with the unerring finishing of Aldridge, energised a new attacking Liverpool: eighty-seven goals resulted in the league in 1987–88, including five in a rout of close rivals Nottingham Forest on 13 April 1988. Some judges argue this to be the best league football performance by the club at home since the war. Praise indeed. Liverpool cantered to the league title in 1988 with ninety points and only two defeats. Lacking the additional pressure from Europe only seemed to make the Reds even more dominant at home. But another domestic league and cup Double was prevented in the FA Cup final when a brutal Wimbledon team (and bad luck) intimidated Liverpool to a shock 0–1 defeat. The old master of planned violence Graeme Souness was probably growling displeasure and contempt somewhere at this sorry Wembley capitulation by the club he had once ruled.

HILLSBOROUGH, 15 APRIL 1989

In the following season, Arsenal would dramatically wrench the league title from Liverpool on goal difference in the final minute of the final league match between the two clubs at Anfield on 26 May 1989. The Liverpool team (and its supporters) was emotionally and physically drained: this was the club's eighth match in twenty-three days, including a charged 3–2 extra time Reds FA Cup final victory over Everton. It was, by any measure, a ridiculous and punitive programme, but placed in its context it was even crueller than this. This was the latest finish by date to a Football League season since Liverpool under George Kay had snatched the title ahead of Stoke City back in June 1947. But the weather in 1989 had been fine. The reason for the delay was much more tragic than mere snow and ice, as it had been just after the war. It was due to another terrible disaster involving the Liverpool Football Club, this time at the Hillsborough Stadium in Sheffield. There, neglect and mismanagement by South Yorkshire Police caused the deaths of 96 Liverpool supporters as a result of events on 15 April 1989 near the start of an FA Cup semi-final meeting with Nottingham Forest. The club and the city were thrown into a vortex of mourning and the defending of its own victim supporters as a result.

As all football supporters should now know – though shamefully many still seem to have different views – the police in Sheffield failed to monitor the Liverpool crowds effectively both inside and outside the ground. Liverpool supporters had been delayed arriving because of roadworks on the M62 motorway, and the Leppings Lane end of the ground had too few turnstiles to properly process these delayed fans in time. The police responded to overcrowding outside by opening an exit Gate C to allow supporters entry, but they then failed to direct arriving Liverpool fans to less crowded pens in the Hillsborough Stadium. As a result, supporters walked into already overcrowded and fatally penned terraced areas of the stadium, where the deadly crushing took place. The police now failed again. The match was halted by referee Ray Lewis at 3.06 p.m., but the police did not respond appropriately or quickly enough to obvious signs of distress among Liverpool supporters who were trapped beneath the police control box in overcrowded pens that had perimeter gates that would not open under crowd pressure. Desperately escaping Reds supporters were even returned to the killing pens because the police initially interpreted crowd panic and suffering as a pitch invasion or the result of hooliganism. In the confusion, only one of the forty-four ambulances that responded to the disaster call was allowed by the police into the stadium. Its crew was overwhelmed by the number of Liverpool supporters requiring treatment on the pitch. The police then compounded all these gross errors by their later disgusting treatment of bereaved families and their attempts to smear Liverpool supporters in a repellent attempt at a cover-up in the national press, viciously led by *The Sun* newspaper.

Historically, as we have seen, English football had long displayed too little care in its treatment of football fans. In the 1950s, grounds were dangerous places that were poorly regulated, and it was only good fortune and the care that supporters showed for each other that had avoided similar disasters since the 1946 tragedy at Burnden Park, Bolton.[9] The 1980s in Britain was a harsher social and economic climate altogether, and football crowds were more volatile, less consensual and rather less caring. Some commentators argued that Hillsborough was symbolic of a general attack by the British state on working-class people in Liverpool and elsewhere.[10] More convincing were those accounts that suggested that the disaster was attributable to a planned general deterioration of public facilities in Britain, a development that had also brought a range of recent disasters on public transport, as Tory policies had prioritised the private sector and devastated areas such as Merseyside.[11] It was difficult to avoid the conclusion that the deaths were also connected to deep-seated problems in terrace cultures and poor relations between some football fans and the police. After all, the Sheffield ground was argued to be one of England's best-appointed stadiums, but this seemed mainly because of the way it was designed to deal with potential hooliganism. The English game had gone down a fatal route and was routinely treating *all* its customers as potential threats.

As the city of Liverpool mourned its huge loss and responded angrily to suggestions that its people, rather than the public authorities, were once again at fault, the Anfield stadium soon became a vast shrine containing flowers and mementos in memory of the dead. The Liverpool players and officials, and the manager Kenny Dalglish and his family, undertook the draining responsibility of attending funerals of dead supporters. Sometimes they attended a number on the same day. The FA discussed abandoning the FA Cup for that season, and the Football League also considered its options for Liverpool FC. Halting the season might have been a sensible response to the scale of the disaster. But after a relatively short period of time, followers of the clubs involved and even some bereaved families seemed to want the league and the FA Cup competitions to continue. Accordingly, after almost three weeks of playing inaction taken up mainly with grieving and showing appropriate respect for the dead, and amidst febrile public debate about where responsibility for the disaster really lay, the Liverpool team played out an emotional friendly match at Glasgow Celtic and then a 0–0 league draw at Everton on 3 May to restart their league campaign. Local followers of the two clubs – some of whom had become rather distanced after the impact of Heysel – were now brought together once again in a communal celebration of their common bond as Merseysiders.

Liverpool then completed their league fixtures, winning the next four to set up yet another league-title bid. They also defeated Forest 3–1 in the replayed FA Cup semi-final at Old Trafford and then Everton 3–2 at Wembley in the final. In the frenzy of the occasion, ticketless supporters tried every means of gaining illegal entry, and fans of both teams invaded the fence-free Wembley pitch, but there was no violence. Removing pitchside fences and converting terraces at major stadiums to seating areas were the key structural outcomes of the official inquiry into the Hillsborough disaster. But at least as important were the new ways that were established of managing football supporters inside grounds. Under a new, more rigorous stadium-licensing system, the police would no longer be responsible for the general organisation of football grounds or for the spectators in them. Instead, football clubs would now be in charge of arrangements for supporters inside grounds, and the police would deal specifically only with matters of hooliganism. A new rhetoric, not centred around issues of control, now began to emerge around football stadiums in England: the job of the new generation of stadium managers, stewards and senior police officers was to ensure, above all else, the safety of their customers. It was a step in a new direction for the national game at last.

The various Hillsborough family supporter groups in the city have since been frustrated by their attempts to make accountable those who were at fault in Sheffield. The inquest into the deaths of supporters insisted that only events up until 3.15 p.m. on 15 April should be considered, even though there was evidence that many of those who died were still alive beyond that point. A private prosecution brought later against senior police officers involved was abandoned when it was decided that the chief superintendent in charge on the day, David Duckenfield, was unfit to face charges. He eventually retired on medical grounds on a full pension. In 1996, the Liverpool supporter and scriptwriter Jimmy McGovern wrote a 90-minute drama-documentary about the disaster and its aftermath, *Hillsborough*, which was screened across the ITV network. It drew huge acclaim for clarifying what had happened, but it also seemed to some critics to present a highly sanitised version of existing football culture in 1989.

Partly as a response to the frustration and sense of injustice felt locally over Hillsborough, over the past 20 years Liverpool supporters have ingested the disaster, the public response to it and the campaigns that have followed as part of the identity of the club itself. For some Reds, this new set of cultural meanings around 'the 96' and the club are even comparable to Celtic FC's historic social heritage and FC Barcelona's socio-political Catalan agenda that proudly proclaims Barça to be 'more than a football club'. No match at Anfield today is complete without the distribution of 'Justice' and 'Don't Buy The Sun' stickers, and on 6 January 2007 for the first six minutes of the televised FA Cup tie against Arsenal the Liverpool Kop displayed a mosaic demanding 'The Truth' about the disaster and Reds supporters repeatedly chanted 'Justice for the 96'. On the 20th anniversary of the disaster in 2009, an extraordinary and unprecedented 28,000 people turned up to hear the Anfield service and to heckle government minister Andy Burnham (an Everton supporter). The British government finally agreed in July of that year that thousands of secret files pertaining to the events in April

1989 be released for public scrutiny under the auspices of a new Hillsborough Independent Panel. Despite this latest development, 20 years on 'the truth' about Hillsborough seemed, for those involved, as distant a goal as it had ever been.

THE LAST GAME?

Back on the football field, on the evening of 26 May 1989 Liverpool Football Club now faced a fresh and determined Arsenal, a club that was obviously outside the Merseyside bubble about Hillsborough and that had been eagerly contesting the league title with few extraneous distractions. This final contest was a strange affair indeed. Liverpool supporters were divided about whether claiming a second league and cup Double would be a fitting memorial to the dead or an insult to those who were still directly suffering because of the impact of Hillsborough. The team seemed caught in the same dilemma, and on some occasions it can be more difficult to defend a position of relative strength rather than be required to go out decisively to win a football match. In the event, Liverpool never really got going, and the Anfield crowd had difficulty responding with the required level of urgency to lift their team's performance. How important was winning yet another league crown, anyway, given what had happened?

As a result, a committed Arsenal pilfered the title by winning 0–2 at Anfield, with future Liverpool man Michael Thomas scoring the decisive and dramatic last-minute goal that eventually divided the clubs. Arsenal won the title only by scoring more goals (73 to 65) than Liverpool. In the directors' box, even as the winning shot ballooned in the net behind Bruce Grobbelaar, Liverpool club secretary Peter Robinson calmly rang down to the Anfield kitchen to get the post-match champagne provided by the sponsors redirected to the visitors' dressing-room.

The Kop was still a standing terrace that night – it would eventually disappear in 1994 – and thousands of Liverpool supporters stayed on to sit on its great steps to applaud the new champions and watch the Arsenal celebrations. Some thought that the wild reactions of the visitors mirrored the distasteful Juventus celebrations of 1985, but this was certainly unfair. And many Liverpool supporters were glad to applaud Arsenal as champions, because the outcome avoided the dilemma of quite how to react to a Reds title win that would have felt like so much ashes in the mouth given the circumstances. Liverpool fans were instead left to reflect soberly on the enormity of what they and their football club had been through over the previous six weeks, and indeed over the past four years. These terrible experiences had probably bonded supporters to the club even more firmly. It had been an emotionally draining journey, with many wonderful highs on the pitch but punctuated by unimaginable, desperate lows off it.

In 1989, the world was changing. Just a few months after Hillsborough the Berlin Wall was breached and Communism went the same way as the Liverpool dominance of European football was heading. Some authors suggest that Hillsborough and this deciding match at Anfield was the key turning point in the post-war history of the sport, the defining moment that moved the game on from its local roots, traditional stadiums and partisan masculine rituals, all of which had given English football both its historic cultural meaning and also deeply scarred it in the hooligan era.[12] There might be something to this idea. After all, Nick Hornby's manifesto for new football, *Fever Pitch*, reached a climax with Arsenal's title win and then went on to sketch out the new, more civilised world for the game. Certainly, the media coverage of those who tragically died at Hillsborough – the sons, daughters, husbands and friends – meant that football supporters would now be more likely to be seen through the prism of the family rather than the usual hooligan lens.

And there was still time in this period of rapid transition for one more Liverpool league title – the 18th – to be collected in 1989–90. By then, the stylish but vulnerable Swedish international Glenn Hysen and the rugged West Midlander David Burrows were in defence, and the still irresistible John Barnes was scoring 22 league goals in 34 appearances. But the cracks were also finally starting to really open up in Liverpool's previously near-invulnerable make-up.

Liverpool FC, league-title winners, 1989–90

	Grobbelaar		
Nicol	Hysen	Hansen	Burrows
Houghton	McMahon	Whelan	Barnes
	Beardsley	Rush	

Liverpool manager Kenny Dalglish reported later on the enormous stress that had been involved for him in the club's return to a 'creepy' Hillsborough to play a league match in November 1989. Liverpool lost 0–2, but few in the Liverpool party wanted to dwell on the result or too long in Sheffield.[13] Crystal Palace were thrashed 9–0 by Liverpool in the league at Anfield in September, and Swansea City were later thumped 8–0 in the FA Cup, so this Reds side could still turn it on and destroy poor opposition. But in the FA Cup semi-final at Villa Park in April 1990 – and this was perhaps the real turning point for the Liverpool team – the rapid but inexperienced Crystal Palace attack made Liverpool's defending look threadbare and inept for once. This shock 3–4 defeat for the Anfield club was a shuddering sign of future struggles to come.

Alan Hansen was now clearly at the end of his wonderful Anfield career, and Kenny Dalglish had started to look strained and drawn in the manager's seat – God knows, he had been through more than any football manager should be forced to endure. The era of the great historic Scottish influence at Liverpool was at its close. Indeed, Liverpool's period of dominance of English football was effectively over. Even as the Reds thrashed Coventry City 6–1 in the last match of the 1989–90 season, with John Barnes and the erratic Israeli striker Ronnie Rosenthal rampant, there was already a sense that this amazing run – eleven league titles and six second-place finishes in eighteen seasons since 1972–73, plus numerous cups won at home and abroad – could not go on. Only a finish of fifth place in the injury-hit season of 1980–81 stood out as a relative failing, and Bob Paisley had still won the European Cup for Liverpool in that year. This fantastic league-and-cup record for one club was now at the end of its supernatural cycle. And English football was about to change radically to try to escape from its recent nightmares.

OLD ROUTES, NEW DIRECTIONS

The depleted and troubled Kenny Dalglish had wanted to resign as manager of Liverpool Football Club in the summer of 1990. He was worn out by the events of the past five years, but especially those of the previous twelve months. He also wanted to buy shares in the club he loved. He was able to do neither. The Liverpool board insisted that he continue as manager and said that there were no shares available, not even for 'King Kenny'. But by Christmas 1990 the huge strain of what had gone before was obvious, and the Liverpool boss was clearly ill and having trouble making decisions, the crucial area of any football manager's job. His signings for Liverpool Football Club had also started to lose their previous assurance and quality: players such as Steve Harkness, Don Hutchison, Jimmy Carter, Nicky Tanner and David Speedie simply could not match the men who had made the club so dominant in the previous two decades. His scouts were letting him down. Also, the sleeping English giants at Arsenal and especially Manchester United had finally got their acts together. There would be no more Liverpool cakewalks in the league. A crazy 4–4 fifth-round FA Cup replay at Everton in 1991, when the manager dithered over making changes as the match see-sawed in front of him, was the moment he chose to make his announcement to resign.

Rather like Bill Shankly before him, Dalglish hinted later that had Liverpool waited over the summer of 1991, while he rested and got his mind straight, he might have returned refreshed and ready to continue in the job. But, as was the case back in 1974, there is seldom time for reflection in football, and – again like in 1974 – Liverpool Football Club felt that they had continuity assured in a more-than-adequate replacement for Kenny. It was one of his old Scottish buddies, the former midfield organiser at Anfield Graeme Souness, who now stepped forward. Souness had been a successful, if controversial, managerial figure at Glasgow Rangers, and the Liverpool hierarchy thought that he would bring back the old reassurance and swagger of the 1980s. But the game had moved on. Kenny Dalglish eventually re-emerged at cash-rich Blackburn Rovers, claiming a Premier League title there as manager in 1995 as Liverpool under Souness, and then Roy Evans, continued to struggle.

Crucially, all this emotional upheaval, disruption and uncertainty for Liverpool Football Club also happened at a critical moment in the development of the modern English game. Liverpool had fallen behind the rest of English football in the 1920s because of tactical inadequacy and in the 1950s because of boardroom penny-pinching. Now it would fall behind again, mainly because of a reluctance to embrace change and because of the baggage of the awful disasters that had so engulfed the club. The old boot-room competitive advantage would no longer work in this new age. The aftermath of Hillsborough had produced an agenda for stadium modernisation in Britain, but it was also a moment when the game itself was completely reconstructed and repackaged in England. This came with the birth of the brassy new FA Premier League in 1992, the rise of satellite TV as a major new funder for English football, and the globalisation of the elite levels of the English game made possible by new technology and new marketing and communication techniques.

'New' football had its doubters, of course, as fans found their voice: Liverpool's excellent local fanzine *Through the Wind and Rain*, for example, routinely poured scorn on the sport's commercial excesses and its empty new promises. Liverpool Football Club had been efficiently and cleverly run by T.V. Williams and later by John Smith and Peter Robinson in football's 'old times'. But the club was hardly best placed now to ride this new commercial and communications wave, especially as it had been immersed for a number of years in the consequences of dealing with two terrible spectator tragedies and focused on avoiding change rather than embracing it. It also lost its guiding figures and some of the crucial domestic advantages it had enjoyed over its close rivals of being continuously involved in European club football. English clubs were banned from Europe for five years, with Liverpool being excluded for six, returning to European action in the UEFA Cup in 1991–92. The glorious boot-room days of Shankly, Paisley, Fagan, Bennett, Moran, Evans and Dalglish were over. Just as the club had lost momentum because of the managerial innovation of Herbert Chapman, and had done so again because of post-war conservatism, now it was falling behind as the game's commercial arm was undergoing a period of rapid and radical revolution.

Liverpool Football Club had, understandably, stressed continuity and stability in its golden years, rather than the sort of transformational and dynamic processes of adaptation that seemed to be required in the new future for the game. One sign of this was that after being regularly thwarted by its local residents and neighbours in its ground redevelopment plans, the club was only able to open its very first executive boxes in August 1992, when a second tier was finally added to the existing Kemlyn Road stand at a cost of £8.5 million. The new Centenary Stand was officially opened on 1 September 1992 – 100 years to the day after Liverpool's first match at Anfield. Suddenly, for things to stay the same in terms of maintaining Liverpool's playing dominance at home and abroad, everything else would have to change.

To be fair, in terms of his policies and his general approach to club management, Graeme Souness was much less of a continuity candidate for the Liverpool manager's job than he might have at first appeared. For example, he lacked the loyalty and the communitarian values of the Shankly/Paisley dynasty. He had left Liverpool in 1984 simply for more money in Italy. He was no Liverpool disciple, and he was a player who was respected rather than loved at Anfield. Dalglish was adored. But Souness came back to the club, supposedly, with a winner's mentality. He rightly realised that Liverpool Football Club urgently required modernisation. He recognised, too, that it was in danger of ossifying by resting on past glories when the world of football was changing so fast. He also thought that some of the club's older stars – John Barnes and Ian Rush among them – were now past their best and obstructing necessary change. Souness altered the Liverpool training regime to finally break the boot-room traditions – players would no longer change at Anfield and travel by coach to Melwood – and he stood accused by some Liverpool supporters and players of trying to alter too much, too soon. The truth was that he took over at probably the most difficult time in the club's recent history. Any new manager might have had difficulty turning Liverpool around at this precise moment, but Souness hardly helped himself, either, with his style of management or his chosen personnel.

In fact, Graeme Souness turned out to be a very poor man-manager and a surprisingly weak judge of players. Some of his key signings – Dean Saunders, Paul Stewart, Nigel Clough, Torben Piechnik, Neil Ruddock and the positively lumpen West Ham skinhead Julian Dicks – were simply not up to past Liverpool standards. The cartoonish Dicks liked to drink two cans of

Coca-Cola before playing matches, and he had regular run-ins with Ronnie Moran during training ('I used to row with Ronnie every day,' he said). Reds coach Steve Heighway clearly thought Dicks was not a typical Liverpool player and refused to talk with him. When Dicks was later dropped to the club's reserve team, the depressed defender got drunk in local pubs in the afternoon before matches.[14]

In the past, senior Liverpool players had made sure that the drinking cliques at Anfield never obstructed the professional responsibilities of the players and also contributed to team spirit. Now the attitudes and values – as well as the football ability – of some of these highly paid new recruits were very questionable. Because of all this gross unprofessionalism, Souness also risked squandering the talents of a rising group of excellent youngsters – the Dalglish signing Jamie Redknapp and two irrepressible and brilliant Scousers, loping winger Steve McManaman and nerveless striker Robbie Fowler among them – as he tried to shape the club for the new era.

An FA Cup final win for Liverpool over Sunderland in 1992 briefly stayed local protest. As George Kay had done in 1950, a pale and drawn Souness attended at Wembley only after a serious illness and hospital treatment. He also faced further fan criticism for crassly selling the story about his illness to the locally hated *Sun* newspaper. A weak sixth-place finish for Liverpool in the new FA Premier League in 1993 – some 25 points behind winners Manchester United – caused further rumblings. It had been preceded by a near-comical UEFA Cup-Winners' Cup exit to Spartak Moscow in November 1992, which had already revived serious doubts about Souness's long-term Anfield future. In the summer of 1993, most Liverpool supporters confidently expected (and hoped) that Souness would be sacked, but with the Liverpool board dithering and divided under the new Liverpool chairman David Moores, a personal friend of the manager and many of the players, Souness managed to hang on. It was a stay of execution only. After a bright start to the 1993–94 league season – but with Liverpool out of Europe once again – things predictably began to deteriorate, and early on in 1994 the critical loss occurred. It was a shattering home defeat to Bristol City in an FA Cup replay. Even the hard man Souness realised that he could not survive this latest lapse, and he resigned before he was sacked.

THE RETURN OF THE BOOT ROOM

Souness was replaced – perhaps reluctantly – by Roy Evans, a boot-room product and a man who could claim 20 productive years' service on the Liverpool coaching staff. Evans was a calmer, much more reflective influence than was Souness, and he vowed to bring the traditions of the Liverpool Way right up to date and, by doing so, to lead the club to a better tomorrow. His personal lineage at the club reached back, reassuringly, to Bill Shankly, and he relied on advice from old Anfield servants, including Tom Saunders, a man who had spotted and raised young talent for the club for many years. The traditional boot-room references delighted the Liverpool fans, but again it looked, possibly, like a return to the past when the future now looked so different for English football. And did the rather kindly Evans really have the necessary ruthlessness of a Shankly or a Paisley to make tough decisions and drive Liverpool on in a new commercial era in front of the all-seated, more pacified, Kop?

With ex-Reds player Doug Livermore, Ronnie Moran and a rejuvenated John Barnes promising a modern version of the traditional Anfield brains trust, Roy Evans constructed a novel and attractive 3–5–2 playing system that briefly threatened to win Liverpool the league title once again in the mid-1990s. With a new, young future international goalkeeper David James and a flexible back three made up of Mark Wright, John Scales and Phil Babb, and flying wing-backs Jason McAteer and Souness signing Rob Jones, it was a slowing John Barnes who now cleverly directed matters from a more withdrawn midfield position. Jamie Redknapp provided some midfield finesse, Steve McManaman offered brilliant wing-play – but in a mazy new channel *across* the pitch – and the left-footed Toxteth urchin genius Robbie Fowler scored goals, seemingly hundreds of them.

This new Liverpool under Evans passed and kept the ball superbly, albeit sometimes at the expense of penetrating weaker opposition and killing off matches. A McManaman-inspired League Cup-final win against Bolton Wanderers in 1995 offered much future promise of returning more silverware to Anfield. Perhaps this renewal of the boot-room ethos was going to work after all? But then Evans helped murder his own dream by making a major mistake, the sort of gaffe that Shankly or Bob Paisley seldom, if ever, made. These earlier bosses checked the character of prospective signings with their scouts as much as they did their football talent. Evans failed to remember this lesson. He signed, for a then record Liverpool fee of £8.5 million, a player whose main focus was palpably not the future of Liverpool Football Club. Evans's new recruit was congenitally programmed to think only about himself, not his teammates, nor his supporters or his employers. The talented, but ultimately corrosive, Stan Collymore joined Liverpool from Nottingham Forest in June 1995. His signing turned out to be the equivalent of a managerial suicide note.

Depending upon who you believed, Collymore was either a football manager's dream or his worst nightmare. He was a player with undoubted ability but also many personal demons that were fully revealed only after he retired as a player. Stan could be brilliant or truly awful, and he often combined these two opposing traits in the same match. But more importantly, Collymore, like an invisible virus, was a stone wall guarantee eventually to destroy the collective unity in any football dressing-room he inhabited. He was the antithesis, in fact, of a 'typical' Liverpool player. According to Robbie Fowler, Stan was 'fucking hopeless' in terms of his attitude to other footballers and building the necessary collective ethos of a successful football dressing-room. He scored 35 goals in 81 appearances for Liverpool, a more than tidy return, but his performance in almost every really significant match that he played for the club was poor, sometimes irresponsibly so. Moreover, he eventually alienated both Fowler and McManaman, his key forward partners. In an era when players' wages soared, Collymore wilfully challenged the authority – and eventually the self-respect – of his caring and much abused manager.

Nevertheless, Liverpool threatened again in the league under Evans in 1995–96 before finally falling away. But the Reds had also powered to the FA Cup final in 1996, fuelled by Fowler's goals, where they met Manchester United. By now the club was haunted by press tales of player excess and a lack of discipline in the dressing-room – the Liverpool 'Spice Boys'. This was unfair on Evans, and the stories were often exaggerated, but it was also clear that the current squad lacked the cold-eyed professional focus of earlier Liverpool sides. This was the infamous 'white suits' final, of course, when the Liverpool players looked both ridiculous and disrespectful in their pre-cup final outfits, and then simply failed to perform in an insipid contest, subsiding to Eric Cantona's late goal. Stan Collymore, Evans's signature signing, was predictably substituted at Wembley, as he would be at half-time in a spineless Reds performance as Liverpool collapsed 0–3 in the UEFA Cup-Winners' Cup semi-final against Paris St Germain in April 1997.

Stan Collymore's brief and unsatisfactory Liverpool career was now effectively over, a football talent carelessly thrown away. He had also done for the manager who had so mistakenly trusted him. A new local star, the much more committed and electric Michael Owen, was about to burst on the Liverpool football scene. Sadly, Roy Evans's entertaining and sporadically promising time as manager of Liverpool Football Club was coming towar its inevitable end. The Liverpool board was about to turn to Europe to t revive its fading league-championship dreams.

CHAPTER 17 REFERENCES

1. Sampson, 'Brussels, 1985', p. 203
2. Kennedy and Williams, *Kennedy's Way*, p. 205
3. Reade, *43 Years with the Same Bird*
4. Foot, *Calcio: A History of Italian Football*, pp. 328–40
5. Jackson, 'The Witnesses'
6. Corbett, *Everton: The School of Science*, p. 261
7. Nicholls, *Scally: The Story of a Category C Football Hooligan*
8. Murden, 'City of Challenge and Change', p. 428
9. Ward and Williams, *Football Nation*, pp. 16–24
10. Scraton, *Hillsborough: The Truth*
11. Taylor, 'English Football in the 1990s'
12. Cowley, *The Last Game*
13. Dalglish, *Dalglish: My Autobiography*, p. 179
14. Blows, *Terminator: The Authorised Julian Dicks Story*, p. 202

18

CONTINENTAL DRIFT
The New Liverpool Technocrats

THIS IS THE MODERN WORLD

Modernisation in English football towards the end of the 1990s increasingly meant looking towards the Continent for inspiration, science, creativity and discipline. These sorts of themes had come and gone in the English game, in one way or another, since before the Hungarian defeat of England back in 1953. But now the new money in English football and a relaxation of the English-are-best mentality meant that club directors were capable – and increasingly willing – to sign up their key men from abroad. They looked for recruits for positions both on and off the field. The previously unknown Arsène Wenger's cerebral coaching success at Arsenal for a while seemed like a signal for the future for almost every top English club. Roy Evans and his staff at Liverpool knew best the English game, of course, and the Bootle-born man had recruited largely British players – his Continental buys had not always been a success.

The club was still well known in football circles for its drinking culture (as was Arsenal before Wenger cleaned it up). Post-match drinking for Reds players had seemed fine in the 1980s, when Liverpool were dominant and the press and supporters were compliant, but now it was beginning to appear outdated and self-indulgent amidst increasing talk about diets and computer analysis of body fat and player performance. The club's supporters were also asking questions about the alleged lack of professionalism at Anfield, where players seemed to be allowed just too much leeway. The Liverpool teams produced by Evans were attractive, sure, but they also indulged in over-passing and had a mental soft centre in critical matches.

Evans's latest major signings to address some of these failings included the hard-nosed England international midfield player Paul Ince and the German European Cup-winner Karl-Heinz Riedle in the summer of 1997. The manager finally lost faith in his 3–5–2 team shape, and in both Collymore and John Barnes, in preparation for a move back to a more conventional 4–4–2 formation, with the ex-Manchester United man Ince supposedly adding the missing steel. The young Michael Owen, every mother's dream, was helping out with the goals while also contributing to the traumas of the 22-year-old injury-hit 'veteran' Robbie Fowler, who was already being written off in some quarters. But was this move back to a more familiar playing system really radical enough to turn things around at Anfield? Owen scored 18 league goals in his first full season, but Liverpool could do no better than third place in the Premier League in 1998.

Perhaps more of a European influence at coaching or managerial level at the club could help get Liverpool back on track and also help Evans develop his management skills? Perhaps a partnership of the old boot room and the new Continental science could finally do the trick? It might also rid the Liverpool dressing-room of some of its bad habits acquired under Souness and not dealt with effectively by Evans. The Liverpool board, and Peter Robinson in particular, scanned the Continent and came up with just the man for the proposed job-share – the French youth academy architect, disciplinarian and confirmed Liverpool Football Club admirer Gérard Houllier.

This was a risky strategy. At the very top level of the game, the Frenchman's record was actually quite patchy, including a last-minute failure to take the French national team to the 1994 World Cup finals. And going for joint football managers – one an Englishman steeped in the Liverpool tradition, the other an internationally known learned French coach, best regarded for developing youth players for the French Football Federation – was never likely to work at Anfield or anywhere else in England. Roy Evans did not want it. But at least it avoided the unpleasantness of sacking the Liverpool manager. The club rarely fired the top man – it was bad form, not the Liverpool Way. The co-manager role would give Houllier a heads-up inside the club before the inevitable outcome of him taking over the first team on his own.

At least Houllier had studied and lived in the city of Liverpool as a trainee teacher, and he loved the traditions and cultures around the club. He liked the working-class fans in the city, the way the terraced houses of Anfield folded around the stadium, and the bond between the supporters and the team, which he likened to the importance of the pass on the pitch. He had respect for what he called the 'Liverpool imaginary'.[1] Here was a boot-room man in French clothing. Or so it seemed.

Houllier's arrival corresponded with the move to Anfield of one of the architects of the cash-cow Premier League, Liverpool fan Rick Parry, after Peter Robinson picked his moment to leave. Parry was a restless advocate of constant change in the game, and he knew Liverpool had suffered in comparison with the recent commercial development of Manchester United. He also knew that the club would have to finance a new stadium to keep up with its competitors. As far back as 1990, a joint all-seated stadium to house both major Merseyside clubs had been proposed on Kirkby golf course at a cost of £125 million, backed by Liverpool City Council. The clubs were scornful, of course, but almost 20 years later Everton were looking again at Kirkby as a location, and neither club would be much advanced in their individual ambitions for stadium relocation. Liverpool FC, for example, were facing a bill of more than £400 million for a venue for which they still had no funding while their rivals had all moved on. But Parry was also wary of the real dangers of going down an ultra-commercialised route for Liverpool Football Club because of the history and values of the club and its cultural importance in the city. In 2002 he said:

> I hate to use the word 'brand', but it's the word that fits. The great thing that Liverpool had never done was to prostitute the brand. And that is terrific. There is a paradox for Manchester United that they are simultaneously the most loved and the most hated brand of all, which is kind of tough from a commercial perspective. The 'brand values' that we have developed for Liverpool, well, the key word for us is 'respect'. In the 1970s and '80s, we were not loved by everybody, but there was always a respect for Liverpool, and that's a value I think is very important.[2]

Liverpool was now a global club, a 'brand' with new markets to serve. The impact of the Internet, club merchandise and satellite TV meant rethinking the whole concept of the fan and seeing the club as an international concern.

Parry favoured the appointment of Gérard Houllier because he liked the attention to detail and the urbanity and strong principles of the new manager, and Parry believed that the Frenchman understood the cultural significance of the Liverpool Way. Houllier thought Parry was the kind of ethical moderniser he could work with. Both men were determined to revolutionise the general approach to organisation and discipline inside the club, and to modernise tactics and player preparation at Melwood. And there was much to do.

THE MEN FROM THE CONTINENT (1)

Gérard Houllier did not like what he saw at Anfield when he arrived in 1998: too much drinking and ill-discipline; too little training tailored to match situations; a training ground that needed rebuilding and modernising; and too little emphasis on scientific preparation in terms of diet, the use of computer technology and specialised coaching. Liverpool had fallen behind its competitors once again. He also thought that Roy Evans was too close, too friendly, with the Liverpool players, some of whom had just too much to say about training and tactics. A manager needed to maintain his distance from his team to properly exercise his authority. In contrast to the great Liverpool dynasties of the recent past, Houllier interpreted players who spoke out of turn as showing a lack of respect. Many would remark later that the new Continental presence at Liverpool lacked something in personal security, but nothing in ego.

Gradually, Houllier asserted himself and his new approach at the start of the 1998–99 season, and in November 1998 Roy Evans realised that this attempt at joint authority could never work in a British football club where players needed to know exactly who the boss was. One Liverpool manager favoured rotating his players, the other sticking to a winning team in the Shankly and Paisley tradition. What exactly *was* the Liverpool policy? After a dressing-room bust-up following a European tie in Valencia, like the honourable man he is Roy Evans took the hint and resigned. Liverpool had finished in the top four in each of his four seasons in sole charge, had won one trophy and played in another major final. With Houllier in lone charge for much of 1998–99, the club slumped to seventh place.

Now the Frenchman acted decisively. He brought in ex-Red Phil Thompson to add some local knowledge and steel, and he started to clear out the players he couldn't work with or who challenged his approach. These included Ince, error-prone goalkeeper David James and defenders McAteer, Wright and Babb. Out, too, went the very moderate foreigners Bjørnebye, Kvarme and Leonhardsen. In a more costly loss, Steve McManaman also opted to join Real Madrid on a Bosman free transfer, the first in England. Houllier began building a new Liverpool team around an emerging core of young local talent he could mould, including the forward prodigy Michael Owen, the young Bootle-born defender Jamie Carragher, the clever midfielder Danny Murphy, and eventually a brilliant youth-team starlet who was beginning to make local waves, a man called Steven Gerrard. Local hero Robbie Fowler seemed truculent and less convinced by the new manager, and was therefore a much more marginal figure.

From abroad for the 1999–2000 season, his first in sole charge, in came the key signings of defenders Sami Hyypiä and Stéphane Henchoz, Dutch goalkeeper Sander Westerveld, fragile but skilful Czech forward Vladimír Šmicer and the excellent German international defensive midfield player Dietmar Hamann.

An elusive but limited African forward Titi Camara and a mysterious young Croat midfielder Igor Bišćan later added a touch of the exotic to this otherwise solid group. It was a mass internationalisation of the Liverpool Football Club playing staff, just as the club's board had hoped and anticipated it would be. The stylish Finnish centre-back Hyypiä and Didi Hamann were the key figures here – powerful and reliable and technically excellent, they would provide much of the Liverpool backbone for the coming campaigns.

This new Liverpool under Houllier was highly functional rather than exciting, with the emphasis on a prosaic brand of counter-attacking football that had little of the romance or style of the Roy Evans era. It was sporadically effective, but it could also be incredibly dull. The new manager also began to insist on the tactical rotation of his squad. It was the end of the period when the sign of a typical Liverpool championship team was six or seven players who had played every league and major cup match. Liverpool's regimented play also contrasted wildly with much of the more sophisticated football now played by Wenger's Arsenal. But Liverpool were broadly competitive in 1999–2000, and the signing of the brawny young England forward Emile Heskey for £11 million from Leicester City in March 2000 was supposed to confirm the club's inevitable passage into the Champions League places. But Heskey had problems settling and scoring, and his presence seemed to unsettle, rather than inspire, his new club. With Fowler now deeply at odds with his manager, the Reds suffered a late-season goal drought and collapse, five winless and scoreless league matches. So it would be the UEFA Cup only for Liverpool in season 2000–01 after all. What an unlikely bonus this turned out to prove.

Landing the experienced German international full-back Markus Babbel on a free transfer in 2000 looked like good business for Houllier, and signing Nick Barmby from Everton kept the local sports scribes happy: Barmby was the first direct Liverpool signing from Everton since Dave Hickson in the 1950s. But the most important Liverpool capture for the 2000–01 season, in a flurry of transfer activity, was a Scot. How fitting. The Coventry City veteran Gary McAllister looked like a retirement case, a man recruited by Houllier mainly to coach, and the midfielder sensed the 'negative vibes' in the camp about him when he signed. But McAllister actually became a key player in an incredible Treble season. He gave the previously stodgy Liverpool side more cleverness, flow and direction from the centre of the field, crucial ingredients. Moreover, the seemingly ageless McAllister would assure himself of a permanent place in Red hearts by scoring an astonishing 44-yard match-winning free-kick against Everton at Goodison Park in a vital Easter 3–2 league win.

Before that, the Reds had stumbled to a League Cup final victory in the

Millennium Stadium in Cardiff, on penalties, over gallant Birmingham City. Michael Owen was left out of the final, while Robbie Fowler scored a stunning goal. Then, after having a peculiarly leisurely route to the later stages, Liverpool – or, rather, two-goal Michael Owen – returned to Wales to positively steal the 2001 FA Cup by 2–1 from under the noses of a dominant Arsenal. This time a crestfallen Fowler was omitted. It was a return to winning ways at last, a triumph for the insight, discipline and hard work of the Liverpool board and for Houllier and his staff. But could it last?

In the league, Liverpool were inconsistent, but they also produced some notable victories: two league wins over Manchester United and a Gerrard-inspired 4–0 rollicking of a classy Arsenal at Anfield, for example. Abroad, the club were also steadily progressing in the UEFA Cup, but making few friends along the way. In the fourth round, the Reds won 2–0 in the Olympic Stadium in Rome, both goals from Michael Owen, which meant a 0–1 loss at home in the second leg against Roma was a very decent result. After they beat Porto in the quarter-finals, next came an especially defensive semi-final display in the first leg in the Nou Camp in Barcelona that produced a ground-out 0–0 draw. It was an excellent result for a side inexperienced at this level, but the manner of the performance saw the Reds accused by some of the European football cognoscenti of 'murdering' the game. Houllier could care less. No one in the Liverpool 4 district complained when McAllister scored the only goal from the penalty spot in the second leg to take Liverpool through.

After all these lean years, it was difficult to take all this in. In this extraordinary season, Liverpool had won two domestic cups already, were still on course to qualify for a chance to win the European Cup once again and were in the club's first major European final for sixteen years – an opportunity to atone at last for all those terrible memories of 1985. And this was Houllier's team, an international combination rapidly rebuilt with a Scouse heart and a new Scottish professor as its brains. What an occasion it was. Fresh from snaffling the FA Cup from Arsenal's grasp, Liverpool now faced the Basques from Alavés in the 2001 UEFA Cup final. On paper, this might have looked like easy meat, and Liverpool were clear favourites. But the Spanish side had destroyed Kaiserslautern 9–2 on aggregate in the semi-finals, so tough competition and goals were on the menu. Tens of thousands of Liverpool supporters made the trip to Dortmund on a damp Ruhr night, a new generation of European football explorers. The flags and songs there made it seem just like old times. But the trip also lacked some of the excesses and the aggression of the 1980s – some hard lessons had been learned.

Liverpool FC, UEFA Cup winners, v. Alavés, 16 May 2001

Westerveld

Babbel   Henchoz   Hyypiä   Carragher

Hamann

Gerrard   McAllister   Murphy

Owen   Heskey

Alavés fans, in their first European final, were charming and hopeful, while Liverpool supporters were, well, just glad to be back on the big stage once more. The city of Dortmund perhaps owed Liverpool a victory after the 1966 Cup-Winners' Cup fiasco, and so it proved. But *what* a struggle! It did not look that way after sixteen minutes, when the Reds were two goals to the good, scored by Babbel and Gerrard. Alavés looked inexperienced and vulnerable, but they came back almost immediately with a goal of their own, from Alonso. Game on – enough to stir Michael Owen to win a penalty, converted by McAllister, who else? A score of 3–1 at half-time ought to have been enough to see this through, but Sander Westerveld was showing the arrogance and sloppiness that would soon cost him his Liverpool career, and danger man Moreno scored twice to level things at 3–3. When a frustrated Robbie Fowler came on for Heskey after 65 minutes and scored with a sublime right-foot shot, most Liverpool supporters would have settled for this romantic ending. But instead Alavés replied again with their third headed goal, from Jordi Cruyff. A final that began as exciting and adventurous was now in danger of just looking defensively naive.

The ridiculous mechanism of the 'golden goal' would now decide this UEFA Cup final. Just three minutes from the end of extra time, as the TV companies were gleefully preparing for penalties, a slithering headed own goal from Geli, after a McAllister free-kick, finally settled matters. Not that many of the Liverpool players knew the rules – they took their signal that the game was over from the Liverpool crowd's delirious response.

The reborn McAllister was voted man of the match in the final (he was man of the season for Liverpool), and there was still time for the Reds to thump Charlton Athletic 4–0 in the final league fixture to clinch a Champions League spot. It was an astonishing return on all four fronts. Gérard Houllier had confounded his critics, who had worried at his management style, conservative tactics and rigid formations. He deserved huge credit in the face of some opposition.

Not everyone even at Liverpool FC – even now – was convinced. Robbie Fowler was the focal point for this group of dissenters. The Scouser hated the new regimentation of it all. He was 'sick to death' of the lack of enjoyment in training and on the field, and the fact that no banter and play-acting was allowed in the camp any more. Even the Liverpool greats of the past would have missed these vital ingredients. Robbie had his sympathisers: Johan Cruyff, the guest of honour at the UEFA Cup final, was no lover of Liverpool's long-ball tactics. He whispered conspiratorially to the striker at his medal presentation, 'Don't let him get you down. You're too good.'[3]

Fowler also despised the way the new manager treated his players like schoolchildren and was depressed by the sheer dullness of many of the new foreign recruits. 'I want the players to be nice,' said Houllier, 'to be good people, to have respect for each other but also respect for the girls in the canteen or the kit manager. I think if you are a nice man, you are a nice player.' This kind of thing was a necessary riposte to the era of Dicks, Ruddock and Collymore, but it also offered a picture of a rather sanitised and authoritarian culture inside the dressing-room. A low point was reached when the young French full-back Grégory Vignal was found sobbing by players in the car park when illness had frustrated his chances of a first-team debut. This was the last straw to some of the local men: a first-team Liverpool player *crying* in front of his teammates! Things had gone too far, and Fowler was bemused and disillusioned. He knew this stage of his Liverpool career was over.

TOTAL ECLIPSE

Emboldened by his successes and lauded by the Liverpool board, Houllier prepared for the new campaign by signing Polish international goalkeeper Jerzy Dudek to replace Westerveld, the veteran Finnish forward Jari Litmanen and a young fitness fanatic, Norwegian left-back John Arne Riise. Liverpool's first match back in Europe's elite club competition after 16 long years away was a tepid 1–1 draw against Boavista. It took place in an eerie Anfield on 11 September 2001 while the rest of Europe looked westwards to the United States. The Twin Towers still smouldered in New York City. No one quite knew that night what lay in wait for the world. Less importantly, no one knew, either, that a different kind of fate would soon strike down the Liverpool Football Club manager near the top of his game and thus change the whole trajectory of his project at Anfield.

Illness hit the Liverpool boss hard, as it had done Liverpool management men before him. Matt McQueen in the 1920s, George Kay in the 1950s and Graeme Souness in the 1990s were all victims of serious illness or accident during their Anfield tenures. Houllier would now have to be added to this list: he suffered a damaged aorta at a match v. Leeds United at Anfield in October 2001, and the Frenchman spent much of the 2001–02 campaign in hospital recovering from serious heart surgery. Nevertheless, Liverpool, under the authority of Phil Thompson and with Steven Gerrard and Jamie Carragher offering on-field leadership, reached the quarter-final of the Champions League and amassed 80 points in the league to finish second only to Arsenal. The players seemed devoted to their recovering leader, and with a little more careful investment surely the ultimate success in the league and Europe would come to Liverpool?

An apparently restored Houllier signed Milan Baroš, a spritely and youthful but essentially heads-down Czech international, and the much coveted Senegalese international pair El-Hadji Diouf and Salif Diao as his final pieces. In, too, came midfield-man Bruno Cheyrou, who joined Liverpool from Lille with glowing references. But critically for the future of their French manager, all of these players, ultimately, failed the test at Anfield.

With Houllier back fully in charge, after a fine 12-match unbeaten league start in 2002–03 Liverpool slid down the table, and they made little progress in the Champions League. The manager fiddled relentlessly with the team. 'Asking Houllier to do nowt,' said keen Reds observer James Lawton in *The Independent* on 16 December 2002, 'to let a group of players grow organically rather than by constant Dr Frankenstein surgery, seems to be too tall a requirement of a passionate, hyperactive man.' He had a point. But the Reds still managed to defeat Manchester United 2–0 in the 2003 League Cup final, some reward in a difficult season that had started to raise new doubts about whether Gérard Houllier could secure the really big prizes for his supporters and players.

Since his illness, Houllier had seemed much less decisive and much too thin-skinned, showing ever-darkening concern about media comment, especially from ex-Liverpool players. Rick Parry certainly thought that the manager had become obsessive, had changed in character, since his heart problem. The quality Australian winger Harry Kewell joined Liverpool from Leeds in July 2003, but the manager had also put his store in recruiting young Continental players at 'bargain' prices, such as Florent Sinama Pongolle and Anthony Le Tallec, who seemed lightweight and ill-suited to the English game. By November, after a run of defeats, his captain Steven Gerrard was already admitting to the press that after just 13 matches Liverpool Football Club could not win the 2004 league title. A pall of paranoia had suddenly settled over Anfield, the manager stalking its corridors like a man plagued by demons. Houllier seemed increasingly lost and befuddled in a fog of statistics, which he now spewed out at every press conference. Journalists had begun to see past his urbanity and were now questioning his managerial capacity – even his sanity. Another Champions League place won in season 2003–04 could not disguise the fact that many of the club's supporters were also losing faith in their manager. Liverpool collected only 60 league points, 30 behind the champions Arsenal. Suddenly, this grand French march seemed to be heading nowhere, and the manager knew it. After brief discussions with the Liverpool board in May 2004, Houllier left the club.

THE MEN FROM THE CONTINENT (2)

On the surface, the new Liverpool manager, the Spaniard Rafa Benítez, seemed very much like the departing Gérard Houllier. He was a technocrat, a coach with no great playing record, a man who laid great store on preparation, tactics and discipline. He favoured scientific assessments of players, and defence more than attack. He liked to keep a rather cold distance between himself and his squad, and he also favoured rotation to keep its members fresh. Unlike Houllier, however, he had enjoyed some club management success in one of the toughest leagues in Europe, twice winning the Spanish title and in 2004 also taking the UEFA Cup with a Valencia side that he had largely inherited.

Despite this incredible recent domestic and European success, Benítez was available because he had fallen out with his employers. They had insisted on the Spanish club model: that the director of football should recruit players who the coach (in this case Benítez) should then prepare. Benítez much preferred the English model, in which the manager chooses his own players and then moulds them into a winning unit. Don't buy me a lamp when I ask for a table, summed up his frustrations with the director of football at the Mestalla. He was glad to leave Spain.

Aware of the growing tensions at Valencia, Liverpool chief executive Rick Parry had rushed to sign up Benítez a matter of days after Houllier had departed. The new man had barely been to Liverpool, but he liked what he was hearing from Parry and his chairman David Moores. He would have the freedom – and the funds – to build his own team with no board interference. He could also bring his Spanish coaching team.

Make no mistake, this signing was a major coup. Benítez was arguably the most prized young coach in Europe at the time, but he knew little about managing in England, where another new young foreign manager, José Mourinho, was already making huge surfer's waves at Chelsea. Winning the Premier League crown would be more difficult than ever. Benítez immediately faced the qualifying rounds of the Champions League (a context in which he excelled), the hard yards of the Premier League (of which he had no experience at all), domestic cup football in England (which he seemed to ignore) and threats from the club's star player and local symbol Steven Gerrard that the young Scouser was leaving, right away, for rivals Chelsea. Clearly, it would not all be plain sailing for the new manager.

Gerrard eventually agreed to stay on at Liverpool, but Michael Owen left – for Real Madrid. The unknown Antonio Núñez joined Liverpool from Madrid to smooth the Owen deal. It was a difficult start. Benítez recruited, in Owen's place, Luis García, a talented if lightweight forward from Barcelona's reserves for £6 million, and also the £10 million 22-year-old midfielder Xabi Alonso from Real Sociedad. Alonso was a quality passer, a game-organiser not unlike Jan Mølby, but a man with much more mobility and tackling verve than the Dane. A man with one name only, Josémi, was also recruited from Málaga in Spain to play right-back, but he never convinced and was soon replaced by a late Houllier signing, the solid and consistent Ireland international defender Steve Finnan. Benítez was also stuck with Djibril Cissé, a forward Houllier had agreed to sign for a then club record fee of £14 million from Auxerre. Cissé was flaky and temperamental, the kind of forward who probably had the look of a pacy, powerful and daunting man in the French League, but who was bullied and clobbered by most British centre-halves he faced. It was a final Houllier mistake that effectively tied the new manager's hands. Benítez tried to loosen the binds in January 2005 by signing Fernando Morientes, a great striker in Spain but half a yard and some courage short for the game in England. Morientes also enjoyed too much the company of physiotherapists.

Initially, Benítez struggled in the league: he tried to rotate his squad in places it should not (and could not) be rotated, underestimating the capacity of any Premier League side at home to mug Liverpool – especially if his own team was stuffed full of still half-baked foreign recruits. It was a lesson the new manager found difficult to learn, especially as Arsenal, Manchester United and the recently funded Chelsea were all candidates now to win the league title. He would also need to learn the importance to English club supporters of the FA Cup: he fielded a weak Liverpool team at bleak Burnley in the third round in January 2005, and the Reds crumbled to a 0–1 reverse, young French full-back Traore scoring a comical back-heeled own goal. There was a near-hysterical reaction in the city to this humiliation and early calls for the manager's head. Better progress came in the League Cup, in which Liverpool eventually made it to the final in 2005 before losing out 2–3 to Mourinho's Chelsea. This rivalry was stoking up nicely: the flamboyant Portuguese versus the unflappable Spaniard – and it had a few miles to run yet.

In contrast to his league travails, Benítez excelled in the European arena, where he had more time to prepare tactically for a specific project in a setting he felt comfortable with and where he was less likely to come up against the sort of bludgeoning approach he was routinely encountering in the British game. There, physical force could smash up well-laid tactical plans. But he still ended up at the rear of the group-stage table in 2004–05, with Liverpool needing to beat the Greeks from Olympiacos by two clear goals at Anfield in the last match to be certain of qualifying for the knockout stages. Actually, Liverpool could barely have chosen more hospitable travellers – the Greeks had rarely secured a decent European result away from home. But the Brazilian master Rivaldo curled home a first-half free-kick, meaning Liverpool now needed three goals in reply and with a team full of inexperienced young players. They got them, the extraordinary Steven Gerrard completing a famous second-half comeback with a rocket past the hopelessly stranded Nikopolidis in the Greek goal.

Next up, Liverpool eased past the Germans from Bayer Leverkusen before an emotional couple of meetings loomed with Juventus, the first time the clubs had met since the terrible events back in 1985. Liverpool and its supporters tried to make their public apologies to the Italians at Anfield, before squeezing through with a 2–1 lead, courtesy of Hyypiä and Luis García, to take to Turin. In Italy, what looked like a tough task proved much hotter off the pitch than on it, with the Reds comfortably holding on for a near risk-free 0–0 draw. Returning from injury, Xabi Alonso was outstanding in organising Liverpool's resistance. It was much the same story at Stamford Bridge in the first leg of the semi-final v. Chelsea, which pitted Benítez against the self-proclaimed 'Special One'. Liverpool played for – and got – a cagey scoreless draw, hoping that the Anfield crowd might subdue a star-studded Chelsea back in the district of Liverpool 4. And this proved to be a magnificent tactical victory for the Liverpool manager over the two legs, little Luis García scoring the famous early 'goal that never was' at the Kop end and then the entire Liverpool crowd screaming cacophonously until the final whistle sounded.

There had been many, many wonderful football occasions at Anfield in the previous 113 years, of course: to celebrate the championship in 1906 against Sheffield United; the joyous scenes for the match against Stoke for another title in 1923; the news reaching Anfield from afar that the Reds had won the league again, in 1947; the 5–0 rout of Arsenal in 1964 to win Shankly's first championship; Inter Milan in 1965; Fairclough's European Cup night against St Etienne in 1977; the 5–0 destruction of Nottingham Forest in 1988; two amazing, gut-wrenching 4–3 evening Premier League matches with Newcastle United in the 1990s; and Gérard Houllier's emotional return from illness as Liverpool beat Roma 2–0 in the Champions League in March 2002. But surely there was nothing quite like this night. There was nothing like the noise and the celebrations and the pinch-yourself-is-it-really-happening exchanges around the city that followed. Twenty years on from the disgrace of Brussels, astonishingly, Liverpool Football Club was back in the European Cup final. There could never be another football night like this one – could there?

THE MIRACLE OF ISTANBUL

Of course, every Liverpool supporter has their own story to tell about Istanbul 2005: where we saw it; how we got there; what we did afterwards in the middle of the night; how we had all given up all hope at half-time. Everyone who was there will remember the chaotic organisation at a stadium built, literally, in the middle of nowhere. How lucky were UEFA that Liverpool won this final, thus deflecting criticism about the European body's continuing contempt for its customers? This epic contest against AC Milan was simply the most dramatic of all European Cup finals, possibly the greatest-ever major final, one that straddled Asia and Europe. It kicked off on one day and finished on another, and had just about *everything* in between. There have even been half-decent books written about this single match.[4] It was a game that raised all the difficult and controversial questions that had been simmering about the Liverpool manager. Should he be considered a tactical genius for turning around a three-goal half-time deficit against one of the best club sides in Europe? Or a stubborn fool for his hubris in making a huge tactical error, one from which he was eventually rescued only by the heart and unwillingness to accept defeat shown by his players? The debate will continue as long as this match is talked about.

Liverpool FC, European Cup-winning team, v. AC Milan, 25 May 2005

Dudek

Finnan (Hamann 46)   Carragher   Hyypiä   Traore

Gerrard   Alonso   Riise

García   Baroš (Cissé 85)   Kewell (Šmicer 23)

There is not much doubt that the vaunted Liverpool manager did err by leaving out Didi Hamann, his most experienced midfield defensive player, from Liverpool's starting line-up for the 2005 Champions League final. This move was so unexpected that when Hamann heard Benítez announce the side, he wondered why *Xabi Alonso* had been left out: the German's mind had blanked the fact that it was *his* name that was missing from his manager's team sheet.

This match had seemed like an unfair contest right from the start because Milan was stuffed with seasoned international stars – Cafu, Seedorf, Shevchenko, Pirlo, Maldini, Crespo, Gattuso, Kaká, Stam – while Liverpool were inexperienced greenhorns by comparison, especially without Hamann. The usually cautious Benítez had seemingly tried to outwit his rivals, who were expecting a dour Liverpool performance focused on counter-attacking. Instead, the Spaniard dispensed with his midfield shield and played the fragile Australian winger Harry Kewell, who had only just returned from injury. It was a typical piece of Benítez conceit, and this tactical gamble failed on all fronts. Kewell broke down in the first half, but Benítez stubbornly stuck to his favoured pattern by bringing on the attacking Czech international Vladimir Šmicer rather than his German midfielder. This woeful mistake simply compounded the manager's earlier selection blunder.

Without the experienced Hamann, Liverpool had no means of coping with the movement of the peerless young Brazilian Kaká, in a match that was far too open for Liverpool to manage. Milan scored in the first minute through Maldini and then ripped through the Reds for a 0–3 half-time lead, with two goals from Crespo, fashioned by Kaká. This looked like humiliation, a possible record scoreline in a major final. This was what some of the fans and key Liverpool players were now thinking: how to face their mates back home. What exactly happened at half-time remains contentious today. Did the Milan players celebrate prematurely, so provoking a murderous response from Liverpool? Did the defiant singing of the Liverpool fans raise the Reds' spirits to launch an irresistible second-half assault? Did Benítez rouse his men to a recovery of Lazarus proportions with a touch of tactical genius and some motivational inspiration? Or did none of these things really happen? Did Liverpool simply decide to 'have a go' at Milan in a typical piece of British football bloody-mindedness, just to see what might transpire when they had nothing left to lose?

Initially, at least, the Liverpool dressing-room seemed to be both devastated and chaotic. The players were in shock. The manager's first plan was to bring on Djibril Cissé for the outclassed Traore, to try to attack his way back into the contest. Who knows what might have happened next if this strategy had actually been followed? The young French full-back was already heading for the shower when it was discovered that the right-back Steve Finnan was injured, so Traore was reinstated. He played a blinding second half. Then Benítez decided to bring on *both* Hamann and Cissé, until it was pointed out that Liverpool now had 12 players in their new system. Some much needed clarity now struck home. Cissé would stay on the bench and Hamann *would* come on; Jamie Carragher would move to the right of what was effectively a back three, with Šmicer supporting in defence when needed. Gerrard would push further forward to support his attackers. At last this looked like a tenable plan, one to offer some scintilla of hope in a hopeless situation. Nobody in the Liverpool camp really believed it would work – except, perhaps, the great unwashed, the Liverpool army of despairing spectators.

But when Benítez restored the German Hamann at the interval, it looked too late; Milan continued to attack, and it seemed like they might score more goals. Benítez had essentially asked his players to try to score and then 'see what happens'. So much for scientific Continental tactics: Liverpool needed some old-fashioned British grit to unnerve their opponents and get back into this uneven contest. They also depended upon the fantastic support of the Reds fans, who just refused to give this up. Captain Steven Gerrard, inevitably, led the charge. Remarkably, Liverpool scored three times – Gerrard, Šmicer and Alonso – in six astounding second-half minutes. 'Six minutes' carries major symbolic importance for the Liverpool club, of course: in 1989, the disastrous Hillsborough FA Cup semi-final lasted only that long. Now the phrase 'six minutes' would have an additional, more joyous, meaning for a new generation of Liverpool supporters.

Visibly rattled, Milan, for all their international experience, could not reply. Dudek, the Liverpool goalkeeper, a modest Catholic man from Polish mining stock, saved point-blank from Shevchenko near the end of normal time and said later that some divine intervention had aided his resistance. Perhaps it also helped him deal with the mental torment of the penalties that followed? He did not need much help. Milan were drained, agog at the Liverpool fightback – it was the usually deadly Shevchenko who missed the vital kick. Liverpool Football Club had come back from the dead to win their fifth European Cup – their first under a foreign manager and with a largely foreign team. It was a miracle, aided from above, some wags claimed, by the Anfield Holy Trinity of Shankly, Paisley and Fagan. But without their two current Scouse rocks, Jamie Carragher and Steven Gerrard, and without the club's extraordinary supporters, none of this would have been remotely possible. Which left one key question: did Liverpool win the 2005 European Cup despite or because of the actions of their manager? Was Benítez inspired or just lucky? In football, history is written by winners.

STILL CHASING A DREAM

What could possibly follow this? Another severe bout of 'Gerrard is going' anxiety in the summer of 2005 and ambitions for winning the Premier League title, of course. In some circles, the Liverpool manager might have been nominated to join the Liverpool greats because of what happened in Istanbul, but he would never be fully accepted into the pantheon until he had conquered *all* the domestic peaks. He climbed another one in 2006. A small mountain, Peter Crouch, was brought in to help him, an unlikely stretched-out target man. Bolo Zenden also arrived, an experienced Dutch midfielder whom the manager tried, unsuccessfully, to sell to the Liverpool crowd by describing him as 'Middlesbrough's best player'. Momo Sissoko was signed up, a destructive Malian midfield player who Benítez had worked with in Spain and who achieved some brief cult status in Liverpool 4. But his poor technique was a vital flaw. Arriving too was a highly promising young Danish central defender called Daniel Munthe Agger from Brondby, though injury blighted his start with the club. Finally, there was even a romantic return to Liverpool for Robbie Fowler, a local folk hero who had been dispatched by Houllier to Leeds United in December 2001 for a crazily inflated £12 million fee and whom Benítez now embraced as a veteran forward option with impeccable Liverpool credentials. All these men had some quality, but some were too late in their careers and none of them were out-and-out successes at Liverpool.

As European champions, Liverpool contested FIFA's invented Club World Championship tournament in Japan in December 2005. The club had lost twice in Japan in the old World Club Championship (in 1981 and 1984) and had barely taken the matter seriously. In 1981, Bob Paisley warned his players to avoid bookings in the fixture because of their impact on much more important league matches. Things had changed in 20 years. Benítez showed something of his deep commitment to the club, and also his rather icy emotional baggage, by staying with his team in Japan even after news of his father's death in Spain. This tournament was a shabby event that intruded badly into the English League season and was palpably more important to the club for marketing purposes than because it had any serious football worth. But who would baulk at the title 'World Champions'? Liverpool lost 0–1 in the final in Yokohama to the South Americans São Paulo. Back in the real football world, meanwhile, the Reds eventually finished behind Chelsea and Manchester United in the Premier League, scoring a paltry 57 goals in the process, despite their new strikers.

But there were compensations. The Liverpool manager out-thought José Mourinho again in an FA Cup semi-final win at Old Trafford on 22 April 2006, immaculately sculpted by Luis García, which led to another Steven Gerrard-inspired dramatic final win in Wales, this time on penalties in the 2006 FA Cup final after a pulsating 3–3 draw with the luckless West Ham United. By now Gerrard was sorting out his gremlins, and he was assuming the mantle of one of the club's greatest-ever players, routinely dredging his team out of seemingly impossible situations, carrying inadequate colleagues and scoring vital goals.

He had every quality – power, technique, vision and coolness in front of goal – even if, as a shy man, he sometimes seemed to lack self-belief. Gerrard was also helping his manager stave off difficult press interviews. Saving the penalty kicks in Wales in 2006 was new Reds goalkeeper Pepe Reina, the Spanish son of a goalkeeper, brought in to replace the heroic – but occasionally slipshod – Jerzy Dudek. Indeed, what had also been astonishing about the 2005 Liverpool European Cup win was that it was the swansong for a group of players recruited under Houllier who had played vital roles in the final. Šmicer, Baroš and Dudek had all left the club immediately after Istanbul, and Hamann and Traore were reduced to minor roles.

In the summer of 2006, Benítez was offered yet more funds for transfers by the Liverpool board, if not (as he liked to point out) the vast sums afforded to those in charge at the two clubs that had just bettered his team in the league. In came Craig Bellamy, an unruly and unpredictable Welsh forward; Fábio Aurélio, a talented but brittle Brazilian full-back Benítez knew from Spain; Mark Gonzalez, a Chilean international winger the manager had chased for two years but who was quite unsuitable for the English game; Dirk Kuyt, a reputable and hard-working striker from Holland; and – a quite startling signing this – the very mundane right-sided forward Jermaine Pennant from the equally ordinary Birmingham City. The superior Argentinian international water-carrier Javier Mascherano joined later in the campaign, on loan from West Ham, to add defensive solidity to the Liverpool cause. He would eventually cost £17 million to keep. Collectively, these players did not seem to be signings designed to build a title-winning team, and although Liverpool again finished third in the Premier League in 2007 they now trailed by 21 points the title-winners Manchester United.

Benítez's counter to local criticism about continuing league failings was again in Europe, where the Reds comfortably saw off PSV Eindhoven, Bordeaux and Galatasaray in the Champions League group stages, won sensationally in Barcelona after Bellamy and Riise had publicly fallen out before the match, the former using a golf club as a preferred weapon, and then thumped PSV again to set up another meeting with Chelsea in the semi-finals. Remarkably, Rafa Benítez outsmarted José Mourinho for a third consecutive occasion in knockout play, with Liverpool winning 4–1 on penalties after each club had secured a 1–0 home win. Pepe Reina in Liverpool's goal was beginning to show all the class and assurance his manager had identified in him, and he was a demon to beat in penalty shoot-outs. But, alas, there was no happy ending, because in a near-chaotic setting in Athens, against the old enemies from 2005 AC Milan, Liverpool eventually lost 1–2.

The Milan side of 2007 was older and definitely weaker than it had been in 2005, which suggested, therefore, that the same might also be true for Liverpool. But a more ambitious approach from Benítez might well have brought another European Cup victory for the Reds, despite the flaws in the 2007 Liverpool squad. The perpetually underperforming Pennant got into great positions but failed to deliver, and leaving Peter Crouch on the bench for seventy-eight minutes, by which time Milan had established a crucial one-goal advantage, was certainly not the cautious Liverpool manager's finest hour.

The reputation of Liverpool's support was also later dragged through the mud by UEFA because of ticketless intrusions into another poorly organised venue. In short, it was business as usual in the European governing body. Two European Cup finals in three years was handsome compensation for failings in the league. But by now things happening off the field at Anfield were beginning to cloud the Liverpool manager's vision of his rightful place at the club. In fact, these developments in the Liverpool boardroom seemed to threaten the entire future of Liverpool Football Club.

CHAPTER 18 REFERENCES

1. Hopkins and Williams, 'Gérard Houllier and the New Liverpool Imaginary'
2. Williams, *The Liverpool Way*, p. 153
3. Fowler, *My Autobiography*, p. 298
4. Williams and Hopkins, *The Miracle of Istanbul*

EPILOGUE

THERE MUST BE SOME WAY OUT OF HERE
The Liverpool Ownership Crisis

THE MONEY GAME

L iverpool Football Club had now acquired an ambitious international manager who seemed imperious in Europe, if rather less certain at home. But the economics at the club still lagged behind developments on the field, and the ailing remnants of the Littlewoods empire could no longer provide the cash to build a new stadium and fund the team. In their search for finance to build a stadium on nearby Stanley Park, club chairman David Moores and chief executive Rick Parry had been keen to try to conserve as much as possible of the cultural heritage, the administration and the 'family ethos' of the Liverpool club. Ideally, the Liverpool Way built patiently over many generations of essentially conservative (and often Conservative) club stewardship, would remain intact and relatively unsullied. But despite this ambition and Liverpool's complex mix of parochialism and historical 'openness' as a city, the realisation that investment in Liverpool Football Club was now being sought from all corners of the globe made some fans – especially locally based supporters – understandably uneasy.

Back in May 2004, the billionaire prime minister of Thailand, Thaksin Shinawatra, had offered a £65-million investment for a 30 per cent stake in the Liverpool club, while a 'hostile' counter-offer of a reported £73 million had been placed on the table from local building magnate Steve Morgan to buy outright control of the club. Both offers were eventually rejected, Shinawatra's possibly because of rising public unease among fans about his alleged human-rights abuses in Thailand. Morgan's offer was at least made up of more local capital, but it was claimed by the Liverpool board to 'undervalue' the club. Morgan also, undoubtedly, posed a threat to the future at Liverpool of both Moores and Rick Parry.

In the light of the obvious difficulties involved in finding suitable new investors or owners for the club, other avenues were also tentatively explored by Liverpool, ones that stressed the local affinities of the club much more clearly. There had been discussions below the surface for some time on the potential for a shared stadium with neighbours and eternal rivals Everton FC. The Goodison Park club were also eyeing several potential sites for relocation (including the vacant King's Dock on the city's waterfront). Predictably, there continued to be vehement objections raised to the idea of a shared stadium from many diehard fans and elements within both club boardrooms, who viewed the proposal as little short of sacrilegious. More prosaically, a shared stadium would cut potential profits as well as costs, and where would the near-destitute Everton club come up with their share of the capital required for such a venture?

More than two years of searching later, Liverpool still had no new investment capital. Then a consortium representing Dubai International Capital (DIC), an arm of the Dubai government and ruling family, reportedly offered a total of £156 million for the purchase of all existing Liverpool shares, plus funds to cover debts and the building of a new stadium on nearby Stanley Park, a total package of around £450 million. The Liverpool board seemed keen to accept the Dubai bid, despite further human-rights concerns. However, just two months later, in February 2007, two American sports and property tycoons, Tom Hicks and George Gillett Jr, men who had never worked seriously together in business, raised the offer for the club to £5,000 a share, or £172 million, plus promised funds for a new stadium. The DIC group had earlier sneered that the 'soccer-phobic' Gillett would not know Liverpool FC from a 'hole in the ground', but it was now publicly furious at the sudden collapse in negotiations, describing the Liverpool board as 'dishonourable' and the club as 'a shambles'.

Liverpool chairman David Moores now had the onerous responsibility of weighing up the pros and cons of the American and Middle Eastern options. He eventually decided to take the plunge and agreed to sell his controlling stake to the US entrepreneurs. Rick Parry was quick to deny that Moores was being swayed by the increased offer for the club shares, saying: 'The price is not a factor in David Moores's mind. He is not after cash for himself, absolutely not. Be assured, the only thing David Moores is concerned about is the club being in the right hands for the future. You can be certain he has done his homework carefully and will make a decision in the best interests of the club.' Moores, himself, was determined to make it clear that he was selling up only to secure the long-term future of the club: 'When you have a decision to make like this and you are so desperate to see the club go into the right hands, then you have to be comfortable with whatever you decide.'

Moores would certainly be 'comfortable': he stood to raise his own cut of the club buyout by some £8 million, to a reported £89.6 million. He was also installed as honorary life president of the club in recognition of his decade-and-a-half service, and he was charged to act as something of a nominal 'boardroom delegate' for astonished Liverpool fans. David Moores might well have favoured passing on his Liverpool shares to the Americans for reasons other than profit. After all, these were two identifiable sports benefactors from across the Atlantic, people who understood the global sports business and who had money to invest, but who also had the club apparently at heart. These might have looked a better bet for a city with strong business and cultural links to the USA than a faceless and rather 'alien' corporate government body from the Middle East. And David Moores was hardly the first football-club chairman in England in the new era to profit from the sale of a club.

But what is more significant is that this profiteering seemed like a complete reversal of the history of the patrician and custodian local funding for Liverpool Football Club. Indeed, it seemed like an inversion of the entire Moores family project of long-term investment in the Merseyside football clubs and in the city of Liverpool itself over more than 70 years. This was a business deal typical of the new age of global liberalisation, one that plainly traduced the core tenets of the Liverpool Way. It was certainly unlikely to endear David Moores to Liverpool fans in 2007, even to those who approved, initially at least, of the American investment over that offered by the men from Dubai.

FISTFULS OF DOLLARS

Two American billionaires, Tom Hicks, owner of the Texas Rangers baseball franchise and the (US) National Hockey League's Dallas Stars, and George Gillett Jr, owner of the Montreal Canadiens and formerly of the Miami Dolphins, had cobbled together in just two months an unlikely alliance to secure a reported £470-million funding package, via a loan from the Royal Bank of Scotland, to buy Liverpool Football Club and to allocate some £215 million to begin work on a new stadium. Hicks, a Texas acolyte and former business partner of President George W. Bush, had made his fortune from raising private equity to fund multimillion-dollar corporate takeovers. Liverpool Football Club was suddenly in the hands of the sort of global sports capitalists who made no secret of their financial motives, their ignorance of 'soccer' or their ambitions to model this highly atypical English football club, commercially, along the lines of an NFL franchise. They openly highlighted the attractions of English football's booming TV monies, the growing Internet income streams for the English game, expanding markets for the Liverpool club in South-East Asia and in South America, stadium naming rights and even their plans for introducing American-style 'bunker suites' into the proposed new Liverpool stadium: underground 'living rooms' where corporate elites could dine in plush splendour and watch banks of TV sets before taking an elevator ride to their match seats. This seemed like 'Americanisation' writ large.

And yet local resistance on Merseyside to this cultural, as well as corporate, takeover of one of the city's core institutions was, for some commentators, surprisingly muted to say the least. This apparently benign reception for the Americans on Merseyside was mainly for four reasons. First, a realist resignation now existed among most Liverpool supporters that in the age of open borders non-local financing was inevitable for any football club with serious pretensions to be competitive for titles at home in England and in Europe. More knowledgeable (and, perhaps, more cynical) Liverpool fans could even make the appropriate historical connections here, about the origins of the club and the commercial hard-headedness of one of its great cultural leaders of the past, as 'Real Deep' told readers of *Through the Wind and Rain* in 2007:

> Haven't we been a plaything for the rich from day one, when we were formed, not for sporting reasons, but to fill a recently vacated Anfield and provide the owner John Houlding with a steady stream of income from both paying customers at the game and the sale of beer in the nearby hostelry? And *he* imported a whole troop of Scottish mercenaries to fill the team. [Bill] Shankly, if he ever stops spinning in his grave (to listen to some people), was quick to threaten to resign when not offered enough money in the transfer market . . . He was also happy to advocate a move away from a dilapidated Anfield.

Second, the cosmopolitan 'city of the sea' of Liverpool was no stranger, of course, to global cultural exchange or, more specifically, to American cultural and commercial investment. Indeed, for much of its history Liverpool had looked west to Ireland and the United States for guidance and inspiration on identity issues more than it had to other English cities. Near its height in the early years of the twentieth century, the port at Liverpool had provided direct employment for up to 60,000 people in the city, much of it in trade involving North America. Even before the First World War, Americans were envied in Liverpool for their supposed modernity and stylishness, and American fashions were imported by Liverpool tailors, who regularly copied clothes brought in by seamen from the eastern seaboard of the USA. Later, this maritime connection

– seamen on the passenger services to the USA were known locally as 'Cunard Yanks' – also fed directly into Liverpool street idioms and language, nightlife and music, with 'the most American of English cities' acting as a site of feverish transatlantic cultural exchange of a sort that allowed the city to take the lead in pop music in the world during the 1960s. In short, the city of Liverpool already had ingrained American sensibilities and sympathies well before Tom Hicks and George Gillett strode into Anfield early in 2007 with their 'good ole boy' homilies about 'tradition' and 'heritage' and their promises to make Liverpool FC the most successful football club in the world. Given the city's distinctive history, the possibility of transatlantic investment and exchange in football did not strike most of its citizens as an especially alien or threatening intrusion.

Third, allied to their obvious commercial savvy, the new Liverpool co-owners were experts in 'selling' themselves to the Liverpool supporters in the set-piece press conferences that followed. They showed little of the arrogance of the Glazer family at Manchester United, for example, who seemed to believe that money was its own explanation for their actions and who had made little attempt to engage with Manchester United fans. 'They are very private people,' said Tom Hicks of Malcolm Glazer and his family. 'I have owned sports teams for 13 years. I gave up my privacy a long time ago, and it is easier for me to be open about these things . . . He showed us how not to do it.'

With the Merseyside press acting largely as enthusiastic cheerleaders, crucially, the general assumption was that the Liverpool buyout would *not* involve the kind of leveraged deal that had loaded more than £600 million worth of Glazer debt onto the Manchester club. Indeed, in the offer document for the Liverpool club the Americans had made it very clear that any loans taken out to secure the deal would be personally guaranteed and that payment of any interest 'will not depend to any significant extent on the business of Liverpool'.

The new owners also cleverly, and rather humbly in this charm offensive, played back to the Liverpool club's supporters some of the familiar and comforting rhetoric about the club's past. 'We are custodians not owners of the franchise,' Gillett said, thus combining the Victorian Britain of John Houlding with the language of late-modern American sport and both reassuring and alarming Liverpool supporters simultaneously. It was left to David Moores to admit, 'I don't think we have maximised our world brand and hopefully they [Gillett and Hicks] will help us get into these areas where we have fantastic fan bases.' And it was George Gillett who coyly told the same group of journalists on 6 February 2007, 'I don't think it's appropriate for Tom or I to try to convince the fans today that we understand the history, the support or the legacy anywhere as well as they do. What we would try to say to the fans is that we have respect. Respect is the way we feel about the history and the legacy of this franchise [sic] . . . I am still learning about the club but I will get it into my blood in every way I can.'

Finally, another familiar device skilfully employed by the Americans and their advisers to mask some of the bleak economics of the deal was the notion of the Liverpool 'family'. The friendly Moores family dynasty – that had followed other Liverpool boardroom families – would now be seamlessly replaced by a transatlantic equivalent, made up of the Gilletts and the Hickses. This message about 'respect' and 'family values' was strongly reinforced in words and images in a commemorative booklet issued by Liverpool FC, carrying pictures of the American buyers and their adult sons at Anfield. It was almost as if the club had been acquired through marriage by some august royal family from a superior and distant culture. Gillett's son Foster would even come over to work inside the club on a day-to-day basis on an executive level with Rick Parry, while Tom Hicks Jr would join the club board. How, exactly, this arrangement would pan out remained a moot point, because it seemed full of potential tensions and conflict. By the end of the 2006–07 season, there were already reports that, smelling who now held the club purse strings, Liverpool manager Rafa Benítez had started to bypass Rick Parry and was talking directly to Foster Gillett in order to expedite transfers and other matters. Parry was now the self-appointed guardian of continuity and the main defender of the 'Liverpool Way' inside the club, but he was already starting to look increasingly and disturbingly isolated in the new Liverpool ownership structure.

THE BACK OF LOVE

This was the background against which, in May 2007, Liverpool had reached the European Cup (Champions League) final for the second time in three years. By the autumn of 2007, it had become clear that the American owners would have to renegotiate a new financial package worth £350 million with the Royal Bank of Scotland and the American investment bank Wachovia in order to pay off their original loans and raise cash to begin work on the Liverpool stadium. Revised plans for the new stadium insisted upon by the new owners had considerably increased its price, so proposals to raise a further £300 million for the funding of the new ground would now have to wait until 2009. Worse, despite their initial denials, the Liverpool owners now reportedly wanted to load the whole of the original acquisition debt of £298 million onto the club's balance sheet, thus replicating core aspects of the Glazer deal at Manchester

United. Gone was the earlier talk about 'respect' and the 'tradition' and the 'heritage' of the Liverpool club. Instead, Hicks chose to compare the purchase of Liverpool Football Club to that of a breakfast cereal company. 'When I was in the leverage buyout business, we bought Weetabix and we leveraged it up to make our return. You could say that anyone who was eating Weetabix was paying for our purchase of Weetabix. It was just business. It is the same for Liverpool: revenues come in from whatever source, and if there is money left over it is profit.'

The first element of the refinancing package was finally agreed in January 2008, with £105 million of the debt saddled on Liverpool and £185 million secured on a holding company, Kop Investment LLC, held in the tax havens off the Cayman Islands and in the US state of Delaware. These were the routine machinations of global capitalism in full flow. The Americans increased their personal guarantees, mainly in the form of credit notes, to around a reported £55 million. This suddenly looked like very deep financial water and not the sort of deal that Liverpool fans – or Moores and Parry – had anticipated. Added to this, a very public row over transfer funds between manager Rafa Benítez and Tom Hicks in November 2007 mobilised Liverpool spectators squarely behind the manager and against the new owners, sparking fan protests. By January 2008, any debates there might have been over the 'politics' of foreign ownership at Anfield had, for some fans, effectively been replaced by a stark pragmatism: broadsheet newspapers carried pictures of Kopites holding up a large home-made banner reading 'Yanks out, Dubai in. In Rafa we Love'. This position hardened still further when it was revealed that Parry, Hicks and Gillett had all secretly met with ex-Germany national coach Jürgen Klinsmann to discuss the managerial position at Liverpool should Benítez's position at the club become 'untenable'. The mood was changed decisively with this revelation. Moreover, despite repeated promises given by the new owners – and this was the main reason, after all, why the club had sought large investors – no visible progress had yet been made on building the proposed new Liverpool stadium.

Finally, as rumours began to circulate early in 2008 that DIC were considering a new £500 million offer for the club, it was clear that Hicks and Gillett were no longer in direct communication with each other nor could they agree on the future of Liverpool Football Club. Gillett looked as if he might be willing to sell his share of the club, possibly to DIC, while Hicks publicly demanded the resignation of the 'failing' Rick Parry. Parry would soon leave as the club began to look like a laughing stock and its borrowings were reported to be some £313 million. David Moores was pronounced to be 'disgusted' at Parry's treatment, and he retired from the Liverpool board in June 2009, saying he was 'heartbroken' at how the new owners had treated the club. At the same time, Merseyside MPs called for the British government to resist an application from the Americans for a loan of £350 million from the majority government-owned Royal Bank of Scotland. Liverpool Football Club, once a model of conservative and unobtrusive stability in the English game, suddenly seemed to be impossibly split, rudderless and constantly in the public eye. Public protests organised by the Spirit of Shankly group continued to occur in the city into the 2009–10 league season, as the Liverpool owners were reputed to be looking for new Middle Eastern investors in the club.

IN TORRES WE TRUST

Despite all this hugely distracting background noise and lack of focus and direction off the field, the Liverpool manager Benítez had soldiered on and had continued to strengthen his team and his squad by bringing in a number of differential quality signings in the summer of 2007. Yossi Benayoun was among them, a skilful and intelligent Israeli wide midfielder. Benayoun had real ability, some speed, mental strength and loads of energy – and he could also score goals. He was the signing Liverpool should so obviously have made when Benítez brought in the soon to be discarded Pennant. The Israeli might even have helped secure a second European Cup for Benítez in 2007.

The much-hyped but pedestrian Brazilian midfield man Lucas Leiva joined from Grêmio in Brazil, having won the coveted Bola de Ouro (Golden Ball) for being the best young player in the 2006 Brazilian championship. He would take time to settle – perhaps he never would. Ryan Babel, another highly rated young star, joined from Ajax for £11.5 million, and he could score extraordinary goals. But the forward seemed destined to be better known for his 'romps' with serial Liverpool 'WAG' Danielle Lloyd than he would be for incisive and courageous play for his club. He lacked technique and heart and seemed destined, at best, for the fringes of the Benítez project.

But the signature signing was the £20-million capture of the Atlético Madrid centre-forward Fernando Torres on a six-year deal in July 2007, with Luis García joining the Madrid club. Benítez had built a successful team at Valencia without a major goalscorer, but his Liverpool side had lacked this sort of flexibility and range of goal contributors. Peter Crouch scored only in spurts, and Dirk Kuyt had reinvented himself as a right midfielder when goals had evaded him in England. So the manager brought in a man who pretty much guaranteed front-end goals. Torres was already a major football figure in Madrid, a man who had been made Atlético captain at 19, so he had some maturity and a sense of responsibility to the collective as well as the necessary selfishness of an authentic frontman. He also had power and threatening pace and was a brilliant finisher. He had turned down a move to Chelsea in 2006, and the only question mark was how he would stand up to the sheer physicality of the English game. Could he stay fit and committed in the hurly-burly of the English Premier League? He showed some early signs that at home, with Liverpool on the front foot, he could be consistently lethal, while away from home he sometimes lost a little enthusiasm if defenders were allowed to buffet him and Liverpool were under the cosh. But this is carping about a player with such talents.

In his first season, and playing in concert with a supporting Steven Gerrard, Torres showed exactly why the Liverpool manager had signed him and why he had joined Pepe Reina and Xabi Alonso as one of Benítez's three gold-standard Liverpool signings. Torres scored 24 goals in 33 league games, the first Red since Robbie Fowler to score 20 or more in the league, and a record for a debut season for a foreign striker in England. In February and March 2008, he became the first Liverpool player since Jackie Balmer in 1946 to score consecutive Anfield league hat-tricks (v. Middlesbrough and West Ham). When he scored the home winner v. Manchester City on 4 May 2008, Torres equalled Roger Hunt's club record of scoring in eight consecutive league matches at Anfield.

The Madrid man ended up by scoring 33 goals in 46 matches in all competitions in his first season, and he could now already be added to the post-war list of truly great Liverpool goalscorers that included Hunt, Rush, Fowler and Michael Owen. This was all good news, of course, but the fitness of Torres seemed an enduring problem. And wider doubts about Benítez and his policies persisted. The manager was at odds, for example, with the club's youth policy, even though Liverpool academy director Steve Heighway had managed to produce *two* recent FA Youth Cup-winning sides out of the Liverpool youngsters. These two men clearly cared little for each other and had very different views on youth team football. Heighway wanted to raise mainly local talent in a caring and supporting environment, and he thought that some of his young stars should have been getting more of a chance in the Liverpool senior squad. How else could you offer incentives to local young players? Benítez, however, wanted to recruit globally and thought the academy was producing sub-standard products ill-prepared for the intensity of the Premier League. Heighway soon left the club, muttering darkly about the loss of important Liverpool FC traditions.

Another low point – and these doubts never fully went away – was when in February 2008 a rotated Liverpool side, excluding Torres and other senior players, abjectly lost 1–2 at home in the FA Cup to the modest Championship club Barnsley. This kind of submission – an invitation to defeat in a competition the club had spent years trying to win – was intolerable for Liverpool supporters who were hungry for more success at home. Benítez seemed to care little for the domestic cups, and his raft of expensively recruited young global squad members seemed little better than the local men who had been patiently raised by Steve Heighway. A number of these imports – the £2-million Argentinian centre-back Paletta among them – represented appalling squander. Later, however, in a generally fretful season, the money-well-spent Fernando Torres almost got Liverpool to another Champions League final with an equalising goal at Stamford Bridge (where else?) in the semi-final second leg in 2008, but at last it was the turn of Chelsea to slide past the Reds to reach the final, only to be defeated in Moscow by Manchester United.

THE TRIALS OF RAFA BENÍTEZ

The Liverpool manager had now assembled his talented Spanish spine – a great goalscorer, a sophisticated midfield organiser and a world-class goalkeeper. Also his key English midfielder Steven Gerrard seemed truly settled for the first time, and the Scouse Carragher was solid at the back. Benítez had signed some centre-back cover in the shape of Martin Škrtel from Zenit St Petersburg in January 2008 for £6.5 million, and the manager was given more money to invest in the summer of that year. At last this was looking like a real championship squad in the making. Some judicious recruitment now and Liverpool would surely run the others very close. But Rafa's spending in 2008 was mysterious and his targets proved, ultimately, to be self-destructive. In some strange ways, chasing the very competent and model professional Gareth Barry from Aston Villa was analogous to Roy Evans signing Stan Collymore in the mid-1990s, because it would eventually have the same sort of corrosive impact on the Liverpool team. Barry was highly rated and an excellent team player, but Benítez crassly let it be known that he was willing to sell the pivotal Xabi Alonso to bring in the Villa man. Not only did it seem like poor management to try to offload his key midfield organiser, but all this took place long *before* Barry was a confirmed capture, and in the end the England international stayed in the West Midlands. Predictably, Alonso decided he would leave Liverpool when the next chance came – which was for Real Madrid in the summer of 2009 for £30 million. Steven Gerrard, for one, was 'devastated' by Alonso's departure.

Benítez compounded this error by signing, for an inflated £20-million fee, Robbie Keane from Spurs to replace the disillusioned and little-used Peter Crouch, then wondering how to fit the Irishman into his Liverpool side. The manager seemed almost immediately unimpressed by what he had bought, and he started to leave the new man out, even after impressive performances.

Stripped of any confidence, the intelligent Liverpool-supporting Keane returned to White Hart Lane soon after for a hefty loss. This left a title-chasing Liverpool squad with little experienced forward cover for the fragile Fernando Torres in the second half of the season. Left-winger Albert Riera joined his Spanish international mates at Anfield, but he had already tried – and failed – to make it in England at Manchester City. Riera seemed to lack pace and a little heart, omissions not recommended in the Premier League.

Finally, Liverpool's first-ever Italian signing, international left-back Andrea Dossena, joined the club from Udinese for around £7 million in July 2008 as a direct replacement for John Arne Riise. On paper, this looked like good business: the top Italians are usually very good defenders, men with a cynical edge. But Dossena seemed to have little of what competent defenders needed in England: he lacked speed, good positional play, height, power and tackling ability. He seemed slightly better going forward than defending, but he also struggled for a decent final ball. Had the Liverpool scouts even been watching the right man? The Italian soon became despondent and virtually sank from view. When Glen Johnson arrived at Anfield in the summer of 2009, it was noted that the England international picked up Dossena's number-2 shirt and the Italian was allocated the rather marginal number 38. He returned to Italy in January 2010.

Despite these problems and misjudgements, this was very nearly a great Liverpool season, and very nearly the league title at last. Benítez still struggled in the domestic cup competitions – falling to Everton in the FA Cup – but in the Champions League there were two famous wins, home and away, against a tepid Real Madrid before Liverpool fell again to Chelsea, despite a 4–4 draw at Stamford Bridge. Only two league matches were lost by the Reds all season, unluckily at Tottenham and predictably at Middlesbrough, where the Reds manager fielded a quite incomprehensible line-up for such an important fixture, including a debut for a raw young French-born Moroccan forward Nabil El Zhar. Liverpool lost 0–2, and Middlesbrough were eventually relegated. Against the other three top-four sides, Liverpool were actually unbeaten, defeating both Chelsea and Manchester United home and away, with the latter being crushed 4–1 at Old Trafford. This sort of away resilience in difficult locations was a major improvement on recent Benítez seasons. But injuries to Torres and an inability to break down the defences of moderate opposition at Anfield cost Liverpool dear. Another extraordinary 4–4 draw, this time at home to Arsenal in April – with the excellent Andrei Arshavin scoring all four goals for the visitors – effectively ended the title race. It was a sobering thought that what Liverpool had spent on the meek and unproven Ryan Babel was very close to what Arsenal had paid for the Russian captain. Meanwhile, Manchester United were now level with Liverpool on 18 league titles won.

A MAN FOR ALL SEASONS?

After six full seasons at Anfield, assessments of Rafa Benítez still varied wildly on Merseyside. For some, his tactical awareness and his achievements in 2005 and 2006 put the manager almost beyond criticism. The duplicity and instability of the new Liverpool owners was also argued to have put the manager in an impossible position; it had on occasions certainly deflected anger that might otherwise have been aimed at the Liverpool boss. For others, Benítez remained just too cautious and too uneven in his judgement of players to ever forge a title-winning squad at Anfield. His substitutions and player selection still mystified. In season 2009–10, Liverpool seemed to have a first XI capable of beating any in the Premier League, but they lacked the sort of depth and squad balance that was now necessary to be truly competitive across a number of fronts. Back-up forwards recruited by Benítez, such as the Ukrainian Andriy Voronin, did little to excite Liverpool fans or suggest that the Liverpool boss yet knew what was required to make a convincing top-level squad in England. How much had really changed at Anfield since 2005 when the manager first came to the city on the bounce from Valencia? Most of those players who now made up the crucial fringes around the Liverpool first XI were Rafa Benítez signings. The new economics of English football also meant that clubs such as Manchester City, Aston Villa and Tottenham would be strongly challenging for top-four places in 2009–10. Things were getting more difficult.

'Big Four' net transfer spending 2004–05 to 2009–10 (millions)

	2004–05	2005–06	2006–07	2007–08	2008–09	2009–10
Liverpool	-31.05	-23.4	-32.85	-23.3	-6.45	-4.95
Chelsea	-87.6	-32.1	-37.7	-13.5	-6.8	-22.0
Manchester United	-20.3	-13.5	- 2.9	-24.0	-33.1	+66.5
Arsenal	-2.55	-5.0	-0.7	+19.9	-20.75	+31.0

Source: Sunday Times, *25 October 2009*

The claims from Benítez that he had simply been outspent by all the other top clubs since 2004 were challenged by the facts. The evidence was that Abramovich's Chelsea was the only major club in England to have outspent

Liverpool over the Benítez era, by £186 million to £122 million, and that Benítez had spent an average of £20 million over income for each season he had been in charge at Anfield. Manchester United's net spend over the same six-season period was just £27 million (after the 2009 sale of Ronaldo), and Arsène Wenger at Arsenal had actually made a net *profit* on deals over this period of around £27 million. What was also different about Benítez was that he had signed a total of 23 players who had cost a fee of £3 million or less, hardly any of whom had succeeded at the club. This attempt at shrewd investment was actually mostly money wasted, and Liverpool were reported to have had as many as sixty-two professional players on the club's books at one stage.

A group stage exit from the Champions League and a crucial failure to qualify for the 2010–11 Champions League also counted against the Spaniard. So too did an attitude to away fixtures that had begun to border on the paranoid. At around 3.45 p.m. on Thursday, 3 June, what had seemed increasingly inevitable finally happened: after six seasons in charge, Rafael Benítez was sacked by the Liverpool board, paid off with a promised £6 million booty.

Few could doubt Benítez's commitment to Liverpool Football Club or indeed the huge problems he had recently faced in managing successfully under his uninterested, absent American owners. But in the end, it was his judgement of players, his incapacity to build and keep a balanced elite squad, Liverpool's increasingly inert showings away from Anfield and perhaps Benítez's personal difficulties in relating effectively to top professional footballers that were his undoing. Xabi Alonso had once said about Benítez that few players really 'enjoyed' being managed by him, but they instantly missed his influence when he left. Perhaps that would be Liverpool's fate and Benítez's legacy: free, for now, from the paralysing disappointments of the recent past, but also facing an increasingly uncertain future in highly unstable times.

In the summer of 2010, Liverpool was at another of those crucial junctures in its eventful history. Having finally moved on, in 1998, from the Anfield boot-room legacy represented by Roy Evans to the age of the foreign technocrat, but with no league titles to show for their adventure, the new Liverpool executive of managing director Christian Purslow and chairman Martin Broughton now had a doubly tough task. They had to sell the club to a rich and responsible buyer *and* recruit a credible new manager. Some foreign talent was briefly reviewed, but the eventual Liverpool solution was to combine in one man some traditional British stability and football knowhow with a convincing Continental veneer.

Roy Hodgson, a 62-year-old multilingual English coach, had done more than Rafa in 2010 by taking lowly Fulham to the Europa League final and he was tipped in some quarters as a likely successor to the faltering Fabio Capello as the next England manager. Hodgson had no Champions League or Premier League title pedigree to talk about, but he had successfully coached abroad and was widely respected in the game and by journalists. He also promised a release from the rather austere man-management approach of Rafa Benítez. Hodgson was something of a football intellectual – he had once compared his career to a painting by the abstract modernist Russian artist Wassily Kandinsky – but he was also more likely than Benítez to put a caring arm around players who needed it and to offer press conferences filled with more than the banalities typically served up by the Spaniard. Finally, Hodgson promised to deliver rather more interesting football. It was a surprisingly sensible managerial choice, one that gently harked back to the more successful traditions of the club.

The avuncular and likeable Hodgson certainly had plenty on his plate. Key Liverpool players were said to be unsure about staying at Anfield and the new Reds manager would have to cope with the financial uncertainty that still mired the club: its debts had risen to over £351 million. Hodgson would need to recruit new coaching staff at Melwood, while rooting out some of the unwanted buys made by Benítez and getting the Liverpool Academy functioning effectively once more. He would need to sell players to bring in his own selections. To all this patient and necessary work would be added the uncomfortable fact that nearly every Liverpool supporter would be crying out immediately for trophies. It was another new direction in the search for what 30 years ago had seemed like the norm: Liverpool football club as league champions. It was difficult not to wish this decent man at the pinnacle of his career a reasonable period of tolerance and a fair wind; he would surely need it.

THE BEST-EVER LIVERPOOL TEAM?

So, how can we wind up this astonishing football story so far? Perhaps by musing about which players, over the entire history of the club, might make up its greatest team. This selection is made much more difficult by the differences between the eras in which these great Liverpool players played. How do you sensibly make comparisons? After all, the brilliant Billy Liddell spent much of his Liverpool career playing in the Second Division. Surely, some will argue, all the real Liverpool greats played in the 1970s and '80s, when the club won title after title and trophy after trophy? Perhaps this is true. Certainly, players of the stature of Souness, Neal, Clemence, Keegan, Rush and Barnes would get into many current Liverpool supporters' best Liverpool side. They all have strong cases, and they all are very close to being in mine.

But the only way to attempt, with any seriousness, this type of entertaining parlour game is to examine, historically, the impact of players from across different eras. We need to look at quality, of course, but also the relationship of players with the Liverpool fans, the longevity of their service to Liverpool Football Club and the opposition they face from other Liverpool greats in their respective positions. That is exactly what I have tried to do here, balancing the whole history of the club against that great period of 1970s and '80s Liverpool dominance.

By looking at the club in this way, it is quite possible to come up with something of an 'alternative' – but I would claim plausible – great Liverpool team to the one that is usually picked by most commentators and supporters today. That is what I have done here – just to get the arguments started. I have selected one current Liverpool player, Steven Gerrard, who seems to me to have been as influential and important over the past decade as any player has been at the club in any period of its existence. Other recent players – Sami Hyypiä, for one – also have their supporters, and Fernando Torres might yet become a Liverpool great. I have selected Bill Shankly as manager over Bob Paisley simply because the former built great Liverpool teams out of the depths of the Second Division in 1959, while the latter inherited and built upon a winning formula. The side set out below can play in a 4–2–4 or a 4–4–2 formation. The dates included here refer to their periods as players at Liverpool Football Club. Have fun with this selection – it might differ a lot from your own.

Liverpool FC's greatest-ever team? 1892–2010

Manager: Bill Shankly; Asst: Tom Watson

E. Scott
(1912–34)

E. Longworth A. Hansen E. Hughes D. McKinlay
(1910–28) (1977–90) (1967–79) (1910–29)

A. Raisbeck S. Gerrard
(1898–1909) (1995–)

I. Callaghan K. Dalglish R. Hunt W. Liddell
(1960–1978) (1977–91) (1959–69) (1939–61)

BIBLIOGRAPHY
Sources and Useful Reading

A'Court, A., *Alan A'Court: My Life in Football*, The Bluecoat Press, 2003

Allt, N., *The Boys from the Mersey: The Story of the Annie Road End Crew*, Milo Books, 2004

Allt, N. (ed.), *Here We Go Gathering Cups in May*, Canongate, 2007

Bale, B., *The Shankly Legacy*, Breeden Books, 1996

Belchem, J. (ed.), *Liverpool 800: Culture, Character and History*, Liverpool City Council and Liverpool University Press, 2006

Belchem, J., 'Celebrating Liverpool', in Belchem, J. (ed.), *Liverpool 800: Culture, Character and History*, Liverpool City Council and Liverpool University Press, 2006

Belchem, J. and MacRaild, D., 'Cosmopolitan Liverpool', in Belchem, J. (ed.), *Liverpool 800: Culture, Character and History*, Liverpool City Council and Liverpool University Press, 2006

Blows, K., *Terminator: The Authorised Julian Dicks Story*, Polar Publishing, 1996

Booth, K., *The Father of Modern Sport: The Life and Times of Charles W. Alcock*, The Parrs Wood Press, 2002

Bowler, D., *Shanks: The Authorised Biography of Bill Shankly*, Orion, 1996

Carter, N., *The Football Manager: A History*, Routledge, 2006

Chinn, C., *Better Betting with a Decent Feller: A Social History of Bookmaking*, Aurum Press, 2005

Collins, T., *Rugby's Great Split: Class, Culture and the Origins of Rugby League Football*, Cass, 1998

Corbett, J., *Everton: The School of Science*, Macmillan, 2003

Corbett, J., 'Shankly: Forgotten Man', in *Observer Sports Monthly*, November 2009

Cowley, J., *The Last Game: Love, Death and Football*, Simon and Schuster, 2009

Dalglish, K., *Dalglish: My Autobiography*, Hodder & Stoughton, 1996

Dohren, D., *The Ghost on the Wall: The Authorised Biography of Roy Evans*, Mainstream Publishing, 2004

Doig, E. and Murphy, A., *The Essential History of Liverpool*, Headline, 2003

Du Noyer, P., *Liverpool Wondrous Place: Music from the Cavern to the Coral*, Virgin Books, 2004

Fishwick, N., *English Football and Society: 1910–1950*, Manchester University Press, 1989

Foot, J., *Calcio: A History of Italian Football*, Fourth Estate, 2006

Fowler, R., *My Autobiography*, Macmillan, 2005

Gill, K., *The Real Bill Shankly*, Trinity Mirror Sports Media, 2006

Hale, S. and Ponting, I., *Liverpool in Europe*, Carlton Books, 1992

Harding, J., *Football Wizard: The Story of Billy Meredith*, Breedon Books, 1985

Hargreaves, I., Rogers, K. and George, R., *Liverpool: Club of the Century*, Liverpool Echo Publications, 1988

Harvey, D., *Football: The First Hundred Years – The Untold Story*, Routledge, 2005

Hewison, D., *The Liverpool Boys Are in Town: The Birth of Terrace Culture*, The Bluecoat Press, 2008

Hey, S., *Liverpool's Dream Team*, Mainstream Publishing, 1997

Hill, D., *Out of his Skin: The John Barnes Phenomenon*, WSC Books, 2001

Hill, J., 'Rite of Spring', in Hill, J. and Williams, J. (eds), *Sport and Identity in the North of England*, Keele University Press, 1996

Holt, O., *If You Are Second You Are Nothing: Ferguson and Shankly*, Macmillan, 2006

Holt, R., *Sport and the British: A Modern History*, Oxford University Press, 1989

Hopcraft, A., *The Football Man*, Cox & Wyman, 1968

Hopkins, S. and Williams, J., 'Gérard Houllier and the New Liverpool Imaginary', in J. Williams et al. (eds), *Passing Rhythms: Liverpool FC and the Transformation of Football*, Berg, 2001, pp. 173–94

Huggins, M. and Williams, J., *Sport and the English: 1918–1939*, Routledge, 2006

Hughes, S., *Secret Diary of a Liverpool Scout*, Sport Media, 2009

Inglis, S., *The Football Grounds of Great Britain*, CollinsWillow, 1985

Inglis, S., *Football Grounds of Britain*, CollinsWillow, 1987

Inglis, S., *League Football and the Men Who Made It*, Willow Books, 1988

Inglis, S., *Played in Manchester: The Architectural Heritage of a City at Play*, English Heritage, 2004

Inglis, S., *Engineering Archie: Archibald Leitch –Football Ground Designer*, English Heritage, 2005

Jackson, J., 'The Witnesses', *The Observer*, 2 April 2005

Jones, C.D. (ed.), *The Social Survey of Merseyside Vol. 3*, Liverpool Corporation, 1934

Jones, S., *Sport, Politics and the Working Class*, Manchester University Press, 1988

Joyce, M., *Football League Players' Records 1888 to 1939*, Soccer Data, 2004

Keith, J., *Shanks for the Memory*, Robson Books, 1998

Keith, J., *Bob Paisley: Manager of the Millennium*, Robson Books, 1999

Keith, J., *Billy Liddell: The Legend Who Carried the Kop*, Robson Books, 2003

Keith, J., *Dixie Dean: The Inside Story of a Football Icon*, Sport Media, 2005

Kelly, S., *Idle Hands, Clenched Fists: The Depression in a Shipyard Town*, Spokesman, 1987

Kelly, S., *The Kop: The End of an Era*, Mandarin, 1993

Kelly, S., *Rotation, Rotation, Rotation*, Heroes Publishing, 2008

Kennedy, A. and Williams, J., *Kennedy's Way: Inside Bob Paisley's Liverpool*, Mainstream Publishing, 2004

Kennedy, D., 'Class, Ethnicity and Civic Governance: A Social Profile of Football Club Directors on Merseyside in the Late Nineteenth Century', *The International Journal of the History of Sport*, Vol. 22 (5), 2005

Kennedy, D., 'Locality and Professional Football Club Development: The Demographics of Football Club Support in Late-Victorian Liverpool', *Soccer and Society*, Vol. 5 (3), 2004

Kennedy, D. and Collins, M., 'Community Politics in Liverpool and the Governance of Professional Football in the Late Nineteenth Century', *The Historical Journal*, Vol. 49 (3), 2006

Kennedy, D. and Kennedy, P., 'Ambiguity, Complexity and Convergence: The Evolution of Liverpool's Irish Football Clubs', *The International Journal of the History of Sport*, Vol. 24 (7), 2007

Kirby, D., 'Rome, 1977', in Allt, N. (ed.), *Here We Go Gathering Cups in May*, Canongate, 2007

Leigh, S., *The Cavern: The Most Famous Club in the World*, SAF Publishing, 2008

Liddell, B., *My Soccer Story*, Stanley Paul, 1960

Liversedge, S., *Liverpool: From the Inside*, Mainstream Publishing, 1995

Liversedge, S., *Liverpool, We Love You!*, Soccer Books Limited, 1997

Lloyd, L., *Larry Lloyd: Hard Man, Hard Game*, John Blake Publishing, 2008

Lupson, P., *Thank God for Football!!*, Azure, 2006

Lupson, P., *Across the Park: Everton FC and Liverpool FC Common Ground*, Sportsmedia, 2009

McGregor, W., 'The League and the League System' (1906), in Leatherdale, C. (ed.), *The Book of Football: A Complete History and Record of the Association and Rugby Games*, Desert Island Books, 1997

Macilwee, M., *The Gangs of Liverpool*, Milo Books, 2006

Macilwee, M., *Tearaways: More Gangs of Liverpool 1890–1970*, Milo Books, 2008

Marne, P., 'Whose Public Space Was It Anyway? Class, Gender and Ethnicity in the Creation of Sefton and Stanley Parks, Liverpool: 1858–1872', *Social and Cultural Geography*, Vol. 2 (4), 2001

Mason, T., *Association Football and English Society 1863–1915*, Harvester, 1980

Mason, T., 'The Blues and the Reds: A History of the Liverpool and Everton Football Clubs', *The History Society of Lancashire and Cheshire*, No. 134, 1985

Matthews, T., *Who's Who of Liverpool*, Mainstream Publishing, 2006

Milne, G., 'Maritime Liverpool', in Belchem, J. (ed.), *Liverpool 800: Culture, Character and History*, Liverpool City Council and Liverpool University Press, 2006

Munck, R. (ed.), *Reinventing the City? Liverpool in Comparative Perspective*, Liverpool University Press, 2003

Murden, J., 'City of Change and Challenge', in Belchem, J. (ed.), *Liverpool 800: Culture, Character and History*, Liverpool City Council and Liverpool University Press, 2006

Nicholls, A., *Scally: The Story of a Category C Football Hooligan*, Milo Books, 2002

Overy, R., *The Morbid Age: Britain Between the Wars*, Allen Lane, 2009

Page, S., *Herbert Chapman: The First Great Manager*, Heroes Publishing, 2006

Pead, B., *Liverpool: A Complete Record 1982–1990*, Breedon Books, 1990

Physick, R., *Played in Liverpool: Charting the Heritage of a City at Play*, English Heritage, 2007

Ponting, I. and Hale, S., *Sir Roger: The Life and Times of Roger Hunt*, Bluecoat Press (undated)

Pooley, C., 'Living in Liverpool: The Modern City', in Belchem, J. (ed.), *Liverpool 800: Culture, Character and History*, Liverpool City Council and Liverpool University Press, 2006

Preston, T., 'The Origins and Development of Association Football in the Liverpool District *c*.1879–*c*.1915', PhD thesis, University of Central Lancashire, 2007

Reade, B., *43 Years with the Same Bird: A Liverpool Love Affair*, Macmillan, 2005

Reed, P., *Football and Fortunes: The Inside Story of the Littlewoods Football Pools, 1923–2003*, Brahm Ltd, 2003

Rippon, A., *Gas Masks for Goal Posts: Football in Britain During the Second World War*, Sutton Publishing, 2005

Rollin, J., *Rothman's Book of Football Records*, Headline, 1998

Rollin, J., *Soccer at War: 1939–45*, Headline, 2005

Rous, S., *Football Worlds: A Lifetime in Sport*, Faber and Faber, 1978

Russell, D., *Football and the English: A Social History of Association Football in England, 1863–1995*, Carnegie Publications, 1997

Russell, D., *Looking North: Northern England and the National Imagination*, Manchester University Press, 2004

St John, I., *The Saint: My Autobiography*, Hodder & Stoughton, 2005

Sampson, K., 'Brussels, 1985', in Allt, N. (ed.), *Here We Go Gathering Cups in May*, Canongate, 2007

Sandbrook, D., *Never Had It So Good: A History of Britain from Suez to the Beatles*, Abacus, 2006

Sanders, R., *Beastly Fury: The Strange Birth of English Football*, Bantam Press, 2009

Scraton, P., *Hillsborough: The Truth*, Mainstream Publishing, 1999

Shankly, B., *Shankly*, Book Club Associates, 1977

Smith, T., *Anfield Iron: The Autobiography*, Bantam Press, 2008

Taw, T., *Football's War and Peace: The Tumultuous Season of 1946–7*, Desert Island Books, 2003

Taw, T., *Football's Twelve Apostles: The Making of the League: 1886–1889*, Desert Island Books, 2006

Taylor, I., 'English Football in the 1990s: Taking Hillsborough Seriously?', in

Williams, J. and Wagg, S. (eds), *British Football and Social Change*, Leicester University Press, 1991

Taylor, M., *The Leaguers: The Making of Professional Football in England, 1900–1939*, Liverpool University Press, 2005

Taylor, M., *The Association Game: A History of British Football*, Pearson Longman, 2008

Taylor, R. and Ward, A., *Three Sides of the Mersey: An Oral History of Everton, Liverpool and Tranmere Rovers*, Robson Books, 1993

Tischler, S., *Footballers and Businessmen: The Origins of Professional Football in England*, Holmes & Meier Publishing, 1981

Ward, A. and Williams, J., 'Bill Shankly and Liverpool', in J. Williams et al. (eds), *Passing Rhythms: Liverpool FC and the Transformation of Football*, Berg, 2001

Ward, A. and Williams, J., *Football Nation: Sixty Years of the Beautiful Game*, Bloomsbury, 2009

Whannel, G., *Fields in Vision: Television Sport and Cultural Transformation*, Routledge, 1992

Williams, G., *The Code War: English Football Under Historical Spotlight*, Yore Publications, 1994

Williams, J., 'Ian Rush', in Stead, P. and Williams, H. (eds), *For Club and Country: Welsh Football Greats*, University of Wales Press, 2000

Williams, J., *Into the Red: Liverpool FC and the Changing Face of English Football*, Mainstream Publishing, 2001

Williams, J., *The Liverpool Way: Houllier, Anfield and the New Global Game*, Mainstream Publishing, 2003

Williams, J. et al. (eds), *Passing Rhythms: Liverpool FC and the Transformation of Football*, Berg, 2001

Williams, J. and Hopkins, S., *The Miracle of Istanbul*, Mainstream Publishing, 2005

Williams, J. and Llopis, R., *Rafa: Rafa Benítez, Anfield and the New Spanish Fury*, Mainstream Publishing, 2007

Wilson, J., *Inverting the Pyramid: A History of Football Tactics*, Orion Books, 2008

Wilson, J., *All Change at Anfield: Liverpool's First Five Seasons*, Now and Then Publications (undated)

Young, P., *Football on Merseyside*, Stanley Paul, 1963

INDEX

Accrington 29, 33
A'Court, Alan 279, 281, 289, 304, 310, 313, 323
admission charges 226, 251
Agger, Daniel 402
AIK (Sweden) 254–5
Ainsley, George 216
Alavés 392–3
Aldridge, John 373–4
Allan, George 64, 68, 70, 75, 76
Alonso, Xabi 397, 398, 399, 401, 413, 414, 418
Anderlecht 327
Anderson, Eric 281
Anfield Road stadium 26–7, 61–2, 101–3, 108, 110, 148, 165, 360
  boys' pen 165, 238, 256
  Centenary Stand 382
  community matches 276
  corporate hospitality 180, 360, 382
  Kemlyn Road redevelopment 324
  Main Stand redevelopment 347
  non-football events 188
  parking 188
  Spion Kop development 193
Arrowsmith, Alf 312, 323, 324, 326, 327
Arsenal 133, 179–80, 207, 374, 378
AS Roma 357, 365
Ashcroft, Charlie 229, 274, 281
Ashworth, David 138, 149, 152, 159, 166, 171–2, 175,

177
Athletic Bilbao 329
Atomic Boys 259
Atyeo, John 277
Aurélio, Fábio 403

Babb, Phil 384, 390
Babbel, Markus 391, 393
Babel, Ryan 412, 415
Bainbridge, Edward 132, 185
Ball, Tommy 181–2
Balmer, Jackie 207, 211, 215, 216, 219, 220, 221, 230, 232, 233–4, 235, 236, 238, 239, 241, 243, 249, 252, 262, 263, 269, 271, 274, 335, 413
Bamber, John 148, 150, 153
Bangerter, Hans 371
Barcelona (FC) 377, 392
Barclay, William 35, 36, 40, 86
Barmby, Nick 391
Barnes, John 374, 379, 380, 382, 384, 388, 418
Baron, Kevin 250, 255, 256, 257, 260, 263, 264–5
Baroš, Milan 395, 399, 403
Barry, Gareth 414
Barton, Harry 198, 199, 201
baseball in Liverpool 65, 146
Bassett, William 95
Bayern Munich 364
Beardsley, Peter 374, 379
Beatles, the 11, 319, 324, 325, 331, 334
Beattie, Andy 304, 333, 345
Becton, Frank 52, 63, 71
Belgian FA 371
Bellamy, Craig 403

Benayoun, Yossi 412
Benítez, Rafa 67, 149, 396–7, 398, 400–1, 402, 403, 404, 412, 415, 417–18
  and American owners 410
  Champions League final mistakes 399–400
  commitment to Liverpool 402
  and domestic cups 414
  and Liverpool Academy 413
  rotation 397
  spending on players 416–17
  support from Liverpool fans 411
  Valencia manager 396
Bennett, Reuben 288, 292, 298, 302, 308, 330, 333, 351, 381
Berry, Edwin 40, 94, 99–100, 145, 168
Bimpson, Louis 277
Blackburn Olympic 26
Bleasdale, Alan 363–4
Blenkinsop, Ernie 206
board at Liverpool FC 94–5, 137, 180–1, 185, 201–2, 268, 271–2
boot room at Liverpool FC 303–4, 351
Bootle 49, 184–5, 225
Bootle FC 25, 28–30, 46, 48
Bootle Rovers 152
Bootle St James 152
Borussia Dortmund 335, 340
Borussia Mönchengladbach 347, 353–4
Boys from the Blackstuff 363
Bradley, Jimmy 96, 99, 100,

104, 164

Bradshaw, Harry 50, 56, 63, 79

Bradshaw, Tom 198, 199, 200, 201

Brierley, Ken 250, 256

British Ladies Football Association 65

Brodie, James Alexander 33

Bromilow, Tom 134, 149, 150, 153, 154, 155, 156–7, 158, 161–2, 167, 170, 173, 174, 182, 184, 235, 335

Buchan, Charles 148–9, 150, 166, 170

Burden Park disaster 226

Burnham, Andy 377

Burrows, David 379

Burslem Port Vale 55–6

Busby, Matt 207–8, 209, 210, 211, 216, 221, 230, 256, 285, 302

Bush, Tom 215, 236

Byrne, Gerry 299, 301, 310, 312, 313, 328, 330, 333–4, 335

Callaghan, Ian 299, 301, 310, 312, 313, 323, 325, 329, 333, 334, 336, 347, 352, 353, 419

Campbell, Kenny 118, 125, 126, 134, 139

Carney, Len 215, 229

Carr, Lance 189, 207

Carragher, Jamie 13, 173, 390, 393, 395, 399, 400, 401, 414

Carter, Neil 268

Cartwright, Harold 273

Cartwright, Walter 168, 180–1, 183, 185, 205–6, 244

Case, Jimmy 351, 352, 353, 359

casuals at Liverpool FC 355

Catton, Jimmy 67

Cavern, the 299, 319

Chambers, Harry 134–5, 140, 149, 152, 154, 155, 156, 157, 167, 168, 169–70, 171,

172, 173, 175, 176, 180, 181, 188, 270, 335

Chapman, Herbert 178–9, 182, 192, 213, 382

Charlton, Jack 310, 333, 334

Chester FC 173

Chorlton, Tom 97, 104

Churchill, Winston 81

Cissé, Djibril 397, 399, 400

Cleghorn, Tom 63–4

Clemence, Ray 344–5, 346, 347, 348, 352, 353, 359, 362, 418

Clennell, Joe 169

Clough, Brian 290, 301, 307, 359

Club Brugge KV 359

Collymore, Stan 384–5, 388, 394, 414

Cologne, FC 329

Connell, Bill 99, 122–3, 133, 159, 167, 174, 192

Cooper, Tom 206, 215, 216, 221

Cormack, Peter 343, 347

Corso, Mario 336

Cox, Jack 76, 81, 82, 83–5, 89, 96, 97, 98, 99, 103, 106, 109, 235, 335

Crompton, Tom 132, 135, 185, 193

Crossley, Russell 274

Crouch, Peter 402, 404, 412, 414

crowds and safety at Liverpool FC 87–8, 98, 119–20, 136, 167–8, 227, 257–8

Cruyff, Johan 394

Crystal Palace 117, 125

Crystal Palace FC 379

Cuff, Will 24, 36, 128

Dalglish, Kenny 206, 357–8, 359–60, 364, 365, 367, 372–4, 376, 379–80, 381, 382, 419

de Mendibil, Ortiz 336

Dean, Bill (Dixie) 154, 170, 180, 187, 190, 195–7, 200,

234

Derby, Lord 129, 150, 182

derby matches on Merseyside 48, 59, 63, 70–1, 73–4, 82, 88–9, 97, 136, 197–8, 259–62, 282, 391

Dermott, John 94

Dick, Alec 29–30

Dick, Kerr's Ladies 146, 275

Dicks, Julian 382–3, 394

Dinamo Bucharest 357

Diouf, El-Hadji 395

Docherty, Tommy 330, 343

Doig, Ted 93, 95, 96, 102, 107, 132, 209

Done, Cyril 213, 216, 220, 221, 232, 233, 234, 235, 238–9, 241, 245–6, 252, 253, 263, 269, 274, 277

Dossena, Andrea 415

drinking at Liverpool FC 360, 367, 373–4, 383

Dubai International Capital (DIC) 406, 411

Duckenfield, David 377

Dudek, Jerzy 394, 399, 401, 403

Dunlop, Bill 63, 83, 84, 96, 97, 99, 100, 103, 104, 105, 109, 235

Eastham, Harry 221, 232, 234, 235, 245

Edwards, Leslie 277, 280, 286, 315

Empire Stadium 117

End, The 355

English, Sam 187

European Capital of Culture 11

European Cup 352–4, 359, 361, 362, 368

European Cup-Winners' Cup 340, 385

Evans, Alun 341, 342

Evans, John 279, 281

Evans, Roy 351, 383–5, 381, 387–8, 390, 391, 414

Evans, William 94

Everton FC 13, 15, 23–8,
34–5, 45–6, 112, 376
fans 55, 126, 151
Goodison Park 35, 74, 103
hooligans 371
shared stadium with
Liverpool 406
shareholders 157

FA, the 17–18, 47, 172
Charity Shield 158
and player discipline 170
Sunday football 299
FA Cup 14, 18, 88, 186, 220,
239, 257, 259–60, 271
FA Cup finals 117–18,
121–7,
defeat by Wimbledon 374
first Liverpool win 332–4
first Merseyside final 373
food 124–5
Hillsborough final (v
Everton) 376–7
kit 262–3
in Liverpool 54–5
and Manchester United
(1977) 353
and Newcastle United
(1974) 347
and social class 118
'Spice Boys' final (1996)
385
and Sunderland (1992) 383
tickets 248, 261, 332
FA Premier League 381
Fagan, Joe 274, 298, 302, 303,
345, 351, 362, 363, 364,
365, 373, 381, 401
Fagan, Willie 215, 219, 220,
221, 230, 232, 233, 235,
238, 239, 241, 242, 243,
255, 257, 258, 259, 265,
269, 274
Fairclough, David 351–2
Fairfoul, Tom 114, 125
Fallowfield 47, 75
female employees at Liverpool
FC 277
Ferguson, Bob 119, 122, 125,

126
Ferns, Phil 326
First Liverpool Regiment 125
FIFA 95, 218, 255
World Club Championship
402
finance at Liverpool FC 110–
11, 158, 164, 361, 410–12
Finnan, Steve 397, 399, 400
floodlights 203, 254–5, 280
folk football 17
Footballer Battalion 127
Football League 28–30, 79, 95,
127–8, 140, 213, 319
Football League Cup 299, 362,
384, 391–2, 395
Football Supporters
Association 373
Forshaw, Dick 134, 149, 150,
154, 155–6, 157, 158, 167,
170, 173, 174, 176, 180,
192
Foulke, Willie 64, 81
Fowler, Robbie 383, 384, 385,
388, 390, 391, 392, 393–4,
402, 413
Fry, C.B. 77
Furnell, Jim 313, 321

García, Luis 397, 398, 399,
402, 412
Gayle, Howard 364
General Strike 308
Gerrard, Steven 80, 390, 392,
393, 395, 396–7, 398, 399,
400–1, 402–3, 413, 414,
419
Gerry and the Pacemakers 325
Gillett, Foster 410
Gillett Jr, George 406–12
Gilhespy, Cyril 148, 154, 168,
174
Gillespie, Gary 373
Glasgow Celtic 376, 377
Goddard, Artie 89, 93, 96, 97,
99, 106, 110, 111
Goldie, Archie 63
Goldie, Bill 83, 84, 235
Gordon, Patrick 50, 56

Graham, Bobby 327, 341
Grand National 54, 240, 259
Great Eastern 102
Grobbelaar, Bruce 362, 365,
370, 373, 378, 379
Gunson, Gordon 198, 199,
200, 201

Hall, Brian 342, 348
Hamann, Didi 13, 390, 391,
393, 399–401, 403
Hampton, Harry 109–10
Hannah, Andrew 41, 51, 56,
62
Hannah, David 62
Hansen, Alan 72, 80, 311, 356,
358, 359, 365, 373, 379,
380, 419
Hanson, Alf 189, 203
Hardaker, Alan 361
Hardy, Sam 95–6, 98, 103,
106, 107, 109, 112, 121
Harley, Jim 221, 223, 230, 235,
240, 241
Harrop, James 109, 112
Harrop, Will 211, 273–4,
282–3
Harrow, Jack 139
Harrower, Jimmy 287
Heighway, Steve 342, 347,
348, 352, 353, 359, 383,
413, 414
Henchoz, Stéphane 390, 393
Henderson, Davy 50, 52, 53
Henri, Adrian 319
Herrera, Helenio 335–6
Heskey, Emile 391, 393
Hewitt, Charlie 105
Hewitt, Joe 96, 99, 103, 105,
106, 107, 192, 314–15
Heysel Stadium disaster 359,
368–72
Hickling, J.G. 203
Hicks, Tom 406–11
Hickson, Dave 291–2, 298,
301, 391
Hill, Clifford 282–3, 310
Hillsborough Independent
Panel 378

Hillsborough Stadium disaster 359, 374–8
Hirst, Brook 257
Hitachi 361
Hobson, Alf 191, 220, 221
Hodgson, Gordon 189, 190, 198, 199, 200, 203, 207, 314
Hogan, Jimmy 178, 278
hooliganism 29, 75, 109–10, 260–1, 262, 279, 284, 365, 368–70
Hooton, Peter 355
Hopcraft, Arthur 12, 339–40
Hopkin, Fred 148, 150, 154, 155, 156, 158, 169, 170, 172, 173, 314
Houghton, Ray 373, 379
Houlding, John 23–5, 26, 30, 33, 34–40, 43, 44, 45, 46, 48, 49, 50, 51, 54, 61, 63, 65, 66, 70, 71, 86, 91, 94, 101, 273, 282, 339, 359, 408
Houlding, William 39, 66, 88, 94
Houllier, Gerard 388–96, 397, 402, 403
 illness 394–5
 and the media 395
 resignation 395–6
 rotation 395
 style of play 391–2
 training methods 390
Howe, Fred 207
Howell, Rabbi 71
Huddersfield Town 133, 178–9, 287
Hughes, Abel 62
Hughes, Emlyn 343–4, 346, 347, 348, 352, 353, 356, 419
Hughes, Laurie 220, 221, 229, 230, 235, 236, 237, 238, 240, 241, 259, 260, 263, 265, 274, 281, 285
Hughes, Simon 341
Hungary 277–8
Hunt, Rev. Kenneth 136–7

Hunt, Roger 290–1, 292, 301, 304, 310, 312, 313, 314, 326, 328, 329, 331, 333, 334, 336, 340, 341, 342, 346, 360, 413, 419
Hunter, John 'Sailor' 83, 84, 89
Hyypiä, Sami 14, 390, 391, 393, 398, 399, 419
Hysen, Glenn 379
Ince, Paul 387, 388, 390
injuries 56, 88, 187, 302–3
Internazionale Milan 335–6

Jack, David 232
Jackson, Brian 281
Jackson, George 215
Jackson, James 187, 196–7, 198, 199, 200
James, David 384, 390
James, Hilda 164
Johnson, David 352, 359
Johnson, Dick 140, 152, 166, 167, 168, 170–1, 172, 173, 174, 180, 181, 182, 270
Johnson, Glen 415
Johnston, Craig 362, 365, 373
Jones, Alan 298, 322
Jones, Bill 221, 230, 235, 236, 240, 241, 242, 243, 260, 263, 265, 274, 281, 290–1, 314
Jones, Joey 351, 352, 353
Jones, Mervyn 274
Jones, Rob 384
Josémi 397
Joseph, Sir Francis 243
Juventus 365–6, 370–2

Kaká 400
Kay, George 208–10, 211, 214, 215, 216, 219, 220–1, 228–9, 230, 233, 236, 240, 242, 245–6, 252, 254, 262–4, 268, 269–70, 280, 359, 375, 383, 394
Kaye, George 220
Keane, Robbie 414–15
Keegan, Kevin 16, 345–6, 347, 348, 351, 352, 353, 355,

358, 360, 418
Keely, Alfred 23
Keetley, Joe 182
Kelly, Theo 229, 230, 248
Kemp, Dirk 191, 215, 221
Kennedy, Alan 350, 357, 361, 365, 370, 373
Kennedy, Ray 198, 331, 350, 351, 352, 353, 359, 367
Kewell, Harry 395, 399, 400
Kirkby 228
Klinsmann, Jürgen 411
Kop Investment LLC 411
Kuyt, Dirk 403, 412

Lacey, Bill 106, 113, 118–19, 121, 125, 134, 139, 153, 154, 155, 156, 157, 168, 173, 174, 176, 177, 182, 235, 335
Lambert, Ray 220, 232, 235, 237, 240, 253, 262, 263, 265, 274, 281
Lancashire Cup 48
Lancashire FA 22
Lancashire League 44–7
Law, Denis 287, 297
Lawler, Chris 312, 323, 324, 327, 333, 347, 351
Lawrence, Tommy 312, 313, 321–2, 326, 328, 333, 336, 340, 341, 344
Lawrenson, Mark 363, 373
laws of football 112
 offside 164, 179
 scrimmage 56
Lawson, Hector 183
Lee, Sammy 363, 364, 365
Leeds City 133
Leeds United 333
Leishman, Tom 293, 310, 312, 313, 321
Leitch, Archibald 102–3, 193
Lewis, Harry 134, 136, 150, 154, 157, 177
Lewis, Kevin 299, 301, 310, 312, 313, 314, 323
Liddell, Billy 13, 206, 215, 216, 219, 220, 221, 229–36,

238–41, 249, 252, 256, 258–60, 262–3, 265, 271, 274, 279–80, 281, 284, 285, 287, 288, 315, 328, 335, 357, 359, 374, 418, 419
autobiography 305–6
BBC reporter 248
changing positions on the pitch 250, 253–4
FA Cup final (1950) 266
Liverpool debut 217–18
penalty taker 280
retires 298, 300–1
Second Division player 269–70
signs for Liverpool 209–10
Liddell, Tom 253
Lindsay, Alec 342, 347, 351
Litmanen, Jari 394
Livermore, Doug 384
Liverpool (city)
accent 163
American links 408–9
cinema 145
and drink 60, 65, 78, 248
gambling 112
gangs 21, 225–6, 275–6
health 138
local football 101–2, 138, 146, 152, 181, 185, 189, 247
Militant politics 363
Orangeism 145
police 49–50, 251
population 147, 372
port 81, 163
post-war reconstruction 228, 247
poverty 43
press coverage 371
puritanism 60–1
'race' rioting 111–12, 134, 250–1, 363
and recession 145, 204
Reynold's Waxworks 163
sectarianism 42, 145
sharp practice 79, 151, 217
teddy boys 284
trams 286

unemployment 111–12, 147–8, 197–8, 199, 372
Liverpool Caledonian FC 42, 46
Liverpool Football Supporters Club 211, 288, 314
Liverpool Rugby Union Club 18, 128
Liverpool Senior Cup 23, 48, 59, 274, 309, 320
Liverpool Shareholders Association 300
Lloyd, Larry 342, 343, 344, 347
Lock, Frank 279, 281
Longworth, Ephraim 113–14, 125, 134, 135, 136, 140, 150, 151, 152, 154, 155, 157, 167, 171–4, 176, 177, 182, 186, 192, 206, 235, 246, 314, 335, 419
Lowe, Harry 122, 125
Lucas, Leiva 412
Lucas, Tom 134, 139, 151, 154, 174, 270

McAllister, Gary 391, 392, 393
McAteer, Jason 384, 390
McBride, Jim 53
McCann, Willie 62
McCartney, John 41
McConnell, Bill 197, 209–10, 222, 228, 230, 231, 239, 241, 243–4, 245–6, 251, 269
McCowie, Alex 73–4
McDermott, Terry 351, 352, 353, 359
McDonald, John 109, 112
McDonald, Kevin 367, 373
McDougall, Jimmy 198, 199, 314
McGovern, Jimmy 377
McGregor, William 28, 29, 40
McInnes, Jimmy 317–18
McKenna, John 22–3, 35, 36, 40, 41, 48, 66, 71, 72, 79, 86, 90, 92, 94, 112, 128, 130, 132, 133, 134, 140,

143–4, 158, 159, 176, 183, 189, 193–4, 208, 282, 339, 359
McKinlay, Donald 113, 123, 125, 126, 134, 140, 151, 152, 154, 155, 159, 165, 173, 176, 177, 183, 206, 235, 335, 419
McLean, Duncan 41, 56
McLeod, Tom 240
McLintock, Frank 310
McMahon Steve 373, 379
McManaman, Steve 383, 384, 385, 390
McNab, Jock 134, 156, 172–3, 180
McNulty, Tom 279
McPherson, Archie 198
McPherson, Bill 103, 104, 105, 107
McQue, Joe 41, 56, 71, 131
McQueen, Hugh 41
McQueen, Matt 41, 55, 56, 137, 143–4, 174–5, 176, 177, 182–3, 187, 192, 394
McRorie, Danny 198
McVean, Malcolm 41–2, 52
Mahon, George 24, 34–6, 46
Manchester United 256, 285–6
as a 'brand' 389
Glazer takeover 409
hooligan rivalry with Liverpool 368
and Munich air disaster 286–7
training facilities 302
marketing at Liverpool FC 253
Martindale, Richard 185
Martindale, Robert Lawson 185, 192, 219, 275–6
Mascherano, Javier 403
mascots at Liverpool 139, 265, 277, 314
match fixing 90, 114, 188
Match of the Day 325
match programmes at Liverpool 61, 207
Matthews, Billy 149

Matthews, Stanley 187, 218, 234, 236–7, 242, 246, 252, 258, 275
1953 FA Cup final 227–8
Meisl, Willy 72
Melia, Jimmy 279, 287, 289, 310, 313, 326
Melwood 274, 278, 285, 304
memorandum of association (LFC, 1906) 94
Mercer, Joe 229, 261, 264, 266–7
Meredith, Billy 83, 90, 105
Mersey Sound, The 324
Mersey tunnel 204
Metcalf, Arthur 125
Middlesbrough Ironopolis 44, 48
Miller, Tommy 114, 119, 120, 125, 126, 136
Milne, Gordon 299, 301, 310, 312, 313, 326, 328, 331, 333, 335, 340
Minshull, Ray 233, 237, 241, 263, 269
Mølby, Jan 367–8, 373, 397
Molyneux, John 285, 289, 298, 301, 312
Moores, David 383, 396, 405–7, 409, 411–12
Moores, John 138, 181, 208, 306–7
Moran, Ronnie 283, 298, 302, 310, 313, 320, 326, 348, 351, 381, 383, 384
Morgan, Hugh 71
Morgan, Steve 405
Morientes, Fernando 397
Morrison, Tom 198, 199, 200
Morrissey, Johnny 287, 321
Moss, Frank 169
Mourinho, José 396, 397, 402, 403
Murphy, Danny 390, 393
Muscular Christianity 20, 23

Neal, Phil 16, 63, 350–1, 352, 353, 359, 365, 418
New Brighton Tower 73, 79

Newcastle United 111
Nicholl, Jimmy 121, 125
Nicol, Steve 331, 363, 365, 373, 379
Nieuwenhuys, Berry 190–1, 207, 215, 217, 220, 231–2, 235, 236, 237, 245, 249
Nigerian Select XI 254
Nisbet, Alexander 94
Norris, Henry 113–14, 133

O'Connor, T.P. 184
Orr, Ronald 107, 109, 111
Orrell, John 26, 34
Orrell, Joseph 61
Owen, Michael 385, 388, 390, 392, 393, 397, 413

Paisley, Bob 214–15, 288, 289, 308, 337, 345, 348, 373, 381, 402, 419
diagnosing injuries 302–3
left out of 1950 FA Cup final 263–4
Liverpool manager 348–62
Liverpool player 219, 221, 222, 229–30, 231, 233, 235, 236, 239, 240, 242, 243, 254, 260, 262, 269, 281
managerial record 362–3
physiotherapist 274
Shankly's assistant 296, 298
World Club Championship 402
Parkinson, John (Jack) 93, 96, 98, 109, 111
Parry, Maurice 80, 83, 85, 96, 97, 99, 103, 154, 192
Parry, Rick 388–9, 395, 396, 405–6, 410–11
Patterson, George 147, 171, 174, 183, 192, 208, 350
Payne, Jimmy 252, 255, 257, 259, 260, 263, 265, 266
Pennant, Jermaine 403, 404, 412
Perkins, Bill 76, 80, 83, 84
Platini, Michel 371

player recruitment at Liverpool FC 144, 187, 220–1, 253, 278
players
earnings 90, 101, 108, 140, 145, 165, 210–11, 226, 248, 286, 308, 361
industrial action 107
and press intrusions 254
union 108, 214, 226, 306
pools companies 138, 181, 208, 223, 225
Pratt, David 174
professionalism 27, 135, 153
public schools and football 17
Pursell, Bob 114, 118, 125

'race' and Liverpool FC 364, 374
Raisbeck, Alex 14, 71–2, 80–4, 86, 89, 92, 96–7, 99, 100, 104, 105, 106, 109, 132, 164, 335, 357, 359, 419
Ramsden, Bernard (Barney) 215, 221, 235, 236, 245
Ramsey, John 94
Raybould, Sam 79–86, 89–91, 93, 96, 97, 98, 99, 104, 105, 164, 335
Reakes, Sydney 282, 293, 307, 310, 312
Real Madrid 286
record defeat for Liverpool FC 281
record win for Liverpool FC 64
Red Star Belgrade 342, 347
Redknapp, Jamie 383, 384
refereeing 51–2, 152, 232, 266, 336
Reina, Pepe 403, 413
Reykjavik, KR 327
Richards, George 243, 271–2, 273
Riedle, Karl-Heinz 387
Riera, Albert 415
Riise, John Arne 394, 399, 403, 415
Riley, Arthur 189, 191, 198,

203, 206, 215, 221
Robertson, John 80, 83, 84
Robertson, Tom 71, 81, 83, 84, 89
Robinson, Peter 346, 347, 349, 351, 359, 378, 381, 388
Robinson, Robbie 92, 96, 107, 110
Rogers, Fred 211
Roosens, Albert 371
Rosenthal, Ronnie 380
Ross, Jimmy 62–3
Ross, Nick 29–30
Ross, Sid 41
Rotherham Town 44, 64
Rous, Stanley 178
Rouse, Jack 192, 211, 214
Royal Bank of Scotland 407, 410, 412
Rudham, Ken 280–1
Rugby Football Union 18, 82, 128
Rush, Ian 16, 358, 360, 365, 367, 373, 379, 382, 413, 418

St Domino's Football Club 24
St Etienne 352
St John, Ian 16, 307–9, 310, 312–13, 314, 322, 326, 328, 330, 331, 333, 334, 336, 342, 346, 355, 356, 360
Salvidge, Archibald 137–8
Sandon Hotel 24, 26, 48
Satterthwaite, Charlie 79, 80, 81, 83, 84
Saunders, Dean 382
Saunders, Tom 384
Savage, Bob 207
Sawyer, Eric 306, 307, 309, 310
Scales, John 384
Scott, Elisha 14, 134, 140, 149, 150, 153–5, 156, 157, 167, 168, 170, 172, 173–6, 182, 184, 185, 188, 191, 199, 200, 229, 290, 335, 348, 357, 359, 419
and Charles Buchan 148,

166
debut v. Newcastle United 113
and Dixie Dean 196–7
leaving Liverpool 204–6
in Liverpool first team 139
and the Liverpool Kop 195–7, 202–3, 206, 296, 340
Scully 364
Seddon, Jimmy 183, 246, 278
Shankly, Bill 67, 177, 187, 241, 270, 322, 329, 331, 355, 362, 364, 381, 384, 408, 412, 419
accepts Liverpool job 292–3
at Anfield 295–8, 299–315, 317, 318, 322–3, 326, 329–30, 333–7, 340, 343–7
and coaching 304–5
European innovation 327–8
influence of the war 305
and injuries 303
at Liverpool AGMs 300, 301–2, 309–10, 320–1
and loyalty to players 341–2
manager at Huddersfield Town 287
and music 332
and performance culture in Liverpool 324–5
and retirement 348–50
signs Liverpool contract 324
and style 311
and training 304
wartime footballer 216
Shannon, Les 251
shareholders at Liverpool FC 201–2, 271–2, 287
Sheldon, Jackie 114, 120, 125, 131, 134, 139
Shelley, Albert 208, 211, 246, 252, 262, 263, 264–5, 270, 278, 288, 302
Shinawatra, Thaksin 405

Shone, Danny 148, 150, 154
Sidlow, Cyril 221, 227, 229, 230, 231, 233, 235, 236, 238, 241, 254, 259, 260, 262, 263, 265, 269, 274, 290
Sissoko, Momo 402
Skrtel, Martin 414
Slater, Bert 290, 301, 313
Šmicer, Vladimír 390, 399, 400, 401, 403
Smith, John 346–7, 359, 361, 371, 381
Smith, Tommy 285, 312, 322, 328, 330, 333, 342, 343, 344, 346, 348, 349, 352, 353, 357, 361
Smyth, Sammy 275
Souness, Graeme 16, 321, 356–7, 358, 359, 363, 364, 365, 367, 368, 374, 381–3, 384, 388, 394, 418
South Africa 188–91, 275, 342, 362
South Liverpool FC 126, 254
Southern League 107–8
Southport Vulcan 133
Speakman, Sam 123
spectator songs at Liverpool 105–6, 325, 334, 354
Spicer, Ted (Eddie) 215, 221, 241, 245, 255, 277
Spion Kop 101–2, 120, 193–4, 196, 202–3, 277, 301, 339, 378
Spirit of Shankly group 412
Steel, Willie 198
Stevenson, General 71
Stevenson, Willie 321, 322, 326, 328, 330, 331, 333, 343, 355
Stewart, Jimmy 109
Storer, Harry 71
Stott, Jimmy 50
Strong, Geoff 327, 333, 334, 342
Stubbins, Albert 222, 230–1, 232, 233, 234, 235, 236, 237, 238, 239, 240, 241,

242, 243, 246, 249, 250–2,
254, 256, 258, 262, 263,
267, 269, 271, 274, 275,
307
supporters at Liverpool FC 52,
86, 93, 119–20, 123–4, 127,
147–8, 199–200, 234, 240,
249–50, 267, 275, 279, 334,
353–4, 400–1
Sutcliffe, Charles 178
Suter, Fergus 19, 22
Swift Chambers, Ben 24

tactics at Liverpool FC 186–7,
246, 256
Taylor, Phil 207
  1950 FA Cup final captain
  266
  Liverpool manager 284,
  290
  resigns as Liverpool
  manager 292
telegraphic address at
  Liverpool FC 95–6
television 228, 264, 298, 320
  and Liverpool FC 216
temperance movement in
  Liverpool 108
Ten Hours Act 21
Tennant, Jack 189
Test matches (football) 56, 63
thefts at Liverpool FC 225–6,
317
Thomas, Michael 378
Thompson, Bobby 322–3
Thompson, Peter 313, 321,
323–4, 326, 330, 331, 333,
340
Thompson, Phil 342, 352, 359,
390
Through the Wind and Rain
381, 408
Torres, Fernando 412–13, 414,
415, 419
Toshack, John 342, 346, 347,
352, 360
training at Liverpool FC 237,
278, 297–8, 389–90

Traore, Djimi 397, 399, 400,
403
Twentyman, Geoff 279, 281,
285, 289, 290, 293, 341,
345, 350, 351, 356
UEFA 329, 361, 368
  ban on English clubs 372
  poor organisation of final
  venues 399, 404
UEFA Champions League
  394–5, 397–8
  final 2005 v. AC Milan
  399–401
  final 2007 v. AC Milan 404
UEFA Cup 343, 347, 351,
391–3
Unsworth, W. Leslie 162

van der Berg, Harman 189
van Himst, Paul 327, 328
Vignal, Gregory 394
Vogts, Berti 353

Wachovia 410
Wadsworth, Harold 134, 139
Wadsworth, Walter 113, 134,
139, 140, 152, 154, 155,
166, 167, 169–70, 173, 174,
176, 177, 182, 188, 235,
270
Walker, John 71, 83, 84, 85
Walker Art Gallery 49
Wallace, Gordon 312, 322, 327
Walsh, Jimmy 182, 183
Walsh, Paul 367
Wark, John 367
wartime football 129–33, 135,
213–20
Watkinson, Bill 241
Watson, Tom 14, 59, 66–8, 69,
70–4, 76, 77, 79, 80–1, 83,
86, 88, 91, 92–3, 94–5, 96,
97, 99, 101, 103, 109, 113,
120, 121, 122–3, 126–7,
128, 131–2, 133–4, 138,
140, 144, 149, 171, 177–8,
419
Watson Cabre, Joseph 102,

193
Welsh, Don 233, 270–1, 272,
277, 280, 283–4, 292
Wenger, Arsène 387, 391, 417
West, Alf 98, 103–4, 109, 164
Westerveld, Sander 390, 393,
394
Wheeler, Johnny 285
Whelan, Ronnie 363, 379,
365, 373
White, Dick 285, 289–90, 301,
312–13
Wilkie, Tom 63, 68
Wilkinson, Algernon 174
Wilkinson, George 281
Williams, Charlie 283–4
Williams, Ronnie 214, 220,
248, 272
Williams, Samuel 153
Williams Tom (T.V.) 210, 274,
282, 283, 287, 293, 295,
304, 306, 307, 309–10, 314,
320, 341, 359
Williams, Walter 153, 159,
165, 173
Wilson, Charlie 79, 83–4, 144,
192, 211
Wilson, Harold 247, 324
Wilton, Robb 240
women fans 28, 258, 319
women's football 12, 65, 146–7,
275, 319
Worcester City 288–90
World Cup 1966 320, 340
Wright, Billy 253
Wright, David 198, 199, 200,
201
Wright, Mark 384, 390
Wyllie, Tom 41, 48

Yeats, Ron 310–12, 313, 314,
323, 327, 328, 330, 332,
333, 334, 336, 341, 342,
355
Young, Percy 210
Younger, Tommy 285

Zenden, Bolo 402